KNOWLEDGE, CONCEPTS
AND CATEGORIES

Studies in Cognition

Editor: Glyn Humphreys
University of Birmingham

Knowledge, Concepts and Categories

Edited by

Koen Lamberts

David Shanks

The MIT Press
Cambridge, Massachusetts

First MIT Press edition, 1997

Library of Congress Cataloguing-in-Publication Data

Knowledge, concepts, and categories/edited by Koen Lamberts
    and David Shanks
  p. cm. — (Studies in cognition)
  Includes bibliographical references and index.
  ISBN 0-262-62118-5 (pbk. alk. paper)
    1. Mental representation.   2. Categorization (Psychology)
  3. Thought and thinking.   I. Lamberts, Loen.   II. Shanks, David R.
  III. Series: Studies in cognition (Cambridge, Mass.)
  BF316.6K66   1997   96-52838
  153.2'3 — dc21   CIP

Cover painting *Odatisque* (tempra) by Ian Hopton

Printed and bound in the United Kingdom by Biddles Ltd,
Guildford and King's Lynn.

Contents

Contributors

Jerome R. Busemeyer, Department of Psychology, Indiana University, Bloomington, IN 47405, USA

Eunhee Byun, Ergonomics Lab, Korea Research Institute of Standards and Science, P.O. Box 102 Yusong Tajeon, 3305-600 South Korea

Nick Chater, Department of Psychology, University of Warwick, Coventry CV4 7AL, UK

Paul De Boeck, Department of Psychology, University of Leuven, Tiensestraat 102, B-3000 Leuven, Belgium

Edward L. Delosh, Department of Psychology, Colorado State University, Fort Collins, Colorado 80523, USA

Thomas Goschke, Departement Psychologie, Universitat Osnabruck, D-4500 Osnabruck, Germany

Ulrike Hahn, Department of Psychology, University of Warwick, Coventry CV4 7AL, UK

James Hampton, Department of Psychology, City University London, Northampton Square, London EC1V 0HB, UK

Evan Heit, Department of Psychology, University of Warwick, Coventry CV4 7AL, UK

Barbara Knowlton, Department of Psychology, Franz Hall, University of California, Los Angeles, CA 90024 1563, USA

Koen Lamberts, School of Psychology, University of Birmingham, Edgbaston Birmingham B15 2TT, UK

Mary E. Lassaline, University of Illinois, Beckman Institute, 405 Mathews Avenue, Urbana, IL 61801, USA.

Mark A. McDaniel, Department of Psychology, University of New Mexico, Albuquerque, NM 87131, USA

Gregory L. Murphy, University of Illinois, Beckman Institute, 405 Mathews Avenue, Urbana, IL 61801, USA.

Larissa K. Samuelson, Department of Psychology, Indiana University, Bloomington, IN 47405, USA

David R. Shanks, Department of Psychology, University College London, Gower Street, London WC1E 6BT, UK

Linda B. Smith, Department of Psychology, Indiana University, Bloomington, IN 47405, USA

Gert Storms, Department of Psychology, University of Leuven, Tiensestraat 102, B-3000 Leuven, Belgium

Bruce W. A. Whittlesea, Department of Psychology, Simon Fraser University, Burnaby, BC V5A 1S6, Canada

Series Preface

Over the past 20 years enormous advances have been made in our understanding of basic cognitive processes concerning issues such as: what are the basic modules of the cognitive system? How can these modules be modelled? How are the modules implemented in the brain? The book series *Studies in Cognition* seeks to provide state-of-the-art summaries of this research, bringing together work on experimental psychology with that on computational modelling and cognitive neuroscience. Each book contains chapters written by leading figures in the field, which aim to provide comprehensive summaries of current research. The books should be both accessible and scholarly and be relevant to undergraduates, postgraduates and research workers alike.

Glyn Humphreys
27 May 1997

Introduction

Koen Lamberts and David Shanks

Few would disagree that the study of mental representation is rightly a central concern in contemporary cognitive psychology or that progress over the last few years in understanding the nature of knowledge, concepts and categories has been considerable. Yet by its very nature this is a difficult subject for students and researchers to get to grips with. Almost every subfield of cognitive psychology can potentially say something about mental representation, and so it is relatively uncommon to find books or review articles attempting to abstract the key conclusions that emerge across different research areas. The present volume is a modest attempt to perform such an abstraction process. We have invited several of the most influential researchers in the field to review their work on knowledge and concepts in the hope of providing a thorough introduction to and overview of the current state of the art.

This volume can be divided into three rather distinct parts. Chapters 1 to 5 each contain a thorough and systematic review of a significant aspect of research on concepts and categories. Together, these chapters aim to give the reader a general introduction to the field. Chapters 6 to 9 are concerned primarily with issues related to the taxonomy of human knowledge. Distinctions such as those between general and specific knowledge, implicit and explicit knowledge, and declarative and procedural knowledge are introduced and critically investigated. Finally, Chapters 10 to 12 discuss formal models of categorization and function learning. The purpose of these three chapters is to provide a few examples of current formal modelling of conceptual behaviour.

To set the scene, we shall briefly review the central issues that are addressed by the various chapters. In early theories of concept learning, it was often implicitly assumed that conceptual knowledge was decomposable in the sense that one could study the acquisition and use of isolated concepts without taking people's prior knowledge or knowledge about other concepts into account. In Heit's chapter, this view is challenged. He discusses a wealth of experimental data which indicate that concept learning depends heavily on prior knowledge. He also explores how models of categorization and concept acquisition can be extended to address the influence of prior knowledge.

Hahn and Chater tackle the old and very important problem of the relation between concepts and similarity. Many theories of concepts and categorization rely on similarity as an explanatory principle. According to these theories, objects belong together in a category (in other words, are instances of the same concept) if they are sufficiently similar to each other. However, similarity itself is defined in terms of concepts. Hahn and Chater discuss this circularity problem in considerable depth, and explore several possible solutions.

Murphy and Lassaline's chapter deals with the hierarchical structure of concepts. Any given object can be categorized at different levels. For instance, the same object can be called a kitchen chair, a chair, or a piece of furniture. This hierarchical organization is a very important characteristic of concepts. In many circumstances, people strongly prefer to label objects at one particular level of the hierarchy. For example, people normally name a Siamese cat as a *cat*, rather than naming it as an *animal* or as a *Siamese cat*. Murphy and Lassaline present an overview of research on this privileged level of categorization, known as the basic level. They discuss different explanations of the basic level, and review its relevance for categorization of various kinds of objects and non-objects (such as emotions, scenes and actions).

Rips (1995) describes how research on concepts has attempted to address two interrelated questions. First, researchers have tried to construct a theory of how people decide whether instances are members of categories. Most chapters in this volume describe research that somehow fits within this category. A second important line of research, however, focuses on how people can understand and produce sentences that contain combinations of concepts. Most people will understand the meaning of complex concepts such as *yellow television* or *squashed tomato* on the basis of their knowledge of the constituent concepts. Hampton, in his chapter, investigates the mechanisms of conceptual combination. He reviews several theories of conceptual combination, and argues that a final account of conceptual combination can be achieved only through a comprehensive understanding of people's everyday knowledge of the world.

There has been some debate recently as to whether concepts should be considered as stable mental representations, or whether they are flexible, temporary, context-dependent constructions. Smith and Samuelson review the evidence for each of these views. They document how the traditional search for constant concepts has not been very successful, and they suggest a unified account of category stability and variability that does not rely on the notion of a fixed, represented concept. They apply this idea to aspects of cognitive development and show how it can explain developmental change in conceptual behaviour.

Shanks' contribution is the first of the taxonomic chapters. He discusses the distinction between symbolic and distributed knowledge representations, and introduces the debate on the status of implicit and explicit knowledge. The past few years have seen an enormous amount of interest devoted to the question of whether (and if so how) information can be represented in an "implicit" form. What is meant by implicit knowledge, and how is it distinguished from explicit knowledge? Although its characterization is controversial, the most common view is that implicit knowledge is simply knowledge that is unavailable to consciousness. A prototypical example (what Chomsky calls "cognizing") concerns the rules of grammar: all competent speakers of a language such as English know (or cognize) the rules of its grammar, but of course they do not (unless they are linguists) know them consciously.

The three chapters that follow Shanks' introduction provide up-to-date discussions of implicit knowledge. Goschke provides a very thorough review of the methodological and theoretical debates related to implicit knowledge, as well as a survey of some of the main experimental findings. He touches on the evidence that distinct brain systems may underlie the acquisition and storage of implicit and explicit knowledge, and this issue is dealt with in greater depth in Knowlton's chapter. She argues persuasively that certain neurological syndromes such as anterograde amnesia are characterized by a selective deficit specific to explicit (declarative) knowledge combined with intact implicit (nondeclarative) knowledge.

Taking a very different approach, Whittlesea considers the possibility that instead of requiring distinct knowledge modules, the experimental evidence may instead be accommodated within a single-system account of knowledge representation. The traditional view exemplified by Knowlton suggests that abstract concepts form part of our implicit knowledge, since amnesics are able, for example, to learn perfectly normally about the prototype of a category. On this view, knowledge of specific events is part of declarative knowledge and is impaired in amnesia. Whittlesea attempts to undermine this abstract/specific dichotomy by presenting the radical argument that all knowledge is based on memory of specific episodes, with apparent sensitivity to the abstract structure of the world being an emergent property of the way specific events are encoded and retrieved. The contrast between these deeply opposing views of knowledge representation serves as an ideal illustration of the difficulty of penetrating the fundamental operations of the mind.

The chapters by Goschke, Knowlton, and Whittlesea relate significantly to another key issue in knowledge representation, namely the question of modularity. Fodor's 1983 book *Modularity of mind* is one of the most influential works of the last 20 years in cognitive psychology. His thesis was that the mind is constructed from a set of processing modules that are informationally isolated from one another, together with a central processor. Each of these isolated modules operates upon its input without any involvement or interference from other modules or from top–down influences from the central processor. Whether any cognitive system, such as the language processor, is truly modular in Fodor's sense remains unclear, and the opposing views taken by Knowlton and Whittlesea on the modular separation of implicit and explicit knowledge show that the debate is still very much alive.

The final three chapters of the book address issues in formal modelling of conceptual behaviour and learning. Lamberts' chapter starts with an introduction to formal modelling in cognitive psychology. He shows how modelling techniques can be used to test experimental hypotheses. In the second part of the chapter, he presents a framework for the time course of categorization. Traditional formal theories of categorization only model the end result of decision making about category membership, but do not provide a detailed description of the underlying cognitive processes. Lamberts reviews several recent attempts to account for the course of processing in perceptual categorization.

In Chapter 11 Busemeyer, Byun, Delosh and McDaniel review models and data about function learning and its relation to category learning. First, they discuss conceptual similarities and differences between category learning and function learning. Next, they summarize the main findings on function learning, and then describe an artificial neural network model of category learning. This model is extended to function learning. As such, Busemeyer et al. provide a very interesting theoretical link between the fields of category learning and function learning.

In the final chapter, Storms and De Boeck present formal models of structure *within* categories. They review the assumptions regarding categorical structure made by different theories of concepts, and show how formal models can be used to identify the structure of categories from empirical data.

As stated previously, our intention in putting this volume together has been to provide an overview of recent research on concepts and knowledge that abstracts across a variety of specific fields of cognitive psychology. Thus readers will find data from many different areas: developmental psychology, formal modelling, neuropsychology, connectionism, philosophy, and so on. Some may regard this enthusiastic mixing of disciplines as unlicensed, but in our view it is a strength rather than a weakness. To the extent that concepts are the basic "alphabet" of cognition, their understanding will be best achieved by a number of convergent approaches.

In putting this volume together, we have been helped by several people, whom we thank warmly: Glyn Humphreys, Andrew Carrick, Rachel Blackman, Roger Jones, Dave Peebles, Noellie Brockdorff, Steve Chong, and Richard Freeman.

REFERENCES

Fodor, J. 1983. *Modularity of mind*. Cambridge, Mass.: MIT Press.
Rips, L. J. 1995. The current status of research on concept combination. *Mind and Language* **10**, 72–104.

CHAPTER ONE

Knowledge and Concept Learning[1]

Evan Heit

It has been remarked of sophisticated computer data bases that "everything is deeply intertwingled" (Nelson 1987). This observation also applies especially well to concept learning by humans. Conceptual knowledge has a highly interrelated nature. What a person learns about a new category is greatly influenced by and dependent on what this person knows about other, related categories.

For example, imagine two people who are learning to drive a manual transmission automobile. In effect, these people are learning about a new concept, *manual transmission cars*. Say that one person has had many years of experience driving cars with automatic transmissions, and the other person has never driven a car before. The first person's learning will be facilitated greatly by previous knowledge of the category *automatic transmission cars*, so that this person will be able to quickly find and operate the steering wheel, brakes, radio, etc. in the new car. Yet this prior knowledge would not be of much help as this person is learning about how to shift gears in manual transmission cars. In fact, all of this experience with automatic transmissions might make it especially difficult to learn to operate a manual transmission. Now imagine the situation of the second person, who has never driven before. Overall, this person will probably learn very slowly compared to the first person, because of this person's lack of relevant prior knowledge. This second person's learning will likely be a drawn-out process with much trial-and-error practice involved. On the positive side, though, the second person might have some advantage over the first person in learning how to shift gears, because the second person would not have to overcome negative transfer from experience with automatic transmissions.

As another example, imagine that you are an explorer visiting a remote island, with the purpose of writing a book about the people that you see there. You bring to this island many forms of prior knowledge that will guide you in learning about these new people. For example, based on your experiences in other places, you would expect to see males and females, younger and older people, shy people and arrogant people. You would also have certain hypotheses at a more abstract level, for example, that the clothes that someone wears may be related to the person's age and gender. (Goodman 1955, referred to such abstract hypotheses as *overhypotheses*.) In a way, these biases resulting from previous knowledge might seem to be undesirable. After all, wouldn't it be better to be a detached, unbiased observer? However, such biases can make learning much more efficient. Without any prior expectations about what the important categories are on this new island, you would likely spend too much time on unimportant information. For example, you might spend the first month of your visit categorizing people in terms of whether they have small ears or large ears, and the second month trying to notice the relation between ear size and how fast people walk. Without the guidance of your prior knowledge, you could spend an interminable amount of time trying to learn about all the possible categories and the relations among categories. Clearly, some use of prior knowledge of old categories would be critical in learning about the new categories on this island. (See Keil 1989, and Peirce 1931–1935, for related arguments.)

The past decade has been an exciting time for categorization research. Our understanding of the "intertwingledness" or interrelatedness of concept learning has been building steadily. There are numerous situations, such as learning about new objects (like manual transmission cars) or visiting new locations (whether they are new islands or just new restaurants) in which category learning is influenced by what is already known. This chapter will review the experimental evidence for the claim that concept learning depends heavily on prior knowledge, and describe the different ways that prior knowledge has an influence. Furthermore, this chapter will discuss current models of categorization and concept learning with the aim of improving these models to address the important influences of prior knowledge. Finally, inductive reasoning and memory, cognitive abilities that are closely related to categorization, will be discussed in terms of effects of background knowledge.

THEORETICAL ARGUMENTS

The seminal paper concerning knowledge effects on concept learning was written by Murphy & Medin (1985). They contrasted two approaches to describing concept learning, which they referred to as *similarity-based* and *theory-based*. According to similarity-based approaches, there is a simple way to tell whether something belongs to a particular category: You assess the similarity between the item and what is known about the category (see also Rips 1989). The more similar item X is to what is known about category C, the more likely you will place X in category C. This similarity-based approach does appear to be a reasonable idea, and it is consistent with several existing accounts of how people learn about categories. For example, take a standard prototype account (Hampton 1993, Rosch & Mervis 1975) of how you might learn about a category such as a novel kind of bird. You would observe members of this species of bird, and remember typical features or characteristics of these birds. These features would be summarized as a prototype, representing the average member of the species (e.g. light brown, fourteen-inch wingspan, lives in treetops). To judge whether another bird belongs to this species, you would evaluate the similarity between this bird and the prototypical list of features.

Murphy & Medin argued that although a similarity-based approach to categorization may be a reasonable start, it will ultimately prove to be incomplete. As illustrated by the earlier example of the explorer visiting an island, there may be so much information available that it will be difficult to simply observe and remember everything. A category learner needs some constraints or biases on what to observe. A related point is that the learner needs to figure out how to describe observations in terms of features. Except perhaps in nature books, birds do not come already labelled with tags such as "light brown" and "lives in treetops". Such descriptions are inferred and applied by the learner. In addition, people have knowledge about the causal relations between these features that would not be captured by a feature list. For example, it is reasonable to expect that smaller birds will tend to live closer to the ground and larger birds would be more likely to live in treetops, because larger birds can better sustain exposure to wind and severe weather.

These critical influences of knowledge are not explained by similarity-based approaches, Murphy & Medin argued. In contrast, theory-based approaches would consider people's knowledge about the world, including their intuitive theories about what features are important to observe and how they are related to each other. The Murphy & Medin article did not propose a particular theory-based model of categorization so much as to lay out the challenges that researchers would face in developing a more complete account of categorization that addresses the influences of knowledge. Much of the categorization research published after Murphy & Medin (1985) has presented experimental evidence for, and more detailed empirical accounts of, knowledge effects on concept learning. Also, some work has begun to develop more complete models of categorization that address some of the issues raised by Murphy & Medin. The next two sections of this chapter will review the empirical work on knowledge and concept learning, and the following section will discuss categorization models that address these experimental results.

EXPERIMENTAL EVIDENCE FOR SPECIFIC INFLUENCES OF KNOWLEDGE

At this point, there is quite a bit of amassed evidence on ways that knowledge influences category learning. Before describing this evidence in detail, it is possible to draw some generalizations about what is known. Perhaps the most fundamental generalization is that in learning about new categories, people act as if these categories will be consistent with previous knowledge. People seem to act with economy, so that previous knowledge structures are reused when possible. This generalization is apparent in a few different ways. In general it is easier to learn a new category when it is similar to a previously-known category, as in the earlier example of learning about manual transmission cars. Also, people's beliefs about new categories include their knowledge from other categories; in effect, there is leakage from one category to another. Likewise, people's strategies in learning new categories are consistent with their beliefs about other categories. For example, an explorer's strategies in studying people on a new island would reflect what the explorer knows about the social structure of other places. In the following sections, four different kinds of experimental results will be described, indicating different effects of prior knowledge.

Integration effects
One of the basic influences of prior knowledge on the learning of new categories is *integration* of prior knowledge with new observations (Heit 1994). That is, the initial representation of a new category is based on prior knowledge, and this representation is updated gradually as new observations are made. For example, imagine that you are walking through some forest for the first time. A nearby forest has large and aggressive birds, so you initially expect the same in the new forest. However, most of the birds you first see are small and unaggressive. As you observe more birds, you gradually revise your beliefs to reflect the

local conditions. After just a few observations, your beliefs about the new category of birds might represent an average of your prior knowledge and what you observe. With an even larger number of observations, your beliefs mostly reflect the data from the new forest (small and unaggressive birds) rather than your previous beliefs based on the other forest (large and aggressive). This process is similar to an *anchor-and-adjust* method of estimation, which Tversky & Kahneman (1974) have argued is a widespread form of reasoning. Also, this process is similar to Bayesian statistical procedures for estimation, in which an initial estimate is revised as new data are encountered (Edwards et al. 1963, Raiffa & Schlaifer 1961).

Recent experiments by Heit (1994, 1995) obtained results that are consistent with an integration account. Instead of being brought to a forest, the subjects in these experiments were shown descriptions of people in a fictional city. Heit assessed subject's initial beliefs about the city as well as their beliefs after they observed members of categories from this city. For example, the subjects learned about a category of joggers. Initially, subjects expected that about 75 per cent of these joggers would own expensive running shoes. Some subjects then saw descriptions of joggers such that 75 per cent did own expensive running shoes, whereas other subjects saw other proportions (0%, 25%, 50%, 100%) of joggers with expensive running shoes. In their final judgements, subjects acted as if they were taking a weighted average of the expected proportion of joggers with expensive running shoes and the observed proportion. For example, subjects who observed 75 per cent expensive running shoes continued to make judgements of about 75 per cent. Subjects who observed only 25 per cent running shoes ultimately made judgements of about 50 per cent. Furthermore, Heit found that subjects who were given a larger number of descriptions of people in the city tended to discount their prior knowledge more, again consistent with the integration account. (For further experimental evidence of integration effects, see Hayes & Taplin 1992, 1995.)

Clinical psychologists sometimes show similar anchoring effects in their categorizations, or diagnoses, of patients (see Mumma 1993, for a review). Clinicians often show *suggestion* effects, so that their diagnoses represent an integration of their previous knowledge and their own observations. A typical source of suggestion effects would be a diagnosis made by a colleague. For example, a clinician might categorize a patient as having borderline personality disorder if another clinician has previously reported this diagnosis, even if the patient's symptoms would fit with a number of other disorders as well. Here, the previous clinician's analysis of the patient serves as an anchor or initial representation when the new clinician learns about the patient.

A critical aspect of integration effects is the initial category representation that people assemble based on prior knowledge. Ward (1994) has developed a technique for studying these initial representations. This work sheds light on how people borrow information from related categories as they begin learning about a new category. Ward's task placed people in a creative situation in which they imagined the members of new categories. For example, subjects were asked to draw pictures of animals that might appear on another planet. These imagined animals were very likely to have familiar appendages such as arms, legs, or wings, and to have sense organs such as eyes and ears. Consistent with the idea of integration, Ward concluded that these initial category representations contained a great deal of specific, borrowed information from established categories of animals on Earth.

Selective weighting effects

Several researchers (Keil 1989, Murphy & Medin 1985, Murphy & Wisniewski 1989) have argued that *selective weighting* effects of prior knowledge are critical in category learning. That is, previous knowledge leads us to selectively attend to certain features or certain observations during concept learning, thereby narrowing the space of hypotheses to be considered. In the earlier example, an explorer could have used previous knowledge to focus on the relation between age and clothing rather than the relation between ear size and speed of walking. Without such selective weighting of relevant information, concept learning would be very slow and difficult.

Pazzani (1991) investigated the issue of selective attention by teaching subjects about categories of balloons. Subjects were instructed either to learn a category of balloons that inflate or to learn a category that was simply labelled "Alpha". A pre-test showed that subjects expected that stretching a balloon would facilitate inflation and that adults would be more successful than children at inflation. It was assumed that subjects in the Inflate conditions (but not in the Alpha conditions) would be influenced by their prior knowledge of what it takes to inflate a balloon. The stimuli in this experiment were pictures of people with balloons. The pictures varied on four dimensions: adult or child, stretched balloon or balloon dipped in water, yellow or purple balloon, and small or large balloon. In some conditions of this experiment, the Inflate (or Alpha) category was defined by a disjunctive rule: these balloons must be stretched *or* inflated by an adult. Note that this rule is relevant to subjects' knowledge about inflating balloons. Pazzani found that category learning was much faster in the Inflate condition than in the Alpha condition. This result may be explained by subjects in the Inflate conditions paying special attention to the age and stretching features. Prior knowledge about these relevant features would be helpful because the concept was defined in terms of age and stretching.

Several other researchers have obtained results that they explained in terms of selective weighting (e.g. Hayes & Taplin 1992, 1995, Keleman & Bloom 1994, Medin, Wattenmaker, & Hampson, 1987, Murphy & Wisniewski 1989, Wisniewski 1995). For example, Medin et al. (1987) used a sorting task to study how people construct categories. Medin et al. found that when people sorted items into groups, they were especially likely to be influenced by pairs of dimensions that were causally related according to prior knowledge. For example, in sorting medical patients who were described by several symptoms, subjects were likely to sort on the basis of a pair of related symptoms such as dizziness and earache, presumably because these dimensions were given extra weight. Considering the theoretical arguments by Keil (1989), Murphy & Medin (1985), and Peirce (1931–1935), it does seem plausible that selective weighting resulting from previous knowledge is a central part of category learning.

Feature interpretation effects

Another important influence of prior knowledge on learning is to help people interpret and represent what they observe. Psychologists such as Asch (1946) made this point with stimuli that describe personality traits. According to Asch's *change of meaning hypothesis*, a feature such as "intelligent" would be interpreted differently in the statements "Sara is friendly and intelligent" and "Mary is ruthless and intelligent". Sara's intelligence is of a quite a different kind from Mary's, because *friendly* or *ruthless* lead us to interpret *intelligent* differently (but see N.H. Anderson 1991, for an argument against this point). If a single adjective can influence interpretation so much, then the rich knowledge that people bring to category learning might well have even stronger effects. A dramatic example of knowledge effects on learning was provided by Lesgold et al. (1988). They studied expert and novice radiologists, on the task of interpreting chest X-rays and making diagnoses. There were numerous interpretation differences between the two groups, attributable to their differences in prior knowledge about human anatomy and X-ray technology. For example, the experts were better able to distinguish the appearance of diseased tissue from the appearance of artefacts on the X-ray film. Also, the experts were more likely than the novices to describe a three-dimensional representation or model of the patient rather than simply focus on simple two-dimensional cues such as a shadow on the film.

Closely related to the work of Lesgold et al. on learning about individual cases, there has been some more recent work on learning about categories. Wisniewski & Medin (1991, 1994a) demonstrated influences of prior knowledge on interpretation of category members. In their studies, the subjects observed drawings done by children. They learned about two categories of drawings, such as drawings done by city children versus farm children, or drawings done by creative children versus non-creative children. The category labels were randomly assigned by the experimenters to a particular drawing and often had a dramatic effect on how features of the drawing were interpreted. For example, one circular configuration of lines on a drawing was interpreted as a purse when the picture was assigned to the city category; in other situations this same configuration was interpreted as a pocket. Similarly, the clothing in another drawing was interpreted as either being a farm uniform or a city uniform depending on the category assignment.

The experiments by Wisniewski & Medin (1991, 1994a) were in some ways ideally suited to study influences of knowledge on feature interpretation, because their stimuli were somewhat ambiguous drawings that indeed needed to be interpreted. In contrast, for many experiments in which subjects learn categories, the features are already given in a much less ambiguous way. For example, in a typical experiment, subjects might learn about lists of features that are familiar medical symptoms, such as runny nose and high fever (e.g. Medin & Schaffer 1978). In such experiments, the representation (simple feature lists) is more or less given to the subject. In contrast, in learning about ambiguous drawings, and probably in many real-word concept learning situations, people must build the representations that would be used to describe category members (see also Goldstone 1994, Murphy 1993, Schyns & Murphy 1994).

Facilitation effects

Some effects of prior knowledge are best described as simply being overall facilitation of learning. It seems plausible that learning about certain kinds of category structures might be more or less facilitated depending on the prior knowledge that is accessed, e.g. depending on the kind of category structure that is expected. Medin & Schwanenflugel (1981) distinguished between two kinds of classification structures, *linearly separable* and *nonlinearly separable*. If a pair of categories, A and B, are linearly separable, then by definition it is possible to classify a new stimulus, X, using a simple linear rule. One such linear rule would be to count whether X has more characteristic features of category A or of category B. In contrast, if A and B overlap to the extent that they are nonlinearly separable, then no linear rule will allow perfect discrimination between members of the two categories. Medin &

Schwanenflugel found that people can learn both kinds of category structures, with no great advantage for one kind of category structure over the other. However, Wattenmaker et al. (1986) investigated the influences of background knowledge on learning these two kinds of structures (see also Nakamura 1985). For example, if your prior knowledge leads you to expect linearly separable categories, would that facilitate the learning of a linearly separable structure?

In the Wattenmaker et al. (1986, Experiment 1) study, half of the subjects learned about linearly separable categories of people and half of the subjects learned about non-linearly separable categories. Also, in the Trait conditions, the stimulus dimensions were labelled to promote remindings of personality categories, such as *honest* versus *dishonest*. For example, some subjects saw person descriptions in terms of behaviours that were either honest (e.g. returning a lost wallet) or dishonest (e.g. pretending to enjoy shopping). The subjects were trained repeatedly on category members until they reached a learning criterion. In the Control conditions, the stimuli were composed of unrelated traits, such as one concerning honesty, one concerning cautiousness, and one concerning co-operativeness, which would not promote the retrieval of coherent prior categories. The first main result was that overall, remindings of prior knowledge helped subjects learn the categories faster: people in the Trait conditions performed better than those in the Control conditions. Making the task more meaningful facilitated category learning (see also Murphy & Allopenna 1994). Secondly, subjects especially showed facilitation from prior knowledge when they learned about a linearly-separable category structure. It appeared that people already had simple linear rules for distinguishing between honest and dishonest people by counting up the number of honest and dishonest behaviours. Thus, learning was most efficient when the structure to be learned was compatible with the structure that was expected according to prior knowledge.

In more recent work, Wattenmaker (1995) has investigated whether these knowledge facilitation effects depend on specific category knowledge or on more general knowledge. That is, when people are facilitated in learning about a new category, is this facilitation the result of a close match between specific information in the new category and specific information in a previously known concept? Or is it a result of a general congruence with an abstract structure, such as the linearly separable structure? Wattenmaker compared category learning using stimuli from two different general domains, social categories and object categories. An overall difference between these two domains might suggest that people apply different general knowledge structures in learning about these two kinds of categories. Indeed, Wattenmaker found that overall, people were facilitated in learning about linearly-separable categories in the social domain, and people learned object categories better when they were non-linearly separable. However, this pattern was only evident when the new categories to be learned closely matched previously known concepts. For example, people favoured learning linearly separable structures for a familiar classification such as introverts versus extroverts, but not for unfamiliar social groupings. Thus it appears that the knowledge facilitation effects reported by Wattenmaker (1995) and Wattenmaker et al. (1986) depended on remindings of rather specific knowledge of particular categories.

The question does remain though, how does more general knowledge influence category learning? Even when someone is not reminded of a specific pre-existing concept, can prior knowledge affect learning?

INFLUENCES OF MORE GENERAL KNOWLEDGE

Children's learning of concepts and names

Perhaps the most dramatic example of concept learning is the performance of young children, who can learn up to 15,000 new words for things by age six (Carey 1978). Of course, learning a new word and learning a new concept are not the same, but they are closely related (Clark 1983). For example, a child's knowing the word "dog" and having the concept of *dog* are two different achievements. Knowing a concept might precede learning its name or alternatively, hearing a name for an object might lead to further investigation of the concept (e.g. Waxman et al. 1991). Early concept learning by children appears to be guided by rather general principles or knowledge structures. Given the large number of concepts learned by children and the systematic biases that are apparent in this learning, it is plausible that the children are being influenced by general knowledge rather than by specific knowledge about other categories.

Markman (1989, 1990) suggested, and reviewed evidence for, certain constraints that would guide category learning by children. First, according to the *whole object assumption*, a novel category label is more likely to refer to a whole object than to its parts. Upon hearing a category label such as "dog" for the first time, a child would assume that this label refers to a dog rather than to some part of a dog such as its wagging tail. Secondly, according to the *taxonomic assumption*, learners will tend to use new words as taxonomic category labels rather than as ways to group things by other relations. For example, after a child has learned about his or her first dog, the child would extend this label to other animals that appear to be in the same taxonomic category – other dogs – rather than extending the label to objects that are otherwise associated with the dog. That is, the child would not call the dog's leash a "dog", or call the dog's owner a "dog". Thirdly, the *mutual exclusivity assumption* would provide further guidance in early category learning. In following this assumption, a child would favour associating particular objects with just one category label. Thus, when learning a new category label, the child would look for some object for which he or she does not already know a label. For example, say that a child already knows the word "dog", and sees a dog being pulled on a leash. Upon hearing the word "leash" for the first time, the child might hypothesize that this term refers to the leash rather than to the dog, because the dog already has a known category label.

These three constraints might seem obvious to an adult who has already learned a language. Yet imagine a child trying to learn thousands of category labels without these assumptions (Quine 1960). In a relatively simple situation of a girl walking in a park with a dog on a leash, the category label "dog" might refer to the girl, the park, the dog, the leash, some part of the girl, the park, the dog, or the leash, or some relation between any of these things. It appears that some application of general knowledge to this potentially confusing situation would be extremely helpful and indeed necessary.

Closely related to Markman's whole object assumption is the *shape bias* (see Landau 1994, and Ward 1993, for reviews). The shape bias is another proposed general constraint on the learning of category labels, such that young children would tend to pay attention to overall shape of an object rather than its texture or size. The shape bias is a kind of selective weighting effect, and as such it fits well with the proposals of Keil (1989) and Murphy & Medin (1985) regarding the selective effects of prior knowledge on category learning. In one study demonstrating the shape bias, Landau et al. (1988) taught young children that some object was called a "dax". When asked to find another "dax", the children tended to choose another object with the same shape even if it had a different size or texture. Likewise, the children tended to reject other objects with different shapes, even if they had the same size and texture as the original "dax". Interestingly, young children seem to limit their use of the shape bias to situations in which new category labels are learned. When the Landau et al. (1988) procedure was repeated except without using the "dax" label, the shape bias was reduced or eliminated. In general, it appears that children are guided by the principle that an object's overall shape is a good predictor of its category label, so children especially pay attention to shapes when learning new labels. However, as the articles by Ward (1993) and Landau (1994) show, the patterns of results for the shape bias, and the underlying general knowledge applied by children in learning category labels, are even more complex and sophisticated than the examples here illustrate.

Knowledge of category essences

In addition to general biases such as the taxonomic constraint and the shape bias that would affect children's learning of category labels, it appears that category learning by children and adults is guided by other rich sources of general knowledge. One set of beliefs, referred to as *psychological essentialism* (Medin & Ortony 1989), seems to be wide-ranging in its influence. The main idea of psychological essentialism is that (at least for the biological domain) people act as if things in the world have a true underlying nature that imparts category identity. Furthermore, this essence is thought to be the causal mechanism that generates visible properties. Therefore, surface features provide clues about category membership. This view is known as *psychological* essentialism because it is concerned with people's *assumptions* about how the world is, not how the world truly is.

Keil (1989) has provided evidence that children are guided by essentialist assumptions as they learn about members of natural kind categories such as animals and precious metals. In one study, Keil described to children how an animal might undergo some superficial transformations, such as transforming a racoon by painting a white stripe on its back and surgically inserting a sac that contains a smelly substance. The key question was whether this transformed animal was a racoon or a skunk. Children as young as age seven tended to maintain the identity of the animal as a racoon, even though it had been given characteristic features of a skunk. Keil's explanation was that children's biological knowledge led them to discount these superficial features, and instead selectively pay attention to other, deeper anatomical properties. For example, a racoon that resembles a skunk would give birth to other racoons rather than skunks. In related research, Keil described to children artefacts, such as pipes and coffee pots, that underwent transformations. Here it seemed that an object's function was critical to its category membership, again pointing to general beliefs that constrain categorization. (However, for a critique of this line of research, especially with regard to artefact categories, see Malt 1993.)

To summarize, people, even young children, appear to have rather deep pools of knowledge about biological categories as well as artefact categories, that are applied to learning about particular category members (see also Carey 1985). One fairly general aspect of this knowledge is that certain categories have essences or essential features that are critical for determining category membership. Psychological essentialism has received a great deal of recent attention (also see Gelman et al. 1994, Medin & Heit, in press, for reviews), but other general knowledge about animals, plants, and people also appears to be critical in guiding categorization and category learning. For example, see work by Springer & Belk (1994) on knowledge of contagion in biological categories, work by Coley (1995) on knowledge about biological and psychological properties, and work by Hirschfeld (1995) on knowledge about racial categories.

IMPLICATIONS FOR CATEGORIZATION MODELS

Why develop models of knowledge effects?

Considering these widespread influences of both specific and general knowledge on category learning, it would be desirable to address and even try to explain these effects in terms of models of categorization. After all, any model of category learning that does not address these influences is not a complete account of category learning (Murphy & Medin 1985). In research on categorization, there is a tradition of implementing theoretical ideas as computational or mathematical models. This development of models of categorization has had multiple purposes. For one, a categorization model is a precise statement of an account of categorization that facilitates communication among researchers. A model of category learning that addresses these influences of knowledge would be an explicit and testable statement of theory. Furthermore, modelling provides a reasoning tool; it is often difficult for a researcher to know what some theory will predict until the theory is implemented as a model (Hintzman 1991). Thus, developing a model of some hypothesized categorization process would facilitate its evaluation in terms of how well it accounts for various experimental results. In this way, a model can provide the link between a psychological account of how knowledge influences category learning and the results of experiments such as those reviewed in this chapter.

Despite the promise and appeal of addressing knowledge effects in categorization with computational models, this issue has only recently begun to receive attention. In fact, in 1993, Murphy suggested that most categorization researchers either work on computational models that do not address prior knowledge effects, or they work on issues in categorization that address the richness of people's background knowledge but do not create formal models! Psychological models of categorization have been applied mainly to studies of category learning in isolated contexts (e.g. J. R. Anderson 1991, Estes 1986, Gluck & Bower

1988, Heit 1992, Kruschke 1992, Medin & Schaffer 1978, Nosofsky 1988, Nosofsky et al. 1994). Typically in these studies, subjects learned isolated categories that were intended by the experimenter to be as unrelated as possible to prior knowledge (e.g. categories of geometric figures or fictional diseases). Of course, categorization researchers have been interested in other important issues in addition to influences of background knowledge, and the strategy of teaching subjects isolated categories would have some value in allowing a researcher to focus on other variables. Therefore, the task of addressing the widespread influences of knowledge on category learning is a new and important challenge for categorization models.

Exemplar models

The *integration* model (Heit 1994) is an exemplar model of categorization (Medin & Schaffer 1978) that addresses some effects of prior knowledge. According to exemplar models, a decision whether to categorize some object X as a member of category A depends on the similarity of X to retrieved exemplars for category A. To the extent that X is similar to category A exemplars rather than to exemplars of alternative categories, X will be classified as an A. The novel assumption of the integration model is that two kinds of exemplars influence judgement of whether some stimulus belongs in a category: exemplars of that category as well as *prior examples* from other related categories. Prior examples are memories from other contexts; in many situations the prior examples would simply be observed members of other categories (Johnson et al. 1993). For example, imagine that you move to a new city and you are looking for friends to join you in jogging. In effect, you are trying to learn about a new category: joggers in this city. Say that you have already met a few joggers in the new city, then you meet a new person and you want to predict whether this person is a jogger. To make this evaluation, you would sum up two sources of evidence, the similarity of the new person to prior examples of joggers from other cities and the similarity of the new person to actual joggers you have observed in the new city.

For several experiments simulating this experience of category learning in a new context, Heit (1994, 1995) found that the integration model gave a good qualitative and quantitative account. Figure 1.1 shows the results of one experiment in which subjects learned about new categories and made judgements about whether some description X belongs in category A. The data points in each graph refer to subjects' average judgements in various conditions. The congruent points refer to test questions that are congruent with prior knowledge, e.g. "How likely is someone with expensive running shoes to be a jogger?" The incongruent points refer to test questions that involve an incongruent pairing, such as "How likely is someone who attends many parties to be shy?" The other variable in the experiment was the proportion of times X actually appeared in category A, e.g. the proportion of people with expensive running shoes who were joggers. The lines in each graph refer to the predictions of the integration model. Note the close correspondence between the data points and the model predictions. As predicted by the integration model, people were influenced by prior knowledge, as indicated by the difference between the congruent and incongruent lines, and they were influenced by what they actually observed, as indicated by the positive slopes of these lines. Also, these two influences appear to combine independently, as evidenced by the parallel pattern of lines. This independence is consistent with the integration model's assumption that people sum up evidence derived from prior knowledge and evidence derived from actual observations.

In addition to the integration of prior examples and observed examples, Heit (1994) developed exemplar models of other possible processes by which prior knowledge might affect category learning. First, prior knowledge may lead to selective weighting of category members so observations that fit prior knowledge are remembered best.

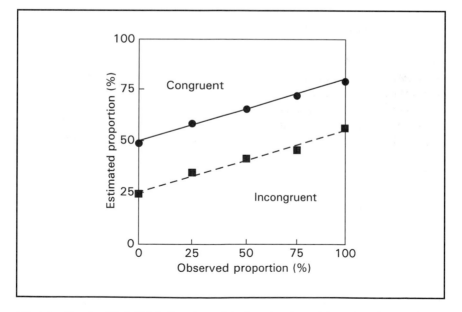

FIG. 1.1.   Results of Heit (1994), Experiment 2, indicated as data points, and predictions of the integration model, indicated as lines.   Reprinted by permission.

For example, you might be more successful at learning about joggers who own expensive running shoes than about joggers who do not. Secondly, prior knowledge may have a distortion effect; for example, a jogger without expensive running shoes might be misinterpreted as a jogger with expensive running shoes or even as a non-jogger. Although these additional processes seem plausible, the results of Heit (1994) could be explained without either of them, i.e. by the integration model alone.

Rule-based models

An alternative scheme for developing models of categorization uses rule-based representations (e.g. Mooney 1993, Nosofsky et al. 1994, Pazzani 1991). These models assume that a decision whether some object X belongs to a particular category A depends on whether X satisfies the conditions of a rule defining category A. Using a complex data base of rules (e.g. Mooney 1993, Pazzani 1991) and probabilistic responding (e.g. Nosofsky et al. 1994) would allow for rule-based models to account for a variety of interesting results in categorization. Furthermore, these rule-based models can readily be extended to address prior knowledge effects. Just as the integration model (which is an exemplar model) assumes that prior knowledge takes the form of prior examples, it would be natural for rule-based models to assume that prior knowledge takes the form of pre-existing rules. For example, Mooney's (1993) *IOU* model of categorization can learn the concept of *cup* after being presented with just a single example of a cup. This cup might be green, owned by Juliana, lightweight, with a flat bottom, and with a handle. Certain of these features, regarding weight, the cup's bottom, and the cup's handle, are critical to the cup category. Mooney's model devotes special attention to these features because they are explainable in terms of pre-existing rules concerning liftability, stability, and graspability. This technique, known as *explanation-based learning*, is a quite powerful way to apply prior knowledge to new category members (see Mooney 1993, and Wisniewski & Medin 1994b, for more extensive reviews of explanation-based learning and for further applications to psychological data).

Pazzani (1991) also developed a rule-based model, known as the *POST HOC* model, that addresses prior knowledge effects. This model, like Mooney's IOU model, begins learning about a new category by accessing rules embodying prior knowledge. These rules may be incorporated into representations of a new category, and in addition, the POST HOC model selectively attends to features that seem especially relevant according to previous knowledge. For example, to account for Pazzani's (1991) experimental results on learning categories of balloons, the POST HOC model would assume that subjects access relevant rules, such as that stretched balloons are more elastic and thus easier to inflate. Then, to learn about the new category members, the model would assume that subjects pay greater attention to goal-relevant features, such as stretching, rather than irrelevant features such as the colour of the balloon. This rule-based model successfully predicted Pazzani's results in term of relative difficulty of the various experimental conditions.

Connectionist models

Finally, it is possible to extend connectionist, or neural network, models of categorization (e.g. Gluck & Bower 1988, Kruschke 1992, Shanks 1991) to address the influences of previous knowledge. (In connectionist models, category learning entails learning a set of associations within a network of nodes. A categorization decision would be performed by assessing which output nodes would be activated after a pattern of inputs is presented to the network.) For example, Choi et al. (1993) have explored connectionist models by assuming that at the beginning of learning, certain connections between inputs and outputs have positive or negative strengths. In effect, a connectionist network would have a head start towards learning, as if the network had already been trained on related stimuli. Choi et al. applied this idea to the result that people tend to learning disjunctively-defined concepts more readily than conjunctively-defined concepts (e.g. Salatas & Bourne 1974). That is, it is generally easier to learn a concept defined in terms of (feature 1 or feature 2 or feature 3. . .) rather than a concept defined in terms of (feature 1 and feature 2 and feature 3. . .). Choi et al. assumed that people begin category-learning tasks with initial hypotheses in mind, e.g. to favour disjunctive rules over conjunctive rules. In terms of connectionist models, these hypotheses could be implemented with negative (or inhibitory) links between nodes corresponding to feature conjunctions and nodes corresponding to category labels. Choi et al. evaluated a few different variants of connectionist models, and were most successful in incorporating prior knowledge into Kruschke's (1992) *ALCOVE* model, which is a hybrid connectionist-exemplar model.

Also, Kruschke (1993) suggested that his *ALCOVE* model could account for prior knowledge effects by varying the attentional strengths on different dimensions at the beginning of learning. This suggestion would be an implementation of selective weighting. Note that this proposal differs from the method applied by Choi et al. (1993), which varied the initial connection strengths between nodes in a network rather than varying selective attention. It would be valuable to investigate Kruschke's suggestion further, because one of the strengths of the *ALCOVE* model is that it can vary attention dynamically over the course of learning. Dynamic attention would correspond to learners having initial hypotheses about which dimensions are relevant to categorization, then adjusting attention as category members are observed (see also Billman & Heit 1988).

Conclusions from modelling efforts

Despite the differences between these exemplar-based, rule-based, and connectionist approaches to modelling the effects of knowledge on concept learning, several themes emerge clearly. Even though the representational details of the models differ, each modelling effort includes two basic kinds of processes. First, in what may be called an *integration* or *anchor-and-adjust* process, the model begins with an initial representation for a new category, then revises this representation as additional information is observed. For example, the connectionist model of Choi et al. (1993) begins a learning task with certain network connections already set with negative or positive values. Then these connections are updated during learning. Secondly, in a *selective weighting* process, the model is directed to pay attention to certain observations or features of observations that seem especially relevant to the task. For example, Pazzani's (1991) rule-based model allocated more resources to learning about whether or not a balloon was stretched compared to whether the balloon was yellow or purple.

Can these categorization models (Choi et al. 1993, Heit 1994, Mooney 1993, Pazzani 1991) address the other effects of prior knowledge, besides integration and weighting effects? These models can also address knowledge facilitation effects, in which it is easier to learn about a new category to the extent that it fits with previous beliefs (e.g. Murphy & Allopenna 1994, Wattenmaker et al. 1986, Wattenmaker 1995). For example, Murphy & Allopenna found that it was easier for people to learn about new categories of vehicles than to learn categories defined in terms of unrelated or conflicting characteristics (e.g. has thick walls, keeps fish as pets, made in Africa, and has a barbed tail). It makes sense that people learning about new vehicles could use previous knowledge about vehicles as a starting point (an integration process) as well as more easily focus on relevant information (a selective weighting process). In contrast, these processes would not help in learning about nonsensical or completely unfamiliar categories. More generally, integration and selective weighting processes are two possible underlying explanations for why people might show knowledge-related facilitation in learning about categories (for additional possible explanations, see Murphy & Allopenna 1994).

Therefore, categorization models with these integration and selective weighting processing assumptions can address three of the basic effects of specific knowledge on learning: integration effects, selective weighting effects, and facilitation effects. That is, when the models are provided with suitable information about what specific facts or prior knowledge would influence the learning of a particular new category, the models can reproduce the general patterns of human performance in category learning. This is a significant feat, considering that most formal models of categorization, without assumptions about integration and weighting, do not address the influences of prior knowledge at all. However, so far these models are incomplete in that the relevant prior knowledge must be specified by the modeller. That is, the models address the processes by which prior knowledge and new observations would be combined, but they do not address the processes by which a learner would determine which prior knowledge is relevant. Such processes might be called *knowledge selection* processes.

For example, Heit (1994) assumed that when subjects learned about joggers in a new city, their prior knowledge consisted of prior examples of joggers from other places. This assumption may be straightforward in the context of a simple laboratory experiment, but knowledge selection processes would necessarily be more complicated in the real world. Imagine that you meet a group of people who are all either British, American, or Belgian, with various occupations and hobbies. What sorts of prior examples or prior knowledge would you use to guide learning about this group? The possibilities seem endless. As another example, imagine that you are learning about a new kind of device that cleans up roadside rubbish with a suction hose, and you have no previous experience with this sort of device (Wisniewski 1995). What prior knowledge would be used here? Note that finding the relevant prior knowledge would be critical for both integration and selective weighting. It appears that assembling the knowledge that is relevant to learning a new concept may require rather sophisticated reasoning processes, in addition to simply retrieving observations from memory. These reasoning processes might include conceptual combination (Hampton, this volume; Murphy 1993, Rips 1995) as well as mechanisms for imagining or imaging possible category members (Ward 1994). A further complexity is that the use of background knowledge and observations might alternate, so that initial beliefs might guide early category learning, which would then lead to the retrieval and perhaps even revision of additional background knowledge. In the terminology of Wisniewski & Medin (1991, 1994b), knowledge and learning would be *tightly coupled* (see Heit 1994, for additional evidence). In principle, these additional processes could be implemented in an even more complete model of categorization, but for the most part this work has not yet been performed.

The final effect of specific knowledge described in this chapter is *feature interpretation* effects, in which the very features that are used to represent category members are themselves learned (e.g. Lesgold et al. 1988, Wisniewski & Medin 1994b). As pointed out by Murphy (1993) and Wisniewski & Medin (1994b), one current limitation of most current models of categorization is that they operate with a fixed, pre-specified representational system. In principle, however, feature learning might be treated as another form of concept learning. Indeed, developing techniques for learning features has been an active area in artificial intelligence research, see Wisniewski & Medin 1994a for a review). Likewise, researchers who develop connectionist models of learning have been concerned with how a model might form internal representations (e.g. Sejnowski & Rosenberg 1985) or develop feature detectors (e.g. Rumelhart & Zipser 1986). Thus, there is good reason to hope that further progress on this issue will be made in the near future.

In contrast to this favourable picture of how current models of categorization can and might address influences of specific knowledge, the day that such models will address effects of more general knowledge seems further off. Consider the sophisticated knowledge representations and processes that must be involved in the taxonomic constraint (Markman 1989), the shape bias (Landau 1994), or psychological essentialism (Medin & Ortony 1989). The knowledge that is relevant to these issues would seem to consist of a richly-connected set of abstract beliefs about categories in general, for example beliefs about relations between the shape of an object and its internal parts. It seems plausible that the simple processes used in explaining effects of specific knowledge (integration and weighting processes) would have some role in explaining the influences of more general knowledge. For example, the shape bias involves selectively paying attention to the contour of an object. However, such simple processes are only part of the story to be told. It remains an open question how much further development will be required to address the effects of more general knowledge with computational models. An optimistic conjecture might be that categorization models will be able to address influences of general knowledge in the same manner as influences of specific knowledge, once representational issues for describing general and specific knowledge are solved. However, even these representational issues are not easy problems.

To return to the point at the beginning of this chapter, it is clear that knowledge about categories is complex and "deeply intertwingled". It is important to keep in mind that although categorization models can presently explain some of the basic phenomena regarding influences of knowledge on concept learning, this is a complex problem that is not going to be solved entirely anytime soon. Yet, these initial, and certainly incomplete, models of knowledge effects on categorization still serve some of the important purposes of computational modelling. That is, these models are explicit implementations of accounts of how background knowledge shapes category learning, allowing these accounts to be compared and applied to psychological data.

RELATIONS TO INDUCTIVE REASONING

Now that the influences of prior knowledge on category learning have been described in some detail, the next two sections will describe research on knowledge effects in two areas of cognitive psychology that are related to category learning: reasoning and memory. After a person has learned about some category, it is natural to ask what this person will do with the category. One important function that categorization serves is to allow inductive inferences or predictions about additional features (J. R. Anderson 1991, Billman & Heit 1988, Estes 1994, Heit 1992, Ross & Murphy, 1996). For example, once you know that someone belongs to the category *salesperson*, you may predict that this person will try to sell you something.

Inductive reasoning is typically studied in the laboratory by presenting subjects with inductive arguments to be evaluated, such as:

Robins are susceptible to a certain disease
_____
How likely is it that ostriches are susceptible to this disease?

Research by Rips (1975) and Osherson et al. (1990) has shown that two kinds of information are critical to inductive reasoning. First, inferences will be stronger to the extent that the premise category (e.g. robin) and the conclusion category (e.g. ostrich) are similar. Inferences between similar categories (e.g. robins and sparrows) are stronger than inferences between less similar categories (e.g. robins and ostriches). Secondly, general knowledge about relations to other categories also has influences. One such influence is that inferences will be stronger to the extent that the premise category is typical of its superordinate category (Rips 1975, Osherson et al. 1990). For example, the knowledge that robins are typical members of the bird category lends strength to inferences from robins to ostriches. On the other hand, if subjects were asked "Given that ostriches are susceptible to a certain disease, how likely is it that robins are susceptible to this disease?" inferences would be relatively weak, because the premise category, ostrich, is not typical of the bird category. (Also see Shipley 1993, for a further analysis of these phenomena and a discussion of their relation to Goodman's 1955, work on overhypotheses.)

Another kind of knowledge about categories that affects inductive reasoning is knowledge about variability. Nisbett et al. (1983) tested subjects on inductive statements of the following form: "Given that you observe that one member of category A has property P, what percentage of the members of category A have property P?" Nisbett et al. found that the strength of inferences was affected by knowledge of how variable this property would be in the category. For example, given that one member of a certain tribe of people is obese, adults subjects estimated that less than 40 per cent of the members of the tribe are obese. But given that one tribe member has a certain colour of skin, subjects concluded that over 90 per cent of the other tribe members would have the same property. Nisbett et al. showed that people make stronger inferences about less variable properties (e.g. skin colour) than about more variable properties (e.g. obesity) for a particular category.

Selective weighting effects, as a result of background knowledge, are also evident in inductive reasoning. Heit & Rubinstein (1994) have found that when people evaluate inductive arguments, they tend to focus on certain features of the categories, depending on what property is being considered in the argument. For example, consider the argument:

Sparrows travel shorter distances in extreme heat

How likely is it that
bats travel shorter distances in extreme heat?

The behavioural property being considered, travelling shorter distances in extreme heat, would lead subjects to compare sparrows and bats in terms of other behavioural features. Because sparrows and bats are similar in terms of flying, this argument was considered fairly strong. On the other hand, consider the argument:

Sparrows have livers with two chambers

How likely is it that
bats have livers with two chambers?

Here, the anatomical property being considered, having a two-chambered liver, would lead subjects to focus on other anatomical properties. Because of the anatomical dissimilarities between sparrows and bats (e.g. one is a bird and one is a mammal), this argument was considered relatively weak. In addition to these results from

Heit & Rubinstein, evidence for selective weighting effects in inductive reasoning has been provided by Gelman & Markman (1986), and Springer (1992). For additional evidence of the influences of knowledge about properties on induction, see Sloman (1994).

Models of inductive reasoning

The category-based induction (CBI) model (Osherson et al. 1990, 1991) is a computational model of induction that addresses some of the influences of categorical knowledge. This model may be applied to complex inductive arguments with multiple premises, such as:

> Category A1 has property P
> Category A2 has property P
> Category A3 has property P
> _____
> How likely is it that
> Category B has property P?

According to the CBI model, two factors influence how people evaluate the inductive soundness of such inferences. First, inferences will be stronger to the extent that the premise categories (A1, A2, . . .) are similar to the conclusion category (B). The second factor in the CBI model is the coverage of the premise, that is the similarity between the category or categories in the premise and members of the superordinate category that encompasses the categories in the premise and conclusion. A few examples should make the idea of coverage clear. Consider again an inductive inference from robin to ostrich. The most specific superordinate category that includes robins and ostriches is *bird*. Now, robin is fairly similar to other members of the category *bird*. Thus, if robins have some property P, it is plausible that all birds, including ostriches, have property P. In the CBI model, the two sources of evaluating inferences, similarity and coverage, are just added together. Category members that are atypical do not contribute much to coverage, for example, ostrich as a premise category would provide little coverage for the superordinate category *bird*. The CBI model also provides an elegant way to evaluate the coverage of arguments with multiple premises. For example, given the premises that both robins and penguins have property P, it seems likely that all birds have property P, because robins and penguins are quite diverse members of the superordinate, birds. On the other hand, the premises that robins and sparrows have some property does not lend as much support to the belief that all birds have the property, because robins and sparrows do not cover the superordinate category birds much better than just robins alone.

The CBI model provides a successful account of several influences of categorical knowledge on inductive reasoning, especially how knowledge about superordinate categories affects reasoning (see Osherson et al. 1990, 1991, for reviews). However, the CBI model does not address the other knowledge effects described here, such as selective weighting effects (e.g. Gelman & Markman 1986, Heit & Rubinstein 1994) or effects of knowledge about variability (Nisbett et al. 1983). In principle, it would be possible to add a selective weighting component to the CBI model, just as it is possible to add selective weighting to categorization models (e.g. Pazzani 1991). That is, it would be possible to have the CBI model focus on different category features depending on which property is being inferred, so that it could begin to address the results indicating selective weighting. However, it might well take a complex reasoning process to figure out which features are relevant to inferring various properties, e.g. which features are relevant to inferring whether an animal travels shorter distances in extreme heat. As mentioned earlier, a challenge for computational models of categorization is to determine which prior knowledge is relevant to a particular situation. Likewise, future computational models of induction will be faced with the challenge of assembling the prior knowledge that is relevant to guiding an inference.

RELATIONS TO MEMORY

There is a strong affinity between research on categorization and research on memory, because categorization and memory are highly interdependent (or "intertwingled") facets of cognition. Two parallels between categorization research and memory research will be drawn here. First, studies of the influences of prior knowledge on category learning are closely related to research on the impact of schemas and stereotypes on memory. Secondly, there are close connections between categorization models and memory models, suggesting that the task of developing categorization models that address knowledge effects is part of a larger enterprise in cognitive modelling.

Influences of knowledge on memory

Research on memory has largely followed two traditions. In the tradition of Ebbinghaus (1885/1964), researchers have focused on precise quantitative relations among various factors that affect memory and various memory tasks (e.g. the effect of amount of study on free recall performance, Underwood 1970). This research tradition has typically used simple verbal stimuli (e.g. nonsense syllables or concrete nouns) with the intent of isolating certain aspects of memory and minimizing the influences of the subject's prior knowledge. Secondly, in the tradition of Bartlett (1932), researchers have focused on the richness of human knowledge and the interesting influences of knowledge on new learning (see Johnson & Sherman 1990, for a review). (Note the similarity to the description of two traditions of research in categorization by Murphy 1993.) To some extent, there may be a trade-off between working in the first tradition and working in the second tradition, but there is plenty of research that draws from both (e.g. Collins & Quillian 1969, Graesser 1981, Smith & Zarate 1992).

As an illustration of work in the second tradition, consider the classic example from Carmichael et al. (1932) in Figure 1.2. When subjects were shown the drawing in Figure 1.2a, their memories of this picture were influenced by their background knowledge. If the picture was originally labelled as glasses, then subjects tended to recall something like Figure 1.2b: their knowledge of glasses influenced their specific memories of the picture. If the picture was originally labelled as a barbell, then subjects tended to recall something like Figure 1.2c. Note that this result is quite like the feature interpretation phenomena for category learning described by Wisniewski & Medin (1991, 1994b), in terms of ambiguous figures being influenced by labelling. Another classic example of the influence of schemas, or general knowledge structures, on memory was provided by Bransford & Johnson (1972). In this study, subjects read a rather abstract paragraph concerning a procedure for arranging items into different groups, going to the proper facilities, etc. Their later recall memory for this passage was poor, unless they had also been told that the passage describes washing clothes. In other words, the subjects' general knowledge about doing laundry facilitated memory for this text. Note the resemblance between this result and the knowledge facilitation

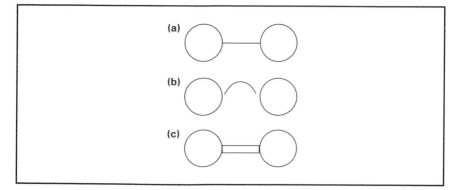

FIG. 1.2.   Illustration of schematic effects on memory, adapted from Carmichael et al. (1932).

results in category learning (e.g. Murphy & Allopenna 1994, Wattenmaker et al. 1986, Wattenmaker 1995).

Researchers in social psychology have also been concerned with influences of knowledge on learning, in particular the influences of social stereotypes on what is remembered about individual people. For example, in a study of the effects of developing gender stereotypes on memory, Stangor & Ruble (1989) showed children television commercials that were either congruent with their stereotypes (e.g. girls playing with toy dolls) or incongruent with their stereotypes (e.g. girls playing with toy trucks). Stangor & Ruble found that the congruent commercials were recalled better. More generally, it appears that what we remember about the people we meet depends on much more than just our direct observations of these people; the influences of social group stereotypes are widespread (see Srull & Wyer 1989, and Stangor & McMillan 1992, for reviews).

Given these similarities between memory phenomena and categorization phenomena, future research on the influences of knowledge on concept learning may be well-informed by considering the related work in memory. For example, the processes proposed in this chapter as influencing category learning have been discussed extensively by theorists in the area of memory as well. Selective weighting influences of knowledge on memory have been emphasized by Alba & Hasher (1983), who discussed how schematic knowledge would operate as a filter either at encoding or retrieval. Similarly, Smith & Zarate (1992) have discussed how a person's goals, recent experiences, and immediate environment would affect selective attention to different social dimensions such as gender, age, ethnicity, or race. In addition to the classic work by Asch (1946) on processes of interpretation and distortion, Taylor & Crocker (1978) have discussed how general knowledge may be used to fill in missing featural information. Finally, integration processes in person memory have been proposed by N. H. Anderson (1991) and Brewer & Nakamura (1984). Work on these topics by memory researchers can certainly guide research on the corresponding issues in categorization. Likewise, categorization research can influence work on memory and social cognition. For example, Rothbart & Taylor (1992) discuss how conceptual knowledge about psychological essentialism and mutual exclusivity might apply to stereotypes and social categories.

Memory models and categorization models
Models of categorization, ideally, will not be isolated accounts of a particular task or experiment but instead will dovetail with other theoretical accounts of cognitive activities such as memory and

reasoning. One example of the potential synergy between categorization models and computational models of memory is the compatibility between exemplar models of categorization and multiple-trace models of memory (Gillund & Shiffrin 1984, Hintzman 1986, 1988). Multiple-trace models assume that a memory judgement, such as a recognition decision, depends on evaluating the total similarity of a test item to memory traces of particular stimuli (see Jones & Heit 1993 for a review). Likewise, exemplar models assume that a decision whether to place a test item in one category or another depends on evaluating the similarity of the test item to memory traces for members of each category. Heit (1993) applied the exemplar models of categorization in Heit (1994) to a set of experiments on stereotype effects on recognition memory (Stangor & McMillan 1992). The simulations in Heit (1993, 1994) provided converging evidence that integration processes can explain a variety of results concerning the influences of prior knowledge on memory as well as categorization. (For a related example of applying exemplar models to categorization and memory tasks, see Smith & Zarate 1992.) Note that such a synergy between categorization models and memory models need not be limited to the common framework of exemplar models and multiple-trace models. For example, connectionist modelling provides another framework for developing general models of categorization and memory.

CONCLUSION

In sum, the interrelated cognitive abilities of category learning, inductive reasoning, and memory are significantly guided by people's background knowledge, including both specific knowledge and more general principles. To an encouraging extent, these influences can be captured by computational models. Yet at the same time these modelling efforts highlight their own incompleteness, in terms of what needs to be explained even further.

The variety of influences of knowledge reviewed in this chapter are if anything an underestimate of the "intertwingled" nature of knowledge and concepts. Theoretical accounts of categorization, whether or not they are in the form of computational models, face a significant challenge in accounting for these influences. Although it has been traditional (e.g. Smith & Medin 1981) to describe accounts of categorization in terms of pure representational formats (exemplar models, prototype models, rule-based models, etc.), it appears that more complex conceptions of representation may be required. These basic forms of representation may well serve as a starting point for future work. In the future, it seems likely that an important question in categorization research will be what sort of complex, multi-modal representational scheme can be used to describe the rich body of conceptual knowledge that is critical to learning. Such a scheme would need to account for knowledge of relations among categories, and knowledge at multiple levels of abstraction. People's knowledge about categories might well include many forms of information such as exemplars, images, and rules and other abstractions (Barsalou 1993, Graesser et al. 1993, Malt 1993). The problem of developing more sophisticated forms of conceptual representation may eventually overshadow comparisons between pure forms of representations, such as experiments intended to address whether exemplar models are better than prototype models.

Although theorists such as Anderson (1978) and Barsalou (1990) have noted that models of cognition must address both representation and processing, in categorization research representational issues have perhaps received more emphasis than processing issues (e.g. see reviews by Komatsu 1992, Medin & Heit, in press; Smith & Medin 1981). In addressing the topic of how previous knowledge guides the learning of new concepts, as well as performing category-based inductive inferences, processing issues are fundamental. The critical questions concern what are the processes by which people assemble relevant knowledge, form the initial representations for new categories, selectively attend to important information, and interpret the category members they observe in light of prior knowledge. It is notable that categorization models with three different representational frameworks (exemplar, rule-based, and connectionist models) are each able to make progress towards addressing knowledge effects by adopting similar sets of processing assumptions. Indeed, these processing assumptions appear more important for fitting various experimental results than the particular representational assumptions of each model.

Another way of going beyond issues of representation to distil highly general principles is to consider various cognitive activities at the computational level (Marr 1982), that is, to consider what computational problems are being solved and at an abstract level how they are being solved. One framework for describing computational-level problems and solutions is provided by Bayesian statistical theory (Edwards et al. 1963, Raiffa & Schlaifer 1961). It is assumed in Bayesian theory that to learn about some new part of the environment (e.g. a novel category or novel property), one begins with an initial estimate based on previous knowledge, then revises this information as new information is encountered. At a very general level, this description can be applied to influences of prior knowledge on concept learning, induction, and memory. We seem to assume initially that new categories will be like old categories, novel properties in inductive arguments will be like familiar properties, and new experiences to be stored in memory will resemble our previous memories. Perhaps future accounts of categorization, inductive reasoning, and memory will receive further guidance from Bayesian statistics (for some examples of Bayesian accounts of cognitive activities, see J. R. Anderson 1990, 1991, Oaksford & Chater 1994).

Although many other issues in categorization will, of course, continue to be important, it is easy to be optimistic about future research on knowledge and concept learning. There have been a large number of recent empirical discoveries and the development of formal models is also beginning to take off. In addition, the importance of prior knowledge in related areas of cognitive psychology, reasoning and memory, is suggestive of the centrality of this issue. It is not possible to know where this line of categorization research will lead, but it appears that it is heading in a promising direction.

REFERENCES

Alba, J. W. & L. Hasher 1983. Is memory schematic? *Psychological Bulletin* **93**, 203–231.

Anderson, J. R. 1978. Arguments concerning representations for mental imagery. *Psychological Review* **85**, 249–77.

Anderson, J. R. 1990. The adaptive character of thought. Hillsdale, New Jersey: Erlbaum.

Anderson, J. R. 1991. The adaptive nature of human categorization. *Psychological Review* **98**, 409–429.

Anderson, N. H. 1991. Stereotype theory. In *Contributions to information integration theory*, vol. ii: *Social*, N. H. Anderson (ed.), 183–240. Hillsdale, New Jersey: Erlbaum.

Asch, S. E. 1946. Forming impressions of personality. *Journal of Abnormal and Social Psychology* **41**, 258–90.

Barsalou, L. W. 1990. On the indistinguishability of exemplar memory and abstraction in memory representation. In *Advances in social cognition*, T. K. Srull & R. S. Wyer (eds), 61–88. Hillsdale, New Jersey: Erlbaum.

Barsalou, L. W. 1993. Structure, flexibility, and linguistic vagary in concepts: Manifestations of a compositional system of perceptual systems. In *Theories of memory*, A. C. Collins, S. E. Gathercole, M. A. Conway (eds), 29–101. London: Erlbaum.

Bartlett, F. C. 1932. *Remembering: a study in experimental and social psychology*. Cambridge: Cambridge University Press.

Billman, D. & E. Heit 1988. Observational learning without feedback: A simulation of an adaptive method. *Cognitive Science* **12**, 587–625.

Bransford, J. D. & M. K. Johnson 1972. Contextual prerequisites for understanding: Some investigations of comprehension and recall. *Journal of Verbal Learning and Verbal Behavior* **11**, 717–26.

Brewer, W. F. & G. V. Nakamura 1984. The nature and functions of schemas. In *Handbook of social cognition*, R. S. Wyer & T. K. Srull (eds), 119–60. Hillsdale, New Jersey: Erlbaum.

Carey, S. 1978. The child as word learner. In *Linguistic theory and psychological reality*, M. Halle, J. Bresnan, & G. Miller (eds), 264–293. Cambridge, Mass.: MIT Press.

Carey, S. 1985. *Conceptual change in childhood*. Cambridge, Mass.: Bradford Books.

Carmichael, L., H. P. Hogan, & A. A. Walter 1932. An experimental study of the effect of language on the reproduction of visually perceived form. *Journal of Experimental Psychology* **15**, 73–86.

Choi, S., M. A. McDaniel, & J. R. Busemeyer 1993. Incorporating prior biases in network models of conceptual rule learning. *Memory and Cognition* **21**, 413–23.

Clark, E. V. 1983. Meanings and concepts. In *Handbook of child psychology*, P. H. Mussen (ed.), 787–840. New York: John Wiley.

Coley, J. D. 1995. Emerging differentiation of folkbiology and folkpsychology. *Child Development* **66**, 1856–74.

Collins, A. M. & M. R. Quillian 1969. Retrieval time from semantic memory. *Journal of Verbal Learning and Verbal Behavior* **8**, 240–47.

Ebbinghaus, H. 1885/1964. *A contribution to experimental psychology*. New York: Dover.

Edwards, W., H. Lindman, & L. J. Savage 1963. Bayesian statistical inference for psychological research. *Psychological Review* **70**, 193–242.

Estes, W. K. 1986. Array models for category learning. *Cognitive Psychology* **18**, 500–549.

Estes, W. K. 1994. *Classification and cognition*. New York: Oxford University Press.

Gelman, S. A., J. D. Coley, & G. M. Gottfried 1994. Essentialist beliefs in children: The acquisition of concepts and theories. In *Mapping the mind*, L. A. Hirschfeld & S. A. Gelman (eds), 341–67. Cambridge: Cambridge University Press.

Gelman, S. A. & E. M. Markman 1986. Categories and induction in young children. *Cognition* **23**, 183–209.

Gillund, G. & R. M. Shiffrin 1984. A retrieval model for both recognition and recall. *Psychological Review* **91**, 1–67.

Gluck, M. A. & G. H. Bower 1988. From conditioning to category learning: An adaptive network model. *Journal of Experimental Psychology: General* **117**, 227–47.

Goldstone, R. L. 1994. Influences of categorization on perceptual discrimination. *Journal of Experimental Psychology: General* **123**, 178–200.

Goodman, N. 1955. *Fact, fiction, and forecast*. Cambridge, Mass.: Harvard University Press.

Graesser, A. C. 1981. *Prose comprehension beyond the word*. New York: Springer.

Graesser, A. C., M. C. Langston, W. B. Baggett 1993. Exploring information about concepts by asking questions. In *The psychology of learning and motivation: categorization by humans and machines*, G. V. Nakamura, R. Taraban, D. L. Medin (eds), 411–36. San Diego: Academic Press.

Hampton, J. A. 1993. Prototype models of concept representation. In *Categories and concepts: theoretical views and inductive data analysis*, I. Van Mechlen, J. Hampton, R. Michalski, P. Theuns (eds), 67–88. San Diego: Academic Press.

Hayes, B. K. & J. E. Taplin 1992. Developmental changes in categorization processes: Knowledge and similarity-based models of categorization. *Journal of Experimental Child Psychology* **54**, 188–212.

Hayes, B. K. & J. E. Taplin 1995. Similarity-based and knowledge-based process in category learning. *European Journal of Cognitive Psychology* **7**, 383–410.

Heit, E. 1992. Categorization using chains of examples. *Cognitive Psychology* **24**, 341–80.

Heit, E. 1993. Modeling the effects of expectations on recognition memory. *Psychological Science* **4**, 244–52.

Heit, E. 1994. Models of the effects of prior knowledge on category learning. *Journal of Experimental Psychology: Learning, Memory, and Cognition* **20**, 1264–282.

Heit, E. 1995. Belief revision in models of category learning. In *Proceedings of the Seventeenth Annual Conference of the Cognitive Science Society*, Pittsburgh, 176–181. Hillsdale, New Jersey: Erlbaum.

Heit, E. & J.Rubinstein 1994. Similarity and property effects in inductive reasoning. *Journal of Experimental Psychology: Learning, Memory, and Cognition* **20**, 411–22.

Hintzman, D. L. 1986. "Schema abstraction" in a multiple-trace memory model. *Psychological Review* **93**, 411–28.

Hintzman, D. L. 1988. Judgments of frequency and recognition memory in a multiple-trace memory model. *Psychological Review* **95**, 528–51.

Hintzman, D. L. 1991. Why are formal models useful in psychology? In *Relating theory and data: Essays on human memory in honor of Bennet*, B. Murdock, W. E. Hockley, S. Lewandowsky (eds), 39–56. Hillsdale, New Jersey: Erlbaum.

Hirschfeld, L. A. 1995. Do children have a theory of race? *Cognition* **54**, 209–252.

Johnson, M. K., S. Hashtroudi, D. S. Lindsay 1993. Source monitoring. *Psychological Bulletin* **114**, 3–28.

Johnson, M. K. & S. J. Sherman 1990. Constructing and reconstructing the past and the future in the present. In *Handbook of motivation and social cognition: Foundations of social behaviour*, E. T. Higgins & R. M. Sorrentino (eds), 482–526. New York: Guilford Press.

Jones, C. M. & E. Heit 1993. An evaluation of the total similarity principle: Effects of similarity on frequency judgements. *Journal of Experimental Psychology: Learning, Memory, and Cognition* **19**, 799–812.

Keil, F. C. 1989. *Concepts, kinds, and cognitive development*. Cambridge, Mass.: MIT Press.

Keleman, D. & P. Bloom 1994. Domain-specific knowledge in simple categorization tasks. *Psychonomic Bulletin and Review* **1**, 390–95.

Komatsu, L. K. 1992. Recent views of conceptual structure. *Psychological Bulletin* **112**, 500–526.

Kruschke, J. K. 1992. *ALCOVE*: An exemplar-based connectionist model of category learning. *Psychological Review* **99**, 22–44.

Kruschke, J. K. 1993. Three principles for models of category learning. In *The psychology of learning and motivation: categorization by humans and machines*, G. V. Nakamura, R. Taraban, D. L. Medin (eds), 283–326. San Diego: Academic Press.

Landau, B. 1994. Object shape, object name, and object kind: representation and development. In *The psychology of learning and motivation* (vol. 31), D. L. Medin (ed.), 253–304. San Diego: Academic Press.

Landau, B., L. Smith, S. Jones 1988. The importance of shape in early lexical learning. *Cognitive Development* **3**, 299–321.

Lesgold, A., H. Rubinson, P. Feltovich, R. Glaser, D. Klopfer, Y. Wang 1988. Expertise in a complex skill: Diagnosing x-ray pictures. In *The nature of expertise*, M. T. H. Chi, R. Glaser, M. J. Farr (eds), 311–42. Hillsdale, New Jersey: Erlbaum.

Malt, B. C. 1993. Concept structure and category boundaries. In *The psychology of learning and motivation: Categorization by humans and machines*, G. V. Nakamura, R. Taraban, D. L. Medin (eds), 363–90. San Diego: Academic Press.

Markman, E. M. 1989. *Categorization and naming in children*. Cambridge, Mass.: MIT Press.

Markman, E. M. 1990. Constraints children place on word meanings. *Cognitive Science* **14**, 57–77.

Marr, D. 1982. *Vision*. San Francisco: W. H. Freeman.

Medin, D. L., R. L. Goldstone, D. Gentner 1993. Respects for similarity. *Psychological Review* **100**, 254–78.

Medin, D. L. & E. Heit, in press. Categorization. In *Handbook of cognition and perception*, D. E. Rumelhart & B. O. Martin (eds). San Diego: Academic Press.

Medin, D. L. & A. Ortony 1989. Psychological essentialism. In *Similarity and analogical reasoning*. S. Vosniadou & A. Ortony (eds), 179–95. Cambridge, Mass.: Cambridge University Press.

Medin, D. L. & M. M. Schaffer 1978. Context theory of classification learning. *Psychological Review* **85**, 207–38.

Medin, D. L. & P. J. Schwanenflugel 1981. Linear separability in classification learning. *Journal of Experimental Psychology: Human Learning and Memory* **7**, 355–68.

Medin, D. L., W. D. Wattenmaker, S. E. Hampson 1987. Family resemblance, conceptual cohesiveness, and category construction. *Cognitive Psychology* **19**, 242–79.

Mooney, R. J. 1993. Integrating theory and data in category learning. In *The psychology of learning and motivation: Categorization by humans and machines* (vol. 29), G. V. Nakamura, R. Taraban, D. L. Medin (eds), 189–218. San Diego: Academic Press.

Mumma, G. H. 1993. Categorization and rule induction in clinical diagnosis and assessment. In *The psychology of learning and motivation: Categorization by humans and machines*, G. V. Nakamura, R. Taraban, D. L. Medin (eds), 283–326. San Diego: Academic Press.

Murphy, G. L. 1993. Theories and concept formation. In *Categories and concepts: Theoretical views and inductive data analysis*, I. V. Mechelen, J. Hampton, R. Michalski, P. Theuns (eds), 173–200. London: Academic Press.

Murphy, G. L. & P. D. Allopenna 1994. The locus of knowledge effects in concept learning. *Journal of Experimental Psychology: Learning, Memory, and Cognition* **20**, 904–919.

Murphy, G. L. & D. L. Medin 1985. The role of theories in conceptual coherence. *Psychological Review* **92**, 289–316.

Murphy, G. L. & E. J. Wisniewski 1989. Feature correlations in conceptual representations. In *Advances in cognitive science*, G. Tiberghien (ed.), 23–45. Chichester, England: Ellis Horwood.

Nakamura, G. V. 1985. Knowledge-based classification of ill-defined categories. *Memory and Cognition* **13**, 377–84.

Nelson, T. H. 1987. *Computer lib; dream machines*. Redmond, Washington: Microsoft Press.

Nisbett, R. E., D. H. Krantz, C. Jepson, Z. Kunda 1983. The use of statistical heuristics in everyday inductive reasoning. *Psychological Review* **90**, 339–63.

Nosofsky, R. M. 1988. Exemplar-based accounts of relations between classification, recognition, and typicality. *Journal of Experimental Psychology: Learning, Memory, and Cognition* **14**, 700–708.

Nosofsky, R. M., T. J. Palmeri, S. C. McKinley 1994. Rule-plus-exception model of classification learning. *Psychological Review* **101**, 53–79.

Oaksford, M. & N. Chater 1994. A rational analysis of the selection task as optimal data selection. *Psychological Review* **101**, 608–631.

Osherson, D. N., E. E. Smith, O. Wilkie, A. Lopéz, E. Shafir 1990. Category-based induction. *Psychological Review* **97**, 185–200.

Osherson, D. N., J. Stern, O. Wilkie, M. Stob, E. E. Smith 1991. Default probability. *Cognitive Science* **15**, 251–69.

Pazzani, M. J. 1991. Influence of prior knowledge on concept acquisition: Experimental and computational results. *Journal of Experimental Psychology: Learning, Memory, and Cognition* **17**, 416–32.

Peirce, C. S. 1931–1935. *Collected papers of Charles Sanders Peirce*. Cambridge, Mass.: Harvard University Press.

Quine, W. V. O. 1960. *Word and object*. Cambridge, Mass.: MIT Press.

Raiffa, H. & R. Schlaifer 1961. *Applied statistical decision theory*. Cambridge, Mass.: Harvard University, Graduate School of Business Administration.

Rips, L. J. 1975. Inductive judgements about natural categories. *Journal of Verbal Learning and Verbal Behavior* **14**, 665–81.

Rips, L. J. 1989. Similarity, typicality, and categorization. In *Similarity and analogical reasoning*, S. Vosniadou & A. Ortony (eds), 21–59. New York: Cambridge University Press.

Rips, L. J. 1995. The current status of research on conceptual combination. *Mind and Language* **10**, 72–104.

Rosch, E. & Mervis, C. B. 1975. Family resemblances: Studies in the internal structure of categories. *Cognitive Psychology* **7**, 573–605.

Ross, B. H. & G. L. Murphy, 1996. Category-based predictions: The influence of uncertainty and feature associations. *Journal of Experimental Psychology: Learning, Memory, and Cognition*, **22**, 736–753.

Rothbart, M. & M. Taylor 1992. Category labels and social reality: do we view social categories as natural kinds? In *Language, interaction and social cognition*, G. Semin & K. Fielder (eds), 11–36. London: Sage.

Rumelhart, D. E. & D. Zipser 1985. Feature discovery by competitive learning. *Cognitive Science* **19**, 75–112.

Salatas, H. & L. E. Bourne 1974. Learning conceptual rules, iii: Processes contributing to rule difficulty. *Memory and Cognition* **2**, 549–53.

Schyns, P. G. & G. L. Murphy 1994. The ontogeny of part representation in object concepts. In *The psychology of learning and motivation* (vol. 31), D. L. Medin (ed.), 305–349. San Diego: Academic Press.

Sejnowski, T. J. & C. R. Rosenberg 1986. *Nettalk: A parallel network that learns to read aloud*. Technical Report jhu/eecs–86/01, Department of Electrical Engineering and Computer Science, Johns Hopkins University.

Shanks, D. R. 1991. Categorization by a connectionist network. *Journal of Experimental Psychology: Learning, Memory, and Cognition* **17**, 433–43.

Shipley, E. F. 1993. Categories, hierarchies, and induction. In *The psychology of learning and motivation* (vol. 30), D. L. Medin (ed.), 265–301. Orlando, Florida: Academic Press.

Sloman, S. A. 1994. When explanations compete: The role of explanatory coherence on judgements of likelihood. *Cognition* **52**, 1–21.

Smith, E. E. & D. L. Medin 1981. *Categories and concepts*. Cambridge, Mass.: Harvard University Press.

Smith, E. R. & M. A. Zarate 1992. Exemplar-based models of social judgement. *Psychological Review* **99**, 3–21.

Springer, K. 1992. Children's awareness of the biological implications of kinship. *Child Development* **63**, 950–59.

Springer, K. & A. Belk 1994. The role of physical context and association in early contamination sensitivity. *Developmental Psychology* **30**, 864–8.

Srull, T. K. & R. S. Wyer 1989. Person memory and judgement. *Psychological Review* **96**, 58–83.

Stangor, C. & D. McMillan 1992. Memory for expectancy-congruent and expectancy-incongruent information: A review of the social and social developmental literatures. *Psychological Bulletin* **111**, 42–61.

Stangor, C. & D. N. Ruble 1989. Differential influences of gender schemata and gender constancy on children's information processing and behaviour. *Social Cognition* **7**, 353–72.

Taylor, S. E. & J. Crocker 1978. Schematic bases of social information processing. In *Social cognition: The Ontario symposium*, E. T. Higgins, C. P. Herman, M. P. Zanna (eds), 89–134. Hillsdale, New Jersey: Erlbaum.

Tversky, A. & D. Kahneman 1974. Judgment under uncertainty: Heuristics and biases. *Science* **185**, 1124–31.

Underwood, B. J. 1970. A breakdown of the total-time law in free-recall learning. *Journal of Verbal Learning and Verbal Behavior* **9**, 573–80.

Ward, T. B. 1993. Processing biases, knowledge, and context in category formation. In *The psychology of learning and motivation: Categorization by humans and machines*, G. V. Nakamura, R. Taraban, D. L. Medin (eds), 257–82. San Diego: Academic Press.

Ward, T. B. 1994. Structured imagination: The role of category structure in exemplar generation. *Cognitive Psychology* **27**, 1–40.

Wattenmaker, W. D. 1995. Knowledge structures and linear separability: Integrating information in object and social categorization. *Cognitive Psychology* **28**, 274–328.

Wattenmaker, W. D., G. I. Dewey, T. D. Murphy, D. L. Medin 1986. Linear separability and concept learning: Context, relational properties, and concept naturalness. *Cognitive Psychology* **18**, 158–94.

Waxman, S. R., E. F. Shipley, B. Shepperson 1991. Establishing new subcategories: The role of category labels. *Child Development* **62**, 127–38.

Wisniewski, E. J. 1995. Prior knowledge and functionally relevant features in concept learning. *Journal of Experimental Psychology: Learning, Memory, and Cognition* **21**, 449–68.

Wisniewski, E. J. & D. L. Medin 1991. Harpoons and long sticks: the interaction of theory and similarity in rule induction. In *Concept formation: Knowledge and experience in unsupervised learning*, D. H. Fisher, M. J. Pazzani, P. Langley (eds), 237–278. San Mateo, California: Morgan Kaufmann.

Wisniewski, E. J. & D. L. Medin 1994a. On the interaction of theory and data in concept learning. *Cognitive Science* **18**, 221–82.

Wisniewski, E. J. & D. L. Medin 1994b. The fiction and nonfiction of features. In *Machine learning* R. S. Michalski & G. Tecuci (eds), 63–87. San Mateo, California: Morgan Kaufmann.

NOTE

1.   Please address correspondence to Evan Heit, Department of Psychology, University of Warwick, Coventry CV4 7AL, United Kingdom. I am grateful to John Coley, Douglas Medin and Gregory Murphy for comments on this chapter.

CHAPTER TWO

Concepts and Similarity

Ulrike Hahn and Nick Chater

CONCEPTS AND SIMILARITY – THE CHICKEN AND THE EGG?

The cognitive system does not treat each new object or occurrence as distinct from and unrelated to what it has seen before: it classifies new objects in terms of concepts which group the new object together with others which have previously been encountered. Moreover, the cognitive system also judges whether new objects are similar to old objects. *Prima facie*, these processes seem to be related, but exactly how they are related is not so clear. This puzzle is important because concepts are thought to be building blocks in terms of which knowledge is represented (e.g. Oden 1987).

One suggestion concerning the relationship between concepts and similarity is that concepts group together objects which are similar. According to this point of view, the reason that "bird" is a useful concept is that birds are relatively similar to each other – mostly having wings, laying eggs, building nests, flying and so on. A hypothetical concept "drib" which grouped together a particular lightbulb, Polly the pet parrot, the English channel and the ozone layer would seem to be a useless, and highly bizarre, concept precisely because the items it groups together are not at all similar.[1] Why is it important that concepts group together similar things – why is "bird" a more coherent concept than "drib"? One suggestion is that birds, being similar, support many interesting generalizations (most birds have wings, most birds fly, and so on); but there seem to be no interesting generalizations to state about dribs. Moreover, on learning that Polly has a beak, it is reasonable to infer that other birds also may have beaks (since Polly is a bird, and birds are similar to each other); on the other hand, it is not reasonable to infer that other dribs may have beaks, since other dribs and Polly have nothing in common. If this view of the relation between concepts and similarity is correct, then similarity is at the very centre of the theory of concepts: a theory of similarity would explain, or at least be an important factor in explaining, why people have the concepts that they do.

There is, however, an alternative view of the relationship between concepts and similarity that also has considerable intuitive appeal. What is it for two objects to be similar? Presumably it is that they have many properties in common – indeed, this point of view is implicit in our discussion above. But to say that birds are similar because, among other things, birds generally lay eggs is the same as saying that birds are similar because, among other things, they are grouped together by the concept "egg-layer". In the same way, the similarity of birds seems to be rooted in the fact that most birds are members of concepts "flyer, has wings", and so on. Thus, it seems that objects are similar because they fall under the same concepts.

Bringing together these intuitively plausible views confronts us with a "chicken and egg" problem. The first point of view suggests that similarity can be used to explain concepts; the second point of view suggests that concepts can be used to explain similarity. This seems dangerously circular, to say the least! The relationship between similarity and concepts is plainly not a straightforward one. As we have seen, it is not even clear which notion should be taken as fundamental. Moreover, unravelling the relationship between concepts and similarity is not merely an entertaining puzzle; it goes to the core of current theories of concepts.

Given this tight connection, it is surprising that there is little research directly integrating the two. Similarity, although frequently employed as an explanatory notion in the concepts literature, is seldom given closer scrutiny. Likewise, models of similarity typically assume given properties, and thus concepts, as a starting point. In both cases, this leaves out the question of whether or not the notion one is building on can actually fulfil its designated role. In this chapter we consider in what ways concepts and similarity are related, and how research in both areas can be brought together. This task is complicated by the fact that just as there are a range of competing theories of concepts, there are also a range of competing views of similarity, none of which is entirely satisfactory. Furthermore, different views of concepts have different roles for similarity, and not all notions of similarity are consistent with all views of concepts.

We begin by establishing the precise role attributed to similarity in current theories of conceptual structure. Subsequently, we investigate the notion of similarity, examining both general issues and current models of similarity. These will be drawn not only from psychology but also from artificial intelligence and computer science. Specifically, we introduce *neural networks, case-based reasoning* (CBR) and a relatively little-known account based on a mathematical notion called *Kolmogorov complexity*. These models are assessed for their adequacy as models of similarity, as only a theory of similarity which is in itself satisfactory can ground a theory of conceptual structure. We then bring these models together with the theories of conceptual structure introduced, examining which models of similarity are compatible with which views of conceptual structure. Finally, leaving particular models and theories behind, we return again to the question of the general relationship between concepts and similarity. We review the empirical evidence and establish along what lines the problem of the "chicken and the egg" might one day be resolved.

CONCEPTS

We begin by giving a brief overview of present theories of concepts in relation to similarity. Current theories of concepts are covered in more detail elsewhere in this volume, and in Komatsu (1992) and Medin (1989). We first outline two theories of concepts, prototype and exemplar theories, in which similarity is directly and explicitly involved. We then consider rule-based and theory-based accounts, which do not explicitly involve similarity, but in which, we argue, similarity plays an important, although indirect role.

Prototype and exemplar views: similarity centre-stage
The common thread linking this family of views is a direct connection between concepts and similarity: categorizing an object involves judging the similarity between that object and some other object(s). Exactly what the new object is compared with, and how that comparison is carried out distinguishes prototype and exemplar views from each other, and identifies different variants of each view. In all cases though, categorization depends on similarity.

Prototype views
The prototype view[2] assumes that each category is associated with a "prototype", a stored representation of the properties that typify

members of that category. The classification of new objects as, for example, birds will depend on how similar that object is to the bird prototype, and also to the prototypes of other categories.

Opinions vary concerning exactly what a prototype is.[3] The simplest view assumes that prototypes are stored mental representations of the same nature as the mental representation of specific objects. It follows from this view that judging the similarity between a specific object to a prototype in classification is exactly the same process as judging the similarity between two objects.

By contrast, some prototype views assume that prototypes are not represented in quite the same way as specific objects, but are specified in somewhat more abstract terms (e.g. Taylor 1989). In its simplest form, this abstract specification could simply list certain properties which have previously appeared in instances of the category (while other features might be ignored entirely – this is what makes the representation abstract). The various listed properties might also have different "weights", reflecting their varying degrees of relevance for category membership. For example, the concept bird might consist of the following list of weighted features:

has wings	0.8
has feathers	0.9
flies	0.5
sings	0.5
lays eggs	0.9

The categorization of a new creature, then, can be divided into three stages: first, which of these features the creature possesses is assessed. Then, using this information, the similarity between the prototype and the new creature must be calculated. Many different measures of similarity, such as addition or multiplication of the weighted features that the creature possesses, have been proposed. Finally, it is necessary to decide whether the creature ultimately is "similar enough" to the bird prototype to count as a bird. This, for example, might involve seeing whether the object is more similar to the bird prototype than it is to any other prototype; again, the possibilities are numerous.

Exemplar views

The exemplar approach also sees classification as involving judgements of similarity to stored representations (see, for example, Brooks 1978, and Medin & Schaffer 1978. For more recent variants, see Kruschke 1992, and Nosofsky 1988, and for an overview, see Komatsu 1992). Instead of judging similarity to a single prototype representing each category, the new object is compared to many stored "exemplars" (specific previously encountered instances) of the category. If the new object is more similar to exemplar birds than to exemplars of any other category, then it will be classified as a bird. According to the exemplar view, the specification of the category is implicit in its instances; no necessary and sufficient features, or even probable features, are abstracted. The concept is learned simply by storing examples of its category members (for experimental investigations on abstraction in category acquisition, see e.g. Homa et al. 1981, Whittlesea 1987, this volume, and Medin et al. 1983).

As with prototype views, there are numerous specific proposals concerning how this framework is fleshed out into a full-blown model of classification. For example, specific models vary according to whether it is the similarity to a single, best-matching exemplar that matters (see, e.g. Hintzman & Ludlam, 1980, and many CBR systems in artificial intelligence, e.g. PROTOS, Porter et al. 1990) or whether a set of exemplars – either a fixed subset or the entire set – is matched (see for discussion, e.g. Homa et al. 1981, Jones & Heit 1993). In all cases, however, similarity assessment is given a central role.

Definitional and theory-based accounts: similarity behind the scenes?
In the last subsection, we considered views of concepts in which similarity is explicitly viewed as central to explaining concepts. Now we turn to rule-based and theory-based views of concepts, which do not make direct reference to similarity. Nonetheless, as we shall see, similarity may play an important, if less visible, role in categorization in these views.

Definitional views
The definitional or "classical" view of concepts holds that concepts possess definitions specifying features necessary and *sufficient* for the concept. This definition is the summary description of the entire class used in every instance of categorization, which proceeds simply by checking for the presence of these features in the entity in question. This view is commonly supplemented by the "nesting assumption" – that a subordinate concept (e.g. "robin") contains nested within in it the defining features of the superordinate ("bird"). The crucial point, in our context, is that concepts are explained without reference to similarity. The definitional view thus requires closer scrutiny.

First and foremost, the definitional view seems inadequate as a theory when transferred from artificial concepts in controlled experiments[4] to our everyday concepts, that is to the concepts for which we typically have words. Of the difficulties faced here, the most serious one is that almost all everyday concepts appear to be indefinable (Fodor et al. 1980). It simply does not seem possible to formulate necessary and sufficient conditions for being, for example, a chair, or a window, or a smile. This is illustrated by the fact that dictionary "definitions" of almost all terms are not really definitions at all. They do not provide necessary and sufficient conditions for category membership – instead they typically do no more than provide some relevant information about category members, which may help the dictionary user identify which concept is intended.[5]

Moreover, even for those concepts which do appear to have definitions, these definitions generally hold only with respect to a range of "background assumptions". Varying these assumptions immediately produces unclear or borderline cases:

> The noun bachelor can be defined as an unmarried adult man, but the noun clearly exists as a motivated device for categorizing people only in the context of a human society in which certain expectations about marriage and marriageable age obtain. Male participants in long-term unmarried couplings would not ordinarily be described as bachelors; a boy abandoned in the jungle and grown to maturity away from contact with human society would not be called a bachelor. (Fillmore, quoted from Lakoff 1987).

Background factors, such as the social conventions concerning marriage, will, in general, hold to varying degrees. Presumably the definition of bachelor can meaningfully be applied if the background conditions are sufficiently similar to the conventions concerning marriage current in the West. This is one way in which similarity can have a "behind the scenes" role in the definitional view – similarity applies to background assumptions underlying the application of necessary and sufficient conditions, rather than being explicitly mentioned in the definition itself.

There is also another way in which similarity would enter the theory of concepts, even if the definitional view were correct. We have so far dealt with the most direct difficulty of the definitional view: that it is difficult or impossible to define almost all concepts. But there is another argument, based on "prototype effects" against the definitional view. This argument, crudely stated is: if category membership is all or none, as the definitional view suggests, why is a robin judged to be (and treated as) a more typical bird than an ostrich? Some theorists have responded by arguing that such effects are attributed to the "identification procedure" for a concept – the procedure used to identify members of that concept; the "core" of the concept, used in reasoning, is still held to consist of a definition (Miller & Johnson-Laird 1976, Osherson & Smith 1981). This two-component account opens the door to similarity – the identification procedure may, for example, be based on prototypes or exemplars, as discussed above, with their direct reliance on similarity.

We have seen that, as a theory of everyday concepts, the definitional view appears to be inadequate. More importantly, the main problems it encounters appear to implicate similarity. Most everyday concepts such as "chair", or "smile" seem to involve networks of related and thus similar instances, but without there being a single set of defining properties. In the other case, similarity of background conditions must hold for a definition to be applicable. Finally, prototype effects, for which an explanation involving similarity suggests itself, must be accounted for.

In experiments on *artificial concept* learning, on the other hand, performance can be modelled accurately by assuming that subjects learn definitional rules. Here, the core problems plaguing the definitional view for everyday concepts are generally ruled out by the design of the materials. Nevertheless, recent research has revealed "intrusions" of similarity where subjects appear to make use of a rule in these contexts as well. For one, Nosofsky et al. (1989) found that the addition of an "exemplar" component to their rule-based account considerably improved the degree to which their model fits the experimental data. Thus, even when using a rule, subjects may also be paying attention to the similarity of new instances to previous instances. More direct evidence comes from Allen & Brooks (1991), who found in many, but not all, experimental conditions that similarity to past instances affected subjects' application of a simple explicit rule, specified by the experimenter. This ongoing influence of similarity to prior episodes, Allen & Brooks argue, may be particularly frequent (because useful) in uncertain situations where rules and definitions have only heuristic value. Incidentally, a similar ongoing role of prior episodes in addition to explicit instructions has emerged in the context of problem solving (Ross 1984, 1987, 1989, Ross et al. 1990, Ross & Kennedy 1990).

In sum, then, the definitional view, while appearing to ignore similarity, actually leaves open a number of ways in which similarity may affect concepts: in determining how definitions are interpreted, as playing a role in a concepts' "identification procedure", and as an additional factor affecting how definitions or rules are applied in actual classification.

Theory-based views

Theory- or explanation-based views of concepts reject exemplar, probabilistic and definitional views and focus instead on the relationship between concepts and our knowledge of, and theories about, the world (Murphy & Medin 1985, Wattenmaker et al. 1986, Lakoff 1987, Medin & Wattenmaker 1987, Wattenmaker et al. 1988, Wisniewski & Medin 1994; see also Heit's chapter in this volume). "Theory", here, can be taken to refer to a body of knowledge that may include scientific principles, stereotypes and informal observations of past experiences (Murphy & Medin 1985, Wisniewski & Medin 1994). Most importantly, properties of objects are not independent and thus not independently assessed in categorization but are embedded within networks of inter-property relationships which organize and link them (Wattenmaker et al. 1988). Accordingly, Lakoff's (1987) "idealized cognitive models" are another expression of the same idea (Medin & Wattenmaker 1987). For example, the concept "bird" cannot be merely a collection of "bird" features such as "has wings", "has feathers", and "has a beak", but must specify how these feature are related (e.g. that the wings are covered in feathers, the beak is not). But not only such relational aspects between features, but also their causal connections can play a crucial role in categorization (Wattenmaker et al. 1988). More fundamentally still, our prior theories influence what features we perceive in the first place (Wisniewski & Medin 1994).

How do theory-based views relate to similarity? It is frequently suggested that theory-based views undermine the role of similarity in theories of concepts. But this is misleading: explanation/theory-based approaches target simplistic views of similarity assessment such as simple counting of shared perceptual features. However, explanations or theories are neither capable of, nor intended to, replace similarity in categorization. What they suggest is that similarity itself, if it is to be relevant to concepts, must be influenced by our theories of, and knowledge about, the world (Lamberts 1994, Wattenmaker et al. 1988). Thus, theory-based views demand a *better* account of similarity, rather than *no* account of similarity, in explaining concepts.

Summary

We have seen that similarity plays an important role in theories of concepts based on prototypes, exemplars, definitions and theories. We now turn to similarity in order to establish whether or not it can really fit the bill.

SIMILARITY

We will begin our investigation of similarity with a treatment of the damning criticisms which have been voiced against similarity as an explanatory notion. With these out of the way, we then turn to specific models of similarity, assessing them for strengths and weaknesses. Finally, we will conclude this section with a discussion of crucial stages of the process of similarity assessment which are outside the scope of all current models of similarity.

Is similarity explanatory: the problem of "respects"

If theories of concepts are to rely on similarity, whether directly or indirectly, then similarity must be a coherent and explanatory notion. Within philosophy, however, grave doubts about the explanatory power of similarity have been expressed (Goodman 1972). If these doubts are well-founded, then the role of similarity in current theories of concepts, and indeed the viability of those theories, must be called into question. In this subsection, we consider Goodman's critique of similarity and how it relates to the theory of concepts.

What does it mean to say that two objects a and b are similar? Intuitively, we say that objects are similar because they have many properties in common. But, as Goodman pointed out, this intuition does not take us very far, because all entities have infinite sets of properties in common (Goodman 1972). A plum and a lawnmower both share the properties of weighing less than 100 kilos (and less than 101 kilos . . . etc.). This seems to imply that all objects are similar to all others! Of course, all entities will also have infinite sets of properties that are not in common. A plum weighs less than one kilo, while a lawnmower weighs more than one kilo (and similarly for 1.1 kilos and 1.11 kilos . . . etc.). Perhaps, then, all objects are dissimilar to all others! Pursuing our intuition about what makes objects similar has led to deep trouble.

Goodman concludes that "similarity" is thus a meaningful notion only as *similar in a certain respect*. Although similarity superficially appears to be a two-place relation, it is really a three-place relation $S (a, b, r)$ – a and b are similar in respect r. Any talk of similarity between two objects must at least implicitly contain some respect in which they are similar.

But, Goodman notes, once "respects" are introduced, it seems that similarity itself has no role to play: the respects do all the work. To say that an object belongs to a category because it is similar to items of that category with respect, for instance, to the property "red" is merely to say that it belongs to the category because it is red – the notion of similarity can be removed without loss. "Similarity", so Goodman says, is a "pretender, an imposter, a quack", "it has, indeed, its place and its uses, but is more often found where it does not belong, professing powers it does not possess" (Goodman 1972: 437). In particular,

Goodman's qualms suggest that similarity may not be an explanatory construct upon which a theory of concepts can rely.

These criticisms have made their way into psychology only fairly recently through authors advocating theory-based approaches to concepts (Murphy & Medin 1985, Medin & Wattenmaker 1987), sparking what has been viewed as the "decline of similarity" within the study of concepts and categorization (Neisser 1987).

Two recent papers (Goldstone 1994a, Medin et al. 1993) have, however, re-evaluated whether Goodman's criticisms really undermine similarity *for psychology*. Perhaps a psychological notion of similarity may not be subject to the points that Goodman raises for similarity in the abstract. Two questions are particularly important. First, are there psychological restrictions on respects, or can simply anything be a respect? Medin et al. (1993) have argued that although similarity is highly flexible as a result of goals, purpose, or context, because respects are by no means fixed, this does not imply that they vary in arbitrary ways. Rather, there is a great deal of systematicity in the variation exhibited with constraints arising both from knowledge and purpose as from the comparison process itself, as we shall discuss in more detail below. Secondly, granting Goodman's claim that similarity involves respects, does this really imply that respects do all of the work, leaving no role for similarity? Goldstone (1994a) argues that people do not usually compare objects only in a single respect such as "size" but along multiple dimensions such as size, colour, shape, etc. Given multiple respects (or, alternatively, a complex respect, such as "colour", or "appearance") the psychologically central issue is how different factors are combined to give a single similarity judgement (Goldstone 1994a). Thus, it seems that respects only do some, but not all, of the work in explaining similarity judgements; in addition, we require an account of how information about different respects is combined to give a single similarity judgement.

While the fact that respects and hence similarity can vary does not render similarity meaningless, Goodman's argument that similarity depends on respects does have important implications for psychology. Most importantly, there will be many different similarity values between objects depending on which respects are considered. Therefore, different types of similarity can be distinguished depending on the respects in question. A number of terms have gradually, and somewhat haphazardly, been introduced to distinguish important types of similarity: *perceptual similarity* is distinguished from similarity based on conceptual properties; *global similarity* which refers to an overall comparison, underlying, for instance, the unspecified feeling that somehow, "John and Bill are very similar", as opposed to similarity centred around one or two specific respects (e.g. size); and, finally, a distinction has been drawn between *surface* and *deep* similarity. This distinction stems from the analogical reasoning literature (Gentner 1983). Here, surface similarity as based on superficial attributes is contrasted with deep or structural similarity based on common relations regardless of the mismatch of superficial attributes. A common example of such a structural correspondence is given by the similarity between Rutherford's model of the atom and the solar system. While planets and electrons do not match at a surface level, they nevertheless have corresponding roles expressed through the relation "orbit around (x, y)". Within each of these types of similarity, of course, there will be further variation, determined by the particular respects that are considered.

This flexibility of similarity has often been ignored when considering the role of similarity in the psychology of concepts. Indeed, it is widespread in the concepts literature to speak merely of "similarity" in a general way, making it necessary for the reader to work out which respects are actually under consideration. In much research, some form of perceptual similarity is assumed. Moreover, many of the criticisms levelled against similarity in the concepts literature are really criticisms of perceptual similarity (e.g. Medin & Wattenmaker 1987).

Finally, there is an alternative reply to Goodman's criticism that also sheds more light on the slightly hazy notion of global similarity. The fact that any two entities have an infinite number of properties in common also ceases to be a problem when similarity is not viewed as an objective relation between two objects but as a relation between mental representations of these objects in a cognitive agent. As mental representations must be finite, computation of similarity between objects can be thought to take place without the need for constraining respects. The crucial issue then becomes one of mental representation, of understanding what is represented and how this is selected. Arguably this is hard, but it is not arbitrary – there is a fact to the matter of what is or is not included in an agent's mental representation.

Different respects correspond to varying representations, varying either in what information is represented or in how it is weighted (or, of course, both). The two notions "similar in a given respect" and "similar in a given representation" are, from this perspective, equivalent. We find, however, that a conceptualization in terms of representation is more natural from a cognitive perspective. The perspective on global similarity then is not one of somewhat unspecified mysterious multiple respects but a comparison between two representations. The above distinctions of types correspond to differences and changes in representation, and the mechanisms of re-representation are given a prominent position both in our general understanding of similarity and of performance differences and variations in difficulty of cognitive tasks. Whatever perspective is chosen, "respects" or "representation", the problem of understanding what material enters a given similarity comparison, how this is selected and weighted, is a crucial part of understanding similarity. We will return to these issues, and the progress psychology has made here, later on in the chapter.

Having considered Goodman's critique of similarity, and suggested that similarity may, nonetheless, be a useful and explanatory notion for the psychology of concepts, we now turn to a range of models of similarity. From psychology, we consider spatial (e.g. Nosofsky 1984) and feature-based models (e.g. Tversky 1977). These models have provided the starting point for most experimental work on similarity. From artificial intelligence, we consider models of similarity used in neural networks and CBR (Bareiss & King 1989). Finally, from computer science, we consider an abstract notion of similarity based on Kolmogorov complexity (Li & Vitanyi 1993).

Spatial models

Theory

Spatial models of similarity represent objects as points in a space, with the distances between objects reflecting how dissimilar they are. These spatial representations can be viewed in two ways: merely as a convenient way of describing, summarizing and displaying similarity data or as a psychological model of mental representation and perceived similarity (Tversky & Gati 1982). In the latter view, objects are viewed as represented in an internal psychological space.[6] Objects are positioned according to their values on the respective dimensions of this space, which are viewed as the properties of the object with psychological relevance. This hypothetical space cannot, of course, be directly investigated. There is, however, a method for constructing putative internal spaces from empirical data on how similar people take objects to be. This empirical data can be of various kinds – for example, it might consist of explicit similarity judgements between pairs of objects, or data concerning how frequently people confuse each object with each of the others. According to the spatial model of similarity, similarity data, of whatever kind, can be interpreted as "proximity data" – i.e. as giving information about the distance between the objects in the internal space. Once similarity data is interpreted in terms of proximities, the problem is to reconstruct an internal space in which the distances between objects reflect, as closely as possible, the given proximity data. The problem is analogous to attempting to derive a map of a country from a table of the distances between each pair of cities. The problem of reconstructing spaces from proximity data can be solved using a set of statistical techniques known as *multi-dimensional scaling* (MDS; Shepard 1980, 1987). By using MDS, a spatial representation can be generated in which the distances between objects correspond as closely as possible to the similarities between objects.

Formally, a traditional MDS-derived model is given by:

$$d_{ij} = [\Sigma_m \ |x_{im} - x_{jm}| \ ^r]^{1/r} \ (2.1)$$

where x_{im} is the psychological value of exemplar i on dimension m; value of r defines the distance metric. A value of $r = 2$ defines the metric as Euclidean (i.e. the shortest line between two points).[7] Other values and thus metrics are possible; $r = 1$, for example, specifies the so-called city-block metric which has also been successfully employed (here the distance between two items equals the sum of their dimensional differences). In general, it seems that it depends both on the stimulus and subject's strategy which value best fits the data (Goldstone 1994a). Stimuli with integral dimensions, that is, dimensions which are perceived together (such as hue, saturation, and brightness for colour) seem better modelled with $r = 2$, whilst stimuli with separable dimensions (size and colour, for instance) are better captured with $r = 1$ (for discussion see Nosofsky 1988; for an overview of differences found between separable and integral stimuli, see Tversky & Gati 1982).

When the spatial approach is used as a psychological model, similarity is often taken not to correspond directly to distance, but is assumed to be an exponential decay function of distance. That is, distance, d_{ij}, is converted to similarity, η_{ij}, via:

$$\eta_{ij} = \exp(-c \cdot d_{ij}^p) \ (2.2)$$

where c is a "general sensitivity parameter"; value of p defines the similarity gradient ($p = 1$ exponential, $p = 2$ Gaussian; Nosofsky 1988). This function is known as the *Universal Law of Generalization* and has been shown to capture the similarity-based generalization performance of both humans and a variety of animals on a range of data sets from colours to morse code signals with striking accuracy (Shepard 1987).

The similarity space on its own does not explain data from cognitive tasks – it must be supplemented with an account of how the similarity space is used. Nosofsky (1984) has developed an account of how similarity spaces could be used in a number of contexts, based on his "Generalized Context Model", which is an extension of Medin & Schaffer's (1978) exemplar account of categorization. This account has successfully fitted subject's performance on recognition, identification, and categorization tasks (e.g. Nosofsky 1988). Relating recognition, identification and categorization results, here, also requires an additional process of selective attention, to capture the fact that subjects focus on different aspects of the stimuli on each of the tasks. This is modelled through additional, flexible, weight parameters on each of the dimensions:

$$d_{ij} = [\textstyle\sum_m w_m \, |x_{im} - x_{jm}|^r]^{1/r} \ (2.3)$$

in which w_m is the "attention weight" given to dimension m $(0 \le w_m; \textstyle\sum w_m = 1)$.

An increase in w_m "stretches" the space along the mth dimension, hence increasing the effect of differences on this dimension on overall similarity; correspondingly, reducing w_m "shrinks" the space on this dimension, making mismatches on this dimension less important. For illustration of this effect one can imagine a graph plotting points according to their value on the x and y axes – e.g. doubling the units per value on the x axis (i.e. 2 inches between levels on x instead of 1) will draw points further apart in the direction of this axis, thus increasing the distance between them. Given this additional mechanism of distorting the space, recognition, categorization and identification performance on this task can be related through an underlying psychological space, which is modified through attention according to the task demands.

The constraint that the weights sum to 1 offers a simple solution to a basic flaw of the unweighted spatial model. The latter fails to incorporate the effect of adding common properties to two stimuli. Intuitively, if two stimuli are modified by adding the same property to each, their similarity should increase. Dimensions, however, on which stimuli have identical values mathematically do not affect the distance between the two, as this is based on dimensional differences only. As far as these two stimuli are concerned this dimension might as well not be represented. This means one could continue to add identical properties to both stimuli indefinitely without this affecting their overall similarity – an intuitively implausible assumption which has also been experimentally invalidated by Gati & Tversky (1982).

This problem arises because the spatial model takes no account of the total number of dimensions of the representations of the objects that are being compared. If two objects are represented by three dimensions, and differ widely on all three, it seems reasonably to assume that they should not be judged as similar. If, on the other hand, they are represented by 10,000 dimensions, and differ only on these three, then it would be reasonable that they are judged to be highly similar. Intuitively, similarity is concerned with the proportion of the properties shared relative to all the properties considered. Spatial models, in their basic form, do not take account of this. By introducing attention weights that must sum to 1, Nosofsky deals with this difficulty, because adding a dimension now implies that the dimension weights for the extant dimensions are reduced. This means that they "shrink", and, hence, the impact of mismatches along the old dimensions is reduced; the new common property, as before, has no impact. The final result is a greater similarity overall.

As a psychological model, these spatial representations of similarity are of additional interest through an emerging link with neural networks. Nets, as will be discussed in more detail below, provide a very simple architecture for storing items in such a way that related items are clustered near or less near to an exemplar, depending on their degree of similarity. The items so stored likewise define a "similarity space" in the network and distance from the prototypical exemplar defines a similarity metric (Churchland & Sejnowski 1992).

Despite the appeal of the spatial approach, in particular its success in fitting a fairly wide range of data, it has come under considerable theoretical and experimental attack.

Problems

The assumptions underlying spatial models of similarity have been criticized, in particular in the work of Tversky, both on theoretical and experimental grounds (Tversky 1977, Tversky & Gati 1978, 1982, Gati & Tversky 1982, 1984, Tversky & Hutchinson 1986). Specifically, it has been argued that the continuous dimensions used by spatial models are often inappropriate, and that spatial models make assumptions about similarity that are not experimentally justified. We consider these issues in turn.

Continuous dimensions

Tversky (1977) argues that dimensional representations used by spatial models do not seem appropriate in many cases. He argues that it is more appropriate and natural to represent, for instance, countries or personality in terms of qualitative features (i.e. something an object does or does not have) rather than in terms of quantitative dimensions. This does not present a decisive argument as MDS and spatial models do not necessarily require continuous dimensions – discrete dimensions are possible and the representation of binary "features" does not automatically present a difficulty (Nosofsky 1990). On the cognitive side, conceptual stimuli might often be structured in a way that gives rise to hierarchical featural groupings or clusters and thus "pseudo-dimensions" (Garner 1978). To take an example of Rosch (1978), an automatic transmission can be treated as a feature that an object has or does not have; once it is decided, however, that the relevant set of objects are cars and that cars must have a transmission, "automatic" and "standard" become two levels on the pseudo-dimension "transmission". This also indicates that dimension vs. feature might be a processing decision that depends on task and occasion (Rosch 1978). Continuous dimensions do, however, have in principle limitations when it comes to nominal variables with several levels: there is no apparent way in which, for instance, "eye colour" which might take on the values blue, green, brown, etc. can be represented, as the different values admit of no meaningful serial ordering, a constraint demanded by the notion of dimension.

Perhaps an even more serious difficulty with representing objects as points in space is that similarity may reflect not just the collection of attributes that an object has, but the relationships in which those attributes stand, as we noted above. Representing such relationships appears to require structured representations of objects, rather than representing objects as unstructured points in space. We shall see that this problem is not limited to spatial models, but also arises for a number of other models of similarity. This problem will be discussed in detail in the context of feature-based models below.

Invalid assumptions.   At the core of spatial models is the notion that similarity can be related to distance in space. Distances, by definition, must be non-negative quantities that obey the so-called metric axioms:

1.   Minimality: $d_{ab} \geq d_{aa} = 0$

2.   Symmetry: $d_{ab} = d_{ba}$

3.   Triangle inequality: $d_{ab} + d_{bc} \geq d_{ac}$

Translating back to similarity, this implies that

1.   Minimality: the similarity between any object and itself is greater than or equal to the similarity of any two distinct objects.

2.   Symmetry: the similarity between objects a and b must be the same as the similarity between and b and a.

3.   Triangle inequality: the similarity of a, b and b, c constrains the similarity of a, c.

Symmetry has been the main focus of attack for critics of spatial models. Similes such as "butchers are like surgeons" vs. "surgeons are like butchers", which differ in meaning with respect to whom they compliment or criticize (example from Medin et al. 1993), appear to indicate that human similarity judgements need not be symmetrical. A number of experiments have demonstrated that this effect is not specific to similes, but occurs with similarity statements ("a is similar to b") and directional similarity judgements (Tversky 1977, Tversky & Gati 1978, Rosch 1978). However, it is possible that such results can be explained not by asymmetry of similarity itself, but by other aspects of the cognitive process being studied. Enhanced spatial models which additionally allow for flexible attention weights on dimensions (Nosofsky 1988), can deal with asymmetries if they are explained in terms of "focusing": the relevant dimensions and their weightings are selected by focusing on the properties of the subject of the comparison – accordingly the space is stretched along the salient dimensions of the subject. For instance, in the comparison "surgeons are like butchers" – "surgeons" is the subject, "butchers" the referent. As the selected dimensions need not be the dimensions most salient in the referent, reversing the direction of the comparison might change the result. A different solution to this problem has been sought through the incorporation of a general notion of bias into spatial models (Nosofsky 1991).

Attempts to show that the other two metric axioms are violated (Tversky 1977, Tversky & Gati 1982) have been even less conclusive. The minimality condition is difficult to investigate because the very idea of the degree of similarity between an object and itself is problematic. The triangle inequality is difficult to test, because the constraint that it places on similarity is extremely weak. Given that similarity and distance are not necessarily the same thing, this axiom does not translate into a specific claim about similarity judgements. Recall that in many models, similarity is assumed to be an exponentially decaying function of distance. According to this assumption, the triangle inequality in distance translates into a much more complex relationship between similarities. The exact nature of this relationship depends on the precise value of exponential decay, which is, of course, not known. But many other assumptions about the relationship between similarity and distance are also possible, the only obvious constraint being that smaller distances correspond to greater similarities. But only when the precise relationship between distance and similarity is specified can the triangle inequality be translated into a claim about similarity. Evidence against the triangle inequality in a constrained case has been claimed by Tversky & Gati (1982). Moreover, there is the further problem of deciding how similarity, which is internal, relates to external behaviour. Therefore, to date, it is not clear to what extent these apparent difficulties really weigh against spatial models.

The chicken and the egg

How does the spatial model relate to the chicken and egg problem with which we began? In the discussion of concepts, we argued that categorization depends on similarity, whether directly or indirectly. According to the spatial model, does similarity depend on categorization? It does because the dimensions in the internal space are assumed to have some meaningful interpretation. Suppose, for example, that faces are classified in some way using an internal space with dimensions such as nose length, eye colour, and so on. To be able to locate a particular face in this space, so that classification can begin, requires classifying the face according to length of nose, colour of eyes, and so on. Hence, similarity depends on categorization. Note that this state of affairs is independent of whether or not we have appropriate labels for these dimensions. Unless the dimensions are meaningful, it is difficult to see how the new object can be assigned a value on each of them. Moreover, even if some way of determining the appropriate location for a new object can be found, it is difficult to imagine how this might occur without determining what properties the object has – i.e. categorizing it. Spatial models of similarity thus require that the apparently circular relationship between concepts and similarity be clarified.

Feature-based models

Theory

Feature-based models, such as Tversky's (1977) contrast model, are designed to overcome the difficulties with the spatial model. The contrast model represents objects not as points in a space with continuous dimensions but as sets of discrete, binary features (note that features need not be limited to perceptual properties). Specifically, according to the contrast model, similarity is defined as:

$$Sim(i,j) = af (I \quad J) - bf (I \cap J) - cf (J - I) \quad (2.4)$$

I, J are the feature sets of entities i and j. a, b, c are non-negative weight parameters; f is an interval scale and $f(I)$ is the scale value associated with stimulus i. This model allows for the violation of all three metric axioms discussed above as being central to spatial accounts.

Basically, similarity is an increasing function of the number of shared features $(I \cap J)$ and a decreasing function of the unmatched features of both objects $(I - J, J - I)$. The weight parameters a, b and c depend on the demands of the task. In particular, varying the focus on either the distinguishing features of I or of J, that is by increasing b over c or vice versa allows the modelling of the asymmetry of directional similarity judgements ("how similar is i to j?"). For tasks which are non-directional, e.g. where the subject is asked "how similar are i and j?" similarity judgements should be symmetrical. In the model, this requires that the parameters b and c are equal.

The scale f reflects the salience or prominence of the various features, thus measuring the contribution of any particular (common or distinctive) feature to the similarity between the objects. The scale value associated with stimulus (object) i is therefore a measure of the overall salience of i, which might depend on, for instance, intensity, frequency, familiarity or informational content (Tversky 1977, Tversky & Gati 1978). Because f, a, b and c can be varied, the contrast model provides a family of measures of similarity, rather than a single measure.

Problems

The contrast model makes the natural prediction that the addition of common properties increases similarity. However, this has an unintuitive consequence of its own: that similarity has no inherent upper bound. The similarity between two items can be increased indefinitely by adding elements without an ultimate value for identity being approximated. In fact, (unless ruled out by definition), the similarity of an item to itself is entirely dependent on the number of features chosen to represent it, again a rather unconvincing property.

Tversky's use of binary features rather than continuous dimensions certainly avoids the difficulties that spatial models can have with discrete properties. But it simply trades one representational problem for another – now continuous dimensions, or even nominal variables with several levels are difficult to represent. Tversky suggests various representational devices which can be used to deal with such cases, albeit somewhat awkwardly. Nominal variables of more than two values can be expressed by making use of "dummy variables" (Tversky & Gati 1982), though this solution introduces otherwise meaningless features. Similarly, ordered attributes (e.g. "loudness" levels) can be expressed through "nesting", that is through the use of a succession of sets each of which is more inclusive than the preceding one, e.g. levels of loudness: as level 1 = (), level 2 = (), and so on, or "chaining" in the case of qualitative orderings (Tversky & Gati 1982).

The representational difficulties with feature-based models do not end here, however. We noted in the discussion of theory-based concepts above that it has been argued that concepts cannot be viewed as mere collections of features. Rather, the relationships between these features must be represented, specifying the relationship of the beak, the eyes, and the tail to the whole bird. A creature with all the right features in the wrong arrangement would not be a bird! But features, as we will see, cannot express relationships. Hence, the feature-based approach to similarity appears to be unworkable from the start. Moreover, relational properties cannot simply be ignored as irrelevant to similarity judgements. Recent experiments have demonstrated that relations play an important role in human similarity judgements (Goldstone et al. 1991, Goldstone 1994b).

The problem is equally serious for spatial models. Dimensions are no more than features with a continuous number of values – these too are unable to represent relationships. If the relationships between features or dimensions are crucial in similarity judgements, not merely the features and dimensions themselves, then both feature-based and spatial models appear to be ruled out automatically as representationally inadequate.

Our most familiar means of representing relationships is natural language. The crucial difference between natural language sentences and collections of features highlights the problem. Natural language sentences have a complex syntactic structure, which can allow a finite vocabulary to be used to express an infinitely large number of statements – language is compositional. Thus, in natural language an infinitely large set of possible relationships, between arbitrary objects, can be expressed using a finite representational system. But compositionality does not appear to be possible in featural or spatial representations (Fodor & Pylyshyn 1988, Fodor & McLaughlin 1990).

Accordingly, artificial intelligence has resorted to a variety of compositional, language-like representational systems, such as *semantic networks* (Collins & Quillian 1972), *frames* (Minsky 1977), *schemata* (Schank & Abelson 1977) and various kinds of visual "sketch" (Marr 1982) in order to store relational information. In psychological terms, such a language-like, structured representation is described as a *propositional code* (Pylyshyn 1973) or *a language of thought* (Fodor 1975).

A mere collection of features is not a language; and neither is a point in a continuous space. So if objects are mentally represented using structured, language-like representations, then neither featural nor dimensional views of similarity will be sufficiently general to be satisfactory. Both approaches require some alternative way in which relationships can be represented using features or dimensions. However, no viable proposals have been put forward, and there are in principle arguments that appear to show that this is not possible (Fodor &

Pylyshyn 1988, Fodor & McLaughlin 1990).[8] The problem of representing relations appears, then, to pose a serious problem for both the psychological models we have considered.

The chicken and the egg

Feature-based views of similarity also share with spatial models their status with respect to the chicken and egg problem. They confront it head on, because features are just concepts by another name. It is no help in this context to argue that these features are different, simpler, concepts than those that were originally to be explained. This provides a solution only if it is possible to arrange concepts in a hierarchy from complex to simple, where the simplest concepts/features are directly given by the perceptual system. This existence of such a hierarchy presupposes a crude empiricism, which has long been rejected as philosophically and psychologically indefensible (Fodor & Lepore 1992). The ways in which this paradox might be resolved will be investigated in the final section of this chapter.

Similarity in neural networks

Theory

Having discussed the major psychological accounts of similarity, we now turn to two important computational ideas which can be used to model cognition, neural networks and CBR. Although these computational approaches are not directly concerned with providing an account of similarity, similarity is central to the way they operate.

Neural networks (alternatively called parallel distributed processing [PDP] models or connectionist models) are a class of computational systems inspired by aspects of the structure of the brain. They consist of large numbers of simple numerical processing units that are densely interconnected, and which operate in parallel to solve computational problems. The relationship with real neurons and synapses is a loose one (Sejnowski 1986) and, within cognitive science, neural networks are generally used as cognitive models without detailed concern for neurobiological issues (Chater & Oaksford 1990). Neural networks have been applied to a range of cognitive domains including speech perception (McClelland & Elman 1986), visual word recognition (Seidenberg & McClelland 1989), learning the past tense of English words (Plunkett & Marchman 1991) and aspects of high-level cognition, including knowledge representation and categorization. For introductions into this ever-growing field the reader is referred to one of the many introductory articles or textbooks available (McClelland et al. 1986,

Bechtel & Abrahamsen 1991, Churchland & Sejnowski 1992, Rumelhart & Todd 1993). Here, rather than attempt to provide a full introduction to neural networks, we shall conduct the discussion at a general level, referring the reader to the literature for further details.

One distinctive aspect of neural networks is their ability to learn from experience. A network can be trained to solve a problem on a series of examples, and will then, if all goes well, be able to generalize to novel cases of the problem to which it has not yet been exposed. A central question in neural network research concerns how this generalization occurs.

Suppose that a neural network is trained on a categorization task (unless indicated otherwise, the network we consider is a standard feed-forward network, with one layer of hidden units, trained by some variant of backpropagation. Many of the points we make apply more generally). That is, the inputs to the network are a set of examples that are to be classified, and the output of the network is to represent the category into which the current input falls. Training involves showing the network examples where the category is specified by the modeller. The network is then tested by presenting new examples and seeing whether they are classified appropriately.

The trained neural network can be viewed as a model of categorization, which, in a sense, presents an alternative to the prototype or exemplar views. Interestingly, neural networks appear to combine some aspects of both views (Rumelhart & McClelland 1985): if a network is trained on a number of distorted examples of a prototype, and then shown the prototype itself, it will classify that prototype as a particularly good example of category (i.e. the output of the network will be particularly high for that category). This is the classic prototype effect (Posner & Keele 1970). On the other hand, neural networks also appear to be sensitive to the specific examples on which they are trained – the classic exemplar effect (see Whittlesea, this volume).

Like prototype and exemplar theories of concepts, neural network categorization depends on similarity (Rumelhart & Todd 1993). But the behaviour of neural networks need not always depend directly on the similarity of the input representations – neural networks are able to form their own internal representations, on the so-called "hidden units". Classification in neural networks is therefore best thought of as determined by similarity in the internal representations of the network – thus similarity in neural networks is flexible because the internal representations are determined by the network itself, in order to provide the best way of solving the problem it has been trained on. Furthermore, each part of the internal representation used by the network need not be treated equally – some parts of the representation may be more strongly "weighted" than others (in the context of a standard feed-forward network with a single layer of hidden units, this has a very direct interpretation in terms of the magnitude of the weights from each hidden unit to the output layer).

How do the internal representations over which similarity is defined in neural networks relate to the representations used by spatial and feature-based models of similarity? Again, neural networks provide a curious combination of aspects of two different views. The internal representations consist of a set of n hidden units, each associated with a numerical value (typically between 0 and 1), its level of activation. The representation associated with the units can therefore be thought of as a point in a continuous n-dimensional space, in which each dimension corresponds to the activity level of each hidden unit. This seems compatible with spatial models of similarity. On the other hand, however, many trained neural networks learn to use a binary (or nearly binary) representation, in that the hidden unit values associated with patterns only take extreme values (i.e. almost 0 or almost 1). In such cases, the neural network can be viewed in terms of binary features, in line with feature-based models of similarity.

These remarks should be enough to suggest that neural networks provide potentially flexible and powerful models of at least some aspects of similarity and categorization, suggesting new perspectives on many issues. Researchers have attempted to exploit the potential of neural networks in a variety of ways (Shanks 1991, Gluck 1991, Kruschke 1992, Hinton 1986, McRae et al. 1993), and it remains to be seen which of these approaches will prove to be the most fruitful.

Problems

Perhaps the most significant area of difficulty for neural network models concerns the representation of relational information. This issue is vast and highly controversial, because it is central to the general debate concerning the utility of neural networks as models of cognition (Chater & Oaksford 1990, Fodor & Pylyshyn 1988, Smolensky 1988). Devising schemes for structured representations in neural networks is a major research topic as they are necessary not only in the context of categorization but for the modelling of language and large areas of reasoning. Numerous approaches have been put forward (e.g. Smolensky 1990, Shastri & Ajjanagadde 1992, Pollack 1990), of which none is wholly satisfactory. The question, thus, remains open.

Another source of problems concerns adapting similarity judgements to take account of "theory-based" effects on similarity judgements. Any effects of background knowledge will be difficult to deal with, because neural networks typically have no background knowledge – their knowledge is restricted to the category instances on which they have been trained. This again, constitutes an important research area, but is at present still in the very early stages (see e.g. Buscmeyer et al., this volume; Choi et al. 1993, Tresp et al. 1993, Roscheisen et al. 1992).

If and how neural networks manage to cope with these problems remains to be seen. They indicate limitations for current network models both of similarity and conceptual structure; any final judgement, however, must be deferred.

The chicken and the egg

Neural networks offer a range of possible perspectives on the chicken and egg relationship between concepts and similarity. One picture mirrors the above discussion for spatial and feature-based models of similarity. The patterns in the inputs and outputs of neural networks can typically be interpreted. For example, the input to a word recognition model might be in terms of perceptual features at different locations, each coded by one or more units in the input to the network. This input itself, like the dimensions in the spatial models, and the features in the contrast model, therefore presupposes a classification. Here, neural networks are nothing new.

Another possibility is that similarity and concepts are mutually constraining, and that neither presupposes the other. This possibility is illustrated (though not using concepts and similarity) by neural networks which involve interactive activation. An example are interactive activation models of word recognition, in which letters and words are recognized simultaneously, so that there are mutual constraints between them (McClelland & Rumelhart 1981). Various tentative hypotheses about which letters are present each reinforce the tentative hypotheses about which words are present with which they are consistent, and inhibit those with which they are inconsistent. At the same time, reinforcement and inhibition flow in the reverse direction from hypotheses about words to hypotheses about letters. The system is designed to settle into a state which simultaneously satisfies these constraints as well as possible. Thus, in an interactive reading system, decisions about which words and letters are present are interdependent. Paradox is avoided, because there is no attempt to recognize words before letters are recognized, or vice versa. Instead, both problems are solved together. It is not yet clear whether a similar approach could be used to provide neural network models which simultaneously calculate similarity judgements and categories, subject to mutual constraint.

There is also a further possibility: that similarity and concepts emerge from a more basic process – given by the way in which the neural network learns from exposure to individual category instances. The way in which the neural network learns will determine both how categorization is carried out and the similarities between individual items. Because the behaviour of neural networks is strongly determined by similarity over the hidden units, this means that, as the network learns, that is, as it learns to form suitable categories over the hidden units, classification and similarity will inevitably be intertwined.

While these various perspectives are suggestive, it is important to stress again that the neural network approach to similarity is still underdeveloped. It is currently difficult to assess to what extent potentially promising directions provided by neural networks will ultimately prove fruitful.

Similarity in case-based reasoning

Theory

Case-based reasoning (CBR) is a computational method in artificial intelligence, from a somewhat different research tradition than neural networks. It is closely linked to both the construction of expert systems and to research on machine learning (see for overviews DARPA 1989, Slade 1991, or Kolodner 1992).

The fundamental idea of CBR is, as the name suggests, that reasoning can be based on past stored cases, rather than on complex chains of inference from stored abstract rules. It therefore requires that past cases relevant to a new situation can be retrieved successfully, and that these cases can be used to guide thinking in the new situation appropriately. Which past cases should be consulted in dealing with a new situation? The cases that are relevant are those that are similar to the new situation. Of course, the notion of similarity may vary depending on the goals and context of the reasoner, in the ways that the discussion of Goodman above suggests. So, if we are reasoning about the just outcome of legal cases, then similarity in matters of legal significance, rather than in the date and place of birth of the people involved in the trial, will be important in determining similarity. If, on the other hand, we were attempting to predict the outcome of the cases by astrological means, the birthdates might be central and the legal details peripheral in determining similarity.

Within artificial intelligence, interest in CBR has been fuelled by the recognition that rule-based approaches to the representation of knowledge encounter severe difficulties. Rule-based systems for representing information presuppose the existence of "strong domain theories" (Porter et al. 1990), that is, theories consisting of facts and abstract rules from which all required solutions can be deduced. But such strong domain theories are rarely available (Oaksford & Chater

1991) – in real-world contexts, all rules, or sets of rules, however elaborate, succumb to countless exceptions. CBR offers an attractive way out of these difficulties. Rather than having to patch up rules with endless sub-rules, to capture endless awkward cases, reasoning takes cases as the starting point. This is appealing not only as a means of building practical artificial intelligence systems, but also a framework for understanding cognition.[9]

CBR is similar in spirit to the exemplar view of concepts – large numbers of examples/cases are stored, and used to deal with the current situation. CBR is much more general, however, in three ways. First, it is concerned with reasoning of all kinds, and not simply with categorization. Secondly, cases in many CBR systems are complex structured representations, rather than points in a space or bundles of features. Therefore, CBR tackles the problem of relational properties by defining a similarity measure over structured representations. Thirdly, many CBR systems make use of prior knowledge such as general knowledge of the domain and explanations of previous cases. Hence, these systems also embody the theory-based view (Porter et al. 1990, Branting 1991).

Approaches to similarity in CBR are too diverse (Bareiss & King 1989) to be described as constituting a theory of similarity – rather, CBR provides a range of accounts, many of which may be of interest in a psychological context. In some systems, similarity requires little or no computation but is implicitly given in the way cases are represented in memory (e.g. Bayer et al. 1992). In others, explicit similarity metrics are used. Here, we find different approaches depending, in particular, on whether cases can be represented exclusively through a set of numerical values or whether symbolic representations are required. Numerical values correspond to "dimensions", which allows Euclidean distance to be used in this context (Cost & Salzberg 1993). Symbolic representations for features and relations on the other hand make use of the traditional artificial intelligence repertoire of frames, scripts or graphs, mentioned above. CBR and machine learning research is, however, continuously evolving new ways of calculating similarities between instances (e.g. Cost & Salzberg 1993). Rather than discussing any of these approaches in detail, we limit our discussion to a few general points.

First, the existence of this wealth of practically useful solutions suggests that psychological theories of similarity have only explored a small range of possible ideas about similarity.

Secondly, paradigms such as CBR and machine learning in general can provide what might be called a problem perspective, that is an understanding of similarity which originates not from high-level considerations about supposed psychological plausibility but from the need to solve a particular problem. Where these problems concern cognitive tasks generally performed by humans such a perspective can greatly contribute to our understanding.

Finally, CBR systems, while subject to limitations of their own (see e.g. Hahn & Chater 1996), provide important empirical support in evaluating models of similarity in real-world domains. While much work remains to be done before conclusions on existing algorithms can be drawn, CBR has already contributed to our understanding of the problem both by highlighting the crucial role of representation and the role of knowledge in matching two items (Porter et al. 1990), illustrating, for example, the need for structured representations, which go beyond current psychological models.

Problems

Approaches to similarity from the point of view of CBR are too various, and also too undeveloped from the point of view of psychological modelling, for a coherent list of problems to be formulated. Individual similarity metrics deserve scrutiny comparable to those provided for spatial models and the contrast model, but this would take a paper of its own. If a general weakness can be claimed, it stems from the fact that the flexibility, the context sensitivity and dependency on goals and tasks that characterizes similarity in human cognition are difficult to achieve. CBR systems are often extremely rigid in what information about a case is represented (Hahn & Chater 1996). Once an initial decision by the modeller has been made, new types of information such as previously unanticipated, novel features cannot be included (a prominent example here is HYPO, Ashley 1990). This, incidentally, is a problem they share with neural networks. In contrast to networks, exceptions to this strait-jacket of uniform representation can be found as well (an example here is given in PROTOS, Porter et al. 1990), although the flexibility of the human cognitive system remains a goal yet to be attained.

It is important to stress, however, that the reason these weaknesses, both of neural networks and CBR systems, become an issue at all, is because they are attempting to tackle a far greater proportion of the job. Spatial models and the contrast model can, because of a considerable number of suitable free parameters, fit much (possibly all) of the flexibility exhibited in human similarity judgements. They do this exclusively, however, by providing *post hoc* fits to the data. The computational models we are discussing here, in contrast, actually attempt to solve the task in question. The vital issue in similarity of what is to be represented and how the individual factors are weighted must thus be addressed in the design and implementation of these models and cannot be left to *post hoc* analysis. These questions, and the answers experiments and modelling have so far provided, will be treated in more detail in the section on feature selection and weighting below.

The chicken and the egg

With respect to the chicken and the egg, CBR offers nothing new. All systems will have a set of basic categories – features, relations, attribute values – with which they operate. Depending on the system, this set can or cannot be extended, possibly also allowing current categories to be further decomposed. At any given point in time, however, some set of categories over which similarity is computed will be treated as given.

Kolmogorov complexity

Theory

We have considered two psychological theories of similarity, spatial and feature-based models, and also the way in which similarity arises in two computational mechanisms, neural networks and case-based reasoners. We now consider an account of similarity which has a computational origin, but which is not specific to any particular computational mechanism. This account has been developed within a branch of computer science and mathematics known as Kolmogorov complexity (see Li & Vitanyi 1993, for a comprehensive introduction). Related ideas are discussed under the headings minimum message length (Wallace & Boulton 1968), minimum description length (Rissanen 1989), and algorithmic complexity theory (Chaitin 1987).

The fundamental idea of Kolmogorov complexity theory is that the complexity of any mathematical object x can be measured by the length of the shortest computer program that is able to generate that object. This length is the Kolmogorov complexity, $K(x)$ of x. The class of objects which can be given Kolmogorov complexities is very broad, including numbers and sets, but also computer programs themselves, and, more generally, representations of all kinds. Anything that can be characterized in purely formal, mathematical terms can be assigned a Kolmogorov complexity. A physical object, such as a chair, cannot, of course be generated by any computer program – and hence Kolmogorov complexity cannot measure the complexity of physical objects. But a representation of a chair (e.g. as a set of features, a point in an internal space, or using a structured representation of some kind) can be assigned a Kolmogorov complexity. An immediate query is that surely the length of the shortest program to describe an object will depend on the nature of the programming language that is being used. This is quite true, although there is a remarkable mathematical result which states that the difference between the Kolmogorov complexities given by different programming languages can differ by at most some constant factor, for any object whatever. This means that, in some contexts at least, the specific programming language under consideration can be ignored, and Kolmogorov complexity can be treated as absolute. Kolmogorov complexity, while easy to define, turns out to have a large number of important mathematical properties and areas of applications, including inductive inference and machine learning (Solomonoff 1964, Wallace & Boulton 1968, Rissanen 1989).

Kolmogorov complexity can be generalized slightly to give a notion of the conditional Kolmogorov complexity, $K(x|y)$, of one object, x, given another object, y. This is the length of the shortest program which produces x as output from y as input. Suppose, for example, that x represents the category "chair," and that y represents the category "bench." $K(x|y)$ will be low, because it is presumably relative easy (i.e. only a short program is required) to transform one representation to the other. This is because many of the aspects of the two representations will be shared, since they have many of the same properties. In particular, the length of the program needed to generate a chair representation from a bench representation will be considerably shorter than length of program required to generate the chair representation from scratch – that is, $K(x|y) < K(x)$. On the other hand, if chair must be derived from, say, whale, then there will presumably be no saving at all in program length – since there are no significant shared aspects of the representation which can be carried over between chair and whale representations.

The intuition is, then, that the conditional Kolmogorov complexity between two representations (i.e. the length of the shortest program which generates the one given the other) will depend on the degree of similarity between those representations. But it is possible to turn this observation around, and use conditional Kolmogorov complexity as a measure of dissimilarity. This gives a simple account of similarity, with a number of interesting properties:

(a)   There is a well-developed mathematical theory in which a number of measures of similarity based on conditional Kolmogorov complexity are developed and studied (Li & Vitanyi 1993).

(b)   Perhaps most importantly, this account applies to representations of all kinds, whether they are spatial, feature-based or, crucially, structured representations. Indeed, it can be viewed as a generalization of the featural and spatial models of similarity, to the extent that similar sets of features (nearby points in space) correspond to short programs.

(c)   The fact that similarity is defined over general representations allows great flexibility, in that goals and knowledge of the subject may affect the representations which are formed. As with the featural model, this flexibility has both advantages, in terms of accounting for the flexibility of people's similarity judgements, and disadvantages, from the point of view of deriving testable empirical predictions.

(d)   Self-similarity is maximal, because no program at all is required to transform an object into itself.

(e)   The triangle inequality holds. The shortest program which transforms z to y concatenated with the shortest program which transforms y to x, is always at least as long as the shortest program that transforms z to x.

(f)   It builds in the asymmetry in similarity judgements: $K (x|y)$ is not in general equal to $K (y|x)$. This asymmetry is particularly apparent when the representations being transformed differ substantially in complexity. Suppose that a subject knows a reasonable amount about China, but rather little about Korea, except that it is "rather like" China in certain ways. Then transforming the representation of China into the representation of Korea will require a reasonably short program (which simply deletes large amounts of information concerning China which is not relevant to Korea), while the program transforming in the reverse direction will be complex, since the minimal information known about Korea will be almost no help in constructing the complex representation of China. Thus, we would predict that $K (China|Korea)$ should be greater than $K (Korea|China)$. This is observed experimentally (Tversky 1977).

(g)   Background knowledge can be taken into account by assuming that this forms an additional input to the program that must transform one object into another. Background knowledge may radically affect the program length required to transform two objects. Whether the effects of background knowledge on human similarity judgements can be modelled in terms of the effects of background knowledge on this program length is an interesting subject for future research.

Measures of similarity based on conditional Kolmogorov complexity have yet to be developed as potential psychological accounts of similarity. This promising direction may be an important avenue of future research.

Problems

Conditional Kolmogorov complexity appears to have a number of difficulties. First, it is psychologically unrealistic, because the general problem of calculating the conditional Kolmogorov complexity between two objects is provably uncomputable (Li & Vitanyi 1993). Psychological judgements of similarity could, however, be based on crude estimates of conditional Kolmogorov complexity, of which a number are available (Rissanen 1989).

Secondly, as in simple, unweighted, spatial models of similarity, conditional Kolmogorov complexity makes somewhat bizarre predictions as common features are added to the representations of the objects being compared. Indeed, similarity decreases as more similar features are added. This suggest that some modification of the approach is required to model human similarity judgements. One obvious suggestion is that the relevant measure of dissimilarity should be given by $K (x|y) / K (x)$. This gives the prediction that objects are judged to be more similar as more and more similar features are added, but it has implications for the other properties discussed above. Whether a measure which is appropriate overall can be found is a topic for future research.

Thirdly, the approach may be insufficiently flexible. Given two representations of objects, it simply gives a global similarity value between those representations. There is no scope for weighting some aspects of the representations more highly than others, or focusing only on sub-parts of the representations. This difficulty can, perhaps, be overcome if it is assumed that the flexibility of similarity in response to changing knowledge and goals is a reflection of the flexibility of the representation of objects in the light of these factors.

The chicken and the egg

This approach appears to break out of the vicious chicken and egg circularity in a radical way. Similarity is measured in terms of program length, which makes no reference to concepts – and hence there is no circularity to explain away. But this is misleading: similarity is defined over representations of the objects being compared; and how an object is represented depends on how it is categorized. It is therefore not clear that Kolmogorov complexity provides any new insights in the apparent interdependence of concepts and similarity.

Feature selection and feature weighting: choosing respects

Leaving our introduction of models and their particular problems behind, we return to the discussion at the beginning of this section, resuming the issue of respects. There, we noted that similarity is relative to respects, rather than an absolute notion. This, we saw, is equivalent to stating that similarity is representation dependent. Fixing the respects for a given similarity comparison can, hence, be described as selecting and, possibly, weighting the factors of interest. How is this reflected in the different accounts of similarity we have described? (For a more thorough account than can be provided here, see Hahn & Chater 1996.)

The short answer is that the feature selection and weighting process is very much outside the scope of all models discussed. Neural networks and CBR systems can capture some of this process. For all other models, it is simply not addressed. The contrast model does not describe how features are chosen, but simply assumes that they are selected from a rich mental representation of the objects concerned, in the light of the task at hand (Tversky 1977). Similarly, spatial models use MDS to establish retrospectively which dimensions were of what importance to a given subject. As a tool for data analysis, this is of utility and importance. As a model of similarity it falls rather short of the mark, given that the selection of factors over which similarity is assessed is the most crucial determinant of similarity.

CBR systems and neural networks depend largely on the input representations chosen by the modeller. To the extent that these systems learn, however, they establish some weighting and selection of features. As we saw above, neural networks can learn their own internal representations, and so can choose the respects in which similarity is appropriately measured for the task on which they have been trained.

At present, however, no computational system exhibits the flexibility of humans. Our similarity judgements are, for instance, highly dependent on contexts, goals or purposes, as is evident not merely from the general considerations of the importance of respects, but also from empirical studies (Roth & Shoben 1983, Sadler & Shoben 1993, Lamberts 1994, Barsalou 1982, 1983, 1987).

Why do current computational systems not mirror this flexibility of human judgements? The answer is, because it is so hard. At a general level, respects appear to be chosen according to whether they are relevant. The general problem of determining relevance is one of the most difficult questions in cognitive science and artificial intelligence (Oaksford & Chater 1991, Chater & Oaksford 1993). Accounting for the features selection and weighting process is, thus, a tall order.

However, experimental investigation has identified a number of factors affecting both selection and weighting, which seem to arise from the way the cognitive system processes similarity judgements (Medin et al. 1993). For example, adding common features, as opposed to relations, to a pair of objects, leads to a greater increase of similarity if common features (as opposed to relations) already dominate in this pair, and vice versa for adding relations. The weight of common features, thus, seems to depend in part on whether two objects share more features or relations (Goldstone et al. 1991). Similarly, the time available for the judgement seems to affect systematically the weight attributed to the dimensions on which comparison is based (Lamberts 1995). Given short deadlines, subjects rely heavily on perceptual properties. With more time, formal category structure exerts the greater role. Including effects of this kind in models of similarity is a far more achievable goal than solving the general problem of what counts as relevant. At present, research on these questions has just begun (Lamberts 1995, Goldstone 1994b).

In summary, the question of which respects are relevant, and how strongly each should be weighted, is fundamental to any complete account of similarity. To the extent that this depends on relevance, the problem is very hard indeed. A more manageable task is presented by constraints arising from the similarity comparison process itself. The question of respects must, however, be a major topic of future research in the literature both on similarity and on categorization.

Conclusions: adequacy of current models of similarity
We have reviewed a range of current models of similarity, from psychology, artificial intelligence and computer science. The two psychological models, spatial and feature-based models, both have important limitations – perhaps most crucially in that they appear to be unable to incorporate relational information. Neural networks, CBR and conditional Kolmogorov complexity provide, on the other hand, an intriguing range of possible models. But these models are not fully worked out and moreover their psychological utility is unproved. Furthermore, we have seen that models of similarity typically leave out a crucial aspect of the psychology of similarity – concerned with choosing which respects, with what weighting, should enter the similarity comparison. Important goals for future research therefore include attempting to apply sophisticated computational ideas concerning similarity to provide better psychological models of similarity, and addressing the question that theories of similarity typically ignore: how respects are chosen.

In the previous section, we considered accounts of concepts. In this section, we have considered accounts of similarity. In the next, we focus directly on how similarity and categorization are related.

CONCEPTS AND SIMILARITY

In introducing the range of theories of concepts, we discussed the role that similarity plays in each. We have considered a range of accounts of similarity. We now reconsider the relationship between concepts and similarity from both a theoretical and an empirical point of view. We ask whether, or to what extent, theories of similarity are able to play the role required of them by theories of concepts. This involves three separate issues. First, we need to investigate how particular models of similarity can be integrated with particular views of conceptual structure, and where this leads to difficulties. Secondly, we must consider the experimental evidence concerning the relationship between similarity and categorization. Finally, it must be shown how the in principle difficulties presented by "the chicken and the egg" relationship might be resolved. We address each of these issues in turn.

Theoretical integration
Table 2.1 shows schematically the extent to which the various theories and models can be integrated. We will take each view of conceptual structure in turn and examine whether the models of similarity discussed above can be fitted in.

TABLE 2.1

	Exemplar	Prototype	Theory	Rule
Spatial	+	+	outside	+
Feature-based	+	+	outside	+
K-distance	+	+	+	-?
Networks	+?	+?	-	+?
CBR	+	+	+	+

As we see, the prototype and exemplar views can basically be reconciled with any view of similarity discussed. While similarity has a central role in either, they do not place any constraints on how similarity is assessed. The only query, for both these views, concerns their compatibility with similarity as found in neural networks. This is, as we recall, because the most standardly used network architectures blur the distinction between both views, showing both prototype and exemplar effects. In this sense, they can be viewed as extensions of prototype or exemplar accounts.

The theory-based view is somewhat less universally compatible. Only in two of the accounts, conditional Kolmogorov complexity and CBR, is some form of theory included directly in the process of similarity assessment. Theories – as some form of general, explicit, but partial knowledge – can affect similarity judgement in both spatial models and the contrast model only through the feature selection and weighting process. But these processes are, as we have seen, beyond the scope of either account. Hence, theory-based views of concepts are compatible, but cannot be integrated with current versions of the spatial and contrast models. Neural networks, at present, fare even worse with theory-based views of concepts, as there is currently no universal mechanism by which networks could represent and use background knowledge (but see Busemeyer et al., this volume). Finally, we noted above that conditional Kolmogorov complexity can be affected by the knowledge, because that knowledge can be used to identify simple transformations between objects, which would not otherwise be available. Conditional Kolmogorov complexity can therefore be used within a theory-based approach. A cautionary note is, nevertheless, required. Allowing knowledge to influence similarity does not guarantee that knowledge influences similarity in a psychologically relevant way – the question of whether conditional Kolmogorov complexity can appropriately capture the effects of "theory" in this respect, needs further investigation.

Finally, the degree to which definitions can be expressed in each of these frameworks again differs. In the spatial model a set of necessary and sufficient features (i.e. a definition) corresponds to a set of dimensions and values to which a point must have zero distance in order to be classified as a member of the category. In the contrast model, a definition becomes a set of specified features which must be shared by the object to be classified. In other words, the terms comprising the distinctive features [i.e. $bf(I - J)$ and $cf(J - I)$] vanish from the equation as irrelevant; the outcome of the comparison must correspond to the weighted total of the definition's features. Likewise, a CBR system can be made to match a set of necessary and sufficient conditions by introducing the constraint that these features be perfectly matched, it is not so clear, however, how definitions can be assimilated in the neural network approach – indeed, the more general question of whether neural networks can follow rules at all is highly controversial in the context of neural network models of language (Christiansen & Chater, 1997; Coltheart et al. 1993, Hadley 1994, Pinker & Prince 1988, Plunkett & Marchman 1991, Rumelhart & McClelland 1986, Seidenberg & McClelland 1989). Finally, the definitional view of concepts does not appear to have any place for the idea that similarity should be measured by conditional Kolmogorov complexity. Although possible connections can be imagined, such as that definitions are short descriptions of sets of objects, and that perhaps there is low conditional Kolmogorov complexity between pairs of objects which are members of such sets, it is not clear whether any account along these, or other, lines could be viable. In our discussion of the definitional view, we also mentioned that recent experimental investigations suggest an "interference" of similarity even where subjects used definitions or similar rules. These effects can be captured by all accounts of similarity as they merely require an ongoing similarity comparison to previous exemplars operating alongside a rule-based classification if we imagine that the former overrides the latter only above certain degrees of similarity match.

In summary, there are partial constraints between current theories of categorization and similarity. These constraints will become more important in modifying theories of concepts and similarity, to the extent that unified accounts of similarity and categorization are developed. We now move on to consider the experimental evidence concerning the relationship between similarity and categorization.

Interpreting the empirical evidence

Empirical evidence concerning the relationship between concepts and similarity comes from a variety of sources. The interpretation of much of this evidence is determined by the theoretical stance taken on concepts and similarity. We have, in passing, already mentioned a great deal of empirical data which can be viewed as support for an intimate connection between both: namely, the empirical evidence that appears to favour either prototype or exemplar views of concepts. Because the prototype and exemplar views assume such a direct and central relationship between concepts and similarity, evidence for these views is automatically evidence that concepts and similarity are closely associated. But we have also already considered evidence from the perspective of rule-based approaches to similarity – that similarity to past examples "intrudes" even on apparently rule-based classification (Nosofsky et al. 1989, Allen & Brooks 1991, Ross 1989, Whittlesea, this volume). Further credibility is lent to the idea that cognition might use similarity to stored examples in categorisation, and in reasoning more generally, by the comparative success of CBR within artificial intelligence. The reason for this was that, in domains without a strong domain theory, rules (or at least rules alone) simply will not work, as there is nothing to tell us what a sufficient set of rules ought to be. The vast majority of real world problems, however, arises in precisely such domains. Here, it is difficult to see what else, if not similarity to cases, could be the driving force.

The theory-based view of concepts, in contrast, has generated a range of experimental studies that appear to cast doubt on the relationships between similarity and categorization (Carey 1985, Keil 1989, Rips 1989,

Wattenmaker et al. 1988, Wisniewski & Medin 1994). However, as we mentioned in reviewing these studies in our discussion of the theory-based view, these studies are not evidence that categorization is not based on similarity; they are evidence that categorization is not based on a simple and rigid notion of similarity, typically conceived as some kind of perceptual similarity. Once it is recognised that similarity need not be rigid, but may itself be influenced by the knowledge that the theory-based view emphasizes, then the necessity for tension between these experimental results and the role of similarity in categorization disappears. Nonetheless, at least one experiment has found a strong dissociation between similarity judgements and categorization – a result which does seem to be inconsistent with a direct link between the two, and hence, between similarity and concepts.

Rips (1989) provides two lines of experiments that undermine a straightforward relationship between similarity and categorization. In one line of experiments, he demonstrates that information such as variability of category members or frequency information differentially affects categorization and similarity judgements. Asked, for instance, whether a three-inch round object is more like a pizza than a quarter (the US coin) subjects prefer the quarter, while nevertheless preferring the classification as a pizza. These results can be explained, with some support from subjects' protocols, by the fact that pizzas allow far greater variability in size than do quarters, a fact which subjects seem to find selectively relevant to classification only. In a second line of experiments, subjects are presented with stories in which the superficial qualities of an animal undergo systematic transformation, creating greater surface similarity with another species. Nevertheless, classification as the original species is preferred. Though effects of the transformation on both categorization and similarity are observed, i.e. no strong dissociation takes place, the impact on similarity judgements nevertheless far outweighs that on categorization. In line with theory-based approaches, Rips argues that our knowledge of "essences" and underlying, non-surface features determines categorization, not superficial resemblance.

A further study, however, has produced results which indicate that strong dissociations between similarity and categorization occur only under special circumstances (Smith & Sloman 1994). Rips' results seem replicable only with sparse descriptions of objects, that is descriptions that contain only what they call "necessary" features with respect to some classification. For objects with descriptions combining necessary and merely characteristic features, categorization tracked similarity. Furthermore, even with sparse descriptions, Smith & Sloman found a dissociation only if subjects were also asked to explain their decisions.

These results are very much in line with the theory-based view. Similarity does play a role, where stimulus materials are sufficiently rich to allow similarity comparisons along dimensions perceived as relevant. Similarity, as stated several times before, is in no way limited to perceptual similarity as Rips suggests.

More generally, this line of experiments also points to the fact that the role of similarity in categorization may differ for different kinds of concepts. Goldstone (1994a) proposes the following ordering in terms of "grounding" by similarity: natural kinds ("dog"), man-made artefacts ("hammer", "chair"), *ad hoc* categories ("things to take out of a burning house"), and abstract schemas or metaphors (e.g. "events in which an act is repaid with cruelty" or "metaphorical prisons"). For the latter, Goldstone suggests, explanations by similarity are almost vacuous:

> an unrewarding job and a relationship that cannot be ended may both be metaphorical prisons, but this categorization is not established by overall similarity. The situations may both conjure up a feeling of being trapped, but this feature is highly specific and almost as abstract as the category to be explained (Goldstone 1994a:149).

At the other end of the scale high within-category-similarity has been shown to characterize at least basic-level objects[10] of many artefacts and natural kinds. At this level, category members share more features as listed by subjects than do the subordinate or superordinate category's members (Rosch 1975).

A slightly different strategy of dissociating categorization and similarity is presented in Rips & Collins (1993). Here, the experimenters aim to establish dissociations between typicality ratings, similarity ratings, and a judgement of the likelihood that a particular instance was a category member. This study, however, fails to provide persuasive data for a number of reasons. Most importantly, similarity is elicited by asking subjects how similar a particular instance is to its category. This is not a well-formed question; "robin" is not similar to "bird", a robin is a bird.[11] Presumably, subjects succeed in making some sense of this question, for example by reformulating it as "how similar is a robin to an average bird", or "to a typical bird", or "to other birds". In lieu of any information on what exactly it is that subjects do, there is no way that the data can be taken to be representative of similarity judgements as assumed to occur in the context of categorization. Additional worries rest on the fact that estimating the likelihood of an item being a category member is not the same as categorizing it (though probabilities may be part of this decision, see e.g. the "Generalized Context Model", Nosofsky 1988); given only the information that Linda is female, it is perfectly possible to judge how likely it is that Linda heads a multinational company. It does not, however, seem possible to categorize Linda, that is, say whether she is or is not head of a multinational company.[12] For this latter question, we simply lack enough information. Given, then, that the measures for the two central notions seem questionable, not much can be made of the results. However, the general strategy of the experiments, searching for differential effects of frequency information on similarity and categorization, does seem a suggestive avenue to pursue.

Clearly, the area requires further research. In particular, the interaction of similarity with "theories", that is prior knowledge, needs further specification. This, we think, requires not only more experimental but also computational work: it is only through the process of building explicit, rigorous models of theory-dependent categorization tasks that the exact need for, and thus role of, similarity assessment can be determined.

The chicken and the egg

We began this chapter by noting that concepts and similarity appear to stand in a "chicken and egg" relationship. Similarity appears to underlie categorization; but belonging to many of the same categories seems to be what makes objects similar. We then argued that this apparently circular relationship actually applies to theories in the psychological literature. We saw that current theories of concepts are all committed to the claim that concepts presuppose similarity, whether directly (for prototype and exemplar views) or indirectly (for rule-based and theory-based views). We then turned to the theories of similarity, and found that these are committed to the claim that similarity presupposes categorization. Spatial, feature-based, CBR and conditional Kolmogorov complexity approaches to similarity all presuppose categorization. We noted that neural network models also frequently presuppose categorization, although we suggested that this may not always be the case. So, our review of current theories of concepts leaves us with the conclusions that, according to current theories, concepts and similarity do stand in a chicken and egg relationship – each seems to presuppose the other.

If we accept that there is a circular relationship between concepts and similarity, how can paradox be avoided? We consider four possibilities.

1. Revise or abandon concepts and similarity. One approach is to attempt to revise the notions of concepts and similarity so that the circular relationship between them is removed. If this is not possible, then perhaps the notions must be abandoned wholesale. While this option cannot be ruled out, it is definitely to be used only as a last resort, given its severe implications for cognitive psychology. Once concepts are abandoned, for example, accounts of how knowledge is represented in memory, how language is produced and understood, what is the output of the perceptual system, and many more fundamental issues in cognitive psychology must be dramatically rethought.

   2. Recursion.   This approach is based on a solution to an even more basic problem of circularity: how a notion can be explained in terms of itself. In computer programming, the notion of recursion is often used to define concepts in terms of themselves in a harmless way. For example, the factorial function can be defined using the following relationships:

factorial (n) = (n) (factorial (n–1)) ·
factorial (0) = 1

   The upper clause involves recursion – factorial is, in a sense, defined in terms of itself. Circularity is avoided because the problem of finding, for example, the factorial of 10 is reduced to the problem of finding the factorial of 9 by applying the recursive clause. But applying the clause again, it is reduced to the problem of finding the factorial of 8, and so on, down to the factorial of 0. Now that a complex problem has been reduced to a simple one, the simple problem can be solved directly, by breaking out of the recursion and applying the lower clause. The important point is that notions can be defined in terms of themselves, by successively reducing complex problems to simple ones of the same form.
   Recursion applies equally well to cases in which there are two interdependent notions to be explained. As before, the important point is that the problems can successively be reduced to simpler problems of the same form. This is the solution to the original "chicken and egg" problem. Each chicken presupposes an egg; and each egg presupposes a chicken. But as evolutionary history is traced back, the ancestor chickens and eggs become simpler and simpler, until there are neither chickens or eggs to be explained at all.
   There are various ways in which this approach might be applied to concepts and similarity. One of these has been discussed already in the context of models of similarity. We noted that concepts could be arranged in a list from most to least complex, and it could be assumed that similarity judgements on which a particular concept depends could only involve simpler concepts. Because recursion has to stop somewhere, some

concepts (or some similarity judgements) would have to be primitives, which are not explained further. Many other possible applications of the idea of recursion can be imagined. It is not clear whether any of these can provide a satisfactory account of concepts and similarity.

3. Mutual constraint.   An alternative approach is that concepts and similarity must be calculated simultaneously by the cognitive system, so that each constrains the other. This was illustrated above, in the discussion of interactive activation neural network models.

Could this approach apply to concepts and similarity? The idea would be that concepts and similarity would be computed simultaneously in a mutually constrained way. That is, decisions about categorization would constrain decisions about similarity, and vice versa, but these constraints would operate simultaneously. This is an attractive idea, although it has not yet been explored.

4. The third factor.   This approach assumes that the relationship between concepts and similarity is to be explained in terms of a third factor, which is more basic than either of them. Consider, for example, the degree to which metals conduct electricity, and the degree to which they conduct heat. These properties co-vary – better heat conductors are better conductors of electricity. This means that it is possible to judge how well a metal will conduct electricity by finding out how well it conducts heat and vice versa. But this does not lead to paradox, because neither notion should be explained in terms of the other. The right explanation is that there is a third factor, the atomic structure of the metal, which determines its conductivity for both heat and electricity. Moreover, this third factor makes it possible to explain why these two properties correlate as they do.

What might an appropriate third factor be in the context of concepts and similarity? A natural approach would be to specify some general goal of the cognitive system, perhaps maximizing expected utility or maximizing the amount of information gained about the environment. The general goal might require the cognitive system to construct categories; and moreover to determine similarity relationships between different objects. The critical challenge for any such approach is to show that the general goal requires concepts and similarity must co-vary, just as a challenge of atomic theory is to explain why conductance of heat and electricity co–vary. In the context of neural networks, the third cause could be the way in which the network learns when it encounters new instances. This learning might produce both classification and similarity as by-products of the change in the hidden unit representations, as we mentioned above.

Summary

We have considered four possible options for dealing with the circular relationship between concepts and similarity. It is not clear which, if any, of them can provide a satisfactory theory of concepts and similarity. But future research must take up the challenge of developing one of these accounts, or devising a different approach to explaining the circular relationship between concepts and similarity. If this is not done, theories of concepts and similarity remain in the perilous position of using explanations which presuppose the very notions that they attempt to explain. Understanding the interrelationship between concepts and similarity is therefore one of the most important, and urgent, problems facing research in both areas.

There is also a more mundane moral to be drawn from the close relationship between concepts and similarity: that it seems likely that the problems that make progress difficult in both areas may be the same. This suggests that it may be fruitful to study concepts and similarity at once, rather than as two separate domains.

CONCLUSION

The major theories of conceptual structure rely more or less heavily on similarity. This seems sound, given the fact that there is significant experimental evidence to support this view. Additionally, computational modelling within artificial intelligence has provided compelling support by highlighting the weaknesses of approaches which make no use of similarity. However, we have also seen that similarity is too complex and difficult a notion for it to be used as an explanatory primitive. Without a model of similarity, much of the problem has simply been swept under the carpet. This is all the more so, as no current model seems fully satisfactory. Furthermore, the difficulties are worsened by the intimate connection of similarity and concepts, which suggest that there are limits to the extent to which they can usefully be studied on their own. Nevertheless, we think, the feeling should not be one of dejection. The material we have reviewed does indicate that many constraints, both on theories of conceptual structure and on models of similarity, have emerged. In short, while no satisfactory solution has yet been found, it has become far clearer what we are looking for. We hope that the review of material in this chapter may provide some useful sources from which further research can begin, and indicate directions which it may prove useful to explore.

REFERENCES

AAAI 1993. *Proceedings of the AAAI–93 Workshop on Case-Based Reasoning.* AAAI Press.

Allen, S. & L. Brooks 1991. Specializing the operation of an explicit rule. *Journal of Experimental Psychology: General* **120**, 3–19.

Ashley, K. 1990. *Modeling legal argument – reasoning with cases and hypotheticals.* Cambridge, Mass.: MIT press.

Bareiss, R. & J. King 1989. Similarity assessment and case-based reasoning. In *Proceedings: Case-Based Reasoning Workshop*, 67–71. San Mateo, California: Morgan Kaufmann.

Barsalou, L. 1982. Context-independent and context-dependent information in concepts. *Memory and Cognition* **10**, 82–93.

Barsalou, L. 1983. Ad hoc categories. *Memory and Cognition* **11**, 211–27.

Barsalou, L. 1987. The instability of graded structure: implications for the nature of concepts In *Concepts and conceptual development: ecological and intellectual factors in categorization*, U. Neisser (ed.), 101–140. Cambridge: Cambridge University Press.

Bayer, M., B. Harbig S. Wess 1992. *Ahnlichkeit und Ahnlichkeitsmasse In Fallbasiertes Schliessen: eine Ubersicht.* Techreport: SEKI Working Paper SWP–92–08.

Bechtel, W. & A. Abrahamsen 1991. *Connectionism and the mind.* Oxford: Blackwell.

Branting, K. 1991. *Integrating rules and precedents for classification and explanation.* PhD thesis, University of Texas, Austin.

Brooks, L. 1978. Nonanalytic concept formation and memory for instances. In *Cognition and categorization*, E. Rosch & B. Lloyd (eds), 169–211. Hillsdale, New Jersey: Erlbaum.

Bruner, J., J. Goodnow, G. Austin 1956. *A study of thinking.* New York: John Wiley.

Carey, S. 1985. *Conceptual change in childhood.* Cambridge, Mass.: Bradford Books.

Chaitin, G. 1987. *Algorithmic information theory.* Cambridge: Cambridge University Press.

Chater, N. & M. Oaksford 1990. Autonomy, implementation, and cognitive architecture: a reply to Fodor and Pylyshyn. *Cognition* **34**, 93–107.

Chater, N. & M. Oaksford 1993. Logicism, mental models and everyday reasoning: reply to Garnham. *Mind and Language* **8**, 72–89.

Choi, S., M. McDaniel J. Busemeyer 1993. Incorporating prior biases in network models of conceptual rule learning. *Memory and Cognition* **21**, 413–23.

Christiansen, M. & N. Chater 1997. Connectionism and natural language processing. In *Language processing*, S. Garrod & M. Pickering (eds). London: UCL Press.

Churchland, P. S. & T. J. Sejnowski 1992. *The computational brain.* Cambridge, Mass.: MIT Press.

Collins, A. & M. Quillian 1972. Experiments on semantic memory and language comprehension. In *Cognition in learning and memory*, L. Gregg (ed.). New York: John Wiley.

Coltheart, M., B. Curtis, P. Atkins M. Haller 1993. Models of reading aloud: dual-route and parallel-distributed processing approaches. *Psychological Review* **100**, 589–608.

Cost, S. & S. Salzberg 1993. A weighted nearest neighbour algorithm for learning with symbolic features. *Machine Learning* **10**, 57–78.

DARPA 1989. Machine learning program plan: case-based reasoning. In *Proceedings: Case-based Reasoning Workshop*, 1–14. San Mateo, California: Morgan Kaufmann.

Fodor, J. 1975. *The language of thought*. New York: Cromwell.

Fodor, J., M. Garrett, E. Walker C. Parkes 1980. Against definitions. *Cognition* **8**, 1–105.

Fodor, J. & E. Lepore 1992. Paul Churchland: State space semantics. In *Holism: a shoppers guide*. Oxford: Blackwell.

Fodor, J. & B. McLaughlin 1990. Connectionism and the problem of systematicity: why Smolensky's solution won't work. *Cognition* **35**, 13–204.

Fodor, J. & Pylyshyn, Z. 1988. Connectionism and cognitive architecture: a critical analysis. *Cognition* **28**, 3–71.

Garner, W. 1978. Aspects of a stimulus: features, dimensions, and configurations. In *Cognition and categorization*, E. Rosch, B. & Lloyd (eds), Hillsdale, New Jersey: Lawrence Erlbaum.

Gati, I. & A. Tversky 1982. Representations of qualitative and quantitative dimensions. *Journal of Experimental Psychology: Human Perception and Performance* **8**, 325–40.

Gati, I. & A. Tversky 1984. Weighting common and distinctive features in perceptual and conceptual judgements. *Cognitive Psychology* **16**, 341–70.

Gentner, D. 1983. Structure-mapping: a theoretical framework for analogy *Cognitive Science* **7**, 155–70.

Gluck, M. 1991. Stimulus generalization and representation in adaptive network models of category learning. *Psychological Science* **2**, 50–55.

Goldstone, R. 1994a. The role of similarity in categorization: providing a groundwork. *Cognition* **52**, 125–57.

Goldstone, R. 1994b. Similarity, interactive activation, and mapping. *Journal of Experimental Psychology: Learning, Memory, and Cognition* **20**, 3–28.

Goldstone, R., D. Medin, D. Gentner 1991. Relational similarity and the nonindependence of features in similarity judgements. *Cognitive Psychology* **23**, 222–62.

Goodman, N. 1972. *Problems and projects*. Indianapolis: Bobbs Merill.

Hadley, R. 1994. Systematicity in connectionist language learning. *Mind and Language* **9**, 247–72.

Hahn, U. & N. Chater 1996. Understanding similarity: a joint project for psychology, case-based reasoning, and law. *Artificial Intelligence Review*, in press.

Hinton, G. 1986. Learning distributed representations of concepts. In *Proceedings of the Eighth Annual Meeting of the Cognitive Science Society*. Hillsdale, New Jersey: Erlbaum.

Hintzman, D. & G. Ludlam 1980. Differential forgetting of prototypes and old instances: simulation by an exemplar-based classification model. *Memory and Cognition* **8**, 378–82.

Homa, D., S. Sterling, L. Trepel 1981. Limitations of exemplar-based generalization and the abstraction of categorical information. *Journal of Experimental Psychology: Learning, Memory, and Cognition* **7**, 418–39.

Hunt, E., J. Marin, P. Stone 1966. *Experiments in induction*. New York: Academic Press.

Jones, C. & E. Heit 1993. An evaluation of the total similarity principle. *Journal of Experimental Psychology: Learning, Memory, and Cognition* **19**, 799–812.

Keil, F. 1989. *Concepts, kinds and development*. Cambridge, Mass.: Bradford Books.

Kolodner, J. 1992. An introduction to case-based reasoning. *Artificial Intelligence Review* **6**, 3–34.

Komatsu, L. 1992. Recent views of conceptual structure. *Psychological Bulletin* **112**, 500–526.

Kruschke, J. 1992. alcove: An exemplar-based connectionist model of category learning. *Psychological Review* **99**, 22–44.

Lakoff, G. 1987. Cognitive models and prototype theory. In *Concepts and conceptual development: ecological and intellectual factors in categorization*, U. Neisser (ed.), 63–100. Cambridge: Cambridge University Press.

Lamberts, K. 1994. Flexible tuning of similarity in exemplar-based categorization. *Journal of Experimental Psychology: Learning, Memory, and Cognition* **20**, 1003–1021.

Lamberts, K. 1995. Categorization under time pressure. *Journal of Experimental Psychology: General* **124**, 161–80.

Levine, M. 1975. *A cognitive theory of learning: research on hypothesis testing*. Hillsdale, New Jersey: Erlbaum.

Li, M. & P. Vitanyi 1993. *An introduction to Kolmogorov complexity and its applications*. New York: Springer.

Marr, D. 1982. *Vision*. San Francisco: W. H. Freeman.

McClelland, J. & J. Elman 1986. Interactive processes in speech perception: the trace model. In *Parallel distributed processing*, vol. 2: *psychological and biological models*, D. Rumelhart & J. McClelland (eds), 58–121. Cambridge, Mass.: MIT press.

McClelland, J. & D. Rumelhart 1981. An interactive activation model of context effects in letter perception, part 1: an account of basic findings. *Psychological Review* **88**, 375–407.

McClelland, J., D. Rumelhart, G. Hinton 1986. *Parallel distributed processing – explorations in the microstructure of cognition*. Cambridge, Mass.: MIT press.

McRae, K., V. de Sa, M. Seidenberg, 1993. Modeling property intercorrelations in conceptual memory. In *Proceedings of the Annual Meeting of the Cognitive Science Society*, 729–34. Boulder, Colorado: Cognitive Science Society.

Medin, D. 1989. Concepts and conceptual structure. *American Psychologist* **44**, 1469–1481.

Medin, D. L. & W. Wattenmaker 1987. Category cohesiveness, theories, and cognitive archaeology. In *Concepts and conceptual development: Ecological and intellectual factors in categorization*, U. Neisser (ed.), 25–62. Cambridge: Cambridge University Press.

Medin, D., G. Dewey, T. Murphy 1983. Relationships between item and category learning: Evidence that abstraction is not automatic. *Journal of Experimental Psychology: Learning, Memory, and Cognition* **9**, 607–625.

Medin, D., R. Goldstone, D. Gentner 1993. Respects for Similarity. *Psychological Review* **100**, 254–78.

Medin, D. & M. Schaffer 1978. Context theory of classification learning. *Psychological Review* **85**, 207–238.

Miller, G. & P. Johnson-Laird 1976. *Language and perception*. Cambridge, Mass.: Harvard University Press.

Minsky, M. 1977. Frame theory. In *Thinking: readings in cognitive science*, P. Johnson-Laird & P. Wason (eds). Cambridge: Cambridge University Press.

Murphy, G. & D. Medin 1985. The role of theories in conceptual coherence. *Psychological Review* **92**, 289–316.

Neisscr, U. 1987. From direct perception to conceptual structure. In *Concepts and conceptual development: ecological and intellectual factors in categorization*, U. Neisser (ed.), 1–20. Cambridge: Cambridge University Press.

Neisser, U. & P. Weene 1962. Hierarchies in concept attainment. *Journal of Experimental Psychology* **64**, 640–45.

Nosofsky, R. 1984. Choice, similarity and the context theory of classification. *Journal of Experimental Psychology: Learning, Memory, and Cognition* **10**, 104–114.

Nosofsky, R. 1988. Exemplar-based accounts of relations between classification, recognition, and typicality. *Journal of Experimental Psychology: Learning, Memory, and Cognition* **14**, 700–708.

Nosofsky, R. 1990. Relations between exemplar-similarity and likelihood models of classification. *Journal of Mathematical Psychology* **34**, 812–35.

Nosofsky, R. 1991. Stimulus bias, asymmetric similarity, and classification. *Cognitive Psychology* **23**, 94–140.

Nosofsky, R., S. Clark, H. Shin 1989. Rules and exemplars in categorization, identification, and recognition. *Journal of Experimental Psychology: Learning, Memory, and Cognition* **15**, 282–304.

Oaksford, M. & N. Chater 1991. Against logicist cognitive science. *Mind and Language* **6**, 1–38.

Oden, G. C. 1987. Concept, knowledge, and thought. *Annual Review of Psychology* **38**, 203–237.

Osherson, D. & E. Smith 1981. On the adequacy of prototype theory as a theory of concepts. *Cognition* **9**, 35–58.

Pinker, S. & A. Prince 1988. On language and connectionism: Analysis of a parallel distributed processing model of language acquisition. *Cognition* **28**, 73–193.

Plunkett, K. & V. Marchman 1991. U-shaped learning and frequency effects in a multi-layered perceptron: Implications for child language acquisition. *Cognition* **38**, 43–102.

Pollack, J. 1990. Recursive distributed representations. *Artificial Intelligence* **46**, 77–105.

Porter, B., R. Bareiss, R. Holte 1990. Concept learning and heuristic classification. *Artificial Intelligence* **45**, 229–63.

Posner, M. & S. Keele 1970. Retention of abstract ideas. *Journal of Experimental Psychology* **83**, 304–308.

Pylyshyn, Z. 1973. What the mind's eye tells the mind's brain: A critique of mental imagery. *Psychological Bulletin* **80**, 1–24.

Restle, F. 1962. The selection of strategies in cue learning. *Psychological Review* **69**, 329–43.

Richter, M., S. Wess, K. Althoff, F. Maurer 1993. Presentations and posters at the First European Workshop on Case-based Reasoning. SEKI Report SR–93–12 (SFB 314).

Riesbeck, C. & R. Schank 1989. *Inside case-based reasoning*. Hillsdale, New Jersey: Erlbaum.

Rips, L. 1989. Similarity, typicality and categorization. In *Similarity and analogical reasoning*, S. Vosniadou & A. Ortony (eds), 21–59. Cambridge: Cambridge University Press.

Rips, L. & A. Collins 1993. Categories and resemblance. *Journal of Experimental Psychology: General* **122**, 468–86.

Rissanen, J. 1989. *Stochastic complexity in statistical inquiry*. New Jersey: World Scientific.

Rosch, E. 1975. Cognitive reference points. *Cognitive Psychology* **7**, 532–47.

Rosch, E. 1978. Principles of categorization. In *Cognition and categorization*, E. Rosch & B. Lloyd (eds). Hillsdale, New Jersey: Erlbaum.

Rosch, E., C. Mervis, W. Gray, D. Johnson P. Boyes-Braem 1976. Basic objects in natural categories. *Cognitive Psychology* **8**, 382–439.

Roscheisen, M., R. Hofman, V. Tresp 1992. *Neural controlling for rolling mills: incorporating domain theories to overcome data deficiency*. Advances in Neural Information Processing 4. San Mateo, California: Morgan Kaufman.

Ross, B. 1984. Remindings and their effects in learning a cognitive skill. *Cognitive Psychology* **16**, 371–416.

Ross, B. 1987. This is like that: The use of earlier problems and the separation of similarity effects. *Journal of Experimental Psychology: Learning, Memory, and Cognition* **13**, 629–37.

Ross, B. 1989. Some psychological results on case-based reasoning. In *Proceedings of the Workshop on Case-based Reasoning*, San Mateo, CA: Morgan Kaufmann.

Ross, B. & P. Kennedy 1990. Generalizing from the use of earlier exemplars in problem solving. *Journal of Experimental Psychology: Learning, Memory, and Cognition* **16**, 42–55.

Ross, B., S. Perkins, P. Tenpenny 1990. Reminding-based category learning. *Cognitive Psychology* **22**, 460–92.

Roth, E. & E. Shoben 1983. The effect of context on the structure of categories. *Cognitive Psychology* **15**, 346–78.

Rumelhart, D. & J. McClelland 1985. Distributed memory and the representation of general and specific information. *Journal of Experimental Psychology: General* **114**, 159–88.

Rumelhart, D. & J. McClelland 1986. On learning past tenses of English verbs. In *Parallel distributed processing*, vol. 2: *psychological and biological models*, D. Rumelhart & J. McClelland (eds), 216–271. Cambridge, Mass.: MIT Press.

Rumelhart, D. & P. Todd 1993. Learning and connectionist representations. *Attention and Performance* XIV, 3–30.

Sadler, D. & E. Shoben 1993. Context effects on semantic domains as seen in analogy solution. *Journal of Experimental Psychology: Learning, Memory, and Cognition* **19**, 128–47.

Schank, R. & R. Abelson 1977. *Scripts, plans, goals, and understanding*. Hillsdale, New Jersey: Erlbaum.

Seidenberg, M. & J. McClelland 1989. A distributed, developmental model of word recognition and naming. *Psychological Review* **96**, 523–68.

Sejnowski, T. 1986. Open questions about computation in the cerebral cortex. In *Parallel distributed processing*, vol. 2: *psychological and biological models*, D. Rumelhart & J. McClelland (eds). Cambridge, Mass.: MIT Press.

Shanks, D. 1991. Categorization by a connectionist network. *Journal of Experimental Psychology: Learning, Memory, and Cognition* **17**, 433–43.

Shastri, L. & V. Ajjanagadde 1992. From simple associations to systematic reasoning: a connectionist representation of rules, variables and dynamic bindings using temporal synchrony. *Behavioural and Brain Sciences* **12**, 456–78.

Shepard, R. 1980. Multidimensional scaling, tree-fitting, and clustering. *Science* **210**, 390–99.

Shepard, R. 1987. Toward a universal law of generalization for psychological science. *Science* **237**, 1317–23.

Slade, S. 1991. Case-based reasoning: a research paradigm. *AI Magazine* **13**, 42–55.

Smith, E. & D. Medin 1981. *Categories and concepts*. Cambridge, Mass.: Harvard University Press.

Smith, E. & S. Sloman 1994. Similarity- versus rule-based categorization. *Memory and Cognition* **22**, 377–86.

Smolensky, P. 1988. On the proper treatment of connectionism. *Behavioral and Brain Sciences* **11**, 1–74.

Smolensky, P. 1990. Tensor product variable binding and the representation of symbolic structures in connectionist systems. *Artificial Intelligence* **46**, 159–215.

Solomonoff, R. 1964. A formal theory of inductive inference, part 1. *Information and Control* **7**, 1–22.

Tanaka, J. & M. Taylor 1991. Object categories and expertise: is the basic level in the eye of the beholder? *Cognitive Psychology* **23**, 457–82.

Trabasso, T. & G. Bower 1968. *Attention in learning: theory and research*. New York: John Wiley.

Tresp, V., J. Hollatz, S. Ahmad 1993. Network structuring and training using rule-based knowledge. In *Advances in Neural Information Processing 5*, C. Giles, S. Hanson, J. Cowan (eds). San Mateo, California: Morgan Kaufman.

Tversky, A. 1977. Features of similarity. *Psychological Review* **84**, 327–52.

Tversky, A. & I. Gati 1978. Studies of similarity. In *Cognition and categorization*, E. Rosch & B. Lloyd (eds), 79–98. Hillsdale, New Jersey: Erlbaum.

Tversky, A. & I. Gati 1982. Similarity, separability and the triangle inequality. *Psychological Review* **89**, 123–54.

Tversky, A. & J. Hutchinson 1986. Nearest neighbour analysis of psychological spaces. *Psychological Review* **93**, 3–22.

Wallace, C. & D. Boulton 1968. An information measure for classification. *Computing Journal* **11**, 185–95.

Wattenmaker, W., G. Dewey, T. Murphy, D. Medin 1986. Linear separability and concept learning. *Cognitive Psychology* **18**, 158–94.

Wattenmaker, W., G. Nakamura, D. Medin 1988. Relationships between similarity-based and explanation-based categorization. In *Contemporary science and natural explanation*, D. Hilton (ed.). Brighton: Harvester.

Whittlesea, B. 1987. Preservation of specific experiences in the representation of general knowledge. *Journal of Experimental Psychology: Learning, Memory, and Cognition* **13**, 3–17.

Wisniewski, E. & D. Medin 1994. On the interaction of theory and data in concept learning. *Cognitive Science* **18**, 221–81.

NOTES

1. Rather *ad hoc* seeming grouping of objects are found as so-called goal derived categories – e.g. "things to take out of a burning house" (Barsalou 1983); these will be discussed later. For "dribs", however, no such unifying goal is in sight.

2. This term is widely used to cover family resemblance (Rosch 1975, Rosch et al. 1976) and probabilistic accounts (Komatsu 1992, Smith & Medin 1981).

3. For example, prototypes can be viewed as abstractions (such as a feature list) or as a particular exemplar (Lakoff 1987). The former is exemplified in notions of central tendency as average properties, modal properties, or modal correlations of properties. Viewing the central tendency as one or a number of particularly representative instances of the category illustrates the latter approach. See Barsalou (1987) for discussion of the numerous ways in which a particular exemplar might be "typical".

4. The definitional view underlies the main psychological research on artificial concepts from 1920 to 1970 (Smith & Medin 1981). Indeed, early empirical research embodied the assumption in the choice of experimental materials used: subjects were typically asked to learn to classify artificial materials, where the "correct" classification was given by a rule formulated by the experimenter (Bruner et al. 1956, Hunt et al. 1966, Levine 1975, Neisser & Weene 1962, Restle 1962, Trabasso & Bower 1968).

5. It is possible to argue that definitions of everyday concepts might exist in an internal "language of thought", even if these definitions could not be given in natural language. While logically possible, this view is unattractive, in the absence of any concrete proposals concerning the nature of this language of thought and how definitions of everyday concepts can be framed in terms of it.

6. In a sense, the notion of psychological space is not particularly well defined: there are no commitments as to what exactly this space is, whether it is a long-term representation or not, nor whether it is explicitly similarity that is represented here or whether the representation of similarity it generates is merely a by-product of a general scheme for the representation of objects.

7. In the Euclidean case, the equation is merely a generalization of Pythagoras' theorem to any number of dimensions: the square of the length of the hypotenuse is equal to the sum of the squares of the lengths of the other two sides. Hence, the length of the hypotenuse equals the square root of this sum. The distance between two points, however, is the hypotenuse of the right-angled triangle defined by the stretch (the differences) between the values of both points on both co-ordinates as the other two sides.

8. It is, of course, true that in a sense anything can be a feature (Tversky 1977) or a dimension, and any relation can also be represented as a feature: the fact that some individual a is the mother of b can make use of the two place relation "mother-of", i.e. mother (a, b), can also be expressed with one-place predicate (i.e. a feature) "mother-of-b", that is mother-of-b (a). This, however, does not solve the problem. The choice between a 1-placed, featural and an n-placed relational representation is not arbitrary as it determines the choice of primitives in the representation of entities. This, in turn, directly affects the similarity between entities as it determines in what ways they can be compared: if representational specificity leads to

"left-eye" and "right-eye" as primitives, one cannot even compare two eyes within the same bird. The problem is one of a general tension between the need for simple features which allow comparison and the need for encoding relations between features. The situation is one of "having your cake and eating it" and it seems that it can only be avoided by using structured representations.

9.   Examples of systems with a primary emphasis on cognitive modelling are to be found in Riesbeck & Schank 1989. Practical applications (e.g. fault diagnosis) can be found in the relevant conference proceedings such as Richter et al. (1993) or AAAI (1993). Examples of commercially available products are ReCall by ISoft S. A. or Remind by Cognitive Systems Inc.

10.   Within a hierarchy of abstraction such as "rocking chair", "chair", "furniture", the basic level – "chair" – is that which seems cognitively privileged in the sense that it is first learned, most freely produced, first accessed, and most quickly confirmed (see, e.g. Murphy & Lassaline, this volume; Rosch 1975, Rosch et al. 1976; see also, e.g. Tanaka & Taylor 1991).

11.   Rips & Collins' own reply that such questions are common in ordinary language as illustrated by questions such as "How similar is Alice to Woody Allen's other movies or how similar is Montreal to European cities?" (1993:483) misses the point as it lacks precisely the element it ought to have: "Woody Allen's other films" are instances, not a superordinate category, of Alice.

12.   This holds for all three accounts of conceptual structure. We cannot tell whether, for examples, a definition of "head of multinational company" applies, for, whatever it may be, it will not contain "male" as a necessary and sufficient definition. In both the exemplar and prototype view, the lack of further detail about Linda makes the necessary similarity computation impossible; again, it need not concern us what exactly exemplars or the prototype of this category look like, because even if "male" was a specified attribute, both accounts, by definition do not require that all attributes are matched. For both, nothing follows from the existence of non-matching (non-necessary) features on their own.

CHAPTER THREE

Hierarchical Structure in Concepts and the Basic Level of Categorization

Gregory L. Murphy and Mary E. Lassaline

Even informal observation of everyday categorization reveals that many objects fit into a number of categories. A single object might be called a *wire-haired terrier, terrier, dog, mammal* or *animal*. On other occasions, it might be called a *pet, friend, guard dog,* or *brute.* At still other times, it might be thought of as *something to be rescued in case of a fire, an expensive gift,* or *a threat to the new shrubs that were just planted.* Part of the power of human thought and reasoning arises from the ability to think of the same thing in different ways, thereby allowing us to access different kinds of knowledge about it (e.g. *mammal* brings to mind certain biological information about the object, whereas *friend* brings to mind very different information). However, this flexibility also presents a problem, in that these different categories must be distinguished and stored in memory, and the appropriate one must be used at a given time.

In this chapter, we will not address all of the possible ways in which an object can be categorized. Instead, we will focus on one particular kind of category organization: the *hierarchical* structure of categories. In the above example, the categories *wire-haired terrier, terrier, dog, mammal* and *animal* form a hierarchy or taxonomy – a sequence of progressively larger categories in which each category includes all the previous ones. That is, dogs include all terriers, which include all wire-haired terriers. The hierarchical organization, which will be described in more detail shortly, has been suggested as a particularly important way of organizing concepts. In fact, when people are asked to categorize an object in a neutral setting, without further instructions, they are very likely to provide one of the hierarchically-organized categories, such as *terrier* or *dog*, rather than a category such as *furry thing* or *something to be rescued in case of a fire*. Thus, these taxonomic categories may be particularly important ones for thought and communication.

In addition to the importance of the hierarchical organization, psychologists have long noted that one particular level of specificity of categories seems to be important. For example, people will normally name a wire-haired terrier as "a dog" rather than calling it "a terrier" or "an animal". There seems to be something about the category *dog* that makes it just the right level of identification. Considerable effort has been expended within the psychology of categorization to identify this especially useful level, called "the basic level of categorization", in a number of different domains. We will be discussing the evidence for such a privileged level of categorization, along with explanations for what gives the basic level its advantages.

HIERARCHICAL STRUCTURE OF CATEGORIES

In order to illustrate the hierarchical structure of categories, we will refer to a category structure in the long-term memory of a fictional person, Emilie, shown in Figure 3.1.

To begin, we need to establish some terminology: The categories that are higher in the hierarchy dominate or are *superordinate* to the lower-level categories; the lower-level categories are *subordinate* to the higher-

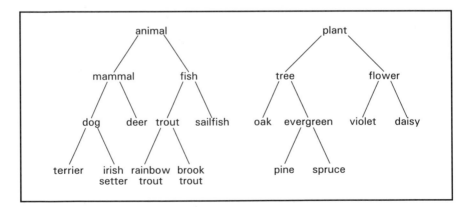

FIG. 3.1.   A simplified conceptual hierarchy. The lines represent IS-A links connecting concepts to their superordinates or subordinates.

level ones. Note that some parts of the hierarchy are "deeper" than others, that is, have more levels. For example, Emilie knows two kinds of dogs but no kinds of deer; therefore, the hierarchy is deeper under the *dog* category. Finally, we should note that in order to save space, we have allowed each category to have only two subordinates. However, this is not an actual rule of hierarchies. In fact, Emilie likely knows many more kinds of animals than are shown in Figure 3.1.

A hierarchy is a kind of network. That is, it has nodes (categories) connected by relations (indicated by lines in Figure 3.1). However, a hierarchy is a special kind of network. To begin with, the only relation allowed between category members is the *set inclusion* relation. For example, the set of animals includes the set of fish which includes the set of trout which includes the set of rainbow trout. Set inclusion is sometimes called the IS-A relation (Collins & Quillian 1969), because the subordinate category "is a" superordinate: An oak IS-A tree, and a tree IS-A plant. In addition, for a network to be a hierarchy, any category can have only one immediate superordinate; no node could have two lines leading to it from above in Figure 3.1. For example, *deer* can have *mammal* as its immediate superordinate, but it cannot also have *fish* as an immediate superordinate.

The nature of the IS-A relation is also important in determining the properties of hierarchies. First, the IS-A relation is *asymmetric*: all dogs are animals, but not all animals are dogs. Secondly, the category relations are *transitive*: all pines are evergreens, and all evergreens are trees; therefore all pines are trees. The transitivity of category membership leads to a similar transitivity of property ascription. Every property true of the members of a category is also true of the category's subordinates. For example, suppose that all animals have blood. If this is true, then all mammals must have blood, and therefore all dogs have blood, and therefore all terriers have blood. This property is directly related to the set-inclusion nature of the links. It is *because* all terriers are animals that the properties of animals must also apply to terriers.

These properties illustrate some of the power of hierarchical descriptions. If Emilie learns something about animals in general, she can now generalize this to all of the many categories that are under *animal* in the hierarchy. Or if she learns that a chow is a kind of dog, she can now generalize everything else that she knows about dogs to chows. Thus, by being able to place a category into its proper place in the hierarchy, one can learn a considerable amount about the category. So, even though Emilie has never seen a chow, she can assume that they have blood, that they bark, and have all the properties common to dogs and other animals. Clearly, this is an important ability to have, since it allows one to immediately access knowledge about new entities that one has had no direct experience with.

Psychological status of hierarchies

People's conceptual structures are widely believed to have the general properties of hierarchies that we have just described (e.g. Markman & Callanan 1983). Indeed, hierarchical structure appears to be a universal property of all cultures' categories of the natural world (Berlin 1992). However, what is not clear is exactly how hierarchies are mentally represented. There are two main possibilities, which are not mutually exclusive. One possibility is that people's concepts are structured in memory much like the diagrams in Figure 3.1. That is, perhaps concepts are connected in hierarchical networks, and the connections are used in order to make inductive inferences and categorization judgements as described in the previous section. For example, in deciding whether a terrier is an animal, one would locate *terrier* in memory and trace upwards in the hierarchy until reaching *animal*. At this point, the sequence of IS-A links would indicate that a terrier is indeed an animal. Furthermore, information true of all animals would be stored with the *animal* concept, and only information distinctive to terriers would be stored at the *terrier* node.

The second possibility is that the hierarchy results from a kind of reasoning process rather than being explicitly stored in memory. Suppose that you know that all Xs are Ys, and all Ys are Zs. Now if you learn that all Zs have six fingers, what does that tell you about Xs? A little thought will reveal that Xs must also have six fingers, since all of them are Zs. Thus, even though you clearly did not have the hierarchy stored in memory (before reading this paragraph), you could use the information about category inclusion to come to the correct answer. This suggests the possibility that people may not have a hierarchy stored in memory but may be able to infer category inclusion and then draw the appropriate inferences (see Randall 1976).

If people did not have the hierarchy stored in memory, how would they know that terriers are dogs and dogs are animals? One suggestion (Rips et al. 1973) is that this information can be computed based on the properties that are known of a category. In a hierarchy, the properties that are generally true of a category are also true of its subordinates; as a result, the more specific categories have the same features as the more general categories, with one or more additional features. Table 3.1 illustrates this. The right column presents the properties (or "features") that are known of each category in the left column, *animal*, *mammal*, and *dog* (clearly, this is just an illustration – people know many more

TABLE 3.1
Hypothetical features of categories that form hierarchical or non-hierarchical sets

Category	Possible hierarchical feature set
Animal	moves, breathes
Mammal	moves, breathes, has fur, gives birth to live young
Dog	moves, breathes, has fur, gives birth to live young, barks, has four legs

things about these categories). As one goes to more specific categories, the list of known features only increases.

The example illustrates how one can look at the properties that are known of two categories and make a judgement about whether they are hierarchical. If X's features are a subset of the features of Y, then X is a superordinate of Y; e.g. the features of *animal* are a subset of the features of *mammal* in the left column of Table 3.1. If X has all the features of Y, plus some additional features, then X is a subordinate of Y; e.g. *dog* has all the features of *animal*, plus some additional ones. If X and Y have the same features, then they are the same category.[1] Note that these rules do not require us to have the IS-A links stored in memory – all we need to know is the properties of the category members, and we can infer the set inclusion relations.

In short, the category hierarchy could be *pre-stored* or it could be *computed* (Smith 1978). If it is prestored, then the links in memory correspond to the IS-A links in Figure 3.1. If it is computed, then hierarchical relations are not stored in memory but are calculated based on the properties of each pair of categories. In the 1970s, many experiments were conducted to discover which of these accounts of conceptual structure was most accurate (e.g. Collins & Quillian 1969, Glass & Holyoak 1975, McCloskey & Glucksberg 1979, Rips et al. 1973; see Chang 1986, or Smith 1978, for reviews). Unfortunately, these experiments were not entirely conclusive. Part of the problem is that it is necessary to make further assumptions about what memory structures and processes are used in any particular experimental task. Since neither theory completely accounted for all of the observed data, each was modified in order to be more complete. The result was that it became difficult to tell the two views apart. We will discuss here three relevant phenomena that have been used to try to distinguish these two views.

If concepts are represented in a hierarchy of the sort shown in Figure 3.1, then accessing conceptual relations should require one to use these hierarchical links. For example, deciding that a pine is a tree, one should first note that pines are evergreens (crossing one IS-A link) and then note that evergreens are trees (crossing another IS-A link). Because of the transitivity of set inclusion, this indicates that pines are trees. If it takes a certain amount of time to cross each IS-A link, Collins & Quillian (1969) reasoned, one could predict the response time to judge the truth or falsity of sentences: subjects should be faster at verifying "a pine is an evergreen" than "a pine is a plant", because the former involves fewer IS-A links than the latter. Similarly, people should be faster at identifying "an evergreen is a plant" than "a pine is a plant". In general, the more IS-A links that need to be traversed in order to verify the statement, the longer it should take people to verify that it is true. (Similar predictions can be made for false statements such as "an evergreen is an oak", but they are a bit more complex.) Collins & Quillian found evidence for this prediction. When a sentence required traversal of only one IS-A link, subjects were faster to verify the statement than when it required traversal of two links. This supported the notion that a taxonomic tree is indeed stored in memory.

Other researchers, however, suggested a different explanation for such results. They argued that if people had stored mental descriptions of each category, then categories closer in the taxonomic tree would generally have more similar descriptions. For example, as Table 3.1 shows, *dog* shares many more features with *mammal* than it does with *animal*. If subjects were using feature lists to decide category relations, perhaps this similarity of the category representations could explain the effect that Collins & Quillian found.

Rips et al. (1973) introduced a new factor, *typicality*, into the statement verification paradigm. They compared category members that were more or less typical or representative of a superordinate category, for example, "a robin is a bird" vs. "an ostrich is a bird". Both judgements would require one IS-A link to be traversed (i.e. both *robin* and *ostrich* would be connected to *bird* as a superordinate), and so both should take about the same amount of time to evaluate. However, Rips et al. found that the sentences including typical terms, such as *robin*, took less time to verify than those including atypical terms, such as *ostrich* or *goose*. Rips et al. also found that for some items, people were faster at verifying category relations that crossed two IS-A links than a less typical category relation that crossed only one IS-A link. For example, people might be faster to verify "a dog is an animal" than "a dog is a mammal", because *dog* is a more typical animal than mammal. These results are inconsistent with the simple taxonomy represented in memory, as shown in Figure 3.1, since it is impossible to verify that a dog is an animal without first going through the *mammal* category. Furthermore, the feature model could explain the typicality effect under the reasonable assumption that atypical members have fewer features on the category's feature list than typical members do (Rosch & Mervis 1975).

Another problem for the pre-stored view of hierarchies is cases of intransitivity. Hampton (1982) has shown that people do not always follow the rules of transitivity that are found in a strict hierarchy. For example, his subjects verified that *car seat* was an example of *chair*. They also agreed that *chair* is an example of *furniture*. But they denied that *car seat* was a kind of *furniture*. If they were simply tracing the links in the IS-A hierarchy, they would not have denied this relation, since each individual link was verified, and that is how all such "long-distance" categorizations are made (e.g. deciding that an evergreen is a plant, as described above). Intransitivity is compatible with the view that hierarchical relations are computed, with a few added assumptions. It seems likely that *car seat* shares some features with *chair* (e.g. having a seat) but perhaps not very many, since it is not very typical. Similarly, *chair* shares some features with *furniture*, but probably different features from those that *car seat* shares with it (e.g. most furniture does not have a seat). As a result, a *car seat* may share very few features with *furniture*, and so subjects may not judge that it is an example (see Hampton 1982, for discussion). Randall (1976) found similar intransitivities in biological categories of a number of different cultures.

As we warned at the outset of this discussion, the evidence in this area is not entirely decisive. There is evidence in favour of the taxonomy stored in the head and in favour of computing taxonomic relations instead. Much of the recent research in the area has involved making more elaborate and sophisticated theories in order to account for a wider variety of data. Such theories are beyond the scope of the present chapter. Our own belief is that the view that taxonomic relations are computed seems to account for the majority of the data most easily (e.g. see McCloskey & Glucksberg 1979). However, a summary would be safe in saying that neither a feature list nor a network by itself may be sufficient to account for all the data. It may be that some category relations are explicitly learned and represented. For example, children may learn that whales are mammals and store this fact explicitly in memory (Glass & Holyoak 1975). However, this does not mean that all such relations are learned. Furthermore, it does seem to be the case that some members of a category are better or more typical than others. This will have to be accounted for either by similarity of the concepts or by different strength of links in the network (see Hampton 1993).

For the moment, we will leave this topic with two important generalizations. First, people are able to learn and use taxonomic relations in order to draw inferences. Secondly, people are able to reason taxonomically about novel materials that have not been previously stored in memory (as in the "All Xs are Ys" kind of example). In the next section, we will discuss some important distinctions that have been made about different levels in the taxonomy.

THE BASIC LEVEL OF CATEGORIZATION

As we described earlier, any object can be thought of as being in a set of hierarchically-organized categories, ranging from extremely general (e.g. *entity*) to extremely specific (e.g. *seventeenth century French upholstered chair*). An unknown object is most likely to be a member of a maximally general category, because members of general categories occur in the world with greater frequency than members of more specific categories. For example, there are more living things in the world than there are cats. Therefore, classification at the most general level maximizes accuracy of classification. Maximally specific categories, on the other hand, allow for greater accuracy in prediction than general categories. Given that something is a cat, you are able to predict more about it (its behaviour, its appearance, its tendency to wake you up in the middle of the night when it knocks over a vase, etc.) than if you know only that it is a living thing (it might or might not have legs, produce leaves, or drink milk). Of all the possible categories in a hierarchy to which a concept belongs, a middle level of specificity, the *basic level*, is the most natural, preferred level at which to conceptually carve up the world. The basic level[2] can be seen as a compromise between the accuracy of classification at a maximally general level and the predictive power of a maximally specific level.

Initial studies of the basic level

Roger Brown (1958) first noted that people seem to prefer to use a consistent middle level of categorization in speech. He noticed that parents speaking to their children tend to use the same short, frequent names for things. For example, a parent might call a sheepdog a *dog* or *doggie*, rather than an *animal* or *sheepdog*. Brown proposed that parents use category names at a level that "anticipates the equivalences and differences that will need to be observed in most. . . dealings with. . . an object" (1958:16), and only supply a different name "in order to identify an immediately important property of the referent" (p. 17). For example, the name *chair* indicates that an object has a seat, a back, and legs, and is used to sit on, but *the new chair* or *the good chair* is in a different class, indicating that it should be treated with care and should probably not be sat on by the child.

It may be that the psychologically basic level of categorization is a reflection of discontinuities in the world, suggesting a connection between the structure in people's concepts and the structure inherent in the world (see Malt, 1995). Berlin (1992, Berlin et al. 1973) studied folk classification by following native speakers of the Tzeltal language (spoken by Mayans in Mexico) through the jungle and asking them to name various plants and animals they came upon. He found that Tzeltal speakers tended to name plants and animals at a single level of scientific classification, that corresponding to the genus (pine, bass), rather than to a more specific (white pine, black bass) or to a more general (tree, fish) level. According to Berlin, people across all cultures have this same basic level, the genus; yet his proposal is perhaps too rigid, as there are exceptions to a universal basic level. First, for people who lack experience with a domain, a higher level may be treated as basic. For example, urban dwellers treated the life form *tree* as basic, rather than the genus (Dougherty 1978, Rosch et al. 1976), presumably because of lesser amounts of interaction with the natural environment. Secondly, people with extensive training may treat a more specific level as basic. We will discuss changes in categorization with expertise in a later section.

Primarily through the work of Eleanor Rosch and her associates (Rosch 1978, Rosch et al. 1976), the empirical paradigms of cognitive psychology were brought to bear on the levels issue, extending the observational work done in linguistics by Brown and in anthropology by Berlin. In a series of influential studies, Rosch et al. developed a number of converging operational definitions of the basic level. First, the basic level of object categories was shown to be the most inclusive level at which category members possess a significant number of common attributes. When subjects were asked to list attributes possessed by categories at the superordinate, basic, and subordinate level (e.g. *clothing*, *pants* and *jeans*)[3] they only listed a few attributes for superordinate categories, and listed significantly more for both basic and subordinate categories. The number of attributes listed for subordinate categories was only slightly more than the number listed at the basic level. Subjects also listed different kinds of attributes at the different levels. The most frequent kind of attribute listed for superordinate categories was functional (e.g. keeps you warm, you wear it). Subjects listed noun and adjective properties at the basic level (e.g. legs, buttons, belt loops, cloth) and additional properties listed at the subordinate level were generally adjectives (e.g. blue).

In a second study, Rosch et al. found that basic level categories are the most inclusive categories for which highly similar sequences of movements are made to category members. In this study, subjects were asked to write down the movements they make when interacting with objects that belong to superordinate, basic and subordinate categories.

As with the attribute listing study, subjects listed many more movements for basic and subordinate level categories (e.g. for *pants*: grasp with hands, bend knee, and raise and extend leg) than for superordinate categories (e.g. for *clothing*: scan with eyes). Similar results were obtained when subjects actually performed the movements associated with each category.

Additional studies were directed at determining the visual similarity of objects at different levels. Rosch et al. found that objects within basic and subordinate level categories had shapes that were more similar than objects within superordinate categories. They determined this by tracing the shapes of pictures of objects, and for pairs of shapes, computing the ratio of the area the two shapes had in common to their total areas. Furthermore, when the pairs of shapes were averaged to create a single shape, subjects could easily identify averages of objects from the same basic and subordinate level concepts, but often could not identify averages of superordinate concepts.

These studies show that members of basic and subordinate level categories are similar in shape, in the movements used when interacting with them, and in attributes they possess. These similarities between basic and subordinate category members have implications for psychological processes involving basic and subordinate concepts. For example, categories that have similar shapes should be easy to represent mentally as images. Rosch et al. tested this idea by presenting subjects with a category name (at either the superordinate, basic or subordinate level) and then asking subjects to identify a briefly-presented picture of an object in that category embedded in visual noise (to make it harder to identify). Basic and subordinate level names helped identification more than superordinate names, suggesting that subjects can construct a mental image representing basic and subordinate categories, but not superordinate categories. In a related study, subjects were faster at verifying that a picture of an object was a member of a basic level category than they were at verifying category membership for either subordinate or superordinate categories. For example, after hearing a category name and seeing a picture of a kitchen table, subjects were faster at verifying that the picture was a *table* than they were at verifying that the picture was *furniture* or a *kitchen table*. This result has been replicated in many other studies (e.g. Jolicoeur et al. 1984, Murphy & Brownell 1985, Murphy & Wisniewski 1989, Smith et al. 1978). Finally, Rosch et al. found that people almost exclusively use basic level names when asked to name pictures of objects.

There is also developmental evidence suggesting that basic level concepts are privileged. Basic level categories are the first categories that children can sort and the first categories that they name. Children are also able to learn novel basic categories before they can learn those at other levels in a category-learning experiment (see Anglin 1977, Horton & Markman 1980, Mervis & Crisafi 1982, Rosch et al. 1976; see also Smith, this volume).

How can the basic level be identified in a category hierarchy? Rosch et al. (1976) suggested that basic level categories maximize *cue validity*, the probability that a particular object belongs to some category, given that the object has a particular feature, or cue. For example, the cue validity for a winged thing being a bird is P (bird | wings), which is the probability that something is a bird, given that it has wings. To calculate the cue validity across all the features possessed by members of a category, you need to know the proportion of the objects possessing each feature that are category members (e.g. how many winged things are birds, how many things with beaks are birds, how many things that live in nests are birds, etc.). The total cue validity for a category would be the sum of the cue validities of all the features possessed by category members: P (bird | wings) + P (bird | beak) + P (bird | lives in nest) +. . . (This category cue validity is no longer a probability, as it can exceed a value of 1.0.)

Rosch et al. (1976) argued that superordinates have lower cue validity than basic categories, because they have fewer common attributes; e.g. animals have fewer things in common than birds do, so there aren't many cues that help you identify something as an animal as help you identify something as a bird. Subordinate categories were said to have lower cue validity than basic level categories because they share more attributes with contrasting subordinate categories than basic categories do with contrasting categories at the same level. For example, knowing that blue jays fly doesn't help much in identifying something as a blue jay, because many other birds fly. As a result, P (blue jay | flies) is quite low. In contrast, knowing that birds fly helps identify something as a bird, because not many other animals fly.

Contrary to Rosch's suggestion, it has been shown that cue validity alone cannot account for the basic level advantage (Medin 1983, Murphy 1982). In fact, the superordinate level, being the most inclusive, actually has the highest cue validity. Because a superordinate includes lower basic level categories, its cue validity can never be lower than that of the category it includes. Consider the feature "has a tail" and the hierarchy of categories, *cat, mammal, animal*. P (cat | tail) is lower than P (mammal | tail), because there are many mammals with tails that aren't cats, like dogs and mice. Since the mammals category includes all cats, as well as other things with tails, if something has a tail you can be surer that it is a mammal than a cat. Likewise, P (mammal | tail) is lower than P (animal | tail), because *animal* includes all mammals as well as other animals with tails that are not mammals, such as lizards and fish. For categories that are nested, cue validity will never be lower for a more general category than for one of the categories it includes. Thus, cue validity is maximized not at the intermediate basic level, but at the most general level, the superordinate (Murphy 1982).

An alternative possibility is that *category validity* can predict which level will be basic. Category validity is the conditional probability of possessing a feature given category membership such as P (wings | bird). The inverse of the argument raised above against cue validity can be raised against category validity as a predictor of the basic level: category validity tends to be highest at the least inclusive or subordinate level (Medin 1983), as more specific categories tend to have less variability in features. For example, P (tail | cat) is greater than P (tail | mammal), since there are proportionally more mammals without tails than cats without tails.

A third probability metric for predicting the preferred level of categorization is *category-feature collocation*, which is the product of cue- and category-validity (Jones 1983). There is some debate as to the validity of collocation in predicting basic categories, but the details of this debate go beyond the scope of this chapter. In part as a response to Jones' model, Corter & Gluck (1992) developed a metric that they call *category utility* and demonstrated that it can correctly predict the preferred level of categorization, as measured by reaction time in picture verification and naming experiments. Category utility combines three kinds of information in one measure: information about the base rate or frequency of occurrence of a category; the category validity of the category's features; and the base rates of each of these features. This measure is higher for categories that are more general (having a higher base rate) and that are very predictive of features. This metric is consistent with psychological explanations for the advantage of the basic level, as will be seen in the next section.

However, one problem with all of these metrics based on the frequencies of features in various categories is that it is often difficult to specify which features should be included (Murphy 1982). In deciding the cue validity of *cat*, should we include such features as "is larger than a beetle", "can be picked up" or "is less than 100 years old"? If not, how do we decide which features are included in the computation and which are not? One cannot simply accept any feature that is above a small frequency in the category, because some very silly features could be highly frequent (e.g. "does not own a raincoat" is true of almost all cats). Perhaps we should only include features that people psychologically represent for the category. However, this approach introduces a certain amount of circularity.[4] The purpose of these metrics was to predict which categories would be psychologically basic, and if we now rely on psychological representations to make this prediction, we are using the representation to predict itself. So far, this difficult question has not been adequately addressed by metrics of the basic level.

Explanations of the basic level

Given that there is good evidence for a preferential level of conceptual representation, a natural question is what accounts for this preference. This is a difficult question to answer, because the evidence is essentially correlational. That is, certain concepts have been found to be preferred, such as *dog, table, shirt* and so on. To explain why these concepts are basic, we need to compare their properties to those of other concepts at different levels, such as *animal, terrier, coffee table, furniture,* etc. The problem is that it is not clear which properties are causes and which are effects.

Let us take one specific example. Basic category names are generally used more frequently, and this may be especially true in speech to children learning language, when such frequency effects could be quite influential (Callanan 1985). We have already mentioned Brown's (1958) observation that parents are much more likely to call a dog a *doggie* than a *German shepherd* or *animal.* Parents' choice of particularly useful names (and their consistency in using the same name over and over) might be influential in vocabulary learning, Brown suggested. Thus, one might argue that basic level concepts are preferred because of their frequency or early age of learning – not because of their conceptual structure. However, such arguments can cut both ways. Why is it that parents decide to use the word *doggie* rather than another? That is, what made them think that this (basic level) name would be particularly helpful? Such preferences and frequency effects may themselves have causes in conceptual structure.

In general, then, a variable that is related to basic-level structure could either be contributing to the basic-level phenomenon or could be a result of such structure. So, perhaps it is basic structure that is causing words to be learned earlier, to be used more often, to be shorter, and so on. In fact, basic concepts generally have many positive characteristics associated with them (e.g. are shorter, more familiar, etc.), which lends some credence to this view. Rather than taking each characteristic as being coincidentally associated with the same concept as the others, it seems more parsimonious to argue that it is some underlying variable that causes the concepts to be the most useful. That is, it is simplest to argue that useful concepts are used more often, learned earlier, have shorter names, are preferred in naming, and have other similar advantages, *because* they are useful.

Psychologists have taken this tack of exploring structural differences between basic and other concepts, with the hope that such differences could eventually explain the basic-level advantage in other measures. We will take the same approach in this section. Furthermore, experiments with artificial categories described below will allow the separate testing of many of these variables.

Differentiation explanation

The most frequently given explanation for the preference for basic concepts is a structural explanation, which we will call the *differentiation explanation*. It is based on a number of related arguments in the literature (e.g. Mervis & Crisafi 1982, Murphy 1991, Murphy & Brownell 1985, Rosch et al. 1976). In this explanation, basic concepts are said to be the most differentiated. Differentiation can be identified with two different properties: *informativeness* and *distinctiveness*.

The informativeness of basic concepts refers to the fact that such concepts are associated with a large amount of information. As a result, when you know what basic concept describes an object, you know a great deal about the object. So, if you know that something is a *dog*, you can infer that it barks, has four legs, has fur, eats meat, is a pet, chases cars, and possesses a host of biological attributes (such as breathing, having a liver, having dogs as parents). Thus, *dog* is a very informative concept, since so many features are associated with it. The distinctiveness of basic concepts refers to the fact that they are different from other categories at the same level. For example, dogs are fairly different from cats, horses, cows, raccoons, and other familiar mammals.

There is descriptive evidence that basic concepts are highly differentiated. As already mentioned, Rosch et al. (1976) showed that subjects list many features for basic concepts, and only a few for superordinates. Thus, basic concepts are much more informative. Mervis & Crisafi (1982) asked subjects to rate the similarity of pairs of categories and found that basic concepts were highly distinctive relative to their contrast categories. That is, they found that people rated *pants* as quite different from other clothing such as *socks* and *shirt*. In fact, Mervis & Crisafi constructed a differentiation scale that combined informativeness and distinctiveness, and they found that basic level categories were higher on this scale than were other categories.

It is worth considering where it is that superordinates and subordinates fall down according to the differentiation hypothesis. Subordinates are quite informative; in fact, they are slightly more informative than their basic concepts, because they are more specific (Rosch et al. 1976). However, they are significantly less distinctive. A kitchen table is not very different from a dining room table, and a coffee table is only slightly more different from both; a sedan is quite similar to a compact car and to a station wagon. In contrast, superordinates are very distinctive. Furniture in general is not very similar to tools or clothing or plants. However, superordinates are very uninformative – clothing differs considerably in its size, shape, material and specific use. Rosch et al.'s subjects could list very few features that were common to superordinate categories. (In fact, the distinctiveness of basic concepts is the same phenomenon as the uninformativeness of superordinate concepts, because superordinates contain multiple distinctive basic concepts.) In short, it is only basic concepts that are both informative and distinctive.

Why is differentiation such an advantage? The informativeness component means that basic concepts are very useful; they communicate a lot of information. However, informativeness comes with a cost: when concepts are too specific, many more of them are needed to cover all the objects in a domain. If informativeness by itself were an unalloyed good, then people would form the most specific categories possible. In the limit, every object would have its own concept, and that would be the preferred level. Rosch (1978) argued that there is a need for *cognitive economy* to counteract the pressure to create ever smaller categories. In short, the conceptual system works better with a few fairly informative concepts rather than a very large number of extremely informative concepts. Distinctiveness works to limit the number of concepts. When objects are quite similar, they tend to be included in the same concept, rather than being split into finer and finer groups. The concepts that are highly distinctive are those that cannot easily be combined without a loss of information. Of course, these principles do not ensure that there are *no* concepts at higher or lower levels than the basic level, but they tend to result in such concepts being less likely to be learned and used. We return to the other levels of categorization later in the chapter.

Experimental evidence for the differentiation explanation

Studies testing explanations of the basic level can best be separated into those using artificial, novel categories and those using common naturalistic categories. We will discuss them separately.

Experiments with artificial categories

One advantage of using artificial materials is that problems with familiarity and frequency of names, age of learning, and the like can be carefully controlled. In contrast, using natural materials requires the experimenter to simply accept the (usually unknown) variation in subjects' experience with different categories and names. An important general finding in experiments using artificial materials is that robust basic-level advantages are usually found (Lassaline et al. 1992, Murphy 1991, Murphy & Smith 1982). This strongly suggests that the preference is caused by the structure of the concepts rather than less interesting causes such as familiarity and characteristics of the names.

Murphy & Smith (1982) taught subjects hierarchies of tool concepts; an example of each basic-level category is shown in Figure 3.2. The hierarchies fit the differentiation explanation's assumptions: the superordinates were uninformative and distinctive; the subordinates were informative but nondistinctive; and the basic concepts were both informative and distinctive. The superordinates in this study were defined primarily by function, as are familiar natural categories such as *furniture* or *vehicle*. Murphy & Smith varied the order in which subjects were taught the different levels in order to discover whether the basic-level advantage could be reduced to a learning order effect. After all the categories were learned, subjects performed a timed categorization task, in which they heard a category name and viewed a picture. They pressed a button to indicate whether the picture was in the category indicated by the name. Rosch et al. (1976, Experiment 7) had found that natural basic categories were the fastest in such a task.

Murphy & Smith found that the basic level concepts that they constructed were indeed the fastest in this task. The subordinate concepts were close behind, but the superordinates were considerably slower. Interestingly, a basic level advantage was found regardless of which category level was learned first. There was an overall finding that categories benefited by being learned first, but this did not change the

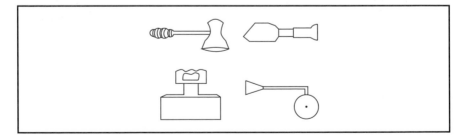

FIG. 3.2.   Artificial tools used as stimuli in the experiments of Murphy & Smith (1982). Each picture is an example from a basic-level category. Members of the same superordinates are shown on each side. Superordinates were largely defined by function: subjects were told that the tools on the right represented cutters and on the left, pounders.

reaction-time ordering of the three levels. Of course, the effect of order of learning in a single experimental session cannot be easily generalized to effects of learning order that take place over months and years in real-world categories, but the fact that the order of learning did not change the relative speeds of the three levels suggests that the basic level cannot be completely reduced to learning order. Murphy (1991) found more support for the differentiation explanation using even more artificial stimuli that did not resemble objects.

Lassaline et al. (1992) performed a similar experiment with hierarchies that contained only two levels. The categories at each level were more complex, and the objects within each category were more diverse than in other experiments of this type. Learning difficulty at different levels in the hierarchy was compared to discover which category levels were easiest. Lassaline et al. also found that the level expected to be basic was learned more quickly. Thus, the finding of basic-level structure has been obtained in many studies and is robust to changes in stimuli.

Mervis & Crisafi (1982) presented experiments with artificial categories that have been interpreted as demonstrating the same point. However, in their experiments, subjects did not actually learn the categories – they made judgements about whether artificial stimuli would be in the same category. The results showed that such judgements parallelled those of the learning experiments. That is, subjects believed that two items from the same (proposed) basic level category should be in the same category, but they were much less consistent in thinking so for superordinates. This result is consistent with the other results cited here, but they do not directly tell us whether such categories would be useful or efficient if they were actually learned.

In summary, direct tests of the differentiation explanation using artificial concepts have generally supported it. Of course, there are inherent limitations in using categories that are artificially constructed and learned within a single experimental session. Nonetheless, it is reassuring that the principles derived from natural categories are able to predict processing advantages in novel category learning in controlled experiments.

Experiments using natural categories

Studies using natural concepts have not always been able to separate the different factors that are proposed by the differentiation explanation. When different concepts are compared, there are always variables other than category level that differ. Nonetheless, the results of such studies are generally quite consistent with the differentiation explanation, as we will now discuss.

Murphy & Brownell (1985) examined atypical subordinates such as *penguin* or *boxing glove* in a picture categorization task. Because such items are atypical, they are in fact quite distinctive: penguins are not similar to other birds, and boxing gloves are quite different from other gloves. Moreover, because they are subordinates, such categories are already informative. Therefore, it seems likely that their members would be more easily categorized into subordinate concepts. That is, contrary to the usual basic-level advantage, *boxing glove* should be preferred to *glove* and *penguin* to *bird*. In fact, this is just what Murphy & Brownell found (see also Jolicoeur et al. 1984). (Note that this result should warn us against taking the word "level" too literally in talking about the basic level of categorization. Although *penguin* and *robin* appear to be at the same level in one sense – both are kinds of birds – the first seems to be much like a basic category and the second is clearly a subordinate. Thus, it is probably best to think of an individual category to be basic or subordinate, rather than an entire "level" of categories.)

Murphy & Brownell further tested the differentiation explanation by experimentally manipulating the distinctiveness of subordinate categories. Consider a subordinate category trial that a subject might see in a typical experiment. First, the name "robin" appears on the screen. After a certain period of time, the name disappears, and a picture of a robin appears. This may appear easy to answer, but the subject now must make sure that the picture is indeed of a robin and not a lark or jay or dove. Because subordinate categories like *robin* are not very distinctive, this decision is rather difficult, even when the picture is indeed the correct one. In contrast, if the category name had been at the basic level, "bird", then no difficult distinction would have been required. That is, if the picture were not a bird, it would have been something that looks quite different (perhaps a dog, a snake or a human). Thus, it is the similarity of *robin* to related subordinates on false trials (i.e. its non-distinctiveness) that makes it a difficult category to verify.

Murphy & Brownell reasoned that the distinctiveness of subordinates could be reduced somewhat by changing the nature of the false trials in this experimental design. In their Experiment 2, the false trials consisted of category names and pictures that were completely unrelated. So, if the category name was "robin", the picture (on the false trial) might be of a car or a hammer. Thus, subjects no longer had to worry about the distinctiveness of subordinates (or any category) in this experiment, because they no longer had to distinguish robins from larks, jays or doves – such false trials never occurred. In this experiment, it takes subjects some time to realize the nature of the false trials that are being used, but by the end of the experiment, subjects were in fact *faster* at the subordinate level than at the basic level. Since subordinates are slightly more informative than basic categories, they actually become fastest when distinctiveness is equated across category levels. Thus, this result suggests that the lack of distinctiveness of the subordinates is responsible for their usual slowness in categorization tasks.

THE OTHER LEVELS

One might wonder why, if the basic level is so advantageous, people form concepts at different levels. Of course, it is not only the ease of thinking about a concept that determines whether it will exist. It is often useful to have extremely technical or detailed concepts that are not of great use on most occasions, but that are important for some specific endeavours. Experts in a field likely require much more specific, detailed concepts than novices do (Rosch et al. 1976). If one becomes an expert on a subclass of insects, one can hardly call all insects *bugs* – precise categories will be necessary. But by the same token, extremely general categories may be useful as well. For example, sometimes one just wants *something to read* without caring whether it is a book, magazine or newspaper. Scientists may find generalities that are true of all *mammals* or *arthropods* or *animals*. Such generalizations require categories that are more general than *dog* or *horse*.

Subordinate level categories
Subordinate categories have not been the subject of much investigation. However, studies comparing all three levels of categorization have suggested some ways in which subordinates differ from the higher levels. As we have already stated, subordinates are more informative than basic categories and are also less distinctive. What additional information is added in going from the basic to the subordinate level? In general, it seems that subordinates differ from their basic category in terms of perceptible details. That is, subordinates share the shape and general function of their basic category but provide additional information about specific details of the object (Tversky & Hemenway 1984). For example, different chairs tend to have the same parts: a back, a seat, legs, and possibly arms. A *dining room chair* tends to have a taller back and to be made out of wood. An *armchair* tends to be upholstered and (obviously) to have arms. An *office chair* tends to swivel rather than to have legs. In each of these cases, the basic shape, function and parts of most chairs are found in the subordinates. However, there is a modification in some part or attribute, along with a consequent minor

modification of function (e.g. an office chair allows you to swivel in order to work at different parts of your office, whereas a dining room chair does not). This is a typical way in which subordinates provide more information than their basic-level categories. This pattern has been proposed as a possible explanation for the basic-level advantage. In particular, it has been suggested that the fact that members of basic categories share distinctive parts (but other levels do not) could explain their processing advantages; see Tversky & Hemenway (1984) and Murphy (1991) for discussion.

Because basic categories are more familiar and more generally helpful, there appears to be a convention in discourse that people name objects by the basic category label unless the information needed in the subordinate label is particularly relevant (Cruse 1977, Murphy & Brownell 1985). For example, if you were to tell someone, "My Jaguar is parked right outside", you would be taken as boasting of owning an expensive sports car. For most purposes, knowing that your *car* is parked outside would be sufficient; it is only when the information added by the subordinate is particularly relevant that it should be used (e.g. "We can't all fit in my Jaguar"). Even when there is no question of boasting, using the subordinate when it is not necessary seems peculiar. For example, if there were only one book on the table and you were to ask "Could you hand me that paperback novel?" your addressee would wonder why you had used this expression rather than "book". Subordinate labels are useful, however, when there is a domain that contains many members of a basic-level category that need to be distinguished. While at the dog show, speakers should not refer to every animal as "dog", or else confusion will result.

In short, subordinates generally indicate changes in the features from those usually expected in the basic category, but they preserve the general parts and functions associated with their basic category. They are useful in making fine distinctions when called for, but otherwise tend not to be used in discourse.

Superordinates

The superordinate level of categorization has been the subject of more research than the subordinate level. Much of this work has come about in the developmental literature, because young children have great difficulty learning superordinate categories (Horton & Markman 1980, Rosch et al. 1976). Although we cannot explore the developmental issues in depth, we will describe some of the results of Ellen Markman's studies of superordinate categories in adults and children. Markman (1985) pointed out a somewhat surprising aspect of superordinate names: they are often mass nouns, rather than count nouns. Count nouns are words like *chair* which can be pluralized and preceded by a number: *five chairs*, *all the dogs*, *some kettles*. In contrast, mass nouns, which usually refer to homogeneous masses or substances, cannot be directly counted or pluralized; all the following are ungrammatical in neutral situations: *five rices*, *all the muds*, *some waters*. (There are actually interpretations of these phrases that are grammatical but they usually require assuming a missing element or an unusual interpretation – such as *waters* referring to oceans.) Mass nouns generally require a *classifier* preceding them in order to be counted, and it is the classifier that is pluralized: *five cups of rice, all the piles of mud, some pails of water*. Typically, mass nouns refer to substances like mud that cannot be easily separated into individual parts, and so are treated as an indistinguishable whole.

Markman's discovery that superordinates are often mass nouns can be illustrated with the following examples from English: *furniture, jewellery, clothing, food*, and *reading material*. Note that one would not say "I have four furnitures in this room", but instead, "I have four pieces of furniture". However, the basic-level names for furniture are almost all count nouns. One can say "I have four chairs/sofas/tables/lamps/beds/stereo sets. . ." That is, examples of furniture are not homogeneous masses like mud, but individual objects; yet, syntactically, *furniture* is a mass noun. This fact is not a quirk of English. In fact, Markman showed that it was true in a wide variety of languages from different language families. For example, 16 of the 18 languages she sampled treated the word corresponding to *food* as a mass noun, but none of the 18 languages treated *egg* as a mass noun, and only one treated *apple* as a mass noun.

Markman argued that this syntactic difference between superordinate and basic-level names reflects the way that superordinate names are normally used. In many cases, superordinates are used to refer to collections of a number of different items. For example, in talking about a single couch, one is very unlikely to refer to it in a form such as "Let's move that piece of furniture". One would be much more likely to use *furniture* in referring to a couch, two tables and some chairs all at once, as in "Let's move this furniture before we begin painting". In fact, this property of superordinates has been verified in written text (Wisniewski & Murphy 1989). Basic level names are most likely to be used to refer to single objects (70% of the time), whereas superordinates are most likely to be used to refer to groups or the entire class of objects (77% of the time). Markman's argument, then, is that this pattern of usage has the effect of making us think of superordinates as referring to multiple objects. She argued in particular that young children might even misunderstand superordinates as referring only to groups of objects. For example, they might think that *clothes* refers to all the clothing they are wearing together, and not to individual shirts or socks. Or they might think that *animal* (even though it is not a mass noun) refers to groups of animals together (e.g. at the zoo).

There are three main pieces of evidence backing Markman's conjecture. First, when young children are taught new superordinates, they learn them slightly better when the superordinate is used as a mass noun during training (Markman 1985). Secondly, young children will sometimes act as if they think that a superordinate name must refer to multiple objects. For example, they might say that a group of animals together can be called *animal*, but will deny this of a single cow. When learning novel superordinates, even older children make this error (Markman et al. 1980). Thirdly, in work on adults, Murphy & Wisniewski (1989) showed that subjects were relatively faster at identifying objects at the superordinate level when they were presented in groups. When objects were presented in isolation, basic categorization was significantly faster than superordinate categorization, as usual. So, a single couch would be categorized faster as *couch* than *furniture*. However, when the couch was shown as part of a living room scene, it was categorized just as fast as *furniture* as *couch*. Thus, it seems that presenting objects together in groups does aid superordinate classification. In sum, there is evidence that the representation of superordinates may be different from that of lower levels of categorization. How these different types of representations are reconciled is not fully known. It does not seem that a hierarchy of the sort shown in Figure 3.1 would represent this difference between superordinates and lower-level categories very well.

Another important difference between superordinates and lower levels has been noted by Rosch et al. (1976) and Tversky & Hemenway (1984). When subjects are asked to list the properties of different categories, they are very likely to list abstract or functional properties for superordinates. In contrast, more specific categories are more likely to have parts and concrete properties listed. In fact, it seems likely that the abstract nature of superordinates may be what encourages children to think of them as referring to groups of objects. For example, if children do not immediately see what is common to all furniture (which differ widely in shape and specific function), they may tend to interpret *furniture* as referring to the collection of sofa, bookshelves, table and chairs in the living room. It is only with greater experience and sophistication that they can perceive the underlying functional properties common to furniture.

In summary, subordinate and superordinate categories are opposites in many respects. Superordinates have only a few features in common, and these tend to be abstract, functional properties. Subordinates have many features in common, but most are also properties of their basic category; their novel properties tend to be minor perceptual or functional modifications of the typical properties at the basic level. These rather different category structures have a similar effect of making the two levels more difficult to use. They are both harder to learn, and children do not seem to know the correct meanings of either level right away. Speakers tend to avoid describing individual objects with names at either level. Nonetheless, both superordinates and subordinates are necessary for people to represent the groupings of entities in some situations.

THE BASIC LEVEL IN NONOBJECT DOMAINS

The notion of a basic level within a hierarchical category structure was initially developed by researchers studying object concepts but has since been applied to a wide variety of nonobject domains, including person categories, emotions, events, and scenes. While in many cases researchers claim to have found strong parallels between object and nonobject domains, there are important differences between object and nonobject categories as well. In the next section, we review research on basic levels in nonobject domains, beginning with those categories that are composed of collections of objects: scenes.

Scenes

Tversky & Hemenway (1983) investigated whether the notion of a basic level could be extended to environmental scenes. Scenes contrast with objects in a number of ways. Both scenes and objects possess a large number of perceptual attributes, but scenes are configurations of objects, providing the background in which objects are set. The configuration of objects within a scene is less constrained than the configuration of parts within an object, so unlike with objects, you might not expect scenes to have a recognizable shape (but see Biederman 1990).

Tversky & Hemenway developed their taxonomy of scene categories by beginning with two categories, *indoors* and *outdoors*, and asking subjects to generate categories and subcategories of indoor and outdoor scenes. They selected the four most frequently generated indoor and outdoor scenes, (*home, restaurant, store, school, mountain, park, beach* and *city*) as well as two subcategories of these. Next they asked subjects to list attributes, actions, or parts for categories at each of their three levels (e.g. *indoors, school, elementary school*). They found that there was a greater increase in the number of attributes, actions and parts in going from the most general to the intermediate level category than in going from the intermediate category to the most specific category.

Tversky & Hemenway also found that people used their intermediate level scene categories most frequently when asked to name pictures of scenes, and when asked to fill in a missing word in a sentence about a scene (e.g. "Since the Hudsons' children were aged 6 and 8, they wanted their new home to be near _____.").

As with object categories, subjects list as many attributes at an intermediate level of scene categorization as at a more specific level, and subjects prefer to use intermediate level categories to label scenes. These results suggest that there is a basic level for scenes, as well as for objects.

Actions and events

Rifkin (1985) tested the idea that event taxonomies have a basic level. He derived his event taxonomy by having a group of subjects generate instances of nine superordinate events (e.g. *meal, entertainment, sports, crime*), and then having a second group of subjects generate superordinate categories (i.e. "This is a type of what?") and subordinate categories (i.e. "What are examples of this activity?") for the instances generated by the first group of subjects. To see if there was a basic level advantage for event categories analogous to that found with object categories, Rifkin then had a third group of subjects list characteristics common to categories at each of the three levels. He found that, as with objects and scenes, there were few attributes listed for superordinate event categories, with more listed for basic categories, and no increase in the number of attributes listed from the basic to the subordinate level.

Morris & Murphy (1990) replicated these results with event categories but also tested a number of other converging operations that had been used by Rosch et al. (1976) to study object concepts, including speeded categorization and free naming. They found that verifying actions as belonging to an event category was fastest at the basic level, and that naming at the basic level was preferred over the other levels. These results are consistent with data from studies of object concepts. In contrast to findings with object categories, however, Morris & Murphy found that superordinate event categories were somewhat informative as well as being distinctive, as measured by similarity judgements. For example, subjects said that events from the same superordinate event, such as *subway travel* and *travel by school bus* were fairly similar (in contrast to object subordinates, such as *rowboat* and *sports car*, which are fairly dissimilar).

Morris & Murphy concluded that there is something like a basic level of events, as shown by most measures of category structure. The differences between object and event superordinates may be due to the fact that event superordinates such as *travel* or *meals* carry important functional and social information, which is central to the nature of the event. This kind of information may not always appear in feature listings, since it is often less tangible than specific actions and objects involved in an event. Thus, the presence and nature of a basic level may depend on the particular domain.

Social and trait categories

People, like objects, can be classified in many ways, including social and occupational role, gender, physical appearance, and personality. Cantor & Mischel (1979) explored the ways in which person classification schemes are fundamentally similar to (or different from) object classification. Person classification serves many of the same functions as does object categorization. As with objects, information can be reduced to a manageable level by using only some characteristics to classify a person, and then making predictions about the person based on their membership in a particular category. For example, having classified someone as a graduate student in psychology, you can make predictions about how they spend much of their time and what kind of lifestyle they lead. Person classification, however, also has the same cost as object categorization. By treating nonequivalent things as equivalent, information about individuals is lost. Not all psychology students are under 30 years old and are warm, caring people, for example, in spite of such stereotypes.

Person categories are fuzzy, like object categories – perhaps even fuzzier, given that person categorization is based largely on human behaviour, which is highly variable even within individuals. In contrast, much object categorization is based largely on perceptual features which are not as variable, such as colour, shape, and size. Also, unlike object categories, the class inclusion relations between person categories themselves can be fuzzy. It is not always clear which categories are subsumed under which other categories, and at what level of generality (e.g. is *extrovert* a superordinate to *salesperson*, or a feature of *salesperson*, or neither?). Another difference between people and natural objects is that the most useful level may shift more with context, purpose, and frame of reference for person categories than for natural object categories.

In addition to the more theoretical goal of understanding how different kinds of concepts are organized, Cantor & Mischel (1979) argued that trying to understand if there is a basic level for person perception has a pragmatic goal, of helping in the selection of the most appropriate unit for studying social behaviour.

Following the attribute listing task used by Rosch and colleagues in their studies of object categorization, Cantor & Mischel had subject list attributes for person categories that varied in level. For example, *emotionally unstable person, committed person,* and *cultured person* were at their highest levels; *criminal madman, religious devotee,* and *patron of the arts* were intermediate categories; and *strangler, Buddhist monk,* and *supporter of community orchestra* were lowest level categories. Like Rosch et al. (1976), Cantor & Mischel found that the gain in number of attributes listed in going from more general to more specific levels was greatest at the intermediate level. Cantor & Mischel also found that there was considerably less overlap in shared attributes across categories at the intermediate level than at the most specific level, but the difference between the intermediate and general level was small. This result is consistent with the hypothesis that categories at an intermediate level are the most differentiated, that is, informative and distinctive. This pattern of attribute listing was consistent for all kinds of features listed (physical appearance, socio-economic status, trait disposition, behaviours).

John et al. (1991) focused more specifically on personality traits. Because traits are usually named by adjectives rather than nouns, they defined hierarchical level for traits as the range of distinct behaviours subsumed by that adjective, such that more specific traits would subsume a smaller number of distinct behaviours. For example, any person who plays on a professional basketball team, performs with a classical ballet company, plays the violin with a local symphony or has published a book of poetry might be classified as *talented*, but of that set of people, only the one who plays the violin would be classified as *musical*. Under John et al.'s definition, then, *talented* is more general than *musical*.

As with person categories, class inclusion for traits can be fuzzy. It is easy to decide which object categories in a taxonomy are more general than others. For example, people agree that a robin is a kind of bird, but that a bird is not a kind of robin. But it is not as easy to decide which traits are more general than others. To understand the problem, consider again the examples of *musical* and *talented*. A skilled musician may be very talented. Yet there are also mediocre musicians who have a great interest in music, but who never reach a high level of technical or artistic accomplishment. One might well think that such people are somewhat musical but not talented. Similarly, other people may lack talent but achieve musical skill through hard work. Thus the large variation in human behaviours and abilities seem to result in trait terms that are not as strictly hierarchically structured.

Traits are different from both objects and persons in that they can be structured both as class inclusion hierarchies and as partonomies (hierarchies in which elements are connected by the PART-OF relation rather than the IS-A relation). For example, one could argue that talent is one component of what one needs to be musical, and so being *talented* would be considered as part of being *musical*. For object concepts, in contrast, two things cannot be related both taxonomically and partonomically. A kitchen chair is a kind of a chair, not a part of a chair, but a leg is part of a chair, not a kind of chair.

While researchers studying object categorization have typically used an attribute listing task to evaluate how informative different object categories are, this is difficult to do with traits, because adjectives do not really have attributes. So instead, John et al. asked subjects to rate a set of traits on how descriptive they were. They defined the basic level of trait categories as the highest level that was descriptive. Then they tested the hypothesis that basic level traits were more useful for personality descriptions than those at other levels by seeing which traits people use in personality descriptions, both of themselves and others. They argued that the basic level for trait categories should be the one that people use most frequently in describing personalities.

Personality descriptions were collected for liked and disliked people, and for desirable and undesirable traits, to see if these variables influenced the preferred level of description. John et al. found that liked people and desirable traits were more likely to be described in basic level terms than disliked people and undesirable traits. John et al. also looked at people's free descriptions of different kinds of people (liked, neutral and disliked) to see which traits they generated (rather than selected), and found an analogous pattern of results. Note that factors like desirability and likeability do not influence the preferred level of description in other domains (so far as is known), and so these results suggest differences between social and object categories.

The influence of desirability and likeability aside, John et al. found a pattern of results that is analogous to data from studies of object concepts, suggesting that there may well be a basic level for trait categories. But because it is difficult to identify the hierarchical organization of social concepts, and because the traits associated with social categories are so variable, a hierarchy may not be the best way, and certainly not the only way, to organize social concepts.

Psychodiagnostic categories

Cantor et al. (1980) took the notion of hierarchically-organized prototype categories from the domain of natural object concepts and applied it to psychiatric diagnostic categories, in part to see if the manner in which the psychiatric categories were used in practice was consistent with the well-defined rule systems that appeared in diagnostic manuals at that time. They asked experienced clinicians to list attributes characteristic of the prototypical patient for a set of diagnostic categories that varied in generality. They measured the number of attributes listed as a function of level (e.g. *functional psychosis, schizophrenia*, and *paranoid schizophrenia*), as well as the amount of overlap in attributes across different categories at the same level (e.g. *paranoid schizophrenic, schizo-affective schizophrenic*, and *chronic undifferentiated schizophrenic*).

Cantor et al. found the greatest increase in the number of listed attributes when moving from their most general level (e.g. *functional psychosis*) to their intermediate level (e.g. *schizophrenic* or *affective disorder*). Also, categories at their intermediate level had fewer attributes that overlapped with other categories at the same level and more attributes that were unique at that level than did categories at their subordinate level (e.g. *paranoid schizophrenic, manic depressive depressed*). These results are consistent with the pattern found for attribute listing with natural object categories and suggest that psychodiagnostic categories can be organized into a meaningful hierarchy with a basic level.

Emotions

Shaver et al. (1987) argue that there is a basic level of emotion categories which is the most useful for making everyday distinctions about emotions. Subjects in their study sorted a list of 135 emotion terms into categories based on their judgements about which emotions were similar to each other. A hierarchical cluster analysis was conducted on the data from the sorting task. Cluster analysis is a method of determining which items are consistently grouped together across subjects. The 135 emotion terms clustered into groups that varied in specificity. There were two clusters at the most general level, corresponding to *positive emotions* and *negative emotions*. At an intermediate level, there were five groups, which they interpreted as corresponding to *love, joy, anger, sadness* and *fear*. At the most specific level, there were 25 clusters (e.g. *cheerfulness, contentment* and *pride* were subsets of the intermediate *joy* cluster). The authors suggested that it is reasonable to consider these five intermediate emotion categories basic, because they conform most closely to sets of emotions identified as primary in other research. For example, people are most likely to use these five emotion terms (and an additional term, "hate") when asked to name emotions (Fehr & Russell 1984). Also, the five basic level emotion categories overlap substantially with the emotions children learn to name first (Bretherton &

Beeghly 1982), and they correspond to the emotions that many theorists have classified as primary.

Shaver et al. (1987) point out that emotion knowledge is probably organized in at least two ways: hierarchically and dimensionally (e.g. high or low intensity, positive or negative emotion), and that these different ways of organizing emotion categories preserve different aspects of emotion knowledge. While the consistency with which emotions are designated as primary across various lines of research is impressive, emotions are like trait categories in that they can be complex combinations of different parts (e.g. *fear* and *sadness* at the same time), and so may be organized in a structure other than a hierarchy.

Programming categories

Adelson (1985) investigated whether concepts from computer programming have a basic level. In an attribute-listing study analogous to that used by Rosch et al. (1976) with concrete object concepts, expert computer programmers were given names of concepts at a general level (e.g. *algorithm* or *data structure*), at an intermediate level (*sort* or *tree*), and at a specific level (*insert* or *binary*) and were asked to list attributes of these concepts. As with object concepts, there were more attributes listed at an intermediate level than at the most general level, and there were not many more attributes listed at a more specific level than at the intermediate level. Adelson also found that subjects in a sorting task chose the intermediate level as the most natural way in which to classify programming concepts. These results suggest that there is a preferred level of conceptualization for programming concepts. Given that this domain is about as distant from object categories as one could get, this result suggests that basic level structure is a general property of the conceptual system.

Conclusions on the basic level in nonobject categories

Investigators have found a basic level in a number of different domains, suggesting that there is considerable generality of the phenomenon and the processes that underlie it. Nonetheless, the results from nonobject categorization are not always as trouble-free as those from object categories. One problem with some of this research is that the category hierarchy and the categories themselves do not always seem to be the ones that people normally use. For example, person categories like *committed person* and *supporter of the community orchestra* may not be particularly widespread, and event categories such as *going to a horror movie* may not be a separate concept for many people. Part of the problem is that categories in some domains may have no fixed names, making it harder to identify and study them. The upshot of this problem is that there may be a basic level in the category hierarchies studied by these investigators, but the hierarchies may not represent the categories that people actually use in everyday life.

Another point to keep in mind when comparing the organization of concepts in object and nonobject domains is that these domains differ in important ways. Objects have many concrete, perceptual features (e.g. is red, has legs), while nonobjects often possess more dispositional, abstract features (e.g. is greedy, is intended to entertain). Similarly, the concepts in these domains may not be organized hierarchically in every case. For example, Vallecher & Wegner (1987) have argued that actions can be conceptualized on different teleological levels. The same action could be thought of as *pressing buttons, making a phone call* or *initiating a friendship*. Such goal-oriented categories do not form the same kind of IS-A hierarchy as found in object concepts: pressing buttons is not a kind of phone call or friendship initiation. Thus, the structures described in this chapter probably cannot account for all the ways people have of thinking about people, events, situations, scenes and other nonobject categories.

EXPERTISE

When Rosch et al. (1976) first proposed the concept of a basic level, they also noted that the location and nature of the basic level might well depend on a subject's expertise in the domain. In particular, they suggested that experts would know much more about categories at specific levels of abstraction. Thus, although categories like *tree* might well be salient for such subjects, more specific categories like *maple* or *birch* would also be quite salient, because experts would know many features that are distinctive to these categories.

Although Rosch et al. did not explicitly test this hypothesis, the anthropological literature provided some evidence to support it. As mentioned earlier, American college students who were in Rosch's experiments had a basic level that was one level higher than that of subjects in non-industrialized societies. Dougherty (1978) compared the development of naming different types of plants in Berkeley, California, children with that observed among the Tzeltal Mayans. She discovered that the American children named plants at a level higher than the biological genus (e.g. they used *tree* rather than *maple*), whereas Tzeltal children used genus-level names (such as *maple*) quite often. She concluded that

> In terms of both the number of distinctions acquired and the specificity to which classifications can be extended, the eight-year old Berkeley child lags well behind the six-year-old Tzeltal child. As Chamber's (n.d.) evidence shows, the ethnobotanical knowledge of urban American adults may develop minimally beyond that of the eight-year-old child (1978:75).

In short, it seems that not only individuals, but whole societies or cultures may differ in their preferred level of categorization (see Malt 1995, for a review). These differences are domain-specific, however. Although urban citizens may well not have elaborate biological categories, they do have elaborate categories of colours, technological devices, legal terms, and so on.

The psychological literature has focused on individual differences in expertise and its influence on conceptual structure. Some of this literature has explicitly addressed the issue of hierarchical classification, but most of it has not. Nonetheless, even the latter has implications for understanding the basic level.

The most complete study of expertise and level of categorization was carried out by Tanaka & Taylor (1991), and we will discuss it in some detail. Their study is of particular interest for two main reasons. First, they examined categorization at the basic, subordinate and superordinate levels. Secondly, they used a within-subject design, in which they tested each subject in an area of expertise and in a domain outside that area. Thus, this study avoids problems relating to irrelevant differences between experts and novices that might explain the results. (For example, perhaps experts are smarter or more dedicated than novices, which could cause better performance in an experimental task.) Their study compared birdwatchers and dog experts in a number of different categorization tasks, finding several interesting differences.

First, their subjects listed features of categories at all three levels (a standard task first used by Rosch et al. 1976). In their novice domain, subjects listed many features at the basic level and fewer at the subordinate level. (For the sake of exposition, we will refer to the category level of *dog*, *bird*, *cat*, etc. as the basic level, even though the results will question whether this level is truly basic for all subjects.) In their domain of expertise, subjects increased the number of features listed at the subordinate level. For example, dog experts did not list more features of *dog* than bird experts did, but they did list more features of *collie*. Secondly, in a free-naming study, Tanaka & Taylor showed subjects pictures of a variety of objects and asked them to give the first name to come to mind. Like Rosch et al. they found that people virtually never use superordinate labels. In their novice domain, subjects produced basic-level names the majority of times (76%). In their expert domain, subjects were fairly likely to produce subordinate names. This tendency was much more pronounced for bird experts, however, who used subordinates 74% of the time, compared to 40% for dog experts (both were higher than the subordinate labelling in the novice domain). We will return to the difference between dog and bird experts a bit later.

Finally, Tanaka & Taylor tested their subjects in a timed categorization task. Such a task is considered an important test of the basic-level advantage, because it is often the only one that shows a distinct disadvantage for subordinate categories. Also, as a speeded perceptual task, its results may be more indicative of automatic processing, rather than conscious strategies that subjects might engage in (e.g. birdwatchers might feel they have to use the most precise name they know in a free naming task). The procedure of the categorization task was quite similar to that described earlier: subjects viewed a category name, followed by a picture. They responded true or false as to whether the object depicted was in the named category.

The results in the novice domain were quite similar to those of Rosch et al. (1976): the basic category was fastest, and the subordinate category slowest. However, in the expert domain, the pattern was quite different: the basic and subordinate levels were equally fast, and the superordinate level was slowest. The primary difference in the results was that the subordinate level became much faster relative to the other levels in the expert domain. Thus, this finding is consistent with the results of Tanaka & Taylor's other experiments, in showing that the subordinate level appears to gain an advantage as a result of expertise.

Tanaka & Taylor point out that this pattern is just what would be expected from the differentiation explanation of the basic level (Murphy & Brownell 1985). According to that explanation, subordinates are usually hampered by being relatively nondistinctive – they do not have many features that are unique. However, Tanaka & Taylor's feature listing results show that experts do know a number of features unique to subordinates – their subordinates *are* fairly distinctive. Furthermore, subordinates are more informative than basic level categories. As a result, experts' subordinates are much like their basic categories from the perspective of category structure. Thus, for experts, there may be no single level of categorization that is "basic" according to the classic definition. Birdwatchers can use the category *bird* quite easily, but they can also easily use *cardinal, crow* or *sparrow*.

Other studies of the relation between expertise and category structure have taken a somewhat different approach, namely, investigating how experts' advanced knowledge might influence their concepts. Chi et al. (1981) examined the categories of physics problems formed by experts and novices. They discovered that novices (students who had done well in the introductory physics course) tended to group the problems based on superficial properties. For example, novices tended to categorize problems with inclined planes together, separately from problems with springs or those involving pulleys. In contrast, experts (advanced physics graduate students) categorized problems according to the physical principle involved in their solution. In some cases, this meant grouping together problems that involved rather different objects, such as a spring and an inclined plane. Although novices had taken the course that involved problems of this sort, they did not seem to have the facility with theoretical knowledge that would allow them to see past the superficial similarities of the problems.

Similarly, Murphy & Wright (1984) examined the feature listings of concepts from psychopathology. Their subjects ranged from complete novices (college undergraduates with no experience with a clinical population) to experts with many years' experience in diagnosing and treating children with psychological disorders. The categories were the three most common ones from child psychopathology, *aggressive–impulsive*, *depressed–withdrawn* and *borderline–disorganized*. Surprisingly, Murphy & Wright discovered that the categories of the novices tended to be more distinctive than those of the experts. The main reason for this was that novices knew only a few features of the category, which were usually superficially related to the category name. For example, they listed features such as "angry" and "hits other kids" for the category *aggressive–impulsive*, and they listed features such as "feels sad" for the *depressed–withdrawn* category. In contrast, experts in clinical psychology listed for more than one category the features that they believe underlie many psychological disorders. For example, all three categories of children were said to have the symptoms "feels sad" and "angry" – not just depressed and aggressive children, respectively.

Together, the Chi et al. (1981) and the Murphy & Wright studies suggest that expertise may not always have the effect of making categories more distinctive, as Tanaka & Taylor's (1991) results might seem to suggest. Murphy & Wright found that experts knew both more distinctive features and more common features than the novices. Chi et al.'s results show that experts may notice underlying similarities between items that appear to be quite different. Thus, the influence of expertise on categorization may be quite complex. Experts may be able to identify objects more readily into specific categories than novices can, but they may also be able to notice commonalities across a domain that novices are not familiar with (e.g. the commonalities that allow spiders, shrimp, insects and crabs to be grouped together as *arthropods*).

Furthermore, some studies of expertise have emphasized that different experts may have somewhat different knowledge about a domain. For example, while biologists would probably categorize fish according to their taxonomic relations, other "fish experts", fishermen, categorize them according to their properties as sport fish and their taste (Boster & Johnson 1989). Similarly, the differences between dog and bird experts noted by Tanaka & Taylor may be due to the different nature of expertise of these two groups. Dog experts often tend to focus on one or two breeds of dogs that they raise and show; bird experts attempt to experience a wide range of birds and to identify different species as quickly and reliably as possible. This difference in the nature of expertise might account for why the bird experts were more likely to supply subordinate-level names in the free-naming task.

In short, there is considerable research still to be done on the nature of expertise and its effect on conceptual organization. It seems likely that expertise will have some influence on the preferred level of categorization, but this influence may well depend on the specific domain and on the nature of the expertise that subjects bring to it.

CONCLUSION

The hierarchical structure of categories is a well-established phenomenon, which has been identified in many different cultures. People rely on such hierarchies in order to be able to generalize their knowledge productively: once you learn that all animals breathe, you do not need to relearn it for dogs, poodles, miniature poodles, and so on. Nonetheless, it is still not fully known whether this hierarchical structure is built into the conceptual system, in the form of taxonomies in the head, or is instead the result of an inferential process. We have suggested that there is considerable evidence opposed to a purely pre-stored hierarchy, but it may well be that there is a mixture of different kinds of conceptual structures. Some categories may be explicitly connected by IS-A links (e.g. *whale* or *mammal*), whereas other hierarchical relations may have to be computed (e.g. *car seat* and *chair*). The field is still awaiting an integrated model of all these phenomena.

The phenomenon of the basic level provides a more consistent set of results. We have concluded that most experiments are consistent with the differentiation explanation of why basic concepts are preferred. This explanation is primarily a structural one – that is, it refers to the number of features known about each category and their overlap with the features of other categories. It can be applied to any domain, once the features of the categories are determined. Thus, it does not depend on complex knowledge structures about a domain, which is one reason why basic-level phenomena can be demonstrated with artificial stimuli. One concern about our explanation, then, might come from the fact that much recent work in concepts has emphasized knowledge and theories about a domain rather than formal rules that apply across wide domains (e.g. Medin 1989, Murphy 1993, Murphy & Medin 1985, Wattenmaker et al. 1986; see the chapter by Heit in this volume). How can these two perspectives be reconciled?

One point to make is that categories cannot be entirely constructed out of pre-existing knowledge structures. Even very "top–down" approaches to concept learning (those relying heavily on people's knowledge) must allow the structure of the stimuli to have some influence, or else concept formation would be a kind of hallucination (i.e. perception without constraints from the environment). As a result, even knowledge-based categorization will be influenced by the structure of the material to be learned. If the category is a very general one, with only abstract commonalities, it will likely be difficult to learn. Similarly, if it is very specific and similar to other categories, it will be difficult to distinguish from the others. Basic categories, which have neither of these problems, will generally be easier to learn. It is clear that knowledge has important effects such as helping to define the features, emphasizing some attributes more than others, or influencing how different kinds of information are combined. Nonetheless, when the stimuli are finally interpreted, some category structures will be easier to learn than others.

A complete explanation of category learning will probably involve both structural and knowledge components. However, the phenomenon of basic-level advantage seems largely to be a structural one. Although gaining knowledge of a domain will influence categorization, the factors of informativeness and distinctiveness will still operate to determine which categories are easy to use, as shown by Tanaka & Taylor's (1991) results with highly knowledgeable experts. In fact, recent evidence has shown that the basic-level advantage is only slightly reduced by priming of knowledge relevant to the subordinate or superordinate level (Lin et al. 1997).

Research outside the area of object categories has been less certain in demonstrating basic-level structure. In general, this does not seem to be a shortcoming of the theory of the basic level but rather a problem in identifying the categories that are actually known and used by subjects in each domain – especially when the categories may not have familiar verbal labels. Also, studies in other domains have often relied on a single task to measure basic-level structure, rather than repeating the process of converging operations used by Rosch et al. (1976). In some cases, studies have simply assumed that the concepts are hierarchically organized, rather than empirically demonstrating this. Thus, a possible goal for future work on basic categories is to elucidate the conceptual structures of new domains in a more complete way.

REFERENCES

Adelson, B. 1985. Comparing natural and abstract categories: a case study from computer science. *Cognitive Science* **9**, 417–30.

Anglin, J. M. 1977. *Word, object and conceptual development*. New York: Norton.

Berlin, B. 1992. *Ethnobiological classification: principles of categorization of plants and animals in traditional societies*. Princeton, New Jersey: Princeton University Press.

Berlin, B., D. E. Breedlove, P. H. Raven 1973. General principles of classification and nomenclature in folk biology. *American Anthropologist* **75**, 214–42.

Biederman, I. 1990. Higher-level vision. In *An invitation to cognitive science*, vol. 2: *visual cognition and action*, D. N. Osherson, S. M. Kosslyn, J. M. Hollerbach (eds), 41–72. Cambridge, Mass.: MIT Press.

Boster, J. S. & J. V. Johnson 1989. Form or function: a comparison of expert and novice judgments of similarity among fish. *American Anthropologist* **91**, 866–89.

Bretherton, I. & M. Beeghly 1982. Talking about internal states: the acquisition of an explicit theory of mind. *Developmental Psychology* **18**, 906–912.

Brown, R. 1958. How shall a thing be called? *Psychological Review* **65**, 14–21.

Callanan, M. A. 1985. How parents label objects for young children: the role of input in the acquisition of category hierarchies. *Child Development* **56**, 508–528.

Cantor, N. & W. Mischel 1979. Prototypes in person perception. In *Advances in experimental social psychology* (vol. 12), L. Berkowitz (ed.), 3–52. New York: Academic Press.

Cantor, N., E. E. Smith, R. de S. French, J. Mezzich 1980. Psychiatric diagnosis as prototype categorization. *Journal of Abnormal Psychology* **89**, 181–93.

Chang, T. 1986. Semantic memory: facts and models. *Psychological Bulletin* **99**, 100–220.

Chi, M. T., P. J. Feltovich, R. Glaser 1981. Categorization and representation of physics problems by experts and novices. *Cognitive Science* **5**, 121–52.

Collins, A. M. & M. R. Quillian 1969. Retrieval time from semantic memory. *Journal of Verbal Learning and Verbal Behavior* **8**, 241–8.

Corter, J. E. & M. A. Gluck 1992. Explaining basic categories: feature predictability and information. *Psychological Bulletin* **111**, 291–303.

Cruse, D. A. 1977. The pragmatics of lexical specificity. *Journal of Linguistics* **13**, 153–64.

Dougherty, J. W. D. 1978. Salience and relativity in classification. *American Ethnologist* **5**, 66–80.

Fehr, B. & J. A. Russell 1984. Concept of emotion viewed from a prototype perspective. *Journal of Experimental Psychology: General* **113**, 464–86.

Glass, A. L. & K. J. Holyoak 1975. Alternative conceptions of semantic memory. *Cognition* **3**, 313–39.

Hampton, J. A. 1982. A demonstration of intransitivity in natural categories. *Cognition* **12**, 151–64.

Hampton, J. A. 1993. Prototype models of concept representation. In *Categories and concepts: theoretical views and inductive data analysis*, I. Van Mechelen, J. Hampton, R. Michalski, P. Theuns (eds), 67–95. New York: Academic Press.

Horton, M. S. & E. M. Markman 1980. Developmental differences in the acquisition of basic and superordinate categories. *Child Development* **51**, 708–719.

John, O. P., S. E. Hampson, L. R. Goldberg 1991. The basic level of personality-trait hierarchies: studies of trait use and accessibility in different contexts. *Journal of Personality and Social Psychology* **60**, 348–61.

Jolicoeur, P., M. Gluck, S. M. Kosslyn 1984. Pictures and names: making the connection. *Cognitive Psychology* **19**, 31–53.

Jones, G. V. 1983. Identifying basic categories. *Psychological Bulletin* **94**, 423–8.

Lassaline, M. E., E. J. Wisniewski, D. L. Medin 1992. The basic level in artificial and natural categories: are all basic levels created equal? In *Percepts, concepts and categories: The representation and processing of information*, B. Burns (ed.), 327–378. Amsterdam: Elsevier.

Lin, E. L., G. L. Murphy, E. J. Shoben. 1997. The effects of prior processing episodes on basic-level superiority. *Quarterly Journal of Experimental Psychology A: Human Experimental Psychology* **50**, 25–48.

Malt, B. C. 1995. Category coherence in cross-cultural perspective. *Cognitive Psychology* **29**, 85–148.

Markman, E. M. 1985. Why superordinate category terms can be mass nouns. *Cognition* **19**, 31–53.

Markman, E. M. & M. A. Callanan 1983. An analysis of hierarchical classification. In *Advances in the psychology of human intelligence* (vol. 2), R. Sternberg (ed.), 325–365. Hillsdale, New Jersey: Erlbaum.

Markman, E. M., M. S. Horton, A. G. McClanahan 1980. Classes and collections: principles of organization in the learning of hierarchical relations. *Cognition* **8**, 227–41.

McCloskey, M. & S. Glucksberg 1979. Decision processes in verifying category membership statements: implications for models of semantic memory. *Cognitive Psychology* **11**, 1–37.

Medin, D. L. 1983. Structural principles of categorization. In *Perception, cognition, and development: interactional analyses*, T. Tighe & B. Shepp (eds), 203–230. Hillsdale, New Jersey: Erlbaum.

Medin, D. L. 1989. Concepts and conceptual structure. *American Psychologist* **12**, 1469–81.

Mervis, C. B. & M. A. Crisafi 1982. Order of acquistion of subordinate, basic, and superordinate level categories. *Child Development* **53**, 258–66.

Morris, M. W. & G. L. Murphy 1990. Converging operations on a basic level in event taxonomies. *Memory & Cognition* **18**, 407–418.

Murphy, G. L. 1982. Cue validity and levels of categorization. *Psychological Bulletin* **91**, 174–7.

Murphy, G. L. 1991. Parts in object concepts: experiments with artificial categories. *Memory & Cognition* **19**, 423–38.

Murphy, G. L. 1993. Theories and concept formation. In *Categories and concepts: theoretical views and inductive data analysis*, I. Van Mechelen, J. Hampton, R. Michalski, P. Theuns (eds), 173–200. New York: Academic Press.

Murphy, G. L. & H. H. Brownell 1985. Category differentiation in object recognition: typicality constraints on the basic category advantage. *Journal of Experimental Psychology: Learning, Memory, and Cognition* **11**, 70–84.

Murphy, G. L. & D. L. Medin 1985. The role of theories in conceptual coherence. *Psychological Review* **92**, 289–316.

Murphy, G. L. & E. E. Smith 1982. Basic level superiority in picture categorization. *Journal of Verbal Learning and Verbal Behavior* **21**, 1–20.

Murphy, G. L. & E. J. Wisniewski 1989. Categorizing objects in isolation and in scenes: what a superordinate is good for. *Journal of Experimental Psychology: Learning, Memory, and Cognition* **15**, 572–86.

Murphy, G. L. & J. C. Wright 1984. Changes in conceptual structure with expertise – differences between real-world experts and novices. *Journal of Experimental Psychology: Learning, Memory, and Cognition* **10**, 144–155.

Randall, R. 1976. How tall is a taxonomic tree? Some evidence for dwarfism. *American Ethnologist* **3**, 543–53.

Rifkin, A. 1985. Evidence for a basic level in event taxonomies. *Memory & Cognition* **13**, 538–56.

Rips, L. J., E. J. Shoben, E. E. Smith 1973. Semantic distance and the verification of semantic relations. *Journal of Verbal Learning and Verbal Behavior* **12**, 1–20.

Rosch, E. 1978. Principles of categorization. In *Cognition and categorization,* E. Rosch & B. B. Lloyd (eds.), 27–48. Hillsdale, New Jersey: Erlbaum.

Rosch, E. & C. B. Mervis 1975. Family resemblances: studies in the internal structure of categories. *Cognitive Psychology* **7**, 573–605.

Rosch, E., C. B. Mervis, W. Gray, D. Johnson, P. Boyes-Braem 1976. Basic objects in natural categories. *Cognitive Psychology* **8**, 382–439.

Shaver, P., J. Schwarz, D. Kirson, D. O'Connor 1987. Emotion knowledge: further explorations of prototype approach. *Journal of Personality and Social Psychology* **52**, 1061–1086.

Smith, E. E. 1978. Theories of semantic memory. In *Handbook of learning and cognitive processes* (vol. 6), W. K. Estes (ed.), 1–56. Potomac, Maryland: Erlbaum.

Smith, E. E., G. J. Balzano, J. Walker 1978. Nominal, perceptual, and semantic codes in picture categorization. In *Semantic factors in cognition*, J. W. Cotton & R. L. Klatzky (eds), 137–68. Hillsdale, New Jersey: Erlbaum.

Tanaka, J. W. & M. E. Taylor 1991. Object categories and expertise: is the basic level in the eye of the beholder? *Cognitive Psychology* **23**, 457–82.

Tversky, B. & K. Hemenway 1983. Categories of environmental scenes. *Cognitive Psychology* **15**, 121–49.

Tversky, B. & K. Hemenway 1984. Objects, parts and categories. *Journal of Experimental Psychology: General* **113**, 169–93.

Vallecher, R. R. & D. M. Wegner 1987. What do people think they're doing? Action identification and human behavior. *Psychological Review* **94**, 3–15.

Wattenmaker, W. D., G. I. Dewey, T. D. Murphy, D. L. Medin 1986. Linear separability and concept learning: context, relational properties, and concept naturalness. *Cognitive Psychology* **18**, 158–94.

Wisniewski, E. J. & G. L. Murphy 1989. Superordinate and basic category names in discourse: a textual analysis. *Discourse Processes* **12**, 245–61.

NOTES

1. For simplicity, we are making the assumption that each category's features are true of all its members. Smith et al. (1984) address the more likely prospect that the features are not necessary in this way. We will have to relax this assumption in explaining intransitivity below.
2. Rosch et al. (1976) made an unfortunate choice of terminology, reflected in their title, of referring to basic level *objects*. However, it should be clear that it is not the object that is basic, but rather the category it is in. The same object is a terrier and a dog and a mammal and an animal, so it cannot be that some objects are basic and others are not. Rather, certain ways of classifying the object (in this case, as a *dog*) are basic and others are not.
3. Note that *pants* in American English corresponds to *trousers* in British English.
4. See Hahn & Chater, this volume, for an extensive discussion of the feature inclusion problem in similarity computation.

CHAPTER FOUR

Conceptual Combination[1]

James Hampton

Human language is compositional. When we construct a sentence in order to make an utterance, we do so by stringing together a series of words from our language in a particular order. The resulting sentence derives its meaning from three sources – the meaning of the individual words that have been selected (in particular the meanings of the "substantive" words such as nouns, verbs and adjectives), the syntactic structure of the sentence which places those words in a logical framework of syntactical roles including the subject, main verb and object, and other parts of the sentence, and finally the context and manner (including intonation and gesture) in which the sentence is uttered, which will determine what the speaker of the sentence actually intends to convey by its utterance on this particular occasion.

Assuming that a large part of our knowledge of the world is structured around the same concepts that underlie the meanings of words, then compositionality must apply equally to knowledge representation.[2] If someone "knows" something then we can describe this knowledge as a belief that some proposition is true. If I know that the sea is rough when there is a storm, then we might assume that this knowledge is represented by a proposition expressed in some symbolic "language" in the mind which maps more or less directly onto our natural spoken language. Corresponding to the words "sea", "rough", and "storm" it is proposed that we have corresponding concepts of *sea*, *roughness* and *storm*, so that propositional knowledge can be represented as a language-like construction in some symbolic form. This proposal is effectively the *language-of-thought* hypothesis proposed by Fodor (1983). It is assumed that a person has a repertoire of available concepts and ways of combining those concepts into higher-order concepts and into propositions. This system allows us to represent a wide range of beliefs, and to construct elaborate representations of considerable complexity.

The process of conceptual combination is at the heart of knowledge representation, in that it asks the basic question – how is the meaning of a complex noun phrase related to the meanings of its component parts? This basic question can also be taken as asking how complex knowledge representations are constructed from simpler concepts. Interest in conceptual combination has arisen within cognitive psychology recently because of research conducted in the 1970s and 1980s into the more fundamental question of how the meanings of individual nouns, verbs and adjectives and the concepts that they represent are represented in a person's memory. One popular theory of conceptual representation, developed by Rosch (1975, 1978) and Mervis (Rosch & Mervis 1975), suggested that the concepts which constitute word meanings for nouns such as "bird" or "chair" are represented in the mind by prototypes. The *prototype theory of concepts* proposed that rather than concepts being represented by an explicit definition which could be used to clearly differentiate when an instance was or was not an example of the concept (as assumed by most linguistic theories of semantics at that time, e.g. Katz & Fodor 1963), concepts are instead represented by an "ideal" or "average" prototype, and whether or not an instance is an example of the concept depends on the similarity of that instance to the prototype for the concept.

This "fuzzy" approach to defining the truth conditions of statements such as "X is a bird" raised the problem of determining the semantics of more complex statements involving logical combinations of concepts – as Osherson & Smith (1981) were first to point out. If the truth conditions of "X is a bird" cannot be determined by a simple set of defining rules, then how is the truth of sentences such as "X is a pet bird" or "X is either a bird or a mammal" to be determined? Osherson and Smith argued that a major advantage of the so-called "classical" approach to concepts, by which each word had a clear-cut definition, was that the problem of assigning truth conditions to complex phrases in the language could be mapped in a direct way onto expressions in standard logic. For example the statement "X is a pet bird" is true (by the standard classical treatment) if both "X is a pet" and "X is a bird" are true. In other words, the truth of the statement is a simple logical conjunction of the truth of the two constituent categorizations. However, if the truth of these constituent categorizations is a matter of degree (as proposed by Rosch and others) then we cannot rely on simple conjunction to provide us with the truth conditions for the complex statement.

The reason for the difficulty comes from the assumption that the truth of categorization statements can be graded.[3] Some categorizations (for example "dogs are animals") are more true than others (for example "bacteria are animals"). If two of these fuzzy truth values are to be combined logically, then a new calculus is needed to determine how the truth of a logical combination is related to the truth of the constituent parts.

The problem of conceptual combination is not only a problem for the prototype theory of concepts.[4] As Rips (1995) has pointed out, the problem is made no more tractable if the simple notion of a prototype is replaced by the currently favoured notion of a schema or "mini-theory" as the representational format for concepts (Murphy & Medin 1985). The *theory view of concepts* is briefly that people represent concepts through a deeper understanding of the causal connections between their observed characteristics. Rather than representing the concept of "bird" as a list of commonly observed characteristics (*flies, has wings, has two legs, builds nests in trees, has feathers*), the theory view proposes that people's concept of "bird" is embedded in a wider set of interlocking theoretical structures corresponding to naïve (and possible fallacious) theories of animal biology, mechanics, etc. Thus, people may understand why birds have wings (to enable them to fly), why they fly (to escape predators and find food), why they nest in trees (because flying enables them to get into the trees in the first place), and so forth. Each characteristic is linked to others with explanatory, causal or goal-directed links.

While the theory view undoubtedly has much to recommend it as a more powerful system for representing conceptual knowledge, when it comes to the problem of conceptual combinations it is less obvious how a set of syntactic rules for combining mini-theories could be formulated. The more powerful the representational medium employed, then the more each example appears to need its own special set of rules for combination, and the more background knowledge appears to be required. Viewed from a philosophical point of view, it has been argued (Fodor 1994) that none of the existing psychological models of concepts is adequate for giving a proper account of compositionality (and hence conceptual combination).

Apart from prototype and theory-based views of concepts, the other main view of conceptual representation is the *exemplar view*. This view holds that concepts are represented in memory by their most common exemplars. Novel instances are then classified by their similarity to the remembered exemplars. This way of modelling concept representations has had best success in accounting for the results of classification learning experiments in which participants have to learn how to sort artifically constructed shapes into different categories (Medin & Schaffer 1978, see also chapters by Heit, Lamberts and Storms in this volume). As a theory of knowledge representation, the exemplar theory would imply that we represent knowledge through particular memories of individual episodes (see e.g. Brooks 1987). This proposal clearly has face validity – there is little doubt that much of our knowledge is heavily dependent on a range of individual remembered experiences. However it cannot work as a complete account, since an exemplar only becomes relevant to a situation when it is analysed. One can only categorize novel instances on the basis of their similarity to remembered exemplars if there is some means of determining similarity of the relevant kind. But this determination of similarity itself presupposes a deeper level of knowledge representation, since not just any kind of similarity may be used. If concepts are represented by exemplars, then conceptual combinations would also have to be represented by exemplars. "Pet birds" would be represented by remembered instances of actual pet birds. As we will see below, such a model accounts well for knowledge of familiar conceptual combinations. There are facts that we know about pet birds (for example that they can talk) which could not be derived from our knowledge of either pets or birds alone, and so must be based on knowledge of exemplars. However, the exemplar view of concepts would have little or nothing to say about how we are able to construct novel unfamiliar conceptual combinations, in the case where we have no remembered instances to recall to mind.

TYPES OF CONCEPTUAL COMBINATION

Conceptual combinations can be broadly divided into three types. First there are combinations of concepts which appear to be broadly intersective in a logical sense. Some adjective noun phrases are intersective – thus a "red apple" is both red and an apple. One can suppose (although empirical evidence might be needed to confirm this – see Hampton 1996) that for most people the category of red apples is simply the overlap of the categories of red things and of apples. Where relative clauses are used for combining concepts the result also appears to be broadly intersective – thus "pets which are also fish" can be understood as the overlap of the categories of pets and fish.

A second type of combination involves an adjective plus noun, or a noun-plus-noun combination where the first word is used to modify the second. The first word is known as the modifier, and the second as the head noun. For example a "corporate lawyer" is a member of the category of lawyers who is concerned with the law appertaining to corporations, while a "criminal lawyer" is a member of the same category of lawyers who works on criminal cases. The difference from the first type of combination should be evident. Criminal lawyers in this sense are not the intersection of the categories of criminals and lawyers (although the intersective reading is also possible and produces an ambiguity in the meaning of the phrase).

The third type is best seen as a subtype of the modifier-head combination. When combinations become familiar and idiomatic they are known as lexical compounds and are typically marked in English by placing stress on the first (modifier) noun. Thus, to use an example from Kamp & Partee (1989), a "*brick* factory" is a factory that makes bricks (a lexical compound), whereas a "brick *factory*" is a factory made from bricks (a novel modifier-head combination). Many lexical compounds have become highly idiomatized so that it is no longer possible to predict their meaning on the basis of their constituent nouns. Rips (1995) cites the example of a "bull ring", which one feels ought to (but does not) mean the ring in a bull's nose. At the extreme, noun–noun compounds can be lexicalized to the point of effectively forming a single lexical unit in the mental lexicon – as in "railway" or "lipstick". Apart from these clearly lexicalized examples, it may not always be simple to distinguish modifier-head constructions from true compounds. It may in fact be better to see both types as falling on a continuum of novelty. Novel combinations such as "butter police" are clearly modifier-head constructions, whereas highly familiar combinations like "patchwork" are clearly compounds. Presumably all compounds started life as novel modifier-head forms, and then gradually became lexicalized through frequent use. A process of chaining can also occur, so that the original meaning can become more and more distant. The best known example of this is Fillmore's example of "topless district" – where the object which is topless is not the district, nor the bars within it, nor the waitresses that serve in them, but the clothing that they wear.

Research on conceptual combination has focused largely on the first two of these types. It can be safely assumed that the understanding of lexicalized compounds involves no new conceptual combination, and so the study of how their meaning relates to the meanings of their constituents is more of interest to students of historical linguistics than to psychologists. Another use of conceptual combinations which will not be explored here is one where the meaning of a conceptual combination is very heavily dependent on the pragmatic context in which the phrase is used. It was stated at the start of the chapter that when people are conversing a major source of meaning comes from the surrounding context, both situational and linguistic. Downing (1977) gives examples of novel noun–noun combinations whose interpretation would be impossible without knowing the prior context. Thus the use of "apple-juice seat" to refer to a place at a table in a restaurant where an order of apple juice had been placed is a case where the communicative context supplies the solution to interpreting the combination. It is probably the case that most novel combinations in actual speech are created in such circumstances, and their novelty may not even be noted by the hearer. Gerrig & Murphy (1992:217) explored this process in a series of experiments in which a novel combination such as "trumpet olive" was rendered meaningful by a prior story context such as the following:

> Peter and Susan watched the skilled old woman with great awe. The woman was carving figures out of stale olives. She had been plying this craft for twenty years. Her work was remarkably detailed. Peter and Susan could see a miniature trumpet appearing out of a new one. Peter said 'Would you like a trumpet olive?'

Their study illustrates very neatly how powerful an influence the discourse or story context can have on the interpretation of a novel phrase. By manipulating the story context, one could cause people to interpret "trumpet olive" to mean a wide variety of things – the olives reserved for the trumpet players for their interval snack at a concert, a kind of olive which is stuffed into a trumpet to keep it in good working order – there is no limit to the creative possibilities. This creativity is possible because the phrase is being used primarily as a referential phrase (Donnellan 1966) to point to some object that has already been established within the story. The context is doing all the work of identifying the relevant object or concept, and the linguistic phrase has merely to point to it in a reasonably distinctive manner. As a result there is little conceptual work for the hearer to do.

For the most part, the study of how people combine concepts has maintained a neutral context so that the effect of manipulating conceptual content can be measured. We will see that people do in fact have the ability to select plausible interpretations for novel combinations in the absence of explicit context, and a number of studies have addressed this capability. In the remainder of this chapter the first two types of conceptual combination – intersective combinations and modifier-head combinations – are considered, and relevant research and theoretical models are reviewed.

INTERSECTIVE COMBINATION

When Rosch and others proposed similarity to prototype as the basis for categorization, it was proposed that one could treat membership in a category as a matter of degree. A ready-made way to model the logic of such gradedness was available in a system known as *fuzzy logic*. Developed by Zadeh (1965), fuzzy logic is a form of set logic in which the truth value of set membership statements can take a continuous value between 1 (true) and 0 (false). For example the statement "John is a tall man" can be taken as being more or less true, depending on how close John is in height to the prototypical tall man. Zadeh's logic proposed an extension of the standard set-logical operators of conjunction, disjunction and negation to include continuous truth values. For example, fuzzy conjunction was defined (for simple cases) with a minimum rule, whereby the truth of the conjunction of two expressions was the minimum of the two individual truth values. Thus "John is both tall and handsome" would be only as true as the least true of the two individual statements "John is tall" and "John is handsome". The minimum rule reduces to the standard classical conjunctive operator in the case that truth values are restricted to just 1 or 0. (A second rule for conjunction was proposed by Zadeh for more complex statements – the rule involved multiplying the two truth values to find the truth of the conjunction, so that the truth of "John is both tall and handsome" would always be less than or equal to the truth of each individual statement. This second set of rules is a direct corollary of the axioms for combining the probabilities of independent events in probability theory.)

Although fuzzy logic had some success in accounting for intuitions about the conjunction of unrelated statements (Oden 1977), it soon became clear, following a key article by Osherson and Smith (1981), that not only the minimum rule, but in fact any rule that takes as input solely the truth value of the two constituent statements is doomed to failure. The reason is that the function of fuzzy conjunction appears to depend also on the degree of relatedness of the two categories being combined. Consider first the case where the two concepts are highly related – as when one is a subset of the other.

(1) X is a kind of poultry
(2) X is a kind of bird
(3) X is a kind of poultry AND a kind of bird

The degree to which (3) is true of some new found specimen creature is likely to be determined largely by the degree to which (1) is true. This is because if (1) is true then (2) is also always true.

Now consider Osherson & Smith's example of two concepts that are generally contradictory.

(4) X is striped
(5) X is an apple
(6) X is a striped apple

An actual apple that had stripes would be a better example of the conjunction "striped apple" than it would be of either of the two constituent concepts – simply because apples do not generally have stripes and striped things are generally not apples. Thus (6) should have a higher truth value than either (4) or (5).

Both of these examples run counter to the principle of the minimum rule for conjunction. A good example of poultry is likely to be a poor example of a bird (since poultry are atypical birds), but still to be a good example of the conjunction "bird which is poultry". Similarly the apple with stripes is a better example of the conjunction than of the constituent concepts – in direct contradiction of the minimum rule.

Smith et al. (1988) took the striped apple example from Osherson & Smith (1981) and collected empirical evidence that it is indeed true that a picture of a brown apple (for example) is considered more typical of the conjunctive concept "brown apple" than it is of the simple concept "apple". The almost trivial nature of this demonstration highlights the failing of the fuzzy logic approach to cope with predictions of typicality in complex concepts. In their *selective modification model*, Smith et al. (1988) adopted a frame formalism (Minsky 1975) for representing a concept such as "apple". In a frame representation, the property information which defines what apples are like (in effect one's knowledge of apples) is represented by a series of attribute slots such as [COLOUR], [SHAPE], [SOURCE], and so forth. Each of these slots can take different values as slot fillers. For example the representation of "apple" in Table 4.1 (loosely taken from Smith et al. 1988) has the following slot:

[COLOUR] = *red (10), green (8), yellow (5), brown (2)*

The weights ($w1$, $w2$ etc.) represent the relative importance of each slot in determining similarity of any instance to the concept. The numbers in parentheses for each slot filler reflect the relative frequency (or typicality) for the different values in the population of apples in the person's experience (they are called *votes* in the selective modification model). Hence red apples are represented as being more typical than green, yellow or brown apples, simply by matching a value with a

TABLE 4.1
Frame representation of the concept "apple"

Weight	Slot	Fillers
w1	COLOUR	red (10), green (8), yellow (5), brown (2)
w2	SHAPE	round (10), stalk at one end (5)
w3	CONTAINS	seeds (15), juice (10)
w4	SOURCE	on apple trees (20)
w5 etc	USED FOR	eating whole (10), apple pies (5), baking (3)

higher number of votes (note that the model was developed in the USA, where red apples are predominant).

When the concept "apple" is modified with a colour such as "brown", to produce the conceptual combination "brown apple", the selective modification model proposes that the representation of "apple" undergoes a selective modification of the [COLOUR] slot of the frame, so that whereas for "apple" [COLOUR] can take values *red, green, yellow* or *brown*, for "brown apple", all the votes for colour are transferred to the value *brown*. In addition the model proposes that the weight of the [COLOUR] slot itself is increased in the frame. Since typicality is determined by similarity to the concept representation (in this they followed the approach adopted by Smith at al. 1974, and by prototype theory), the model proposed that typicality was determined by a weighted function of matching and non-matching features (Tversky 1977), computed across the frame representation. Hence by increasing the weight for the [COLOUR] slot, the influence of colour on typicality is increased in the case of "brown apple" relative to "apple".

The selective modification model predicts correctly that brown apples are more typical of "brown apple" than of "apple", whereas a regular apple is more typical of "apple" than of "brown apple". However, it should be noted that the model is overspecified for even this relatively straightforward prediction. It incorporates two mechanisms (transfer of votes to *brown*, and increase in the weight of the [COLOUR] slot) whereas the first alone would produce the same prediction. It is also highly problematic as a model of categorization in complex categories (as opposed to the determination of typicality).

To understand the problem, a brief digression is necessary to explain the difference between graded membership as measured by typicality and graded membership as it relates to categorization. Rosch's prototype model simply proposed that concept categories are graded, and this gradation could be seen both in variation in typicality (for example sparrows are typical examples of the category of birds, whereas ostriches are atypical), and also in the existence of borderline cases, where items are so atypical as to render their category membership questionable (as in whether carpets are furniture, or a lift is a vehicle – see Hampton & Gardiner 1983, and McCloskey & Glucksberg 1978, for copious examples in British and American English respectively). The prototype model proposed that both variation in typicality and the occurrence of borderline cases (whose gradedness is reflected in their probability of categorization across a sample of people or occasions), are driven by the same underlying dimension – namely similarity to the concept prototype. However, they do not have to follow similarity according to the same function.[5] It is clear that both sparrows and ostriches are birds (all 44 subjects agreed on a positive categorization in the Hampton & Gardiner 1983 study), but whereas sparrows are universally considered highly typical in England, ostriches are considered highly atypical. So typicality can vary widely even when categorization is constant. This apparent anomaly is easily resolved by assuming that categorization is derived from similarity via a threshold criterion. Once similarity is above some level, then categorization is certain, although there will continue to be variations in rated typicality (see Hampton 1993, 1995, for a more formal explication of the prototype model). In effect, categorization probability reaches its ceiling well before similarity to the prototype reaches its maximum.

Returning to the selective modification model, we can see how it is primarily a model for determining typicality rather than categorization. For example, for "red apple", the weight of the colour slot is boosted and all the votes are transferred to the colour *red*. An actual red apple is then more similar to the concept "red apple" than it is to the concept "apple", and so should be rated as such. The weight of the colour slot needs to be boosted in the model so that the colour of an object counts as much as its "appleness" in determining its typicality. A well formed brown apple – which has all the other slots of the concept fully matching – should not be considered a better example of a "red apple" than an oddly shaped and unusually small red apple.

The effect of giving high weight to the colour slot, however, will be to make other red fruits like strawberries or tomatoes also highly similar to the "red apple" concept, since they will capture all the red votes on the highly weighted colour slot, as well as matching many of the fruit properties. If colour is weighted to the point where it counts as much as appleness in determining similarity, then it follows that other fruits with the right colour red but low appleness should be as similar to the "red apple" concept as apples that are not red. It is extremely unlikely therefore that the selective modification model would allow the concept representation for "red apple" to correctly categorize red apples from all other fruits, and indeed

Smith et al. at the end of their article qualify their model as applying only to typicality judgements, and restate the earlier arguments (Osherson & Smith 1981, 1982) with regard to categorization – that is that categorization must depend on a well-defined core of features, rather than on similarity to prototype.

An alternative model which does attempt to account for the range of conceptual logical functions such as conjunction, disjunction and negation while maintaining a similarity-based model of conceptual categorization is to be found in my own work (Hampton 1987, 1988a, 1988b, 1996). The initial aim was to examine the degree to which people's conjunctive concepts do in fact closely follow the logical function of set intersection. An earlier study (Hampton 1982, see also Kempton 1978, Randall 1976) had thrown up the possibility that people's semantic categorizations were only loosely modelled by set logic. For example, people were willing to accept that chairs are a type of furniture and that car seats are a type of chair, but would then deny that car seats are a type of furniture. The relation between people's use of categorization statements and the mathematician's notion of class inclusion is therefore not a direct mapping.

Hampton (1988b, Experiment 1) extended this demonstration of intransitivity to subsets of categories defined by modifier-head combinations. Consider for example "school furniture" or "office furniture". The selective modification model, and most other accounts of conceptual combination, take it as given that the complex concept forms a proper subset of the head noun concept. There are a number of well-known exceptions involving privative modifiers such as "fake", "counterfeit" and "alleged", which do not follow this rule (a "fake dollar" is not a dollar), and there are also cases such as "stone lion" or "chocolate rabbit" where the modifier has the effect of changing the reference of the head noun to objects with the shape and appearance of the original objects (Franks 1989, Wisniewski 1996). But these examples clearly do not apply to the "school furniture" example, which could be paraphrased with a simple thematic IN relation (Levi 1978) – "furniture that is found in schools", or possibly a USED-FOR relation – "furniture that is used for schools".

Hampton (1988b, Experiment 1) asked subjects to classify a number of objects such as desks, chairs and blackboards either as being "furniture" or as being "school furniture", and found that there were a number of cases that mirrored the earlier intransitivity result – not all objects classed as school furniture were also included in the category of furniture. When asked to classify school furniture as a type of furniture, they were happy to do so. In a follow-up test, however, the respondents were asked to choose between two alternative statements:

(a) All school furniture is also furniture

(b) Some school furniture is not furniture

When faced with this choice, many people chose (b), indicating that there was no inconsistency in their minds between claiming both that school furniture is a kind of furniture, and that there are kinds of school furniture which are not furniture. Once a concept has been modified, it appears that the resulting class of objects is only an approximate subset of the head noun class.

In subsequent experiments, Hampton (1988b) made the modifier relation more explicitly conjunctive by using a relative clause construction. Thus the phrase "sports which are also games" certainly appears *prima facie* to involve taking the head noun class ("sports") and then identifying the subset of the head noun category that are also in the class of "games". However, this is not how subjects responded. Where an activity was a very typical example of one category (for example "chess" is a typical game) then it was more likely to be classified in the conjunction ("sports which are games") than in the other constituent concept ("sports"). Across a number of pairs of overlapping concepts, the general rule seemed to apply that the likelihood of being classed in the conjunction was some average of the two constituent categorization probabilities (see Huttenlocher & Hedges 1994, for an attempt to provide a purely statistical account of this result). Furthermore, three reliable but unexpected results emerged. One was a concept dominance effect such that one of the two concepts had a greater influence on the conjunction than the other. For example, membership in the conjunction "sports which are games" was more heavily determined by membership of the games category than membership of the sports category – regardless of which was taken as head noun (see Storms et al. 1993, for further studies of the dominance effect). The second result was non-commutativity – the two forms of the conjunction "sports which are games", and "games which are sports" were not identical in either typicality or membership. The third was overextension. People were more likely to overextend the conjunction to include items that were judged not to be in one or the other constituent category than they were to underextend it by omitting items that were judged to be in both constituent categories. None of these phenomena is readily accounted for by purely statistical effects.

Overextension has since also been found in visually defined concepts such as coloured letters and cartoon faces (Hampton 1996a). In this study, I found additional evidence against a purely statistical account. Stimuli in one part of the experiment were cartoon faces which varied in their features so that they could be classified along two dimensions. Some looked happy while others looked sad, and orthogonal to this distinction, some looked like adults while others looked like children. Subsets of stimuli were selected in the critical condition that were clear members of one category (for example, all looked like children), and borderline cases of the second category (for example, they were at the borderline in terms of looking happy or sad). Categorization in the conjunction "happy children" was then measured. It was found that variation in typicality in the first category "children" (where probability of categorization was at ceiling) was correlated with categorization in the conjunction. The link between similarity (as measured by typicality variation amongst clear category members) and categorization probability in the conjunction shows that typicality in one category can compensate for borderline status in the other. No models that propose that the conjunction is categorized through application of a rule of the kind {X is an AB if and only if X is an A and X is a B} where the two constituent categorization decisions are made independently (see for example Huttenlocher & Hedges 1994) can account for this kind of compensation.[6]

An interesting corollary of the overextension effect is to be found in work by Tversky & Kahneman on probability judgements. Tversky & Kahneman (1983) showed that people will on occasion consider it more likely that an individual falls in the conjunction of two classes than in one of the individual classes alone, even although this breaks a basic axiom of probability theory. For example, they told people a story about a person Linda who had been quite radical in her views when at college. When asked to rank-order a set of statements in terms of their likelihood, people tended to rank "Linda is a feminist bank teller" as more probable than "Linda is a bank teller", even though there could be no situations in which the first was true but the second was false.

Tversky & Kahneman's account of their result was based on the notion of "representativeness". If the conjunctive concept appears to be a closer description of the individual than the single constituent concept, then people judge the individual more likely to belong in the conjunction. There is clearly a close parallel between overextension of conjunctions of semantic categories and this reasoning fallacy. Both the judgement of categorization (Hampton 1988b) and of probability (Tversky & Kahneman 1983) depend on an assessment of similarity of the instance to the representation of the conjunctive category, and a corresponding tendency to over-extend the boundaries of the conjunction, or over-estimate the probability that an individual belongs to it.

The model which Hampton (1987) developed to account for these results followed the same approach as the selective modification model

(Smith et al. 1988) in rejecting fuzzy logic formulations of conceptual combination in favour of representations involving intensional or attribute information (an approach advocated by Cohen & Murphy 1984). Unlike the selective modification model however, the composite prototype model (Hampton 1987) was intended to account for both typicality and membership in conjunctively defined categories. The model proposed that when forming a concept such as "pets that are also birds", people take their prototype representation of "pet" and "bird", and combine the prototypes into a composite to represent the conjunction. Membership and typicality in the conjunction are then determined by similarity to the composite prototype, with a criterion threshold being used to determine membership as in standard prototype theory. The way that this works can again best be represented using a frame representation with an attribute-value structure. Each attribute has certain values for one concept and certain values for the other. The composite prototype will then inherit its own attribute values from one or other constituent parent according to certain principles. To take an example, the [LOCATION] slot for "pet" has the value "in the home", while the same slot for "bird" has the value "in the wild". "Pet bird" inherits the value from "pet" rather than "bird" – pet birds live in the home and not in the wild. On another attribute, however, the composite would inherit the value from "bird" – for example for the slot [COVERING] the most common "pet" value would be "furry", but "pet bird" would take the value "feathered" which it inherits from "bird".

Having proposed that inheritance of slot values from the constituent concepts is not complete, but that conflicting values may compete to occupy the slot for the composite concept, it is then necessary to determine the principles by which the inherited value is chosen. To investigate this process, Hampton (1987) obtained attribute property listings from different groups of respondents for each constituent of a combination such as "birds which are pets" and for both ways of expressing the conjunction ("birds which are pets", and "pets which are birds"). The attributes listed were then all combined into a single list, which was given to further groups of subjects who made a judgement about how important each attribute was for categorizing an instance as a member either of a constituent class ("birds", or "pets") or of the conjunctive class ("pets which are birds", or vice versa). This procedure was followed for six different conjunctions. The importance ratings were then analyzed to see just how the process of attribute value inheritance works.

It appears that the choice of which value is inherited for any attribute is determined initially by the importance of the attribute for each constituent. Regression equations showed that a high proportion of variance in the importance of an attribute for the conjunction could be predicted from the importance for the respective constituents. (There was also a concept dominance effect which appeared to mirror closely the concept dominance effect found for typicality judgements by Hampton 1988b.) In addition to this overall effect, there was also an effect of the centrality or mutability of a property for the constituent concept. Where a property was considered a central "necessary" feature of a constituent (the top end of the "importance" scale), then it was also considered central for the conjunctive concept. Similarly where a property was considered "impossible" for a constituent (the bottom anchor point on the importance scale), it was also considered impossible for the conjunction.

In the final study, Hampton (1987) demonstrated that the degree to which an attribute value was inherited by the conjunction was also determined by the amount to which it conflicted with all the attributes of the opposing constituent. For example, one attribute of "birds" was "migrates". This was judged to be in conflict with many of the attributes of being a pet, and so was not judged to apply to the conjunction of "pets which are birds". Degree of conflict entered significantly into the regression equation, predicting additional variance after the two constituent importance ratings had been entered.

The result of the interaction of the two concepts in determining which attribute values are inherited is that the composite prototype representation of the conjunction will be a hybrid of the two constituents – bearing resemblance in some respects to one constituent and in other respects to the other. It is therefore easy to see how an instance class could be more similar to the composite prototype than to either of the constituent classes (the original problem identified by Osherson & Smith 1981). Furthermore if membership of the conjunctive class is determined by how similar an instance is to the composite prototype, then it is relatively straightforward to demonstrate that one would therefore expect a pattern of overextension and/or underextension, rather than the application of a "logical" intersection rule. (The relative proportion of each would depend on where the threshold criterion for similarity to the composite prototype is placed. Empirically it appears that people place the criterion quite low, so that the conjunctive class ends up with a greater number of instances than expected on the basis of constituent class membership.)

The study of attribute inheritance (Hampton 1987) also threw up an interesting number of attributes which were considered true of the conjunction but not true of either constituent. These were termed emergent properties and included the properties of "pet birds" that they live in cages and can talk – aspects not considered true of "pets" or "birds" alone. These properties are particularly interesting since they appear to break the basic compositionality of conceptual combination (see for example Murphy 1988, 1990). It appears that a major source of emergent properties is simply knowledge of the world – or "extensional feedback" as Hampton (1987) described it. We use the words "pet" and "bird" to identify the conjunctive class of pet birds, retrieve some familiar instances, and then proceed to describe them. We cannot expect any model of conceptual combination to account directly for such effects, as they clearly relate to information that is obtained from another source – namely familiarity with the class of objects in the world (Rips 1995, refers to this as breaking the "no peeking principle"). The exemplar approach (representing a combination through its exemplars) is the only account that will explain such emergent attributes. A study by Medin & Shoben (1988) highlights the importance of this level of exemplar knowledge. They showed that typicality of items in conjunctive categories could vary as a function of the kinds of exemplar found in those categories. For instance, for the combination "small spoon", metal spoons were judged to be more typical than wooden spoons, whereas for the combination "large spoon", the reverse relation was found. Without some experiential knowledge of actual spoons, their sizes and their materials, this kind of effect would be impossible to explain. In effect then, one cannot ask theories of conceptual combination to predict such effects, nor should one take failure to predict such effects as a criticism of any theory.

A second source of emergence, however, may be considered fair game for models of conceptual combination. These are emergent features that appear in novel or unfamiliar concept conjunctions. A well-known example of this notion is the concept of a "beach bicycle". Given the opportunity to reflect on this concept (expanding the modifier-head form into a more explicit conjunction such as "a bicycle which is used for riding on the beach"), people typically consider the problem of riding on a beach – that the wheels would sink in the sand – and so suppose that a beach bicycle would be equipped with particularly wide tyres. Since there is no information about wide tyres in either the bicycle or the beach concepts alone, and no knowledge of actual instances to retrieve (indeed many people may never have tried riding on a beach), then this emergent feature must have been the result of an appeal to background "theory", and in particular to naive understanding of the mechanics of bicycles and beaches. (There can be no exemplar-based account of this result if a person has never before encountered an exemplar of the concept.)

The best available source of evidence for theory-based emergent features currently lies in the domain of social stereotype categories. Kunda et al. (1990) investigated conjunctions such as "a Harvard-educated carpenter", and found (in a relatively informal way) that subjects created quite complex and detailed stories in order to explain how an individual might end up in such a conjunction (see also Hastie et al. 1990). Hampton (1997a) reviewed the frequency of emergent attributes across a series of studies, and confirmed that theory-based emergence is more easily found in social categories than in object or activity categories. Emergent attributes in novel or unfamiliar concept conjunctions are supportive evidence for Murphy & Medin's (1985) view that concepts are deeply embedded in theories of the world (see also Murphy 1993). People have to use more abstract theoretical understanding to resolve the conflicting attribute values in constructing the composite prototype. In another domain, Hampson (Casselden & Hampson 1990, Hampson 1990) investigated the combination of incongruent personality traits (following the pioneering work of Asch 1946). Although there were interactions among traits in the pattern of inheritance, there was in fact little or no evidence for emergent properties in her studies.

Evidence for the importance of background knowledge on social cognition came from another study (Hampton & Dillane 1993) in which conjunctions of social categories were judged from different points of view. Manipulation of point of view was originally introduced by Barsalou & Sewell (described in Barsalou 1987). They showed that typicality in a category varied systematically when people were asked to make the judgements from the point of view of others – be they stereotypical groups like housewives versus farmers, or familiar groups like faculty members versus students. In the study by Hampton & Dillane, people were asked to generate and rate attributes about two contrasting social categories – for example an Oxford graduate and a factory worker – and to take the point of view of either an Oxford graduate or a factory worker while completing the task. Other groups were asked to perform the same tasks for the conjunction "an Oxford graduate who is a factory worker", or its converse – again taking one or the other point of view. Manipulation of the point of view had a huge effect on the attributes that were considered true of the conjunction. The most common pattern to emerge was one of conflict. When adopting one point of view, people judged people in the conjunction to have the same (mostly unpleasant) properties as the other category. Thus from an Oxford graduate's point of view, the graduate factory worker was mostly like other factory workers, whereas from the factory worker's point of view he was most like other Oxford graduates (the scenarios were all about men in this study).

In a second unpublished experiment (Hampton & Oren), in addition to point of view, the sex of the person described was also manipulated.

Each pair of concepts contained one male and one female stereotype (for example "a fighter pilot who is also a child minder"). Half the respondents were asked to consider males while the other half considered females. Thus, for example, one set of groups judged females who were either fighter pilots or child minders or both, from the point of view of either a female fighter pilot or from the point of view of a female child minder. Other groups performed the same task taking a male's point of view about males. (The sex of the subject making the judgements was not manipulated but varied randomly across groups.) The results were particularly interesting. There was a considerable number of emergent attributes, as one would expect from the Kunda et al. (1990) study. What was especially striking was the difference between the male and female points of view. Consider for example the combination "a car mechanic who reads romantic fiction". When taking a female's point of view about a female, both points of view produced positive emergent attributes such as ambitious, broad-minded, clever, easygoing, charming and caring. When taking a male's point of view about a male, the emergent attributes were far more negative, such as dissatisfied, elusive, unreliable, lonely, and soppy. Overall the male stereotypes also generated far more patterns of conflict – whereby someone in the conjunction had none of the positive attributes of one's own group. The female stereotypes in contrast were more likely to show a pattern of complementarity. Even though the two stereotypes were strongly inconsistent, female points of view about females tended to consider someone in the conjunction as having the positive elements of both stereotypes. The implications of these results for social psychology have yet to be explored. It is clear that social categories provide a very rich source of materials for exploring the processes of conceptual combination. Almost any two social categories can in principle overlap – there are very few ontological constraints of the kind found in artefact and natural kind categories.

Hampton (1997a) also reported a study in which a technique was developed for forcing people to come up with emergent attributes for object categories. The technique was to take two noun classes that are quite disjoint and ask people to imagine an object that falls in both classes. Imagine for example a "fish that is also a vehicle". Some respondents failed to find a solution that truly matched the task requirements (drawing, for example, a car with a fish's head and tail modelled at either end), but many were able to find ingenious solutions to the problem. Successful solutions frequently involved stretching of concept categories (whales and dolphins were treated as fish – presumably because their greater intelligence could be used to good effect), and many emergent features were produced, only loosely based on existing vehicles (for example a control mechanism that involved electrodes implanted in the unfortunate animal's brain). Theory-based reasoning in conceptual combination can therefore be elicited within the domain of object categories, although many of the combinations caused considerable difficulty for the subjects in the study. (See Ward 1994, 1995, for examples of how even when urged to come up with novel solutions to problems such as designing a new creature, people will usually stay very close to existing familiar concepts.)

MODIFIER-HEAD COMBINATIONS

The study of "intersective" combinations has revealed a range of non-compositional effects, including over-extension of conjunctive categories and emergent properties that are true of a conjunction but not of either constituent. These effects are however relatively marginal, in the sense that people can still appreciate that intersective combinations approximate to the logical function of set intersection. When we turn to consider modifier-head constructions, then non-compositional effects come to the fore.

Murphy (1988) views conceptual combination as a highly creative process in which the end result of any combination may involve the introduction of deep theoretical knowledge and a wide range of facts about the world. Murphy's data depend largely on familiar modifier-head combinations. For example, Murphy (1988) showed how for a range of noun–noun combinations there are properties which emerge as being true of the combinations which are not true of either of the constituent parts. Casual things are not pulled over the head, and neither are shirts, but yet casual shirts are pulled over the head.

The number of examples of "emergent" properties of this kind is large, and demands an explanation in any theory of conceptual combination. The most direct explanation involves what was referred to above as "extensional feedback" (Hampton 1988b) or the "no peeking principle" (Rips 1995). Many of Murphy's emergent features could never be predicted or derived from the constituents, because they are contingent facts about the world. The term "casual shirt" identifies a known category of objects in the world, and it is through examination of this extensional set ("peeking" at the world outside) that the emergent properties are identified. Thus it is that we know that pet birds sometimes talk (Hampton 1987), that stop signs are hexagonal or that boiled eggs are hard whereas boiled potatoes are soft.

As Rips (1995) rightly argues, such examples do not rule out the possibility of a computational account of conceptual combination in the way Murphy seems to suggest. While it is clear that these examples implicate background knowledge in the understanding of phrases such as "boiled eggs", it can be argued that there is little conceptual work being done when understanding such phrases. In effect the concept of a "boiled egg" already exists as a subset of the concept "egg" (along with scrambled, poached and fried eggs), and we simply retrieve what we know about the complex concept from our memory.

In a second experiment, Murphy (1988) considered how the meaning of an adjective changes as a function of the noun with which it is combined in a range of adjective-noun combinations. For example, adjectives such as "long" or "new" or "open" can take a wide range of different meanings when modifying different nouns. Thus an "open year" was a flexible one, "open people" were revealing of their thoughts, an "open world" was one full of opportunity, while an "open hand" was a card hand dealt face up. This demonstration points to a second source of information that people use in interpreting conceptual combinations – the polysemy of many words (and particularly of high frequency adjectives). An adjective such as "open" has a highly extendable meaning, based on some very abstract schema of openness. In different domains the word's meaning has been taken and given meanings that are very specific to that domain. While this process can probably be used creatively, it is also likely that such specialized meanings are simply learnt as alternative meanings of the term by anyone learning the language. (In fact such extended uses cannot always be translated with the same adjective in another language.)

In order to assess the processes of conceptual combination "in the raw" it is necessary to consider novel combinations – combinations that are unfamiliar to the subject both as objects and as linguistic expressions. The influence of background knowledge and theories on the processes of conceptual combination can then be assessed. For noun–noun combinations this can be achieved by combining sets of nouns in novel ways and asking subjects for interpretations. Gagne & Shoben (1997) conducted a study of this kind. They took the corpus of naturally occurring compounds collected by Levi (1978) and selected a set of head and modifier nouns. All possible combinations were then considered and those that had a reasonably clear immediate interpretation were selected. Typically, novel noun–noun or adjective–noun combinations were interpreted using one of about 12 semantic relations, which they termed thematic relations. For example a "mountain magazine" was interpreted with the ABOUT relation as "a magazine about mountains". In a subsequent reaction time study, Gagne & Shoben carefully selected combinations in which the common interpretation involved a thematic relation which was either (a) high frequency for both head and modifier,

(b) high frequency for the head but not the modifier, or (c) high frequency for the modifier but not the head. Comprehension times for the combinations indicated that the critical variable for determining speed of comprehension was the frequency of the relation for the modifier. Provided the relation was that normally expected for the modifier, the phrase was understood equally fast, regardless of whether the head noun commonly appeared in that relation or not. On the other hand, where the relation was uncommon for the modifier, it was slower to comprehend – again regardless of the fact that it was a common relation for the head noun.

This result is consistent with the left to right ordering of modifier and head in English. Assuming that the modifier is read first, then its common thematic relation could be retrieved and applied to the head noun. Only in the case where the resulting combination fails to make sense would the common thematic relation for the head noun be retrieved as an alternative interpretation. The result is not however a comfortable one for Smith et al.'s (1988) selective modification model. Although that model makes no processing assumptions, it would seem to imply a computational process model in which the head noun frame is set up in working memory first, and the modifier is retrieved second. The model would therefore be more consistent with a stronger influence of the head noun relation frequency over the comprehension time than with the obtained result.

Gagne & Shoben (1997) examined the influence of "preferred" thematic relations on processing speeds. Wisniewski (1996), however, took a different approach to studying modifier-head combinations. He selected a set of nouns from different taxonomic categories, such as animals, artefacts and substances, and then combined them pair-wise into eight different kinds of combination (he omitted substance–substance pairs). Subjects in his experiment were asked to paraphrase the concept "combination", in order to explicate its meaning. The different paraphrases were then examined to see what kinds of relation were generated, as a function of the taxonomic categories of the head and modifier nouns. Wisniewski found that contrary to previous assumptions (Levi 1978, Gagne & Shoben 1997), modifier-head constructions are not always interpreted through the generation of a thematic relation whereby the modifier modifies a slot of the head noun (as in the "mountain magazine" example). In a high proportion of cases – and particularly in the animal–animal case – the interpretation offered for the combination involved what Wisniewski termed "property mapping". In property mapping a highly salient property of the modifier was taken and mapped directly onto the head noun. To understand the difference between "slot filling" (as he termed the use of a thematic relation) and property mapping, consider a concept combination such as "tiger hound". By generating a likely thematic relation, one might paraphrase this as "hound used to hunt tigers". In Wisniewski's terms, the representation of "hound" has a slot [USE FOR HUNTING] which could be filled with values such as "foxes", "deer", "boar" and so forth. Because "tiger" can plausibly fill this slot, the interpretation is seen as plausible. The alternative, property mapping, strategy is to take a salient property of tigers – for example their stripes – and apply this to overwrite the corresponding property of hounds in order to come up with the paraphrase "hound with stripes".

Property mapping requires both that the modifier noun has a highly distinctive property, and that the alignment of the two concepts is sufficiently close that the property can easily be mapped across. This would predict that the more similar two nouns are (within the same ontological category), then the more likely it is that property mapping will occur, and Wisniewski (1996) was able to confirm this prediction. In a further study by Davidson & Stevenson (1995), it was reported that combinations composed of two natural kinds were more likely to produce property mapping than those composed of two artefacts or a mix of an artefact and a natural kind. Similarity however did not have a major effect in this experiment, in that pairs of natural kinds and pairs of artefacts were judged equally similar. It may therefore be the case that there is an additional constraint when property mapping can occur. When two artefact terms are combined, it could be that direct property mapping is prevented by the fact that the head noun property which is to be replaced is also very central to the meaning of the head noun. For most pairs of natural kinds this constraint may be absent.

Wisniewski (1996) also noted two further strategies for interpretation of novel combinations which occurred in his data. First, when two objects were highly similar, people could form a hybrid of the two. Thus a "horse cow" could be some hybrid creature that was half horse and half cow. This strategy could be seen as an extension of property mapping, although it also implies a more symmetrical relation between the two concepts than is found in straight property mapping (where the combination is still considered to be in the head noun concept class). The second strategy was the construal of one or other of the two nouns to refer metonymically to a part or other related aspect of the concept itself (Nunberg 1979). For example a "tiger chair" was interpreted as a chair covered with tiger skin (use of the noun to refer to a part), and an "artist collector" was interpreted as someone who collects the works of artists. This interpretation strategy uses a more general linguistic strategy by which complex referential phrases can be shortened. So we can speak of "a Monet" and refer not to a member of Claude Monet's family, but to one of his paintings. Subjects using the construal strategy were looking for plausible, complex phrases that could have been shortened in a similar way.

A final plausible strategy for interpreting novel combinations is through analogy with already familiar combinations. Recognizing a good analogy commonly requires property mapping and alignment of features. In this case however, if the novel combination reminds us of a familiar combination with the same head or modifier noun, then we might adopt the same thematic relation to provide an interpretation. For example we could interpret "tiger hound" by analogy with "fox hounds", or alternatively by analogy with "tiger shark" depending on the availability of such more familiar combinations. Existing familiar combinations would then be recruited to aid in the search for an interpretation. Although linguistic intuition suggests that established combinations can be extended to novel ones in just this way, there has as yet been no direct experimental test of this notion.

CONCLUSIONS

We have seen that conceptual combination covers two rather distinct sorts of psychological process. The first involves the way in which conjunctions of prototype concepts are formed. The conceptual combination in this instance remains approximately intersective, although there appear to be systematic non-intersective effects, particularly when social stereotype categories are involved. Emergent attributes can be found arising from knowledge of the instances in the conjunctive category, and more rarely arising from the theory of the domain in which the concepts are embedded.

The second form of conceptual combination is perhaps specific to particular languages, and involves the interpretation of novel noun–noun modifier head constructions. (Dutch and German also allow noun–noun constructions to be generated in a free way, whereas French requires semantic marking of the thematic relation with a preposition such as *à, de* or *en*.) It involves a search for an interpretation which can be likened to a problem solving or constraint satisfaction process. Two different strategies for interpretation have been identified by Wisniewski as slot filling and property mapping, and according to Gagne & Shoben, the speed of comprehension in slot filling depends to a large extent on how commonly the modifier enters into the thematic relation by which it is modifying the head noun.

Research on conceptual combination is still at a relatively early stage of development. However, considerable progress has been made in the last 15 years towards understanding how concepts as expressed through word meanings interact when placed together in phrases. It is clear that no simple set of compositional rules will be adequate to the task of a full description of the meaning of a complex concept. However, by separating out the effects of familiarity, and by explicating the strategies that can be employed in combining concepts, we are now closer to the goal of explaining how the meaning of phrases relates to that of their constituent parts. It has become clear that the process of achieving this goal must depend heavily on an understanding of knowledge representation, and of knowledge revision. The strong conclusion that can be draw from the work of Medin, Murphy and others is the degree to which many of the phenomena of conceptual combination can only be properly understood in the context of a fuller theory of the knowledge and naïve theories of the world in which concepts are embedded.

REFERENCES

Asch, S. E. 1946. Forming impressions of personality. *Journal of Abnormal and Social Psychology* **41**, 258–90.

Barsalou, L. W. 1987. The instability of graded structure: implications for the nature of concepts. In *Concepts and conceptual development: Ecological and intellectual factors in categorization*, U. Neisser (ed.), 101–140. Cambridge: Cambridge University Press.

Barsalou, L. W. 1993. Structure, flexibility, and linguistic vagary in concepts: manifestations of a compositional system of perceptual symbols. In *Theories of memory*, A. C. Collins, S. E. Gathercole, & M. A. Conway (eds), 29–102. Hillsdale, New Jersey: Erlbaum.

Brooks, L. R. 1987. Nonanalytic cognition. In *Concepts and conceptual development: Ecological and intellectual factors in categorization*, U. Neisser (ed.), 141–74. Cambridge: Cambridge University Press.

Casselden, P. A. & S. E. Hampson 1990. Forming impressions from incongruent traits. *Journal of Personality and Social Psychology* **59**, 353–362.

Cohen, B. & G. L. Murphy 1984. Models of concepts. *Cognitive Science* **8**, 27–58.

Davidson, O. & R. Stevenson 1995. Interpretation of noun-noun compounds. Paper presented to Conference of the British Psychological Society, Cognitive Section, Bristol.

Donnellan, K. 1966. Reference and definite description. *Philosophical Review* **75**, 281–304.

Downing, P. 1977. On the creation and use of English compound nouns. *Language* **53**, 810–842.

Fodor, J. A. 1983. *The modularity of mind*. Cambridge, Mass.: MIT Press.

Fodor, J. A. 1994. Concepts – a pot-boiler. *Cognition* **50**, 95–113.

Franks, B. 1989. Concept combination: towards an account of privatives. In *Papers from the 1989 Edinburgh Round Table on the Mental Lexicon*, G. Dunbar, B. Franks, T. Myers (eds), 85–109. Centre for Cognitive Science, University of Edinburgh.

Gagne, C. & E. J. Shoben 1997. Influence of thematic relations on the comprehension of modifier–noun combinations. *Journal of Experimental Psychology: Learning, Memory and Cognition* **23**, 71–87.

Gerrig, R. J. & G. L. Murphy 1992. Contextual influences on the comprehension of complex concepts. *Language and Cognitive Processes* **7**, 205–230.

Hampson, S. E. 1990. Reconciling inconsistent information: impressions of personality from combinations of traits. *European Journal of Personality* **4**, 157–72.

Hampton, J. A. 1982. A demonstration of intransitivity in natural categories. *Cognition* **12**, 151–64.

Hampton, J. A. 1987. Inheritance of attributes in natural concept conjunctions. *Memory and Cognition* **15**, 55–71.

Hampton, J. A. 1988a. Disjunction of natural concepts. *Memory and Cognition* **16**, 579–91.

Hampton, J. A. 1988b. Overextension of conjunctive concepts: evidence for a unitary model of concept typicality and class inclusion. *Journal of Experimental Psychology: Learning, Memory, and Cognition* **14**, 12–32.

Hampton, J. A. 1993. Prototype models of concept representation. In *Categories and concepts: theoretical views and inductive data analysis*, I. Van Mechelen, J. A. Hampton, R. S. Michalski, P. Theuns (eds), 67–95. London: Academic Press.

Hampton, J. A. 1995. Testing the prototype theory of concepts. *Journal of Memory and Language* **34**, 686–708.

Hampton, J. A. 1996. Conjunctions of visually based categories: overextension and compensation. *Journal of Experimental Psychology: Learning, Memory, and Cognition* **22**, 378–96.

Hampton, J. A. 1997a. Emergent attributes in conceptual combinations. In *Conceptual structures and processes: emergence, discovery and change*, T. B. Ward, S. M. Smith, & J. Viad (eds), 83–110. Washington DC: American Psychology Association.

Hampton, J. A. 1997b. Psychological representation of concepts. In *Cognitive models of memory*, M. A. Conway & S. E. Gathercole (eds). Hove, UK: Psychology Press.

Hampton, J. A. & M. Dillane 1993. Taking a point of view on attributes inheritance. Paper presented to the 34th Annual Convention of the Psychonomic Society, Washington DC.

Hampton, J. A. & M. M. Gardiner 1983. Measures of internal category structure: a correlational analysis of normative data. *British Journal of Psychology* **74**, 491–516.

Hastie, R., C. Schroeder, R. Weber 1990. Creating complex social conjunction categories from simple categories. *Bulletin of the Psychonomic Society* **28**, 242–7.

Huttenlocher, J. & L. V. Hedges 1994. Combining graded categories: membership and typicality. *Psychological Review* **101**, 157–65.

Kamp, H. & B. Partee 1989. *Prototype theory and compositionality*. Unpublished manuscript.

Katz, J. J. & J. A. Fodor 1963. The structure of a semantic theory. *Language* **39**, 170–210.

Kempton, W. 1978. Category grading and taxonomic relations: a mug is a sort of cup. *American Ethnologist* **5**, 44–65.

Kunda, Z., D. T. Miller, T. Clare 1990. Combining social concepts: the role of causal reasoning. *Cognitive Science* **14**, 551–78.

Levi, J. 1978. *The syntax and semantics of complex nominals*. New York: Academic Press.

McCloskey, M. & S. Glucksberg 1978. Natural categories: well-defined or fuzzy sets? *Memory and Cognition* **6**, 462–72.

Medin, D. L. & M. M. Schaffer 1978. Context theory of classification learning. *Psychological Review* **85**, 207–238.

Medin, D. L. & E. J. Shoben 1988. Context and structure in conceptual combination. *Cognitive Psychology* **20**, 158–90.

Minsky, M. 1975. A framework for representing knowledge. In *The psychology of computer vision*, P. H. Winston (ed.), 211–277. New York: McGraw-Hill.

Murphy, G. L. 1988 Comprehending complex concepts. *Cognitive Science* **12**, 529–62.

Murphy, G. L. 1990. Noun phrase interpretation and conceptual combination. *Journal of Memory and Language* **29**, 259–88.

Murphy, G. L. 1993. Theories and concept formation. In *Categories and concepts: theoretical views and inductive data analysis*, I. Van Mechelen, J. A. Hampton, R. S. Michalski, & P. Theuns (eds), 173–200. London: Academic Press.

Murphy, G. L. & D. L. Medin 1985. The role of theories in conceptual coherence. *Psychological Review* **92**, 289–316.

Nunberg, G. 1979. The non-uniqueness of semantic solutions: Polysemy. *Linguistic and Philosophy* **3**, 143–84.

Oden, G. C. 1977. Integration of fuzzy logical information. *Journal of Experimental Psychology: Human Perception and Performance* **3**, 565–75.

Osherson, D. N. & E. E. Smith 1981. On the adequacy of prototype theory as a theory of concepts. *Cognition* **11**, 35–58.

Osherson, D. N. & E. E. Smith 1982. Gradedness and conceptual conjunction. *Cognition* **12**, 299–318.

Randall, R. A. 1976. How tall is a taxonomic tree? Some evidence for dwarfism. *American Ethnologist* **3**, 543–53.

Rips, L. J. 1995. The current status of research on concept combination. *Mind and Language* **10**, 72–104.

Rosch, E. 1975. Cognitive representations of semantic categories. *Journal of Experimental Psychology: General* **104**, 192–232.

Rosch, E. 1978. Principles of categorization. In *Cognition and categorization*, E. Rosch & B. Lloyd (eds), 27–48. Hillsdale, New Jersey: Erlbaum.

Rosch, E. & C. B. Mervis 1975. Family resemblances: studies in the internal structure of categories. *Cognitive Psychology* **7**, 573–605.

Smith, E. E., D. N. Osherson, L. J. Rips, M. Keane 1988. Combining prototypes: a selective modification model. *Cognitive Science* **12**, 485–527.

Smith, E. E., E. J. Shoben & L. J. Rips 1974. Structure and process in semantic memory: a featural model for semantic decisions. *Psychological Review* **81**, 214–241.

Storms, G., P. De Boeck, I. Van Mechelen, D. Geeraerts 1993. Dominance and non-communativity effects on concept conjunctions: extensional or intensional basis? *Memory and Cognition* **21**, 752–62.

Tversky, A. 1977. Features of similarity. *Psychological Review* **84**, 327–52.

Tversky, A. & D. Kahneman 1983. Extensional versus intuitive reasoning:the conjunction fallacy in probability judgement. *Psychological Review* **90**, 293–315.

Ward, T. B. 1994. Structured imagination: the role of category structure in exemplar generation. *Cognitive Psychology* **27**, 1–40.

Ward, T. B. 1995. What's old about new ideas? In *The creative cognition approach*, S. M. Smith, T. B. Ward, R. A. Finke (eds), 157–78. Cambridge, Mass.: MIT Press.

Wisniewski, E. J. 1996. Construal and similarity in conceptual combination. *Journal of Memory and Language* **35**, 434–453.

Zadeh, L. 1965. Fuzzy sets. *Information and Control* **8**, 338–53.

NOTES

1. I would like to acknowledge the help of a number of colleagues who contributed in various ways to the development of the ideas and research described in this chapter. In particular I should like to thank Lawrence Barsalou, Nick Braisby, Herbert Clark, Margaret Dillane, Danièle Dubois, Bradley Franks, Janellen Huttenlocher, Frank Keil, Iven van Mechelen, Douglas Medin, Helen Moss, Gregory Murphy, Laura Oren, Lance Rips, Edward Shoben, Gert Storms, Jean-Pierre Thibaut, Thomas Ward and Edward Wisniewski.

2. There will of course be kinds of knowledge which do not involve language-like symbolic representations such as motor skills used in a tennis serve or golf swing, the ability to recognize faces or musical themes, and episodic memory for particular events. The representation of knowledge through concepts based in language is just one form of knowledge representation, and one whose interface with other forms of memory representation is far from understood (Barsalou 1993).

3. The notion of truth here is one of psychological acceptability – how willing are people to accept the statement as true. This notion should not be confused with a metaphysical or ontological notion of truth – of what is actually the case in the world.

4. Space does not permit a full description of different theories of concepts here. For a fuller treatment see Hampton (1997b).

5. It is also quite likely that similarity itself may be computed using different weights for the different dimensions in the case where typicality is being judged as opposed to the case where category membership is being decided. In the latter case more weight may be accorded to dimensions that are most diagnostic of category membership, whereas in the former, weight may be also given to dimensions that are representative of the most central examples. Allowing weights to change between tasks in an unconstrained manner however does introduce a large number of free parameters to the prototype model which could seriously undermine its predictive value as a model.

6. The results were actually more complex. While typicality as an adult or a child influenced categorization in the conjunction for stimuli with borderline emotional expressions, the reverse pattern was not found. Typicality as a happy or sad face did not compensate for borderline values of the adult/child dimension. See Hampton (1996) for details and further discussion of this result.

CHAPTER FIVE

Perceiving and Remembering: Category Stability, Variability and Development

Linda B. Smith and Larissa K. Samuelson

> . . . no two ideas are ever exactly the same, which is the proposition
> we started to prove. The proposition is more important theoretically
> than it at first sight appears (William James 1890:235).

Traditional theories of categorization concentrate on the stability of cognition, how it is that people perform the same cognitive act over and over despite varying local circumstances. For example, each time a person encounters a frog, whether in a pond or in a comic strip, the encountered object is understood to be the same kind of thing – a frog. Traditional theory explains this stability by positing stable mental representations. According to this view, the reason that people understand the frog in the pond and the frog in the comic strip to be the same sort of thing is that in both cases they access the same representation, the same concept of frog.

Figure 5.1 portrays an act of knowing in this view: a sensory event makes contact with the concept of frog and it is at the instant of contact – when perceiving activates permanent knowledge stores – that the individual may be said to "know" that it has seen a frog. Thus knowledge, in the form of relatively permanent representations, is distinct from knowing which consists of momentarily activated representations. Most research on categories has been concerned with the structures of these stable representations presumed to underlie moments of knowing.

The problem, of course, is that as empirical scientists we have only individual moments of knowing as our window onto knowledge. And

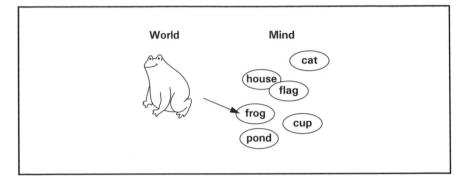

FIG. 5.1.   The traditional view of a moment of knowing: an object makes contact with a represented concept.

these, unlike the presumed constant concepts that underlie them, are highly variable. For example, when we encounter two frogs on two different occasions, we do not think exactly the same thing. Barsalou (1987) demonstrated this empirically; he found that when people read the word *frog* in isolation, they do not think "eaten by humans". But when *frog* is read in the context of "French restaurant", "eaten by humans" does come to mind. What is "known" in a real moment of knowing depends on the context. As William James noted in the opening quote, this fact has profound theoretical consequences. We pursue these consequences in the following three parts of this chapter.

Part 1 briefly reviews the traditional search for constant concepts in the face of variable moments of knowing. It is not a history of success (see Barsalou 1989, 1987, Komatsu 1992, Goldstone et al. in press; and Jones & Smith 1993).

Part 2 explores how the processes, perceiving and remembering, that make individual acts of knowing also make categories. These results suggest a unified account of category stability and variability that does not make use of the idea of a represented concept.

Part 3 applies these ideas to category development and demonstrates the potential value of James' insight that "no two ideas are ever the same", for explaining developmental change.

PART 1: THEORIES ABOUT CONCEPTS

What makes it convenient to use the mythological formulas is the whole organization of speech, which, as was remarked a while ago, was not made by psychologists, but by men who were as a rule only interested in the facts their mental states revealed. They spoke of their states as *ideas of this or of that thing*. What wonder, then, that the thought is most easily conceived under the law of the thing whose name it bears! (William James, 1890:236).

The traditional framework depicted in Figure 5.1 makes sense when one thinks about the stability of human categories in the face of a highly variable world. We regularly recognize quite diverse things as instances of the same kind: we know pond frogs and restaurant frogs and poison-dart frogs to all be frogs. A permanently represented concept has been seen by many to be necessary to explain this stability. For example, Keil (1994) wrote

> Shared mental structures are assumed to be constant across repeated categorizations of the same set of instances and different from other categorizations. When I think about the category of dogs, a specific mental representation is assumed to be responsible for that category and roughly the same representation for a later categorization of dogs by myself or by another (1994:169).

Thus, "repeated categorizations based on the same mental representation [are] the launching point for most psychological investigations of what concepts are".

The traditional framework depicted in Figure 5.1 also fits the understanding of categories found in logic. This conceptualization, the logic of classes, distinguishes between the *extension* of a class and the *intension* of a class. The extension is all the possible members of a class. Thus the extension of the class "triangle" is all possible triangles. The intension is the rule that picks out all and only members of the class, for example, the intensional definition of a triangle might be "a closed figure having three sides". Psychological theories of categories reflect these ideas of fixed extensions and intensions. In psychology, the extension is the "repeated categorizations" that people make, i.e. the data to be explained. The intension is the hypothesized concept that determines the extension, the mental structure that causes people to categorize objects the way that they do.

These foundational ideas of stable categories and stable concepts, however, have led to little progress. Instead a steady succession of theories of concepts have been offered, rejected, resurrected, and rejected again.

From criterial properties to essences
In the 1960s, research on concepts concentrated on psychological intensive definitions that were lists of necessary and sufficient features.

This approach came to be rejected on both theoretical and empirical grounds. First, there was no psychological basis for determining the features that form the primitives of such concepts (Murphy & Medin 1985, Fodor 1977). Secondly, no successful version of the theory was ever formulated – no one could find the defining properties of such everyday categories as dog or cow or game (see Smith & Medin 1981, Wittgenstein 1953, Katz 1972, Rosch & Mervis 1975). Thirdly, there were data that directly contradicted the idea of necessary and sufficient features. Specifically, if category membership is determined by necessary and sufficient properties then all members of the category are equally good. People, however, consistently and systematically judge some instances of a category to be better than others (Rosch 1973). A robin, for example, is a better bird than a blue jay.

Thus, in the 1970s, the field turned to probabilistic theories of concepts (Smith & Medin 1981). Concepts became lists of characteristic rather than defining features (or in exemplar models, lists of the features of each experienced instance). These probabilistic theories derived from and readily explained graded category judgements. However, probabilistic theories came to be rejected for the same reasons that the defining-feature theories were rejected. First, there is no principled basis for determining the features that comprise representations (see Murphy & Medin 1985). Secondly, no one has yet offered a successful accounting of any natural category. And, thirdly, people make category judgements that are not in accord with probabilistic feature representations. Specifically, people *believe* that categories are organized by defining features that are necessary and sufficient. For example, along with judging robins to be better birds than blue jays, people also believe that all birds possess some property possessed by all and only birds (Rips 1989, Keil 1994). Moreover, people will maintain that an object that does not look or act at all like a bird, but instead looks and acts like an insect with elongated, transparent wings and antennae, nonetheless "really is a bird". They do so if they are also told that this insect-like organism has birds for parents and has bird DNA (e.g. Rips 1989). In such judgements, being a bird seems to depend criterially on special properties that are causally related to the origins of the entity.

In light of these data, theories of concepts in the 1980s turned from feature-based (or similarity-based) representations to theory-like (or explanation-based) representations (Murphy & Medin 1985). Many researchers studying people's beliefs about what "really makes something what it is" proposed that relevant representations are more like naïve theories than lists of criterial or probabilistic features (Keil 1989). In this view, concepts are domain-specific belief systems about the causal relations among properties and among concepts. Thus, the reason that an organism that looks and acts nothing like a bird might still "really be a bird" is because the organism possesses the essential property, the biological structure, that *causes* the outward manifestations characteristic of birds. These ideas resurrect the criterial-property concepts of the 1960s. However, by the more contemporary view, it is not that all instances of a category share an "essence" but that people believe that they do and use that belief when they decide whether something is or is not a member of a category.

Unfortunately, concepts as naïve theories have the same problems as previous theories about concepts. First, there is no consensus as to what naive theories are, how they are mentally represented, or what kinds of knowledge are included. There is no principled or psychological basis for deciding what counts as a "theory" and what does not (see Keil 1994). Secondly, there is no well-formulated account of any natural category within this framework. Thus, once again, there is no demonstration that this kind of theory can actually do the job of explaining human category judgements. Thirdly, and even amidst the vagueness of these accounts, naïve theories clearly do not explain all the data. For example, they offer no account of why robins are psychologically better birds than blue jays.

One contemporary response to this state of affairs is to propose that concepts are composed of multiple parts, with some parts organizing categorization in some tasks and other parts organizing category judgements in other tasks (see Keil 1994). Specifically, probabilistic feature associations have been proposed to be involved in the identification of instances as members of a category and theory-like knowledge has been proposed to underlie people's reasoning about categories. Figure 5.1 thus becomes Figure 5.2. However, recent evidence suggests that explaining human categorization may require a more radical departure from old ideas about concepts, certainly more radical than piecing together old theories into a "two-part" hybrid.

Variable categories

Malt (1994) contrasted the liquids people label *water*, how much of the psychologically essential property (H_2O) these potential instances of "water" had, and the typicality of each as an instance of the category "water". The principal result is that none of these category judgements aligned (see also Rips 1989, Rips & Collins 1993). Tea, for example, which is not called water at all, is judged to have a higher percentage of the essential property (H_2O) than ocean water which is uniformly called water and is judged to be highly typical of the category "water". Mineral water, in contrast, is called water, is judged to have a high percentage of H_2O, but is also judged to be an atypical instance of the

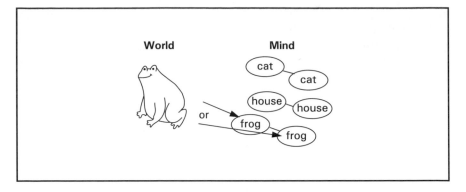

FIG. 5.2.   Hybrid concepts: one part is about causes and essences and is accessed in some tasks and the other part is probabilistic feature lists (of experienced exemplars) and accessed in other tasks.

category "water". In brief, Malt's evidence suggests three distinct patterns of category judgements over the same domain of instances – one in naming tasks, one in judging the percentage of "pure water", and one in judging category typicality. Is it sensible to suppose that there are parts of a single concept devoted to each of these tasks?

Lakoff's (1987) analysis of the word "mother" poses the same problem for the idea of a single cohesive and coherent concept. By Lakoff's analysis, people sometimes use the word "mother" to refer to the person who gave birth; other times to the nurturing female adult; other times to the wife of the father. These various meanings are mutually contradictory as seen in such statements as, "She's not my real mother, all she did was give birth to me", and "I searched for my real mother because I wanted to know my genetic origins". Similar to Malt's findings about water, Lakoff's analysis of "mother" suggests contradiction, context-dependency, and multiplicity in the place of coherence, stability, and singularity.

Other evidence suggests shifts in category membership occur with quite small and seemingly non-meaningful shifts in contexts. For example, Rips (1989) found that people judged a three-inch diameter object to be a more likely member of the category "pizza" than the category "quarter" – a judgement that seems to contradict the greater intuition that three-inch objects are more similar to quarters than to typical pizzas. Rips justified subjects' judgements by pointing to the fixed size of quarters determined by the process of minting them. He posited that subjects' concepts were theory-like accounts of the origins of things. Recently, however, E. Smith and Sloman (1994) replicated Rips' study with one small change. Rips had told subjects about only one property of the to-be-classified item, that it was three-inches in diameter. Smith & Sloman, in contrast, told subjects about two properties, that the to-be-classified object was three inches in size and silver-coloured. Everything else about the two studies was the same; but the results were just the opposite. In the Smith & Sloman study, people did not make use of their knowledge about the set sizes of quarters but instead judged category membership by overall similarity (that is, a three-inch silver object is judged to be a quarter and not a pizza).

Altogether Malt's, Lakoff's, and Smith & Sloman's results suggest that the fundamental assumption made by theories of concepts, what Keil called "shared representations" that make "repeated categorizations", is not quite right. Acts of categorization are not simply repeated; they vary. Different tasks and contexts seem to create different categories.

The plausibility of this last idea is demonstrated in Barsalou's (1983) elegant studies of *ad hoc* categories, Barsalou asked adults to determine "all the things on a desk that could be used to pound in a nail". Subjects readily formed novel and contextually-coherent categories. These *ad hoc* categories were not based on a previously represented concept; nonetheless, they show the same performance characteristics as more ordinary categories, that is, well-organized typicality judgements, graded category membership, and characteristic features. These findings present a strong challenge to the traditional view of knowing shown in Figure 5.1; they suggest that individual acts of categorization do not require an already represented concept.

Can a theory of concepts be saved?

Together these data revive James' earlier criticism of concepts as potentially "mythological entities". Two responses to the growing concern about the very idea of a concept argue that the notion of concept should be retained. One response asserts that categories, the data notwithstanding, are not variable. In this view, the existence of fixed taxonomies through which people understand their world is a self-evident truth; that psychologically, individual entities either are or are not water, either are or are not mothers. This position can be held if one assumes that some of the tasks that psychologists have considered to be category-judgement tasks are not really category-judgement tasks at all. Armstrong et al. (1983), Gelman & Coley (1991), Soja et al. (1991), and Rips (1989) have all argued that careful introspections by subjects about category membership reveal the fixed taxonomy through which people represent the world. Other judgements such as object recognition, typicality judgements, naming, and similarity judgements, in contrast, are not really category judgements in that they do not rely on the represented taxonomy. The problem with this argument is that it dismisses as irrelevant rather than explains the findings of category variability.

A second response arguing for the idea of a concept has been offered by Medin & Ortony (1989). They argue that stable concepts might be inputs to the processes that create variable categories. Medin & Ortony wrote

> we think care has to be taken not to equate instability in outputs or behaviours with underlying or internal instability. Might it be that underlying concepts are in fact stable (whatever that might mean) and that the apparent instability is an artifact of the processes that operate on these stable representations? (1989:191).

This view is pictured in Figure 5.3. We have a single coherent concept of, for example, frog that we access whenever we encounter or think about frog – when we recognize a frog, when we introspect about the essential properties of frogs, when we make typicality judgements, and when we reason about frogs in ponds versus frogs in restaurants. In this view, real-time processes of perceiving, remembering and responding to specific task demands make individual acts of categorization different. But underneath all the variability of individual acts is the very same concept.

This proposal explicitly recognizes two main facts about human categorization that need to be explained: the stability across individual acts of categorization and the uniqueness of individual acts. Before we consider further the viability of this idea, there is a third fact about human categories that needs to be explained.

Category development
Acts of categorization do not just vary from task to task, they also vary over developmental time. Eighteen-month-old children, but not adults,

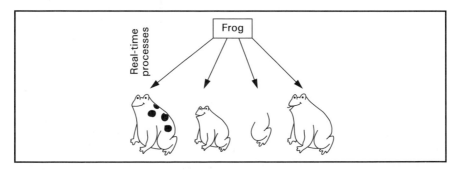

FIG. 5.3.   Medin & Ortony's idea of a constant concept that gives rise to variable performance.

sometimes classify goats with dogs by calling a goat "doggie" (Mervis 1987). Pre-school children, but not older children and adults, maintain that the category "island" includes landmasses with beaches and palm trees that are not surrounded by water (Keil 1989). Three-year-olds, but not adults, call objects "comb" that look like combs even if they are made from materials that cannot possibly untangle hair (Landau et al. submitted).

Given the theoretical framework of concepts, the principal question developmentalists have asked about these kinds of results is whether immature intensive definitions are fundamentally different from more mature ones. In the 1960s, research focused specifically on whether pre-school children's categories were based on illogical complexive definitions in contrast to the presumed criterial property structure of mature concepts (Inhelder & Piaget 1964). In the 1980s and 1990s, the question shifted to whether young children's concepts are organized by probabilistic clusters of perceptual properties in contrast to the presumed theory-based concepts of adults (Keil 1989).

Just as there is no strong evidence for any single kind of concept in the adult literature, there is no strong evidence for a developmental shift from one particular kind of concept to another. Indeed, although children's category judgements are different from adults, they appear to be like adults' category judgements in being contextually and task determined. One compelling set of findings on the contextual nature of young children's categories are those of Imai et al. (1994). In one task, they presented three-year-old children with an exemplar object, for example, a picture of a birthday cake and then asked the children which of three test objects "go with" the exemplar: (a) a same shaped object (a wide-brimmed hat); (b) a taxonomically-related object (a pie); or (c) a thematically-related object (a birthday gift). Children predominantly chose the thematically related object. In a second task, children were asked to generalize a novel "dinosaur talk" name. For example, they were told that in dinosaur talk, the birthday cake was called "dax". The children were then asked which of the three test objects was also called "dax". The children primarily chose the same shaped object, the hat. In this same task, older children and adults extended the novel name to the taxonomically related object. Although Imai et al. did not elicit taxonomic-category judgements from these children, evidence from other researchers strongly suggests that if the children had been asked to feed the dinosaur, they would have chosen the cake and the pie (Bauer & Fivush 1992). Altogether, this evidence suggests that children categorize objects differently when making "goes with" judgements, when naming, and when making functional judgements (see also, Landau et al., submitted; Smith et al., 1996). In brief, children's categories, like those of adults, are contextually variable. But critically, they are also contextually variable in different ways than those of adults.

In light of this evidence, reconsider Medin & Ortony's suggestion, illustrated in Figure 5.3, that stable concepts serve as input to variable processes. How would such a model explain concept variability both across tasks and across development? The theoretical problem is illustrated in Figure 5.4. The figure depicts a represented concept at two points in development and the variable performances that emerge from these two representations. In this picture, two distinct kinds of variability need to be explained – change in concepts with development and changes in individual acts of categorization across contexts and tasks. In Part 2, we lay the groundwork for an alternate solution, one in which the very same processes that make variability across individual acts of categorization make variability across developmental time.

Summary
Theories of concepts have concentrated on the stability of categories – on the fact that people treat quite diverse entities as equivalent and that they do so in globally similar ways across contexts and tasks. However, the evidence suggests that on closer inspection categories are variable as well as stable. Further, people appear able to create categories on the spot. Category variability and in task category creation are facts not well explained by the idea of a concept. In the next section, we seek insights into these phenomena from what is known about processes of perceiving and remembering.

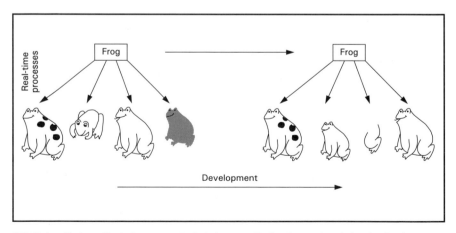

FIG. 5.4.   Cartoon illustrating concepts that change with development and also that lead to con-textually-variable performances.

PART 2: PERCEIVING AND REMEMBERING

For an identical sensation to recur it would have to occur the second time in an *unmodified brain*. But as this, strictly speaking, is a physiological impossibility, so is an unmodified feeling an impossibility (William James 1890:232–3).

. . . brains use *processes that change themselves* – and this means we cannot separate such processes from the products they produce. In particular, brains make memories, which change the ways we'll subsequently think. *The principal activities of brains are making changes in themselves.* (Minsky 1986:288).

Figure 5.1 with which we began this chapter presents one picture of knowing: seeing a frog activates a stored knowledge representation that provides the meaning of the sensory event. This picture foregrounds the role of stored knowledge in knowing. Backgrounded are the processes – perceiving and remembering – that realize that knowledge in a particular moment of knowing. In this part, we turn to the considerable evidence on processes of perceiving and remembering for insights into the stability and variability of categories. This extensive literature points to three fundamental truths about cognitive processes:

(1) they depend broadly on the immediate input and its larger context;

(2) they are temporally extended with real rise times and decay times such that activity at any moment depends on and emerges out of preceding activity;

(3) they change as a direct consequence of their own activity.

In this section we review the evidence. We then show how the stability and variability of human categories arise naturally from these facts.

The immediate context

The first fact about perceiving and remembering is contextual dependency. This context dependency is at direct odds with classic psychophysical approaches to perception (see Marks 1993, Schyns & Rodet, in press). The classic work sought to map invariant components of the physical world that gave rise to invariant percepts – the wavelength that specified a colour, the voice onset times that specified a phoneme, the features that specified a letter. We now know that perception is much messier than this; there may be no finite set of primitives out of which perceptions are built, no 1:1 map from specific inputs to specific percepts. Instead, perception is relative, and contextually determined: the reflected wavelengths seen as red when they emanate from firetrucks are the not the same as the ones seen as red when they emanate from hair (Halff et al. 1976); the voice onset times that signal a certain consonant are not fixed but depend on other aspects of the stimulus including the rate of talking (Kelly & Martin 1994); the relevant features for letter perception shift radically with the font (Sanocki 1991).

Figure 5.5 illustrates several more classic examples of the role of context in perception. Panel a shows how the perceived size of an object depends on surrounding objects: an object looks smaller than it really is when surrounded by objects that are much larger yet looks larger than it really is when surrounded by objects just slightly larger than itself. Panels b and c show how the perceived similarity of two objects depends on other perceptually present objects. In Panel b, the perceived similarity of objects 1 and 2 is low but the perceived similarity of these same two objects in Panel c is high (for more relevant data on the context-dependency of perceived similarity see Goldstone et al. 1991). Finally, Panel d shows how the addition of a constant line, a small change in context, radically transforms shape and perceived similarity (Palmer 1989).

The importance of these textbook facts about the context-dependent nature of perception should not be underestimated. They mean that the psychological object, the object to be categorized, is not itself a fixed

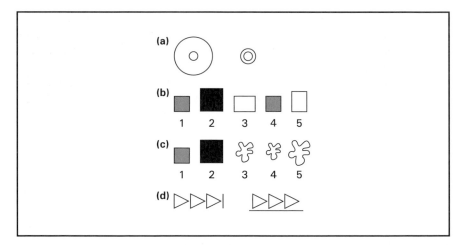

FIG. 5.5.   Illustrations of context effects in perception: a – perceived size of centre circle depends on size of surrounding circle; b and c – perceived similarity of objects 1 and 2 depend on other objects in the comparison set; and d – the perceived shape and orientation of triangles depends of the perceived frame.

entity with one objectively correct description. Rather, psychological objects, like the categories in which we place them, depend in a chameleon-like way on the surrounds.

The contextual malleability of general cognitive processes is also seen in many memory phenomena. Light & Carter-Sobel's (1970) classic demonstration of encoding specificity provides one good example. They showed that the word "jam" encountered in the context of traffic does not lead to the same memory as the word "jam" encountered in the context of strawberry. Further, the to-be-remembered word, jam, is better recognized by subjects in the context that matches the original learning (the word "traffic") than one that is different. The importance of context goes far beyond this paradigm (see Tulving & Thomson 1973). Evidence from a variety of memory tasks indicates that what is remembered depends critically on a holistic match between the quite general context of the original event and the context of the moment. Thus, Godden & Baddeley (1980) found that scuba divers who learned lists of words underwater remembered them better when tested underwater than on land. Similarly, Butler & Rovee-Collier (1989) found that babies who had learned to kick to make a mobile bounce in a crib with a particularly patterned crib sheet and bumper, remembered days later what they learned when the crib sheet and bumper were the same but not when they were different. Other evidence shows that the particular room, the particular voice of a speaker, and even the mood of the subject matter in what is remembered and what is recalled (S. Smith 1986, Palmeri et al. 1993, Eich 1985). In sum, what we remember depends broadly on the moment of learning and the moment of retrieval.

These facts about perceiving and remembering have profound implications for theories of categories. Objects can not map stably into a set taxonomy because the objects of mental life are not themselves stable entities. These facts also mean that mental events are naturally adapted to context – thoughts about frogs in restaurants differ appropriately from thoughts about frogs in ponds because the perceived object and the remembered knowledge are made in and from the context of the moment.

Continuity with the just-previous past

The second fact about perceiving and remembering is that these processes are extended in time. Because the information-bearing events that comprise perceiving and remembering take time and endure, mental activity at any point in time will be a mixed result of immediate input and just-past activity. This is readily seen in tongue twisters. The difficulty in saying "Peter Piper picked a peck of pickled peppers" lies not in saying "pickled" but in saying "pickled" after "picked". The journals and textbooks of cognitive psychology are filled with many more examples.

One such example is the ubiquitous phenomena of "priming": within a narrow time frame, the perception of a prior word (or object) facilitates the perception of subsequent words (or objects) that are similar in some way. Thus perceiving the word "doctor" facilitates perceiving "nurse". Phenomena of "priming" are widespread in lexical processes, picture perception, object recognition, and motor behaviour (see for example, Klatzky 1980, Rosenbaum 1991, Harris & Coltheart 1986).

All theories of priming, in one way or another, posit that the internal activity that gives rise to the recognition of the first item (e.g. doctor) persists and thus facilitates processing of the second. The basic idea is that the pattern of activity associated with the first item overlaps in kind with the pattern underlying the perception of the second item and thus puts the second in a state of partial activation and readiness. Priming shows without a doubt that the thoughts we have at one moment grow out of those just before.

The temporal reality of cognitive processes, the shaping of the present by the just-previous past is also everywhere evident in perception. One class of relevant phenomena are adaptation effects: the repeated presentation of an event alters the perception of subsequent events. Such adaptation effects are seen in what one might think of as the primitive sensations of colour, loudness and pitch (e.g. Anstis & Saida 1985, Marks 1993), but also in the more complicated perceptions of musical chords (e.g. Zatorre & Halpern 1979), shapes (e.g. Halpern & Warm 1984), speech sounds (e.g. Remez et al. 1980) and faces (O'Leary & McMahon 1991). For example, prolonged staring at curved lines causes physically straight lines to be perceived as curved (Gibson 1933). The repeated presentation of a sound can cause subsequent sounds to be perceptually assimilated to it or to be perceptually pushed away from the adapting event (Marks 1993). The repeated presentation of one stimulus event can even shift what might seem to be preset category boundaries. For example, Remez (1979) shifted the boundary between whether sounds were perceived as a vowel or a buzz by the repeated presentation of an |a| sound.

These ever-present adaptation and priming effects, like the pervasive context effects, mean that mental states are extremely unlikely ever to be repeated. They mean, as James put it in the opening quote of this chapter, that we never have the same idea twice. These ideas also mean that there is a pull for coherence from one thought to the next one, for the meaning of an event to depend on its place in a stream of events. If we think first about eating and then about frogs we will think differently than if we think first about ponds and then about frogs.

A history of individual acts of knowing

The third fact about processes of perceiving and remembering is that they change themselves. An act of perceiving or remembering causes not only transient changes but also longer lasting, near permanent, changes. We know long-lasting changes must happen or we would have no memories of the individual events of our own lives and no connectedness with our own past. Empirical evidence suggests further that the power of a single processing event to alter subsequent knowing can be quite remarkable. We mention two such examples.

One example is Jacoby et al.'s (1989) ability to make people famous overnight. They had subjects read a list of names that included all non-famous people, names such as Samuel Weisdorf. Twenty-four hours later they gave subjects a list of famous and non-famous names and asked subjects to pick out the famous people. Subjects picked out Samuel Weisdorf along with Minnie Pearl and Christopher Wren. Having read the name once was sufficient to create a lasting degree of familiarity – one sufficient for a categorization of the name as "famous".

A second example is Perris et al.'s (1990) equally dramatic demonstration of toddlers' memory of a single experimental session that occurred in their infancy. The original experimental event was designed to test infants' use of visual cues to control reaching. To do this Perris et al. (1990) taught six-month-old children to reach in the dark for different-sized objects. The different sizes were signalled by different sounds (e.g. bells for big objects, squeaks for little ones). One to two years after the original experiment, Perris et al. brought these children back to the laboratory. At this point, the children were between 18 and 30 months of age. At this test session, the lights were simply turned off, the sounds played and the children's behaviour was observed. Perris et al. found that the children who had been in the experiment as babies reached in the dark for the sounding objects; control children who had not participated in the infant study did not. Thus, the one-time experience at six months permanently changed these children, altering the likelihood of behaviours one and two years later.

There are many more such demonstrations of long-lasting facilitatory effects in the literature – of the benefits of a single prior processing experiences (with units as small as single words) that have effects days, weeks, years later (e.g. Jacoby 1983, Salasoo et al. 1985, Rovee-Collier et al. 1985, Brooks 1987). These results indicate that each act of perceiving and remembering changes us.

Critically, the accrual of these long-term changes provides a source of stability in a continually changing system. If there are statistical regularities, patterns, in our experiences that recur over and over again, then as each moment of knowing is laid on the preceding moments, weak tendencies to behave and to think in certain ways will become strong tendencies – sometimes so strong that they will not be easily perturbed and thus might seem fixed.

There is considerable evidence that people are ready learners of statistical regularities. Indeed, people appear to learn whatever sorts of regularities are presented to them (Kelly & Martin 1994, Hasher & Zacks 1984, Coren & Porac 1977, Saegert et al. 1973, Shapiro 1969, Ashby et al. 1993, Lewicki et al. 1989, Reber et al. 1980). Examples include the pervasive effects of word frequency on word recognition (Harris & Coltheart 1986), typicality judgements which often reflect the most commonly-experienced instances (e.g. robin) and the strong effect of the frequency with which a face or brandname has been experienced on the likeability of that face or brandname (Zajonc 1968). Other evidence includes adults' remarkable sensitivity to the frequencies of events in the world – from the lethality of different events (Lichtenstein et al. 1968) to the frequency of fast food restaurants (Shedler et al. 1985; see Kelly & Martin 1994, for a review).

Still other evidence indicates that even very young children are highly sensitive to statistical regularities and, moreover, that these regularities play a demonstrable role in their category boundaries. For example, Sera et al. (1988) showed two-year-olds series of objects varying widely in size – for example, sneakers that varied from doll size to US men's size 18, buttons that varied from dots to platter size, and plates that varied from button size to several feet in diameter. In each case the children were asked individually about each object whether it was big or little. For each category, sneakers, buttons, and plates, the children imposed a sharp boundary between the sizes designated big and those designated little. For each category, that boundary fell at the (likely) most commonly experienced size by the child for that category – their own shoe size for sneakers, the size of a shirt button for buttons, and the 12 inch standard dinner plate size for plates. Apparently, children's everyday experiences with specific objects – putting on their own shoes, having their shirts buttoned, sitting at the dinner table – create in aggregate quite good knowledge about the specific sizes of specific kinds of things.

Other evidence suggests that regularities, correlations among multiple properties, may shape category judgements in unexpected ways. For example, Sera et al. (1994) asked speakers of Spanish and English to "cast" an animated film in which everyday objects came to life. The subjects' specific task was to decide whether the voices for these animated objects should be male or female. Spanish and English speakers provided quite different castings. For example, the Spanish speakers classified arrows and wheels along with ballerinas and queens as female voices but classified ice cream and shoes along with kings and giants as male voices. In contrast, English speakers cast arrows and wheels as male voices, ice cream as a female voice and shoes as possibly either. Critically, the Spanish speakers' judgements were predictable from the grammatical gender of the lexical item. Apparently, the association of shoes and ice cream with kings and men via the determiner "*el*" (as opposed to "*la*") makes shoes and ice cream more manly for Spanish than English speakers.

Widespread sensitivity to all forms of regularities and patterns seems likely to play a crucial role in categorization generally. As Kelly & Martin (1994:107) wrote, "the world is awash with stuff best described as 'tendencies', 'maybes', 'estimates', and 'generally speakings'". No individual regularity may be enough to explain the stability and context sensitivity of categories, but the combination of the many imperfect relationships in the world may. Consistent with this idea, Lakoff (1987) suggested that grammatical gender categories stably emerge and are productive because they are made of imperfect mixtures of imperfect cues – biological gender, cultural associations, the perceptual properties of objects, phonological properties of the word. Similarly, Kelly (1994) argued that parsing speech into word units may be dependent on a complex web of prosodic, phonological, and morphophonemic cues.

Statistics, however, may not be everything. The history, or specific order of events in a learner's past may be a critical determiner of what is learned. One provocative demonstration of this idea is Schyns & Rodet's (in press) study of how category learning may create new perceptual features. In their study, adults learned about two different types of cells from a Martian creature; Cell type A or Cell type AB, illustrated in Figure 5.6. Cell type A was defined in terms of a single feature, illustrated by the arrow in the figure. Instances of cell type A differed in other components but all possessed this critical feature. Cell type AB was defined by the more complex feature indicated by an arrow in the Figure. The critical manipulation was which specific category, type A or type AB, was learned first. The critical question was whether subjects defined cell type AB by a single feature that spatially conjoined the two parts or by two potentially separable features. After familiarization with the two categories, subjects were presented with test cells that spatially separated the two possible parts of the complex feature as illustrated in Figure 5.6. Subjects who learned cell type A first said the test cells were instances of type AB because they contained the two critical parts. Subjects who learned cell type AB first said test cells were instances of type A because they contained the A feature but not the complex B feature. Apparently learning A first had enabled

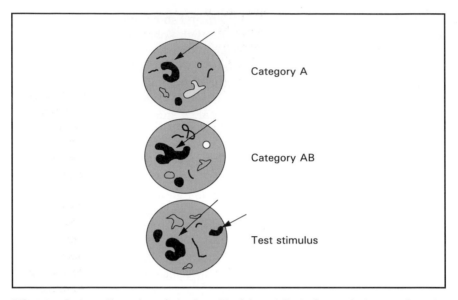

FIG. 5.6.   Redrawn illustrations of stimuli used by Schyns & Rodet (in press). Arrows point to the critical features.

the subjects to parse the complex AB feature into two parts – the feature defining A and a new feature.

What is important about these results is that they show that what one knows depends not just on the total aggregate of learning experiences but their order. (See Regier 1995, for a computational model which provides a similar demonstration in the domain of spatial terms.)

How these facts may make categories

The extensive evidence on the contextual nature of perceiving and memory, the temporal groundedness of cognition in preceding activity, and its sensitivity to the history of its own activity provide a solution to the problem of how categories are both globally stable and locally variable, how novel categories may be created on-line, and how categories change over the life of an individual. Consider again the individual act of categorization that occurs upon seeing a frog and recognizing it as such. One's thoughts upon seeing the frog will be the combination of the immediate input in its full complexity, one's just preceding cognitive activity, and one's lifetime history of activity. The compression of all these sources of information in a single act means that what we know at a moment is an adaptive mix of the same stable regularities that also form other moments of knowing and the idiosyncrasies of this moment.

We can see these ideas at work in three recent studies of how categories adapt themselves on-line. In one study, Goldstone (1995) asked subjects to judge the hue of objects by adjusting the colour of one object (the target) until it matched precisely another (the standard). The individual objects were letters and numbers and they were presented in a random order to the subjects to be judged. Unbeknown to the subjects, Goldstone had arranged for the colours and objects to be correlated across trials as shown in Figure 5.7. Specifically, the letters tended to be redder than the numbers. This fact strongly influenced subjects' judgements. Specifically, they judged presented letters (e.g. the "L" in Figure 5.7) to be redder than numbers of the exact same hue (e.g. the "8" in Figure 5.7). Apparently, subjects' lifetime history of experience with letters and numbers caused same category members to influence each other in the here and now. Long-term category knowledge combined with the transient effects of seeing redder letters than numbers and with the sensory information presented by the single to-be-judged object. Processes operating over different timescales combined in a single moment of knowing to make an individual letter look a particular degree of red.

The semantic congruity effect provides a second example of how knowing in a moment is made in the combination of long-term changes, transient in-task effects, and the immediate input. The semantic congruity effect refers to the finding that in comparative judgements, people are faster when comparing objects on a quantitative dimension when the direction of comparison is congruent with the location of the stimuli on the continuum. For example, when asked to make judgements about the size of animals, subjects are faster to choose the larger of two relatively large animals (e.g. elephant versus hippopotamus) than to choose the larger of two relatively small animals (e.g. hamster versus gerbil). Conversely, subjects are faster to choose the smaller of two small animals than to choose the smaller of two relatively large animals (Banks & Flora 1977). This general and robust effect clearly depends

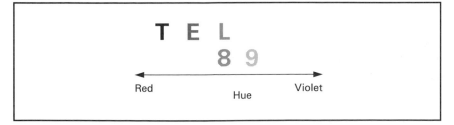

FIG. 5.7.   Illustration of the correlations instantiated in Goldstone's (1995) experiment on colour perception.

on people's long-term and stable knowledge about the sizes of things. Banks & Flora originally suggested that people represent "elephant" as "very big" and therefore can answer questions about bigness directly. By this account, judging that an elephant is small (in comparison to say a whale) is difficult because it requires one to override the represented attribute "very big".

This account, however, cannot be the whole story. Our long-term knowledge about the sizes of things is not all that matters in the semantic congruity effect. For example, Cech & Shoben (1985) showed that the direction of the semantic congruity for a pair such as "rabbit–beaver" changes depending on the other pairs being judged in the task. In the context of other pairs of animals varying widely in size (from elephants to mice), "smaller than" judgements were faster than "larger than" judgements for the pair "rabbit–beaver". However, when this same pair was judged in an experiment in which rabbits and beavers were the biggest animals judged, the reverse semantic congruity was found: subjects were faster at judging which member of the rabbit–beaver pair was larger rather than smaller. Subsequent experiments have shown that the direction of semantic congruity for a given pair will shift in the course of an experiment as the sizes of the objects judged prior to the pair shift in one direction or the other (Cech et al. 1990). Thus, the semantic congruity effect is not dependent solely on the absolute value of a given item nor our long-term knowledge of the sizes of things. Rather, how fast one answers the question "Is this bigger than that?" depends on long-term knowledge, the preceding items just judged, and the immediate question asked.

The creation of transient "concepts" that meld the information from immediate input, from just-previous activity, and from a lifetime of activity seems fundamental to intelligence. One final example that makes this point is Sanocki's research on people's ease of recognizing letters in quite different fonts (1991, 1992; see also McGraw & Rehling 1994). The traditional approach to letter recognition (as we saw in the traditional approach to category recognition generally) is to try to specify the features that specify a particular letter – the features for example that enable one to recognize all the various letter "ys" in Figure 5.8. Sanocki's results, however, suggest a single set of represented and abstract features are not what enables us to recognize the letters of distinct fonts. The evidence against such an idea is that people are faster to recognize letters in familiar than in novel fonts and are faster to recognize letters consistent with the fonts of just previously seen or surrounding letters – even when the fonts are very well known. Altogether, the results suggest that people adjust their definition of features on-line to fit the font they are reading; for example, a specific

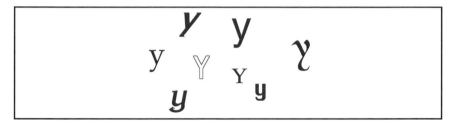

FIG. 5.8.   The letter "y" in various fonts.

"y" that is difficult in one context is easy in another. Again, what we perceive when presented with a particular letter depends all at once on the immediate character of that letter, the character of the just-previously-perceived letters, and one's long-term experience of perceiving particular fonts.

We believe that these three examples – the influence of category knowledge on colour perception, the semantic congruity effect, the perception of letter categories – provide the key to understanding human categorization more generally. They suggest that categories exist only as the products of mental activity – in individual mental events with real-time durations that are themselves the product of their own lifetime of activity, the just-previous activity, and the immediate input. Categories that are this – the on-line product of complex processes of perceiving and remembering – will be dynamically stable, adaptive and, given an idiosyncratic mix of past and present, inventive. These ideas offer an alternative to the dualistic treatment of category stability and variability in Figure 5.3 and the dualistic treatment of real time processes and development in Figure 5.4.

We depict the new framework schematically in Figure 5.9. The activity of many heterogeneous and interacting subsystems that comprise a moment of knowing is represented by $*t$. The material causes of the activity at a single moment of knowing are the immediate input, the just-previous activity, and the nature of the cognitive system itself. The immediate input to the system at a particular moment in time is represented by I_t. The multiple processes of perceiving and remembering are indicated by arrows between the input and the individual moment of knowing and between one moment of knowing and the next. Importantly, since the activity at $*t$ is in part determined by the activity at $*t - 1$, it is also partly determined by the activity at $*t - 2$, $*t - 3$... $*t - n$. Each moment of knowing thus brings with it the history of its own past activity. Further, since each act of knowing permanently changes processes of perceiving and remembering, the accrued activity changes the cognitive system itself. It will not be the

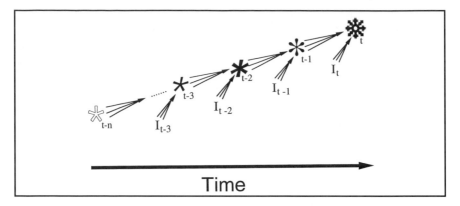

FIG. 5.9.   Illustrations of how individual moments of knowing (*) combine immediate input (I), just-previous activity, and the history of activity.

same at t as it was at $t_{(n-1)}$. Thus real time and developmental time are unified; the very processes that make categories vary from moment to moment also make development.

PART 3: LEARNING NAMES FOR THINGS

> . . . our brain changes, and that, like aurora borealis, its whole internal equilibrium shifts with every pulse of change. The precise nature of the shifting at a given moment is a product of many factors. . . . But just as one of them certainly is the influence of outward objects on the sense-organs during the moment, so is another certainly the very special susceptibility in which the organ has been left at that moment by all it has gone through in the past. (William James, 1890:234).

In this section, we show how the ideas illustrated in Figure 5.9 both fit and are supported by data on children's category formation. We focus specifically on young children's initial generalization of a novel noun to new instances. Told that one object is, for example, a "dax", what other objects do children take to also be a "dax"? The now considerable evidence on this categorization task is critical to theories of categorization generally for three reasons. First, very young children in this task, like the subjects in Barsalou's *ad hoc* category experiments, appear to form coherently structured categories *on line*. Secondly, these categories seemingly created on the spot from hearing one object named once are often right, smart from an adult point of view. Thirdly, these phenomena seem central to the origins of lexical categories such as bird, frog, water – the ones that dominate the adult literature on concepts.

The critical results derive from studies employing an artificial word learning task. For example, in one such study, Landau et al. (1988) presented two- and three-year-old children with a small, blue, wooden inverted U-shaped object. They told the children that this exemplar object "is a dax". They then asked the children what other objects were also "a dax".

Figure 5.10 depicts the exemplar and the test objects. Given these stimuli, the children systematically generalized the name only to test objects that were the same shape as the exemplar – as if they already knew that objects of this shape (but necessarily a particular colour or material) were the same kind of thing. This result has now been replicated many times in many laboratories. Importantly, however, in these tasks children do not just form categories organized by shape. The nature of the categories they form depends on the immediate context, the just-previous events, and the child's history of naming things.

Contextual factors

Young children form well-organized categories specifically in word learning tasks. They do not do so generally in other kinds of categorization tasks. For example, given the objects in Figure 5.10, two- and three-year-olds do not categorize by shape when asked to make similarity judgements (Landau et al. 1988). Instead, they form categories based on holistic similarity or changing criteria. In a further

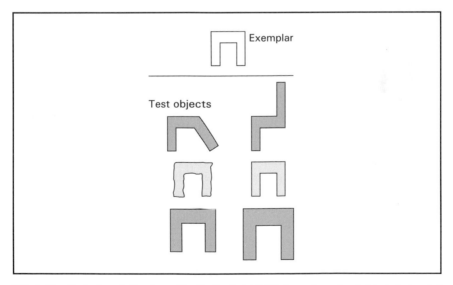

FIG. 5.10.   Illustration of stimuli used by Smith et al. (1988): three-dimensional objects that varied in shape, size, and material (wood, sponge, and wire mesh).

study, Landau et al. (submitted) showed that children also classify differently when asked the names of things as against when asked to make judgements about function. For example, in one experiment, they used stimuli shaped like those in Figure 5.10, except now the exemplar and some of the test objects were made of sponge. The exemplar was named ("this is a dax") and then the experimenter spilled water on the table and wiped it up with the spongy exemplar. The children systematically generalized that name to same-shaped objects but when asked about function, these same children selected objects made of sponge when asked to wipe up water. The finding that systematic categorization by shape given stimuli like those in Figure 5.10 is specific to the task of naming has been replicated a number of times in several laboratories (e.g. Imai et al. 1994, Soja 1992). These findings tell us that stimulus properties alone do not compel the categories children form.

The stimulus properties, however, do matter. Children spontaneously form lexical categories by shape only when presented stimuli like those in Figure 5.10; changes in several kinds of properties change the categories children form. If the named objects have eyes, for example, children form lexical categories organized by shape and texture (Jones et al. 1991). If the objects are made of non-rigid substances (e.g. shaving cream with gravel in it), children form lexical categories organized by colour and texture (Soja et al. 1991).

What process creates these context effects on children's category formation in the task of generalizing a newly-learned word? Smith (1995, see also Jones & Smith 1993) suggest that it is a mix of here-and-now and learned forces on selective attention. The specific proposal is that memories of novel words are formed which include the properties of the object (and context) that children attend to at the time of hearing the novel word. The properties that children attend to will depend on the intrinsic salience of specific object properties and past attentional learning. This last point is a critical part of the proposal. One hundred years of research on attention suggests that the regular association of contextual cues with attention to some property leads to automatically increased attention to that property in that context. The language learning task presents the child with many statistical regularities which can guide attention and thus also guide language learning itself. There are perhaps associative relations between the syntactic frame "this is a _____" and specific object properties and also associative relations among object properties. In this view, the categories children form upon hearing a novel object named seem right from an adult point of view because they reflect, at least in part, statistical regularities in how words map to objects.

In sum, children's systematic generalizations of novel words used to label a novel object suggest that when children hear a novel object name, they form a category on the spot. Moreover the nature of the formed category appears to be influenced by a number of contextual factors – the task, the objects, and the linguistic context in which the novel word is embedded.

Continuity with the just-previous past

A growing literature indicates that young children's interpretation of novel words are also strongly influenced by the events occurring just prior to hearing the novel object named (see e.g. Baldwin 1991, Baldwin & Markman 1989, Tomasello & Kruger 1992, Olguin & Tomasello 1993, Tomasello et al., 1996). In one series of experiments, Akhtar et al. (1996) created a naturalistic novel word learning situation that consisted of a sequence of events. First, the child (a 24 month old) along with three adults was introduced to three novel objects. The objects were played with successively until the child was highly familiar with each of them; however, none of these objects was ever named. Secondly, the three now familiar objects were placed in a transparent box along with a novel fourth object, the target object. The adults looked generally at the transparent container (but not at any individual object) and said, "Look, it's a modi. A modi." During the third event, the child and adults played successively with each of the four objects but the adults did not name any of them. The fourth event was the test: the four objects were placed on table and the child was asked to indicate "the modi." Although, all four objects had been present when the novel name was supplied, the children had no trouble determining the referent. The children chose the target object (the most novel of the four when the name was first supplied) when asked to get "the modi". This result fits the idea that in the moment of hearing a novel name children link that name to the object that most demands attention. The object most demanding of attention at a particular moment, in turn, depends on its novelty which depends on prior events.

A second experiment by Akhtar et al. demonstrated the role of context in the sequence of events organizing attention. First, the child and three adults played successively with three novel objects, thus making all these objects familiar to the child. Secondly, two of the adults left the room and a novel fourth object, the target object, was introduced. The child and the remaining adult played with this novel toy but the remaining adult never named the object. By one description, then, one that centres only on the object and not the context, the target object is at this point equivalent to the other three in familiarity for the child. Thirdly, the three original toys and the target object were placed together in the transparent box and the two other adults returned. While looking generally at the transparent box, the two returning adults said "Look, a gazzer. It's a gazzer." Fourthly, all participants played with the four objects. Fifthly, on the test trial, the four objects were presented and the child was asked to indicate "the gazzer". The children chose the target object.

These results fit what we know about the contextual nature of memories; with the fact that what is remembered depends on the holistic match between the general context of the original event and the context of the moment. This fact suggests the following description of events in Akhtar et al.'s second experiment. In Event 1, three memories are formed, each consist of the object (Oi) and the context of three adults playing and attending (C1): the memories formed thus are O1 + C1, O2 + C1, O3 + C1. Event 2 consists of a different object, the target OT, and a different context, one that does not contain two of the adults. Thus the memory stored of the second event will be OT + C2. In the critical Event 3 when the novel name is offered, all objects are presented in the transparent box and all four adults are present. This context, C1', is thus more similar to the original context than is C2. By this analysis, then, the target object is the most novel in the context when the name is offered and thus the one attended to most and most likely to be associated with the novel name.

There are many other results in the literature that show that the interpretation of a novel name applied to a novel object is a mental event that grows out of and is continuous with just-previous mental activity: children interpret novel words as referring to novel objects with novelty determined by just-preceding events (Markman 1989, Merriman & Bowman 1989); children are more likely to map a word to an object and form a well-organized category if the sound of the word has been highlighted by recently hearing other similar words (Merriman & Marazita 1995, Schwartz et al. 1987); and finally, presenting children with an array of test objects (and thus the variation among potential category members) prior to naming the exemplar alters the formed category (Merriman et al. 1991). Clearly, children's category formation in the context of interpreting a novel object name is a mental event created in the context of ongoing processes of perceiving and remembering.

A history of individual acts of knowing

This is considerable evidence that supports Smith's (1995) proposal that the smartness of children's category formation upon hearing a novel object derives from learned associations among linguistic contexts and the properties of novel objects. The fact that in many stimulus contexts children form categories organized by shape similarities makes sense from this point of view. In English, the common nouns that name common concrete objects refer to categories of things of similar shape (Rosch 1978, Biederman 1987).

Jones et al. (1991) proposed that children learn to attend to shape as a consequence of learning words that refer to similar things. They reasoned that if attention to shape in the context of naming rigid objects was the product of statistical regularities in the language then it should emerge only after some number of names for rigid things have been learned. They tested this hypothesis in a longitudinal study of children from 15 to 20 months. During this time span, the number of concrete nouns in the children's productive vocabularies increased from an average of five to over 150. The children were tested once a month in an artificial word learning task much like the artificial word learning task described earlier. The principle result is that the children did not systematically generalize novel nouns to new instances by shape until after they had 50 nouns in their productive vocabulary. This result is consistent with the idea that the shape bias in naming is a product of learning words that refer to objects of similar shape.

The importance of the child's personal history of forming categories is also seen in the growing evidence for cross-linguistic differences (Imai & Gentner in press; Gopnik et al. in press; Waxman et al. in press; Choi & Bowerman 1991, Sera et al. 1991). Several of these cross-linguistic studies focused on children's naming of objects versus substances. Lucy (1992) predicted cross-linguistic differences in the categorization of these two kinds because languages differ in how they mark countable and non-countable entities – in what kinds of nouns called "count nouns" take the plural and numerical determiners (e.g. "two dogs") and what kinds called "mass nouns" do not (e.g. "some sugar"). English maps the distinction between count nouns and mass nouns on to that between rigid objects versus substances (see Lucy 1992). The work of Soja et al. (1991) cited earlier suggests that very young children learning English generalize names for objects and substances differently – a result that suggests that the object–substance distinction could be universal and independent of language.

However, other languages divide up countable and non-countable things differently and in ways that ignore the distinction between rigid things of constant shape and malleable substances of variable shape. For example, in some languages only categories referring to humans (brother, wife, priest) receive plural marking. In others, the division between kinds of entities that are syntactically marked or not marked for number is between animate things and inanimate things. Lucy specifically argued that the potency of the contrast between rigidly-shaped things and substances might be specific to languages like English which map the count–mass distinction on this contrast; languages which map the distinction on, for example, animates versus inanimates might not direct attention away from the contrast between rigid and non-rigid things.

To test this idea, Lucy (1992) examined the classifications of adult speakers of Yucatec Mayan, a language in which nouns for all inanimate things (rigid objects and non-solid substances) are treated like English mass nouns and do not take the plural. Consistent with Lucy's prediction, Yucatec-speaking adults, in marked contrast to English-speaking adults, classify rigid objects by material and not by shape. For example, given a cardboard box, a wooden box, and a piece of irregularly shaped cardboard, Yucatec speakers classify the cardboard box with the piece of cardboard; English speakers classify the two boxes together. More recent evidence (Lucy 1996) suggests further that these differences in classification between English-speaking and Yucatec-speaking individuals increase with development – as they should if they are created by the statistical regularities in a language and the individual's history of category judgements.

Imai & Gentner (1993) provided further evidence for the developmental growth of cross-linguistic differences. Their subjects were English-speaking and Japanese-speaking children. In Japanese, like Yucatec, inanimate nouns (names for rigid things and non-rigid substances) do not take the plural; all are syntactically like English mass nouns. Imai & Gentner showed that this difference matters for how children generalize novel names to new instances. Specifically, American children formed lexical categories consistent with an object–substance distinction. Japanese children's categorizations were better described by a complex-shape versus simple-shape distinction rather than rigidity *per se*. Moreover, these differences were evident at age two but increased dramatically between the ages of two and four years, and were most marked in adults. These results demonstrate that category formation in the moment – the kind of things children assume to have the same name – is moulded by the kinds of categories that children have formed in the past.

Putting it together

Young children learn names for things rapidly. They are so adept at this learning that they seem to know the category of objects a word refers to from hearing it name a single object. The evidence reviewed above strongly fits the picture in Figure 5.9. Children's word learning is smart because children create categories on-line out of their history of experience, the transient effects of preceding activity, and the details of the moment. The wisdom of the past is fit to the idiosyncracies of the here and now. This is a powerful idea. It means that children can form novel categories – think thoughts never thought before – that are adaptive. This can happen because the categories created on-line will be a unique mix of past and present.

How this mixture can cause both stability and variability is illustrated in one final study of children's novel word generalizations. Smith et al. (1992) examined young children's interpretations of novel nouns versus novel adjectives. The objects in all conditions were made of wood and varied in shape and colour. The colours of the named objects were realized by putting glitter in paint. In the noun condition, an exemplar was labelled with a novel count noun "is a dax"; in the adjective condition, the exemplar was labelled with a novel adjective, "is a dax one". Critically, the experiment was performed twice: once when the objects were presented under ordinary lighting conditions and once when the objects were presented in a darkened chamber under a spotlight. The effect of the spotlight was to make the glitter sparkle and the colours thus attention-grabbing.

The key result is that the categories that children form depend on both syntactic context and room illumination. Under ordinary illumination the children generalized both novel nouns and novel adjectives only to objects the same shape as the exemplar. Colour was ignored. In the spotlight condition, in contrast, children generalized novel nouns and novel adjectives differently. Children again generalized the novel noun by shape, ignoring colour. But they generalized the novel adjective on the basis of the sparkling colour.

These results show that knowledge of language and local idiosyncratic forces on attention combine in a moment to invent categories. It is unlikely that these children possessed any specific rules about adjective categories and sparkling versus non-sparkling glitter. Rather, children's variable interpretation of novel adjectives is best explained in the here-and-now mix of past learning about adjectives and the context of sparkling colours just as the stability of children's interpretations of novel nouns is explained by the mix of past learning about nouns and the present task context. In brief, the processes that make stability and variability may be the same.

WHAT ABOUT CONCEPTS?

Experience is remolding us every moment, and our mental reaction on every given thing is really a resultant of experience of the whole world up to that date. (William James 1890:234).

Children's category formation in the context of hearing a novel object named is sometimes considered apart from categorization in adults and as reflecting mechanisms perhaps specific to language learning (see Markman 1989). However, category formation by children in the service of word learning looks very much like categorization by humans generally. Wise stability is coupled with street-smart variability. The stability and the variability seem to directly fall out of basic truths about processes of perceiving and remembering: their context-dependency, the extended duration of real-time processes, and finally and most critically, that these are processes which change themselves by their own activity. Moments of knowing, be they interpreting a novel word, reasoning about quarters and pizzas, judging the essential properties of water – may be wisely stable and smartly variable all at once precisely because each moment of knowing combines intelligence across multiple timescales – the fast time of on-line processes, the slower time of developmental change, and in the non-changing aspects of perceptual and memorial processes, the very slow scale of change over evolutionary time. A successful theory of categories thus might require that we give up timeless abstractions such as concepts.

One might ask whether it is, nonetheless, useful to keep the idea of concept, just alter its meaning. Barsalou (1993) proposed such a new conception of concepts, one in which the word concept is used to refer to not to internal representations but to the thought made in the moment. James (1890:246) took the opposite stand, "I shall avoid the use of the expression concept altogether".

REFERENCES

Akhtar, N., M. Carpenter, M. Tomasello, 1996. The role of discourse novelty in early word learning. *Child Development*, **67**(2), 635–645.

Anstis, S. M. & S. Saida 1985. Adaptation to auditory streaming of frequency-modulated tones. *Journal of Experimental Psychology: Human Perception and Performance* **11**, 257–71.

Armstrong, S. L., L. R. Gleitman, H. Gleitman 1983. What some concepts might not be. *Cognition* **13**, 263–308.

Ashby, F., M. Gregory, W. Todd 1993. Relations between prototype, exemplar, and decision bound models of categorization. *Journal of Mathematical Psychology* **37**, 372–400.

Baldwin, D. A. 1991. Infant's contribution to the achievement of joint reference. *Child Development* **62**, 857–90.

Baldwin, D. A. & E. M. Markman 1989. Establishing word-object relations: a first step. *Child Development* **60**, 174–82.

Banks, W. P. & J. Flora 1977. Semantic and perceptual processes in symbolic comparisons. *Journal of Experimental Psychology: Human Perception and Performance* **3**, 278–90.

Barsalou, L. W. 1983. Ad hoc categories. *Memory and Cognition* **11**, 211–27.

Barsalou, L. W. 1987. The instability of graded structure: implications for the nature of concepts. In *Concepts and conceptual development*, U. Neisser (ed.), 101–40. Cambridge: Cambridge University Press.

Barsalou, L. W. 1989. Intraconcept similarity and its implications for interconcept similarity. In *Similarity and analogical reasoning*, S. Vosniadou & A. Ortony (eds), 76–121. Cambridge: Cambridge University Press.

Barsalou, L. W. 1993. Challenging assumption about concepts [commentary]. *Cognitive Development* **8**, 169–80.

Bauer, P. J. & R. Fivush 1992. Constructing event representations: building on a foundation of variation and enabling relations. *Cognitive Development* **7**, 381–401.

Biederman, I. 1987. Recognition by components: a theory of human image understanding, *Psychological Review* **94**, 115–47.

Brooks, L. R. 1987. Decentralized control of categorization: the role of prior processing episodes. In *Concepts and conceptual development*, U. Neisser (ed.), 141–74. Cambridge: Cambridge University Press.

Butler, J. & C. Rovee-Collier 1989. Contextual gating of memory retrieval. *Developmental Psychobiology* **22**, 533–52.

Cech, C. G. & E. J. Shoben 1985. Context effects in symbolic magnitude comparisons. *Journal of Experimental Psychology: Learning, Memory, and Cognition* **11**, 299–315.

Cech, C. G., E. J. Shoben, M. Love 1990. Multiple congruity effects in judgements of magnitude. *Journal of Experimental Psychology: Learning, Memory, and Cognition* **16**, 1142–52.

Choi, S. & M. Bowerman 1991. Learning to express motion events in English and Korean: the influence of language-specific lexicalization patterns. *Cognition* **41**, 83–121.

Coren, S. & C. Porac 1977. Fifty centuries of right-handedness: the historical record. *Science* **198**, 631–2.

Eich, E. 1985. Context, memory, and integrated item/context imagery. *Journal of Experimental Psychology: Learning, Memory, and Cognition* **11**, 764–70.

Fodor, J. D. 1977. *Semantics: theories of meaning in generative grammar*. New York: Crowell.

Gelman, S. A. & J. D. Coley 1991. Language and categorization: the acquisition of natural kind terms. In *Perspectives on language and thought: interrelations in development*, S. A. Gelman & J. P. Byrnes (eds), 146–96. Cambridge: Cambridge University Press.

Gibson, J. J. 1933. Adaptation, after effect and contrast in the perception of curved lines. *Journal of Experimental Psychology* **16**, 1–31.

Godden, D. & A. Baddeley 1980. When does context influence recognition memory? *British Journal of Psychology* **71**, 99–104.

Goldstone, R. L. 1995. Effects of categorization on color perception. *Psychological Science* **6**, 298–304.

Goldstone, R. L., D. L. Medin, D. Gentner 1991. Relational similarity and the non-independence of features in similarity judgements. *Cognitive Psychology* **23**, 222–62.

Goldstone, R., D. Medin, J. B. Halberstadt, in press. Similarity in context. *Memory and Cognition*.

Gopnik, A., S. Choi, T. Baumberger, in press. Cross-linguistic differences in early semantic and cognitive development. *Cognitive Development*.

Halff, H. M., A. Ortony, R. C. Anderson 1976. A context-sensitive representation of word meanings. *Memory and Cognition* **4**, 378–83.

Halpern, D. F. & J. S. Warm 1984. The disapperance of dichoptically presented real and subjective contours. *Bulletin of the Psychonomic Society* **22** (5) 433–6.

Harris, M. & M. Coltheart 1986. *Language processing in children and adults: an introduction*. London: Routledge & Kegan Paul.

Hasher, L. & R. T. Zacks 1984 Automatic processing of fundamental information: the case of frequency of occurrence. *American Psychologist* **39**, 1372–88.

Imai, M. & D. Gentner, 1993. Linguistic relativity vs universal ontology: cross-linguistic studies of the object substance distinction. *Proceedings of the Chicago Linguistic Society* 1993.

Imai, M., D. Gentner, N. Uchida 1994. Children's theories of word meaning: The role of shape similarity in early acquisition. *Cognitive Development* **9**, 45–75.

Inhelder, B. & J. Piaget 1964. *The early growth of logic in the child*. New York: Norton.

Jacoby, L. L. 1983. Perceptual enhancement: persistent effect of an experience. *Journal of Experimental Psychology: Learning, Memory, and Cognition* **9**, 21–38.

Jacoby, L. L., C. Kelley, J. Brown, J. Jasechko 1989. Becoming famous overnight: limits on the ability to avoid unconscious influences of the past. *Journal of Personality and Social Psychology* **56**, 326–38.

James, W. 1950. *The principles of psychology*, vol. 1. New York: Dover Publications [original work published 1890. New York: Henry Holt & Co.

Jones, S. S. & L. B. Smith 1993. The place of perceptions in children's concepts. *Cognitive Development* **8**, 113–40.

Jones, S. S., L. B. Smith, B. Landau 1991. Object properties and knowledge in early lexical learning. *Child Development* **62** (3), 499–516.

Katz, J. 1972. *Semantic theory*. New York: Harper & Row.

Keil, F. C. 1989. *Concepts, kinds, and cognitive development*. Cambridge, Mass.: MIT Press.

Keil, F. C. 1994. Explanation, association, and the acquisition of word meaning. *Lingua* **92**, 169–96.

Kelly, M. H. & S. Martin 1994. Domain-general abilities applied to domain-specific tasks: Sensitivity to probabilities in perception, cognition, and language. *Lingua* **92**, 105–40.

Klatzky, R. L. 1980. *Human memory: structures and processes*, 2nd edn. San Francisco: W. H. Freeman.

Komatsu, L. D. 1992. Recent views of conceptual structure. *Psychological Bulletin* **112**, 500–26.

Lakoff, G. 1987 Cognitive models and prototype theory. In *Concepts and conceptual development*, U. Neisser (ed.), 63–100. New York: Cambridge University Press.

Landau, B., L. B. Smith, S. S. Jones 1988. The importance of shape in early lexical learning. *Cognitive Development* **3**, 299–321.

Landau, B., L. B. Smith, S. Jones 1995. *Object shape, object function and object name.*

Lewicki, P., T. Hill, I. Sasaki 1989. Self-perpetuating development of encoding biases. *Journal of Experimental Psychology: General* **118**, 323–37.

Lichtenstein, S., P. Slovic, B. Fischoff, M. Layman, B. Combs 1978. Judged frequency of lethal events. *Journal of experimental Psychology: Human Learning and Memory* **4**, 551–78.

Light, L. L. & L. Carter-Sobel 1970. Effects of changed semantic context on recognition memory. *Journal of Verbal Learning and Verbal Behavior* **9**, 1–11.

Lucy, J. A. 1992. *Grammatical categories and cognition: a case study of the linguistic relativity hypothesis*. Cambridge: Cambridge University Press.

Lucy, J. A. 1996. The impact of language-specific categories on the development of classification behaviour. *International Journal of Psychology* **31** (3–4), 5623.

Malt, B. C. 1994. Water is Not H_2O. *Cognitive Psychology* **27**, 41–70.

Markman, E. M. 1989. *Categorization and naming in children: problems of induction*. Cambridge, Mass.: MIT Press.

Marks, L., E. 1993. Contextual processing of multidimensional and undimensional auditory stimuli. *Journal of Experimental Psychology Human Perception and Performance* **19**, 227–49.

McGraw, G. & J. Rehling 1994. *Roles in letter perception: human data and computer models*.

Medin, D. & A. Ortony. 1989. Psychological essentialism. In *Similarity and analogical reasoning*, S. Vosniadou & A. Ortony (eds), 179–95. New York: Cambridge University Press.

Merriman, W. E. & L. L. Bowman 1989. *The mutual exclusivity bias in children's word learning*. Monograph 54 (p. 130), Society for Research in Child Development.

Merriman, W. E. & J. M. Marazita 1995. The effect of hearing similar-sounding words on young 2-year-olds' disambiguation of novel noun reference. *Developmental Psychology* **31**, 973–84.

Merriman, W. E., J. M. Schuster L. B. Hager 1991. Are names ever mapped onto preexisting categories? *Journal of Experimental Psychology: General* **120**, 288–300.

Mervis, C. B. 1987. Child-basic object categories and early lexical development. In *Concepts and conceptual development*, U. Neisser (ed.), 201–233. Cambridge: Cambridge University Press.

Minsky, M. 1986. *The society of mind*. New York: Simon & Schuster.

Murphy, G. L. & D. L. Medin 1985. The role of theories in conceptual coherence. *Psychological Review* **92**, 289–316.

O'Leary, A. & M. McMahon 1991. Adaptation to form distortion of a familiar shape. *Perception and Psychophysics* **49**, 328–32.

Olguin, R. & M. Tomasello 1993. Twenty-five-month-old children do not have a grammatical category of verb. *Cognitive Development* **8**, 245–72.

Palmer, S. G. 1989. Reference frames in the perception of shape and orientation. In *Object perception: structure and process*, B. E. Shepp & S. Ballesteros (eds), 121–64. Hillsdale, NJ: Erlbaum.

Palmeri, T. J., S. D. Goldinger, D. B. Pisoni 1993. Episodic encoding of voice attributes and recognition memory for spoken words. *Journal of Experimental Psychology: Learning, Memory, and Cognition* **19**, 309–28.

Perris, E. E., N. A. Myers R. K. Clifton 1990. Long-term memory for a single infancy experience. *Child Development* **61**, 1796–1807.

Reber, A. S., S. M. Kassin, S. Lewis G. Cantor 1980. On the relationship between implicit and explicit modes in the learning of a complex rule structure. *Journal of Experimental Psychology: Human Learning and Memory* **6**, 492–502.

Regier, T. 1995. A model of the human capacity for categorizing spatial relations. *Cognitive Linguistics* **6**, 63–88.

Remez, R. E. 1979. Adaptation of the category boundary between speech and nonspeech: a case against feature detectors. *Cognitive Psychology* **11**, 38–57.

Remez, R. E., J. E. Cutting, M. Studdert-Kennedy 1980. Cross-series adaptation using song and string. *Perception and Psychophysics* **27**, 524–30.

Rips, L. J. 1989. Similarity, typicality, and categorization. In *Similarity and analogical reasoning*, S. Vosniadou & A. Ortony (eds), 21–59. Cambridge: Cambridge University Press.

Rips, L. J. & A. Collins 1993. Categories and resemblance. *Journal of Experimental Psychology: General* **122**, 468–86.

Rosch, E. 1973. On the internal structure of perceptual and semantic categories. In *Cognitive development and the acquisition of language*, T. E. Moore (ed.), 111–44. San Diego, California: Academic Press.

Rosch, E. 1978. Principles of categorization. In *Cognition and categorization*, E. Rosch & B. Lloyd (eds), 28–46. Hillsdale, New Jersey: Erlbaum.

Rosch, E. & C. B. Mervis 1975. Family resemblances: studies in the internal structure of categories. *Cognitive Psychology* **7**, 573–605.

Rosenbaum, D. A. 1991. *Human motor control*. San Diego, CA: Academic Press.

Rovee-Collier, C., P. C. Griesler, L. A. Earley 1985. Contextual determinants of retrieval in three-month-olds infants. *Learning and Motivation* **16**, 139–57.

Saegert, S., W. Swap, R. B. Zajonc 1973. Exposure, context, and interpersonal attractors. *Journal of Personality and Social Psychology* **25**, 234–42.

Salasoo, A., R. M. Shiffrin, T. C. Feustel 1985. Building permanent memory codes: codification and repetition effects in word identification. *Journal of Experimental Psychology: General* **114**, 50–77.

Sanocki, T. 1991. Intra- and inter-pattern relations in letter recognition. *Journal of Experimental Psychology: Human Perception and Performance* **17**, 924–41.

Sanocki, T. 1992. Effects of font- and letter-specific experience on the perceptual processing of letters. *American Journal of Psychology* **105**, 435–58.

Schwartz, R. G., L. B. Leonard, D. M. Frome-Loeb, L. A. Swanson 1987, Attempted sounds are sometimes not: an expanded view of phonological selection and avoidance. *Journal of Child Language* **14**, 411–18.

Schyns, P. G. & L. Rodet, in press. Categorization creates functional features. *Journal of Experimental Psychology: Learning, Memory & Cognition*.

Sera, M. D., C. A. H. Berge, J. D. C. Pintado 1994. Grammatical and conceptual forces in the attribution of gender by English and Spanish speakers. *Cognitive Development* **9**, 261–92.

Sera, M. D., E. L. Reittinger, J. D. C. Pintado 1991. Developing definition of objects and events in English and Spanish speakers. *Cognitive Development* **6**, 119–42.

Sera, M. D., D. Troyer, L. B. Smith 1988. What do two-year-olds know about the sizes of things? *Child Development* **59**, 1489–96.

Shapiro, B. J. 1969. The subjective estimation of relative word frequency. *Journal of Verbal Learning and Verbal Behaviour* **13**, 638–43.

Shedler, J. K., J. Jonides 1985. *Availability: plausible but questionable*. Paper presented at the 26th Annual Meeting of the Psychonomic Society, Boston.

Smith, E. E. & D. L. Medin 1981. *Categories and concepts*. Cambridge, Mass.: Harvard University Press.

Smith, E. E. & S. A. Sloman 1994. Similarity- versus rule-based categorization. *Memory and Cognition* **22**, 337–86.

Smith, L. B. 1995. *Self-organizing processes in learning to learn words: development is not induction*. The Minnesota Symposia on Child Psychology, vol. 28: Basic and applied perspectives on learning, cognition, and development (1–32). Hillsdale, New Jersey: Erlbaum.

Smith L. B., S. S. Jones, B. Landau 1992. Count nouns, adjectives, and perceptual properties in children's novel word interpretations. *Developmental Psychology* **28**, 273–86.

Smith, L. B., S. Jones, B. Landau, 1996. Naming in young children: a dumb attentional mechanism. *Cognition* **60**, 143–171.

Smith, S. M. 1986. Environmental context-dependent recognition memory using a short-term memory task for input. *Memory and Cognition* **14**, 347–54.

Soja, N. 1992. Inferences about the meanings of nouns: the relationship between perception and syntax. *Cognitive Development* **7**, 29–46.

Soja, N., S. Carey, E. Spelke 1991. Ontological categories guide young children's inductions of word meanings: object terms and substance terms. *Cognition* **38**, 179–211.

Tomasello, M. & A. C. Kruger 1992. Joint attention on actions: acquiring verbs in ostensive and non-ostensive contexts. *Journal of Child Language* **19**, 311–23.

Tomasello, M., R. Strosberg, N. Akhtar, 1996. Eighteen-month-old children learn words in non-ostensive contexts. *Journal of Child Language* **23**, 157–176.

Tulving, E. & D. M. Thomson 1973. Encoding specificity and retrieval processes in episodic memory. *Psychological Review* **80**, 352–73.

Waxman, S. R., A. Senghas, S. Benveniste, in press. *A cross-linguistic examination of the noun-category bias: evidence from French- and Spanish-speaking preschool-aged children*.

Wittgenstein, L. 1953. *Philosophical investigations*. New York: Macmillan.

Zatorre, R. B. 1968. Attitudinal effects of mere exposure. *Journal of Personality and Social Psychology*, *Monograph Supplement* **9**, 1–29.

Zatorre, R. J. & A. R. Halpern 1979. Identification, discrimination, and selective adaptation of simultaneous musical intervals. *Perception and Psychophysics* **26**, 384–95.

CHAPTER SIX

Distributed Representations and Implicit Knowledge: A Brief Introduction[1]

David R. Shanks

In this chapter my goal is to provide a brief introduction to two topics in knowledge representation that have attracted particular interest in recent years. The first goes under the various names of "connectionism", "parallel distributed processing", and "neural networks", and refers to the idea that certain mental representations are *distributed*. The meaning and significance of this term will become clearer below, but the essential idea is that much of the traditional language of cognition ("symbols", "rules", "modularity", etc.) should be abandoned in favour of a style of theorizing which concentrates on complex interactions between patterns of excitatory and inhibitory activation distributed across many simple processing elements. As anybody interested in knowledge representation will appreciate, recent work on connectionist networks has raised a number of controversial issues concerning mental representation. In this chapter I shall briefly review some of these issues: are distributed representations fundamentally different from the traditional symbolic representations assumed in language-of-thought theories of cognition (and if so, how)? Are distributed representations adequate from a cognitive point of view? And what do connectionist systems have to say about explicit rules?

The second area I shall briefly discuss concerns so-called "implicit" or "tacit" knowledge, that is, knowledge we possess and use but which we are unable to consciously reflect upon or articulate. For example, anyone who can ride a bicycle tacitly knows many laws of dynamics and kinematics which they apply when cycling but which they are unlikely to be aware of. Similarly, any competent speaker of English tacitly knows many complex rules of syntax such as how *wh-* words (what? who?) can be moved in the construction of sentences, but unless the speaker happens to be a student of linguistics, these rules will again be unconscious and unreportable. As with connectionism, implicit knowledge has a number of important implications concerning knowledge representation.

My aim in this chapter is not to provide an extensive overview of either area (implicit knowledge is the focus of Chapter 8 by Goschke). Rather, I shall pursue the more modest goal of trying to show that they are linked in very important and fundamental ways. Each of these two topics is now the focus of substantial research efforts in cognitive psychology, but the speed with which they have become prominent means there has not yet been much reflection on the relationship between them. Research on connectionism has proceeded almost entirely independently from that on implicit knowledge, but I shall try to argue that they are inextricably linked. Each is an exciting field of enquiry in its own right, but in combination, they constitute a small revolution in the way we think about cognitive processes.

CONNECTIONISM AND KNOWLEDGE REPRESENTATION

As a starting point, let us begin by asking what types of representation there are. Most researchers would cite three rather contrasting representational formats (see Haugeland 1991). First, language, logic, and computer programs rely on what we can broadly call *symbolic* representations. The key attribute of these is that elementary symbols can be combined according to certain syntactic rules to create sentences whose meaning is a direct function of the symbols and the way they are combined. In contrast, images, pictures, maps, and other objects represent the world *iconically*. Such representations are characterized by the property that some aspect of the internal structure of the representation mirrors directly an aspect of the represented object. Finally, in most connectionist networks information is represented in a *distributed* fashion. It is the latter that is our concern here.

I shall not provide here a detailed description of the behaviour of any specific connectionist systems (see Bechtel & Abrahamsen 1991, or Quinlan 1991, for an introduction) but will instead just give a rough outline of how such systems operate. The key idea is that a network consists of very many elementary units or nodes each of which can take on a certain level of activation. The units receive inputs from the outside world and from other units and provide outputs to the world. Usually, the activation level of a unit is some non-linear function of the sum of all its inputs. The activation a of one unit affects that of another via a modifiable or weighted connection between them: if the weight is w, then the receiving unit typically receives an input of magnitude $a.w$ from the sending unit which adds to the input it receives from all other units transmitting to it.

The units in the network receive inputs and transmit outgoing signals to other units. In many networks, the pattern of connectivity is entirely unidirectional so that the output of a unit never gets to influence its own input. In this case, a single pass through the network is sufficient to allow an output pattern to be generated from the input pattern provided. In contrast, networks in which there are feedback loops between the units may take many "cycles" to reach a stable output, because the activation of a particular unit affects that of others to which it is connected, which in turn alters the signals they send to the original unit, which changes its activation, and so on.

The weights on the connected links can be modified in response to a training regime imposed on the network. A learning rule such as the "backpropagation" algorithm (Rumelhart et al. 1986) adjusts the weights in the network such that with sufficient exposure to the input patterns, correct outputs are reliably produced. As a result, the weights come to represent knowledge about the statistical relations between co-occurring elements (Stone 1986), a point to which I shall return later.

An example of an application of such a system is in the domain of object classification. Humans have the ability to accurately classify millions of objects such as cups, dogs, cars, trees, faces, and so on, and we acquire this ability via prolonged instruction. As is the case with children, connectionist networks can be trained to classify objects (e.g. Knapp & Anderson 1984). A description of the object is presented to one set of units in a network, and activation spreads to a set of output units that correspond to the possible categories. An external teacher provides information about the correct category of each object, effectively telling the network "this is a face" or "this is a cup". Eventually, the network learns which object features tend to be predictive of the different categories and is hence able to classify objects accurately, even if those objects are new. This ability to generalize knowledge to novel objects or stimuli is a crucial achievement of networks, because generalization is clearly a central aspect of the flexibility of mental representations. And as we shall see below, the key feature of generalization in distributed systems is that it depends on *similarity*: similar inputs tend to cause similar outputs.

What counts as a "representation" in a network of connected units? There are two possibilities, the pattern of unit activations at a given moment in time and the matrix of weights on the connections. The matrix of weights is fairly stable and only changes gradually with time as learning proceeds and new knowledge is acquired. Thus the weights can best be thought of as the long-term memory of the system. In contrast, the pattern of momentary activations of the units represents something more like the content of working memory, the set of representations that is evoked by the particular input pattern presented. Just as the content of working memory changes moment-by-moment as new stimuli are presented and new information is retrieved from long-term memory, so the current activations of the units change continuously as a function of new inputs and the existing weights.

What are the main characteristics of connectionist representations? Probably the key distinction, as van Gelder (1991) and others have argued, is that whereas symbols are localized representations which occupy a single element of the computing resources, connectionist representations are *distributed*. A good analogy is with holograms. A holographic image is stored on a photographic plate in such a way that if the plate is broken in half, the entire image is still recoverable (although it will be somewhat degraded in form). Hence it is not the case that different parts of the image are stored on different parts of the plate; rather, the whole image is stored to some degree at every part of the plate. Moreover, a plate can store many holograms simultaneously, each being evoked by incident light of a separate wavelength. In this case, every part of the plate stores not only every part of a given image, but also stores many different images. Van Gelder (1991) has broken the concept of distributedness into two more specific notions by distinguishing between the property of being *superposed* (many images are stored in a combined form) from the stronger property of *equipotentiality* (each part of the storage medium plays the same functional role with regard to storing images).

Let us unpack these notions of superposition and equipotentiality a bit further. Representations are superposed when they occupy the same storage resources. For instance, in vector or matrix models of memory (e.g. Eich 1982, Humphreys et al. 1989, Murdock 1982) the memory system is conceived as a high-dimensional vector or matrix. When a new memory is added to the system, it is merely blended in with the original vector (or matrix) in such a way that it can be retrieved given an appropriate retrieval cue. But the vector (or matrix) has exactly the same dimensions after the memory is added that it had before. The memory is superposed on top of all the other memories stored in the system and occupies the same representational substrate. In connectionist systems a similar means of storage is used, but in this case the mechanism consists of a large set of weighted connections between units in the network. When a new memory is added to the network, some or many weights may change but the actual representational medium (the number and connectivity of units) does not. The memory is again just superposed on top of all others. As an aside, it is important to bear in mind that just because knowledge is stored in a superposed form does not mean that it is impossible to analyze the way in which a network is solving a problem. Numerous methods exist for describing the character of superposed representations in more abstract terms (e.g. Cleeremans 1993).

What about the concept of equipotentiality? Here, the idea is that all of the parts of the representational medium are alike in their functional role with respect to storage. The left and right halves of a broken holographic plate, for example, are capable of retrieving exactly the same images. In a connectionist system, equipotentiality is seen in the following manner. Suppose we have a standard back-propagation network which has been trained to map a set of input patterns onto a set of output patterns via a large number of internal hidden units, and suppose that we then split the hidden units into two halves and remove one or other half. Although performance is likely to be very considerably poorer in the damaged than in the intact system, correct outputs will still tend to be generated. Importantly, it is unlikely to make any major difference which half of the hidden units are removed; the overall pattern of outputs for the input patterns will be largely similar. What most definitely will not happen is that removal of one half of the units leads to incorrect outputs for just some input patterns (with the remainder of the inputs leading to correct outputs) while removal of the other half leads to the opposite pattern. Of course, in some symbolic, non-distributed systems this is exactly what would happen: for example, if half of the disc on which this chapter is stored gets overwritten, then half of the chapter will be lost.

Van Gelder's (1991) analysis of the notion of what characterizes a distributed representation is an important contribution, not least because it is somewhat counter-intuitive to think of knowledge in terms of superposition and equipotentiality. In fact, van Gelder actually argues that superposition rather than equipotentiality is more central from the point of view of connectionist networks, on the grounds that no storage medium is likely to be truly equipotential when analyzed at a sufficiently microscopic level. Be that as it may, the important thing to realise from his analysis is that it underlines the radical difference between distributed and symbolic representations.

STRUCTURED REPRESENTATIONS

So much for the basic operations of connectionist systems. I now turn to the central issue for our present purposes, namely an assessment of some of the main representational issues raised by the startling successes of such models in accounting for human cognitive processes. The most significant issue concerns the fact that connectionist systems abandon the idea that thought involves symbol manipulation. Jerry Fodor (1976) and other philosophers are committed to the view that the central processor manipulates symbolic representations structured according to a language of thought. On this view, mental representations such as beliefs exhibit a property called *constituent structure*, which is to say they are decomposable via a set of syntactic rules into the primitive elements (symbols) of which they are formed. In an extremely provocative article, Fodor & Pylyshyn (1988; see also Fodor & McLaughlin 1990) presented three arguments for the constituent structure of thoughts and combined this with an argument that distributed representations typically do not manifest such structure. The first of Fodor & Pylyshyn's arguments is that we are able to entertain an infinite number of thoughts and beliefs using finite resources. This seems to require that the finite resources available (i.e. symbols) can be combined recursively, which in turn requires a set of syntactic rules of composition. The second argument for the constituent structure of thought derives from the notion of systematicity. According to Fodor & Pylyshyn, anyone who can understand the proposition JOHN LOVES MARY must be capable of understanding the proposition that MARY LOVES JOHN – the very nature of the process of understanding a proposition entails an understanding of its obvious inferential affordances. But this can only be the case if the two mental representations are made of the same parts. In other words, the symbols JOHN, LOVES, and MARY must be the same in and of themselves in the two propositions; it is merely their structure that differs.

The third argument for constituent structure concerns another aspect of inference. It is trivial for humans, say, to infer from "P & Q is true" that "P is true" (to infer from "x is an American philosopher" that "x is a philosopher"). Such inferences are abundant in our daily lives, but seem to require some coherent relationship between the two propositions. Such a relationship is immediately provided if, again, propositions have constituent structure.

These arguments make a powerful case for the constituent structure of thought. Why is this such a controversial claim? The problem is that the way knowledge is typically represented in connectionist networks does not seem to preserve the constituency of structure, and hence such systems would appear to be inadequate as models of cognition. In a nutshell, Fodor & Pylyshyn's (1988) claim is that either connectionist systems are inadequate in that they are unable to represent knowledge in the same way as the cognitive system, or else they can achieve adequacy merely by implementing symbolic systems. Fodor & Pylyshyn would probably be happy to concede that input and output modules may be accurately characterized in terms of connectionist systems, but they strongly denounced the notion that the central system is understandable in anything other than symbol-manipulating terms.

There are two different responses one can make to Fodor & Pylyshyn's provocative claims. The first is to accept them as correct, in which case it must be concluded that knowledge is represented in symbolic terms in the sort of way envisaged by language-of-thought theories of mind. This renders connectionist models largely uninteresting from a psychological point of view. Note that this is true even if it is possible to construct connectionist systems that implement symbolic systems. Although such systems (e.g. Touretzky & Hinton 1988) do manifest constituent structure, they present no interesting challenge to Fodor & Pylyshyn in that they can merely be conceived of as realizations of symbol-manipulating machinery in brain-like hardware. Nobody disputes that when one goes down to a sufficiently low level of analysis, the computations of the brain are carried out via the transmission of excitation and inhibition along weighted connections. What is at issue is whether these processes can be accurately described, from a higher level, as involving symbol manipulation.

The second response to Fodor & Pylyshyn's (1988) argument that mental representations cannot be distributed is to claim that although most connectionist systems do not manifest constituent structure in Fodor & Pylyshyn's sense, they do often manifest what we might call "weak" constituent structure. This claim can then be combined with a further view, namely that thoughts do not truly have constituent structure, and from these two ideas emerges the conclusion that distributed systems are ideal models of knowledge representation.

What does it mean to say that mental representations manifest "weak" constituent structure? Smolensky (1988; see also van Gelder 1990) has contrasted constituent structure with the notion of "micro-featural" overlap. Suppose we take a concept such as CUP WITH COFFEE, represented in some distributed fashion as the activation of a large number of units each of which codes some tiny part or micro-feature of it. What we would like is for there to be some natural relationship between this concept and the concept COFFEE. The problem, at first sight, is that the CUP WITH COFFEE representation will consist of a pattern of micro-features in some distributed representation, and although the COFFEE representation may overlap with it in terms of some of those micro-features, it will be different on many micro-features as well. Moreover, to the extent that there is overlap, it does not seem in any way to be systematic. The concept CUP WITH COFFEE may have the same overall degree of overlap or similarity with the concept COFFEE as with the concept GLASS WITH BEER, but from a constituent view it is only COFFEE that shares compositional structure with CUP WITH COFFEE. GLASS WITH BEER may be similar to CUP WITH COFFEE, but it does not share any constituent structure with it.

Smolensky's view is that, although connectionist systems may not manifest true constituent structure, they reveal enough to get by. At the same time, concepts and thoughts are not truly compositional either. In reflecting the similarity between concepts in terms of micro-feature overlap, connectionist systems manifest all of the structure that is necessary. We do not really want COFFEE to have any privileged connection with CUP WITH COFFEE over and above micro-feature overlap, because it is in fact mistaken to believe that the concept COFFEE is the same when it appears in isolation as when it appears as an element of a more complex concept. The reason for this is that mental representations are inevitably context-dependent in a way that is not naturally dealt with in the symbolic theory: the sense of JOHN in the propositions JOHN LOVES MARY and MARY LOVES JOHN are subtly different. In the same way, in a distributed representation the concept COFFEE may be subtly different when part of the concept CUP WITH COFFEE than when represented alone.

There are a variety of lines of evidence for this context-dependency view (see Goschke & Koppelberg 1990, 1991). For example, typicality judgements for members of a category are highly variable even within a given person. In one context, a category exemplar will be judged highly typical of the category while in a different context it will be judged atypical. A cow is judged highly typical of the category ANIMAL in the context of milking but not in the context of riding, whereas the converse pattern would be seen for the exemplar "horse" (Roth & Shoben 1983). Also, it appears that lexical access is sensitive to context. Tabossi (1988) presented subjects auditorily with statements such as "to follow her diet, the woman eliminated the use of butter", and presented a visual target word (FAT) at the offset of "butter." Subjects made a lexical decision to the target word. Tabossi found that reaction times were faster in such sentences–where the context primed a relevant aspect of "butter" – than in control sentences such as "to soften it, the woman heated the piece of butter", in which an inappropriate aspect (i.e. its softness) was primed. This suggests that on different occasions that a concept is activated, its internal structure or meaning can differ depending on the context. Goschke & Koppelberg (1990, 1991) review other types of evidence demonstrating that context-invariant constituency may be the exception rather than the rule.

In order for mental representations to have true constituent structure, the constituents in question must be context-free. That is, the atomic constituents of thought must bear roughly the same properties regardless of the context. In Fodor & Pylyshyn's (1988:42) words, "a lexical item must make approximately the same semantic contribution to each expression in which it occurs". If the properties of a constituent varied significantly from one context to another, then it is hard to see how it could be identified as one and the same constituent. But according to Goschke & Koppelberg, it is very hard to identify any concepts whose meaning is not context-sensitive.

The argument to this point is that mental representations may not manifest the sort of constituent structure demanded by language-of-thought theories of cognition. In a variety of ways, knowledge and thought may instead have the properties of distributed systems. But this approach treats mental representations as being of only one sort. Perhaps some representations are accurately characterized as distributed while others have internal constituent structure? Evidence from studies of implicit learning suggests that this may be the correct approach.

IMPLICIT AND EXPLICIT KNOWLEDGE

A recent study by Roberts & MacLeod (1995) shows that under some circumstances mental states do have constituent structure, but under other circumstances they do not. These authors questioned whether circumstances exist in which a conjunctive concept such as P & Q might function atomically and hence not license inference to its individual elements P and Q. Roberts & MacLeod trained their subjects to identify coloured shapes (e.g. red parallelograms) with a given concept. In the training phase of the experiment, exemplars and non-exemplars of this category were presented, the subject judged for each item whether it was a member of the target category or not, and corrective feedback was given. Then in the critical test phase, monochrome shapes were presented and the subject was asked to say whether each shape could be a member of the target category, if it was coloured appropriately. Thus to judge that a monochrome parallelogram could be a member of the category defined by red parallelograms, the subject's target concept must be decomposable into the separate elements red and parallelogram. The test evaluated the extent to which "all concept exemplars are P" could be inferred from "all concept exemplars are P & Q".

Under normal training conditions, subjects performed reasonably well in the initial training phase (making 69 per cent correct classifications by the end of that stage) and made the correct inference in the decomposition phase on 78 per cent of trials. Thus to a good degree, the concept P & Q tended to allow one of its elements, P, to be inferred. A second group of subjects, however, had to perform a taxing digit-memory task during the training phase (but not during the decomposition test). This attention-demanding task meant that subjects were unlikely to be able to form and test hypotheses about the target concept as easily as subjects in the normal training group. To compensate for this, more trials were given in the training phase for dual-task subjects, and this ensured that performance at the end of the classification phase (68 per cent) was about the same as in the normal training group. Despite this, dual-task subjects were significantly worse at making correct decompositional judgements (62 per cent correct). Thus although training under dual-task conditions had not rendered subjects any less able to apply the concept P & Q, it did make them poorer at inferring P and Q. Roberts & MacLeod's (1995) data therefore suggest that – contrary to Fodor & Pylyshyn's assertion – mental representations need not always have constituent structure.

Distributed knowledge has much more of a procedural than of a declarative flavour. It follows from this that if the procedural/declarative dichotomy captures an important distinction at the level of mental representations, then distributed systems may turn out to be perfectly suited to describing procedural knowledge, but there may be other representations (i.e. declarative ones) which are not distributed. So to the extent that knowledge really can be represented in declarative or rule-like form, connectionist systems might seem to be inadequate. In this section I shall briefly review some further evidence for a distinction between procedural (implicit) and declarative (explicit) knowledge (a fuller review is provided in Goschke's chapter). I shall concentrate on evidence from a single experimental task, artificial grammar learning. Evidence from other fields for the distinction between a rule-based and a similarity-based process has been reviewed by Herrnstein (1990), Nosofsky et al. (1994), Regehr & Brooks (1993), Shanks & St. John (1994), and Sloman (1996).

In a typical experiment, subjects are presented in the acquisition phase with strings of letters generated from a simple finite-state grammar such as that shown in Figure 6.1, originally created by Brooks & Vokey (1991). The grammar is entered at the left and links are traversed until the grammar is exited at the right-hand side, and as a

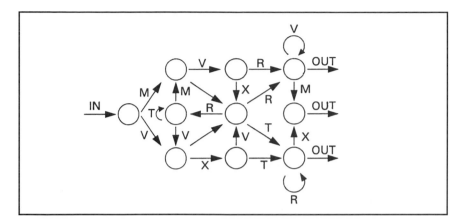

FIG. 6.1:   The artificial grammar used by Brooks & Vokey (1991) to generate letter strings.

link is traversed a letter is picked up and added to the string. In this way, strings such as MVRVM and VXVRMVXR can be generated from the grammar shown in Figure 6.1. The grammar specifies certain constraints that exist in the order of string elements, much as exist in natural languages. For instance, strings can only begin with M or V. Subjects are shown a series of "grammatical" training strings, but are not told about the rules of the grammar: usually, they are asked simply to memorize the strings for some later memory test. At the end of the learning stage, subjects are informed of the existence of a set of rules governing the structure of the training items and are then presented with a set of test items all of which are novel; some however are grammatical and others ungrammatical (i.e. they cannot be generated from the grammar). The subject's task is to discriminate the grammatical from the ungrammatical items.

A large number of studies have shown that subjects can perform at levels significantly above chance, despite having been given minimal exposure to the study items and despite having received no instructions during the study phase regarding the later test. Typically, about 60–70 per cent of test items are correctly classified.

In recent years a number of adaptations of the basic artificial grammar learning (AGL) task have been explored which seem to provide evidence for two rather distinct modes of learning which can be broadly labelled "implicit" and "explicit". I shall focus on the "explicit" account of artificial grammar learning later, but for present purposes it suffices to think of an explicit system as one which in a deep sense acquires knowledge about the rules of the grammar. Such a system would be uninterested in whether a novel test string happens to be similar to one of the training strings: instead, it would simply determine whether the test string can be created from the rules of the grammar.

In contrast, the "implicit" account proposes that what subjects learn when exposed to study items in an AGL experiment is simply the frequency statistics of the surface elements (i.e. the letters) from which the strings are constructed. These statistics could cover anything from simple knowledge of which letters occur at the beginning or end of strings to more sophisticated knowledge of the legal string positions of different n-grams (string fragments of length n). In the former case, the subject might simply learn that strings only ever commence with M or V, and on this basis reject novel test items beginning with other letters; in the latter case, the subject might in addition know which bigrams, trigrams, etc. are permissible and where in the string they can occur. When presented with a new test string to classify, an implicit system would determine whether the string possesses a high proportion of the surface elements which it has learned are characteristic of grammatical strings. Clearly, performance very much better than chance can be achieved simply by learning something of the statistical distribution of the surface elements from which the training strings are constructed. The critical point is that this sort of learning is exactly what would be expected from a connectionist system forming a distributed representation of the structure of the grammar. As we saw previously, a weight between two nodes in a connectionist system is a reflection of the statistical relationship between the features coded by the units. Consistent with this, connectionist models have been quite successful at accounting for human performance in these experiments (e.g. Dienes 1992).

What is the evidence favouring this implicit learning process? A number of studies have provided support which I shall briefly review. First, and most straightforwardly, Reber & Allen (1978) asked subjects to retrospectively describe their learning experience and concurrently to justify their grammaticality judgements. While subjects reported using a variety of types of information in making their grammaticality judgements, the violation or non-violation of expected bigrams was the most common justification, especially concerning the initial and terminal bigrams of a string. Violations of expectations about single letters, particularly the first or last letter of a string, and about trigram or longer sequences were also reported. Thus subjects plainly know a considerable amount about the frequency statistics of different n-grams in the training strings.

Perruchet & Pacteau (1990, Experiment 3) asked their subjects in the training phase to memorize strings generated from a grammar and then gave them a recognition test on letter pairs either present or absent in the training strings. Subjects performed quite well: only three out of 25 old pairs were judged less familiar than any new pair and the correlation between recognition scores and the frequency of occurrence of pairs in the training strings was 0.61. By the results of this test, then, subjects were aware of the relative frequencies of letter pairs.

In another experiment, Perruchet & Pacteau (1990, Experiment 2) took a rather different approach. They constructed test strings that either contained illegal orders of legal bigrams or contained illegal bigrams. If subjects only had information about legal bigrams on which to judge the grammaticality of test strings, then strings containing illegal bigrams should have been rejected, but strings comprising legal bigrams in an illegal order should have been mistakenly accepted as grammatical. In accordance with this pattern, Perruchet & Pacteau found that items containing illegal bigrams were much more likely to be rejected than ones containing legal bigrams in illegal orders. Perruchet & Pacteau then constructed a model that used bigram frequency information to make grammaticality judgements. The model produced the same level of performance as subjects, except in one particular: subjects were sensitive to the beginnings and endings of strings, but the model was not.

Finally, Perruchet & Pacteau (1990, Experiment 1) trained one group of subjects in the normal way on strings generated from the grammar but trained another group on just the letter pairs comprising those strings. When subsequently required to discriminate grammatical and ungrammatical strings, the performance of the two groups was indistinguishable so long as test items containing an illegal initial letter were dropped from the analysis. Subjects trained on the letter pairs would have had no opportunity to learn which initial letters were permissible, so this procedure is not unreasonable. Perruchet & Pacteau concluded that subjects primarily knew letter pairs, but also had some positional information, namely of which pairs could legally start and end strings.

Probably the most convincing evidence for the operation of an implicit, similarity-based mechanism comes from a recent study by Meulemans & van der Linden (1997, Experiment 2a). These authors arranged for grammatical and ungrammatical test strings to be equated in terms of the frequency distribution of bigrams and trigrams. Thus, subjects were unable to decide the true grammatical status of a test string simply by seeing whether it contained a high or low proportion of the bigrams and trigrams that had occurred in the study strings. Under these conditions, subjects were unable to discriminate grammatical and ungrammatical strings: whatever learning process was being applied, it was incapable of learning the true rules of the grammar. Instead, and in accordance with a similarity-based mechanism, subjects tended to call a string "grammatical" if it contained a high proportion of the bigrams and trigrams present in the training strings, regardless of whether it was truly grammatical or not.

So much for the evidence for the operation of an implicit system in artificial grammar learning. What sort of evidence is there that under other conditions people can learn about explicit rules? The important feature of the studies mentioned above is that learning proceeded under incidental conditions in which during the acquisition stage subjects had no reason to try to work out the rules of the grammar. But when the nature of the learning stage is changed, genuine rule learning becomes possible. As an example, Shanks et al. (1997) created strings conforming to a rather different set of rules. Specifically, we used a biconditional grammar based on strings of six consonants (D, F, G, K, L and X) which were arranged in two sets of four letters separated by a dot, e.g. DFGK. FDLX. There were three biconditional rules linking letters in positions 1 and 5, 2 and 6, 3 and 7, and 4 and 8, such that where there was a D in one linked position there should be an F in the paired position (i.e. D↔F), G was paired with L (G↔L), and K was paired with X (K↔X). Like Meulemans & van der Linden (1997), we arranged that grammatical and ungrammatical test items could not be distinguished on the basis of their overlap with the training strings in terms of bigrams or trigrams (or indeed any other n-gram). Apart from the type of grammar we used, the other major change was that we trained subjects in the learning phase to work out the rules of the grammar. Specifically, subjects were told that strings were formed according to a set of rules and were shown flawed examples of grammatical strings. They had to indicate which letters they thought created violations of the grammar, and were then given feedback about their accuracy. Strings contained between one and four incorrect letters and subjects adopted a hypothesis-testing strategy to determine the underlying rules used to generate grammatical strings.

Under these conditions we found that at least some subjects were able to work out the rules of the biconditional grammar such that at test they made nearly 100% correct grammaticality decisions. The implication is that they formed a mental representation in the form of a symbolic rule and applied this to the test items. A connectionist system creating a distributed representation of the frequency statistics of the training items would have no means of making correct decisions in the test stage. Hence a plausible hypothesis is that humans possess two learning systems capable of creating distinct forms of mental representation. One system is effectively a symbolic rule mechanism of the sort advocated by Fodor and

Pylyshyn (1988), while the other is a connectionist mechanism that creates distributed representations.

CONCLUSION

Distributed representations have a number of properties that distinguish them from symbolic ones. First and foremost, they do not have internal structure – a distributed representation cannot be decomposed into simpler atomic representations concatenated via syntactic rules. Secondly, connectionist systems tend to respond on a "similar inputs cause similar outputs" basis. From the point of view of human knowledge representation, both of these properties are significant. We have seen that Fodor & Pylyshyn (1988) made a strong argument against distributed representations on the grounds that thoughts do have internal structure, but this view is challenged by the results of psychological experiments demonstrating the context dependency of concepts. This context dependency means that it is quite difficult to find atomic concepts whose properties are identical regardless of how they are combined with other concepts.

Moreover, implicit learning experiments provide a good deal of support for the notion that the application of knowledge depends fundamentally on similarity (see Goldstone 1994, for a fuller evaluation of this view). People seem to learn about complex domains by accumulating information about the frequency statistics of the stimuli they encounter, and respond to new events on the basis of their featural overlap with stored representations. This is exactly what one sees in connectionist systems in which the weights on connections between units reflect the degree of statistical relatedness of the elements represented by the units. The "similar inputs cause similar outputs" rule characterizes aspects of the behaviour of both humans and connectionist networks.

These experiments, however also suggest that under some circumstances learning is governed by a rather different, explicit, mechanism. The key (and perhaps unsurprising) finding is that people can in appropriate conditions learn about abstract structure in a way that is not captured by simple frequency statistics. In this case it does seem as if a symbolic, rule-based system is applied. Hence there may be room in a complete theory of the cognitive system for both distributed and symbolic representations. Of course, if this view of mental representation is correct, then it becomes important to specify how the symbolic and distributed systems interact. As yet, little can be said about this, but I shall briefly mention two possibilities representing opposite ends of the spectrum. One view would be that the systems are essentially independent, each operating on its inputs and generating outputs, and without any direct communication between them until the response selection stage, at which point one system "wins". On this view the systems are modules that are informationally encapsulated from each other. The cognitive architecture proposed by Hayes & Broadbent (1988) seems accurately characterized in this way, and "dual-route" models have also been proposed to deal with certain phenomena in language acquisition (e.g. Coltheart et al. 1993).

On the other hand, the two systems may have a much more intimate, non-modular relationship. For instance, it may be the case that the distributed system acts to identify those regularities in the world which the rule system can then reason about. A number of so-called "hybrid systems" in which a connectionist system passes information to a symbolic one typify this view of the cognitive system. A good example is provided by Lamberts' (1990) model of how people solve physics problems. In this model, the distributed system is capable of solving simple problems by itself, but when a problem proves too difficult it assists the symbolic system by providing it with memories of previously-encountered problems. The synergistic relationship between the systems means that problems can be solved which the systems in isolation would be unable to deal with. Plainly, it remains an important goal for future research to describe in more detail the way in which distinct distributed and symbolic representational systems might interact.

REFERENCES

Bechtel, W. & A. Abrahamsen 1991. *Connectionism and the mind: an introduction to parallel processing in networks*. Oxford: Blackwell.

Brooks, L. R. & J. R. Vokey 1991. Abstract analogies and abstracted grammars: comments on Reber (1989) and Mathews et al. (1989). *Journal of Experimental Psychology: General* **120**, 316–23.

Cleeremans, A. 1993. *Mechanisms of implicit learning*. Cambridge, Mass.: MIT Press.

Coltheart, M., B. Curtis, P. Atkins, M. Haller 1993. Models of reading aloud: dual-route and parallel-distributed-processing approaches. *Psychological Review* **100**, 589–608.

Dienes, Z. 1992. Connectionist and memory-array models of artificial grammar learning. *Cognitive Science* **16**, 41–79.

Eich, J. M. 1982. A composite holographic associative recall model. *Psychological Review* **89**, 627–61.

Fodor, J. A. 1976. *The language of thought*. Brighton: Harvester.

Fodor, J. A. & B. P. McLaughlin 1990. Connectionism and the problem of systematicity: why Smolensky's solution doesn't work. *Cognition* **35**, 183–204.

Fodor, J. A. & Z. W. Pylyshyn 1988. Connectionism and cognitive architecture: a critical analysis. *Cognition* **28**, 3–71.

Goldstone, R. L. 1994. The role of similarity in categorization: providing a groundwork. *Cognition* **52**, 125–57.

Goschke, T. & D. Koppelberg 1990. Connectionist representation, semantic compositionality, and the instability of concept structure. *Psychological Research* **52**, 253–70.

Goschke, T. & D. Koppelberg 1991. The concept of representation and the representation of concepts in connectionist models. In *Philosophy and connectionist theory*, W. Ramsey, S. P. Stich, D. E. Rumelhart (eds), 129–61. Hillsdale, New Jersey: Erlbaum.

Haugeland, J. 1991. Representational genera. In *Philosophy and connectionist theory*, W. Ramsey, S. P. Stich, D. E. Rumelhart (eds), 61–89. Hillsdale, New Jersey: Erlbaum.

Hayes, N. A. & D. E. Broadbent 1988. Two modes of learning for interactive tasks. *Cognition* **28**, 249–76.

Herrnstein, R. J. 1990. Levels of stimulus control: a functional approach. *Cognition* **37**, 133–66.

Humphreys, M. S., J. D. Bain, R. Pike 1989. Different ways to cue a coherent memory system: a theory for episodic, semantic, and procedural tasks. *Psychological Review* **96**, 208–33.

Knapp, A. G. & J. A. Anderson 1984. Theory of categorization based on distributed memory storage. *Journal of Experimental Psychology: Learning, Memory, and Cognition* **10**, 616–37.

Lamberts, K. 1990. A hybrid model of learning to solve physics problems. *European Journal of Cognitive Psychology* **2**, 151–70.

Meulemans, T. & M. van der Linden, 1997. The associative chunk strength in artificial grammar learning. *Journal of Experimental Psychology: Learning, Memory, and Cognition*, **23**.

Murdock, B. B. 1982. A theory for the storage and retrieval of item and associative information. *Psychological Review* **89**, 609–26.

Nosofsky, R. M., T. J. Palmeri, S. C. McKinley 1994. Rule-plus-exception model of classification learning. *Psychological Review* **101**, 53–79.

Perruchet, P. & C. Pacteau 1990. Synthetic grammar learning: implicit rule abstraction or explicit fragmentary knowledge? *Journal of Experimental Psychology: General* **119**, 264–75.

Quinlan, P. T. 1991. *Connectionism and psychology: a psychological perspective on new connectionist research*. Hemel Hempstead, England: Harvester Wheatsheaf.

Reber, A. S. & R. Allen 1978. Analogic and abstraction strategies in synthetic grammar learning: A functionalist interpretation. *Cognition* **6**, 189–221.

Regehr, G. & L. R. Brooks 1993. Perceptual manifestations of an analytic structure: the priority of holistic individuation. *Journal of Experimental Psychology: General* **122**, 92–114.

Roberts, P. L. & C. MacLeod 1995. Representational consequences of two modes of learning. *Quarterly Journal of Experimental Psychology* **48A**, 296–319.

Roth, E. M. & E. J. Shoben 1983. The effect of context on the structure of categories. *Cognitive Psychology* **15**, 346–78.

Rumelhart, D. E., G. E. Hinton, R. J. Williams 1986. Learning internal representations by error propagation. In *Parallel distributed processing: explorations in the microstructure of cognition*, vol. 1: *foundations*, D. E. Rumelhart, J. L. McClelland, and the PDP Research Group (eds), 318–62. Cambridge, Mass.: MIT Press.

Shanks, D. R., T. Johnstone, L. Staggs 1997. Abstraction processes in artificial grammar learning. *Quarterly Journal of Experimental Psychology*, **50A**, 216–252.

Shanks, D. R. & M. F. St. John 1994. Characteristics of dissociable human learning systems. *Behavioural and Brain Sciences* **17**, 367–447.

Sloman, S. A. 1996. The empirical case for two systems of reasoning. *Psychological Bulletin* **119**, 3–22.

Smolensky, P. 1988. On the proper treatment of connectionism. *Behavioural and Brain Sciences* **11**, 1–74.

Stone, G. O. 1986. An analysis of the delta rule and the learning of statistical associations. In *Parallel distributed processing explorations in the microstructure of cognition*, Vol. 1: foundations. D. E. Rumelhart, J. L. McClelland and The PDP Research Group (eds), 444–59. Cambridge, Mass.: MIT Press.

Tabossi, P. 1988. Effects of context on the immediate interpretation of unambiguous nouns. *Journal of Experimental Psychology: Learning, Memory, and Cognition* **14**, 153–62.

Touretzky, D. S. & G. E. Hinton 1988. A distributed connectionist production system. *Cognitive Science* **12**, 423–66.

van Gelder, T. 1990. Compositionality: a connectionist variation on a classical theme. *Cognitive Science* **14**, 355–84.

van Gelder, T. 1991. What is the "d" in "pdp"? A survey of the concept of distribution. In *Philosophy and connectionist theory*, W. Ramsey, S. P. Stich, D. E. Rumelhart (eds), 33–59. Hillsdale, New Jersey: Erlbaum.

NOTE

1.   The writing of this chapter was supported in part by grants from the Biotechnology and Biological Sciences Research Council and the Economic and Social Research Council.

CHAPTER SEVEN

Declarative and Nondeclarative Knowledge:
Insights From Cognitive Neuroscience

Barbara Knowlton

INTRODUCTION

In the past twenty years, cognitive neuroscience has emerged as a discipline in its own right (see Gazzaniga 1995). This area has witnessed technological advances such as functional brain imaging, sensitive electrophysiological measurement of evoked potentials, and the rigorous study of patients with neuropsychological deficits. In the past, the field of cognitive psychology has remained somewhat insulated from findings in systems-level neuroscience. Neuroscientific studies using animal models could provide insight into basic psychological mechanisms but could not be readily applied to questions about topics like language and consciousness. Researchers in cognitive psychology have concentrated on the analysis of behaviour to study the mind, and without doubt, this approach continues to be extremely important in that the workings of the mind are still far from being understood. However, precisely because of the difficulty of the questions in cognitive psychology, it makes sense to draw information from all available sources, including information about human brain function. Cognitive neuroscience can provide important constraints on psychological models.

Historically, a danger in integrating psychology and neuroscience is the fact that these different levels of analysis may produce models that do not map on to each other directly. For example, a psychological construct like working memory does not necessarily correspond to a particular brain structure. However, keeping in mind the fact that the mapping between different levels of analysis might be fairly indirect, this caveat should not preclude an earnest attempt at employing findings from cognitive neuroscience to inform theories of cognitve structure. In this chapter I will describe how our rapidly increasing understanding of human brain function is currently shaping theories of the organization of knowledge systems.

THE RELATIONSHIP BETWEEN KNOWLEDGE AND MEMORY

The concepts of knowledge systems and memory systems are closely linked. Knowledge is acquired through learning and is assessed through memory performance. The proposal of a knowledge system does not necessarily require that there is a corresponding learning or memory system. For example, a single acquisition system could store information in a number of distinct knowledge systems, and a single retrieval system could access information from a number of different knowledge systems. However, knowledge of brain organization does induce one to view the process of acquisition and retrieval as linked to a particular knowledge system. If a knowledge system maps on to a brain system, corresponding acquisition and retrieval systems would arise from brain circuitry integrating the knowledge system with sensory input and behavioural output structures. Thus, if we assume that knowledge systems are based on distinct brain systems, and there is specificity as to the inputs and outputs of these brain systems, then it follows that acquisition and retrieval processes should be thought of as specific to particular knowledge systems. Thus, based on a brain systems approach, it seems most natural to consider memory and knowledge systems as linked.

DECLARATIVE AND NONDECLARATIVE KNOWLEDGE

In this chapter, I will focus on evidence for the idea that knowledge is stored in a declarative system, or in one of multiple nondeclarative knowledge systems. The term *declarative knowledge* was first used in cognitive psychology in the 1970s, and refers to the fact that some knowledge can be "declared", and is thus accessible to conscious awareness (Anderson 1976). In the study of artificial intelligence "declarative" refers to information stored as a set of facts, rather than emerging from the execution of a procedure (Winograd 1972, 1975). It had been a topic of controversy as to whether knowledge was represented in a declarative or procedural form. However, it became clear that it was impossible to strictly distinguish between the two types of knowledge based on their representations alone. More recently, the term "declarative knowledge" has become identified with a brain systems perspective (Cohen & Squire 1980, Squire 1982) and has become identified with the type of knowledge that is acquired poorly in amnesia. Global amnesia results after damage to circumscribed brain areas, including the hippocampus and associated regions (Mayes 1988, Squire 1986). Patients with damage in these regions exhibit a severe deficit in the conscious recollection of information about facts and events. These memories are declarative in that subjects can consciously "declare" the contents of these memories. Figure 7.1 gives an example of the performance of an amnesic patient on a declarative memory test. Declarative memories are what we typically think of when we think about memory: one retrieves declarative knowledge when one remembers a fact that was learned yesterday, or remembers what one had for breakfast this morning, or the experience of visiting a friend last week. The deficits in conscious recollection are exhibited by amnesic patients as both impaired recognition and recall of information. As I will discuss later, there are a collection of memory abilities that are spared in amnesia, and the knowledge retrieved in these cases is not necessarily accessible to awareness, and is thus "nondeclarative". The distiction between declarative and nondeclarative knowledge maps on to the explicit/implicit distinction quite well (Roediger 1990, Schacter 1987, Schacter et al. 1993). Both dichotomies are based on differences in awareness of knowledge. Subjects are aware that they have learned explicit knowledge and unaware that they have acquired implicit knowledge. Implicit knowledge has also been more broadly defined as knowledge that one has without awareness of the source of this knowledge (e.g. semantic knowledge). More typically, though, it is identified with nondeclarative knowledge. In the case of semantic knowledge, one might be aware that one has learned something although unaware of the circumstances of that learning. The term "nondeclarative" has an the advantage over the term "implicit" in that it makes clear the idea that this knowledge is defined negatively, by the fact that it does not depend on conscious awareness, rather than by positive criteria. As such, nondeclarative knowledge does not refer to a single system, but rather multiple implicit knowledge systems that may have different properties (see Squire et al. 1993).

In human subjects one can a priori define the knowledge acquired in a task as either declarative or nondeclarative, depending on whether subjects are aware of what is being learned. In an attempt to link studies of human subjects and experimental animals, the term "declarative" has been applied to tasks that are failed by animals with lesions to the

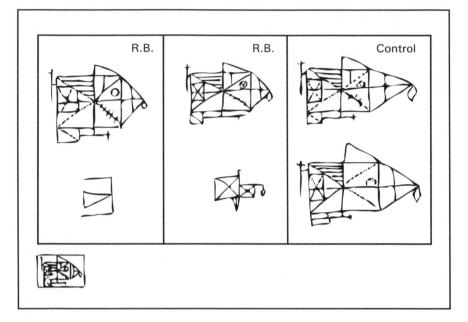

FIG. 7.1.   The left-most panel shows the performance of an amnesic patient (R.B.) when copying a complex figure (above) and when attempting to reproduce it from memory 12 minutes later (below) six months after the onset of his amnesia. The centre panel shows his performance 23 months after the onset of amnesia, and the right-most panel shows the performance of a control subject at copying and reproducing the figure from memory. From Zola-Morgan et al. 1986.

hippocampal region (Kim et al. 1995, Squire & Zola-Morgan 1991, Wiig & Bilkey 1994). However, describing memory abilities in animals as declarative is problematic in that it is impossible to define "declarative" in nonverbal organisms that cannot "declare". Thus, the use of the term "declarative" is circular when applied to research with experimental animals.

Despite the fact that for humans subjects, tasks can be defined as declarative or nondeclarative a priori, it is still often difficult to do so. For example, subjects' verbal report may underestimate the knowledge acquired in a particular task. Subjects may be aware of what they have learned, but they may not be able to put it into words. Also, in some tasks, it is a matter of speculation as to what information is actually being learned. For example, in some tasks, subjects could acquire knowledge of a set of complex rules to solve the task. If subjects were unable to describe these rules, an experimenter might conclude that they had acquired nondeclarative knowledge of these rules. However, perhaps subjects are solving the task based on a simple heuristic that results in good performance. Subjects might be able to verbalize this heuristic, but the experimenter might not consider this knowledge as relevant to task performance. Shanks & St. John (1994) have stressed that it is critical that awareness must be assessed for the actual information subjects are employing to perform the task in order to determine if performance is based on nondeclarative knowledge.

DECLARATIVE KNOWLEDGE AND AMNESIA

Partly because the a priori analyses of the information learned in different tasks are often ambiguous, the dissociations found in studies of neuropsychological data are particularly useful in classifying knowledge systems. Certainly, analyzing neuropsychological dissociations alone is inadequate because it does not provide any insight into the functional characteristics of knowledge systems. However, in cases in which the behavioural data from normal subjects are ambiguous, the performance of patient groups can help to segregate tasks. For instance, suppose that amnesic patients exhibit normal acquisition on a task in which it is unclear whether the acquired knowledge is declarative. This would suggest that this task is similar to other nondeclarative tasks performed normally by amnesic patients, and thus would strongly suggest that the task also does not depend on the acquisition of declarative knowledge.

As mentioned earlier, amnesia results from damage to structures in the medial temporal lobe, including the hippocampus, or diencephalic brain structures including the anterior and dorsomedial nuclei of the thalamus (Mair et al. 1979, Parkin 1984, Squire 1986, Victor et al. 1971). The best-studied amnesic patient (H.M.) had most of the medial temporal lobes removed in order to treat epilepsy that was intractable to other treatments. After surgery, it became apparent that patient H. M. exhibited a severe memory impairment. He was unable to remember events that happened only a short time previously, and he needed to be re-introduced to people each time they met (Corkin 1984, Scoville & Milner 1957). For the most part, this deficit was for the acquisition of new information. Information that he had learned prior to the surgery (retrograde memory) was relatively intact, especially remote memories from childhood (Marslen-Wilson & Teuber 1975).

NONDECLARATIVE SKILL LEARNING

Despite the profound learning deficit in acquiring declarative knowledge, patient H.M. was shown to be capable of some kinds of learning. He improved on successive trials of a motor skill task, rotor pursuit learning (Corkin 1968). In this task, subjects must keep a hand-held stylus in contact with a rotating disk. Patient H.M. did not remember the experience of practising the task despite his improvement across trials. He also showed learning in a perceptuo-motor mirror-tracing task in which he observed his hand tracing a figure in the reflection of a mirror (Milner 1962). Again, patient H.M. did not recollect having experience with the apparatus. Other amnesic patients exhibit similar dissociations between motor skill learning and memory for training episodes. These data were some of the earliest indications that amnesia might be specific for declarative memory, yet would spare the learning of motor skills in which the actual information learned is not necessarily available to consciousness. It has been shown subsequently that other amnesic patients exhibit normal or fairly normal learning in perceptual-motor tasks (Brooks & Baddeley 1976, Cermack et al. 1973, Cohen & Squire 1980, Tranel et al. 1994). Figure 7.2 shows normal performance in a perceptual skill learning task by a group of amnesic patients. Intuitively, awareness of what is being learned does not seem necessary for motor skill learning to occur. As one learns to ride a bicycle, for example, one might not be aware of the changes in one's actual body position as performance improvement occurs. The knowledge pertaining to skill performance, or "knowing how" has been described as procedural knowledge (Anderson 1976, Cohen & Squire 1980). Procedural knowledge, such as knowledge of how to perform particular skills, is one type of nondeclarative knowledge. When the term "declarative" was first used, all knowledge that was not declarative was considered procedural. However, because as we shall see there are many differences and dissociations that can be produced within nondeclarative memory, it seems that such a dichotomy falls short. There are some nondeclarative memory abilities (such as priming, see below) that are not easily described as procedural.

DISSOCIATIONS IN SKILL LEARNING

As discussed earlier, the knowledge that is acquired during skill learning is nondeclarative and is acquired normally by amnesic patients, who nevertheless have impaired memory for specific training episodes. There is also evidence for a double dissociation between skill learning and declarative memory. Patients with Huntington's disease or Parkinson's disease exhibit deficits in acquiring perceptual and motor skills, such as rotor-pursuit learning and learning to read mirror reversed text, although their declarative memory is

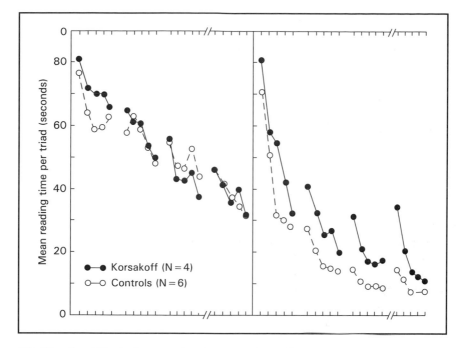

FIG. 7.2.   Acquisition by four amnesic patients with Korsakoff's disease and six control subjects of a mirror-reversed reading skill. The x-axis indicates performance on five trials in three daily sessions, followed by a final session three months later. From Cohen & Squire, 1980.

not as poor as that of amnesic patients (Harrington et al. 1990, Heindel et al. 1988, Martone et al. 1984, O'Brien et al. 1995; although see Jordan & Sagar 1994 for a demonstration of normal motor skill learning by patients with Parkinson's disease). These patients have damage to a part of the brain called the basal ganglia. One difficulty with measuring perceptuo-motor skill learning in these patients is that they exhibit motor problems that lead to a different baseline level of performance in many of these tasks. Thus, these subjects perform worse than control subjects at the beginning of training, making comparisons of improvement somewhat difficult to interpret. Nevertheless, it does appear that the acquisition of nondeclarative knowledge in the form of motor programs is impaired in these patients. In patients with Huntington's disease, the cognitive deficits are not specific to perceptuo-motor skill learning. Among other deficits, these patients exhibit impaired declarative memory, although the deficits are typically not as severe as those seen in the patients with amnesia that have been studied (Josiassen et al. 1983). Patients with Parkinson's disease generally do not exhibit

profound declarative memory deficits, so they provide a better dissociation between the acquisition of skills and the acquisition of declarative knowledge.

PRIMING

Amnesic patients have also been shown to exhibit preserved learning
abilities in non-motor tasks. This has been studied most extensively in
the domain of priming. In a number of priming paradigms, the prior
presentation of a stimulus results in that stimulus being processed more
rapidly and accurately when it is subseqently presented (Schacter et al.
1993, Shimamura 1986, Richardson-Klavehn & Bjork 1988). In other
paradigms, priming is demonstrated by the increased probability that
a partial stimulus can elicit a previously presented stimulus. Priming
can be shown using a variety of different stimuli. One kind of priming,
perceptual priming, refers to priming based on the surface features of
the stimulus (see Schacter 1994). One example of a perceptual priming
task is word-stem completion. In this task, subjects are presented with
a set of words, and then sometime later asked to complete a set of three-
letter word stems (such as MOT. . .) with the first word that comes to
mind. Subjects exhibit a tendency to complete these stems with the
previously presented words. For instance, if the word "motel" had been
on the list, then subjects who had seen the list of words would be more
likely to complete MOT. . . with "motel" than subjects who had not been
presented with the word list. In a sense, the words on the list had become
"primed" and thus more available to come to mind in the completion
task. Amnesic patients exhibit this priming effect to the same degree
as subjects without brain damage (Graf et al. 1984; see Warrington &
Weiskrantz 1974, for an early interpretation of this effect). Figure 7.3
shows an example of normal priming by amnesic patients.

Normal perceptual priming in amnesic patients can also be
demonstrated using the perceptual identification paradigm (Cermak et
al. 1985, Haist et al. 1991, Hamann et al. 1995). In this paradigm,
subjects are presented with a list of words and then later asked to
identify words that are flashed briefly on a computer screen. Subjects
are able to identify the previously presented words with greater accuracy
than words that had not been presented previously.

Perceptual priming can also be demonstrated for non-verbal
materials. The objects depicted in line drawings that were presented
previously can be named more quickly than objects in new line drawings.
Both amnesic patients and normal subjects exhibit this effect (Cave &
Squire 1992, Mitchell & Brown 1988).

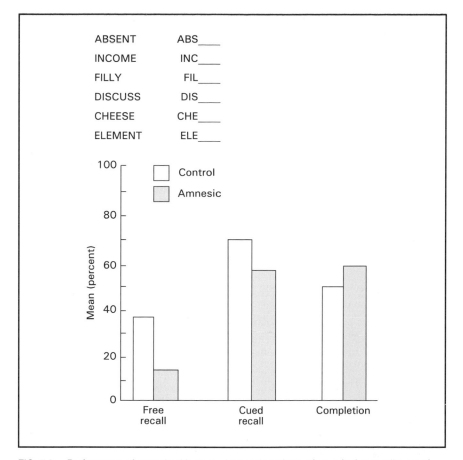

FIG. 7.3.   Performance of control subjects and amnesic patients when asked to recall a set of study words (free recall), when asked to recall study words using 3-letter stems as cues (cued recall), and on a priming measure in which subjects were asked to complete word stems with the first word that comes to mind without reference to the study items (completion). From Graf et al. 1984.

In all of these tasks, priming is considered to be perceptually based because changes in the surface features of the stimuli between the presentation phase and the test phase will decrease the amount of priming. For example, if a set of words are presented in one font, and then word stems are presented in a different font, there will be less priming than if the same font was used at study and test (Graf & Ryan 1990, Jacoby & Hayman 1987, Roediger & Blaxton 1987). Also, presenting a different picture of an object at study and test will decrease priming for that object picture (Biederman & Cooper 1991,

Cave & Squire 1992). An early view of perceptual priming was that it resulted because the presentation of a stimulus activated a pre-existing representation of the stimulus, and this activation would allow the stimulus to be processed more fluently when it was subsequently seen (Diamond & Rozin 1984). However, it has been shown more recently that priming can occur when novel materials are presented a second time, such as random line patterns or non-words, which subjects would not be expected to have experienced before (Gabrieli et al. 1990, Haist et al. 1991, Musen & Treisman 1990; Figure 7.4). In other studies, amnesic patients and normal subjects read a novel prose passage more rapidly after pre-exposure to this particular passage (Musen et al. 1990), and read lists of novel non-words more rapidly after pre-exposure (Musen & Squire 1991). It seems that priming can occur for newly-created representations, not just pre-existing ones. Importantly, amnesic patients can exhibit normal priming for novel and familiar materials, suggesting that both types of priming are independent of declarative knowledge.

PRIMING AND BRAIN IMAGING

The results of brain imaging studies are consistent with the idea that pre-exposed stimuli are processed more fluently than stimuli that had not been recently pre-exposed. Brain activity during priming has been measured using the positron emission tomography (PET) technique. PET

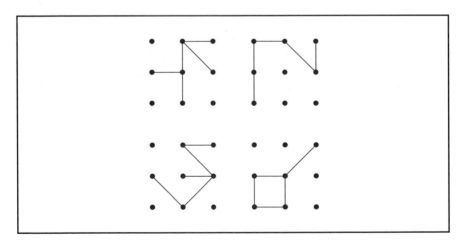

FIG. 7.4.   Examples of study items used to demonstrate priming for novel information. Subjects were able to reproduce such patterns more accurately when they had been presented previously. From Musen & Triesman, 1990.

measures the amount of blood flow to different regions of the brain, which is correlated with neural activity in those regions. Using this technique, it has been shown that the second presentation of visual stimuli elicits less blood flow in visual areas of the brain than when the stimuli were presented the first time (Buckner et al. 1995, Schacter et al. 1996, Squire et al. 1992). The result is consistent with the idea that primed stimuli require fewer processing resources, and as such, they can be processed more fluently.

CONCEPTUAL PRIMING

In addition to perceptual information, conceptual information can also be primed. For example, when subjects are presented with examples of a particular category (e.g. apple, banana, orange), they are likely to produce these particular examples when later given a category (e.g. fruit) and asked to name the first examples that come to mind. Priming is indicated by the fact that subjects who were presented with the target words are more likely to later produce them than subjects who had not been presented with these words. Amnesic patients exhibit normal conceptual priming (Graf et al. 1985). It is possible that this phenomenon also depends on fluency. Fewer processing resources may be required to bring the target words to mind because of their prior presentation. This fluency difference probably operates at the level of semantic or lexical representations in higher order brain areas responsible for more elaborate levels of processing.

PRIMING AND RECOGNITION

How are priming and recognition related? The representation that leads to priming is nondeclarative in that subjects are not necessarily aware that they have acquired this representation, and this knowledge emerges through performance of a priming task. Subjects can show priming for stimuli even though they do not remember having been presented with the stimuli before. In contrast, recognizing is accompanied by the awareness that the item was experienced before. One could imagine that both priming and recognition access the same representation. For instance, the presentation of a word could leave a neural trace that could be accessed as a memory and would also lead to fluent processing the second time the stimulus was presented. However, the evidence suggests that the nondeclarative knowledge leading to priming and the declarative knowledge leading to recognition are separate. First, the nature of the two representations is different. Perceptual priming is based on surface features and appears insensitive to the level of processing at encoding (Graf & Mandler 1984, Jacoby & Dallas 1981). Thus, a subject will exhibit about the same amount of priming if he or she was thinking about the meaning of each word (deep encoding) as it was pre-exposed, or whether he or she was just counting the number of vowels in each word (shallow encoding). In some studies a levels-of-processing effect was found in that there was more priming when a deeper level of encoding was performed at study (e.g. Challis & Brodbeck 1992). One possible explanation for these results is that subjects are using some explicit memory on the priming task. For example, in a word-stem completion task, subjects might realize that many of the test items could be completed with study words, and they might try to explicitly retrieve these words. This idea finds some support in a recent study that demonstrated virtually no level-of-processing effect in perceptual priming by amnesic patients under the same conditions in which an effect was obtained with normal control subjects (Hamann & Squire 1996). The lack of a level-of-processing effect appeared to be due to the fact that amnesic patients were unable to effectively use an explicit memory strategy.

In contrast to perceptual priming, recognition memory is very sensitive to the level of processing at study, with superior performance resulting with deep encoding during study (Craik & Lockhart 1972, Richardson-Klavehn & Bjork 1988). So it appears that in this case the declarative and nondeclarative knowledge have different characteristics. Brain imaging data also support the idea that these two kinds of knowledge are distinct, in that priming results in activity decreases in fairly early perceptual areas of the brain, whereas recognition memory results in activity in higher-order processing areas. Also, the fact that amnesic patients are able to acquire knowledge capable of supporting priming, but not knowledge capable of supporting recognition, points to the idea that priming is based on a knowledge system distinct from the one that is involved in recognition.

Some recent data suggest that a double dissociation between priming and recognition can be obtained. There has been a report of a patient M.S., who sustained a lesion in visual association areas on the right side of the brain. This patient exhibits a deficit in visual perceptual identification and word-stem completion priming, although his visual recognition memory for words presented during the study phase was normal (Gabrieli et al. 1995; Figure 7.5). Thus, this patient exhibits a dissociation pattern that is opposite to that of the amnesic patients. These double dissociation data provide additional evidence that different knowledge bases are required to perform the recognition and word-stem

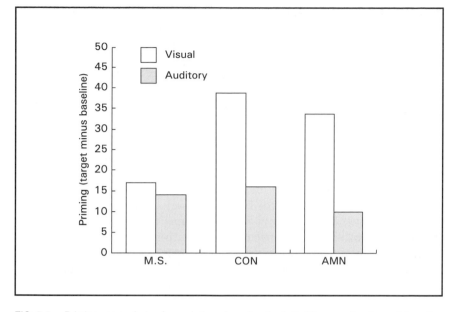

FIG. 7.5.   Priming scores (rate of completion of previously studied items - rate of completion of unstudied items) for patient M.S., normal control subjects, and a group of amnesic patients. Note that patient M.S. exhibits normal priming when the study words are presented in the auditory modality. From Gabrieli et al. 1995.

completion tasks. Without evidence for a double dissociation, one could interpret the data from single dissociations as measuring a sensitivity difference between two tasks. For example, the dissociation between priming and recognition seen in amnesic patients could be consistent with a single knowledge system giving rise to both abilities, if one supposes that priming is a more sensitive measure of existing knowledge and the impairment in amnesia is not complete. However, the fact that patient M.S. exhibits the opposite dissociation between the two abilities is most consistent with the idea that they rely on independent knowledge systems.

It is important to keep in mind that the term "nondeclarative knowledge" does not describe a single entity. Rather, there are many kinds of nondeclarative knowledge that have different characteristics. Even within the domain of priming, perceptual and conceptual priming can be dissociated. Patient M.S. exhibits impaired perceptual priming, but his conceptual priming is intact (Gabrieli et al. 1995). Patients with Alzheimer's disease exhibit the opposite dissociation; intact perceptual priming with impaired conceptual priming (Keane et al. 1991). This pattern of results is consistent with the idea that these patients have damage to higher-order cortical association areas, while lower-level cortical areas involved in perception are relatively spared in this disease.

SEQUENCE LEARNING

Sequence learning is a type of skill learning that does not appear to necessarily result in declarative knowledge. In one sequence learning task, subjects see a series of lights appearing in different locations, and their task is to press a key on a computer keyboard that corresponds to the location of the light. Unbeknown to the subject, the lights are appearing in the locations in a fixed sequence, not in random locations. Subjects become faster and faster at pressing the correct keys with training. Subjects show that they have learned the sequence at some level because, when the lights are switched to a random sequence, their reaction time increases (Nissen & Bullemer 1987). The reaction times for the random sequence may be shorter than the reaction times at the beginning of training, which suggests that non-specific (not sequence-dependent) learning is taking place in addition to learning about the sequence. Despite the sensitivity to the sequence that subjects display by their perfomance speed-up, subjects are not necessarily aware of this sequence. Thus, it appears that in these subjects, this knowledge is nondeclarative, because conscious awareness of this knowledge is not necessary for performance (Cohen et al. 1990, Willingham et al. 1989). Data from amnesic patients also fit with this view, in that these patients exhibit normal learning of a sequence as assessed by reaction-time speed-up, yet exhibit little or no recognition of the sequence (Nissen & Bullemer 1987, Reber & Squire 1994). In contrast to the amnesic patients, patients with Huntington's disease, and to a lesser extent patients with Parkinson's disease, exhibit difficulties in acquiring nondeclarative knowledge of the sequence (Ferraro et al. 1993, Jackson et al. 1995, Knopman & Nissen 1991; see also Pascual-Leone et al. 1993). These patients may give faster reaction times with successive trials, but they do not show normal speed-up that is specific to the fixed sequence. Again, as with the perceptuo-motor skill learning tasks, these patient groups start with a different baseline level of performance than normal subjects in that they start out responding more slowly. Nevertheless, it appears that sequence learning measured by reaction time speed-up might involve the acquisition of motor programs as in the case of motor skill learning. Such motor programs would represent a form of nondeclarative knowledge.

CATEGORY-LEVEL KNOWLEDGE

Another area in which nondeclarative knowedge acquisition has been studied is category learning. As a subject is exposed to a series of examples of a category, he or she might learn about each individual example, but he or she would also learn about the items as a group, or what has been termed "category-level knowledge". In some situations, these two kinds of knowledge map on to the declarative/nondeclarative distinction. Subjects would be consciously aware that they had learned about specific examples: when asked, they would be able to recognize the old examples as part of the past. However, category-level knowledge can be different, in that subjects may not be aware that they are acquiring this knowledge, and they are not always able to describe it well. Such category knowledge only emerges when the subject is confronted with new examples of the category, and is asked to classify them. For example, suppose a person hears several different études by Chopin. The subject would be consciously aware that he or she had heard each piece. However, the subject might not be aware that he or she had also learned something about the pieces as a group, or what is common among these études. Later, the subject could listen to a different Chopin étude and would correctly classify it as being in the same category as the pieces that he or she had heard earlier. The subject might not be able to describe the basis for his or her classification judgement well, but would rather say something like "I know Chopin when I hear it". This distinction between knowledge of specific examples and knowledge of a category has been explored in amnesic patients, and these data also support the notion that these two kinds of knowledge are distinct. In the following sections I will describe the evidence for nondeclarative category learning in amnesia.

ARTIFICIAL GRAMMAR LEARNING

The artifical grammar learning paradigm has been extensively studied, first in normal subjects and more recently in amnesic patients. In these studies, letter strings are said to be part of a single category ("grammatical") if they follow a set of rules. These rules allow only certain letters to follow other letters. Figure 7.6 shows examples of artificial grammar rule systems. After viewing a series of letter strings that follow these rules ("grammatical" letter strings) subjects are told for the first time that all of the letter strings that they had seen belonged in a single category, and that their task would be to decide for a new set of letter strings whether or not each one was also a member of that category. Although subjects typically cannot describe the basis for their judgements well, and they seem to have little idea of the underlying rules, they are able to classify new letter strings at a level significantly above chance (see Reber 1989 for a review). The knowledge about the artificial grammar that is acquired thus appears to be nondeclarative because subjects are not aware of what they have learned, and their knowledge only manifests itself through performance of the classification task. The neuropsychological evidence confirms this view. Amnesic patients are able to acquire the necessary information about the artifical grammar normally, in that they can discriminate grammatical from non-grammatical items as well as normal subjects after training (Figure 7.7). As expected, however, these patients are impaired at recognizing the specific letter strings that were used during training (Knowlton et al. 1992, Knowlton & Squire 1996).

The fact that membership in the grammatical category is defined by a set of rules does not necessarily mean that subjects are acquiring nondeclarative knowledge about these rules. Subjects may be acquiring nondeclarative knowledge that is correlated with the grammatical rules and would allow for good discrimination performance. It has been shown that subjects will endorse as grammatical letter strings that contain

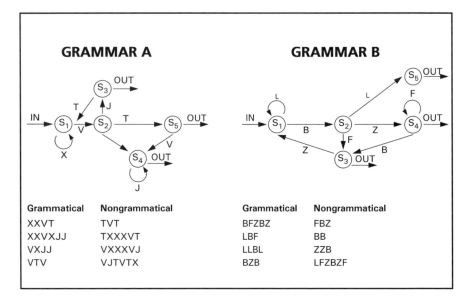

FIG. 7.6.   Two artificial grammar rule systems. "Grammatical" letter strings are generated by traversing the diagram from the input node to the output node, picking up a letter at each transition. Beneath each grammar are shown examples of letter strings that are formed according to the grammatical rules and letter strings that violate these rules. From Knowlton et al. 1992.

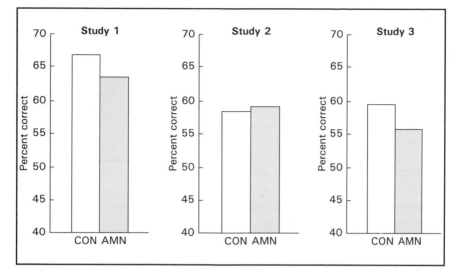

FIG. 7.7.   The results from three different studies showing normal artificial grammar learning performance by amnesic patients.From Squire & Knowlton, 1995.

letter bigrams and trigrams that are repeated frequently in the training strings. Subjects may be learning the frequencies of these "chunks", and use this information to classify new items (Knowlton & Squire 1994, 1996). Like rule knowledge, this chunk frequency knowledge does not appear to be declarative because subjects are not aware of it, and amnesic patients learn it as well as normal subjects do. Thus, nondeclarative information can take the form of fairly concrete, stimulus-specific information. Consistent with this idea is the fact that after viewing grammatical letter strings, subjects can identify new grammatical strings better than non-grammatical strings when they are briefly presented (Buchner 1994). Thus, some sort of priming-like mechanism based on the bigrams and trigrams that were presented during training would allow the grammatical items to be perceived more fluently. Non-grammatical items, which typically contain illegal chunks that were not presented during training, would not benefit as much from perceptual fluency, which may be a mechanism whereby nondeclarative stimulus-specific information could influence grammaticality judgements

Although chunk frequency plays a role in grammaticality judgements, it is also clear that subjects are learning some kind of abstract, rule-based information about the artificial grammar. The strongest evidence for this statement is the fact that both amnesic patients and normal subjects are able to transfer their knowledge of an artificial grammar to strings formed with new letters (Gomez & Schwaneveldt 1994, Knowlton & Squire 1995). That is, if the subject was trained using letter strings that were made up of the letters X, J, T and V, he or she would be tested using items made up of the letters B, F, L and Z. In order to exhibit transfer between letter sets, subjects must have aquired some fairly abstract knowledge about the rules that govern the relationship between the letters in order to show transfer. For example, such rules might be something like "letter strings often start with a repeat", or "two letters cannot alternate more than twice". It should be kept in mind that the transfer effect is small, and subjects perform consistently better when the same letter set is used at study and test. These findings suggest that both concrete, stimulus-specific information, and more abstract, rule-based information are learned in the artifical grammar task. Because amnesic patients exhibit the same pattern of results as normal subjects (i.e. positive letter-set transfer, but better same letter-set performance), it appears that both types of knowledge are nondeclarative. Recently, it has been shown that there is a correlation between the degree of declarative knowledge subjects have about the grammatical rules and their performance on letter-set transfer (Gomez & Schwaneveldt 1994). However, the fact that amnesic patients exhibit the same degree of letter-set transfer as control subjects suggests that abstract information can be acquired implicitly. The correlation between declarative knowledge and letter-set transfer could have arisen from the influence of a third factor, such as level of attention during training.

FUZZY CATEGORIES

In addition to rule-based category learning, there is some evidence that the learning of fuzzy, or naturalistic, categories is also nondeclarative. In these categories, membership is not determined by adherence to a set of rules, but rather by the resemblance of an item to a central tendency, or prototype, of the category. Items that are similar to the prototype are classifed most readily as being in the category, while items that are further from the prototype are classified less readily as being in the category. Eleanor Rosch found that subjects were quicker to call a robin a bird than they were a chicken or a penguin (see Rosch 1973). According to one view, experience with category exemplars results in a representation of the prototype (or average of the exemplars) to be formed (Franks & Bransford 1971, Posner & Keele 1968). Knowledge of such a prototype is generally thought to be nondeclarative because subjects are not necessarily aware that they have acquired such knowledge.

Posner and Keele (1968, 1970) studied learning of fuzzy categories using dot pattern stimuli. Subjects were presented with dot patterns that belonged to one of three categories. Each category was formed by generating a random dot pattern (the category prototype), and then generating distortions of this prototype to form category examples. The subjects did not see the category prototypes during training, only the examples. When the subjects were asked one week later to classify new patterns into the three categories, they classified the prototypes the most accurately, followed by the low distortions of the prototypes, then the

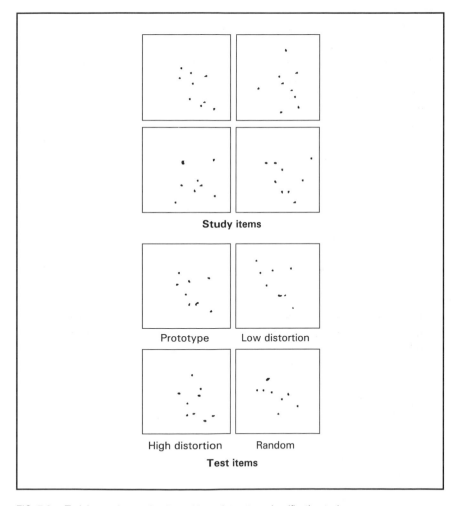

FIG. 7.8.   Training and test stimuli used in a dot pattern classification task.
From Knowlton & Squire, 1993.

high distortions of the prototypes (although the training items were comparable high distortions). Thus it appeared that subjects were abstracting a prototype, or a central tendency for each of the three categories during training. More recently, it has been shown that amnesic patients are capable of acquiring normal category level knowledge in paradigms similar to the one used by Posner & Keele (Knowlton & Squire 1993, Kolodny 1994; Figures 7.8 and 7.9). The amnesic patients exhibit the same pattern of results as normal subjects, in that they endorse the prototype and low distortions as being in the category, although they were shown high distortions during training. These data support the idea that acquisition of category-level information does not require the declarative system. Despite the good

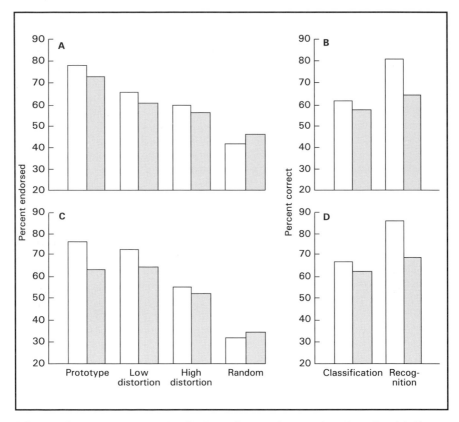

FIG. 7.9.   Data showing normal classification performance by amnesic patients. Panel A: The percentage of each type of test item endorsed as being in the category by control subjects and by amnesic patients. Panel B: The percent correct score for classification and recognition of training dot patterns. Panels C and D show similar data using different materials.
From Knowlton & Squire, 1993.

categorization performance shown by amnesic patients, they exhibit a significant impairment in recognizing specific dot patterns. Such recognition would rely on declarative knowledge, because subjects are consciously recollecting the past. In contrast, in classification, the subject is merely reacting to a stimulus without consciously accessing a stored category representation. Subjects are able to make judgements, and show the prototype abstraction effect, without being aware necessarily of what the category prototype is.

One plausible mechanism of prototype abstraction is related to priming and perceptual fluency. One could imagine that as the exemplars are presented, they each induce an activation trace in visual cortical areas. The prototype of the category would activate the average of these neural representations, just as aligning glass panes with etched patterns would reveal a pattern that corresponds to the invariance, or commonalities, across the patterns (St. John & Shanks 1996). In a similar fashion, the neural activation corresponding to the average of the exemplars would result in a trace that is stronger than any individual exemplar, and thus the prototype pattern, which corresponds to this trace, would be processed more fluently than other patterns, even training patterns.

One difficulty for the perceptual fluency explanation is that amnesic patients show normal category learning even when they must concurrently learn three categories, as in the Posner & Keele studies (Kolodny 1994). The perceptual fluency view has trouble dealing with this fact because it requires that there be some mechanism whereby the different examples become neurally segregated. This aspect of category learning would appear to be declarative, because subjects would be conscious of learning the category labels, even if they were not able to describe well the criteria for membership in each of the three categories. The normal performance of amnesic patients on the classification task when three categories are used suggests that declarative knowledge of these category labels is not required for the examples to be segregated during training.

EXEMPLAR-BASED MODELS

The finding of a prototype abstraction effect does not necessarily mean that category-level knowledge in the task exists as an abstracted prototype. An important development in the field of category learning was the demonstration that an exemplar-based representation can, and readily does, give rise to a prototype abstraction effect (Hintzman 1986, Medin & Schaffer 1978, Nosofsky 1992). In these models, the individual examples are stored, rather than an abstracted prototype. When the subject makes classification judgements, he or she makes comparisons with each of the stored members of the category. If the test item is similar to a large number of stored exemplars, then the item will be classified as being in the category. If, however, the item is dissimilar from most of the exemplars, it will not be classified as being in the category. These models account for the prototype abstraction effect because the prototype is in general similar to a large number of examples because it is the central tendency of all of the examples. Thus, the prototype, and items that are near the prototype, will be classified most readily as being in the category because they are similar to the most stored examples.

From these models, it seems most parsimonious to hypothesize that the same knowledge base (individual exemplars) is used for both recognition and classification judgements (Nosofsky 1991). However, the finding that amnesic patients can exhibit normal classification performance in the face of severely impaired recognition memory challenges this notion. Exemplar-based models can only account for this dissociation if the stored exemplars that lead to recognition (and are penetrable to awareness), are distinct from the stored exemplars that lead to classification (which are stored as nondeclarative knowledge).

The perceptual fluency view discussed above could be seen as a compromise between the prototype view and an exemplar-based view. By the perceptual fluency view, all category-level information exists as stored exemplars, and the prototype is not stored as a separate entity. However, by this view, the prototype can be said to emerge as a property of the way in which the exemplars are stored, and as such it could be said to involve a representation. By this view, this representation, and the representation of the exemplars that comprise it, would be nondeclarative. The declarative representation of exemplars that would lead to recognition would involve higher-order brain structures and more elaborate processing.

In the real world, category learning is undoubtedly not uniform, and the processes and knowledge representations involved probably differ depending on the exemplars and the training procedure used. In some cases, when individual examples are not memorable or distinctive, subjects may form a prototype representation. However, when the individual examples are distinctive, or if there are not enough of them to tax memory capacity, then subjects may use exemplar-based knowledge for classification. Under some circumstances, subjects may be using declarative knowledge of examples to make classification judgements. In the study by Kolodny, amnesic patients were impaired at learning to classify Renaissance paintings by artists after viewing a few examples of each of three artists (Kolodny 1994). In this experiment, the recognition memory for each of the training paintings was excellent for the normal subjects, so it is quite possible that in this case subjects were making similarity comparisons with examples stored in declarative memory.

AMNESIA AS A STORAGE DEFICIT

One means to interpret the data from amnesic patients is to assume that their brain damage results in a deficit in a certain type of information processing, rather than in storage of information as declarative knowledge. Perhaps the deficit in amnesia is one of conscious access to stored memories, and not one of storage of information as conscious memories. For example, in word-stem completion priming, amnesic patients cannot access the representation of a previously presented word when asked to recognize it, but they can still indirectly access the representation in a priming task. By this view, it does not make sense to think of declarative and nondeclarative knowledge systems, because information is stored in a single representation that is accessed in multiple ways. This view makes the assumption that the brain damage leading to amnesia interrupts retrieval and not storage. If amnesia were a storage deficit, then it would appear that a particular kind of representation (declarative) would not be formed, and that any spared learning abilities would arise from different representations that would be formed normally in these patients. Thus, the systems view depends on the idea that amnesia results because declarative information cannot be stored. Can cognitive neuroscience provide any data to support either view? The bulk of evidence concerning what we know about the hippocampus and other brain structures damaged in amnesia supports the storage view. In the following sections I will describe the evidence supporting the idea that amnesia is a deficit in information storage.

CONSOLIDATION

Some of the most compelling evidence supporting this view comes from studies showing that the hippocampus has a time-limited role in memory. In animals, lesions of the hippocampus made soon after training severely disrupt memory, while lesions made after increasing post-training delays are increasingly less effective (Cho et al. 1993, Kim & Fanselow 1992, Zola-Morgan & Squire 1990; Figure 7.10). A similar phenomenon can be seen in human amnesic patients, who typically exhibit what has been termed a gradient of retrograde amnesia (Barbizet 1970, Ribot 1881, Squire et al. 1989). Memories acquired in the months or years before the patient sustained brain damage are typically lost, while more remote memories are spared. These data suggest that the hippocampus is involved in consolidating memories and that after these memories have become consolidated, they become independent of the hippocampus. These data are most consistent with the idea that the hippocampus is involved in forming memories and that amnesic patients do not form declarative memories normally. It is possible that the retrograde gradient could be accounted for by a retrieval deficit in amnesia if newer memories were retrieved by the hippocampus and older memories are retrieved some other way. Nevertheless, even if the retrograde gradient can be explained by changes in retrievability, the single system view must explain why changes in the retrievability of memories holds only for declarative access, and not for access by other processes, as there is typically no gradient of retrograde amnesia for nondeclarative memories.

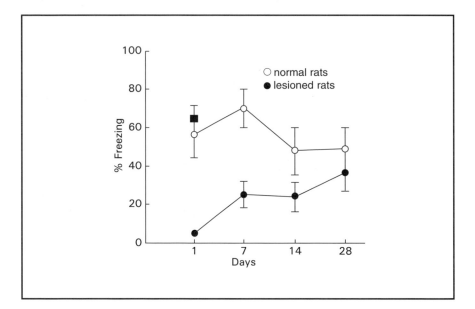

FIG. 7.10.   The performance of normal rats and lesioned rats on a test of memory for a context in which the rats received foot shock. Memory is indicated by the percentage of time the rat spent freezing in that context (Y axis). Along the X axis is the interval between training and the creation of a lesion in the rat's hippocampus. Note that the lesion results in virtually no memory when performed one day after training, but has no significant effect on memory when performed 28 days after training. The square indicates the performance of rats in which the cortex overlying the hippocampus was lesioned one day after training. From Kim & Fanselow, 1992.

FUNCTIONAL IMAGING OF HIPPOCAMPUS

Another set of data that support the idea that the hippocampus is involved in storage comes from studies showing that the hippocampus is active during memory storage. Studies using PET, which measure blood flow, show that the hippocampus is active during both the encoding and retrieval of information in memory tasks (Roland & Gulyas 1995). These data are consistent with the idea that the hippocampus is involved in both storage, and subsequent retrieval of information. As such, these data support the idea that amnesic patients are not storing declarative information.

ELECTROPHYSIOLOGICAL DATA

Some very preliminary evidence from electrophysiological studies in monkeys provides the strongest support for the idea that the hippocampal region is necessary for forming representations. In these studies, monkeys were trained to associate together several fractal patterns into pairs. As these associations were acquired, neurons in the temporal lobe of the cerebral cortex showed learning-dependent changes. For example, there was an increase in neuronal firing during the delay after one element of a pair was presented and before the monkey selected the associated pattern. In other cases, a neuron that had responded to only one element of a pair before training would later respond to the associated pattern after training (Sakai & Miyashita 1991). Figure 7.11 shows examples of training pairs used in these studies. The critical finding is that a unilateral lesion to the rhinal cortex, which is the major input to the hippocampus, along with a lesion of the fibres that interrupted the connections between the two brain hemispheres, resulted in an absence of these learning-related changes in the cortex on the same side as the compromised hippocampus (Miyashita et al. 1994). These results suggest that the hippocampal system and immediately associated cortical areas are crucial for setting up declarative representations. It follows that amnesic patients, who have damage to the hippocampus or to structures closely associated with it, have difficulty in setting up declarative representations, not solely in retrieving them. Thus, spared memory abilities reflect the storage of information in nondeclarative representations. Although these results are quite preliminary, such data potentially could be useful for supporting a systems view of memory organization.

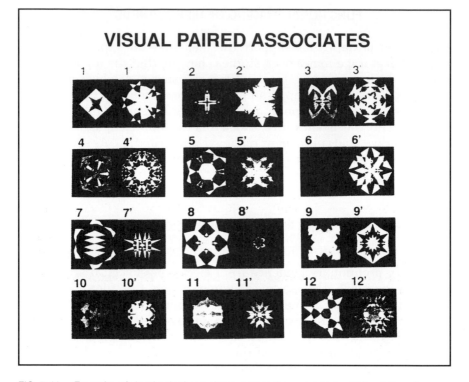

FIG. 7.11.   Examples of visual-paired associates used in the experiments of Miyashita and colleagues. From Miyashita, 1994.

CONCLUSION

Cognitive neuroscience is a fairly young field, and will continue to gain influence apace with technological advances, especially in the realm of functional imaging. The rising influence of cognitive neuroscience does not mean that studies restricted to cognition are no longer relevant. In fact there is much to be learned about how knowledge is represented, and what form these representations might take. Cognitive studies have been quite successful in addressing these questions, while cognitive neuroscience is most effective for producing dissociations and distinctions based on brain localization. The questions surrounding the study of the mind are complex enough that it seems prudent to use all available information to shape and constrain theories. The study of knowledge systems, and in particular the idea that there is a declarative knowledge system and nondeclarative knowledge systems owes much to both the cognitive and cognitive neuroscience approaches.

REFERENCES

Anderson, J. R. 1976. *Language, memory, and thought.* Hillsdale, New Jersey: Erlbaum.

Barbizet, J. 1970. *Human memory and its pathology.* San Francisco, CA: Freeman.

Biederman, I. & E. E. Cooper 1991. Evidence for complete translational and reflectional invariance in visual object priming. *Perception* **20**, 585–93.

Brooks, D. N. & A. Baddeley 1976. What can amnesic patients learn? *Neuropsychologia* **14**, 111–22.

Buchner, A. 1994. Indirect effects of synthetic grammar learning in an identification task. *Journal of Experimental Psychology: Learning, Memory and Cognition* **20**, 550–66.

Buckner, R. L., S. E. Petersen, J. G. Ojemann, F. M. Miezen, L. R. Squire, M. E. Raichle 1995. Functional anatomical studies of explicit and implicit memory retrieval tasks. *Journal of Neuroscience* **15**, 12–29.

Cave, C. B. & L. R. Squire 1992. Intact and long-lasting repetition priming in amnesia. *Journal of Experimental Psychology: Learning, Memory, and Cognition* **18**, 509–20.

Cermak, L. S., R. Lewis, N. Butters, H. Goodglass 1973. Role of verbal mediation in performance of motor tasks by Korsakoff patients. *Perceptual and Motor Skills* **37**, 259–63.

Cermak, L. S., N. Talbot, K. Chandler, L. Wolbarst 1985. The perceptual priming phenomenon in amnesia. *Neuropsychologia* **23**, 615–22.

Challis, B. H. & D. R. Brodbeck 1992. Level of processing affects in word fragment completion. *Journal of Experimental Psychology: Learning, Memory, and Cognition* **18**, 595–607.

Cho, Y. H., D. Beracochea, R. Jaffard 1993. Extended temporal gradient for the retrograde and anterograde amnesia produced by ibotenate entorhinal cortex lesions in mice. *Journal of Neuroscience* **13**, 1759–66.

Cohen, A., R. I. Ivry, S. W. Keele 1990. Attention and structure in sequence learning. *Journal of Experimental Psychology: Learning Memory and Cognition* **16**, 17–30.

Cohen, N. J. & L. R. Squire 1980. Preserved learning and retention of a pattern-analyzing skill in amnesia: dissociation of knowing how and knowing that. *Science* **210**, 207–10.

Corkin, S. 1968. Acquisition of motor skill after bilateral medial temporal excision. *Neuropsychologia* **6**, 255–65.

Corkin, S. 1984. Lasting consequences of bilateral medial temporal lobectomy: clinical course and experimental findings from H. M. *Seminars in Neurology* **4**, 249–59.

Craik, F. I. M. & R. S. Lockhart 1972. Levels of processing: a framework for memory research. *Journal of Verbal Learning and Verbal Behavior* **11**, 671–84.

Diamond, R. J. & P. Rozin 1984. Activation of existing memories in anterograde amnesia. *Journal of Abnormal Psychology* **93**, 98–105.

Ferraro, F. R., D. A. Balota, L. T. Connor 1993. Implicit memory and the formation of new associations in nondemented Parkinson's disease individuals and individuals with senile dementia of the Alzheimer type: a serial reaction time (srt) investigation. *Brain & Cognition* **21**, 163–80.

Franks, J. J. & J. D. Bransford 1971. Abstraction of visual patterns. *Journal of Experimental Psychology* **90**, 65–74.

Gabrieli, J. D. E., D. A. Fleischman, M. M. Keane, S. L. Reminger, F. Morrell 1995. Double dissociation between memory systems underlying explicit and implicit memory in the human brain. *Psychological Science* **6**, 76–82.

Gabrieli, J. D. E., W. Milberg, M. M. Keane, S. Corkin 1990. Intact priming of patterns despite impaired memory. *Neuropsychologia* **28**, 417–27.

Gazzaniga, M. (ed.) 1995. *The cognitive neurosciences*. Cambridge, Mass.: MIT Press.

Gomez, R. L. & R. W. Schwaneveldt 1994. What is learned from artificial grammars? Transfer tests of simple association. *Journal of Experimental Psychology: Learning, Memory, and Cognition* **20**, 396–410.

Graf, P. & G. Mandler 1984. Activation makes words more accessible, but not necessarily more retrievable. *Journal of Verbal Learning and Verbal Behaviour* **23**, 553–68.

Graf, P. & L. Ryan 1990. Transfer-appropriate processing for implicit and explicit memory. *Journal of Experimental Psychology: Learning, Memory, and Cognition* **16**, 978–92.

Graf, P., A. P. Shimamura, L. R. Squire 1985. Priming across modalities and priming across category levels: extending the domain of preserved functioning in amnesia. *Journal of Experimental Psychology: Learning, Memory and Cognition* **11**, 385–95.

Graf, P., L. R. Squire, G. Mandler 1984. The information that amnesic patients do not forget. *Journal of Experimental Psychology: Learning, Memory and Cognition* **10**, 164–78.

Haist, F., G. Musen, L. R. Squire 1991. Intact priming of words and nonwords in amnesia. *Psychobiology* **19**, 275–85.

Hamann, S. B. & L. R. Squire 1996. Level-of-processing effects in word-completion priming: A neuropsychological study. *Journal of Experimental Psychology: Learning, Memory, and Cognition*, **22**, 933–947.

Hamann, S. B., L. R. Squire, D. L. Schacter 1995. Perceptual thresholds and priming in amnesia. *Neuropsychology* **9**, 3–15.

Harrington, D. L., K. Y. Haaland, R. A. Yeo, E. Marder 1990. Procedural memory in Parkinson's disease: impaired motor but not visuoperceptual learning. *Journal of Clinical and Experimental Neuropsychology* **12**, 323–39.

Heindel, W. C., N. Butters, D. P. Salmon 1988. Impaired learning of a motor skill in patients with Huntington's disease. *Behavioural Neuroscience* **102**, 141–7.

Hintzman, D. L. 1986. "Schema abstraction" in a multiple-trace memory model. *Psychological Review* **93**, 411–28.

Jackson, G. M., S. R. Jackson, J. Harrison, L. Henderson, C. Kennard 1995. Serial reaction time learning and Parkinson's disease: evidence for a procedural learning deficit. *Neuropsychologia* **33**, 577–593.

Jacoby, L. L. & M. Dallas 1981. On the relationship between autobiographical memory and perceptual learning. *Journal of Experimental Psychology: General* **110**, 306–40.

Jacoby, L. L. & C. A. G. Hayman 1987. Specific visual transfer in word identification. *Journal of Experimental Psychology: Learning, Memory, and Cognition* **13**, 456–63.

Jordan, N. & H. J. Sagar 1994. The role of the striatum in motor learning: dissociation between isometric motor control processes in Parkinson's disease. *International Journal of Neuroscience* **77**, 153–65.

Josiassen, R. C., L. M. Curry, E. L. Mancall 1983. Development of neuropsychological deficits in Huntington's disease. *Archives of Neurology* **40**, 791–6.

Keane, M. M., J. D. E. Gabrieli, A. C. Fennema, J. H. Growden, S. Corkin 1991. Evidence for a dissociation between perceptual and conceptual priming in Alzheimer's disease. *Behavioral Neuroscience* **105**, 326–42.

Kim, J. J., R. E. Clark, R. F. Thompson 1995. Hippocampectomy impairs the memory of recently, but not remotely, acquired trace eyeblink conditioned responses. *Behavioral Neuroscience* **109**, 195–203.

Kim, J. J. & M. F. Fanselow 1992. Modality-specific retrograde amnesia of fear. *Science* **256**, 675–7.

Knopman, D. S. & M. J. Nissen 1991. Procedural learning is impaired in Huntington's disease: evidence from the serial reaction time task. *Neuropsychologia* **29**, 245–54.

Knowlton, B. J., S. J. Ramus, L. R. Squire 1992. Intact artificial grammar learning in amnesia: dissociation of classification learning and explicit memory for specific instances. *Psychological Science* **3**, 172–9.

Knowlton, B. J. & L. R. Squire 1993. The learning of categories: parallel brain systems for item memory and category knowledge. *Science* **262**, 1747–9.

Knowlton, B. J. & L. R. Squire 1994. The information acquired during artificial grammar learning. *Journal of Experimental Psychology: Learning, Memory and Cognition* **20**, 79–91.

Knowlton, B. J. & L. R. Squire 1996. Artificial grammar learning depends on implicit acquisition of both rule-based and exemplar-specific information. *Journal of Experimental Psychology: Learning, Memory and Cognition* **22**, 169–181.

Knowlton, B. J. & L. R. Squire 1996. Artificial grammar learning depends on implicit acquisition of both abstract and exemplar-specific information. *Journal of Experimental Psychology: Learning, Memory and Cognition* **22**, 169–81.

Kolodny, J. A. 1994. Memory processes in classification learning: an investigation of amnesic performance in categorization of dot patterns and artistic styles. *Psychological Science* **5**, 164–9.

Mair, W. G. P., E. K. Warrington, E. L. Weiskrantz 1979. Memory disorder in Korsakoff psychosis: a neuropathological and neuropsychological investigation of two cases. *Brain* **102**, 749–83.

Marslen-Wilson, W. D. & H. L. Teuber 1975. Memory for remote events in anterograde amnesia: recognition of public figures from news photographs. *Neuropsychologia* **13**, 353–64.

Martone, M., N. Butters, M. Payne, J. Becker, D. Sax 1984. Dissociations between skill learning and verbal recognition in amnesia and dementia. *Archives of Neurology* **41**, 965–70.

Mayes, A. R. 1988. *Human organic memory disorders*. New York: Cambridge University Press.

Medin, D. L. & M. M. Schaffer 1978. Context theory of classification learning. *Psychological Review* **85**, 207–38.

Milner, B. 1962. Les troubles de la mémoire accompagnant des lesions hippocampiques bilatérales. In *Physiologie de l'hippocampe*. Paris: Centre National de la Recherche Scientifique.

Mitchell, D. B. & A. S. Brown 1988. Persistent repetition priming in picture naming and its dissociation from recognition memory. *Journal of Experimental Psychology: Learning, Memory and Cognition* **14**, 213–22.

Miyashita, Y. 1994. Two mechanisms of visual long-term memory in the primate inferotemporal cortex: timing and association. *IBRO News* **22**(3), 6–7.

Miyashita, Y., S. Higuchi, X. Zhou, H. Okuno, I. Hasegawa 1994. Disruption of backward connections from the rhinal cortex impairs visual associative coding of neurons in inferotemporal cortex of monkeys. *Society for Neuroscience Abstracts* **20**, 428.

Musen, G., A. P. Shimamura, L. R. Squire, 1990. Intact text-specific reading skill in amnesia. *Journal of Experimental Psychology: Learning, Memory, and Cognition* **16**, 1068–76.

Musen, G. & L. R. Squire 1991. Normal acquisition of novel verbal information in amnesia. *Journal of Experimental Psychology: Learning, Memory, and Cognition* **17**, 1095–1104.

Musen, G. & A. Treisman 1990. Implicit and explicit memory for visual patterns. *Journal of Experimental Psychology: Learning, Memory, and Cognition* **16**, 127–37.

Nissen, M. J. & P. Bullemer 1987. Attentional requirments of learning: evidence from performance measures. *Cognitive Psychology* **19**, 1–32.

Nosofsky, R. M. 1991. Tests of an exemplar model for relating perceptual classification and recognition memory. *Journal of Experimental Psychology: Human Perception and Performance* **17**, 3–27.

Nosofsky, R. M. 1992. Similarity scaling and cognitive process models. *Annual Review of Psychology* **43**, 25–53.

O'Brien, S., D. L. Harrington, K. Y. Haaland, N. Hermanowicz 1995. Perceptual-motor learning deficits in Parkinson's disease. *Journal of the International Neuropsychological Society* **1**, 153.

Parkin, A. J. 1984. Amnesic syndrome: a lesion-specific disorder? *Cortex* **20**, 479–508.

Pascual-Leone, A., J. Grafman, K. Clark, M. Stewart, S. Massaquoi, J-S. Lou, M. Hallett 1993. Procedural learning in Parkinson's disease and cerebellar degeneration. *Annals of Neurology* **34**, 594–602.

Posner, M. I. & S. W. Keele 1968. On the genesis of abstract ideas. *Journal of Experimental Psychology* **77**, 353–63.

Posner, M. I. & S. W. Keele 1970. Retention of abstract ideas. *Journal of Experimental Psychology* **83**, 304–8.

Reber, A. S. 1989. Implicit learning and tacit knowledge. *Journal of Experimental Psychology: General* **118**, 219–35.

Reber, P. J. & L. R. Squire 1994. Parallel brain systems for learning with and without awareness. *Learning and Memory* **1**, 217–29.

Ribot, T. 1881. *Les maladies de la mémoire*. New York: Appleton-Century-Crofts.

Richardson-Klavehn, A. & R. A. Bjork 1988. Measures of memory. *Annual Review of Psychology* **39**, 475–543.

Roediger, H. L. 1990. Implicit memory: retention without remembering. *American Psychologist* **45**, 1043–56.

Roediger, H. L. & T. A. Blaxton 1987. Effects of varying modality, surface features, and retention interval on priming in word-fragment completion. *Memory and Cognition* **15**, 379–88.

Roland, P. E. & B. Gulyas 1995. Visual memory, visual imagery, and visual recognition of large field patterns by the human brain: functional anatomy by positron emission tomography. *Cerebral Cortex* **5**, 79–93.

Rosch, E. H. 1973. On the internal structure of perceptual and semantic categories. In *Cognitive development and the acquisition of language*, T. E. Moore (ed.), 111–44. New York: Academic Press.

Sakai, K. & Y. Miyashita 1991. Neural organization for the long-term memory of paired associates. *Nature* **354**, 152–5.

Schacter, D. L. 1987. Implicit memory: history and current status. *Journal of Experimental Psychology: Learning, Memory and Cognition* **13**, 501–18.

Schacter, D. L. 1994. Priming and multiple memory systems: perceptual mechanisms of implicit memory. In *Memory systems*. 1994. D. L. Schacter & E. Tulving (eds), 233–68. Cambridge, Mass.: MIT Press.

Schacter, D. L., N. M. Alpert, C. R. Savage, S. L. Rauch, M. S. Albert 1996. Conscious recollection and the human hippocampal formation: evidence from positron emission tomography. *Proceedings of The National Academy of Sciences, (USA)* **93**, 32–325.

Schacter, D. L., C.-Y. Chiu, K. N. Ochsner 1993. Implicit memory: a selective review. *Annual Review of Neuroscience* **16**, 159–82.

Scoville, W. B. & B. Milner 1957. Loss of recent memory after bilateral hippocampal lesions. *Journal of Neurology, Neurosurgery, and Psychiatry* **20**, 11–21.

Shanks, D. L. & M. F. St. John 1994. Characteristics of dissociable human learning systems. *Behavioral and Brain Sciences* **17**, 367–447.

Shimamura, A. P. 1986. Priming effects in amnesia: evidence for a dissociable memory function. *Quarterly Journal of Experimental Psychology* **38**, 619–44.

Squire, L. R. 1982. The neuropsychology of human memory. *Annual Review of Neuroscience* **5**, 241–73.

Squire L. R. 1986. *Memory and brain*. New York: Oxford University Press.

Squire, L. R., F. Haist, A. P. Shimamura 1989. The neurology of memory: quantitative assessment of retrograde amnesia in two groups of amnesic patients. *Journal of Neuroscience* **9**, 829–39.

Squire, L. R. & B. J. Knowlton 1995. The organization of memory. In *The mind, the brain, and complex adaptive systems*, H. L. Morowitz & J. L. Singer (eds), 63–97. Reading, Mass.: Addison-Wesley.

Squire, L. R., B. J. Knowlton, G. Musen 1993. The structure and organization of memory. *Annual Review of Psychology* **44**, 453–95.

Squire, L. R., J. G. Ojemann, F. M. Miezen, S. E. Petersen, T. O. Videen, M. E. Raichle 1992. Activation of the hippocampus in normal humans: a functional anatomical study. *Proceedings of the National Academy of Sciences* **89**, 1837–41.

Squire, L. R. & S. Zola-Morgan 1991. The medial temporal lobe memory system. *Science* **253**, 1380–86.

St. John, M. F. & D. R. Shanks 1996. Implicit learning from an information processing standpoint. In *How implicit is implicit learning?* D. Berry (ed.). Oxford: Oxford University Press.

Tranel, D., A. R. Damasio, H. Damasio, J. P. Brandt 1994. Sensorimotor skill learning in amnesia: additional evidence for the neural basis of nondeclarative memory. *Learning and Memory* **1**, 165–79.

Victor, M., R. D. Adams, G. H. Collins 1971. *The Wernike–Korsakoff syndrome*. Philadelphia: Davis.

Warrington, E. K. & L. Weiskrantz 1974. The effect of prior learning on subsequent retention in amnestic patients. *Neuropsychologia* **12**, 419–28.

Wiig, K. A. & D. K. Bilkey 1994. Perirhinal cortex lesions in rats disrupt performance_ in a spatial dnms task. *Neuroreport* **5**, 1405–08.

Willingham, D. B., M. J. Nissen, P. Bullemer 1989. On the development of procedural knowledge. *Journal of Experimental Psychology: Learning, Memory, and Cognition* **15**, 1047–60.

Winograd, T. 1972. *Understanding natural language*. New York: Academic Press.

Winograd, T. 1975. Frame representations and the declarative/procedural controversy. In *Representation and understanding*, D. G. Bobrow & A. Collins (eds), 185–210. New York: Academic Press.

Zola-Morgan, S. & L. R. Squire 1990. The primate hippocampal formation: evidence for a time-limited role in memory storage. *Science* **250**, 288–90.

Zola-Morgan, S., L. R. Squire, D. G. Amaral 1986. Human amnesia and the medial temporal region: enduring memory impairment following a bilateral lesion limited to field ca1 of hippocampus. *Journal of Neuroscience* **6**, 2950–67.

CHAPTER EIGHT

Implicit Learning and Unconscious Knowledge:
Mental Representation, Computational Mechanisms, and Brain Structures[1]

Thomas Goschke

1. INTRODUCTION: PHENOMENA, TASKS, AND QUESTIONS

1. 1. What is implicit learning?

The human mind has a strong tendency to make the world intelligible by conceptualizing it in terms of dichotomies. There is no exception to this general rule when the mind reflects about its own functioning. Both our folk psychology and our scientific theories about how we perceive, learn, think, and act are often grounded in the idea of an opposition between two fundamentally different modes of mental functioning. Among the dichotomies that have been proposed throughout the history of psychology are those between perceptive versus apperceptive, analytic versus holistic, rational versus experiential, logical versus intuitive, verbal versus imaginal, propositional versus analogue, symbolic versus subsymbolic, abstract versus specific, willful versus automatic, or declarative versus procedural processes. Ever since Freud (1901) distinguished between primary and secondary processes in his book on the interpretation of dreams, probably the distinction that has produced most fascination and controversy is the one between conscious versus unconscious mental processes (cf. Epstein 1994). Whereas Freud conceived of the unconscious in terms of dynamic processes driven by emotional conflicts and repressed wishes, most recent conceptualizations of the unconscious have, however, been developed independently of, or even deliberatively in opposition to, psychodynamic views. It has become common to use the term "cognitive unconscious" to denote forms of information processing that occur automatically and outside of awareness, but which are not necessarily related to unconscious conflict and motivated repression (e.g. Greenwald 1992, Kihlstrom 1987, Velmans 1991).

The notion of the cognitive unconscious has also become a central topic in research on knowledge representation. In particular, the question whether complex knowledge can be acquired and expressed unconsciously has attracted considerable attention. We all know from everyday experience that conscious knowledge and the mastery of a skill are very different things. The ability to give a brilliant lecture about the laws governing the dynamics of moving masses is of little help when it comes to playing good tennis. Conversely, it is no pre-condition for becoming a tennis champion to be able to solve differential equations. Likewise, some of us can immediately discriminate guitar solos by Prince and Keith Richards or diagnose a defective engine from the noise it makes, without being able to verbally describe the perceptual invariances exploited in making these judgements.

In the 1960s, Arthur Reber initiated a research programme on what he termed *implicit learning* to denote a form of learning that occurs in the absence of an intention to learn and that results in a form of knowledge that is expressed in performance, but is difficult to verbalize and not accessible to consciousness. Reber (1967, 1969) and his co-workers investigated the acquisition of relatively complex rule systems by presenting their subjects a number of meaningless letter strings such as XVVCMS that were generated by an *artificial grammar* (AG); (see the next section for details). Subjects were not informed about the existence of a rule system, but were instructed to process the stimuli under some orienting task (for instance, memorizing the letter strings). The remarkable finding was that when asked to classify novel letter strings as being grammatical or non-grammatical, subjects typically performed well above chance level, even though they frequently appeared to have no conscious or verbalizable knowledge about the underlying rules. Since the early studies on artificial grammar learning, a variety of other tasks have been used to investigate implicit learning which will be described in the following section. The common rationale behind these tasks is to show that exposure to, or processing of, a set of stimuli instantiating a rule system or a co-variation pattern improves task performance, thereby indicating that knowledge about the rules or co-variations has been acquired, while at the same time subjects have no conscious or verbalizable knowledge about these rules or covariations (see Berry & Dienes 1993, Reber 1989, Seger 1994, Shanks & St. John

1994, for reviews).[2] At this point we have to make an important distinction between two aspects of the term *implicit*.

Incidental acquisition

With respect to the process of learning, the term "implicit" denotes that knowledge is acquired incidentally as a result of an exposure to a set of stimuli or performance on some task. Ideally, subjects have no intention to learn or to discover rules and use no analytical strategies such as conscious hypothesis-testing. In addition, some researchers have suggested that implicit learning may even occur when attention is distracted by a secondary task or when the relevant stimuli are ignored.[3]

Unconscious knowledge

With respect to the product of learning, the term "implicit" denotes the idea that the acquired knowledge is unconscious and difficult to verbalize. Although at first sight this may appear to be a straightforward point, it has turned out to be extremely difficult to reach a consensus as to which operational criteria indicate the presence or absence of conscious knowledge (see section 2).

The distinction between explicit and implicit learning was a major catalyst for the return of the unconscious in human information-processing psychology, as is documented by an already vast experimental literature. Interest in implicit learning was particularly boosted by new methodological techniques for investigating unconscious learning in the laboratory, which have revealed sometimes intriguing dissociations between explicit and implicit forms of knowledge. In addition, the study of brain-damaged patients in clinical neuropsychology as well as the exciting recent developments of new functional brain-imaging techniques have opened a window to the neural structures underlying implicit and explicit learning. However, the impressive number of new findings and ingenious methodological innovations is balanced by an equally remarkable amount of unresolved and controversial theoretical issues. In fact, the field is still dominated by the aim of demonstrating that implicit learning exists at all (or that it does not). Only recently have attempts been made to investigate the boundary conditions, mechanisms, and brain systems underlying implicit learning. In this chapter I will give a tutorial, albeit selective, review of this research, including some of my own recent work. The chapter is organized along five major theoretical questions. After an overview of tasks and methods, I will discuss the following issues:

(1) Does implicit learning actually lead to unconscious knowledge, and if so, how can (un)conscious knowledge be measured?

(2)   Does implicit learning require attention or is it automatic?

(3)   Does implicit learning lead to abstract knowledge?

(4)   What are the computational mechanisms underlying implicit learning?

(5)   Does implicit learning involve specific brain systems?

1.2. Overview of implicit learning tasks and basic findings

In order to render the term "implicit learning" more vivid, it will be useful to start by briefly describing a number of typical implicit learning tasks and some basic findings. I will focus on four classes of tasks, which I will term *incidental concept learning*, *sequential contingency*, *simultaneous co-variation*, and *dynamic system control* tasks.

Incidental concept learning tasks

In incidental concept learning tasks subjects are presented a number of stimuli that instantiate a structural regularity or rule system. For instance, subjects may be presented with a set of dot patterns or line drawings of imaginary animals that unbeknown to them are exemplars of a common category. Category membership may be defined by some combination of features or by the overall similarity of exemplars to an abstract prototype (Homa 1979, Posner & Keele 1968). In a test phase, subjects are typically asked to decide whether new stimuli do or do not belong to the same category as the study items. The incidental concept learning task that has been studied most extensively is artificial grammar (AG) learning introduced by Reber and his co-workers (Reber 1967; see review in Reber 1989, 1993). In a typical AG experiment, subjects first study a list of meaningless letter strings (e.g. XVCCMT) under some orienting tasks (for instance, subjects may be instructed to memorize the strings or to judge their pleasantness). Unbeknown to the subjects, all strings were generated by a finite state grammar. Such a grammar consists of a set of states (represented by numbered circles), which are connected by labelled arrows. Legal strings are generated by following a sequence of arrows from the start to the end state. Each time one passes from one state to another, the symbol on the connecting arrow is written. The set of strings that can be generated this way is called a language and the strings of this language are termed grammatical. After the learning phase, subjects are informed that the strings were generated by a complex rule system, but no specific information about the grammar is provided. They are then presented new strings, some of which are generated by the same grammar (grammatical strings), whereas others are constructed from the same letter set, but do not conform to the grammatical rules because they contain one or more violations (non-grammatical strings). When subjects are asked to judge whether the new strings are grammatical or not, they are usually able to classify new strings significantly better than chance (approximately 60 to 70 per cent of items are classified correctly). Subjects are often not able to describe the underlying rules and sometimes indicate that they made their decisions on an intuitive basis. These findings were initially interpreted as evidence that subjects must have acquired knowledge about the abstract rules of the grammar and that this knowledge must be unconscious. Reber and Allen (1978:191) spoke of "an unconscious abstraction process which maps veridically the intrinsic structure of the environment". As will be discussed in sections 3 and 5, both the unconscious nature and the abstractness of the acquired knowledge have become topics of intense controversy.

Sequential contingency tasks

In these tasks subjects are presented a sequence of stimuli the order of which is determined by a more or less complex rule. For instance, in Lewicki's matrix search task (1986, Lewicki et al. 1988) subjects have to locate a target stimulus (for instance, a digit) in a matrix of flanker stimuli (irrelevant digits). Unbeknown to them, the location of the target depends on the sequence of previous events according to a set of rather complicated rules. Subjects usually show a decrease of search times in the course of training as well as a substantial increase in response time when the contingencies are suddenly changed.

A particularly popular task in this category is the *serial reaction task* introduced by Nissen & Bullemer (1987). On each trial a stimulus is presented in one out of four possible locations arranged horizontally in a visual display and the subject has to press one of four response buttons that corresponds to the location of the stimulus. When the sequence of locations follows a repeating pattern, reaction times typically decrease with practice faster than in a condition in which subjects respond to a random sequence. When the repeating sequence is unexpectedly switched to a random sequence after prolonged training, there is usually a marked increase in response times. Performance increments in this task have been observed even for subjects who were not able to verbalize the sequence after training and who performed poorly in a cued recall test of the sequence. This suggests that subjects can acquire procedural knowledge about sequential structures incidentally and in the absence of conscious knowledge about the sequence (e.g. Cohen et al. 1990, Curran & Keele 1993, Willingham et al. 1989). As with AG learning, it is currently debated what kind of knowledge underlies performance increments in sequence learning tasks and whether this knowledge is really unconscious (see section 3).

Simultaneous co-variation tasks

Co-variation learning experiments are similar to sequential learning tasks in that subjects are also exposed to stimuli instantiating some kind of co-variation. The difference is that the co-variation holds between different simultaneously presented stimuli or between features of a complex visuo-spatial stimulus. The critical co-variation is usually chosen to be non-salient or intuitively improbable in order to prevent subjects' from becoming aware of it. For instance, Lewicki (1986) presented his subjects photographs of women with short or long hair together with brief descriptions depicting them either as kind or capable. There was a co-variation between the personality trait and hair length (for instance, long-haired women were always kind). In a test phase, subjects made judgements about the personality of unfamiliar women. Although subjects apparently had not noticed the co-variation, their judgements were nevertheless influenced by it. The effect of implicit knowledge about such co-variations has also been investigated in the context of social judgements (see Greenwald & Banaji 1995, for an overview).

Dynamic system control

In these tasks subjects are presented with a computer simulation of a dynamic system, for instance, a fictitious sugar factory or city transport system (Berry & Broadbent 1984, Broadbent et al. 1986, Hayes & Broadbent 1988). The subject receives feedback about one or more state variables (e.g. the current number of workers in a factory, the amount of sugar output) and the task is to maintain a specified level of a target value (e.g. sugar output). To this end, the subject can manipulate one or more input variables (e.g. the number of workers). After each manipulation the next state of the system is computed according to a set of linear equations, which map the current (or sometimes a previous) state of the system in combination with the subject's input to a new state. What caused researchers to become fascinated with these tasks was the observation that subjects sometimes achieved high proficiency at controlling the system (indicated by their ability to produce the desired target value), although on a post-experimental questionnaire they exhibited little or even misleading declarative knowledge about the regularities governing the system. Conversely, verbally instructing subjects how to attain the target value sometimes improved their questionnaire performance but had no effect on actual control performance (Berry & Broadbent 1984). This pattern of findings was considered as evidence that subjects had acquired a tacit knowledge base that allowed them to make correct responses intuitively and in the absence of a conscious or rational justification.

Summary
Despite differences in stimulus types and response modalities (see Seger 1994, for discussion) the common rationale behind all of these tasks is to have subjects process stimuli under some cover task in which the stimuli instantiate some kind of regularity, structure, contingency, or co-variation. At least two different dependent variables must be measured, one indicating that implicit knowledge has been acquired and the other indicating lack of conscious knowledge of the relevant regularity, contingency, or co-variation. Among the performance measures that have been used as indicators of implicit knowledge are judgements of grammaticality or category membership, response times, and accuracy. With respect to the measurement of explicit knowledge, there is an ongoing controversy whether *verbal reports* (in the form of post-experimental questionnaires or interviews) or *discriminative behaviour* and *forced choices* (such as recognition tests) are better suited to infer the existence or non-existence of conscious knowledge. This controversy will be discussed in some detail in section 2.

1.3 Open questions
The remaining part of this chapter will be organized around five central theoretical questions which concern

(1) the unconscious nature,

(2) the attentional preconditions,

(3) the abstractness,

(4) the computational mechanisms, and

(5) the neurological basis of implicit learning and knowledge.

Question 1: Does implicit learning lead to unconscious knowledge?
The claim that implicit learning can produce knowledge which is inaccessible to consciousness rests on dissociations between task performance and measures of conscious knowledge. However, various reseachers have proposed instead that performance in these tasks reflects the acquisition of fragmentary conscious knowledge about aspects of the stimulus material (cf. Dulany et al. 1984, Perruchet

1994a, Shanks & St. John 1994, see section 3). Moreover, it has turned out to be far from trivial to specify operational criteria to justify why performance in a given task (e.g. grammaticality judgements) should be attributed to unconscious knowledge, whereas performance in some other task (e.g. free recall) should be interpreted as evidence for conscious knowledge (see section 2).

Question 2: Does implicit learning occur automatically and without attention?

This question concerns the second defining criterion of implicit learning according to which implicit learning occurs incidentally, without intention or attention. This question has two aspects. First, we can ask whether implicit learning occurs even if stimuli are processed in a passive, incidental fashion (as compared to an active, intentional rule-discovering strategy). Secondly, one can ask whether implicit learning is possible even when the relevant stimuli are ignored or one's attention is distracted (for instance, when a concurrent secondary task must be performed; see section 4).

Question 3: Does implicit learning lead to abstract knowledge?

Given that implicit learning does exist, a fundamental question is how sophisticated it can be (Loftus & Klinger 1992). Some have argued for a smart unconscious capable of abstraction of rules, full semantic processing, and even creative problem-solving. In a review of research on the cognitive unconscious in the journal *Science*, Kihlstrom (1987:1450) states: "One thing is now clear: consciousness is not to be identified with any particular perceptual-cognitive functions. . . *All of these functions* can take place outside of phenomenal awareness. Rather consciousness is an experiential quality that may accompany any of these functions" (emphasis added). Similar views have been expressed with respect to implicit learning. Concluding from his work on implicit co-variation learning, Lewicki states "Our conscious thinking needs to rely on notes. . . or computers to do the same job that our nonconsciously operating algorithms can do instantly and without external help" (Lewicki et al. 1992:798). Likewise, Reber observes that implicit knowledge is "deep, abstract, and representative of the structure inherent in the underlying invariance patterns of the stimulus environment" (1989:226). This image of implicit learning as a mechanism capable of unconscious rule abstraction, that may be even more powerful than our slow and capacity-limited conscious strategies of knowledge acquisition, contrasts sharply with an alternative view according to which implicit learning relies on elementary cognitive operations such as the storage in memory of specific exemplar stimuli or the

learning of event frequencies and conditional probabilities (e.g. Perruchet 1994a; see also Greenwald 1992, see section 5).

Question 4: What are the computational mechanisms underlying implicit learning?

The first wave of implicit learning research was dominated by attempts
to demonstrate replicable dissociations between performance measures
and conscious knowledge in order to prove the existence of implicit
learning. More recently, interest in underlying processing mechanisms
has increased and various computational models of implicit learning
have been explored with the aid of computer simulation (e.g. Dienes
1992, Cleeremans 1993, Haider 1990, Mathews 1991, Servan-Schreiber
& Anderson 1990; see section 6).

Question 5: What brain systems are involved in implicit learning?

Finally, we can ask whether explicit and implicit forms of learning and
knowledge are mediated by separate brain systems or networks of
systems, and whether different forms of implicit learning are subserved
by a single system or whether there are separable brain systems
underlying different forms of unconscious learning. Although findings
from clinical neuropsychology and functional brain imaging have to date
yielded only fragmentary answers to these questions, they provide
additional constraints that help to decide between competing theories,
which are sometimes difficult to distinguish on the basis of behavioural
data alone (see section 7).

2. DISSOCIATIONS AND OPERATIONAL CRITERIA

The trajectory of the concept of the unconscious through the history of
experimental psychology resembles that of a pendulum periodically
swinging from fascination and almost uncritical acceptance to
methodological scepticism and even radical rejection. For many people
the intuitive appeal of implicit learning resides in its allegedly
unconscious status. The idea that not only basic processes like pattern
recognition or peripheral motor control, but also complex cognitive
processes may occur outside of consciousness, fascinates researchers and
lay people alike. On the other hand, sceptical doubts have been raised
throughout the history of psychology as to whether unconscious
cognition in general and implicit learning in particular do exist at all.
Attempts to resolve this controversy empirically are plagued by various
methodological and conceptual problems. It is no accident that the
current controversy about implicit learning is in many respects a

recapitulation of the debate about subliminal perception in the 1960s (see Dixon 1971, Eriksen 1960, Greenwald 1992, Holender 1986).

Virtually all arguments for the existence of implicit learning are based on dissociations between performance in direct tasks supposedly tapping explicit, conscious knowledge and indirect tasks supposedly measuring implicit, unconscious knowledge (cf. Reingold & Merikle 1990). Such dissociations can take one of two forms.[4]

Quantitative dissociation

A quantitative dissociation is present when performance in an indirect test cannot be fully accounted for by conscious knowledge as revealed by a direct test. Erderlyi (1986) has expressed this condition in terms of a simple unequality: the amount of knowledge revealed in a direct test (E) must be less than the amount of knowledge revealed in an indirect test (I), that is, $E < I$. In the extreme case, E equals 0. For instance, when subjects in an AG experiment classify new letter strings better than chance, but cannot verbalize the rules guiding their decisions, this is considered as evidence that classification performance must have been based on implicit knowledge. Likewise, when subjects in a sequence learning experiment show reaction time increments when they respond to a structured sequence of stimuli as compared to a random sequence, but cannot recall segments of the sequence, this is considered as evidence that subjects' knowledge about the sequence structure is implicit. In many cases, however, subjects are able to verbalize at least fragments of the stimulus structure or some of the rules guiding their decisions. In such cases one must show that this fragmentary conscious knowledge is not sufficient to fully account for the performance increments in the allegedly indirect test, a requirement that – as we will see – can be very difficult to fulfil.

Qualitative dissociations

Qualitative (sometimes termed *functional*) dissociations are present when an independent variable has an effect on performance in task A, but not on task B, or when a variable even has opposite effects on the two tasks (one speaks of single and double dissociations, respectively). For instance, consider an AG experiment in which subjects study a list of letter strings either with their full attention focused on the strings, or with their attention distracted because they have to perform an attention-demanding secondary task. If the secondary task impairs the ability to consciously recall letter strings but has no effect on the ability to judge the grammaticality of new letter strings, this would constitute a single dissociation. When a further variable (for instance, a certain type of brain damage) would impair implicit learning but leave conscious knowledge intact, this would constitute evidence for a double dissociation. Unfortunately, whereas qualitative dissociations have become an empirical cornerstone for distinguishing between implicit and explicit memory, they have received far less attention in implicit learning research.

A closer look reveals various problems with the logic of dissociations, especially with respect to quantitative dissociations (see Reingold & Merikle 1990, Shanks & St. John 1994). I will consider seven such problems in order to highlight the conceptual and empirical intricacies inherent in the study of implicit learning. The first three problems concern the interpretation of dissociations between tasks allegedly measuring explicit and implicit knowledge. The final four problems concern the operational criteria for explicit and implicit knowledge and the question of how one can be sure that performance in a given task was in fact unconscious and not mediated by conscious knowledge.

(1) Explanatory (in)sufficiency problem

The explanatory sufficiency problem concerns the question of how one can be sure that performance increments in an allegedly indirect task cannot be fully accounted for by explicit knowledge as revealed by a direct test. For instance, consider subjects in an AG task who are better than chance in judging the grammaticality of new letter strings and who also report fragmentary conscious knowledge about the permissibility of letter pairs. In order to attribute subjects' above-chance performance in the classification test to implicit learning, one would have to show that their conscious knowledge is not sufficient to explain the level of accuracy in the classification test. As we will see later, in many implicit learning experiments it is unclear whether this criterion has been satisfied.

(2) Causal necessity problem

Although the explanatory insufficiency of explicit knowledge justifies the conclusion that at least part of the acquired knowledge must be implicit, the reverse does not hold. Even if explicit knowledge as revealed by a direct task is in fact sufficient to account for performance in the indirect test, this does not necessarily imply that learning was *not* implicit. To establish this conclusion one must further show that the explicit knowledge was *in fact* causally effective in mediating performance in the indirect test. For instance, when a subject in an AG experiment can consciously recall permissible letter pairs from study strings, this does not show that the ability to make above-chance judgements of the grammaticality of novel strings was causally mediated by conscious recollections of letter pairs. Rather, it is possible that grammaticality judgements and free recall reflect learning in two parallel, independent learning systems. It may even be that explicit knowledge is the result of a reflection about one's own implicit or procedural knowledge. By now it may seem impossible in principle to demonstrate that explicit knowledge was or was not causally efficacious. However, I will argue later that the study of brain-damaged patients provides an important source of constraint that may help to decide this issue. The point is that if patients can be identified who lack the ability to retain new explicit, declarative knowledge but nevertheless show normal performance increments in some implicit learning task, this suggests that explicit knowledge is not a necessary cause for the observed learning effects.

(3) Backward inference problem

The third problem is in some sense the mirror image of the causal necessity problem. As Shanks et al. (1994) have recently pointed out, virtually all attempts to infer the unconscious nature of implicit learning rely on a backward inference from a later direct test to the previous learning task. This raises the concern that explicit knowledge that was available and perhaps causally relevant during the learning task may be subject to rapid forgetting and therefore go undetected in a later direct test. For instance, many people serving as subjects in the serial reaction task described earlier have from time to time – especially early in training – the impression that they are able to anticipate the next stimulus or experience a fleeting awareness that some stimuli follow others in a regular fashion. However, at this stage, even a slight distraction of attention can cause forgetting of this knowledge. Thus, even if subjects were probed immediately afterwards, they might not be able to verbalize their impressions. The point is that such fleeting pieces of fragmentary conscious knowledge, although they will not be stored in declarative long-term memory, may nevertheless be a necessary condition for initial performance increments to occur. It is difficult to test this possibility, because probing subjects' conscious knowledge at various points during the training task has the unavoidable side-effect of directing subjects' attention to stimulus structures and thus altering their task strategy (Shanks et al. 1994). Although this may also have the flavor of an unresolveable dilemma, I will later discuss recent attempts to overcome this problem by using event-related brain potentials as a non-obtrusive online measure of explicit knowledge in a sequence learning task (Eimer et al., in press).

(4) Information criterion

I now turn to the second class of problems which relate to the question of how to measure explicit and implicit knowledge. Most researchers seem to agree that any empirical approach to the problem of implicit knowledge must rely on a *third-person* perspective. This means that we do not have direct access to subjective phenomenal states of other persons (these states are called *qualia* in philosophy). Rather we have to infer the presence (or absence) of conscious knowledge from observable behaviour, where I understand behaviour in a broad sense as including choice reactions, verbal report, psychophysiological indicators, and neurophysiological measures of brain activity.[5] In a recent review of the implicit learning literature, Shanks & St. John (1994) formulated two important criteria that behavioural tests must satisfy to count as valid measures of explicit knowledge. According to what they term the *information criterion*, a direct test must tap the very knowledge that was in fact responsible for performance in the indirect test (this criterion is related to, but not identical to, the explanatory sufficiency problem). Consider a subject in an AG learning task who is able to classify novel letter strings as grammatical or non-grammatical significantly better than one would expect by chance, but who is not able to report any of the rules of the artificial grammar. According to Shanks & St. John this does not suffice to show that his or her grammaticality judgements were not based on explicit knowledge. The reason is that a different type of knowledge may have governed classification performance. For instance, the subject may have classified novel strings on the basis of their similarity to previously presented strings, and this knowledge may well be accessible to consciousness, but will not be reported if it is not specifically asked for.

(5) Sensitivity criterion

A second problem discussed by Shanks & St. John (1994) is that direct and indirect tests may simply differ in their sensitivity, that is, knowledge revealed in a direct test may not exhaust all conscious knowledge that a subject actually has. For instance, when a subject is asked to classify letter strings as grammatical or non-grammatical, she or he may rely on conscious hypotheses about what makes a string grammatical. However, when these hypotheses are associated with very low subjective confidence, the subject may refrain from reporting them, because he or she may set a strict criterion as to how confident one must be that a given rule is correct to consider it worth reporting. By contrast, the subject may set a more lenient criterion in the case of grammaticality judgements, especially when explicitly forced to guess, and thus perfomance on this test will be influenced even by low-confidence knowledge.[6]

(6) Subjective and objective criteria

The two criteria discussed by Shanks & St. John relate to an important distinction between subjective and objective criteria for consciousness. This distinction was introduced in research on subliminal perception by Cheesman & Merikle (1984, Holender 1986, Merikle 1982). Stimuli are said to be below a subjective threshold when a subject shows above-chance discriminative responding but denies being aware of the relevant information mediating their discriminations (for instance, when subjects guess better than chance the identity of tachistoscopically-flashed words, although they deny having seen the words at all). Stimuli are below objective threshold when subjects actually respond at chance level in a forced-choice discrimination task (that is, when subjects perform at chance in deciding whether a word was presented or not). According to a strict conception of the term unconscious, only stimuli below an objective threshold are unconscious.

To a considerable degree, the controversy surrounding implicit learning derives from one's preference for either a subjective or an objective criterion for unconscious knowledge. For instance, Shanks & St. John (1994) have raised serious doubts as to whether verbal reports meet the Sensitivity and the Information Criterion and recommend the use of an objective criterion of unconsciousness and discriminative behaviours as measures of conscious knowledge. According to their view, in order to convincingly establish that knowledge in an implicit learning task is unconscious it is necessary to show that subjects perform at chance level in forced choice tests intended to measure conscious knowledge. For instance, subjects in a serial reaction task may be said to have no conscious knowledge about a structured event sequence when they cannot discriminate better than chance between old and new sequences.

However, as Berry & Dienes (1993:15) rightly point out, performance cannot be at chance on all discriminative tests, otherwise no measure would remain to demonstrate the existence of implicit learning. Thus a distinction has to be made between those discriminative tasks which are to be used to establish the non-existence of explicit knowledge and those discriminative tasks which are intended to reveal the existence of implicit knowledge. But how can we decide a priori which kind of discriminative behaviour indicates conscious knowledge and which reflects implicit knowledge?

At this point we are faced with a fundamental problem that must be solved before we can even start to apply the sensitivity and information criteria. The logic of task dissociations presupposes that we already have an operational criterion that allows us to distinguish direct and indirect tests, indexing explicit and implicit knowledge, respectively. Once we have such a criterion, dissociations between indirect and direct tasks may be considered as evidence for implicit learning. But a dissociation between two tasks in itself provides no information about the implicit or explicit nature of the dissociated tasks. This becomes clear when one considers the fact that our interpretation of task dissociations is often inconsistent (see Allport 1988, for a thoughtful discussion of this point). Consider the behaviour of blindsight patients who as a result of a certain type of brain damage are obviously blind in a specific area of the visual field. Although these patients may report seeing nothing in the "blind" field, they are sometimes able to discriminate in a forced-choice test whether or not a stimulus was presented or they may even be able to grasp the "unseen" object (Weiskrantz 1986). Many people are inclined to interpret such non-verbal behaviour as an expression of *implicit* knowledge. However, compare this case with a split-brain patient[7] who is presented an object in the left visual field such that the information reaches the right hemisphere. Right-handed patients will usually be unable to name the object, because the information has no access to left hemispheric structures necessary for speech production. It has been shown, however, that such patients are nevertheless able to choose the correct object from a set of hidden test objects on the basis of tactile information with their left hand (which is controlled by the right hemisphere). Such observations have sometimes been interpreted as showing that the right hemisphere is conscious of the object, but cannot express its knowledge verbally (see Puchetti 1985, and peer commentary for discussion). In this case non-verbal discriminative behaviour is taken as evidence for conscious knowledge, although the patient – like the blindsight patient – cannot verbally express what he or she perceives or knows.

Let us consider a number of solutions that may be proposed to resolve such inconsistencies. First, one might think that the problem will be resolved once we know more about the underlying neurophysiological processes. However, in principle the question under which conditions discriminative behaviour does or does not indicate conscious knowledge returns on the neurological level itself. We have no better criteria to decide whether a brain process is associated with consciousness than we have in the case of overt behaviour. If anything, the available neurophysiological evidence suggests that there is no single brain system in which unitary visual representations are formed and which serves as the basis for both conscious perception and intentional control of action (cf. Damasio 1989, Dennett 1991, Kinsbourne 1988). Rather the ability to make verbal judgements about visual objects and the ability to perform goal-directed motor actions with the same objects appear to be mediated by neuro-anatomically separate systems (Goodale 1993).

Secondly, it has been suggested taking into account the complexity, sophistication, or flexibility of a given piece of behaviour as a criterion. In the case of simple discriminations or preference judgements (as in the example of the blindsight patient), we are inclined to consider the underlying knowledge as unconscious. If behaviour is complex and shows transfer to various tasks (for instance, when one can use an object for various purposes), we are more willing to ascribe conscious knowledge about the object to the behaving agent. Although this is a reasonable heuristic, it runs the danger of being circular. The reason why we want operational criteria for implicit and explicit knowledge is that we want to investigate empirically the functional characteristics of the two forms of knowledge. Using the complexity or flexibility of behaviour as a criterion to distinguish explicit and implicit knowledge means presupposing functional characteristics of the two types of knowledge, which should instead be revealed by empirical research based on some independent operational criterion.

Thirdly, it is tempting to conceive of being conscious of something as being able to voluntarily repond to this something (in contrast to guessing or automatic responding). The problem then becomes one of how to distinguish voluntary from involuntary behaviour. A common operational criterion for voluntary action is that the corresponding behaviour can systematically be modulated by verbal instructions (for instance, a subject's key press in response to a stimulus is considered as voluntary, when it would not occur unless the subject was instructed to respond in this way). However, at this point we are back at accepting subjects' verbally expressed understanding of our instructions and their consent to follow these instructions as the criterion for conscious knowledge.

A task-content criterion.   The conclusion I want to draw from this discussion is that it is difficult if not impossible *not* to rely on subjects' verbal report or consent to verbal instructions as a criterion for conscious knowledge. This does not invalidate the importance of Shanks & St. John's (1994) Sensitivity and Information Criteria. It may often be true that free recall or verbal reports do not exhaust what a subject is conscious of and that forced-choice judgements are more sensitive measures of conscious knowledge. This fact does not, however, solve the problem of how to decide whether a test measures explicit or implicit knowledge. For instance, whether performance in a forced-choice recognition test does or does not express explicit knowledge depends on whether the subject bases his or her recognition judgements on conscious recollections or whether he or she is guessing. A subject who is simply guessing may nevertheless perform better than chance, but I see no reasons why such performance should be considered as an expression of conscious knowledge. Thus the only way to make it plausible that subjects perform a task on the basis of what they are subjectively conscious of is either to instruct them to do so or to rely on their verbal report that they have done so. What justifies us in interpreting a test as a test of explicit and not of implicit knowledge is not whether the task requires verbal reports or discriminative behaviour, but the crucial point is the *semantic content* of the task *instruction* and the subject's *intention* to follow this instruction.[8] In this sense forced-choice responses, even non-verbal ones, constitute speech acts that express a subject's belief about the information in question (for instance, a key-press may express the belief "I have seen this letter string before" or "grammatical strings never start with an X").

Note that this conclusion does not invalidate the use of additional convergent criteria. For instance, in lack of better knowledge, it is a reasonable heuristic to take into account the complexity or flexibility of behavioural responses as a criterion for conscious knowledge. We should be aware of the possibility that there are simply no clear-cut a priori operational criteria for conscious and unconscious knowledge, but that the distinction will be continuously refined as the network of relevant observations, interpretations, and constraints from many levels of explanation evolves.

(7) Contamination problem

Up to this point I have considered the problem of how to measure conscious knowledge as the problem of how to specify criteria to classify tasks as measuring implicit and explicit knowledge. I have thus presupposed that there are such tasks. However, a final problem that we have to consider is that this assumption may just be wrong because performance in many tasks will reflect both explicit and implicit knowledge. For instance, recognition judgements may reflect a mixture of conscious recollections and feelings of familiarity that need not be accompanied by conscious recollection (Jacoby 1991, Mandler 1980). The converse holds as well: performance in an allegedly indirect test may be contaminated by explicit knowledge and conscious memories (Schacter et al. 1989). Serious doubts have been raised as to whether there are process-pure measures of either explicit or implicit knowledge at all (cf. Jacoby 1991).

Two solutions to this problem have been proposed. The first is to rely on qualitative rather than quantitative dissociations. If it can be shown that an independent variable has different or even opposite effects on performance in an implicit learning task and on measures of conscious knowledge, this suggests that performance in the two tasks is mediated by different types of knowledge and/or processes (although even this conclusion is not unambiguous; see Dunn & Kirsner 1988). Unfortunately, in contrast to implicit memory research, to date there are only a few examples of qualitative dissociations in the study of implicit learning (see section 3.2).

A second solution for the contamination problem is the so-called *process dissociation method* that was proposed by Jacoby (1991) and that also has primarily been used in implicit memory research. I will defer a discussion of this method until section 3.3, where I summarize recent results from our own work (Goschke & Stürmer, in preparation) in which we applied this method to an implicit learning task.

3. QUESTION (1): DOES IMPLICIT LEARNING LEAD TO UNCONSCIOUS KNOWLEDGE?

Having sharpened our awareness of the conceptual and methodological problems inherent in the attempt to demonstrate implicit learning and unconscious knowledge, we can now turn to the first theoretical question formulated in the introduction.

3. 1 Artificial grammar learning
In their studies on AG learning, Reber and his associates have frequently used verbal reports as indicators for conscious knowledge. In terms of the distinction between objective and subjective criteria for unconsciousness they adhered to the latter criterion. For instance, in one such experiment Reber & Allen (1978) asked subjects to justify their grammaticality judgements and reported that subjects often referred to aspects of the letter strings such as "... first and last letters, bigrams, ... trigrams and recursions" (Reber & Allen 1978:202). However, according to the authors such retrospective reports of rule-like pieces of knowledge "yielded few data of value" (Abrams & Reber 1988:432) and contained only few correct and often even incorrect descriptions of the underlying grammar (cf. Reber & Lewis 1977).

According to the criteria formulated in section 2 this conclusion is valid only insofar as the reported fragmentary rules were insufficient to account for the level of accuracy of the (less than perfect) grammaticality judgements. Therefore Mathews et al. (1989) trained subjects with grammar strings over a period of four weeks and asked them to report any rules that would help one to distinguish grammatical from nongrammatical strings. These protocols were used to instruct a different group of yoked subjects, who had not been trained with the letter strings and who were asked to use the rules provided by the experimental subjects as guidelines to classify novel letter strings. The yoked subjects performed well above chance, but significantly worse than the experimental subjects who had been trained on the letter strings. The authors interpreted this finding as evidence that verbal reports do not exhaust the knowledge that actually mediated the experimental subjects' classification performance, suggesting that part of this knowledge must have been implicit.

The instruction method, however, suffers from several weaknesses. Among other things, the yoked subjects may have had problems in applying the rules correctly or may not have used them consistently or exhaustively. In fact, even subjects who were given complete information about the rules underlying the behaviour of a simulated dynamic system showed far from perfect performance when subsequently trying to control the system themselves (Stanley et al. 1989). To overcome these problems Dienes et al. (1991) performed an AG study in which they used the rules that had been verbalized by their subjects as the basis for a computer simulation of the classification task. Simulated classification performance was still worse than subjects' performance, indicating that even when the verbalized rules were applied exhaustively and in an error-free way, they were not sufficient to fully account for subjects' classification performance.

In summary, when one accepts a subjective criterion for determining awareness of knowledge, AG studies suggest that at least part of the acquired knowledge is implicit and not accessible to verbal report. This conclusion has been challenged, however, by those who prefer an objective criterion of (un)awareness. As was discussed earlier, according to Shanks & St. John (1994) verbal reports may not be sensitive enough to reveal all conscious knowledge subjects have, especially when they set a strict criterion for what they consider worth reporting. Various researchers have therefore used discriminative or forced-choice tasks as more sensitive measures for conscious knowledge. In one important AG study, Dulany et al. (1984) had their subjects underline those parts of each test string that they thought would make the string grammatical or non-grammatical. The authors interpreted the marked letters as the expression of fragmentary conscious rules which, for example, may be verbally paraphrased as "strings may not begin with an X" or "strings frequently contain an RV". The authors could show that these miniature rules (which they termed a "correlated grammar") predicted subjects' actual classification performance without substantial residue. The authors concluded that AG learning does not involve unconscious rule abstraction, but is rather based on the acquisition of conscious fragmentary knowledge.[9]

Although these results are interesting in their own right because they suggest what kind of knowledge may underlie AG learning, they are not conclusive with respect to the consciousness issue. First, it is not clear to what degree Dulany et al.'s data suffer from the Contamination Problem, because subjects' marks may well reflect implicit influences. That is, subjects may subjectively believe they are guessing or may mark letters on a purely "intuitive" basis, in which case it seems odd to consider the marks as an expression of conscious knowledge. Secondly, the instruction to underline critical letters may have forced subjects to reflect about their own performance and to (re)construct explicit knowledge that was not necessarily causally mediating their spontaneous grammaticality judgements (it is thus unclear whether the Causal Necessity Criterion was satisfied; see Dulany et al. 1985 and Reber et al. 1985, for further discussion).

In summary, the available evidence indicates that part of the knowledge acquired in AG learning appears to be below a subjective threshold. Knowledge elicited in free reports appears to be insufficient to fully account for classification performance, even if the knowledge was applied exhaustively and error-free by means of computer simulation. By contrast, researchers using forced-choice measures of explicit knowledge have sometimes reported that the elicited knowledge was sufficient to account for the level of accuracy in subjects' grammaticality judgements. However, it is not fully clear how far forced-choice measures are contaminated by implicit knowledge and whether conscious fragmentary knowledge about bigrams is actually causally effective in making grammaticality judgements. In the light of the Causal Necessity Problem the fact that subjects acquire some explicit knowledge which may be sufficient to account for their grammaticality judgements, does not necessarily show that the explicit knowledge was causally relevant for their performance. In adult humans it may be very difficult to establish conditions in which performing a task produces no explicit knowledge at all. This does not exclude the possibility, however, that explicit and implicit learning systems operate in parallel and independently from each other. Of course, this hypothesis would be empirically empty if it was impossible in principle to test whether conscious knowledge does or does not play a causal role in implicit learning. Therefore, recent studies of AG learning in amnesic patients are particularly important because they provide suggestive evidence that conscious memory for study strings or bigrams is in fact not necessary for AG learning to occur (see section 7).

3.2 Dynamic system control tasks

Dissocations between verbalizable knowledge and task performance have also been observed in dynamic system control tasks. Berry & Broadbent (1984, cf. Broadbent et al. 1986) found that practice with these systems (e.g. the sugar production system described earlier) improved control performance, but had no effect on the amount of explicit knowledge as revealed in a post-experimental questionnaire in which subjects were asked about the relationships governing the system. In addition, there was no positive correlation between control performance and verbal knowledge. In fact, subjects who performed better in controlling the system showed even less accurate knowledge about the system in the questionnaire. Moreover, providing subjects with advance information about how to control the system improved their explicit knowledge in the questionnaire, but did not change their actual level of performance in controlling the system.

In contrast to these observations, a number of recent studies have found positive correlations between verbal reports and control performance, at least under certain conditions (e.g. McGeorge & Burton 1989, Sanderson 1989). However, in most cases the evidence appears compatible with the assumption that explicit knowledge emerges later than increments in control performance (this conclusion receives further support from studies with amnesic patients discussed in section 7). For instance, Stanley et al. (1989) had their subjects practise a control task and asked them to explain verbally how to control the system. An analysis of the learning curves showed that control performance improved before subjects were able to verbally explain how one could control the system. From such findings it has been concluded that control performance and verbal reports do not reflect access to a common knowledge base, but that there are partially independent knowledge systems underlying action and conscious knowledge.

Further evidence for this conclusion was reported by Hayes & Broadbent (1988). In each trial, subjects pressed one of 12 keys indicating 12 possible attitudes toward a computer-simulated "person" (ranging from "very unfriendly" to "loving"). The computer person would then in turn respond with one of the 12 attitudes. Subjects' task was to maintain the computer person's responses at a "friendly" level. In a so-called salient condition, the computer's response in each trial was a function of the subject's attitude in that trial minus 2, plus a random number r being either -1, 0, or 1. In the non-salient condition, the computer behaved according to the same equation, but responded to the subject's response in the next-to-last trial. After subjects in both conditions had attained a specified level of success in controlling the computer person, a transfer phase followed in which the equations governing the computer responses were changed by replacing the -2 with a $+2$. When subjects worked on these tasks under single task conditions, performance in the non-salient condition was worse than in the salient condition after the unexpected change in the underlying equations. By contrast, in a dual task condition, in which subjects had to generate random letters or numbers while they were working on the computer person task, the salient group showed worse relearning after the contingency change as compared to the nonsalient group. Hayes & Broadbent interpreted these findings as evidence for two different learning systems. According to this interpretation, learning in the non-salient condition proceeds via an unselective learning system which stores all contingencies between stimuli in a passive way, but which produces knowledge that is inflexible and not verbalizable. Unselective implicit learning is assumed to operate independently from working memory and should thus not be affected by the secondary task. By contrast, learning in the salient condition proceeds via a selective learning system mediating explicit learning of a small number of salient contingencies. The selective system produces knowledge which is amenable to verbal report and which can be used in a flexible way to change one's responses after the change in the contingencies in the transfer phase. Selective learning is assumed to engage a limited-capacity working memory system and should thus be impaired under dual task conditions.

These findings are noteworthy because they constitute a *double dissociation* between the two tasks and thus provide evidence for the assumption of two independent learning systems. However, in a replication study, Green & Shanks (1993) failed to obtain the critical interaction between salient versus non-salient conditions and single versus dual tasks. These authors consistently found that both with and without a secondary task, subjects showed better performance after the rule change in the salient control task than in the non-salient task. They suggest that the two tasks simply differ with respect to their difficulty.

Further doubts about the original interpretation of system control studies are raised when one considers the Explanatory Sufficiency Criterion. For instance, with respect to the computer person task, one may question whether subjects actually have to learn the underlying regularities to be able to master the task, not to speak of the assumption that the implicit learning system extracts *all* contingencies in the environment (Hayes & Broadbent 1988). Various researchers (Buchner 1993, Haider 1990, Sanderson 1989) have shown that very simple strategies will often produce a relatively high level of performance, especially with non-salient systems. Examples for such simple but efficient strategies in the computer person task are, for instance, choosing only responses in the "friendly" range or constantly pressing the key 9. If subjects use such strategies, it is not very suprising that their task performance does not correlate with their verbal description of the underlying system, because they neither need this knowledge in order to perform at a reasonable level, nor do they explore the state space of the system sufficiently exhaustively to even have a chance to acquire such knowledge (cf. Buchner 1993). Furthermore, Dienes & Fahey (1995) have recently shown that participants can learn to control a non-salient dynamic system simply by storing instances of previously successful trials on the task. Whereas participants had a tendency to repeat the same response for situations in which they had previously been correct, they performed at chance on new situations dissimilar to old ones. This shows that learning in system control tasks need not reflect unconscious abstraction of rules, but can be explained by a simple "look-up table" model.

3.3 Sequence learning

Dissociations between performance increments and conscious knowledge have also been observed in sequence learning tasks. In a number of studies a reliable speed-up of reaction times in the serial reaction task described in section 1.2 has been reported for subgroups of subjects who were not able to verbalize the sequence structure after training or who had not even noticed that there was a structure (e.g. Cohen et al. 1990, Curran & Keele 1993, Reed & Johnson 1994, Stadler 1993, Willingham et al. 1989, Willingham et al. 1993). Analogous results were obtained with the matrix search task (Lewicki et al. 1988). Moreover, subjects showed reliable learning in the serial reaction task even if their performance in a subsequent prediction task, in which they had to predict on each trial at which location the next stimulus would appear, was not superior to that of control subjects who had been trained on a random sequence (e.g. Cohen et al. 1990, Hartman et al. 1989, Stadler 1989, Willingham et al. 1989). From the fact that subjects performed at chance level in the prediction task, but nevertheless showed reliable performance increments in the sequence learning task, or from the fact that performance in the prediction task was uncorrelated with the response times in the sequence learning task, it has been concluded that the knowledge acquired in the serial reaction task is (partly) implicit.

Perruchet & Amorim (1992) have recently questioned the usefulness of the prediction task as a measure of conscious sequence knowledge. They noted that in almost all previous studies subjects had not been explicitly instructed that the sequence of events in the prediction tasks was the same as in the previous serial reaction task. This and other methodological arguments led them to the conclusion that conscious sequence knowledge can be better assessed with recognition and free recall tasks. In one of their own experiments, they had subjects first perform the serial reaction task with a 10-trial sequence that was repeated 10 times. After this task one group of subjects received a recognition task in which they had to decide whether four-item sequences were part of the previously presented sequence or not. Another group received a free recall task in which subjects were instructed to reproduce the training sequence, using the same keys as in the serial reaction task. Subjects performed well above chance in both the recognition and free recall test. Even more remarkable, there were impressively high correlations (ranging from 0.63 to 0.98) between reaction time benefits in the serial reaction task and both recognition and recall of partial sequences. The authors concluded that learning in the serial reaction task is mediated by the acquisition of conscious knowledge about small chunks of three or four successive sequence elements.

Although these results suggest that explicit knowledge may play a more prominent role in sequence learning than was previously thought, the issue is far from settled. First, a dissociation between explicit knowledge and reaction time benefits in the serial reaction task has recently been reported even though a recognition test was used (Willingham et al. 1993; but see Perruchet & Gallego 1993, for a critical discussion). Secondly, in the light of the Contamination Problem it is not clear whether tasks like recognition or recall are process-pure measures of explicit knowledge or whether they are influenced by implicit knowledge (Cohen & Curran 1993). For instance, even subjects having the subjective impression of simply guessing in the recall task may nevertheless perform better than chance due to the influence of implicit knowledge.

Process-dissociation

We have recently made an attempt to tackle the Contamination Problem and to separate conscious and unconscious knowledge in sequence learning (Goschke & Stürmer, in preparation). Subjects performed the serial reaction task either with a repeating 12-element sequence or with a pseudo-random sequence. At various points during the task, subjects performed a sequence production task in which they were asked to self-generate a 100-trial sequence using the same keys as in the serial reaction task. The novel feature of our study was that we did not consider the sequence production task as a process-pure measure of explicit knowledge, but we tried to separate the influences of implicit and explicit knowledge within this task. To this end we adapted the process-dissociation method that was proposed by Jacoby (1991, Jacoby et al. 1993) in the field of implicit memory. This method is based on the idea of setting intentional (explicit) and automatic (implicit) processes in opposition to each other. This is done by comparing performance in a so-called *inclusion* and an *exclusion* condition. In our *inclusion condition* subjects were instructed to try to remember and reproduce as accurately as possible the previous training sequence. Only when they were not able to recollect the old sequence were they allowed to guess and press any key that would "feel" correct (this condition is called inclusive because performance reflects both conscious knowledge and mere guessing). By contrast, in the *exclusion condition*, subjects were instructed to produce a random sequence and not to reproduce the training sequence. In both conditions, we computed how often subjects produced chunks of lengths two to 12 that were contained in the training sequence.

We reasoned that a subject with perfect explicit knowledge of the training sequence should produce *only* chunks from the training sequence in the inclusion condition, whereas she or he should produce *no* chunks from the training sequence in the exclusion condition. In this case sequence production would be under complete intentional control. By contrast, a subject possessing no explicit knowledge at all has no intentional control over performance and should thus produce an equal number of chunks from the training sequence in the exclusion and inclusion conditions. When a subject in the exclusion condition produces more chunks from the training sequence than a subject who had been trained on a random sequence, this difference can be attributed to unconscious influences of the previous exposure to the structured sequence. The reason is that if the subject had conscious knowledge about the training sequence he or she would avoid producing chunks from the training sequence in the exclusion condition. By the same logic, the amount of truly conscious knowledge of the sequence can be estimated by subtracting recall performance in the exclusion condition from performance in the inclusion condition (thereby correcting recall performance for implicit influences). Jacoby et al. (1993) have described how separate quantitative measures of conscious and unconscious influences can be derived from performance in the two conditions by way of simple algebra.[10]

Using this method, we obtained a number of noteworthy findings. First, we showed that sequence recall is in fact contaminated by implicit knowledge, as indicated by the fact that subjects trained on a structured sequence produced more chunks from the training sequence in the exclusion condition than one would expect by chance. That is, although subjects intentionally tried not to reproduce the training sequence, they were unable to avoid doing so. Secondly, the process-dissociation method allowed us to track the time course of the development of explicit and implicit knowledge. Whereas early in training, subjects showed above-chance probability of producing chunks from the training sequence both in the exclusion and inclusion conditions, after prolonged training they showed an increasing tendency to produce chunks from the training sequence in the inclusion condition only, and sometimes showed even below-chance frequency of chunks in the exclusion condition. Thirdly, we obtained a dissociation between performance increments in the serial reaction task and process-dissociation estimates of explicit knowledge. Although subjects showed virtually no intentional control over the production of chunks from the training sequence early in training (the number of correctly recalled old chunks in the exclusion and inclusion conditions did not differ significantly from each other), they already showed a reliable speed-up of response times in the serial reaction task after no more than five repetitions of the structured sequence. Finally, subjects whose attention was distracted during the serial reaction task by a concurrent secondary task showed lower estimates of explicit knowledge, whereas the index of implicit knowledge was unaffected by the distraction. These findings demonstrate that the process-dissociation method can profitably be applied to implicit learning research in order to separate implicit and explicit knowledge.

Event-related brain potentials and sequence learning

In the introduction I discussed a further problem in measuring conscious knowledge which I termed the Backward Inference Problem (Shanks et al. 1994, Shanks & St. John 1994). This problem results from the fact that explicit knowledge is usually measured after the training phase and thus fragmentary explicit knowledge that was available during the serial reaction task may simply have been forgotten. Moreover, probing subjects' conscious knowledge has the unavoidable side-effect of directing their attention to the structure inherent in the stimuli and thereby altering their subsequent strategy in the serial reaction task.

In search of an on-line measure of explicit knowledge that can be obtained unobtrusively and concurrently with the serial reaction task, we turned to electrophysiological indicators of subjects' brain activity (Eimer et al., in press).

Event-related brain potentials (ERPs)[11] were recorded while subjects performed a modified variant of the serial reaction task, where in each trial one of four letters (A, B, C, D) was presented at fixation, each of which was mapped to one out of four response keys. Subjects were presented two blocks, each consisting of 54 repetitions of an ambiguous 10-letter sequence. At unpredictable points in the standard sequence, *deviant* letters were inserted, that were not allowed to occur at that specific position within the regular sequence. In two experiments we found that reaction times for deviant stimuli were significantly slower than for standard stimuli, this difference becoming more pronounced in the course of training. Subjects clearly had acquired knowledge about the sequential structure. Verbal reports and a recognition test for parts of the training sequence showed that some subjects had acquired partial explicit knowledge about segments of this sequence. These subjects produced larger reaction time differences between deviant and standard trials than subjects showing no explicit knowledge. Most important, sequence learning was also reflected in electrophysiological measures. When we computed ERPs separately for regular and deviant items, we obtained an enhanced negativity in the range of 200 milliseconds post-stimulus for deviant as compared to regular items. This "N2" effect tended to be larger in the second part of the experiment. Moreover, the degree to which subjects became aware of the sequence was reflected in the ERP data. Subjects possessing at least some explicit knowledge produced a larger N2 effect than subjects lacking explicit knowledge. For subjects with explicit knowledge the N2 effect increased in the course of the experiment, while for the other subjects this increment was smaller or even absent. This suggests that N2 enhancements elicited by deviant stimuli may be an indicator of the amount of consciously available, explicit knowledge about the stimulus sequence. Interestingly, there was a dissociation between electrophysiological and behavioural indicators of sequence learning. Subjects unaware of the sequence and showing no reliable N2 effect nevertheless showed considerable reaction time benefits for standard as compared to deviant stimuli. It is conceivable that these reaction time effects may be as a result of implicit learning processes that are reflected neither in verbal reports nor in electrophysiological measures. Recent results from brain-imaging studes using positron emission tomography (PET) indicate that procedural learning of a motor skill may involve modifications in some of the same brain areas which are also involved in the execution of the skill, including subcortical structures like the basal ganglia (see section 7). Learning-related neural activity in such subcortical brain structures is not easily tapped with electrophysiological measures obtained from the surface of the head. Thus, it is an interesting possibility that the dissociation between the N2 effect and reaction time benefits may be because the N2 in explicit learners reflects the detection of deviances from a sequential structure on the basis of explicit knowledge, while reaction time benefits in implicit learners are partly as a result of the development of new or more efficient motor programs in subcortical brain areas. However, at present we cannot rule out the alternative possibility that behavioural, verbal and electrophysiological measures tap the same type of knowledge, but simply differ in their sensitivity. Further studies are clearly needed to decide this issue.

Despite this reservation, ERPs should play an important role in future research on implicit learning. In contrast to behavioural measures, ERPs hold the promise of serving as a non-reactive on-line measure of the development of conscious knowledge that does not depend on the subject's overt responding and that can be obtained concurrently with the serial reaction task without having to inform subjects about the existence of a structure. Moreover, if our N2 effect turns out to be replicable, it would validate the backward inference from subjects' verbal reports to the processes underlying learning in the serial reaction task. The fact that the N2 effect was present only for subjects showing explicit knowledge about the sequence, but not for subjects having no explicit knowledge, indicates that subjects in both groups were matched in their ability to remember or verbalize sequential knowledge after the training phase. Rather, the N2 effect provides suggestive evidence that the acquisition of sequential knowledge in explicit and implicit learners was indeed mediated by different underlying brain processes. Hopefully, further investigations of the time course and topography of ERP waveforms in response to deviant and regular events in sequential learning tasks will yield new insights concerning the neurophysiological basis of sequence learning.

3.4 Conclusions

What conclusions can be drawn from the available evidence as regards the unawareness of implicit knowledge? Knowledge acquired in implicit learning tasks appears at least under certain conditions (especially when attention is distracted or when knowledge is probed early in training) to be below a subjective threshold. Subjects show performance increments in artificial grammar, system control, and sequence learning tasks, even when they are not able to verbally report the grammatical rules, the regularities governing dynamic systems, or the structure of event sequences. In most studies, lack of verbalizable knowledge was not complete, however, but frequently subjects reported fragmentary rules or contingencies. After pro-longed training, positive correlations between task performance and verbal knowledge have often been reported. At present it must be considered as an unresolved issue whether these findings indicate the existence of two independent learning systems operating in parallel or whether verbal reports and task performance simply differ in their sensitivity to low-confidence knowledge represented in a common knowledge base.

The use of forced-choice tests for explicit knowledge has usually led to much more sceptical conclusions as regards the unconscious nature of knowledge in implicit learning tasks. As will be shown in more detail in section 5, in almost all of these tasks it has been shown that the level of performance typically achieved by subjects can be accounted for by the assumption that subjects acquire fragmentary knowledge (for instance, knowledge about permissible letter pairs in artificial grammar learning, about co-varations between input–output values in a very restricted range of the state space in system control tasks). Moreover, such knowledge is often revealed in forced-choice measures such as recognition. This has been interpreted as evidence that performance in implicit learning tasks is not mediated by unconscious rules, but by conscious fragmentary knowledge. However, at present it seems premature to exclude the possibility of truly implicit learning. First, using forced-choice measures suffers from the problem that test performance may be contaminated by implicit knowledge. Recent attempts to separate implicit and explicit influences by means of the process-dissociation method (Goschke & Steiner, in preparation), suggest that knowledge may be implicit in early phases of sequence learning. Secondly, findings with amnesic patients to be discussed in section 7 also support the assumption that performance increments in various learning tasks do not rely on brain systems necessary for conscious recollection of prior episodes, but that one or several implicit learning systems may operate independently from conscious memory.

4. QUESTION (2): DOES IMPLICIT LEARNING REQUIRE ATTENTION OR IS IT AUTOMATIC?

Whereas the last section concerned the unconscious status of the *products* of implicit learning, I now turn to the role of attention and consciousness in the learning *process*. According to the second meaning of the term implicit, implicit learning is assumed to occur incidentally, independent of intention and attention. Learning processes can be implicit in at least two different ways. First, learning may occur without an intention to discover rules and in the absence of conscious hypothesis testing strategies. Secondly, learning may occur even though the relevant stimuli (or contingencies between stimuli) are ignored or processed outside of focal attention.[12] Given that explicit memory usually does depend on attention (e.g. Eich 1984), evidence that implicit learning requires no, or minimal, attention would be theoretically important because it implies a qualitative dissociation between implicit and explicit learning.

4.1 Implicit learning with unattended stimuli

Negative evidence for co-variation learning without attention was obtained by Carlson & Dulany (1985) in a category learning task. In a training phase, subjects were presented with a number of arrays consisting of three lines of five letters each. There were two categories of lines which were defined by the presence of either an R or an S in the centre of the line. R- and S-lines differed with respect to the probabilities with which letters appeared at the remaining positions of the line. For instance, the letter F appeared with 0.7 probability in R-lines, but only with 0.3 probability in S-lines (these remaining letters were termed "diagnostic features" by the authors). There was thus a statistical co-variation between the letters R and S, which defined the category, and the diagnostic features. The authors adapted Sperling's (1960) partial report technique to manipulate attention. In each trial, one line was cued and subjects had to report the letters from this line. In the attended condition, the critical letter R or S as well as the diagnostic features appeared on the cued line. In the unattended condition, the defining letters R or S also appeared on the cued line, but the diagnostic features appeared on a line adjacent to the cued line and were thus processed outside of focal attention. After 40 displays had been presented, subjects were informed about the existence of a category structure. They were presented 40 old and 40 new displays in which the central position was blank. Subjects were asked to indicate whether the missing letter should be an R or an S. There was no evidence that subjects in the unattended condition had learned anything about the relation between diagnostic features and category membership, and they classified test items at chance level. By contrast, subjects in the attended group classified both old and new test stimuli with greater-than-chance accuracy. This result appears to show that unattended contingencies were not learned. It should be noted, however, that the diagnostic letters in the uncued condition were not only presented outside of focal attention, but also on a different line than the defining letters R and S. It is therefore not clear whether differences between attended and unattended conditions may in part be due to the spatial segregation of the critical letters and the diagnostic features. Perhaps the co-variation would have been learned in the non-attended condition when both the diagnostic features and the category letter had been presented in the same (unattended) line.

Further negative evidence for learning of non-attended sequential dependencies stems from a sequence learning study by Willingham et al. (1989, Experiment 3). They had their subjects respond to four different colours which could appear at one of four locations. In a condition in which the sequence of colours followed a repeating pattern while the locations were determined at random, reliable sequence learning was obtained. By contrast, when the sequence of colours was random while the sequence of locations followed a repeating pattern, no learning was obtained in the training phase. Assuming that the instruction to respond to the colours has distracted attention from the locations, this result is compatible with the interpretation that sequential contingencies between locations are not learnt when they are neither actively attended to nor task-relevant.

However, contrasting results have been obtained by Mayr (1996) who presented geometric figures which could occur at different locations on the computer monitor. Both the sequence of objects and the sequence of locations followed a regular pattern and both sequences were completely uncorrelated. Although subjects had to respond to the identity of the objects, they nevertheless showed reliable learning of the sequence of locations. When the sequence of locations was switched to a random sequence there was a reliable increase in response times. One may suspect that the discrepancy between the two studies was because of the fact that in Mayr's study the distance between the different spatial locations was much larger (the locations formed the corners of a square with a side length of 20 cm) than in the experiment of Willingham et al. (the locations were separated by 4.8 cm). Thus, in Mayr's study eye movements may have been a critical factor in learning the unattended sequence of locations. However, using a different sequence learning task, Goschke (1996) showed that two uncorrelated sequences of letters and locations were learnt simultaneously even when subjects had to fixate on a central fixation point and trials with eye movements were excluded from the analyses.

Further positive evidence for learning of contingencies between ignored stimuli was reported by Buchner (1993, Experiment 3) in an experiment which combined AG and sequence learning techniques. In each trial, two letters were presented. One of the letters was presented in light grey, the other one in dark grey. Different groups of subjects were instructed to attend either only to dark or light letters and to decide as fast as possible whether it was a vowel or a consonant. Unbeknown to subjects, the sequence both of attended and ignored letters was determined by two finite state grammars. In a subsequent test phase new sequences were presented that were generated either by the attended or the ignored grammar. In contrast to the study phase, in each trial only a single letter was presented and some of the sequences were non-grammatical in that they contained irregular letters. Reaction times for irregular as compared to regular letters were reliably longer, irrespective of whether sequences were generated by the attended or the unattended grammar. Obviously, subjects had acquired knowledge about sequential dependencies between the ignored letters. Further analyses showed that this finding was not as a result of learning that occurred in the test phase. Moreover, the reaction time difference between grammatical and nongrammatical letters was also present in a subgroup of subjects who were not able to recall any of the letters of the ignored sequence.

Finally, learning of unattended contingencies has also been reported in a recent study by Musen & Squire (1993) who used the Stroop task, in which subjects have to name the ink colour in which a colour word is written. If colour word and ink colour are incongruent (e.g. the word RED written in blue), this produces interference as reflected in longer naming latencies. Musen & Squire (1993) established a co-variation between word identity and ink colour and found that subjects named the ink colour increasingly faster when ink colour and word identity covaried. When the relationships were changed after a series of trials, this caused a disruption in subjects' responding. As it is plausible that subjects in the Stroop task actively try to ignore the identity of the words, these results also suggest that co-variations involving ignored stimuli can be learnt.

In summary, in light of the discrepant empirical findings, at present the evidence for learning of co-variations between unattended stimuli must be considered as inconclusive. Whether co-variation learning occurs in the absence of attention probably depends on subtle details of the experimental procedure and the dependent variables employed. There appears to be a trend that learning of unattended co-variations does not show up when subjects have to make classification judgements, whereas positive evidence was obtained when more indirect measures such as response times were used. Moreover, some findings suggest that implicit learning of unattended contingencies may be more probable when subjects have to respond to the critical stimulus feature.

4.2 Dual task studies

A number of researchers have used dual task techniques to investigate the role of attention in implicit learning. In these studies, subjects perform some implicit learning task while their attention is distracted by having them perform a concurrent secondary task.

Sequence learning

Most studies on the role of attention in implicit learning have been performed with the serial reaction task (SRT). Nissen & Bullemer (1987) had their subjects count tones of a high pitch and ignore tones of a low pitch that were presented in each interval between a response and the next stimulus in the SRT. Subjects performing this tone-counting task showed virtually no evidence for sequence learning.

Nissen & Bullemer concluded that sequence learning requires attention (although they assumed that learning can result in unconscious knowledge). In a subsequent study, Cohen et al. (1990) showed that the effect of the tone-counting task depends on the complexity of the sequence. They distinguished between *ambiguous* sequences, in which each element is followed by different successor elements depending on the position within the sequence (e.g. 1–3–2–3–1–2), *unique* sequences, in which each element can be perfectly predicted by its immediate predecessor (e.g. 1–5–2–4–3), and *hybrid* sequences, which contain both unique and ambiguous transitions. The tone-counting task impaired only the learning of ambiguous sequences, whereas subjects in the dual task condition still learned unique and hybrid sequences. Moreover, Curran & Keele (1992) showed that distraction not only interfered with the acquisition of sequential knowledge, but also with its expression. When subjects performed the serial reaction task in the initial training phase without distraction and a secondary task was added after the training phase, they no longer expressed knowledge about ambiguous transitions. Conversely, when sequence knowledge was tested under dual-task conditions, the degree of expressed knowledge did not differ depending on whether subjects had performed the training phase with or without distraction. The authors considered their results as evidence for two qualitatively different learning mechanisms. According to this interpretation, unique and hybrid sequences can be learned by a simple associative learning mechanism that operates independently of attention. By contrast, ambiguous sequences can only be learned if they are parsed into a hierarchical representation which presumably requires attention. Although the results were consistent with this interpretation, Cohen et al. (1990:28) themselves conceded that their data provided no direct evidence for the postulated hierarchical parsing process. The necessity of postulating two qualitatively different learning mechanisms has been challenged by Cleeremans & McClelland (1991, Cleeremans 1993), who proposed a connectionist model to account for the learning of both unique and ambiguous sequences (see section 6).

One limitation of many dual-task studies is the relatively unspecific use of the term "attention". The detrimental effects of the tone-counting task on the learning of ambiguous sequences have by and large been attributed to the fact that the secondary task reduces attentional resources. However, in order to develop models of the processes underlying sequence learning, it is necessary to specify which subprocesses are selectively impaired by a given secondary task (cf. Stadler 1995). In a recent series of experiments I have tried to test such a model of sequence learning in which I distinguish two subprocesses (Goschke 1992a, b, 1994). According to this model subjects in the serial reaction task form anticipations of the immediate consequences of their responses by comparing in each trial the anticipated next event with the actual next event (see also Hoffmann 1993, for an extended discussion of the role of anticipations in sequence learning). Because subjects receive feedback about which response is followed by which event, they will gradually form associations between responses and their consequences. Such anticipations reduce the number of possible response alternatives in the next trial, thereby producing faster responses. The second postulated subprocess is the short-term retention of a limited number of previous sequence events. This *context memory* is a precondition to generate context-dependent anticipations and to learn higher-order contingencies, in which the probability of an event is determined by more than one preceding event. This is the case for ambiguous transitions, in which the same event can have different successors depending on its serial position within the sequence (e.g. 1–3–2–4–3–6).

Assuming that the two processes operate at different points of time within a given trial of the serial reaction task, I tried to selectively interfere with one of the processes while leaving the other one unimpaired, by having subjects perform a secondary task at different points of time within each trial (see Frensch et al. 1994, for a similar manipulation). In the secondary task a random letter was presented in each trial and subjects had to count the number of occurrences of a specified target letter. In an *inter-trial distraction* condition, subjects had to perform the secondary task in each interval between a response and the presentation of the next event. In an *intra-trial distraction* condition, subjects had to perform the secondary task concurrently with the presentation of each sequence element, but no distraction occurred in the response-stimulus interval. In three experiments using both hybrid and ambiguous sequences I found no evidence for sequence learning in the inter-trial distraction condition. This finding is consistent with the assumption that distracting subjects' attention in the interval between response and next event interfered with the formation of response-stimulus associations and impaired the ability to anticipate the next event. By contrast, in the intra-trial distraction condition, reliable sequence learning was obtained in all experiments. However, a fine-grained analysis of response times for individual transitions in the sequence indicated that subjects learned only first-order transition probabilities. Sequence events which could be perfectly predicted by their immediate predecessor produced larger response-time benefits than events which could only be predicted on the basis of two context elements. In addition, response times for events which could be predicted perfectly on the basis of two elements did not differ from events which could only be predicted with 0.5 probability. Obviously, in the intra-trial distraction condition it was still possible to form response-stimulus associations, but the secondary task interfered selectively with the retention of previous sequence events in context memory. Consequently, information about the context of the current response was no longer available and thus only first-order conditional probabilities were learned. In conclusion, different patterns of interference were obtained although in both conditions an identical secondary task was used that differed solely with respect to the point in time at which attention was distracted. Thus, the detrimental effects of a secondary task on sequence learning cannot be attributed to a reduction in nonspecific attentional resources, but instead these effects depend on the exact timing of the interference and on the specific subprocesses affected. More specifically, the formation of response-consequence anticipations and context-retention appear to be two separable submechanisms in sequence learning.

Other studies

In one study of AG learning using a dual task technique, Dienes et al. (1991) had their subjects generate a random number every two seconds while they were memorizing grammatical letter strings. Subjects in the dual task group classified the grammaticality of novel test strings worse than control subjects and showed less knowledge of the rules of the grammar in their verbal reports. In particular, random generation selectively eliminated knowledge about the permissible locations of bigrams within letter strings. This finding corresponds to the result in sequence learning studies, in which an attentional distraction also appeared to interfere selectively with the formation of higher-order, context-dependent contingencies.

Effects of a secondary task on dynamic system control were investigated in the study by Hayes & Broadbent (1988) which was discussed in detail in section 3 and will therefore not be recapitulated here. Suffice it to say that this study provided evidence that the acquisition of conscious knowledge about salient contingencies was impaired when attention was distracted by a random letter generation task. By contrast, implicit learning of non-salient contingencies which involved a time-lag was less affected by the secondary task and thus appears to operate independently from attention or working memory. However, as was discussed in section 3, this rather remarkable finding was not replicated in a more recent study (Green & Shanks 1993), and a number of additional problems called into question the original interpretation of system control studies in term of two qualitatively different learning modes.

4.3 Conclusion: Differentiating attentional subsystems in implicit learning

The findings discussed in this section paint no simple picture of the role of attention in implicit learning. Although there have been several studies in which no evidence for implicit learning was obtained, when relevant stimuli or contingencies were ignored or when attention was distracted by a secondary task, it seems that implicit learning is at least less dependent on attention than explicit learning. It is important to note, however, that different implicit learning tasks appear to require different amounts of attention and may involve different attentional subsystems. It will therefore be important in future research to go beyond unitary constructs like attentional resource or unspecific processing capacity and to develop explicit models of the submechanisms involved in various forms of implicit learning on the basis of detailed task analyses. Furthermore, it seems particularly promising to integrate the study of implicit learning more closely with the neuropsychology of attention. There is an emerging consensus that the distinction between automatic and attentional processes does not constitute a single dichotomy, but that the different criteria that were originally proposed to distinguish automatic and attentional processes (such as intentionality, consciousness, or capacity-limitations) do not converge. It thus seems more appropriate to conceive of the differences between automatic and attentional processing in terms of a multi-dimensional continuum (Allport 1989, Bargh 1989, Goschke 1995, Neumann 1984, 1992). This view is corroborated by recent progress in the neuropsychological differentiation of functionally distinct attentional systems. On a gross neuro-anatomical level, there is now evidence for distinct posterior and anterior attentional subsystems mediating spatial orienting, vigilance, and target detection. Within the posterior system, further distinctions have been suggested between subsystems for disengaging, shifting, and engaging attention (Posner & Peterson 1990; but see Farah 1994, for an alternative view). It will be an important area for future investigations whether different forms of implicit learning (for instance, learning of sequences of stimulus locations, objects, and motor responses) involve experience-dependent modifications in different attentional subsystems (Goschke 1996). The same holds for the role of working memory in implicit learning. As in the field of attention, there has been a transition from a unitary concept of a single short-term store to a multi-component working memory consisting of functionally specialized subsystems (Baddeley 1986). It can thus be asked whether the context memory that appears to be involved in sequence learning consists of various subsystems involved in the learning of sequential structures in different modalities (spatial, auditory, symbolic). Indirect evidence for this possibility stems from the above-mentioned studies of Mayr (1994) and Goschke (1996) who found that subjects were able to learn two simultaneously-presented sequences of objects and locations without any indications of interference. Future studies should systematically investigate whether the amount of interference caused by a secondary task depends on whether the secondary task has to be performed in the same or a different modality from the implicit learning task.

5. QUESTION (3): DOES IMPLICIT LEARNING LEAD TO ABSTRACT KNOWLEDGE?

5. 1 Theoretical alternatives

We can now turn to the third issue raised in the introduction, that is, the question of how sophisticated implicit learning is. The recent controversy surrounding this issue has been centred around the question of how abstract implicitly acquired knowledge is.

Abstractionist view

Some researchers consider implicit learning as a process for the induction of abstract rules (e.g. Reber 1989). The product of implicit learning is conceived of as an unconscious representation of the abstract pattern of co-variations within a stimulus domain. To avoid misunderstandings with respect to this view, it is important to discuss in more detail what is meant by the term "abstract". First it should be noted that even the most decided proponents of the abstractionist view probably do not believe that subjects in implicit learning experiments actually form a representation of a finite-state grammar or of a system of linear equations governing the behaviour of a dynamic system. Rather, two more realistic versions of the abstractionist position have been argued for.

(1) According to Reber (1993:120/121): "an abstract representation is assumed to be derived yet separate from the original instantiation. Abstract codes contain little, if any, information pertaining to the specific stimulus features from which they were derived; the emphasis is on structural relationships among stimuli". The prime examples for this kind of abstract representations are *non-instantiated rules*. In the case of AG learning a non-instantiated rule specifies relational features of letter strings and its content can be formulated without reference to the specific surface form of individual strings, but it refers to stimulus *types*. Reber (1993:121)

gives a concrete example of a letter string TPPPTXVS, which could be coded in the form of "a single occurrence of letter-type 2 followed by three occurrences of letter-type 1, another single occurrence of type 2 and single occurrences of types 5, 4, and 3". Judgements about novel stimuli are made by comparing "the abstract coding of each of the novel test strings with the previously established deep representations" (Reber 1993:121).

(2) A second form of abstract representation that has been proposed are *prototypes*. Here the idea is that a representation of the central tendencies of the configuration of feature values across a set of specific exemplars is induced. For example, in the simplest version of this view, exposure to a large number of birds will lead to the formation of a representation of an "average bird" whose properties are the central tendencies of the properties of all previously encountered birds. Judgements about novel stimuli are made by computing some measure of the similarity between the new stimulus and the prototype (see Smith & Medin 1981, for a detailed discussion). Note that a prototype representation is abstract in a different sense from a non-instantiated rule. The prototype is abstract in that it does not contain information about individual exemplars, but represents only the central tendency of a set of exemplars. However, whereas non-instantiated rules specify relational features of stimulus types, prototypes represent the central tendencies of the specific properties of *token* stimuli.

Non-abstractionist models

According to the non-abstractionist view, implicit learning does not involve unconscious abstraction, but is based on more elementary processes like the storage in memory of specific stimuli or fragments of stimuli (e.g. letter pairs in AG learning), or the formation of specific associations (e.g. between adjacent events in sequence learning experiments), or the acquisition of information about the probability or frequency of specific events (cf. Shanks & St. John 1994). As Perruchet (1994a:830) in a recent critical evaluation of implicit learning research put it: "nonconscious processes are operative in the use of specific knowledge, while conscious processes can deal with both specific and abstract knowledge". Within the non-abstractionist camp one can also distinguish two different positions.

According to *whole exemplar* models, subjects store individual stimuli they encounter during the learning task (Brooks 1978, Vokey & Brooks 1992). The important point is that stimuli are stored not in terms of *types*, but the encoding of each individual instance or *token* stimulus produces a separate memory trace. This stands in contrast to the abstractionist view according to which property information is centralized, that is, each property is represented only once and further encodings of instances of the same category strengthen the links between properties of the abstract representation (Barsalou 1990). A second important point is that in exemplar models the encoding of novel instances can in principle occur without changing representations of already stored instances. In abstraction models each newly-encoded exemplar will lead to a revision of the generic representation of property strengths.

According to *fragmentary exemplar* models subjects do not store whole exemplars, but partial stimuli. One version of this view holds that subjects store small chunks of information. These chunks can consist of bigrams or trigrams in AG, or of partial sequences of two or three successive events in sequence learning (Dulany et al. 1985, Perruchet & Pacteau 1990). When subjects process novel test stimuli, for instance, when they are asked to judge the grammaticality of letter strings in an AG experiment, they are assumed to check whether test stimuli contain one or more of the chunks stored in memory and use the resulting chunk overlap or match as the basis for their judgements.[13]

How can one decide between abstractionist and non-abstractionist views on the basis of observable behaviour? What are the boundary conditions that favour one or the other mode of processing? At an operational level, many researchers have assumed that abstraction implies transfer. A person can be said to have abstract knowledge about the regularities instantiated in a set of stimuli when she or he is able to respond adaptively not only to previously encountered stimuli, but also to novel stimuli instantiating the same regularity (as we will see later, the situation is actually more complex because certain types of non-abstractionist models can also account for transfer effects). Two kinds of transfer can be distinguished.

Instantiated transfer
In the simplest case, novel stimuli do not only instantiate the same regularity as the training stimuli, but they are also constructed from the same surface features. For instance, in an AG learning experiment, instantiated transfer refers to the ability to judge better than chance the grammaticality of novel letter strings which are constructed from the same set of letters as the study strings.

Non-instantiated transfer
A second type of transfer refers to situations in which novel stimuli instantiate the same deep structure, but differ in their surface features

from study stimuli. For instance, in AG learning, non-instantiated transfer refers to the ability to judge as grammatical novel letter strings that are generated by the same underlying AG, but where the terminal symbols of the grammar are mapped to a different set of concrete letters (e.g. CXVVCL may become MLTTMU). Another example of non-instantiated transfer would be a shift from letter strings to tone sequences, where letters are consistently mapped to tones of different frequencies and the tone sequences are generated by the same abstract grammar as the letter strings.

Are rules in the head?

It appears plausible to assume that whenever an individual shows non-instantiated transfer to a novel stimulus domain he or she must have formed a representation of the abstract rules underlying the construction of the stimuli. In fact, one fundamental assumption of mainstream cognitive science has been that our ability to use complex rule systems such as language can only be explained by assuming that the mind manipulates symbolic representations with a syntactic constituency structure according to formal rules (Fodor & Pylyshyn 1988, Pylyshyn 1984). However, other philosophers have maintained that behaviour *conforming* to rules can be brought about by systems which are not literally *governed* by rules (Dennett 1987). An often-used example is the motion of the planets which can be described by systems of differential equations, although to our knowledge planets do nothing remotely similar to solving differential equations. Within cognitive science, connectionist theorists in particular attempt to show that behaviour that may be described formally by symbolic rules can be produced by dynamic networks of simple, neuron-like processing units whose internal workings do not – at least not in any literal sense – involve symbolic rules or representations (Goschke & Koppelberg 1990, 1991, Rumelhart & McClelland 1986, Smolensky 1988). Although in the present chapter I can barely touch the complexity of this controversy, it is important to keep in mind that non-instantiated transfer performance may in principle be produced by an information-processing system that is "non-abstractionist" in the sense that it does not have an explicit representation of abstract rules (see section 6 for further discussion).

Can assumptions about internal representations be empirically tested?

Before discussing the empirical evidence on the issue of abstract versus specific representations we must briefly consider a fundamental difficulty with respect to the inference from behavioural data to mental representations. In principle, assumptions about internal representations can only be tested in conjunction with assumptions about the processes operating over these representations (Anderson 1978, Palmer 1978). The problem thus is that it will often be possible to account for a given set of data equally well with abstractionist and exemplar models, provided one makes the right process assumptions (Barsalou 1990).

For instance, exemplar models have been proposed which store individual instances, but which compute average frequencies of properties (or co-occurrences of properties) across all stored exemplars at the retrieval stage. For instance, when learning about birds, such a model might store information about each individual bird in the form of a list of features. When the model has to decide whether a new animal is a bird or not, it will compute the average over all feature values of all the birds it has stored and compare these average values with the feature values of the new animal. Although such a model does not literally store abstract rules or prototypes, its categorization behaviour will be indistinguishable from that of abstractionist models which form abstract representations at encoding (cf. Estes 1986). Conversely, as shown by Barsalou (1990), given suitable processing assumptions, abstractionist models can reconstruct information about individual exemplars from an abstract representation. In conclusion, non-abstractionist and abstractionist representations will often be computationally equally powerful depending on process assumptions (Barsalou 1990).

Some researchers have tried to distinguish between different types of representations on the basis of more subtle empirical data such as response times. For instance, it appears plausible that a system that already stores an abstract prototype will judge the prototypicality of a new exemplar faster than a system in which typicality must first be computed from a set of exemplars. However, when this computation is implemented in the exemplar model as a parallel resonance process (cf. Hintzman 1986, Ratcliff 1978), the model may produce essentially the same response times as an abstractionist model. After having considered various apparent differences between exemplar and abstractionist models, Barsalou notes:

> "It is therefore impossible to conclude from behavioural research on category learning that people represent categories with exemplars or abstractions. Instead we can only conclude that particular models (i.e. representation-process pairs) are either supported or rejected" (1990:63; cf. Seger 1994:179).

This conclusion should not be taken to imply that it is futile to investigate empirically which type of mental representation is acquired in implicit learning. Rather the point is that assumptions about representation can only be tested in conjunction with assumptions about processes, an insight that still receives too little attention in implicit learning research. Only recently have researchers begun to formulate explicit computational models of implicit learning (see section 6). Moreover, irrespective of the question of *how* implicit knowledge is represented, the experiments discussed later have yielded important information about what information is implicitly acquired.

5.2 Transfer to novel stimuli with the same surface structure

Most of the evidence concerning the abstractionist versus non-abstractionist controversy stems from the investigation of transfer in AG learning (see Reber 1989, 1993, for review). Perhaps the most general and well-established finding in AG learning is that after exposure to a set of grammatical letter strings subjects are able to judge the grammaticality of novel strings constructed from the same letter set reliably better than chance. However, as was discussed earlier, positive transfer to novel stimuli as such does not necessarily imply that subjects have learned abstract rules. More direct evidence supporting the abstractionist view was provided by Reber & Lewis (1977). After studying a set of letter strings generated by a finite-state grammar subjects were asked to solve "anagrams", that is, they were presented scrambled versions of novel grammatical letter strings and had to rearrange them into grammatical strings. The authors correlated the frequencies of bigrams contained in the strings that subjects had produced in the anagram task with the frequencies of bigrams in (a) the set of training strings and (b) the complete set of grammatical strings that could be generated by the grammar. They found that the latter correlation was higher and concluded that subjects must have learned something about the grammar that is more abstract than the information contained in the specific training set.

This interpretation has been called into question, however, by Perruchet et al. (1992), who argued that the relative frequencies of specific bigrams were lower in the set of learning exemplars than in the set of strings used for the anagram task, which may have produced an artefactual correlation. Perruchet et al. (1992) presented subjects only bigrams in the study phase and nevertheless obtained higher correlations between the frequencies of bigrams in subjects' anagram solutions with the complete set of grammatical strings than with the frequencies of bigrams in the study set. The authors concluded that, because subjects had studied isolated bigrams, the difference between these correlations cannot be as a result of the fact that subjects acquired abstract knowledge.

A general problem with many AG studies is that it has not been proven that in order to produce above-chance performance with new stimuli it is really necessary to learn the abstract rule system the experimenter used to generate the stimuli. Proponents of a non-abstractionist view have thus attempted to demonstrate that the level of performance usually observed in implicit learning studies can be accounted for by the assumption that subjects simply memorize whole or partial letter strings.

In one important study, Dulany et al. (1984) asked their subjects to mark which part of each test string they thought made the string grammatical or non-grammatical. The authors considered the marked letters as an expression of fragmentary rules (which they termed "correlated grammars"). These miniature rules predicted subjects' classification performance without residue, from which the authors concluded that AG learning does not involve rule abstraction, but is rather based on fragmentary knowledge about permissible letter chunks. Although the results are consistent with this interpretation, it should be noted that the fact that subjects can indicate which part of a letter strings makes the string grammatical or non-grammatical does not exclude the possibility that subjects have also learned something more abstract. As Weinert (1991) notes, competent speakers of a language are able to indicate which part of an ungrammatical utterance is incorrect, but one would not want to infer from this fact that this exhausts what one knows about the syntax of one's native language.

More compelling evidence for the role of isolated bigrams in AG learning comes from a study by Perruchet & Pacteau (1990). In their first experiment, one group of subjects studied whole letter strings, whereas subjects of a second group were presented isolated letter pairs taken from grammatical strings (the frequency of letters and pairs was matched in both groups). Although subjects in the pairs group were never exposed to complete letter strings, they were nevertheless able to classify novel test strings significantly above chance, albeit at a lower level than the group exposed to whole strings. When all items were eliminated from the analysis in which non-grammaticality was because of a non-permissible initial letter (because these items were particularly easy to classify for subjects in the whole strings group, but impossible to classify for subjects in the pairs group), the two groups showed virtually the same level of performance. In a second experiment, subjects studied whole strings and were tested on two types of novel non-grammatical strings containing either non-permissible bigrams or permissible bigrams at a non-permissible location within a string. Whereas subjects judged the grammaticality of strings containing non-permissible bigrams significantly above chance, they showed very poor sensitivity in detecting permissible bigrams at non-permissible locations. Finally, in Experiment 3, subjects' explicit memory for bigrams was tested with a recognition test. A computer simulation showed that the level of accuracy in subjects' grammaticality judgements could be accounted for on the basis of subjects' explicit memory for isolated bigrams. From these findings, the authors conclude that subjects in AG learning acquire primarily knowledge about permissible bigrams and that this knowledge is more important for their grammaticality judgements than either knowledge about whole strings or knowledge about positional dependencies of bigrams within strings.

The generality of this conclusion is challenged, however, by a number of findings indicating that subjects do acquire additional information about the positions within whole strings at which bigrams may or may not occur. In the Mathews et al. (1989) study (described in section 3) subjects' verbal protocols about what they thought made strings grammatical or non-grammatical often contained information about beginnings or endings of strings, about runs and their positions, about the position of bigrams within a string, as well as "not"-rules specifying that certain strings are non-grammatical. In a critical comment on the Perruchet & Pacteau (1990) study, Mathews (1990) noted that the strings used by Perruchet & Pacteau had arbitrary endings (that is, any letter was allowed at the final position) and were much shorter than in the Mathews et al. (1989) study (5.0 versus 9.5 letters on average). These properties of Perruchet & Pacteau's stimulus material may have discounted the usefulness of positional information for grammaticality judgements.

In order to investigate more directly whether subjects acquire knowledge about legal positions of substrings, Dienes et al. (1991) developed a new sequential dependency task. After studying grammatical strings, subjects were presented with stems of new grammatical strings differing in length from zero to five letters. Subjects had to rate for each letter in the grammar how confident they were that a given letter would be a legal completion of the stem. Subjects judged permissible bigrams correctly as grammatical above-chance only when the bigrams appeared at a legal location within the string. Thus subjects had obviously acquired some knowledge about positional dependencies of bigrams within strings.

Related to the question whether subjects learn only isolated bigrams or also positional dependencies is the question whether subjects learn only partial strings (bigrams or trigrams) or memorize whole strings (what I termed whole and fragmentary exemplar views). In order to investigate this issue, Vokey & Brooks (1992, cf. Brooks 1978, McAndrews & Moscovitch 1985) varied the grammaticality of test strings independently from their similarity to whole individual learning strings. To this end, they constructed grammatical and non-grammatical test strings that were either similar or non-similar to one of the study strings. The results showed that both factors influenced grammaticality judgements, that is, grammatical strings were judged as grammatical more often than non-grammatical strings, and similar strings were classified as grammatical more often than non-similar strings. Both factors were additive and of approximately the same magnitude.

That the similarity of test strings to individual study strings influenced grammaticality judgements does not in itself, however, constitute unequivocal evidence that subjects memorized whole letter strings. The reason is that usually the similarity of whole test items to study items will be confounded with the degree to which test and study strings have partial strings in common. Test items which are similar to study items will on average also contain bigrams or trigrams that appear more frequently in the study set than is the case for non-similar test items. Re-analyses of the materials used by Vokey & Brooks (1992) showed that this "chunk overlap" was in fact larger for similar than for non-similar items (Perruchet 1994b). It is thus a plausible alternative hypothesis that grammaticality judgements are dependent on the frequency with which chunks in a given test string occur in the study set. Test items containing bigrams or trigrams that occur with high frequency in the study set have a higher probability of being classified as grammatical than test items containing few overlapping chunks.

In a recent study, Knowlton & Squire (1994, Experiment 2b) have unconfounded the similarity of test strings to study strings and the overlap of partial strings. As in the Vokey & Brooks, study, the authors manipulated the similarity of test items to study items independently from their grammatical status. Similar items were defined as test items that differed from a specific study item by only one letter, non-similar items differered from all study items by at least two letters. The important new point was that the authors constructed their material in such a way that test strings that were either similar or non-similar to specific study items had the same average overlap of chunks with the strings of the study set. Thus similar and nonsimilar test strings were equated with respect to the overlap of chunks between the test set and study set (of course, grammatical test strings still contained more chunks that also appeared in the set of study strings than non-grammatical test strings). Under this condition both normal subjects and amnesic patients still classified test strings better than chance. However, with the overlap of chunks between study and test strings held constant for similar and nonsimilar strings, the similarity of test strings to study strings had no longer any effect on grammaticality judgements.

It is thus not the similarity of whole test items, but the overlap of chunks that appears to be crucial for grammaticality judgements.

In conclusion, studies on AG learning suggest that classification of novel strings from the same letter set depends on knowledge about specific chunks and their frequencies in the set of study items. In addition, to a limited degree subjects appear to acquire information about positional dependencies of bigrams within whole strings. Although it is too early to draw firm conclusions, it should be noted that the finding that fragmentary chunks rather than whole exemplars are memorized has interesting theoretical implications. Whole versus fragmentary exemplar views suggest quite different hypotheses concerning the nature and possible adaptive functions of implicit learning. In particular, the fragmentary view fits with the more general idea that implicit learning involves mechanisms specialized for the extraction of invariances across a large number of single episodes (for instance, frequently-recurring chunks in a set of letter strings), whereas explicit declarative memory serves to retain single episodes in their spatio-temporal context in order to deal effectively with exceptions and unexpected deviations from a rule structure (cf. Sherry & Schacter 1987).

5.3 Transfer to stimuli with a different surface structure

The results discussed so far suggest that subjects in AG tasks acquire relatively specific information about permissible letter chunks and, to a limited degree, about positional dependencies. However, when drawing theoretical conclusions from these findings, one should not lose sight of the fact that in these studies (e.g. Vokey & Brooks 1992) a reliable effect of the grammaticality of test strings was found that was independent from the similarity of test strings to study strings. At first sight it is difficult to account for this effect in terms of specific knowledge about chunks. Even more important are studies which have investigated performance on transfer tasks in which test stimuli were used that instantiated the same deep structure, but differed in their perceptual surface characteristics. If subjects show positive transfer to such stimuli, this constitutes *prima facie* evidence that they must have acquired knowledge that is more abstract than stored exemplars or chunks.

Probably the first transfer experiment along these lines was reported by Reber (1967). Subjects first memorized grammatical letter strings. In a second session, one group of subjects had to memorize novel strings that consisted of the same letters as in the first session, but that were constructed by using a different grammar (same vocabulary/different syntax). In another group the same grammar as in the first session was used to generate the strings, but a new set of letters was used (different vocabulary/same syntax). In addition, there were groups in which neither or both of these aspects were altered. The main finding was that changing the grammar led to worse performance in memorizing the strings, whereas changing the vocabulary had small or no effects on performance.

Analogous findings were reported by Mathews et al. (1989), who trained subjects with grammar strings over a period of four weeks. In each session, subjects studied a list of 20 grammatical strings. They were either instructed to memorize the strings or to figure out the rules governing the construction of the strings. In the subsequent test phase, subjects received 200 forced-choice trials, in each of which one grammatical together with four non-grammatical strings were presented. Rule-discovery subjects were instructed to choose the string that conformed to the set of rules, whereas memory subjects were told to choose the string that was most similar to one of the memorized strings. Half of the subjects in each group studied in each session strings generated from a new letter set but conforming to the same underlying grammar, whereas the other half of the subjects studied strings from the same letter set in sessions 1 to 3. Both groups were presented strings from a novel letter set in session 4. Ignoring a number of details of the rather complex design of this experiment, the main findings relevant for the abstractness issue were as follows. Memory-instructed subjects who were exposed in each session to a changing letter set performed worse in the forced-choice task than subjects receiving the same letter set. There was no difference, however, between same and different letter set groups for the rule-instructed subjects. Moreover, in session 4, when subjects in all groups received strings from a changed letter set, both memory- and rule-instructed subjects showed substantial transfer. This indicates that they had learned something about the grammar that allowed them to perform clearly above chance even when the surface structure of the stimuli was changed.

Recently, Gomez & Schvaneveldt (1994) added an important piece of evidence to the debate about the abstractness of implicit knowledge. They reasoned that the crucial test for the role of bigram information in AG learning involves transfer to novel letter sets. If subjects acquire only knowledge about permissible bigrams contained in the original training set, they should lack higher level knowledge necessary for transferring the ability to make above-chance grammaticality judgements to new letter strings with a different surface structure. By the same token, when subjects studying whole strings do acquire essentially the same knowledge as subjects studying only isolated bigrams, both groups should show equal amounts of transfer to a new letter set. In Gomez & Schvaneveldt's first experiment, subjects either studied whole strings or lists of bigrams, in which the frequency of each bigram equalled the frequency with which it appeared in the set of whole study strings. Subjects who had studied only bigrams showed no transfer to a new letter set and classified test strings which contained bigrams in non-permissible locations no better than chance. These subjects only showed a marginally significant sensitivity to non-permissible bigrams. By contrast, subjects who had studied whole strings were sensitive to both non-permissible bigrams and permissible bigrams at non-permissible locations. Most importantly, the latter subjects also showed reliable positive transfer of their ability to make above-chance grammaticality judgements for both types of strings to test strings that were constructed from a changed letter set. Thus subjects studying whole strings obviously learned more than subjects studying only isolated bigrams. Subjects exposed to strings, but not subjects exposed to bigrams, learned something about the legal positions of bigrams within strings. Subjects exposed to strings showed significantly larger sensitivity to violations because of non-permissible letter pairs, even though subjects who studied isolated bigrams had been exposed to information that was in principle sufficient for acquiring the same level of performance. In conclusion, subjects in the string group apparently did not base their grammaticality judgements on bigram information alone.

Taken together, AG experiments in which transfer to novel strings from a new letter set has been investigated suggest that to a certain degree transfer performance is mediated by knowledge that goes beyond memory for specific training strings or chunks. Subjects appear to be able to use knowledge acquired in the study phase to make above-chance grammaticality judgements to novel letter strings, even if the surface structure (the "vocabulary") is changed. The crucial question is, of course, whether this fact justifies the conclusion that implicit learning involves the abstraction of unconscious rules. In fact, two alternative explanations for the observed transfer performance appear worth considering.

According to the first explanation, subjects use simple conscious rules to map relational features of study strings to transfer strings. For instance, assume that a subject has formed rules such as "the same letter never appears in the first and last position of a string" and "identical letters are allowed to occur at positions 1 and 2". When the subject has learned that XVVCML is a grammatical string, these rules would enable him or her to classify the transfer string LMMGTU as grammatical and to reject the string LMXGTL as non-grammatical. It has not been investigated systematically whether such simple mapping rules are sufficient to explain transfer to novel stimuli with a different surface form. Likewise, assuming that such rules do play a role in transfer tasks, we do not know whether they are actually conscious or whether they are acquired and applied implicitly. Indirect evidence relevant to this point stems from the AG study of Mathews et al. (1989) that was described in section 3. In this study, subjects' verbal protocols contained statements indicating that only specific beginning and ending patterns or runs in the middle of strings were allowed. Such rules may allow for a limited degree of transfer to a new letter set. If subjects apply such rules consciously, transfer performance should improve when subjects have an opportunity to consciously figure out the mapping between study and transfer stimuli (that is, which letters correspond to which). Interestingly, transfer to different letter sets in Experiment 3 of Mathews et al. (1989) was much better when subjects received feedback during the transfer phase as to whether their grammaticality judgements were correct or not. This is consistent with the assumption that transfer to stimuli with a new surface structure was mediated by explicit rules specifying a mapping between features of study and transfer strings. However, further research will be necessary to establish this conclusion firmly.

A second, not mutually incompatible, interpretation of transfer effects to a new letter set has been suggested by Brooks & Vokey (1991). The basic idea is that transfer performance is based on the perceived similarity between transfer strings and specific study strings with respect to the correspondence of within-item relations between letters (the authors speak of *abstract analogies*). For instance, the strings XCLLLX and BKVVVB could be perceived as similar because both strings share certain relations among letters in specific positions. The authors conducted an AG experiment in which the similarity of test items to specific training items was varied independently from the grammaticality of the test items. In addition, they tested subjects with same-letter and changed-letter items. Similarity had a significant effect on classification performance even when test items were constructed from a changed letter set, indicating that transfer performance was at least partly mediated by abstract analogies to specific training items.

In closing this section it should be noted that most of the studies in which transfer to stimuli with different surface structures has been investigated in other implicit learning tasks have yielded negative results. In particular, in dynamic system control, positive transfer from one control task to another instantiating the same set of linear equations was obtained only when both tasks had a similar "semantic surface" (for instance, when both were either transport system or person interaction tasks), but not when the cover story was changed (Berry & Broadbent 1988, Squire & Frambach 1990). Even informing subjects that both systems were governed by the same set of equations did not improve transfer performance.

5.4 Learning of miniature languages

Studies on AG learning are limited in their diagnosticity as regards the abstractness issue, because relatively simple finite-state grammars are used to generate stimuli. These grammars specify permissible transitions between letters from a restricted vocabulary. Thus, it may come as no surprise that subjects primarily learn bigrams and trigrams, perhaps together with information about their positions within whole strings, as well as simple relational features as described at the end of the previous section. As compared to the complexity of the task of learning a natural language, these systems may just be too simplistic to induce truly abstract learning. I will therefore briefly discuss studies in which more complex rule systems have been used, in particular *phrase structure grammars*. These grammars specify legal transitions and positional dependencies between *classes of terminal symbols*. For instance, in the case of natural language, such a rule may specify that verbs follow nouns in simple sentences. In order to learn such rules, it does not suffice to learn transitions between terminal symbols (for instance, that MAN is followed by EATS or CAT is followed by SLEEPS). Because there is an unlimited number of possible instantiations of this rule, the learner must figure out the abstract form class to which a terminal symbol belongs (that MAN and CAT are nouns) and learn legal transitions and positional dependencies between these form classes.

Laboratory studies on the learning of miniature languages have shown that simple positional rules are easily learned. That is, subjects quickly learn that stimuli from a given category are only allowed at specific positions within a stimulus string. By contrast, it appears to be extremely difficult if not impossible to learn positional dependencies between formally-defined *classes* of symbols, when a form class is defined solely by the pattern of co-occurrences of symbols within complex expressions. In other words, subjects apparently do not learn to which class a symbol belongs when symbols within a given class have nothing else in common but the fact that they appear only at specific positions within a whole string (cf. Braine 1966). To make this somewhat abstract point more vivid, consider a study by Smith (1969) who had subjects learn pairs of letters which belonged to one of four categories ("M", "N", "P", and "Q"-letters). N-letters always followed M-letters, whereas Q-letters always followed P-letters. Subjects learned relatively fast at which positions different letters occurred. However, they were not able to learn contingencies between letter classes as indicated by the observation that they frequently made errors consisting of PN or MQ pairs (see also Braine et al. 1990).

Analogous findings were obtained in the already described AG study of Mathews et al. (1989). In their Experiment 4, Mathews et al. used a so-called bi-conditional grammar that consisted of three rules specifying which letters must occur in corresponding positions within the first and the second half of eight-letter strings. The three rules specified that an X at a specific position goes with a T at the corresponding position in the other half string, that a P goes with C, and that an S goes with V. Thus, TPPV. XCCS is a grammatical string, whereas TPPV. CXXP is non-grammatical. Across all valid strings, each letter appeared in each position with the same frequency. As a consequence, strings generated by this grammar have a much lower degree of family resemblance than strings generated by a standard finite state grammar. In contrast to the results from experiments with conventional finite state grammars, there was no evidence that subjects implicitly learned these bi-conditional rules. Subjects who had memorized letter strings performed near chance level when they had to discriminate grammatical and non-grammatical strings. By contrast, subjects who had been instructed to figure out the rules of the grammar by explicit hypothesis-testing and who received feedback about the correctness of their hypotheses were able to discriminate grammatical from non-grammatical strings better than chance. A substantial proportion of subjects in the latter, but not the former group, were able to verbalize some of the rules. This suggests that implicit learning may lead to the induction of family resemblances or co-variation patterns in a set of structured stimuli, but that explicit or analytic processes are necessary to induce structural regularities when the stimuli do not exhibit patterns of family resemblances.

From a more general view, this conclusion casts doubt on the idea that implicit learning involves an unselective mode of learning in which *all available co-variations* are picked up (Hayes & Broadbent 1988). Subjects have great difficulty in learning contingencies that hold between arbitrary categories of stimuli, where category membership is defined solely by the distribution of positional co-occurrences between stimuli. Note that in the experiments discussed earlier, the co-occurrence information contained in the study stimuli was in principle sufficient to induce the relevant formal categories as well as the positional contingencies between these categories.[14] The finding that subjects nevertheless consistently fail to implicitly acquire structural regularities on the basis of co-occurrence information alone casts serious doubts on the idea of implicit learning as a mechanism that automatically induces all possible contingencies and co-variations contained in the input information.

Does this mean that implicit learning of complex structures such as miniature languages does not exist at all? An interesting novel perspective on this issue is opened by the suggestion that implicit learning depends essentially on whether the stimulus information contains perceptual surface cues that point to the underlying rule structure. For instance, it is much easier to learn positional dependency relations between formal classes of artificial words, when words from the same abstract form class share a common phonological feature (for instance, when all words in a given class have the same ending such as *salum*, *tilum*, *kelum*, whereas words from a different class have a different ending, such as *fenid*, *lubid*, *tabid*). The same holds for the learning of higher-order syntactic structures, which can be learned much more easily when the stimulus input contains *correlated cues* indicating relevant form classes or structural boundaries (cf. Braine et al. 1990, Morgan et al. 1987).

The role of such surface cues in implicit learning has recently been explored in a series of ingenious miniature-language learning experiments by Weinert (1991, 1992). Subjects had to memorize 12 auditorily-presented sentences that consisted of artificial words (e.g. DEROS) and that were generated by a simple phrase structure grammar. Words belonged to one of several abstract form classes and words within one class shared the same ending (e.g. *OS* or *UM*). For one group of subjects the sentences were spoken with a monotonous prosody without segmentations. In a second group the sentences contained prosodic cues which marked boundaries between phrases in accordance with the underlying phrase structure. A third group heard sentences that were spoken with an irregular phonology which was uncorrelated with the underlying phrase structure. In the subsequent test phase, subjects had to judge the grammaticality of new sentences. In several experiments adults as well as pre-schoolers showed above-chance performance only when they had been exposed to sentences containing prosodic cues to the underlying phrase structure.[15] Implicit learning (at least of sequential structures) obviously depends in important ways on the availability of perceptual surface cues which are correlated with the underlying deep structure. Presumably, such cues serve to direct attention to relevant segmentations, thereby making it easier to detect elementary constituents and to parse linear structures into hierarchical representations.[16]

5.5 Conclusions

The considerations in the previous section shed a new light on the debate concerning abstract versus specific knowledge. As was discussed in the introduction to this section, it has often been assumed that behaviour that conforms with abstract rules and that is sensitive to structural regularities requires the acquisition of an internal representation of the rules or regularities. In the case of complex structures such as language, this would indeed be a remarkable task for an implicit learning system. On the other hand, those who view implicit learning as a relatively elementary process such as storing chunks, have often concluded that true abstraction is only possible via explicit, conscious hypothesis testing. An alternative to these two positions holds that relatively simple learning principles may produce behaviour that is sensitive to structural regularities and that conforms with abstract rules, provided the input information contains surface cues to facilitate the extraction of deep-structural contingencies. Cues that point to the relevant structural boundaries presumably make the learning task a much simpler one. Rather than having to learn an abstract rule system, the task becomes one of acquiring a much simpler set of contingencies (for instance, as discussed earlier, phonological surface cues transform the task of inducing abstract form classes into one of learning much simpler co-variations between phonological features and form classes; cf. Weinert 1991, for further discussion.)

In closing this section, it should be noted that it is probably too simplistic to ask for the type of information (rules, exemplars, chunks) that is acquired in implicit learning tasks. It appears more realistic that different types of knowledge are acquired depending on the requirements of the learning situation as well as individual differences. For instance, there is evidence that study conditions in which subjects' attention is focused on individual exemplars (for instance, paired-associate learning or exposure to a small number of stimuli) increase the tendency to classify stimuli on the basis of their similarity (Reber & Allen 1978, McAndrews & Moscovitch 1985). By contrast, when a large number of strings is processed in a more passive manner, subjects seem to have a stronger tendency to acquire more abstract information (cf. Reber 1989:228). Similar findings have been reported in studies of concept acquisition. When exemplars of a to-be-learned category (e.g. cartoon faces) were presented under incidental learning conditions or when subjects' attention was distracted by a concurrent secondary task, subjects showed a stronger tendency to classify stimuli according to their holistic family resemblance. By contrast, under intentional study conditions and with undivided attention, subjects tended to make more analytical categorizations based on a single criterial attribute (Kemler-Nelson 1984, Smith & Shapiro 1989). Kemler-Nelson suggested that a holistic, similarity-based form of category learning is a "fall-back" mode of processing, characteristic of young children and of adults under time-pressure or distraction. Moreover, the dominance of analytic or holistic forms of processing appears to be modulated by emotional states and personality dispositions (Isen 1987, Kuhl 1995). Research is needed to systematically investigate the moderating effects of these almost completely neglected variables on implicit learning.

6. QUESTION (4): WHAT ARE THE COMPUTATIONAL MECHANISMS UNDERLYING IMPLICIT LEARNING?

Recently various computational models of possible mechanisms underlying implicit learning have been developed. Because of space restrictions I will provide only two brief examples to give a flavour of this kind of theorizing[17] (for more extended reviews see Cleeremans 1993, Dienes 1992, 1993).

6. 1 Competitive chunking

Servan-Schreiber & Anderson (1990) developed a so-called competitive chunking model which is based on the assumption of a constantly operating, relatively automatic process of creating and applying chunks to the perceptual input. In this model continuing exposure to a set of structured stimuli will lead to the formation of increasingly higher-order chunks as the result of the combination of more elementary chunks. For instance, when subjects in AG learning are presented letter strings such as MVXXCML, they will initially encode the strings in terms of elementary chunks already stored in memory (in this case, elementary chunks consist of individual letters). In the next step, more complex chunks such as (MV), (XXC), or (CML), are created and stored in memory with a given probability. Repeated exposure will lead to the creation of even more complex chunks such as ((MV) (XXC)). Chunks that occur frequently in the set of training strings will be strengthened more often than infrequent chunks, because each time a chunk is used to encode an input string its memory representation is strengthened. The model is called competitive because chunks in memory compete with each other to be applied to the encoding of the current stimulus. The outcome of the competition depends on the so-called support of the *competing* chunks, where the support of a chunk is a function of the average strength of its constituency chunks. Chunks with greater support will be retrieved with greater probability and thus further strengthened. This process of creation, competition, and strengthening of chunks can in principle continue until a stimulus is represented by a single chunk.

In order to apply their model to AG learning, the authors assume that the number of higher-level chunks that is needed to represent a letter string is related to the experienced *familiarity* of the string. The fewer chunks are necessary at the highest level to represent a new string, the more familiar it will appear, and the stronger will be the tendency to judge the string as grammatical. In other words, higher-order chunks allow for a more compact representation of the perceptual input, and the more compactly a string is represented, the more familiar it will appear.

Servan-Schreiber & Anderson formalized and implemented these assumptions in a computer simulation. With parameters in the model set at suitable values, they were able to reproduce empirical results from an AG experiment by Reber (1967) as well as new data from their own experiments. The model not only accounted for the level of classification performance of human subjects, but also exhibited a number of more fine-grained properties that were similar to the behaviour of the subjects. For instance, the model was less sensitive to rule violations in the middle of test strings and it was more sensitive to non-permissible chunks than to valid chunks in non-permissible locations within a string. A major limitation of the model in its present form is that it cannot account for transfer to strings from a new letter set, because the chunks represent only surface-specific information. In order to account for the positive transfer to strings from a new letter set observed in human subjects, it would be necessary to equip the model with some means of applying mapping rules or abstract analogies (cf. Vokey & Brooks 1992).

6.2 Connectionist networks

Probably one of the most important developments in cognitive science during the last decade has been the renaissance of connectionist or neural network models as an alternative type of computational modelling (for an introduction and overview see Rumelhart & McClelland 1986). In contrast to more traditional symbolic information-processing architectures (such as production systems; cf. Anderson 1983, Newell 1973), connectionist networks consist of a large number of simple processing units which are interconnected by weighted (excitatory or inhibitory) connections. Units do not represent real neurons, but are abstract computational devices that have some features in common with real neurons. Each unit sums the activation it receives from all other units it is connected to and transforms this net input into a new output (usually according to a non-linear function). In most networks units are organized in several layers, in particular, an input layer, an output layer, and one or more intermediate layers of so-called hidden units. Networks with hidden units are computationally much more powerful than networks consisting only of input and output units (Rumelhart et al. 1986).

The state of a network at a given point in time is characterized by the activation pattern over its units. If one conceives of each unit as a dimension in a co-ordinate system and of the activation of a unit as a value on the corresponding dimension, the units of a network define an n-dimensional state space. Each point in this space corresponds to a possible activation state of the network. The dynamic behaviour of the network can thus be described as the transformation of activation vectors into new activation vectors, i.e. as a trajectory through the state space.

One important distinction is between *local* and *distributed* representation. In a local representation single units can be interpreted as indicating the presence of a conceptual entity (for instance, there may be one unit representing the letter B). By contrast, in distributed networks conceptual entities are represented as patterns of activation over a large number of units (for instance, the letter B may be represented by a *pattern of activation* over several units encoding the elementary graphemic feature of the letter).

What makes connectionist networks attractive as candidate models of implicit learning is the fact that they can learn to map a set of input patterns to a set of output patterns, or to extract regularities and invariances from a set of inputs. Learning consists in a change of the connection weights between units. These changes are not controlled by some supervisory process, but the connection weights change in a self-organizing manner depending on the activation state of the units and feedback from the environment. I will briefly discuss two applications of connectionist models to implicit learning.

Pattern associators and AG learning

Dienes (1992) has explored the performance of various pattern associator networks in the AG task. A pattern associator is a network that maps activation patterns over the input units to activation patterns over the output units. In each trial of his simulations, Dienes (1992) presented a letter string as an input to the network and the task of the network was to reproduce the same string over its output units. In the simplest case, each letter in each position of an input string was coded by the activation of one single input unit. Thus a whole letter string corresponded to a pattern of activation, in which for each letter in each position the corresponding input unit was turned on (Dienes explored various encoding schemes and network architectures, which I cannot discuss here). The idea behind this simulation was that in order to reproduce the input strings, the network must acquire knowledge about the co-occurrences and contingencies between letters in different positions, that is, the network must adjust its connection weights in a way that allows it to predict each letter from the other letters in a given string. When the network attempts to reproduce a novel letter string it has not encountered before, it will do this by exploiting the co-occurrence constraints it has acquired in the training phase. When strings conform to the constraints of the study set (that is, when they are grammatical), the network should be more accurate at reproducing them as compared to non-grammatical strings. Dienes speculated that an analogous process may take place in human subjects performing the AG task.

The most successful simulation of the empirical data was obtained when Dienes trained the auto-associator network with the so-called *Delta rule* (Widrow & Hoff 1960). According to this rule, connection weights are changed depending on the error the network produces. On each trial, the actual output of the network is compared to the desired output and all weights are changed in such way that, if the same input were to be presented again, the overall error would be slightly reduced. For instance, if the activation of an output unit was too high, all connection weights from active units feeding into this unit would be slightly reduced. This is done simultaneously for all output units. Across many trials the network will gradually develop a connectivity that allows it to optimally map input patterns to the desired output patterns.

Dienes presented his model with 20 strings taken from an experiment by Dienes et al. (1991), and connection weights were changed according to the Delta rule. Subsequently the network was tested with 25 new strings. The network not only achieved a similar overall level of performance as the human subjects, but it also showed a similar ranking of test strings with respect to their difficulty as did the subjects. For this analysis, Dienes ranked test strings according to the number of experimental subjects that had correctly classified them and he ranked strings according to how well the network had reproduced them. The correlations between the rank orders ranged between 0.32 and 0.69 for different variants of the model. Interestingly, neither connectionist models using other learning rules such as the popular Hebb rule, nor various exemplar memory models were successful at predicting the difficulty rank order. It should be noted, however, that like the competitive chunking model, the pattern associator model in its present form is not capable of generalizing knowledge to transfer strings from a new letter set.

Recurrent networks and sequence learning

A second interesting application of connectionist models has been developed by Cleeremans & McClelland (1991), who used a simple recurrent network (SRN; Elman 1991) to model sequence learning. The SRN consists of input, output, hidden, and context units. In each trial, a stimulus activates input units, which propagate their activation to the hidden units, which feed into the output units. The special feature of the SRN is that in each training cycle the activation of the hidden units is copied back to the context units. In the next trial, both the input units and the context units feed their activation into the hidden units. Because the activation pattern over the context units represents the network's previous internal state, context units supply the SRN with a kind of short-term memory for previous inputs. The SRN thus processes a given stimulus in the context of previous events.

Cleeremans & McClelland (1991) compared the performance of human subjects with the performance of an SRN with 15 hidden units on a sequence learning task. In the experiment with the human subjects, on each trial a stimulus appeared at one of six locations and subjects had to press one of six buttons corresponding to the six locations. The sequence of locations was generated by a finite state grammar, but in a small number of trials, the stimulus appeared at an unexpected location that was not allowed by the grammar. In the course of 20 sessions involving a total of 60,000 trials, subjects increasingly responded faster to grammatical stimuli than to deviant stimuli, thereby showing that they had acquired knowledge about the sequential structure of the stimuli.

In a computer simulation, the same sequence of events was presented to the SRN. The six stimulus locations were represented by the activation of different input units. In each trial, the task of the network was to predict the next location. Connection weights were changed according to a generalized version of the Delta rule (the so-called Backpropagation-of-Error rule).[18] The SRN gradually improved its ability to predict the next location. In order to compare the SRN with the data from the human subjects, Cleeremans & McClelland (1991) assumed that the response time speed-up in their subjects was based on the ability to make increasingly valid predictions of the next stimulus location. They thus transformed the prediction accuracy of the SRN into simulated response times. A slightly modified variant of the SRN accounted for about 80 per cent of the variance in the data from the human subjects. Detailed analyses showed that both the responses of the human subjects as well as the predictions of the SRN were influenced by up to three context events.

What is particularly interesting about the SRN is that although the network processed only a single event at a time, it nevertheless learned to use the temporal context in which events occurred to predict their successors. The SRN was thus able to adapt its behaviour in a context-sensitive manner to the sequential structure of the sequence, although it did not explicitly represent previous elements (see Cleeremans 1993, for a detailed discussion of the kind of internal representation of sequential structures that these networks develop). Moreover, it has been shown that SRNs can also induce the structural regularities of more complex sequences such as sentences generated by a phrase structure grammar (Elman 1991).

In closing this section, I would like to note that the architecture of the SRN fits with the analysis of subprocesses in sequence learning described in section 4 (Goschke 1992a,b, 1994). There I concluded on the basis of dual-task experiments that sequence learning involves (a) the comparison of anticipated and actual events and (b) context-memory for previous events. Analogously, learning in the SRN is also driven by the match or mismatch between anticipations of the next event and the actual successor event, and context units serve as a memory for temporal context.

6.3 Conclusions

Although there are probably other models, including models based on symbolic representations, that may account for empirical data from implicit learning task, the models discussed in this section have a number of common features that make them *prima facie* plausible explanations of implicit learning (cf. Cleeremans 1993). First, the models learn in a self-organizing manner (by slight changes in connection weights or by the probabilistic creation and strengthening of chunks) and the acquisition of knowledge is a by-product of processing stimuli. Secondly, learning occurs in an incremental fashion. Thirdly, both the competitive chunking and the various connectionist models are particularly sensitive to statistical co-variation patterns in the stimulus information. Finally, especially in connectionist models, knowledge is not represented in terms of a well-structured set of symbolic rules, but knowledge is instantiated in a distributed manner in the connectivity of the network. This connectivity allows the network to produce rule-conforming behaviour that is sensitive to regularities in the environment. At least on a level of gross analogies, this fits with the fact that implicitly acquired knowledge is often difficult to verbalize. Some authors have speculated that the products of processing in these models (for instance, retrieved chunks or activation patterns over output units) correspond to the contents of consciousness in human subjects, whereas quantitative parameter values (for instance, the strengths of chunks or connection weights) correspond to information that is not amenable to verbal report, but expressed in performance or intuitive feelings of familiarity. However, at present such hypotheses must remain highly speculative, because almost nothing is known about the relation between phenomenal consciousness and the format in which knowledge is internally represented.

A major shortcoming shared by all of the models discussed in this section is that they cannot account for transfer performance to novel stimuli with a new surface structure. One might argue that it is to date an open question whether such transfer in human subjects actually reflects implicit knowledge, or whether it is due to the application of conscious mapping rules (see section 5). If transfer effects reflect conscious rule knowledge rather than implicit abstraction, the above models – insofar as they are intended as models of implicit learning – would not be required to account for these effects.

This point relates to more fundamental questions concerning the representation of complex structures. It has been forcefully argued that the ability to use syntactically-structured rule systems such as natural language can only be explained by systems that have internal representations which consist themselves of syntactically-structured symbol systems (Fodor & Pylyshyn 1988). In contrast, connectionists have argued that only external symbol systems like language or logic have a syntactic constituency structure, but that this need not be the case for the internal representations underlying the ability to use such symbol systems (for discussion see Clark 1989, Goschke & Koppelberg 1990, 1991, Smolensky 1988, van Gelder 1990). At present, this controversy is essentially unresolved and the topic of an ongoing debate. It will be of central theoretical importance for theories of implicit learning and mental representation to investigate the role of implicit learning and nonsymbolic representations in the acquisition and use of external symbol systems.

7. QUESTION (5): DOES IMPLICIT LEARNING INVOLVE SPECIFIC BRAIN STRUCTURES?

Despite the vast number of experimental findings on implicit learning, some of which were discussed in the previous sections, it is still an open issue whether explicit and implicit forms of learning are mediated by qualitatively different systems, or whether they reflect different processes within a single learning system (cf. Roediger 1990, Schacter & Tulving 1994). Some researchers have even argued that it is in principle impossible to infer the existence of different types of knowledge representation or separate learning systems on the basis of behavioural data alone, because any set of data may be as well accounted for by a unitary learning system, given that the right process assumptions are made (cf. Anderson 1978, Barsalou 1990, Palmer 1978). Against this background, it has sometimes been argued that data from neuropsychology and neurophysiology may provide the desperately needed constraints for deciding between competing theories. In fact, some of the most compelling pieces of evidence in favour of multiple learning systems differing with respect to their processing characteristics, phenomenal status, and anatomical substrate, stem from neuropsychological investigations of brain-damaged patients and lesion studies in animals (for reviews see Goschke, in press, Schacter & Tulving 1994, Markowitsch 1992, Moscovitch 1994, Schacter 1994, Squire 1994, Squire et al. 1993). In this section I will briefly summarize some pertinent findings on what is known about the brain systems mediating implicit forms of learning.

Before discussing the evidence, a note of caution is in order. In interpreting the consequences of brain damage it is important to realize that impairments as well as spared functions are the result of the operation of the residual brain. From the fact that damage of a specific structure produces an impairment of a specific cognitive function, one cannot conclude that the damaged structure was the anatomical locus of this function (cf. Farah 1994). To use a somewhat crude analogy, from the fact that a TV set no longer generates pictures on the screen when the plug has been damaged it does not follow that the normal function of the plug was to generate pictures. It is thus of great importance that findings using relatively novel functional brain imaging technologies with normal subjects provide converging evidence for conclusions drawn from the careful testing of brain-damaged patients.

7.1 Implicit learning in amnesic patients

Neuropsychological investigations have documented a large number of functional dissociations between implicit and explicit forms of processing in a variety of domains, including perception, language, memory, and learning (e.g. Milner & Rugg 1992, Schacter et al. 1988). As regards implicit learning, the most relevant findings concern the amnesic syndrome.[19] Although amnesia is a cover term for a variety of different impairments, it is now relatively well established that damage to a number of localizable brain structures usually impairs the ability to encode and retain new information in declarative long-term memory. In particular, the medial-temporal lobe and diencephalic structures appear to be necessary for intact declarative memory. Lesion studies with non-human primates suggest that the hippocampus and related areas (entorhinal, perirhinal, and parahippocampal cortex) and the diencephalon (especially the medial thalamus) are crucial "bottleneck" structures for the formation of declarative memories (Kolb & Wishaw 1990, Markowitsch 1992).[20]

One well-studied amnesic patient who has reached tragic fame is H.M. who was neurosurgically treated for epilepsy in 1953, when large portions of the temporal lobes (including the anterior part of the hippocampus) were removed. After the operation, H.M. showed normal intelligence, perception, and language and was able to remember events that had happened some time prior to the operation. However, he had almost completely lost the ability to remember newly-learned facts or events as shown by his extremely bad performance on standard explicit memory tests (Kolb & Whishaw 1990, Milner et al. 1968). Despite his severe impairment of explicit memory, H.M. was still able to acquire various motor skills. For instance, he showed almost normal learning curves on the pursuit rotor task and a mirror tracing task. Similar findings have been obtained with other patients, even though the patients often denied ever having performed the task before (Cohen & Squire 1980, Moscovitch et al. 1986, Soliveri et al. 1992, Squire et al. 1993).

A number of more recent studies suggest that not only the acquisition of motor and cognitive skills, but also the acquisition of knowledge in typical implicit learning tasks may be spared in amnesic patients. These findings indicate that at least some forms of implicit learning are independent from the brain structures underlying explicit declarative memory.

Sequence learning

In the serial reaction task, patients suffering from Korsakoff's disease whose conscious episodic memory was severely impaired showed a reliable speed-up of response times when the sequence of stimuli followed a repeating pattern and an increase in response times when the sequence was unexpectedly switched to a random sequence (Nissen & Bullemer 1987). This performance increment was still present one week later (Nissen et al. 1989). Moreover, while the control subjects usually noted the repeating pattern, there was no evidence for conscious knowledge in the group of amnesic patients. Analogous findings were obtained with patients suffering from Alzheimer's disease (Knopman & Nissen 1987), who (as a group, but not in each individual case) showed normal sequence learning despite their impaired declarative memory and lack of awareness of the repeating sequence. In a more recent study, Reber & Squire (1994) found intact sequence learning in amnesic patients in a test block *after* the patients' explicit knowledge had been probed and shown to be at chance. Taken together, these results suggest that performance increments in the serial reaction task are mediated by brain systems different from those underlying explicit memory for sequential structures.

Dynamic system control

Analogous findings have been reported in system control tasks. Squire & Frambach (1990) used Berry & Broadbent's (1984) sugar factory task in which subjects have to attain a pre-specified level of sugar production by hiring different numbers of workers on each trial. In early stages of learning, amnesic patients showed normal learning. However, later in training normal subjects outperformed the patients, presumably because the normal subjects began to acquire declarative knowledge about the system, which was not available to the amnesic patients (see also Glisky et al. 1986).

Concept learning and artificial grammar learning

In a study of concept learning, Knowlton & Squire (1993) presented amnesic patients and control subjects with random dot patterns, which were distortions of a common prototypical pattern (the prototype pattern itself was not presented). During the test phase, the prototype pattern, novel distortions of the patterns, and novel random patterns were shown and subjects had to judge whether the test patterns were members of the same category as the training patterns. Like the control subjects, the amnesic patients classified the prototype and new distortions of the prototype more frequently as belonging to the same category than novel random patterns, thereby indicating that category learning may proceed in the absence of declarative, episodic knowledge about the training exemplars.

Similar findings have been reported for AG learning. Knowlton et al. (1992) found that amnesic patients in a standard AG learning task were able to classify novel test strings as grammatical or non-grammatical at the same level of accuracy as normal subjects. However, compared to control subjects, the amnesic patients were severely impaired in an episodic recognition test, in which they had to indicate whether letter strings had appeared in the study phase. In a follow-up study, Knowlton & Squire (1994) tested 12 amnesic patients (six with damage to the diencephalon, six with hippocampal damage as confirmed by magnetic resonance imaging) and 12 normal subjects matched for age, education, and intelligence. In the study phase, subjects were twice presented 23 grammatical strings, each for three seconds, with the instruction to immediately reproduce each string. Five minutes later subjects were informed about the existence of a rule system and asked to classify new items according to whether they conformed to this rule. Non-grammatical strings contained violations from permissible letters at one position within the string. Subjects were encouraged to base their judgements on their "gut feeling" and not to try to figure out what the rules were. Both control subjects and amnesic patients classified strings significantly above chance (58.3 per cent versus 59.1 per cent, respectively) and did not differ significantly in their classification performance. Obviously, AG learning in amnesic patients is mediated by brain systems different from those necessary for declarative memory. Moreover, as was discussed in section 5, Knowlton & Squire (1994) could convincingly show that their subjects' grammaticality judgements depended on the overlap of letter bigrams between study and test strings. Taken together, these findings add an important new aspect to our discussion of exemplar models in section 5. Given that a substantial portion of the knowledge acquired in AG tasks consists of letter chunks, the findings with amnesic patients show that such chunks need not be consciously recollected to mediate grammaticality judgements. Rather, stored chunks appear to influence grammaticality judgements implicitly, perhaps in a manner similar to priming effects in implicit memory.

Conclusion
Neuropsychological studies of amnesic patients suggest that various forms of implicit learning are independent from the medial-temporal and diencephalic brain systems which appear to be necessary for conscious, episodic memory (Squire 1994). Squire et al. (1993) have suggested that implicit learning of rules in AG learning or the induction of prototypes from exemplars may be based on the formation of associations between stimulus features and categories and perhaps involve similar processes as the acquisition of habits. Such a view shares some aspects with the idea mentioned in section 5 that implicit learning involves a system specialized for the extraction of invariances across a large number of single episodes, whereas the declarative memory system is necessary for the retention of single episodes in an autobiographical spatio-temporal context (cf. Sherry & Schacter 1987).

7.2 Neuropsychology of implicit learning
If implicit learning is independent from medial-temporal/diencephalic declarative memory systems, what brain structures are involved in it? The pertinent empirical evidence is still very sparse and prohibits firm conclusions. If anything, there are some indications that different forms of implicit learning involve modifications in different brain structures, in particular, structures which are also involved in the initial performance of a given task.

This conclusion is primarily supported by studies of skill acquisition and sequence learning. Patients suffering from Parkinson's or

Huntington's disease, who show pathological degenerative changes in brain structures mediating motor behaviour (such as the basal ganglia and neostriatal structures), are impaired in the acquisition of sensori-motor skills and procedural learning tasks (Butters et al. 1990, Heindel et al. 1988). Likewise, when tested with sequence-learning tasks such as the serial reaction task, patients with Huntington's disease (Knopman & Nissen 1991) and Parkinson's disease (Ferraro et al. 1993) also show impairments.[21] In contrast, despite somewhat impaired declarative memory performance, these patients performed better on standard explicit memory tests than amnesic patients, while the amnesics performed better on sensori-motor learning tasks.

Functional-brain-imaging techniques provide additional support for the assumption that the acquisition of procedural skills (and perhaps implicit sequence learning) involves cortico-striatal circuits related to motor behaviour. Grafton et al. (1992) obtained PET scans while subjects performed a pursuit rotor task in which they had to keep a stylus in contact with a target on a rotating disk. In order to obtain brain activation due to the execution of the motor behaviour, they subtracted scans in the tracking condition from a control condition in which subjects merely had to track the target with their eyes. This subtraction showed a relative increase in brain activity in a network consisting of various motor-related areas (e.g. motor cortex, supplementary-motor area, left pulvinar in the thalamus, part of the basal ganglia and the cerebellum) as well as areas in the occipital cortex related to visual information processing. In order to isolate specific effects of *learning* the skill, scans that were obtained in successive stages in the course of training were subtracted from each other. The largest learning-dependent increase in brain activity was observed in left motor cortex, left supplementary-motor area and left thalamus. The authors conclude that the acquisition of a skill involves modifications in those brain areas which also underly the original execution of the skill.

Particularly interesting brain-imaging results were recently reported by Grafton et al. (1994) who studied sequence learning in the SRT task with PET. When subjects performed the SRT together with a distracting secondary task, they developed no explicit knowledge about the sequence and learning-related increases of cerebral blood flow were observed in various brain areas related to the control of motor performance (including contra-lateral motor cortex, supplementary-motor area, and putamen). These results are consistent with the conclusion of Grafton et al. (1992) that the implicit acquisition of a motor skill occurs in brain areas controlling the original execution of the skill. However, when subjects performed the SRT without a secondary task, and when most of the subjects acquired conscious sequence knowledge, learning-related increases of cerebral blood flow were obtained in a very different network of brain structures (the right dorsolateral prefrontal cortex, right premotor cortex, and parieto-occipital cortex). On the basis of other findings suggesting that dorsolateral prefrontal and parietal areas may be involved in spatial working memory, these findings indicate that explicit sequence learning may involve working memory systems, whereas implicit motor learning is based on a different network of motor-related brain areas.

Further evidence for a distinction between explicit and implicit modes of sequence learning was reported in another PET study in which participants performed the serial reaction task under single task conditions (Rauch et al. 1995). To investigate implicit learning, PET scans were obtained during an early phase in training after which participants showed no reliable explicit knowledge of the sequence. After the implicit learning phase, subjects were informed of the 12-element sequence and given an opportunity to observe three repetitions of the sequence. Further PET scans were then obtained during additional training blocks after which subjects showed reliable explicit knowledge of the sequence. Implicit sequence learning activated right-sided cortico-striatal areas including ventral premotor cortex, ventral striatum, and thalamus, as well as bilateral visual association cortex. Although partly different components of the striatum were activated as compared to the Grafton et al. (1995) study, both studies converge in that they suggest the involvement of a cortico-striatal system in implicit motor sequence learning. In the explicit learning condition, Rauch et al. (1995) obtained learning-related activation in language and visual areas, including left Broca's area, bilateral temporo-parietal cortex, and bilateral primary visual cortex. The activation of Broca's area may reflect the fact that response keys were labelled with letters and that subjects in the explicit condition probably used these labels to maintain parts of the sequence in working memory. In contrast to the Grafton et al. study, no activation of the dorsolateral prefrontal cortex was found. This and other differences in the pattern of brain activity in the explicit conditions of the two PET studies presumably reflect differences in the procedures as well as in the sequence structures used.

Given the few available studies, it would be premature to draw conclusions as regards the neurological basis of different forms of implicit learning. However, the evidence on procedural and sequence learning suggests three interesting hypotheses. First, neural structures can be directly modified as a result of processing sensory information or performing some task, and implicit learning may involve modifications in brain structures which are also involved in the initial performance of a given task. Secondly, to the degree that this is correct, one should expect that different types of implicit learning depend on modifications in different brain systems. In fact, double dissociations between different groups of patients with respect to performance on different skill learning tasks (e.g. mirror reading, Tower of Hanoi, motor skill learning, SRT) have been reported (see Soliveri et al. 1992, for review). Finally, brain-imaging findings indicate that explicit and implicit modes of learning in the same task are mediated by different networks of brain structures, although the precise anatomy and functional role of these networks remains to be elucidated. In particular, the available studies show that the activation of brain areas in explicit learning conditions depends in subtle ways on details of the procedures and materials.

8. CONCLUSIONS

8.1 Functional properties of explicit and implicit knowledge

Although at present there is no general agreed-upon theory of implicit learning, there are now numerous replicated findings that suggest a number of functional differences between implicit and explicit forms of learning. These differences may serve as constraints for the development of an integrated theory of the functional architecture of different forms of learning and memory.

Modality and material specificity

Whereas explicit knowledge is usually robust against changes in perceptual surface features of stimuli, implicit knowledge shows only limited transfer to stimuli that instantiate the same deep structure, but differ in the perceptual surface. Knowledge acquired in dynamic system control or serial reaction tasks appears not to transfer to tasks governed by the same structural regularities, when these regularities are mapped to a different sensori-motor surface or semantic cover scenario. The most convincing evidence for abstract implicit knowledge stems from AG learning, where reliable transfer effects have been reported for changed letter sets or shifts in presentation modality. However, as was discussed, these transfer effects may not reflect abstract implicit knowledge, but rather be because of the application of relatively simple conscious mapping rules and analogies.

Interestingly, limited transfer to stimuli with changed perceptual surface features is also characteristic of implicit memory. Repetition priming effects in indirect tests like word-fragment completion are strongly attenuated when perceptual features such as type font or presentation modality are changed between study and test (Jacoby &

Hayman 1987, Jacoby & Dallas 1981, Kirsner et al. 1983). It remains a topic for future research whether this similarity reflects a deeper relationship between implicit learning and memory.

Response specificity

Implicit knowledge is often bound to specific tasks or response channels and shows up primarily in a speed-up, priming, or bias in specific response systems. By contrast, explicit knowledge can be flexibly applied to a wide variety of response systems and modalities. These findings bear some analogy to what is known about the acquisition of procedural skills, which also appear to be based on the formation of very specific invariant stimulus–response mappings (Shiffrin & Schneider 1977) or the accumulation in memory of similar instances of such mappings (Logan 1988).

Informational isolation

Implicit knowledge is relatively isolated from subjects' general knowledge, beliefs, and intentions. For instance, an amnesic patient may show intact sequence learning or priming effects in recognizing previously presented faces. However, he or she will not be able to integrate the knowledge expressed in such priming effects with further knowledge (e.g. about the person whose face produces a priming effect), and he or she will not be able to use this knowledge for the intentional control of actions. In contrast, conscious declarative knowledge can in principle be integrated and connected with any other piece of knowledge and used for the planning of arbitrary intentional actions.

Intentional impenetrability

Implicit learning appears to be relatively insensitive for intentional influences. Although the evidence on this point is not conclusive, at least some forms of implicit learning appear not to require one's full attention. Moreover, instructing subjects to deliberately search for rules or to explicitly test hypotheses does not improve (in fact sometimes impairs) implicit learning in AG tasks (Reber 1976). Likewise, performance on more complex types of dynamic system control tasks is not improved by providing subjects with explicit information about the rules governing the system (Berry & Broadbent 1988). Again, this parallels findings from implicit memory research, where it has been shown that encoding variables such as depth of processing or elaboration, which improve recall and recognition performance, usually have no or even reverse effects on indirect memory tests (at least when so-called data-driven tests are considered; e.g. Roediger & Blaxton 1987, Roediger et al. 1989; for review see Richardson-Klavehn & Bjork 1988).

Robustness

Implicit knowledge has sometimes been shown to be very durable. For instance, Allen & Reber (1980) retested subjects who had participated in an earlier experiment on AG learning (Reber & Allen 1978) two years later. Despite the two-year delay, subjects still classified letter strings as grammatical or non-grammatical significantly above chance. This long-term retention of knowledge was especially pronounced for knowledge acquired in an "implicit mode", whereas conscious knowledge appeared to be more fragile. Good retention of implicit knowledge over longer time intervals ranging from days to even years has been reported in a number of studies (e.g. Fendrich et al. 1991, Mathews et al. 1989, Nissen et al. 1989, Squire & Frambach 1990). Moreover, amnesic patients who are unable to recall new information after longer retention intervals show normal long-term retention of implicit knowledge.

Conclusions

On the basis of these observations, some researchers (e.g. Reber 1993, Sherry & Schacter 1987, Squire 1987) have conceived of implicit learning and memory as evolutionary old forms of knowledge acquisition that are more basic than our more recently-evolved capacities for declarative knowledge and symbolic thought. According to this view, implicit learning evolved as a means to adapt the behaviour of organisms to invariant, repeating, or regular patterns of stimulation in the environment. This would explain why implicit learning is closely tied to specific perceptual and response systems. In the further course of evolution, learning and memory have increasingly been decoupled from the immediate control of behaviour. Specific brain structures evolved which were not directly involved in perception and action, but which served for the acquisition and representation of declarative knowledge and episodic memories. This form of memory enabled organisms to store internal representations of individual, spatio-temporally localized experiences as well as general knowledge about the world independently from the immediate control of action and from the direct modification of perceptual and motor systems. This form of knowledge is the basis for mental planning and control of arbitrary types of future actions (Goschke 1995, in press, Neumann 1990, Prinz 1983).

8.2 Final remarks

What probably strikes a reader patient enough to follow me through the sometimes inconsistent and complex field of implicit learning is the remarkable discrepancy between the apparently overwhelming evidence for unconscious cognition in everyday life and the immense difficulties one encounters when trying to demonstrate implicit learning in the laboratory. Everyday life appears to abound with examples of unconscious learning of rule systems, which are often considerably more complex than the AG or event sequences used in the laboratory. That children learn a language without having conscious access to syntactic rules, or that non-experts can learn to discriminate piano pieces by Ravel and Debussy in the absence of any formal training in music analysis, appears to prove beyond doubt that we possess a powerful implicit learning system that enables us to acquire complex rule systems and intuitive knowledge. This impression notwithstanding, the unconscious has turned out to be remarkably resistant to attempts to prove it experimentally. In a sense, the return of the unconscious under the terminological cover of implicit cognition has mobilized similar methodological and conceptual defences that led to the partial repression of the unconscious during the first wave of research on subliminal perception in the 1950s. Perhaps this is as it should be in good science, as participants on both sides join the second round of the controversy with refined conceptual arguments and clearly improved methodological tools that allow us to investigate in much more detail the operating principles of implicit forms of learning.

Rather than recapitulate conclusions concerning the specific topics of the previous sections, I would like to close this chapter with three general issues that in my view have been neglected in implicit learning research.

The first issue concerns the complexity of the rule structures that have been investigated. Although AGs or matrix search tasks may seem relatively complex when compared to standard materials in experimental psychology, it is an open question how far the learning principles observed in these tasks can be generalized to the acquisition of rule systems such as language or music. Techniques are needed that allow us to investigate under controlled conditions the acquisition of much more complex rule structures such as music, for which learning by means of conscious strategies appears less plausible.

Secondly, there has to date been little integration between the field of implicit learning and other manifestations of implicit knowledge. Although occasionally implicit learning and memory are discussed in relation to phenonema such as intuition (Bowers et al. 1990, Kuhl 1990, Perrig 1990), incubation in problem solving (Dorfman et al. 1996, Mandler 1994), implicit representations in motivation and emotion (Jacoby & Kelley 1990, Kuhl 1994, McClelland et al. 1985), or personality differences in cognitive styles (Kuhl 1995), there is very little systematic experimental research on these topics. In most cases, there are not even well-developed tasks to study the phenomena under question.

Finally, a deeper understanding of unconscious cognition will probably only be attained when we also make progress in understanding the role of consciousness in functional and neural models of learning, memory, and knowledge. At the beginning of this chapter, I discussed the conceptual and methodological problems that arise in the attempt to operationalize the distinction between conscious and unconscious knowledge. To a substantial degree these methodological problems are surface reflections of fundamental philosophical problems concerning the concept of consciousness.

I have discussed findings suggesting that explicit forms of memory and learning rely on medial-temporal/diencephalic brain structures which are separate from those mediating nondeclarative forms of memory. This observation may account for functional dissociations between the two forms of knowledge, but it does not answer the question of why some forms of memory and knowledge are and others are not accompanied by a subjective quality of knowing or remembering (cf. Moscovitch 1994), not to speak of the question why and in virtue of which properties some brain states are correlated with consciousness *at all* (what in philosophy is called the problem of qualia; cf. Bieri 1992, Flohr 1991). Sometimes an additional separate system responsible for the emergence of conscious representations is postulated. Being well aware that this is little more than a theoretical placeholder for future explanations, Schacter (1989) has termed this structure the "conscious awareness system", into which information from perceptual input modules must be transferred in order to become conscious. Others have critized a systems account of consciousness, arguing that the neurological evidence speaks against the existence of a highest integrative centre in the brain where all the information comes together. According to this view, component aspects of perceptions and memories (colour, motion, location, identity, etc.) are represented in separate areas and form a distributed network of segregated pieces of knowledge (Damasio 1989, Dennett 1991). Rather than postulate a consciousness system, it has been suggested that consciousness is a property of specific brain states. For instance, it has been hypothesized that neuronal activation patterns must remain stable for at least some hundred milliseconds to give rise to a conscious experience, or that a specific form of synchronized neural firing is the substrate of the binding together of segregated features into a unitary conscious percept (cf. Crick & Koch 1990, Flohr 1991). Fascinating as such proposals are, at present they must remain speculative and we have to admit that almost nothing is really known about the neural representation of conscious and unconscious knowledge. One important long-term motivation behind an interdisciplinary approach to implicit learning is thus the prospect that this research will help to shed light on the relations between knowledge representations, phenomenological states, and neural structures.

REFERENCES

Abrams, M. & A. S. Reber 1988. Implicit learning: robustness in the face of psychiatric disorders. *Journal of Psycholinguistic Research* **17**, 425–39.

Allen, R. & A. S. Reber 1980. Very long term memory for tacit knowledge. *Cognition* **8**, 175–85.

Allport, D. A. 1988. What concept of consciousness? In *Consciousness in contemporary science*, A. J. Marcel & E. Bisiach (eds), 159–82. Oxford: Oxford University Press.

Allport, D. A. 1989. Visual attention. In *Foundations of cognitive science*, M. I. Posner (ed.), 631–81. Cambridge, Mass.: MIT Press.

Anderson, J. R. 1978. Arguments concerning representations from mental imagery. *Psychological Review* **85**, 249–77.

Anderson, J. R. 1983. *The architecture of cognition*. Cambridge, Mass.: Harvard University Press.

Anderson, J. R. 1987. Skill acquisition: Compilation of weak-method problem solutions. *Psychological Review* **94**, 192–210.

Baars, B. J. 1988. *A cognitive theory of consciousness*. Cambridge: Cambridge University Press.

Baddeley, A. D. 1986. *Working memory*. Oxford: Oxford University Press.

Bargh, J. 1989. Conditional automaticity: varieties of automatic influences in social perception and cognition. In *Unintended thought*, J. S. Uleman & J. A. Bargh (eds), 3–51. New York: Guilford Press.

Barsalou, L. W. 1990. On the indistinguishability of exemplar memory and abstraction in category representation. In *Advances in social cognition*, vol. 3: *content and process specificity in the effects of prior experiences*, T. K. Srull & R. S. Wyer (eds), 61–88. Hillsdale, New Jersey: Erlbaum.

Berry, D. C. & D. E. Broadbent 1984. On the relationship between task performance and associated verbalizable knowledge. *Quarterly Journal of Experimental Psychology* **36**, 209–231.

Berry, D. C. & D. E. Broadbent 1988. Interactive tasks and the implicit-explicit distinction. *British Journal of Psychology* **79**, 251–72.

Berry, D. C. & Z. Dienes 1991. The relationship between implicit memory and implicit learning. *British Journal of Psychology* **82**, 359–73.

Berry, D. C. & Z. Dienes 1993. *Implicit learning: theoretical and empirical issues*. Hillsdale, New Jersey: Erlbaum.

Bieri, P. 1992. Was macht Bewusstsein zu einem Rätsel? *Spektrum der Wissenschaft* (October), 48–56.

Bowers, K. S., G. Regehr, C. Balthazard, K. Parker 1990. Intuition in the context of discovery. *Cognitive Psychology* **22**, 72–110.

Braine, M. D. S. 1966. Learning the positions of words relative to a marker element. *Journal of Experimental Psychology* **72**, 532–40.

Braine, M. D. S., R. E. Brody, P. J. Brooks, V. Sudhalter, J. A. Ross, L. Catalano, S. M. Fisch 1990. Exploring language acquisition in children with a miniature artificial language: effects of item and pattern frequency, arbitrary subclasses, and correction. *Journal of Memory and Language* **29**, 591–610.

Broadbent, D. E., P. FitzGerald, M. H. P. Broadbent 1986. Implicit and explicit knowledge in the control of complex systems. *British Journal of Psychology* **77**, 33–50.

Brooks, L. 1978. Nonanalytic concept formation and memory for instances. In *Cognition and categorization*, E. Rosch & B. B. Lloyd (eds), 169–211. Hillsdale, New Jersey: Erlbaum.

Brooks, L. & J. Vokey 1991. Abstract analogies and abstracted grammars: comments on Reber (1989) and Mathews et al. (1989). *Journal of Experimental Psychology: General* **120**, 316–23.

Buchner, A. 1993. *Implizites Lernen*. Weinheim: Psychologie Verlags Union.

Butters, N., W. C. Heindel, D. P. Salmon 1990. Dissociation of implicit memory in dementia: neurological implications. *Bulletin of the Psychonomic Society* **28**, 359–66.

Carlson, R. A. & D. E. Dulany 1985. Conscious attention and abstraction in concept learning. *Journal of Experimental Psychology: Learning, Memory, and Cognition* **11**, 45–58.

Cheesman, J. & P. M. Merikle 1984. Priming with and without awareness. *Perception and Psychophysics* **36**, 387–95.

Clark, A. 1989. *Microcognition: philosophy, cognitive science, and parallel distributed processing*. Cambridge, Mass.: MIT Press.

Cleeremans, A. 1993. *Mechanisms of implicit learning*. Cambridge, Mass.: MIT Press.

Cleeremans, A. & J. L. McClelland 1991. Learning the structure of event sequences. *Journal of Experimental Psychology: General* **120**, 235–53.

Cohen, A. & T. Curran 1993. On tasks, knowledge, correlations, and dissociations: comment on Perruchet and Amorim (1992). *Journal of Experimental Psychology: Learning, Memory, and Cognition* **19**, 1431–7.

Cohen, A., R. I. Ivry, S. W. Keele 1990. Attention and structure in sequence learning. *Journal of Experimental Psychology: Learning, Memory, and Cognition* **16**, 17–30.

Cohen, N. J. & L. R. Squire 1980. Preserved learning and retention of pattern-analyzing skill in amnesia: dissociation of "knowing how" and "knowing that". *Science* **210**, 207–9.

Crick, F. & C. Koch 1990. Towards a neurobiological theory of consciousness. *Seminars in the Neurosciences* **2**, 263–75.

Curran, T. & S. W. Keele 1993. Attentional and nonattentional forms of sequence learning. *Journal of Experimental Psychology: Learning, Memory, and Cognition* **19**, 189–202.

Damasio, A. R. 1989. Time-locked multiregional retroactivation: a systems-level proposal for the neural substrates of recall and recognition. *Cognition* **33**, 25–62.

Dennett, D. C. 1987. *The intentional stance*. Cambridge, Mass.: MIT Press.

Dennett, D. C. 1991. *Consciousness explained*. Boston, Mass.: Little, Brown.

Dienes, Z. 1992. Connectionist and memory-array models of artificial grammar learning. *Cognitive Science* **16**, 41–80.

Dienes, Z. 1993. Computational models of implicit learning. In *Implicit learning: theoretical and empirical issues*, D. C. Berry & Z. Dienes (eds), 81–112. Hillsdale, New Jersey: Erlbaum.

Dienes, Z., D. E. Broadbent, D. Berry 1991. Implicit and explicit knowledge bases in artificial grammar learning. *Journal of Experimental Psychology: Learning, Memory, and Cognition* **17**, 875–87.

Dienes, Z. & R. Fahey 1995. Role of specific instances in controlling a dynamic system. *Journal of Experimental Psychology: Learning, Memory, and Cognition* **21**, 848–62.

Dixon, N. F. 1971. *Subliminal perception: the nature of a controversy*. London: McGraw-Hill.

Dorfman, J., V. A. Shames, J. F. Kihlstrom 1996. Intuition, incubation, and insight: implicit cognition in problem solving. In *Implicit cognition*, G. Underwood (ed.), 257–96. Oxford: Oxford University Press.

Druhan, B. & R. Mathews 1989. THIYOS: a classifier system model of implicit knowledge of artificial grammars. *Proceedings of the 11th Annual Conference of the Cognitive Science Society*. Hillsdale, New Jersey: Erlbaum.

Dulany, D. E., R. A. Carlson, G. I. Dewey 1984. A case of syntactical learning and judgement: how conscious and how abstract? *Journal of Experimental Psychology: General* **113**, 541–55.

Dulany, D. E., R. A. Carlson, G. I. Dewey 1985. On consciousness in syntactic learning and judgement: a reply to Reber, Allen, and Regan. *Journal of Experimental Psychology: General* **114**, 25–32.

Ebbinghaus, H. 1885. *Uber das Gedächtnis [On memory]*. Leipzig: Duncker & Humblot.

Eimer, M., B. Stürmer, F. Schlaghecken, T. Goschke, in press. ERP indicators of explicit and implicit learning in a serial reaction time task. In *Mapping cognition in time and space: combining EEG, MEG with functional brain imaging*, H-J. Heinze, G. R. Mangun, T. F. Münte, Elger & Scheich (eds).

Elman, J. L. 1991. Distributed representation, simple recurrent networks, and grammatical structure. *Machine Learning* **7**, 195–225.

Epstein, S. 1994. Integration of the cognitive and the psychodynamic unconscious. *American Psychologist* **49**, 709–24.

Erderlyi, M. H. 1986. Experimental indeterminacies in the dissociation paradigm of subliminal perception: comment on Holender 1986. *The Behavioral and Brain Sciences* **9**, 30–31.

Eriksen, C. W. 1960. Discrimination and learning without awareness: a methodological survey and evaluation. *Psychological Review* **67**, 279–300.

Estes, W. K. 1986. Memory storage and retrieval processes in category learning. *Journal of Experimental Psychology: General* **115**, 155–74.

Farah, M. J. 1994. Neuropsychological inference with an interactive brain: a critique of the "locality" assumption. *Behavioral and Brain Sciences* **17**, 43–104.

Fendrich, D. W., A. F. Healy, L. E. Bourne 1991. Long-term repetition effects for motoric and perceptual procedures. *Journal of Experimental Psychology: Learning, Memory, and Cognition* **17**, 137–51.

Ferraro, F. R., D. A. Balota, L. T. Connor 1993. Implicit memory and the formation of new associations in nondemented Parkinson's disease individuals and individuals with senile dementia of the Alzheimer type: a serial reation time (srt) investigation. *Brain and Cognition* **21**, 163–80.

Flohr, H. 1991. Brain processes and phenomenal consciousness. *Theory and Psychology* **1**, 245–62.

Fodor, J. A. & Z. W. Pylyshyn 1988. Connectionism and cognitive architecture: a critical analysis. *Cognition* **28**, 3–71.

Frensch, P. A., A. Buchner, J. Lin 1994. Implicit learning of unique and ambiguous serial transitions in the presence and absence of a distractor task. *Journal of Experimental Psychology: Learning, Memory, and Cognition* **20**, 567–84.

Freud, S. 1901. *Zur Psychopathologie des Alltagslebens*. Gesammelte Werke (Vol. 4) (1954). Frankfurt: S. Fischer.

Glisky, E., D. Schacter, E. Tulving 1986. Computer learning by memory impaired patients: acquisition and retention of complex knowledge. *Neuropsychologia* **24**, 313–18.

Gomez, R. L. & R. W. Schvaneveldt 1994. What is learned from artificial grammars? Transfer tests of simple association. *Journal of Experimental Psychology: Learning, Memory, and Cognition* **20**, 396–410.

Goschke, T. 1991. Die Bedeutung impliziten Wissens für die Modellierung menschlicher Expertise. In *Dortmunder Expertensystemtage '91*, H. Heinz (ed.), (37–61). Köln: Verlag TÜV Rheinland.

Goschke, T. 1992a. The role of attention in implicit learning of event sequences. *International Journal of Psychology* **27**, 110 [abstract].

Goschke, T. 1992b. Aufmerksamkeit und implizites Lernen regelhafter Sequenzen. In *Bericht über den 38 Kongress der Deutschen Gesellschaft für Psychologie in Trier 1992*, L. Montada (ed.), 166–7. Göttingen: Hogrefe.

Goschke, T. 1994. *Mechanisms of implicit sequence learning: evidence from dual task-studies and event-related brain potentials*. Poster presented at the 1994 European Summer Institute for Cognitive Neuroscience, Nijmegen, The Netherlands.

Goschke, T. 1995. Wille und Kognition: zur funktionalen Architektur der intentionalen Handlungssteuerung. (Volition and cognition: the functional architecture of intentional action control). In *Enzyklopädie der Psychologie Serie iv, Band 4: Motivation, Volition und Handeln*, H. Heckhausen & J. Kuhl (eds), 583–663. Göttingen: Hogrefe.

Goschke, T. 1996. *Implicit learning of stimulus and response sequences: evidence for independent learning systems*. Paper presented at the Max-Planck Institute for Cognitive Neuroscience, Leipzig, Germany.

Goschke, T. in press. Gedächtnis und Lernen: mentale Prozesse und Hirnstrukturen. In *Was der Geist über das Gehirn wissen kann*, G. Roth & W. Prinz (eds). Heidelberg: Spektrum Akademischer.

Goschke, T. & D. Koppelberg 1990. Connectionist representation, semantic compositionality, and the instability of concept structure. *Psychological Research* **52**, 253–70.

Goschke, T. & D. Koppelberg 1991. The concept of representation and the representation of concepts in connectionist models. In *Philosophy and connectionist theory*, W. Ramsey, D. E. Rumelhart, S. Stich (eds), 129–62. Hillsdale, New Jersey: Erlbaum.

Graf, P. & S. Komatsu 1994. Process dissociation procedure: handle with caution! *European Journal of Cognitive Psychology* **6**, 113–29.

Graf, P. & D. A. Schacter 1985. Implicit and explicit memory for new associations in normal and amnesic subjects. *Journal of Experimental Psychology: Learning, Memory, and Cognition* **11**, 501–18.

Grafton, S. T., E. Hazeltine, R. Ivry 1995. Functional mapping of sequence learning in normal humans. *Journal of Cognitive Neuroscience* **7**, 497–510.

Grafton, S. T., J. C. Mazziotta, S. Presty, K. J. Friston, R. S. J. Frackowiak, M. E. Phelps 1992. Functional anatomy of human procedural learning determined with regional cerebral blood flow and PET. *Journal of Neuroscience* **12**, 2542–8.

Green, R. E. A. & D. R. Shanks 1993. On the existence of independent explicit and implicit learning systems: an examination of some evidence. *Memory and Cognition* **21**, 304–17.

Greenwald, A. G. 1992. New look 3: unconscious cognition reclaimed. *American Psychologist* **47**, 784–7.

Greenwald, A. G. & M. R. Banaji 1995. Implicit social cognition: attitudes, self-esteem, and stereotypes. *Psychological Review* **102**, 4–27.

Haider, H. 1990. *Explizites versus implizites Wissen und Lernen*. PhD Dissertation, Psychology Dept. Universität der Bundeswehr Hamburg.

Hartman, M., D. S. Knopman, M. J. Nissen 1989. Implicit learning of new verbal associations. *Journal of Experimental Psychology: Learning, Memory, and Cognition* **15**, 1070–82.

Hayes, N. A. & D. E. Broadbent 1988. Two modes of learning for interactive tasks. *Cognition* **28**, 249–76.

Heindel, W. C., N. Butters, D. P. Salmon 1988. Impaired learning of a motor skill in patients with Huntington's disease. *Behavioral Neuroscience* **102**, 141–7.

Hillyard, S. A. & M. Kutas 1983. Electrophysiology of cognitive processing. *Annual Review of Psychology* **34**, 33–61.

Hintzman, D. L. 1986. "Schema abstraction" in a multiple-trace memory model. *Psychological Review* **93**, 411–28.

Hintzman, D. L. & A. L. Harty 1990. Item effects in recognition and fragment completion: contingency relations vary for different subsets of words. *Journal of Experimental Psychology: Learning, Memory, and Cognition* **16**, 955–69.

Hirsh-Pasek, K., D. G. Kemler-Nelson, P. W. Jusczyk, K. W. Cassidy, B. Druss, L. Kennedy, 1987. Clauses are perceptual units for young infants. *Cognition* **26**, 269–86.

Hoffmann, J. 1993. *Erkenntnis und Vorhersage*. Göttingen: Hogrefe.

Holender, D. 1986. Semantic activation without conscious identification in dichotic listening, parafoveal vision and visual masking: a survey and reappraisal. *The Behavioral and Brain Sciences* **9**, 1–23.

Homa, D. 1979. Abstraction of ill-defined form. *Journal of Experimental Psychology: Human Learning and Memory* **4**, 407–16.

Isen, A. M. 1987. Positive affect, cognitive processes, and social behaviour. In *Advances in experimental social psychology* (vol. 20), L. Berkowitz (ed.), 203–253. New York: Academic Press.

Jacoby, L. 1991. A process dissociation framework: separating automatic from intentional uses of memory. *Journal of Memory and Language* **30**, 513–41.

Jacoby, L. L. & M. Dallas 1981. On the relationship between autobiographical memory and perceptual learning. *Journal of Experimental Psychology: General* **110**, 306–40.

Jacoby, L. L. & C. A. G. Hayman 1987. Specific visual transfer in word identification. *Journal of Experimental Psychology: Learning, Memory, and Cognition* **13**, 456–63.

Jacoby, L. L. & C. M. Kelley 1990. An episodic view on motivation. In *Handbook of motivation and cognition*, vol. 2: *foundations of social behaviour*, E. T. Higgins & R. M. Sorrentino (eds), 451–81. New York: Guilford Press.

Jacoby, L. L., J. P. Toth, A. P. Yonelinas 1993. Separating conscious and unconscious influences of memory: measuring recollection. *Journal of Experimental Psychology: Learning, Memory, and Cognition* **122**, 139–54.

Joordens, S. & P. M. Merikle 1993. Independence or redundancy? Two models of conscious and unconscious influences. *Journal of Experimental Psychology: Learning, Memory, and Cognition* **122**, 462–7.

Kemler-Nelson, D. G. 1984. The effect of intention on what concepts are acquired. *Journal of Verbal Learning and Verbal Behavior* **23**, 734–59.

Kihlstrom, J. F. 1987. The cognitive unconscious. *Science* **237**, 1445–52.

Kinsbourne, M. 1988. Integrated field theory of consciousness. In *Consciousness in contemporary science*, A. J. Marcel & E. Bisiach (eds), 239–56. Oxford: Oxford University Press.

Kirsner, K., D. Milech, P. Standen 1983. Common and modality-specific processes in the mental lexicon. *Memory and Cognition* **11**, 621–30.

Knopman, D. & M. J. Nissen 1987. Implicit learning in patients with probable Alzheimer's disease. *Neurology* **37**, 784–8.

Knopman, D. & M. J. Nissen 1991. Procedural learning is impaired in Huntington's disease: evidence from the serial reaction time task. *Neuropsychologia* **29**, 245–54.

Knowlton, B. J., S. J. Ramus, L. R. Squire 1992. Intact artificial grammar learning in amnesia: dissociation of classification learning and explicit memory for specific instances. *Psychological Science* **3**, 172–9.

Knowlton, B. J. & L. R. Squire 1993. The learning of categories: parallel brain systems for item memory and category knowledge. *Science* **262**, 1747–9.

Knowlton, B. J. & L. R. Squire 1994. The information acquired during artificial grammar learning. *Journal of Experimental Psychology: Learning, Memory, and Cognition* **20**, 79–91.

Kolb, B. & I. Q. Wishaw 1990. *Fundamentals of human neuropsychology* [Chapter 15]. New York: W. H. Freeman.

Kuhl, J. 1990. Intuition und Logik der Forschung in der Psychologie. In *Max-Planck Institut für Psychologische Forschung* Erinnerungen, Würdigungen, Wirkungen, H. Heckhausen (ed.). Heidelberg: Springer.

Kuhl, J. 1994. Motivation and volition. In *International perspectives on psychological science: the state of the art* (vol. 2), G. d'Yderwalle, P. Eelen, P. Bertelson (eds), 311–40. Hillsdale, New Jersey: Erlbaum.

Kuhl, J. 1995. Wille und Freiheitserleben: Formen der Selbststeuerung. In *Enzyklopädie der Psychologie Serie IV, Band 4: Motivation, Volition und Handeln*, H. Heckhausen & J. Kuhl (eds). Göttingen: Hogrefe.

Lahav, R. 1993. What neuropsychology tells us about consciousness. *Philosophy of Science* **60**, 67–85.

Lewicki, P. 1986. *Nonconscious social information processing*. New York: Academic Press.

Lewicki, P., T. Hill, E. Bizot 1988. Acquisition of procedural knowledge about a pattern of stimuli that cannot be articulated. *Cognitive Psychology* **20**, 24–37.

Lewicki, P., T. Hill, M. Czyzewska 1992. Nonconscious acquisition of information. *American Psychologist* **47**, 796–801.

Loftus, E. F. & M. R. Klinger 1992. Is the unconscious smart or dumb? *American Psychologist* **47**, 761–5.

Logan, G. D. 1988. Toward an instance theory of automatization. *Psychological Review* **95**, 492–527.

Mandler, G. 1980. Recognizing: the judgement of previous occurrence. *Psychological Review* **87**, 252–71.

Mandler, G. 1994. Hypermnesia, incubation, and mind popping: on remembering without really trying. In *Attention and performance XV: conscious and nonconscious information processing*, C. Umilta & M. Moscovitch (eds), 3–33. Cambridge, Mass.: MIT Press.

Markowitsch, H. J. 1992. *Neuropsychologie des Gedächtnisses*. Göttingen: Hogrefe.

Mathews, R. 1990. Abstractiveness of implicit grammar knowledge: comments on Perruchet and Pacteau's analysis of synthetic grammar learning. *Journal of Experimental Psychology: General* **119**, 412–16.

Mathews, R. C. 1991. The forgetting algorithm: how fragmentary knowledge of exemplars can abstract knowledge. *Journal of Experimental Psychology: General* **120**, 117–19.

Mathews, R. C., R. R. Buss, W. B. Stanley, F. Blanchard-Fields, J. R. Cho, B. Druhan 1989. Role of implicit and explicit processes in learning from examples: a synergistic effect. *Journal of Experimental Psychology: Learning, Memory, and Cognition* **15**, 1083–1100.

Mayr, U. 1996. Spatial attention and implicit sequence learning: evidence for independent learning of spatial and nonspatial sequences. *Journal of Experimental Psychology: Learning, Memory and Cognition* **22**, 350–364.

McAndrews, M. P. & M. Moscovitch 1985. Rule-based and exemplar-based classification in artificial grammar learning. *Memory and Cognition* **13**, 469–75.

McClelland, D. C., R. Koestner, J. Weinberger 1985. How do self-attributed and implicit motives differ? *Psychological Review* **96**, 690–702.

McClelland, J. L., B. L. McNaughton, R. C. O'Reilly 1995. Why there are complementary learning systems in the hippocampus and neocortex: insights from the successes and failures of connectionist models of learning and memory. *Psychological Review* **102**, 419–57.

McGeorge, P. & M. Burton 1989. The effects of concurrent verbalisation on performance in a dynamic systems task. *British Journal of Psychology* **80**, 455–65.

Mehler, J., P. Jusczyk, G. Lambertz, N. Halsted, J. Bertoncini, C. Amiel-Tison 1988. A precursor of language acquisition in young infants. *Cognition* **29**, 143–78.

Merikle, P. 1982. Unconscious perception revisited. *Perception and Psychophysics* **31**, 289–301.

Milner, A. D. & M. D. Rugg 1992. *The neuropsychology of consciousness*. London: Academic Press.

Milner, B., S. Corkin, H-L. Teuber 1968. Further analysis of the hippocampal amnesic snydrome: 14-year follow-up of H.M. *Neuropsychologia* **6**, 215–34.

Mishkin, M. & T. Appenzeller 1987. The anatomy of memory. *Scientific American* **256**, 62–71.

Morgan, J. L., R. P. Meier, E. L. Newport 1987. Structural packaging in the input to language learning: contributions of prosodic and morphological marking of phrases to the acquisition of language. *Cognitive Psychology* **19**, 498–550.

Moscovitch, M. 1994. Memory and working with memory: evaluation of a component process model and comparison with other models. In *Memory systems* 1994, D. L. Schacter & E. Tulving (eds), 269–310. Cambridge, Mass.: MIT Press.

Moscovitch, M., G. Winocur, D. McLachlan 1986. Memory as assessed by recognition and reading time in normal and memory-impaired people with Alzheimer's disease and other neurological disorders. *Journal of Experimental Psychology: General* **115**, 331–47.

Musen, G. & L. R. Squire 1993. Implicit learning of color–word associations using a Stroop paradigm. *Journal of Experimental Psychology: Learning, Memory, and Cognition* **19**, 789–98.

Neumann, O. 1984. Automatic processing: a review of recent findings and a plea for an old theory. In *Cognition and motor processes*, W. Prinz & A. F. Sanders (eds), 255–94. Berlin: Springer.

Neumann, O. 1992. Theorien der Aufmerksamkeit: von Metaphern zu Mechanismen. *Psychologische Rundschau* **43**, 83–101.

Newell, A. 1973. Production systems: models of control structure. In *Visual information processing*, W. G. Chase (ed.), 463–526. New York: Academic Press.

Nissen, M. J. & P. Bullemer 1987. Attentional requirements of learning: evidence from performance measures. *Cognitive Psychology* **19**, 1–32.

Nissen, M. J., D. Willingham, M. Hartman 1989. Explicit and implicit remembering: when is learning preserved in amnesia? *Neuropsychologia* **27**, 341–52.

Palmer, S. E. 1978. Fundamental aspects of mental representation. In *Cognition and categorization*, E. Rosch & B. B. Lloyd (eds), 259–303. Hillsdale, New Jersey: Erlbaum.

Perrig, W. J. 1990. Implizites Wissen: eine Herausforderung für die Kognitionspsychologie. *Schweizerische Zeitschrift für Psychologie* **49**, 234–49.

Perruchet, P. 1994a. Learning from complex rule-governed environments: on the proper functions of nonconscious and conscious processes. In *Attention and performance XV: conscious and nonconscious information processing*, C. Umilta & M. Moscovitch (eds), 811–35. Cambridge, Mass.: MIT Press.

Perruchet, P. 1994b. Defining the knowledge units of a synthetic language: comment on Vokey & Brooks (1992). *Journal of Experimental Psychology: Learning, Memory, and Cognition* **20**, 223–8.

Perruchet, P. & M. A. Amorim 1992. Conscious knowledge and changes in performance in sequence learning: evidence against dissocation. *Journal of Experimental Psychology: Learning, Memory, and Cognition* **18**, 785–800.

Perruchet, P. & J. Gallego 1993. Association between conscious knowledge and performance in normal subjects: reply to Cohen and Curran (1993) and Willingham, Greeley, and Bardone (1993). *Journal of Experimental Psychology: Learning, Memory, and Cognition* **19**, 1438–44.

Perruchet, P., J. Gallego, C. Pacteau 1992. A reinterpretation of some earlier evidence for abstractiveness of implicitly acquired knowledge. *Quarterly Journal of Experimental Psychology* **44A**, 193–210.

Perruchet, P. & C. Pacteau 1990. Synthetic grammar learning: implicit rule abstraction or explicit fragmentary knowledge? *Journal of Experimental Psychology: General* **119**, 264–75.

Posner, M. I. & S. Keele 1968. Retention of abstract ideas. *Journal of Experimental Psychology* **83**, 304–8.

Posner, M. I. & S. E. Peterson 1990. The attention system of the human brain. *Annual Review of Neuroscience* **13**, 25–42.

Puchetti, R. 1985. Experiencing two selves: the history of a mistake. *Behavioral and Brain Sciences* **8**, 646–747.

Pylyshyn, Z. W. 1984. *Computation and cognition: towards a foundation for cognitive science.* Cambridge, Mass.: MIT Press.

Ratcliff, R. 1978. A theory of memory retrieval. *Psychological Review* **85**, 59–108.

Rauch, S. L., C. R. Savage, H. D. Brown, T. Curran, N. M. Alpert, A. Kendrick, A. J. Fischman, S. M. Kosslyn 1995. A PET investigation of implicit and explicit sequence learning. *Human Brain Mapping* **3**, 271–86.

Reber, A. S. 1967. Implicit learning of artificial grammars. *Journal of Verbal Learning and Verbal Behavior* **5**, 855–63.

Reber, A. 1969. Transfer of syntactic structures in synthetic languages. *Journal of Experimental Psychology* **81**, 115–19.

Reber, A. S. 1976. Implicit learning of synthetic languages: the role of instructional set. *Journal of Experimental Psychology: Human Learning and Memory* **2**, 88–94.

Reber, A. S. 1989. Implicit learning and tacit knowledge. *Journal of Experimental Psychology: General* **118**, 219–35.

Reber, A. S. 1993. *Implicit learning and tacit knowledge: an essay on the cognitive unconscious.* Oxford: Oxford University Press.

Reber, A. S. & R. Allen 1978. Analogic and abstraction strategies in synthetic grammar learning: a functionalist interpretation. *Cognition* **6**, 189–221.

Reber, A. S., R. Allen, S. Regan 1985. Syntactical learning and judgement, still unconscious and still abstract: comment on Dulany, Carlson, and Dewey. *Journal of Experimental Psychology: General* **114**, 17–24.

Reber, A. S. & S. Lewis 1977. Implicit learning: an analysis of the form and structure of a body of tacit knowledge. *Cognition* **5**, 333–61.

Reber, P. J. & L. R. Squire 1994. Parallel brain systems for learning with and without awareness. *Learning & Memory* **1**, 217–219.

Reed, J. & P. Johnson 1994. Assessing implicit learning with indirect tests: determining what is learned about sequence structure. *Journal of Experimental Psychology: Learning, Memory, and Cognition* **20**, 585–94.

Reingold, E. M. & P. M. Merikle 1990. On the inter-relatedness of theory and measurement in the study of unconscious processes. *Mind and Language* **5**, 9–28.

Richardson-Klavehn, A. & R. A. Bjork 1988. Measures of memory. *Annual Review of Psychology* **39**, 475–543.

Roediger, H. L. 1990. Implicit memory. Retention without remembering. *American Psychologist* **45**, 1043–56.

Roediger, H. L. & T. A. Blaxton 1987. Effects of varying modality, surface features, and retention interval on priming in word fragment completion. *Memory and Cognition* **15**, 379–88.

Roediger, H. L., M. S. Weldon, B. H. Challis 1989. Explaining dissociations between implicit and explicit measures of retention: a processing account. In *Varieties of memory and consciousness: essays in honour of Endel Tulving*, H. L. Roediger & F. I. M. Craik (eds), 3–41. Hillsdale, New Jersey: Erlbaum.

Rumelhart, D. E. & J. L. McClelland, 1986. *Parallel distributed processing: explorations in the microstructure of cognition*, vol. 1. Cambridge, Mass.: MIT Press.

Rumelhart, D. E., G. E. Hinton, R. J. Williams 1986. Learning internal representations by back-propagating errors. *Nature* **323**, 533–6.

Sanderson, P. M. 1989. Verbalizable knowledge and skilled task performance: association, dissociation, and mental models. *Journal of Experimental Psychology: Learning, Memory, and Cognition* **15**, 729–47.

Schacter, D. L. 1987. Implicit memory: history and current status. *Journal of Experimental Psychology: Learning, Memory, and Cognition* **13**, 501–18.

Schacter, D. L. 1989. On the relation between memory and consciousness: dissociable interactions and conscious experience. In *Varieties of memory and consciousness*, H. L. Roediger III & F. I. M. Craik (eds), 355–90. Hillsdale, New Jersey: Erlbaum.

Schacter, D. L. 1994. Priming and multiple memory systems: perceptual mechanisms of implicit memory. In *Memory systems 1994*, D. L. Schacter & E. Tulving (eds), 233–68. Cambridge, Mass.: MIT Press.

Schacter, D. L., J. Bowers, J. Booker 1989. Intention, awareness, and implicit memory: the retrieval intentionality criterion. In *Implicit memory: theoretical issues*, S. Lewandowsky, J. C. Dunn & K. Kirsner (eds), 47–66. Hillsdale, New Jersey: Erlbaum.

Schacter, D. L., M. P. McAndrews, M. Moscovitch 1988. Access to consciousness: dissociations between implicit and explicit knowledge in neuropsychological syndromes. In *Thought without language*, L. Weiskrantz (ed.), 242–78. Oxford: Oxford University Press.

Schacter, D. L. & E. Tulving (eds) 1994. *Memory systems 1994*. Cambridge, Mass.: MIT Press.

Seger, C. A. 1994. Implicit learning. *Psychological Bulletin* **115**, 163–96.

Servan-Schreiber, E. & J. R. Anderson 1990. Learning artificial grammars with competitive chunking. *Journal of Experimental Psychology: Learning, Memory, and Cognition* **16**, 592–608.

Shanks, D. R., R. E. A. Green, J. Kolodny 1994. A critical examination of the evidence for unconscious (implicit) learning. In *Attention and performance XV: conscious and nonconscious information processing*, C. Umilta & M. Moscovitch (eds), 837–60. Cambridge, Mass.: MIT Press.

Shanks, D. R. & M. F. St. John 1994. Characteristics of dissociable human learning systems. *Behavioral and Brain Sciences* **17**, 367–95.

Sherry, D. F. & D. L. Schacter 1987. The evolution of multiple memory systems. *Psychological Review* **94**, 439–54.

Shiffrin, R. M. & W. Schneider 1977. Controlled and automatic human information processing, II: perceptual learning, automatic attending, and a general theory. *Psychological Review* **84**, 127–90.

Shimamura, A. P. 1986. Priming effects in amnesia: evidence for a dissociable memory function. *Quarterly Journal of Experimental Psychology* **38A**, 619–44.

Smith, E. E. & D. Medin 1981. *Categories and concepts*. Cambridge, Mass.: Harvard University Press.

Smith, J. D. & J. H. Shapiro 1989. The occurrence of holistic categorization. *Journal of Memory and Language* **28**, 386–99.

Smith, K. H. 1969. Learning co-occurrence restrictions: rule induction or rote learning? *Journal of Verbal Learning and Verbal Behavior* **8**, 319–21.

Smolensky, P. 1988. On the proper treatment of connectionism. *Behavioral and Brain Sciences* **11**, 1–74.

Soliveri, P., R. G. Brown, M. Jahanshahi, C. D. Marsden 1992. Procedural memory and neurological disease. *European Journal of Cognitive Psychology* **4**, 161–93.

Sperling, G 1960. The information available in brief displays. *Psychological Monographs: General and Applied,* **74**, 1–28.

Squire, L. R. 1987. *Memory and the brain*. New York: Oxford University Press.

Squire, L. R. 1992. Memory and the hippocampus: a synthesis from findings with rats, monkeys, and humans. *Psychological Review* **99**, 195–231.

Squire, L. 1994. Declarative and nondeclarative memory: multiple brain systems supporting learning and memory. In *Memory systems 1994*, D. L. Schacter & E. Tulving (eds), 203–232. Cambridge, Mass.: MIT Press.

Squire, L. R. & M. Frambach 1990. Cognitive skill learning in amnesia. *Psychobiology* **18**, 109–117.

Squire, L. R., B. Knowlton, G. Musen 1993. The structure and organization of memory. *Annual Review of Psychology* **44**, 453–95.

Squire, L. R., J. G. Ojemann, F. M. Miezin, S. E. Peterson, T. O. Videen, M. E. Raichle 1992. Activation of the hippocampus in normal humans: a functional anatomical study of memory. *Proceedings of the National Academy of Sciences* **89**, 1837–41.

Stadler, M. A. 1989. On learning complex procedural knowledge. *Journal of Experimental Psychology: Learning, Memory, and Cognition* **15**, 1061–69.

Stadler, M. A. 1993. Implicit serial learning: questions inspired by Hebb (1961). *Memory and Cognition* **21**, 819–27.

Stadler, M. A. 1995. Role of attention in implicit learning. *Journal of Experimental Psychology: Learning, Memory, and Cognition* **21**, 674–85.

Stanley, W. B., R. C. Mathews, R. R. Buss, S. Kotler-Cope 1989. Insight without awareness: on the interaction of verbalization, instruction and practice in a simulated process control task. *Quarterly Journal of Experimental Psychology* **41A**, 553–77.

Tulving, E. & D. L. Schacter 1990. Priming and human memory systems. *Science* **247**, 301–5.

Tulving, E., D. L. Schacter, H. A. Stark 1982. Priming effects in word-fragment completion are independent of recognition memory. *Journal of Experimental Psychology: Learning, Memory, and Cognition* **8**, 336–42.

Van Gelder, T. 1990. Compositionality – A connectionist variation on a classical theme. *Cognitive Science* **14**, 355–84.

Velmans, M. 1991. Is human information processing conscious? *Behavioral and Brain Sciences* **14**, 651–726.

Vokey, J. R. & Brooks, L. R. 1992. Salience of item knowledge in learning artificial grammars. *Journal of Experimental Psychology: Learning, Memory, and Cognition* **18**, 328–44.

Warrington, E. K. & Weiskrantz, L. 1970. Amnesic syndrome: Consolidation or retrieval? *Nature* **228**, 629–30.

Weinert, S. 1991. *Spracherwerb und implizites Lernen*. Berne: Huber.

Weinert, S. 1992. Deficits in acquiring language structure: the importance of using prosodic cues. *Applied Cognitive Psychology* **6**, 545–71.

Weiskrantz, L. 1986. Blindsight: a case study and implications. Oxford: Oxford University Press.

Widrow, C. & Hoff, M. E. 1960. *Adaptive switching circuits*. Institute of Radio Engineers, Western Electronic Show and Convention, Convention Record 4, 96–104.

Willingham, D. B., T. Greeley & A. M. Bardone. 1993. Dissociation in a serial response time task using a recognition measure: Comment on Perruchet and Amorim (1992). *Journal of Experimental Psychology: Learning, Memory, and Cognition* **19**, 1424–30.

Willingham, D. B., M. J. Nissen & P. Bullemer 1989. On the development of procedural knowledge. *Journal of Experimental Psychology: Learning, Memory, and Cognition* **15**, 1047–60.

NOTES

1. Part of this chapter was written during a stay at the Institute for Cognition & Decision Sciences at the University of Oregon at Eugene, which was supported by a grant from the German Academic Exchange Council (DAAD). I would like to thank Steve Keele for his hospitality and numerous stimulating discussions on implicit learning during my stay.

2. Implicit learning is usually distinguished from implicit *memory* which is investigated with so-called *indirect* memory tests (Graf & Schacter 1985). In an indirect test the subject is not asked to consciously recall or recognize previously presented stimuli, but memory for prior experiences is inferred from the fact that the processing of a stimulus is facilitated by a previous encounter with the same stimulus *(repetition priming)*. For instance, in a test in which subjects have to complete word fragments (e.g._E_OR_) with the first word that comes to mind, previously presented words are correctly completed with higher probabilities then unstudied words (e.g. Tulving et al. 1982). In the late 1960s neuropsychologists made the exciting observation that amnesic patients who were severely impaired in their ability to recall or recognize previously presented material as a result of damage to medial-temporal or diencephalic parts of the brain nevertheless showed normal repetition priming effects in indirect memory tests (Warrington & Weiskrantz 1970; for review see Shimamura 1986; Squire 1992; Tulving & Schacter 1990). Similar dissociations have been reported for normal subjects (for reviews see Richardson-Klavehn & Bjork 1988; Roediger 1990; Schacter & Tulving 1994). These observations suggest that implicit memory is a form of memory in which "vanished mental states give indubitable proof of their continuing existence even if they themselves do not return to consciousness at all" Ebbinghaus (1885:2). Whereas implicit memory refers to priming effects of a single encounter with a stimulus on later processing, the term implicit learning is usually used in relation to tasks in which performance increments result from repeated practice or from exposure to a series of stimuli which instantiate a rule structure or co-variation. At present it is an unresolved issue whether implicit learning and implicit memory are separate phenomena, or whether they share underlying structures and mechanisms (see Berry & Dienes 1991; Buchner 1993). Because to date implicit learning has been investigated relatively independently from implicit memory, I will restrict my discussion to the field of implicit learning.

3. Note that this criterion distinguishes implicit learning from skill acquisition. Like implicit knowledge, well-practised skills such as tennis or riding a bike are difficult to describe verbally and can be executed without conscious control of the details of the action. However, whereas implicit learning is defined as the acquisition of knowledge without an intention to learn and without the encoding of conscious rules, the acquisition of skills usually starts with an intention to learn and is based on the encoding and subsequent practice of verbally stated rules (cf. Anderson 1987).

4. In implicit memory research a third type of dissociation is discussed, which is based on the stochastic independence between performance in two memory tasks (cf. Tulving et al. 1982, Hintzman & Hartry 1990). As stochastic independence has to date not been systematically investigated in implicit learning research, I will not discuss it further.

5. In discussions about consciousness the view is often expressed that conscious and unconscious processes differ in their functional, computational, or causal properties. For instance, it has been suggested that conscious knowledge is more flexible and globally available for the intentional control of arbitrary action, whereas unconscious knowledge is more rigid and only expressed in specific response channels (e.g. Baars 1988, Lahav 1993). In interpreting such statements it is important to note that we have no way of finding out whether it is the phenomenal state of knowledge *as such* that is causally relevant for the observed functional properties of that knowledge. That is, we do not know whether conscious knowledge has the properties it has *by virtue of its being conscious*, or whether the fact that knowledge is associated with subjective phenomenal properties is merely epiphenomenal and causally inert (cf. Bieri 1992, Dennett 1991, Eimer et al., in press). All we can hope for is to find systematic *correlations* between certain functional properties and internal states that we depict by some operational criterion as conscious or unconscious. In this chapter, I will therefore make no attempt to show that conscious and unconscious knowledge have different causal roles or computational functions, but rather will try to answer the more modest question of whether there are systematic functional differences between knowledge that we classify as conscious or unconscious on the basis of observable behaviour.

6. As one way to increase the probability that the sensitivity criterion will be met, Shanks & St. John (1994:373) suggest making cues in the direct and indirect tests as similar as possible and only varying the instructions for the subjects. They assume that under such conditions "... it is unlikely that the performance test would retrieve more conscious information than the awareness test when the latter has provided subjects with a stronger motivation to do so." However, even with cues in direct and indirect tests being identical, an explicit judgement ("Was this letter string in the study set?") may still be associated with a stricter criterion than an indirect judgement ("Does this string feel right?").

7. Split-brain patients have undergone a neurosurgical operation in which the corpus callosum, the major connection between the two cerebral hemispheres, has been cut. Such operations have been undertaken as an *ultima ratio* in untractable cases of epilepsy.

8. Note that the present argument presupposes that something like conscious knowledge does exist and that it makes sense to try to measure it. A more radical response would be to give up the idea of a unitary conscious representation underlying our intentional actions. According to such a view, consciousness is not a unitary phenomenon at all, but we have to distinguish different forms of consciousness depending on how we measure it (cf. Allport 1988).

9. Further evidence for the importance of knowledge about permissible bigrams was reported by Perruchet & Pacteau (1990) and will be discussed in section 5.

10. The probability of reproducing a chunk from the training sequence in the inclusion test equals the sum of the probability of consciously remembering a chunk (E) and the probability of producing a chunk as a result of implicit knowledge (I) without consciously remembering it *I (1 – E): Inclusion = E + I (1 – E)*. In the exclusion test a chunk from the old sequence will only be produced when it is not consciously recognized as old but is produced automatically: *Exclusion = I (1 – E)*. The probability of consciously recollecting and producing a chunk from the old sequence can thus be determined as *E = Inclusion – Exclusion*. The probability of automatically producing a chunk from the old sequence that is not consciously recollected can thus be determined as *I = Exclusion / (1 – E)*. The term *I* in the last equation reflects both automatic or implicit influences as a result of the training phase with the repeating sequence as well as the baseline probability of producing a chunk from the training sequence when that sequence was not presented before. Thus, in order to obtain an estimate of the influence of the prior training phase on the recall task one has to subtract this baseline probability from the estimate of *I*.

It should be noted that the process-dissociation method is based on the assumption that automatic or unconscious and intentional or conscious effects are *independent*. This assumption has been called into question by Joordens & Merikle (1993; see also Graf & Komatsu 1994), who derive a different index for *unconscious* influences. However, there is consensus among these authors that the process-dissociation procedure is in any case useful to estimate *conscious* influences.

11. ERPs are obtained by recording voltage-time waveforms from electrodes located at different points on the scalp. Waveforms obtained from a large number of trials are averaged, time-locked to the presentation of a stimulus or the execution of a response. As a result of the averaging procedure, random fluctuations of the spontaneous electroencephalogram (EEG) cancel each other out and the waveform deflections specific for the processing of a given stimulus become visible. ERPs triggered by a specific combination of a task and a stimulus typically consist of a relatively regular sequence of positive and negative voltage deflections which differ in their latencies, amplitudes, and scalp topography. ERP components are labelled according to their latency or order of occurrence and the direction of the voltage deflection (e.g. P300 denotes a positive-going deflection that occurs with a peak latency of about 300 milliseconds; N200 denotes a negative-going component peaking around 200 milliseconds post-stimulus; P3 and N2 denote the third positive and second negative component respectively). It is generally assumed that ERPs or their components reflect specific patterns of neural activity mediating perceptual, cognitive or motor processes (cf. Hillyard & Kutas 1983).

12. A third meaning of implicit is that learning may occur even when the relevant stimuli are presented sublimally. However because of space restrictions I will not discuss the relevant evidence in this chapter (for a review of implicit learning with sublimal stimuli see Seger 1994:175).

13. A somewhat different type of fragmentary exemplar model is the *competitive chunking* model of Servan-Schreiber & Anderson (1990), which will be described in section 6. In this section, I will also discuss neural-net or connectionist models of implicit learning, which in some sense fall in between the distinction of abstractionist and exemplar models.

14. This point is clearly illustrated by the fact that a special class of connectionist networks (so-called *simple recurrent networks*; see section 6) are capable of inducing abstract form classes and positional dependencies solely from information about the co-occurrences of words within sentences (Elman 1991).

15. Interestingly, phonological segmentation cues appear to be used very early in ontogenetic development. Infants just a few days old are already sensitive to intonational patterns in speech (Mehler et al. 1988), and after only a few months infants appear to become sensitive to perceptual cues to syntactic boundaries (Hirsh-Pasek et al. 1987; for implications for natural language learning, see Morgan et al. 1987, Weinert 1992).

16. Interestingly, a similar principle seems to hold for more elementary forms of sequence learning. In the serial reaction task, learning is facilitated when the sequence contains at least some unique transitions, which serve as anchoring points to parse the sequence into sub-sequences. In the absence of such segmentation cues, learning is more difficult and attention-demanding (Cohen et al. 1990, Goschke 1994).

17. In particular, I will not discuss the classifier model of AG learning by Druhan & Mathews (1989).

18. Backpropagation of error is a generalization of the Delta rule for networks with hidden units that was developed independently by different researchers (e.g. Rumelhart et al. 1986). In each learning trial, the actual output activation is compared to the desired output and a measure of the error produced by the network is computed. This error term is then propagated back through the network. In a first step the connection weights from the hidden layer to the output layer are slightly changed such that the overall error is slightly reduced, if the same input is presented again. This step is then repeated for the next lower level, that is, an error term is recursively computed for the hidden units, and this error term is then used to adjust the connections from the input to the hidden units. Across many learning trials, the network will gradually develop a connectivity that corresponds to a (local) minimum of the error function.

19. Amnesia is a cover term for memory impairments resulting from brain damage caused by fractures of the skull, strokes, infections such as encephalitis, or degenerative changes as in Alzheimer's or Korsakoff's disease. Amnesia can also be the result of surgical destruction or removal of brain tissue that sometimes is performed as an *ultima ratio* in extreme cases of epilepsy. Transient amnesia can occur after electroconvulsive therapy (ECT) or some forms of pharmacological treatment. The term *retrograde amnesia* denotes an impairment of memory for facts and events that were acquired or experienced prior to the brain damage, whereas the term *anterograde amnesia* is used when the ability to remember new events is impaired. In most cases, some memories remain intact and complete amnesia is rare. Amnesic patients can show entirely normal intelligence, language, and an intact short-term memory.

20. The role of the hippocampus in explicit memory has recently been supported by a PET-study (Squire et al. 1992) which showed increased activation of the (right) hippocampus when subjects performed a cued recall task. There is, however, some controversy over whether the amygdala, a limbic structure adjacent to the hippocampus and involved in emotional processing, also plays a role in episodic memory (cf. Mishkin & Appenzeller

1987, Squire 1992). Furthermore, it should be noted that the hippocampus and related structures are probably not the anatomic *locus* at which long-term memory traces are stored. This is shown by the observation that amnesic patients as well as animals with hippocampal lesions often (though not always) exhibit a temporal gradient of forgetting, that is, the longer before the lesion an event was experienced, the better it is remembered (cf. Squire 1987). It has been speculated that for a transient period the retrieval of newly-learned information is dependent on intact medial-temporal/diencephalic structures. During this time, consolidation processes take place which finally lead to the formation of permanent memory traces in neocortical sites, which – once established – can be retrieved in a content-addressable manner without requiring further participation of hippocampal structures (McClelland et al. 1995).

21. It should be noted, however, that in the study of Knopman & Nissen (1991), only some of the subjects (five from 13) actually showed an impairment of sequence learning, whereas the group as a whole showed normal response time savings in a re-test after a delay of 20 to 60 minutes.

CHAPTER NINE

The Representation of General and Particular Knowledge

Bruce W. A. Whittlesea

People are sensitive not only to the particular events they have experienced, but also to the characteristics of those events taken as classes. There is general agreement about the principles governing the representation of information about particular events. We encounter objects in some context and for some purpose: the processing of the event is directed and constrained by the similarity of the current event to previous ones, the nature of the current task, the affordances of the object and the availability of attentional and processing resources. Memory stores a representation of the event, as the object was experienced in that context and task.

However, people's sensitivity to the properties of classes is more puzzling. Research of the last twenty years has made it clear that in dealing with novel events, people respond more readily to events that are typical of their class or category, or contain high-frequency, regular or common features. For example, people classify a typical fruit, such as an apple, faster than an atypical fruit, such as a fig (Rosch & Mervis 1975); orthographically regular words are identified more efficiently than orthographically irregular words (Wheeler 1970). The puzzle is that the person never directly encounters these characteristics that apparently drive their performance: frequency, typicality and regularity are attributes that emerge across a succession of events, but are not present in any one of them. They are abstract properties of events taken as classes, not properties that could be directly apprehended in any actual encounter with an object.

Two major theories of memory structure and function have arisen to explain this sensitivity to abstract properties. Both of these theories build on a broad cross-section of the psychological literature, both are capable of explaining a wide variety of phenomena, and each is incompatible with the other. Deciding which is the better alternative is important. Memory structure and function are at the heart of all psychological activities: with the possible exception of reflexes, all of human performance is directed or influenced by memory. Theory construction in all fundamental areas of psychological investigation, including attention, perception, learning, and social interaction, is predicated on assumptions about how memory works. The success of work in applied areas, such as the education of medical experts, the creation of remedial reading courses, the understanding of syndromes such as multiple personality and hidden memory, the development of effective therapies for memory disorders in clinical and ageing populations, and the development of artificial intelligence, is dependent on deciding on the appropriate theory of memory.

In trying to understand how memory can be sensitive to general properties of experience, researchers have made use of two major metaphors. One is that memory is a store, a repository for information. This metaphor treats knowledge as a collection of facts held in memory. People appear to possess two kinds of facts, those about particular experiences ("I stroked my cat today") and those about general concepts ("a cat is a small, furry mammal with non-circularly-constricting irises"). The existence of two kinds of knowledge implies two different ways of acquiring knowledge, and two different stores to hold the knowledge. The metaphor thus challenges the investigator to explain how this dichotomy of knowledge types arises out of experience.

The second metaphor, given by Paul Kolers (e.g. 1973), is that memory is a set of skills, practised activities that can be fluently re-enacted if called upon. The skill metaphor treats knowledge as a collection of procedures. It focuses on the operations involved in encountering objects for various purposes, including identifying the object as a member of a class and acting appropriately toward it as an individual entity in a particular context. This metaphor suggests limitless variability in the ways that people process particular objects for specific purposes, and challenges the investigator to think of a reasonably small number of general principles to capture the variability of interactions between memory and the stimulus environment.

The older theory of representation, which I will call a *separate systems account*, uses the store metaphor. It points to the evidence that people are sensitive to the abstract structure of classes of events. It takes the common-sense approach that if memory is sensitive to the general, abstract structure of experience, then memory itself must contain a representation of that information. Because that information is distributed across events, there must be some mental mechanism that abstracts that knowledge across a person's experiences. Because the person is unaware of performing this abstraction, it must be an unconscious activity. Because the person, being unaware of performing this function, does not direct it, it must be an automatic function. Further, because this mechanism abstracts information out of memory codes for particular events, and because the abstract knowledge it accumulates is qualitatively different from the knowledge one has about particular events, it must constitute a second memory system, independent of the memory that is responsible for keeping track of the events themselves.

In summary, according to the separate systems account, people have two memories. One is devoted to recording particular events, and is responsible for remembering those events on a later occasion. That system preserves the detail of particular experiences, obeys the principles of encoding variability and encoding specificity, and is responsible for performance in reflective tasks, such as recognition and recall. The other system is committed to abstracting commonalities across events. That system preserves structural and conceptual knowledge in an organized network, operates by spreading activation, and is responsible for performance in non-reflective tasks, such as classification and identification.

This separate-systems account has been promoted by many investigators, studying quite different aspects of performance, including dissociations between remembering and identification (Tulving et al. 1982), implicit learning (Reber 1969, 1989), concept acquisition (Rosch 1978), semantic priming (Meyer & Schvaneveldt 1971), word identification (Wheeler 1970) and many other phenomena. It is currently the dominant theory of memory representation, as demonstrated by the fact that it is taught, in all of its ramifications, in most of the current textbooks, with only minor acknowledgement of an alternative.

The newer theory of representation, which I call an *episodic-processing account*, also recognizes the importance of the abstract structure of experience, but denies that people acquire knowledge about the general properties of classes in a different way than they learn about individual events. It argues that memory does not need to compute a direct representation of the general, abstract properties of experience in order to respond to those properties. Instead, it assumes that sensitivity to the general properties of classes is an emergent phenomenon, arising from the encoding of many specific events.

The episodic-processing theory assumes that memory encodes the detail of each event in a person's life, *as those events were experienced* given the processing performed on those occasions; that that is all that memory contains; and that all interactions with objects in the world are governed by a single set of memory principles. This account focuses on the specific activities required to perform particular tasks on particular objects, and emphasizes the variability of processing and consequent experience that is possible given slight changes in the task, stimulus, context and subject's prior experience (the assumption of encoding variability). It assumes that memory preserves the specific experience of each event, as it was processed, without additionally computing an abstract summary across similar experiences (distributed and processing-specific representation). It explains variations in subsequent performance through the representation of specific aspects of prior experiences, and through the specific cues currently available to access earlier experiences (transfer-appropriate processing). Fundamentally, it assumes that all knowledge, whether general or particular, consists of the potential to perform appropriately toward stimuli in some task; that is, memory consists of a set of processing skills, not a set of static facts. Unlike facts, which naturally divide into knowledge about general or particular properties of experience, these processing skills vary tremendously, from the skill of locating a feature to attend to the skill of decoding the meaning of an abstract word such as BEAUTY: in fact, any operation that a person can perform on a stimulus can be regarded as a skill. These skills can be combined in infinitely various ways, in response to the demands of particular tasks and the affordances of particular stimuli. They cannot be captured in any classification scheme based on type of knowledge, but they can be described through their operating principles. Of particular importance, these skills each consist of some actual past experience of processing some stimulus in some way: although with much practice people appear to develop "general skills" for processing common types of stimuli, their ability actually depends on the simultaneous cuing of many specific prior experiences.

The episodic-processing account argues that every encounter with an object occurs in some context and for some purpose. The object itself possesses some set of features, which can be processed in various ways, at various levels of abstractness and extensiveness. The context and purpose determine the particular cognitive and perceptual operations that the person begins to perform on the structural affordances of the object. In addition, this processing begins to interact with memory: the particular operations the person is performing cue prior experiences of processing similar structures in similar ways, and those experiences begin to guide and modify current processing. The entire processing episode is thus highly interactive: the final product is determined by the way the physical properties of the stimulus are organized and interpreted, given the initial purpose, the context of the event, and the specific prior experiences that are cued by current stimulus processing. Memory retains a record of the episode, consisting of the experience of the current object, as it was processed on that occasion. In effect, the person has just acquired a new mini-skill, consisting of the ability to process a specific structural organization in a particular way. This skill becomes a new resource, available to be cued in a subsequent encounter with another object.

The important point in this account is that memory does not store or retrieve stimuli as such, and does not compute average or summary information about categories of events, but instead encodes and applies experiences of organizing selected stimulus properties in particular ways, for particular purposes on particular occasions. In consequence, the effect of prior experience in processing a current stimulus depends on the specific operations performed on stimulus properties on both current and past occasions, and on the similarity of the structure-as-processed between the two events. For example, imagine a person encountering the same word, SHOE, on two occasions, but on one occasion using it to compute an anagram (HOSE), and on the subsequent occasion judging whether it is a synonym of BOOT. Although the nominal structure of the stimulus is identical on the two occasions, the analysis-and-recombination performed on the first occasion creates an organization of structure with little, if any, similarity to the organization needed to perform the second. In contrast, an earlier experience of reading SHOE as a whole item would facilitate the later judgement, because both events involve integral organization of the stimulus components, even though their formal purposes differ. However, if the later task were to name the letters in SHOE as rapidly as possible, then the analytic activity involved in anagram production would be more similar to what is required in the later task, and would influence the second event to a greater degree than would an earlier experience of reading the word.

Thus, according to the episodic-processing account, memory only ever preserves information about particular processing experiences. The distinction between general and specific knowledge does not reflect a dichotomy of systems or stores, abstracting general knowledge out of particular knowledge, and storing it separately. Instead, the distinction between those two forms of knowledge lies in the selectivity with which prior experiences are cued in particular tasks. If the cues made available in encountering an object are sufficiently distinctive and extensive, they may be able to cue a particular prior experience selectively. The selective retrieval of processing and contextual detail about that event permits the person to recognize that they have encountered that particular stimulus on a particular occasion in the past. However, if the cues are less distinctive and extensive (as in the usual classification or identification test), then performance may be controlled by the mass of prior experiences in parallel. In that case, performance will exhibit sensitivity to general properties of the mass, such as the typicality of the stimulus for its class.[1]

I contend that there is no positive evidence for a dedicated mental apparatus that abstracts general, summary properties across particular experiences, or that conceptual knowledge is represented in a separate memory system, organized according to different principles than those governing the encoding of particular events. In this chapter, I will attempt to substantiate that claim, using examples from my own work on classification, implicit learning, word and object identification and conceptual processing.

Point: Sensitivity to the general structure of a domain does not require that subjects abstract a summary representation of that structure. Distributed representation and parallel access can also produce sensitivity to general properties of a domain.

Example: Typicality effects in family resemblance categories.

Wittgenstein (1953) pointed out that natural categories have an internal coherence, or family resemblance, consisting of the fact that each member of the category overlaps with some other members on a number of features. For example, the set {ABCD, CDEF, EFGH} is held together by the overlap of features between items, even though no single feature is found in every item. Moreover, given that the category is defined by featural overlap, there exists the possibility that some items, such as CDEF in the example, share features with more other items than do others.

Rosch (e.g. 1977, 1978) demonstrated that people are sensitive to this formal structure of categories. For example, Rosch & Mervis (1975) asked subjects to list the attributes of members of the FURNITURE category, and also to rate their typicality for the category. They observed that the typicality rating that subjects assigned to an item could be predicted from the overlap of the list of attributes for that item with other members of the category. Thus subjects rated CHAIR as highly typical of the FURNITURE category, and the list of attributes they produced for CHAIR overlapped considerably with the lists for other members, such as COUCH, TABLE and DESK, whereas a member like BED, whose list of attributes overlapped little with other members, was judged to be atypical of the category. Rosch concluded that subjects' judgements about members of categories must be controlled by their knowledge of the distribution of attributes across the category, and that category learning must consist of internalizing the formal, objective structure of the category.

Numerous investigators, including Rosch (1978), argued that this knowledge of the distribution of features across the category could be captured through a prototype, or most typical example of the category. Posner & Keele (1968) demonstrated that the prototype enjoys a special status, being as well classified as any member of the category that subjects had actually seen, and better classified than novel items. Many other investigations have substantiated the special status of the prototype, showing that it is classified more accurately, more confidently and more quickly than other members of the category (e.g. Franks & Bransford 1971, Neumann 1974, Rosch et al. 1976).

The fact that the prototype held this special status convinced investigators that it must be abstracted across the subjects' experience of category members (e.g. Rosch 1977, 1978, Homa et al. 1981). That is, in encountering successive exemplars of a category, the subjects were thought to keep a running summary of the frequency with which various features occurred within the exemplars. Because people are not aware of computing this summary, it must be computed unconsciously, through an automatic process of abstraction.

In order to succeed in organizing categories, this abstractive process would have to be sensitive to the abstract, structural properties of stimuli, and completely insensitive to their contexts, their specific physical manifestation and the tasks in which they were encountered. For example, people encounter exemplars of a category such as BIRD in many different colours and shapes, in many different settings, while performing various activities, and the encounters may be widely separated in time, during which the person encounters exemplars of many other categories. The unconscious formation of a prototype of the category therefore requires that the memory system responsible for category learning is sensitive to whatever properties are stable across experiences of category members, and to those properties only. That memory system was clearly different from the one responsible for remembering particular events involving category members, because remembering is sensitive to small variations in the original encounter with an object (e.g. the levels-of-processing effect; Craik & Lockhart 1972) and at test (the encoding specificity effect; Tulving & Thompson 1973).

The idea that concepts are represented in memory by prototypes, automatically abstracted across instances of the category and preserving only summary information about the structural properties of the instances, achieved the status of orthodoxy. It is still propounded in almost every undergraduate textbook as the major explanation of concept acquisition. However, an alternative explanation of the effects of typicality was proposed by Brooks (1978) and Medin & Schaffer (1978). Those investigators suggested that the effects explained by abstraction of a prototype could be as well explained if subjects simply encoded each exemplar of a category, and test items were classified with speed, accuracy and confidence proportional to their similarity to the set of encoded instances. They pointed out that a test item that is similar to the prototype is also, necessarily, similar to a large number of instances, because the prototype is the average of the instances. Similarly, a test instance far from the prototype must necessarily consist of atypical features, and would consequently be dissimilar to most presented instances. Essentially, they pointed out, all of the evidence in favour of representation by abstracted prototypes was correlational; although it was certainly consistent with that possibility, it was equally consistent with representation of the category through codes of the exemplars themselves.

This argument raised the problem of pre- versus post-computed sensitivity to general properties of experience. Performance will be most efficient toward a stimulus that represents the average of a set of stimuli if the subject has already computed the average of the set, and has a prepared representation of that average. However, it will also be most efficient for that stimulus if the subject has simply encoded each presented member of the set, and those representations simultaneously assist performance in processing any incoming stimulus. Consider the stimulus set {011, 101, 110}. Each of those stimuli is more similar to their average, {111}, than any one is to another. In consequence, if the set is encoded as it is presented, and test items receive assistance in processing to the extent of their similarity to the whole set, then the novel test item {111} will be processed more efficiently than any one of the items that was actually presented previously, even though the average was not computed prior to the test. Thus, whenever a subject is found to be sensitive to some regular, average or typical property in the world, the psychologist has the problem of deciding whether that sensitivity means that the subject has a prepared summary of their prior experience, or alternatively that they have simply encoded their prior experiences, and those experiences are now directing performance in parallel. This issue must be decided empirically: the observation of a correlation between structure and performance is not sufficient to conclude that performance is controlled by a pre-computed summary of the general structure of the category.

There is thus no direct evidence that people automatically and unconsciously abstract the prototype of a category. However, there is a great deal of evidence that they retain information about the specific instances that they encounter, and that that information influences their decisions in categorization tasks. For example, Whittlesea (1987) created a domain consisting of two categories, based on two prototype strings, FURIG and NOBAL. The instances of the categories were distortions of these prototypes, of varying typicality for their category. For instance, FYRIG, FYRIP and FYKIP were all instances of the FURIG category, differing from the prototype by one, two and three features. In the training phase of one experiment, subjects were shown five items from each category, items that differed from their prototype by two features. For the FURIG category, this consisted of the set {FEKIG, FUTEG, PURYG, FYRIP, KURIT}. Across this set, the prototypical letters {F, U, R, I, G} appear three times each, and the nonprototypical letters only once each in any location. Items of the two categories were shown in random sequence. Subjects were instructed to pronounce each stimulus, and copy it. This training provided the subjects an opportunity to learn about the categories, either by developing a prototype or by encoding the presented instances.

In the test phase, subjects were shown two types of stimuli, both of which were novel. One type (e.g. FUKIP) differed from the prototype by two features, and also differed from the most similar training item (FEKIG) by two features. The other type (e.g. PEKIG) differed from the prototype by three features, but from the most similar training item (FEKIG) by only one feature. This pair of test items provides a critical test, pitting the typicality of test instances (their similarity to the prototype) against their similarity to particular training instances. The result was that subjects were more likely to identify a test instance correctly if it was more similar to a training instance rather than more typical, contrary to the predictions of prototype theory, but consistent with the predictions of instance theory.

Other experiments in that series demonstrated that performance on test stimuli is not controlled only by the most similar training instance, but by the simultaneous similarity of the test instance to each of the training instances. For example, one study used two types of test instance (e.g. FUKIG and PEKIG) that are of identical similarity to the nearest training instance (FEKIG). If only the nearest instance controlled performance, the test instances would be identified equally well. However, FUKIG is more similar to other members of the training set (shown earlier) than is PEKIG. In consequence, if performance on test instances is controlled by the set of training instances in parallel, performance would be more accurate on FUKIG than PEKIG. It was. In general, across seven experiments, the subjects' performance on any test item was directly predictable from that item's simultaneous similarity to the set of training items.

Taken together, the principles of distributed representation and parallel access to encoded exemplars can explain the finding that originally motivated the prototype-abstraction hypothesis, that prototypical items can be identified with greater accuracy and confidence than items that the subject actually encountered previously. Because the prototype instance is more similar to the set of training instances than any other instance, including the training instances themselves, it receives more influence from previously encoded instances than does any other test instance. To demonstrate that principle, I compared the subjects' ability to identify a novel, highly typical item (e.g. FUKIG) and a less typical item (e.g. FEKIG) that had actually been shown in training. The critical variable was the relative similarity of those test items to the entire set of training items: this was manipulated through the distribution of other training items. When the previously-exposed item was more similar to the training set, it was identified more accurately than the novel, more typical item; but when the novel item was made more similar to the training set by the addition of new training stimuli, it was more accurately identified than the old item. This reversal shows that neither typicality nor prior presentation of an item dictates how well it will be processed. Instead, performance is controlled by the similarity of the item to the set of exemplars that the subject has already encoded.

These experiments demonstrate that the observation of a "prototype effect" does not necessitate that subjects have abstracted a representation of the prototype. In domains with many exemplars, typical items are likely to be more similar to the set of previously-encountered items than less typical items, so that typicality will ordinarily be a good predictor of performance. However, typicality is insufficient to explain all of the effects observed with family-resemblance categories. When critical comparisons are conducted, it is apparent that the subjects retain specific representations of the particular items they encounter, and access those representations in parallel in processing further exemplars of the domain.

Point: Depending on the induction task, subjects may encode category members either as whole units or as collections of separate features. Whereas the former type of encoding makes them indirectly sensitive to the general structure of the domain, the latter makes them directly sensitive to that structure. However, coding the separate features does not entail computation of an abstract, summary representation of the structure of the category.

Example: Speeded identification of letters in pseudo-words.

The last section demonstrated that subjects can become sensitive to the general properties of a domain simply by encoding the instances as individual entities. However, the episodic-processing account does not claim that people always encode the instances as wholes. Instead, it assumes that people process stimuli in whatever way satisfies current demands, and encode the experience of processing the items in that way. In consequence, it predicts that if subjects are led to process category members as collections of separate features instead of as individual items, they will encode the features separately, and fail to encode the relationships among features that define the items. In consequence, their later performance will be controlled by the typicality of the various features constituting test items, and not by the holistic similarity of a test item to particular training items.

This form of representation grants the subject direct sensitivity to the typicality structure of the category. If each feature of each training exemplar is encoded with some probability, then the subject will have more records of typical than atypical features. When shown items at test, records of the various features will contribute independently to assist the subject in identifying the stimulus. Items more typical of the category will have more typical features, and hence will be identified more efficiently.

Because it applies directly to the typicality structure of the category, this form of representation appears to qualify as general knowledge: taken as a set, the subjects' representations of the features will be highly representative of the abstract structure of the domain. However, this form of encoding is not the same as the computation of a summary representation such as a prototype.[2] Although the features are abstracted out of the presented items, there is no presumption that memory organizes that knowledge into a compact, summary representation of the category as a whole, or that the act of abstraction is performed as a chronic function of memory. Instead, it is assumed that the subjects abstract the features in response to specific demands of the task, and retain information about the features in distributed representations of the various experiences of encountering them. In fact, this form of representation has more in common with the encoding of whole instances discussed in the last section than it does with the structural-abstraction assumptions of the separate-stores account. In both cases, the subject is thought to simply encode whatever aspects of the stimuli (features or identities of whole items) they were led to process by the induction task, without performing any automatic organization of information across items.

To illustrate this form of encoding, Whittlesea & Brooks (1988) presented subjects with items taken from the FURIG and NOBAL categories introduced earlier, using the same training items as those earlier experiments. The critical manipulation was that some subjects were required to pronounce and copy the training strings, whereas others were required to compare each stimulus to its category prototype (displayed above the item on the computer screen), and to copy matching letters on one page and non-matching letters on another. The intent of the first manipulation was to cause the subject to treat the training stimuli as individual entities, and code them as wholes, whereas the second manipulation encouraged the subject to analyze the stimulus into its component features, and encode those separately.

In the subsequent test, subjects were shown a mixture of old and novel but similar items. These items were displayed for 30 ms, then masked. A caret (^) was then placed under the location where one of the letters had been, indicating that the subject was to report the letter that had been there. The target letter was always one of the ten letters used to create the prototypes of the categories. Intermixed with these trials, subjects were shown single letters, again for 30 ms, and required to report them. These letters were the same as those used as targets when presenting strings. A baseline test, with no pre-training, was also conducted.

Subjects in the baseline condition achieved identification accuracy of approximately 49 per cent, whether target letters were presented in strings or alone. Relative to that condition, the "pronounce and copy" training assisted subjects to report a letter presented in a test string (69 per cent accuracy), but did little to assist identification of the same letters presented alone (52 per cent). That is, after that training, success in identifying a letter depended on reinstatement of the context in which it had been seen earlier. That means that the letters of the training strings had been integrated to some degree in encoding, resulting in representations of the items as separate, whole entities. In contrast, after the "analyze and copy" training, performance in both test conditions was facilitated relative to the baseline condition, but presentation of the test letter in a string or by itself made no difference to the success of identification (about 61 per cent in both cases). That means that subjects did form a record of the perceptual manifestation of the letters during the training phase, which resulted in better-than-baseline performance; but that the letters were coded separately, not integrated within items. More critically, it meant that the typical features were not integrated into a summary representation of the category prototype. Each of the test strings possessed several prototypical letters, and the target letter was always a prototypical letter. If the subjects had pre-computed a summary representation of the prototype during the training phase, we should have observed some interdependence among the prototypical letters at test, resulting in superior performance on letters presented within strings over letters presented alone. Instead, it is clear that in this case, the subjects learned about the individual features of training stimuli, but encoded them in a distributed fashion.

This distributed encoding of features can make subjects directly sensitive to the typicality structure of a domain. As an illustration, Whittlesea (1987) required some subjects to encode training items in the "analyze and copy" fashion just described, while others performed the "pronounce and copy" training. The test compared success in identifying typical but novel stimuli versus less typical items that had been shown in training. Following the "pronounce and copy" training, old stimuli were better identified than novel, more typical stimuli, but after the "analyze and copy" training, the reverse effect was observed: now the novel, more typical items were identified more effectively than the old, less typical ones.

The cause of this reversal is fairly obvious: when subjects pronounced and copied stimuli, they integrated the letters of each stimulus, treating it as a whole item. The resources they had in memory, on which to draw when classifying test items, consisted of a set of integrated wholes. In consequence, a test item that was structurally similar to a particular training item was more similar to what the subjects had encoded than was an item that was more similar to the category prototype. In contrast, when subjects were required to analyze the stimuli, they encoded the stimuli as a collection of separate letters. In consequence, a test item that was more similar to the average properties of the training stimuli was more similar to what the subject had encoded, producing direct sensitivity to the typicality of stimuli without computation of a summary prototype.

Point: Memory does not apprehend stimulus structure directly. The acquisition of knowledge about structure is mediated by the specific processing applied to members of the domain, and by the subjects' interpretation of the task.

Example: Implicit learning of rule-based categories.

The separate-systems account assumes that memory is directly sensitive to the structure of a stimulus domain, and automatically abstracts that knowledge out of the particular instances of the category that the subject experiences. This assumption is required to explain the further assumption that an abstract representation of the general structure develops across time and exemplars, without the subject's awareness of, or intention to, compute regularities across the stimuli. In consequence, this account predicts that the acquisition of sensitivity to general structure is broadly stable, developing in much the same way regardless of the specific activity performed on encountering the instances of the category. In contrast, the episodic-processing account assumes that subjects encode processing experiences, not knowledge structures; and that sensitivity to general aspects of structure is usually a by-product of encoding the structure of particular instances for some specific purpose, which dictates what aspects of the stimulus will be processed, and the organization in which they are encoded. In consequence, this account predicts that small changes in the task in which the subject encounters members of a category will have a large influence on the subjects' later sensitivity to aspects of the general structure of the domain.

The importance of this difference in assumptions is demonstrated in the ongoing debate over the nature of implicit learning. Extensive research on this topic has been conducted using the "artificial grammar paradigm", pioneered by Reber (e.g. 1969). In this paradigm, stimuli are generated from a grammar (a set of structural rules dictating the sequence and repetition of stimulus elements; see Figure 9.1), generating items such as MTTV, VXTVT and VXVRXRM. Subjects are exposed to these stimuli, without informing them about the method of generation. The subjects are then required to judge the "goodness" of

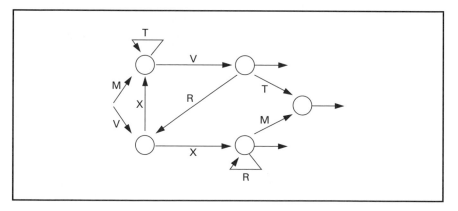

FIG. 9.1.   The Markov grammar used by Reber & Allen (1978). Items are generated by starting with either M or V, and picking up letters along successive paths until exiting at the right.

novel items, discriminating legal (rule-preserving: e.g. MTTVT) from illegal (rule-violating: e.g. MTVRT) items.

Reber (e.g. 1969, Reber & Allen 1978) observed that memorizing the training items made subjects sensitive to the general structure of the domain, without knowing it existed: they could discriminate novel legal items from novel illegal items with some accuracy, although they could say little about the rules governing the structure of the set. Reber concluded that the subjects had learned the general structure of the domain (the generating rules), without motive or awareness of doing so, and that this implicit learning demonstrated an automatic function of the unconscious mind to abstract the general structure of the environment.

This conclusion touched off a storm of controversy. Clearly, Reber's subjects had learned about some aspect of the structure of the domain: but it was less clear how abstract or unconscious the learning was. Brooks (1978, 1987, Vokey & Brooks 1992) argued that the subjects were simply encoding the presented instances, and discriminating legal from illegal items on the basis that legal items were generally more similar to training items than were the illegal items. Dulany et al. (1984) argued that the subjects were learning rules, but not the general rules used to construct stimuli. Instead, they argued, subjects encoded salient units such as VXTT_ or _TTV_, that captured the effect of the rules; and that the subjects were quite aware of having this knowledge. Reber (1989) and Mathews et al. (1989) argued that the subjects' learning was not tied to the surface structure of the stimuli, because it could transfer to stimuli following the same sequence and repetition rules as training items, but consisting of novel components. Instead, they argued that subjects pick up mini-rules, pieces of the abstract, deep structure of the set, coded in terms of repetition patterns, and that this learning was implicit. Perruchet & Pacteau (1991) argued that subjects might be encoding no more than bigrams from the stimuli. Even that would enable them to discriminate legal from illegal items, because illegal items often contain pair-wise violations, and legal items do not.

The big question behind this controversy is "What level of the structure of a domain do people incorporate, when they do not realize the domain has general structure?" The framing of this question presupposes that memory has some basic, preferred organization, that makes it directly and automatically sensitive to some level of organization of information in the world. The primary goal of research on implicit learning has been to identify that preferred level of organization, and thereby work out the form of the basic, stable cognitive structures in memory.

Whittlesea & Dorken (1993) instead applied the skill metaphor of memory to the problem of implicit learning. We changed the question to "What do people learn to do with stimuli, when they do not realize the domain has general structure?" In our first experiment, we created two grammars, and required subjects to spell the items of one grammar and to pronounce the items of the other. This procedure pits the assumption of stable acquisition of a preferred level of structure against the assumption of task-dependent variations in encoding structure. If implicit learning consists of automatic encoding or abstraction of some level of the structural organization of the categories, then the activity that the subjects performed on them (spelling versus pronouncing) should have no effect on their later performance. In contrast, if implicit learning, like explicit learning, consists of encoding the structures of items the way they were processed, then the difference in processing demands might influence their later performance on structurally-related items.

After the training, we explained to subjects that the items had actually consisted of two categories, created through two sets of rules. We then showed subjects novel items taken from the two grammars, and asked them to classify the items as belonging to the category they had spelled earlier, or to the category they had pronounced earlier. Before making that decision, we asked them to spell or pronounce the test item; this test-time activity was crossed with what they had done earlier with similar items, so that all four combinations of training and test activity were explored. This task gave the subjects an opportunity to experience the ease with which they could perform that type of activity on that item.

The logic of this test procedure is similar to the logic of the "encoding specificity" tests used by Tulving (e.g. Tulving & Thompson 1973) and others to explore explicit learning and remembering of unrelated events. Tulving argued that if performance in a memory test is facilitated by reinstating the context in which an item was first encountered, then the effective code permitting recognition of the item must preserve information about the context, not just the item. We extended that principle to the implicit learning of structured items, and the later classification of novel category members. If classification of a novel item is superior when it is processed in the same way as a structurally similar training item, then we would argue that the representation sponsoring classification does not simply retain the abstract structure of training items (either individually or as a set), but instead preserves the specific experience of processing the structure of the training items in a particular way.

The subjects had some ability to discriminate the test items of the two categories: Overall, their accuracy was 64 per cent, against a chance rate of 50 per cent. However, their success in classifying the test items depended on whether the task they performed on the test items (spelling or pronouncing) was the same as the task they had earlier performed on other members of that grammar. When the processing at test matched that at training, their success in classification was 67 per cent, but when the tasks were different, their success was only 61 per cent.

In a second experiment, the test task was changed, from discriminating between the categories of grammatical items to discriminating grammatical items (of either category) from nongrammatical items. Again, subjects spelled or pronounced novel test items before classifying them, and the test task was congruent with the training task for half of the grammatical test items. The subjects showed excellent ability to discriminate legal from illegal test items: overall, they claimed grammatical items to be legal on 57 per cent of trials, and nongrammatical items on only 27 per cent. However, once again we observed that the match between training task and test-processing task was important. The subjects correctly classified novel items as grammatical on 66 per cent of trials when the training and test tasks matched, and on only 48 per cent of trials when they did not.

These results demonstrate that subjects encode the structures of category members in specific ways dictated by the purpose for encountering the items, rather than having free receptivity to the abstract structure of the world. However, in those experiments we told the subjects how to act toward the stimuli. It is therefore possible that if subjects are merely exposed to a set of stimuli, and not specifically told how to process them, they might drop into a "free receptivity" mode, and automatically encode some default level of structure.

Whittlesea & Wright (1997) provided further evidence that subjects in implicit learning experiments are not passive recipients of stimulus structure, but instead actively adapt to the learning situation. Two groups of subjects were exposed to a set of items created according to a set of abstract rules. The two groups received the same stimuli, and both groups were instructed to memorize the items in anticipation of a memory test. The only difference between the groups was the sequence in which items were presented (see Table 9.1). This difference does not affect the overall rule structure of the category, or the identity of particular instances, or the frequency of bigrams or letter clusters across the set; in fact, it does not affect any aspect of abstract category structure. However, the groups learned quite differently. When asked to classify novel items as legal or illegal, the group that had received order A based their decisions on the structure of the first half of each stimulus, whereas subjects in group B used the second half of each stimulus. The reason for this is obvious: the training order for group A

TABLE 9.1
Stimuli used by Whittlesea & Wright (1997)

Group A stimuli	Group B stimuli
RMCMTXTV	RMCMTXTV
RMCMTVXT	RMCCTXTV
RMCMXXTV	MCRMTXTV
RMCMXVVT	MRRCTXTV
RMCCTXTV	RMCMTVXT
RMCCTVXT	RMCCTVXT
RMCCXXTV	MCRMTVXT
RMCCXVVT	MRRCTVXT
MCRMTXTV	RMCMXXTV
MCRMTVXT	RMCCXXTV
MCRMXXTV	MCRMXXTV
MCRMXVVT	MRRCXXTV
MRRCTXTV	RMCMXVVT
MRRCTVXT	RMCCXVVT
MRRCXXTV	MCRMXVVT
MRRCXVVT	MRRCXVVT

massed items by the repetition pattern in the first half of the stimuli, whereas the training order for group B massed items by the pattern in the second half. Clearly, the subjects picked up on this relationship between items, and strategically focused their learning on those aspects of the stimuli that appeared to be rich in useful information.

In a related experiment, Whittlesea & Wright (1997) created a new grammar (see Figure 9.2). The rules of this grammar are that one begins at any node, and continues around the circle, picking up either (but only one) element along each succeeding path, until one has five letters, such as the item HKQLP. The only structure this grammar contains is the sequence of letters, for example the knowledge that either K or Z can follow either H or V. There is no repetition in the set, and the location of elements within a string is unimportant. Items from this grammar were given to a group of subjects, with instructions to memorize them for a later test.

The same stimuli were given to a second group, in a slightly modified form. Each item was expanded through repetition of one or two elements. For example, the item HKQLP became HKQQLP, and VKNTB became VVKNNTB. This set contained exactly the same sequence information as the previous set, but additionally presented repetitions of some elements. This group was also asked to memorize the set for a later test.

In the transfer test, subjects were shown novel items, half of which were legal (e.g. HKQLB) and half illegal (e.g. HKLBV), as defined by the sequence rules. None of the test items contained repetition. The

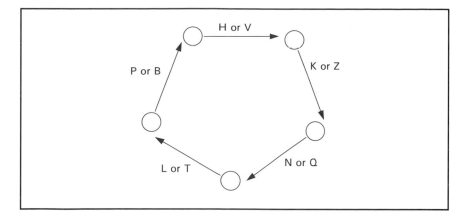

FIG. 9.2.   The sequential grammar used by Whittlesea & Wright (1997). Items are generated by starting at any node, picking up either letter over each successive path, until the stimulus is five letters long.

question was whether subjects who had trained on the set containing repetition as well as sequence would perform as well as the group exposed to sequence information only. If memory is directly sensitive to the structure of a domain, then there should be no difference between the groups. In contrast, if repetition is a naturally salient type of information, and subjects selectively attend to and learn about the repetition at the expense of sequence information, then we might expect to see a difference between the groups.

The result was that subjects trained on the stimuli without repetition achieved 63 per cent accuracy in discriminating legal from illegal items, whereas subjects shown items containing repetitions achieved only 55 per cent, reliably less than the first group. Clearly, the presence of the repetition in the training stimuli led those subjects to focus selectively on that aspect of structure, and to fail to encode the sequence aspect, although subjects not shown repetition were able to encode sequence information. We concluded that acquisition of structural information is not an automatic function of memory, and that memory is not directly sensitive to any particular level of structural information. Instead, what subjects learn about the structure of a domain depends on the specific way that they process particular items, controlled by the explicit or implied demands of the encoding task.

Point: The application of general versus particular knowledge is not co-ordinated by the demand to judge items as particular entities or examples of general sets. Instead, it is controlled by the specific operations performed on test stimuli, given the test task.

Example: Selective application of knowledge in family resemblance categories.

According to the separate-systems account of representation, general and particular knowledge are not only acquired by different principles and retained in different stores, but are also applied under different circumstances. Information about particular items is selectively applied in tasks that require a judgement about items as individual entities, whereas general knowledge about structure is applied in tasks that treat the stimulus as an example of a class. The level of the task demand (item versus class) should be the dominant factor controlling whether the subject accesses particular or general knowledge, because those levels correspond to the major distinction between the stores. In contrast, according to the episodic-processing account, both item-level and class-level information are encoded as a by-product of satisfying the specific demands of current tasks, rather than as a systemic function, and similarly either level of knowledge can be cued by the specific processes engaged in the course of encountering further stimuli. The level of the task demand should have some effect on which form of knowledge is accessed, but many other specific aspects of the task, including the perceptual organization of test stimuli and the demands of concomitant tasks, should also act as cues to select one form of knowledge over the other.

To test these assumptions, Whittlesea et al. (1994) used the family-resemblance domain described earlier, based on the FURIG and NOBAL prototypes. The one change was that the FURIG stimuli were now presented to subjects as artificial nouns, indicated by an -ISM suffix (e.g. FEKIGISM, KURITISM), and members of the NOBAL category were presented as artificial verbs, taking an -ING suffix (e.g. NEKALING, KOBATING). In all experiments of this series, subjects were trained twice on the same stimuli before being tested. In one training phase, they were required to pronounce and copy each whole stimulus (complete with suffix), thus encoding each item as a unique entity. In the other training phase, they were told the class of each stimulus (noun or verb) but shown only the stem (the FEKIG part), and asked to judge how typical each letter was for its class. This encouraged the subjects to learn about the typicality of each letter for its category. In effect, under instructional control, the subjects computed the running summary across items that the separate-systems account assumes is a chronic and unconscious function of memory. There was thus no question about the subjects' initial learning of the categories: they had both general information about the domain as a whole, in terms of the typicality of the various stimulus components, and also information about individual training instances. The question was which form of knowledge, general or particular, the subjects would apply when they had both, and could use either to perform the required test task.

In the first experiment, we tested one group of subjects in an item-verification task, showing them a stimulus like PEKIGING and asking whether it was completed with the correct suffix. Another group was shown only the stem (PEKIG), and asked whether it was a verb. The critical test of which type of information the subject applied was a comparison of two types of items, one (e.g. PEKIG) that was more similar to a particular training instance (FEKIG) but less typical of the whole set, and another (e.g. FUKIP) less similar to any training instance but more typical of the category (with proto-type FURIG). When subjects were tested on the whole-item verification task, they relied on their knowledge about particular prior exemplars; but when subjects were asked to verify the stem as a noun or verb, the reverse pattern was observed, the subjects relying on knowledge about the separate features.

This result is what would be expected under the separate-systems account. The subjects demonstrated selective usage of item-level and category-level knowledge, depending on whether the task implied an item-level or category-level judgement. However, in four succeeding experiments, we observed that the subjects' application of those forms of knowledge was also critically influenced by a variety of minor and incidental characteristics of the task. In one study, subjects were offered a forced choice: two novel stimuli, complete with suffixes (e.g. FEKIGING and NEKALING), were presented simultaneously, and the subjects were asked to decide which had the correct suffix. For half of the subjects, the stimuli were presented side by side; for the other half, the stimuli were presented one above the other. This apparently trivial change was enough to switch subjects from reliance on similarity to particular training items, in the former case, to reliance on separate features in the latter. In another study, we presented a category name (e.g. VERB) and a whole item (e.g. NEKALISM), asking subjects to verify that the stem belonged to that category. Half the subjects received the category name in advance of the item; half received the item before the category name. Again, this apparently trivial change determined which type of knowledge subjects applied. When the category name was supplied first, they focused on the category-relevant features of the stimuli; when the item was presented first, they based their decision on the specific similarity of that item, as a whole unit, to particular training items.

These studies demonstrate that the kind of knowledge that subjects will apply on subsequent encounters with members of a domain is not controlled exclusively, or even primarily, by the demand to treat the items as individual entities or examples of a class. This contradicts the assumption of the separate-systems account that memory is functionally organized around a distinction between knowledge about particular events versus general knowledge of classes. Instead, the two types of knowledge appear to have been selectively cued by the perceptual organization and cognitive operations that the subject imposed on the stimuli on first encountering them. For example, side-by-side presentation made it easier to encode the stimuli as whole items for purposes of comparison, whereas vertical presentation made it easier to encode and compare them a letter at a time: those organizations of the stimuli were respectively more similar to representations of whole training items or of separate features, and selectively cued those resources, regardless of the kind of judgement demanded by the task. Similarly, when the name of the class to be verified is presented first, it cues retrieval of information about classes, and causes subsequent processing of the item to be guided by that knowledge; whereas presenting the item first cues retrieval of similar items, and causes subsequent activity to rely on that basis, even though the task is to verify the item's class.

In general, it appears that access to representations in memory is controlled by the similarity between the structure of current stimuli, as organized by the perceptual and cognitive operations the person is currently performing, and the structure of previous stimuli, as encoded given the operations that were performed at that time. That means that the fundamental organization of memory, the effective organization of memory that dictates which representations will control current processing, is in terms of the specific experiences of processing preserved within the representations, not in terms of an epistemological distinction between events and classes.

Point: Traditionally, it has been assumed that the ability to identify members of familiar domains is controlled by general knowledge, developed slowly through abstraction over hundreds or thousands of experiences of the category. Contrary to that assumption, a single, brief experience can permanently modify performance. Finding that performance in some familiar domain is correlated with aspects of general structure does not mean that the original learning of that domain proceeded through abstraction of that structure, or that performance in that domain is now controlled by abstracted structure. To find out what controls people's performance on members of a domain, it is necessary to observe new learning.

Example: Word and object identification.

Investigators studying people's ability to identify familiar words and objects have been impressed with the degree to which performance can be predicted by describing an item in terms of its abstract properties. For example, words that are orthographically (Wheeler 1970) or phonologically (Glushko 1979) regular, of high frequency (McClelland & Rumelhart 1981) or from a high-density neighbourhood (i.e. words that differ from many other words by only one letter; Andrews 1992) are easier to identify than other words. Such observations led many researchers to conclude that these general properties directly control the act of identification.

According to many researchers, words are identified by one of two routes (e.g. Paap & Noel 1991). Familiar words have a representation in a "lexicon", a mental table connecting the perceptual manifestations of particular words with their pronunciation codes. These "lexical" entries correspond to prototypes in the category literature: They are representations of the abstract structure of the word, summarized across thousands of particular experiences of that word. In consequence, a word such as WORD is represented only in terms of the compound of its features {W, O, R, D}; no information about the variations in letter size, font, handwriting style or text context in which the word has been encountered is included in the representation. Unfamiliar words are thought to be identified through the other route, consisting of a set of spelling-to-sound rules that can be used to construct a pronunciation for a letter compound not found in the lexicon. This hypothetical set of rules corresponds to the rule-abstraction hypothesis popular in the implicit learning paradigm (discussed earlier). The evidence that people have such rules for constructing pronunciations, even though they cannot describe them, is the same as the evidence for the abstraction of rules from items created by artificial grammars: the subjects' performance is predictable from a knowledge of the rules.

However, the conclusion that subjects possess a lexicon and a set of spelling-to-sound rules suffers from the same problems as the prototype- and rule-abstraction hypotheses: they are based on correlational evidence. The fact that subjects behave the way they would if they had rules does not prove they have educed the rules. Whittlesea & Brooks (1988) pointed out that the orthographic regularity of a word is confounded with its similarity to all of the occurrences of words that the person has encountered. That means that there exists an alternate possibility: rather than possessing any abstract knowledge about words (either lexical representations or spelling-to-sound rules), people may simply encode their individual experiences of processing words.[3] In that case, a high-frequency word would have very many similar representations encoded in memory; processing of moderate-frequency words in dense neighbourhoods would be influenced by the mass of similar neighbours; and unfamiliar words could be sounded out by their analogy to representations of the experience of pronouncing structurally similar words. In consequence, the orthographic-regularity effects would occur regardless of whether people have a lexicon and a stock of pronunciation rules, or only preserve a record of each encounter with a word.

The problem in deciding between those alternatives is that investigators of word identification have primarily manipulated stimulus aspects that correspond to abstract properties of the subjects' experience, such as the orthographic or phonemic regularity of the stimuli. The problem is that both distributed-representation and pre-computed abstraction accounts predict the same effects for those variables. The major, and critical, difference between the accounts is that the distributed-representation account assumes that each occurrence of a word will be encoded *as it was experienced,* meaning that if the subject attended to the context, the font, or other aspects of the word that are definitionally irrelevant to naming it, those aspects would be incorporated into the representation, and would influence later interactions; whereas the pre-computed abstraction account argues that the effective knowledge controlling identification, whether a lexical entry or a spelling-to-sound rule, consists only of abstract information about the interrelationships among features. In consequence, if the abstraction account is correct, and identification of words depends only on their structure, then performance in identification tasks should be stable. A single specific experience of a word that has been seen many times in the past should not greatly affect identification of that word on a later occasion. In contrast, if performance depends on the similarity of the current stimulus to prior processing episodes, then identification performance should be highly modifiable, simply by providing one new but distinctive experience.

Whittlesea & Brooks (1988) investigated the influence of context on word identification. In a study phase, we presented common words either in isolation (e.g. BLACK) or in a simple phrase (e.g. BIG STEEL BOX). The question was whether one further presentation of a common word, in a specific context, would have an effect on the subjects' ability to identify that word later. In the subsequent test phase, we crossed the conditions: Some of the words originally shown in isolation were now presented in phrases, and some of the words originally presented in phrases were now shown alone; the remainder were presented in their original contexts (i.e. in isolation or in a phrase). Each test word or phrase was presented for 30 milliseconds, and followed by a pattern mask. The location of the target word was marked by a caret, whether the word was presented alone or in a phrase: the subjects were instructed to report whatever word had been in that location. We observed that the efficiency of naming depended on the match between the contexts of training and test: words presented alone at test were identified more accurately if they were presented in isolation (41 per cent accuracy) than if they had been shown in a phrase (31 per cent), and words tested in phrase were more accurately reported if presented earlier in a phrase (56 per cent) than if shown alone (30 per cent). These effects demonstrate that the subjects had learned new information about these familiar words during the training phase, and that this new information, consisting of the context in which they occurred, had a critical effect on their ability to identify the words later. We concluded that memory preserves specific experiences of words in particular contexts, and that word identification is influenced by these particular prior-processing experiences, not just by the average, abstract structural properties of the mass of prior experience.

Whittlesea (1989) showed that context-specificity effects can be observed in reading, as well as in identification of single words. Text passages about 150 words long were randomly scrambled twice, producing two scrambled versions. Subjects read one or the other version aloud, as fast as possible. Later, they read either the same version or the alternative one. They were reliably faster in reading the same version than the alternative. Because the texts were scrambled, but consisted of the same words, the advantage could not have come from use of long-established orthographic, lexical, syntactic or semantic structures. Instead, the effect demonstrates fast acquisition of some aspects of the specific contexts of the words of the passage, even though those contexts consisted of random words.

In addition to context, the specific way in which a stimulus is processed can be learned on a single exposure. Whittlesea & Brooks (1989) showed subjects slides of common objects, and asked them to verify questions involving either a noun or a verb concept. For example, shown a slide of a teddy bear, the subject might be asked to verify the question "Is it for a child?" or alternatively "Is it for playing?"; a spoon would be accompanied by the concepts "soup" or "eating". On a first pass, half of the slides were exposed with noun questions, half with verb questions. Total exposure to each item was about half a second. On a second pass, 24 hours later, half of the slides were accompanied by the same question as on the first day, the other half presented with the alternative question. We observed a perfect cross-over interaction of question type by familiarity: for both types of propositions, receiving the same question given 24 hours before caused a 50 ms advantage over answering the novel question.

These specificity effects contradict the idea that the effective representation supporting identification of familiar items consists of an abstract structural representation. That idea predicts that modification of the subjects' efficiency in identification of familiar words and objects should be slow, requiring many experiences of a novel form of presentation to outweigh the response tendencies built up over many previous experiences. In contrast to that idea, the data just described demonstrate that a single further experience can have a crucial effect on the efficiency of identification, if the specific characteristics of that experience are reinstated on a later occasion. This leads to the conclusion that the effective representation sponsoring identification of common words and objects, just like the effective representation supporting classification of members of family-resemblance and rule-based categories, preserves the particular way in which those items were experienced on the multitude of occasions on which they were encountered.

The results also pose a warning to investigators interested in the source of performance in domains in which subjects have much relevant experience, such as words. In such domains, it is tempting to try to deduce the basis of performance by comparing the subjects' ability to perform on stimuli differing on set-wise properties, as for example orthographic regularity or neighbourhood density. However, such studies are inherently correlational, and cannot determine whether the dimension varied is actually the source of performance variations, or only correlated with the true source. A better way to determine the direct cause of performance is to investigate what it takes to modify the subjects' performance on the same stimuli, as illustrated by the experiments earlier, or even better to observe the development of the ability to perform on stimuli, beginning with new learning in a new domain, as illustrated by the classification experiments reported earlier. This approach reduces the threat of concluding that subjects' performance is controlled by the broad, abstract structure of a domain, when they are actually recapitulating specific processing operations.

Point: Semantic relationships between stimuli influence subjects' efficiency in processing those stimuli. This has been taken as evidence that conceptual knowledge is represented in a network organization, operating through a spreading-activation mechanism. In conflict with that idea, experiences of semantic relationships produce enduring specificity effects. Sensitivity to conceptual properties does not require that memory possesses an abstract organization any more than does sensitivity to general physical structure.

Example: Semantic priming, semantic verification.

Many theorists have postulated that concepts are represented in an abstract network of semantic relations. For example, Anderson (e.g. 1980, Anderson & Bower 1973) suggested the propositional network. In this model, concepts are represented through nodes, each of which is connected to some others. The meaning of any concept is given by the set of concepts to which it is linked. These linkages are not mere associations: instead, concepts are linked together to form whole propositions, or statements about some aspect of general knowledge. These propositions form the basic units of the network. For example, a simple proposition, carrying one piece of a person's knowledge about the world, might be CATS EAT BIRDS. This proposition involves three concepts, CATS, EAT and BIRDS, and specifies the three-way relations among the concepts: CAT is the agent of the proposition, BIRD the object, and EAT the specific action relating agent to object. The proposition forms part of what one knows about CATS: the rest is carried by a series of other propositions, such as CATS DRINK MILK, ARE PETS, HAVE FUR, etc. Similarly, the meaning of BIRD is given in part by the fact that BIRD is the object of EATING by the agent CAT.

As stated so far, the model incorporates only general knowledge about various concepts: it permits the subject to define CAT, but not to report a particular experience involving a particular cat. The concept nodes, as such, cannot participate in any propositions about specific events, because the information about the specific event would then become part of one's general knowledge about other concepts. For example, if in my house yesterday, MY CAT DIED, then DEAD would become part of the general knowledge about the agent of EATING BIRDS. Anderson's (e.g. 1980) solution was to make a distinction between concept nodes, or types, which participate in the semantic connections with other concept nodes and thus provide general semantic knowledge, and instance nodes, or tokens, which participate in propositions about particular events. The nodes which participate in a proposition about an individual event are all instances (tokens) of the concepts to which they refer. Thus in the proposition MY CAT ATE A BIRD YESTERDAY, the ideas CAT, ATE, BIRD and YESTERDAY all refer to specific instances of general concepts, rather than to the general concepts themselves. These token nodes can be interrelated through the same kinds of relationships as types (e.g. through agent, object, "has-as-part" and "is-a" connections), and can additionally be related to tokens referring to specific contexts (e.g. time, YESTERDAY; place, IN MY YARD). Each general type can give rise to multiple corresponding tokens, each referring to a distinct example of the concept. Thus in the event MY CAT ATE A BIRD BUT YOUR CAT DID NOT, the two occurrences of CAT are represented by two separate tokens in the episodic proposition, and refer to two distinct objects, although both refer to the general concept CAT.

In principle, this propositional network provides an elegant means of registering all of a person's knowledge, both general and episodic. However, it gains its power through redundant systems, coding all of a person's experiences through instances of a concept (the token system), and coding them again in the abstract, through the context-free propositions summarizing the relationships between concepts that are generally true across events (the type system). It may thus grant memory more power than is necessary to explain its performance. Further, as indicated by earlier sections, it is questionable whether a dichotomy between episodic and conceptual knowledge is in any way fundamental to the architecture of human memory, although it is clearly fundamental to the way psychologists approach the classification of knowledge.

In contrast, the episodic-processing theory argues that there is no fundamental distinction between conceptual and episodic knowledge. According to this theory, conceptual knowledge, like episodic knowledge, is acquired on particular occasions, and preserved in representations of those particular experiences. If, on different occasions, one learns that a CAT HAS FUR, that CATS EAT BIRDS, and a CAT IS A PET, then those pieces of information will be registered in separate traces. More fundamentally, the knowledge summarized in the proposition CATS EAT BIRDS is likely to be distributed across experiences of seeing various cats eat birds on different occasions, and the name CAT itself will be encoded across multiple experiences of applying that name to different cats, having various but similar perceptual manifestation. The general knowledge of the concept is thus distributed across the set of experiences in which the nominal stimulus has been encoded in some way; the general meaning of that stimulus exists as a potential to retrieve those representations, and the effective meaning of that stimulus consists of those representations that are actually cued in a particular interaction with the stimulus, and which control performance on that occasion. Thus according to episodic-processing theory, the only difference between conceptual and episodic knowledge is whether one's later purpose is to retrieve information about what occurred on some specific occasion in the past, or to retrieve properties that have been generally true of a stimulus in the past. Which of these occurs, and the breadth or specificity of the set of representations that assist current processing, depends on the cue properties presented by the current stimulus, and the task in which it is processed.

The propositional network and episodic-processing accounts thus differ on whether the abstract relationships that define concepts have been pre-computed, and are represented separately from episodic representations, or whether that knowledge is computed on-line from those same traces. This difference generates some testable implications. One concerns the "semantic priming" effect (Meyer & Schvaneveldt 1971), consisting of the observation that subjects are faster to identify a probe word (e.g. NURSE) after seeing a related prime (DOCTOR) than an unrelated prime (BREAD). The effect has been taken as evidence for network representation of concepts: the explanation is that identification of the prime causes its type node to become activated, and that this activation spreads to nodes of related concepts along the semantic linkages, thereby preparing the subject to identify them. The episodic-processing account can also explain this effect, but argues that the direction of the effect is reversed: instead, it suggests, the prime is encoded as an experience, and the attempt to identify the probe benefits from the availability of the prior experience as a resource to assist in identification.

In the ordinary test of semantic priming, the effect of the prime on processing the probe is inferred from the latency with which the subject can name the probe. Whittlesea & Jacoby (1990) instead measured the effect indirectly, through the effect of experiencing a related prime-probe pair on the identification of a third stimulus. We presented three stimuli in rapid succession on each trial: the first, or "prime", was presented for 60 milliseconds, the second, or "probe", for 150 milliseconds, and finally the third, or "transfer" stimulus was presented until the subject named it. Immediately following the trial, the subject was asked to report the probe, to ensure that the probe was actually identified. Various aspects of the situation were manipulated for control purposes. On the trials of interest, the prime and transfer target were the same word (e.g. GREEN), and the probe was semantically related to the prime (e.g. PLANT). The critical manipulation was that the probe was presented in uniform upper case on some trials, but in mixed case on other trials (e.g. pLaNT).

The spreading-activation explanation of semantic priming requires that it be unconditional: presentation of the prime pre-activates all related words, regardless of whether or how they will be presented. By that account, the prime (GREEN) pre-activates the node representing the probe (PLANT); in turn, identification of the probe should reciprocally activate the node representing GREEN, so that node is activated again, just prior to presentation of that word as the transfer target. This sequence of activities will occur automatically, whether the probe is degraded or not; the only uncertainty is whether degraded presentation of PLANT will reduce its reciprocal activation of GREEN, resulting in slower identification of the transfer target, or whether the probe pre-activates the transfer target to the same degree when it is easy or difficult to identify. In consequence, the spreading-activation assumption predicts that the transfer stimulus will be identified more slowly when preceded by a degraded probe, or that identifying the transfer stimulus will be unaffected by our manipulation.

Neither of these predictions is correct: the transfer target was identified about 25 milliseconds faster when the probe was degraded. We concluded that the assumption of spreading activation, the major assumption of network accounts, is incorrect. Instead, our results suggest that the trace of the prime is more available after identifying a difficult presentation of the probe; in turn, that suggests that the prime is more extensively processed when the probe is difficult. That means that the processing relationship between the prime and probe is variable, conditional on the need for assistance in identifying the probe. Further, it means that the direction of control is from the probe back to the prime, rather than from the prime forward to the probe: the prime exists as a resource for processing the probe, to be retrieved if necessary, rather than automatically activating the probe. This backward-acting, conditional processing could occur through a variety of mechanisms, similar to semantic matching (Neely & Keefe 1989) or cue-compounding (Ratcliff & McKoon 1988). For current purposes, it is sufficient that the effect cannot be explained through spreading activation.

One of the primary functions that network representation is supposed to accomplish is the ability to understand the abstract, meaningful relationship between concepts, for example, one's knowledge that "a shark is a fish". Network theories of all kinds assume that one's knowledge of this relationship is represented through linkages between concept nodes. Where a direct linkage does not exist, the relationship can still be inferred, by tracing the connection between two concepts through other nodes to which both are connected. Thus, for example, a person could infer that "a pencil is an artifact", even if the person had never thought of that relationship before.

This idea of mediated connections is central to network representation. The basic evidence for that assumption was provided by Collins & Loftus (1975). They asked subjects to verify the truth of class-inclusion propositions such as "a robin is a bird" and "a robin is an animal". In terms of class inclusiveness, the second proposition is less direct than the former, because the class "bird" intervenes between the classes specified in the proposition. Collins & Loftus observed that this difference is important for performance: subjects identified the more direct propositions faster than the less direct ones. They concluded that concepts are represented in memory by nodes interrelated by semantic links, that concepts that are more closely related semantically are connected by stronger or more direct connections, and that the number or strength of intervening links determines the rate at which activation spreads from one node to another, thus controlling the latency of verification.

If semantic verification is controlled by a network of abstract, summary representations of concepts, then performance in that task should be stable, influenced only by the mass of the subjects' life-long experience. It should not be affected by a single, specific experience of the relationship in question.

Whittlesea & Brooks (1989) tested the stability of applying concept knowledge. We presented subjects with propositions containing more and less directly related concepts, and observed the same effect that Collins & Loftus (1975) did. However, we tested our subjects again 24 hours later. Again, half of the propositions involved more direct class-inclusion relations, and half less direct; the critical variable was that half of each were ones that had been tested 24 hours earlier, and half were novel. The latter were novel only in the pairing of concepts within propositions; both concepts in the proposition had been presented in propositions tested the day before, but not within the same proposition. On this occasion, we again observed a benefit for direct over indirect relationships; but we also observed that propositions repeated from the day before were verified faster than new propositions at the same level of directness.

This means that the subjects retained a record of processing specific semantic relationships, and used these specific records in verifying propositions on the second day. This contradicts several intuitions that have supported network models of concept representation, including the ideas that effective learning about concepts proceeds slowly, that any effects of particular experiences involving concepts will be short-lived, and that a task requiring a purely conceptual decision will be accomplished through access to abstract semantic knowledge. Instead, the results suggest that knowledge about semantic relationships is preserved in episodic representations, that can be retrieved by specific cues on a later occasion.

One interesting implication of this idea is that concepts do not have stable meanings: instead, the meaning of a concept depends on the context in which the concept is cued. A pair of stimuli CAT and LAP will retrieve a different subset of representations of experience than CAT and BIRD. The common meaning of CAT across the former subset is COMFORT (if you like cats), whereas the meaning of CAT across the second is CRUELTY. This instability of meaning corresponds to the obvious fact that people selectively think of different aspects of concepts at different times, and that which they think about depends on the cue properties of other available stimuli. For example, in considering how people form friendships, subjects generally agree (on different occasions) with both of the aphorisms "opposites attract" and "birds of a feather flock together", depending only on which is available as a cue for retrieving past experience. This fundamental instability is an important property of conceptual processing, and a strong clue about the nature of representation.

CONCLUSIONS

The title of this chapter, "The representation of general and particular knowledge", suggests that the reader is about to learn about a dichotomy of representation systems, one for general knowledge and one for knowledge of particular events. However, as demonstrated by the experiments in this chapter, memory is not organized around a dichotomy of knowledge types. Moreover, the problem of general knowledge breaks down into two sub-problems: the acquisition of knowledge that is truly general, and the development of sensitivity to general structure without acquisition of general knowledge. General knowledge about a domain (knowledge about the abstract relationships among its members) can be acquired through direct comparison of its members, either physically present or recalled from memory. This learning is not mysterious: it involves the same processes and encoding principles as any other occasion on which the subject attends selectively to some stimulus characteristics. However, such general knowledge is not acquired automatically, incidental to processing the members as individual entities. In contrast, sensitivity to the general structure of the domain can develop incidental to such instance-wise processing: encoding the global structure or individual features of each of a series of related stimuli can provide the person with resources to perform related operations on similar stimuli, and parallel access to those representations can enable the subject to perform more efficiently on novel stimuli that are regular or typical of the domain.

People are not restricted to processing stimuli as individual entities or examples of classes: they have a huge number of options about what to do when they encounter a stimulus. Taking a word as an example, a person could name it, try to memorize it, mentally rotate it, separate it into syllables, learn it as an exception to a spelling rule, attempt to recall a previous occasion of seeing it, check it for repetition of letters, generate a rhyme or semantic associate, compare its structure or meaning with that of other words in memory, rate its concreteness or pleasantness, classify it as a part of speech, and so on. These activities differ in abstractness, elaborateness, integration or analysis of the stimulus components, the amount of the stimulus structure actually processed, the amount of prior experience in performing the task on similar stimuli, and the memory resources needed to perform the task. However, the evidence is that memory always works in the same way: regardless of how the person processes the stimulus, memory simply preserves the experience of whatever the person did on that occasion. That representation will support later interactions with other stimuli to the extent that the specific operations performed on the earlier occasion can be applied to the new stimuli, given their structure and the task to be performed on them.

Memory has no interior structure: it is not divided into subsystems, nor is abstract, conceptual knowledge preserved in a qualitatively different fashion than representations of experiences of particular events. Instead, memory has a latent organization, in terms of the contents of its representations. Each representation preserves the experience of processing some stimuli in some particular way: further interactions with other stimuli cue those representations broadly or narrowly, depending on the cues made available in the later encounter. In turn, those cues depend on the structure of the stimuli, organized in some way that is appropriate for current purposes, and the processing context, including both the physical presence of other stimuli and the demands of the task itself. The organization of memory is thus in the potential of future events to cue selected subsets of the representations of particular events in memory.

REFERENCES

Anderson, J. R. 1980. *Cognitive psychology and its implications*. San Francisco: W. H. Freeman.

Anderson, J. R. & G. H. Bower 1973. *Human associative memory*. Washington DC: Winston.

Andrews, S. 1992. Frequency and neighbourhood effects on lexical access: lexical similarity or orthographic redundancy. *Journal of Experimental Psychology: Learning, Memory, and Cognition* 18, 234–54.

Brooks, L. R. 1978. Non-analytic concept formation and memory for instances. In *Cognition and categorization*, E. H. Rosch & B. B. Lloyd (eds), 169–211. Hillsdale, New Jersey: Erlbaum.

Brooks, L. R. 1987. Decentralized control of categorization: the role of prior processing episodes. In *Concepts and conceptual development: ecological and intellectual factors in categorization*, U. Neisser (ed.), 141–74. Cambridge: Cambridge University Press.

Collins, A. M. & E. F. Loftus 1975. A spreading-activation theory of semantic processing. *Psychological Review* 82, 407–28.

Craik, F. I. M. & R. S. Lockhart 1972. Levels of processing: a framework for memory research. *Journal of Verbal Learning and Verbal Behavior* **11**, 671–84.

Dulany, D. E., R. A. Carlson, G. I. Dewey 1984. A case of syntactical learning and judgement: How conscious and how abstract? *Journal of Experimental Psychology: General* **113**, 541–55.

Franks, J. J. & J. D. Bransford 1971. Abstraction of visual patterns. *Journal of Experimental Psychology* **90**, 65–74.

Glushko, R. J. 1979. The organization and activation of orthographic knowledge in reading aloud. *Journal of Experimental Psychology: Human Perception and Performance* **5**, 674–91.

Homa, D., S. Sterling, L. Trepel 1981. Limitations of exemplar-based generalization and the abstraction of categorical information. *Journal of Experimental Psychology: Human Learning and Memory* **2**, 322–30.

Kolers, P. A. 1973 Remembering operations. *Memory and Cognition* **12**, 347–55.

Mathews, R. C., R. R. Buss, W. B. Stanley, F. Blanchard-Fields, J. R. Cho, B. Druhan 1989. Role of implicit and explicit processes in learning from examples: a synergistic effect. *Journal of Experimental Psychology: Learning, Memory, and Cognition* **15**, 1083–1100.

McClelland, J. L. & D. E. Rumelhart 1981. An interactive-activation model of context effects in letter perception, Part 1: an account of basic findings. *Psychological Review* **88**, 375–407.

Medin, D. L. & M. M. Schaffer 1978. Context theory of classification learning. *Psychological Review* **85**, 207–38.

Meyer, D. E. & R. W. Schvaneveldt 1971. Facilitation in recognizing pairs of words: evidence of a dependence between retrieval operations. *Journal of Experimental Psychology* **90**, 227–34.

Neely, J. H. & D. E. Keefe 1989. Semantic priming in the lexical decision task: roles of prospective prime-generated expectancies and retrospective semantic matching. *Journal of Experimental Psychology: Learning, Memory, and Cognition* **15**, 1003–19.

Neumann, P. G. 1974. An attribute frequency model for the abstraction of prototypes. *Memory and Cognition* **2**, 241–8.

Paap, K. R. & R. W. Noel 1991. Dual-route models of print to sound: still a good horse-race. *Psychological Research* **53**, 13–24.

Perruchet, P. & C. Pacteau 1991. Synthetic grammar learning: implicit rule abstraction or explicit fragmentary knowledge? *Journal of Experimental Psychology: General* **119**, 264–75.

Posner, M. I. & S. W. Keele 1968. On the genesis of abstract ideas. *Journal of Experimental Psychology* **77**, 353–63.

Ratcliff, R., & G. McKoon 1988. A retrieval theory of priming in memory. *Psychological Review* **95**, 385–408.

Reber, A. S. 1969. Transfer of syntactic structure in synthetic languages. *Journal of Experimental Psychology* **81**, 115–19.

Reber, A. S. 1989. Implicit learning and tacit knowledge. *Journal of Experimental Psychology: General* **118**, 219–35.

Reber, A. S. & R. Allen 1978. Analogic and abstraction strategies in synthetic grammar learning: a functionalist interpretation. *Cognition* **6**, 193–221.

Rosch, E. H. 1977. Human categorization. In *Advances in crosscultural psychology* (vol. 1), N. Warren (ed.), 1–49. London: Academic Press.

Rosch, E. H. 1978. Principles of categorization. In *Cognition and categorization*, E. H. Rosch & B. B. Lloyd (eds), 27–48. Hillsdale, New Jersey: Erlbaum.

Rosch, E. H. & C. B. Mervis 1975. Family resemblances: studies in the internal structure of categories. *Cognitive Psychology* **7**, 573–605.

Rosch, E, H., C. Simpson, R. S. Miller 1976. Structural bases of typicality. *Journal of Experimental Psychology: Human Perception and Performance* **2**, 491–502.

Tulving, E., D. L. Schacter, H. A. Stark 1982. Priming effects in word-fragment completion are independent of recognition memory. *Journal of Experimental Psychology: Learning, Memory, and Cognition* **8**, 336–42.

Tulving, E. & D. M. Thompson 1973. Encoding specificity and retrieval processes in episodic memory. *Psychological Review* **80**, 352–73.

Vokey, J. R. & L. R. Brooks 1992. The salience of item knowledge in learning artificial grammars. *Journal of Experimental Psychology: Learning, Memory, and Cognition* **18**, 328–44.

Wheeler, D. D. 1970. Processes in word recognition. *Cognitive Psychology* **1**, 59–85.

Whittlesea, B. W. A. 1987. Preservation of specific experiences in the representation of general knowledge. *Journal of Experimental Psychology: Learning, Memory, and Cognition* **13**, 3–17.

Whittlesea, B. W. A. 1989. Perceptual encoding mechanisms are tricky but may be very interactive: comment on Carr, Brown and Charalambous. *Journal of Experimental Psychology: Learning, Memory, and Cognition* **16**, 727–30.

Whittlesea, B. W. A. & L. R. Brooks 1988. Critical influence of particular experiences in the perception of letters, words, and phrases. *Memory and Cognition* **16**, 387–99.

Whittlesea, B. W. A. & L. R. Brooks 1989. *Processing the slightly unconventional: enduring influence of particular experiences in propositional verification, classification and object identification*. Unpublished manuscript.

Whittlesea, B. W. A., L. R. Brooks, C. Westcott 1994. After the learning is over: factors controlling the selective application of general and particular knowledge. *Journal of Experimental Psychology: Learning, Memory, and Cognition* **20**, 259–74.

Whittlesea, B. W. A. & M. D. Dorken 1993. Incidentally, things in general are particularly determined: an episodic-processing account of implicit learning. *Journal of Experimental Psychology: General* **122**, 227–48.

Whittlesea, B. W. A. & L. L. Jacoby 1990. Interaction of prime repetition with visual degradation: is priming a retrieval phenomenon? *Journal of Memory and Language* **29**, 546–65.

Whittlesea, B. W. A. & R. Wright 1997. Implicit (and explicit) learning: acting adaptively without knowing the consequences. *Journal of Experimental Psychology: Learning, Memory and Cognition* **23**, 181–200.

Wittgenstein, L. 1953. *Philosophical investigations*. Oxford: Blackwell.

NOTES

1. On some occasions, the person's purpose for encountering an object may lead them to treat the object as a member of a class, and thereby to process and encode class-level properties. However, such abstraction across items

is by no means a chronic activity, nor an activity that is performed automatically or unconsciously; nor is the knowledge produced available independent of the processing characteristics of the original and later events. Instead, like all other knowledge, it is supported, constrained and cued by an interaction of current demands, context, stimulus structure and representations of prior experiences.

2. Again, this does not mean that people cannot compute a prototype if they try to do so, by recalling and comparing various members of the category. They can. The computation itself is an episode, and will be represented like any other, and can exert influence on later events like any other episode. The CONTENTS of an episode may be abstract, if the person was performing abstraction during that episode. However, the EPISODE exists as a representation of an experience like any other, and will exert influence on future performance like any other episode: it is not freely available, independent of the particular characteristics of current processing, but instead is cued by the particular characteristics of the context, task and structural features of the object, as processed for current purposes. Here I only mean to argue that the computation of a summary representation, such as a prototype, is not an automatic function of memory.

3. Obviously, no representation system, not even the human brain, can encode a mass of information such as every word that a person says, or every occasion of saying a word, and preserve each record separate from each other. As thousands of similar experiences build up, the system becomes less sensitive to idiosyncratic properties, and more sensitive to average properties of the experiences: in effect, the mass of experience begins to act like a prototype. However, that development occurs through accretion of representations of particular experiences, not through any dedicated computation of abstract properties. The basic experience-coding mechanism of the system is shown by the fact that one further, but distinctive, encounter with a well-known word shows large specificity effects. Although the system is saturated with representations of that word, it still has the capacity to learn about one further occurrence as though it were a wholly novel event.

CHAPTER TEN

Process Models of Categorization[1]

Koen Lamberts

Categorization is basic to all our intellectual abilities (Estes 1994). It is the process of assigning objects (of whatever kind) to categories (which are collections of objects that are grouped together for some purpose). Contemporary theories provide excellent formal accounts of many aspects of categorization (e.g. Ashby 1992, Estes 1994, Medin & Schaffer 1978, Nosofsky 1986). However, most theories have little to say about the time course of categorization processes. Traditionally, experimental categorization research has been focused on the *outcome* of categorization processes, without paying too much attention to the details of the processes themselves. The theories that emerged from this tradition provide only a general characterization of these processes.

Recently there has been some interest in true process models of categorization. Several theories have been proposed that aim to provide a detailed description of the time course of categorization processes. In this chapter I will review this recent work. I will first present a theoretical framework for perceptual categorization. Next I will describe different process theories, and I will try to indicate how they fit within the general framework.

This chapter also has another purpose. I will attempt to give a brief overview of the basic principles of formal, mathematical modelling in psychology. There are several reasons why such an overview seems appropriate in a chapter on categorization theories. The most important reason is that I found it nearly impossible to discuss recent work on categorization, without referring to formal modelling methods. In recent years, formal modelling techniques have been used extensively in the study of categorization, and perhaps more often than in many other areas of psychology. One of the reasons for the prominence of formal modelling in categorization research is that earlier work on learning and memory, with its traditional emphasis on mathematical model construction (e.g. Atkinson et al. 1965, Atkinson & Estes 1963, Shepard 1958), has inspired many contemporary theories of categorization and category learning (e.g. Estes 1994, Gluck & Bower 1988, Nosofsky 1986). Formal theories of categorization have also been developed in other disciplines, such as data analysis or computer science, and these efforts have inspired recent work in psychology (e.g. Medin et al. 1987). As a result of these developments, current research on categorization provides an excellent illustration of how mathematical model construction can be used to understand and analyze various aspects of cognitive processes. Unfortunately, much of the literature on formal modelling has not been very accessible to experimental psychology. The key publications usually appear in journals that address an audience of experts in formal methodology. Of course, many issues in the field of mathematical modelling are very complex, and require sophisticated formal treatment. However, in the third section of this chapter, I will attempt to show that very useful results can be achieved with just a few fairly simple techniques. Readers who are familiar with formal modelling can easily skip this part of the chapter.

A FRAMEWORK FOR PERCEPTUAL CATEGORIZATION

Perceptual categorization is a complex process, that involves several stages. Figure 10.1 shows the flow of information through the cognitive system, from the initial presentation of an object to the final category decision. First, the object needs to be processed by the perceptual system. I will assume that objects can be represented by a set of dimensions, on which they have certain values (see Garner 1978). Perceptual processing involves the identification of the object's values on different dimensions. For instance, if the object is an apple, perceptual

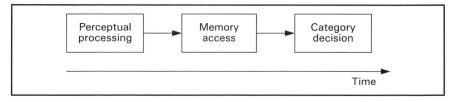

FIG. 10.1.   Processing stages in perceptual categorization.

processes will establish that its colour is red, that its shape is roughly circular, and that it has a little stem on top.

For any object, the number of dimensions that can be used to describe it is in principle unlimited. The apple could also be described as weighing half a pound, being juicy, smaller than a house, larger than a fly, not as bright as the sun, and so forth. In most circumstances, however, people seem to base their category decisions only on a small number of stimulus dimensions, either because they have insufficient time to investigate a stimulus on a large number of dimensions (e.g. Lamberts 1995), or because they simply do not need the information from certain dimensions to make a valid decision. To classify the object as either an apple or a pear, for instance, it is not relevant to know whether it is green or not, because both apples and pears can be green. In this decision context, shape is probably the most important dimension. Usually, constraints on relevant dimensions are provided by background knowledge or the decision context (see Hahn & Chater, this volume; Murphy & Medin 1985).

In the second stage, information stored in long-term memory needs to be retrieved. The perceptual representation of the object guides this retrieval process. A considerable part of research on concepts and categorization in the last 20 years has been devoted to the nature and the form of category information in memory. Traditionally, three different hypotheses about category representations have been distinguished (see Smith & Medin 1981, Storms & De Boeck, this volume). Not all theories of categorization adhere strictly to one of these hypotheses, but most theories somehow incorporate elements from one or two of them.

The oldest hypothesis is that categories are represented by a set of formal decision rules. A membership rule for the "car" category could state, for instance, that the object has four wheels, can be driven on the road and has an engine. According to this view, category decisions depend on the retrieval of the appropriate rule from memory, and on the subsequent comparison of the object with the membership conditions specified in the rule. If the object fulfils all conditions, it is assigned to the category. Although this view has some intuitive appeal, it is certainly not universally applicable. Many categories have no clearly defining features at all, and if they do have them, people do not necessarily use them in making category decisions.

The second hypothesis is that categories are represented by their prototype (e.g. Hampton 1993). Prototypes can be considered as averages or summaries of the representations of category members. For instance, a prototypical "car" will have four wheels, passenger seats, a roof, and so forth. Classification of an object takes place by comparison of the object with category prototypes. The more similar an object is to the prototype of a category, the more likely it is that the object will be assigned to that category. Prototypes do not define a category in the strict sense of a formal rule. Rather, they provide a basis for probabilistic, similarity-driven category assignment. Although a prototypical car probably has a roof, a cabriolet will be classified as a car by most people, because it has so many other features in common with the prototype.

The third view on category representations is the most recent (Estes 1986, 1994, Hintzman 1986, Lamberts 1994, Medin & Schaffer 1978, Nosofsky 1986). According to this view, categories are not represented by summary descriptions such as rules or prototypes, but rather by sets of exemplars. Exemplar theories assume that categorization of an object involves comparisons between that object and many, many exemplars stored in memory. The probability of classifying an object as a member of a given category depends on the similarity of the object and the category members stored in memory. Thus, if the object is very similar to many exemplars stored as "cars", there is a good chance that the object will be classified as a car. Exemplar theories differ radically from the other theories, because they do not assume that abstract category representations are important at all. Intuitively, exemplar models may seem rather implausible. People certainly do not have the experience that they remember every single object or event they encounter, and that they classify new objects or events by computing similarities to known instances. However, such subjective impressions can be very misleading. The exemplar view does not imply that people should be able to recall or retrieve every single instance in memory. It merely states that instances leave traces in memory, and that these traces are accessed in categorization. No claims are made about whether access to stored exemplars is a conscious process or not.

In the third stage of perceptual categorization, the information retrieved from memory is used to make a decision about category membership. How the decision process is described will depend on the assumptions that are made about the representation of category information in memory. A rule-based theory would state that decision making involves the application of membership rules. If an object matches all the conditions of a rule, its category membership can be established in a deterministic and unambiguous manner. In prototype theories, the decision would depend on the similarity of the object to the prototypes of different categories. Either the category with the most similar prototype is chosen, or the similarity information enters a probabilistic decision-making process. In the latter case, the probabilities of the choice alternatives can be determined in different ways. Usually, however, some form of Luce's (1963) choice rule is applied:

$$Probability\ (Response_{J})|\ Stimulus_{i}) = \frac{Similarity\ (Stimulus_{i}, Prototype_{J})}{\sum_{K} Similarity\ (Stimulus_{i}, Prototype_{K})}\textbf{(10.1)}$$

The probability that a stimulus $_i$ is classified in a category $_j$ is thus a function of the stimulus' similarity to the prototype of that category, and of its similarity to the prototypes of all other categories under consideration. In most situations, only a few choice alternatives are relevant, so the choice process can be very simple and requires little effort. In other situations, however, the number of choices is potentially very large, and the decision process will therefore demand more cognitive resources.

Most exemplar theories also use the choice rule to describe the decision process (Medin & Schaffer 1978, Nosofsky 1986). Exemplar theories postulate that choice probabilities depend on the summed similarities of a stimulus and the exemplars from different categories:

$$Probability\ (Response_{J}\ |\ Stimulus_{i}) = \frac{\sum_{j \in J} Similarity\ (Stimulus_{i}, Exemplar_{j})}{\sum_{K} \sum_{j \in K} Similarity\ (Stimulus_{i}, Exemplar_{j})}\textbf{(10.2)}$$

in which $_{j \in J}$ refers to all exemplars that belong to category $_J$, and $_K$ is the set of relevant categories.

The simple serial model of perceptual categorization in Figure 10.1 is probably somewhat idealized, because it is likely that some information flows in both directions. The perceptual processes in the first stage, for instance, might be influenced by information stored in memory (e.g. Goldstone 1994). Another possibility is that the three stages are not really successive, in the sense that processing at a given stage can start before the previous stage is completed (this would be an example of processes in cascade, McClelland 1979). Nevertheless, a serial model is quite sufficient as a framework in which different theories of the time course of perceptual categorization can be situated. Before I present these theories, however, I will first discuss some of the basics of formal modelling in psychology.

PRINCIPLES OF FORMAL MODELLING

Estimating model parameters

Assume that we carry out a simple categorization experiment in which photographs of cats and dogs are shown on a computer screen. For every photograph, the subjects have to indicate whether they believe they saw a cat or a dog. The photographs differ in resolution; some of them are of really good quality, with a very high resolution, others photographs are poor, and show very little detail. Suppose further that we have a simple mathematical model, that tells us how people's classification performance depends on the resolution of the stimulus. Specifically, suppose that the model states the following:

$$P\ (correct) = 0.5 + \frac{R^q \times a}{2} \quad \textbf{(10.3)}$$

According to this expression, the probability of a correct response is a function of the resolution of the stimulus R, and the amount of attention paid to the task a. Both R and a can have values between 0 and 1. If R is 1, the resolution is maximal, showing even the smallest details, and if R is 0, the resolution is very poor. If a is 1, the subject is really concentrating on the task, and if a is 0, the subject is paying no attention at all. Therefore, if either R or a is 0, the probability of a correct response is only 0.5 (which is the chance level, because there are only two response alternatives). The probability will increase with increasing R and a. If both R and a are 1, the subject will always give a correct response. The q parameter (which can take any value greater than or equal to 1) determines the shape of the relation between R and the probability of a correct response. If q is 1, the relation is linear; otherwise, P (correct) is a non-linear function of R.

Now suppose that we have carried out the experiment with one subject, and that we want to test whether our model about the relation between resolution and performance is correct. Normally, a theory is tested by deriving predictions from it, and by comparing these predictions with observed data. However, the problem with our simple categorization model is that it does not make any specific predictions about the responses of a given subject. Although we know R, the resolution, of each stimulus, we don't know the values of a and q for a particular subject (let us assume that a and q are constant for each subject throughout the experiment). Yet, prediction of performance in the task would require that a and q are somehow fixed at particular values. If the model is correct, then each parameter will have a "true" value for each subject. Unfortunately, the true values that apply in a given situation are unknown. It is likely that these values will differ between subjects, for instance. Such differences can be interesting in some other context, but they are not really relevant if the real interest is in finding out whether resolution has the effect on categorization prescribed by the model. It would not be fair to arbitrarily fix the model's parameter values, and then reject the model because its predictions are very different from the observed data. The model can only be fairly rejected, if there is no combination of parameter values that yields predictions that fit the data well. In applying the model to an individual subject's categorization data, one would therefore have to ensure that the parameter values are somehow optimal, by fixing them at values that provide the best possible estimates of the true, unknown values. If the model is correct, and if the parameter estimates are good, this procedure will guarantee that the model accurately predicts the data.

The question is, of course, what counts as "good" parameter estimates. If there are no a priori criteria for preferring certain values to others (as in the case of the cat–dog categorization experiment, where we have no idea about a particular subject's attention level or about the value of q), the best estimates can be obtained by looking at the observed data, and trying to find a set of parameter values that maximizes the correspondence between these observed values and the values predicted by the model. This process is called *model optimization*. It can be very complicated, and many different techniques for estimating parameters from data have been developed. Most techniques rely on a measure of goodness-of-fit, which describes how well observed values correspond to the predictions generated by the model. Optimization then implies that a search is carried out for a combination of parameter values that produces predictions that maximize the chosen goodness-of-fit function.

Which measure of goodness-of-fit is appropriate in a given situation depends on different factors, such as whether the data are discrete (such as error frequencies) or continuous (such as response times), which assumptions can be made about the distribution of noise in the data, whether one is interested in comparing different models, and so forth. However, model parameters are almost always chosen on the basis of a maximum-likelihood criterion. For any combination of parameter values, one can work out the probability that the data would have occurred, given that the model is true. In parameter estimation, this probability is called *the likelihood of the parameters*, given the data. Maximum-likelihood parameter estimates are those that make the data most likely to have occurred, given that the model is true.

Sometimes it is possible to compute exact likelihood values and use the likelihood function directly as a goodness-of-fit function in model optimization. To illustrate how exact likelihood values can be computed, assume that the cat–dog categorization experiment yielded the results shown in Table 10.1. These are the data for one subject, who received 100 stimuli at each resolution (yielding a total of 500 stimuli). Table 10.1 lists the number of correct responses at each resolution.

The categorization model would generate five probabilities of a correct response, one for each resolution. The probabilities would depend on the

TABLE 10.1
Ficititious data for cat–dog categorization experiment

Resolution	Number correct
0.5	53
0.6	61
0.7	67
0.8	79
0.9	92

model's parameter values. Using these probabilities, the likelihood of the data set can be worked out, because the response frequencies will have a joint binomial distribution (see, e.g. Hays 1988, or another introductory statistics text). The likelihood is:

$$L = \prod_{j=1}^{J} \binom{F_j}{f_j} p_j^{f_j}(1-p_j)^{F_j-f_j} \quad \textbf{(10.4)}$$

In this expression, J is the number of data points (in this case, $J = 5$), f_j is the observed number of correct responses at resolution j, F_j is the total number of responses for resolution j (always equal to 100 in the current experiment), and p_j is the probability of a correct response at j, as stated by the model. Because likelihood values computed in this way can become very small, causing undesirable underflow and round-off errors in the computation, it is often more convenient to compute the logarithm of the likelihood (called the log-likelihood) and use that in optimization. The logarithm is a monotone transformation, which implies that the parameter values that maximize log-likelihood also maximize likelihood. For the example, the log-likelihood function becomes:

$$\ln L = \sum_{j=1}^{J} [\ln F_j! - \ln f_j! - \ln (F_j - f_j)! + f_j \ln p_j + (F_j - f_j) \ln(1 - p_j)]$$
$$\textbf{(10.5)}$$

The product is replaced by a sum, which can be computed more accurately (also, if an analytic method is used to compute maximum-likelihood parameter estimates, a sum is easier to differentiate than a product). Returning to the categorization experiment, assume that we arbitrarily decide to set the value of q at 2 and the value of a at 1. The model then predicts the response probabilities shown in Table 10.2.

Inserting these predictions into the log-likelihood equation, yields a value of -16.552. If we had assumed that q was 1 and a was 1 instead, the model's predictions would have been worse, as shown in column 4 of Table 10.2. This is confirmed by a lower log-likelihood value (-48.899, to be precise).

TABLE 10.2
Observed choice frequencies and predicted choice proportions for
cat–dog categorization experiment

Resolution	Number correct	P(correct) q=2, a=1	P(correct) q=1, a=1	P(correct) q=2.696, a=1
0.5	53	0.63	0.75	0.58
0.6	61	0.68	0.80	0.63
0.7	67	0.75	0.85	0.69
0.8	79	0.82	0.90	0.77
0.9	92	0.91	0.95	0.88

The goodness-of-fit measure discussed so far applies to discrete data (such as choice frequencies). When data are continuous, or nearly continuous (such as response times measured in milliseconds), other indices of goodness-of-fit are more appropriate. One such measure is the residual sum of squares (RSS). It is defined as follows:

$$RSS = \sum_{j=1}^{n} (obs_j - pred_j)^2 \quad \textbf{(10.6)}$$

in which n is the number of observations, obs_j is the observed value j, and $pred_j$ is the corresponding value predicted by the model. It is easy to see that large values of RSS indicate that the model predictions do not correspond well to the observed values. When RSS is used in model optimization, parameter values are chosen such that RSS becomes as small as possible. Parameter estimates obtained in this way are maximum-likelihood estimates, if each observed data point can be described as a sum of a value predicted by the model, and an error value, drawn at random from an independent normal distribution with mean zero and fixed variance (see e.g. Borowiak 1989, for a proof).

Another measure of goodness-of-fit, which is closely related to RSS, is the coefficient of variation, commonly called R^2:

$$R^2 = 1 - \frac{RSS}{TSS} \quad \textbf{(10.7)}$$

in which the total sum of squares, TSS, is given by

$$TSS = \sum_{j=1}^{n} (obs_j - \overline{obs})^2 \quad \textbf{(10.8)}$$

R^2 can have values between zero (indicating very poor fit) and one (when predicted values correspond exactly to observed values).

Once a goodness-of-fit measure has been chosen, the next step is to find the parameter values that maximize the goodness-of-fit. For some types of models, best-fitting parameter values can be found analytically. This is achieved by taking the partial derivatives of the goodness-of-fit function with respect to each parameter, setting the partial derivatives equal to zero, and solving the resulting set of equations simultaneously. Illustrations of this method can be found in any textbook of mathematical statistics (see also Riefer & Batchelder 1988, Wickens 1982). For many models, however, this method does not work, either because the goodness-of-fit function cannot be differentiated, or because the resulting set of equations cannot be solved. In those cases, the only solution is to carry out a direct search for the best-fitting parameter values, using a computer. Depending on the number of parameters, the nature of the model, the goodness-of-fit function and the required precision of the solution, this can be a very complex and time-consuming process. The underlying principle of numerical optimization is always the same. The goodness-of-fit function is evaluated for different combinations of parameter values, until a combination is found that yields the best possible fit to the data. Optimization techniques differ in how they determine the "promising" directions for search in the parameter space. Numerical optimization is an important and large subdiscipline of computer science, and a treatment of optimization methods is beyond the scope of this chapter. A good introduction can be found in Wickens (1982), and an accessible discussion of numerous methods is provided by Press et al. (1989). Fortunately, several statistical software packages (and even some popular spreadsheet programs) have built-in optimization sub-routines, that work quite well and do not require much technical knowledge from the user.

To illustrate the estimation procedure, I carried out a computer search to find the optimal parameter values for the dog–cat categorization experiment, using an optimization method called the "downhill simplex method" (see Press et al. 1989). The best-fitting parameter values were $q = 2.696$ and $a = 1$. For these values, the log-likelihood value was -13.434. The model's predictions are shown in the right-most column of Table 10.2.

Comparisons between model versions

Formal model construction in psychology can have several different purposes. First, it can be used to test a particular theory about a particular process. If the theory can be translated into a formal model, application of the model to a data set will tell the investigator whether the theory is useful or not. Tests of overall goodness-of-fit are specifically designed to answer such questions; they will be discussed in the next section. Secondly, formal modelling can also be used to incorporate theoretical assumptions in data analysis (Riefer & Batchelder 1988). Particular formal models, such as the model that I proposed for the cat–dog categorization experiment, can be used to test various hypotheses about parameter values, in much the same way as general-purpose techniques such as analysis of variance test hypotheses about parametric differences between conditions.

To illustrate how this can be accomplished, let us return to the cat–dog categorization study again. Assume that we tested another subject in exactly the same conditions as the first subject. The data are shown in Table 10.3 (for convenience, the data from subject 1 are also included in the table).

If we want to model these data, we have several options. We can apply the model separately to the data from each subject, but we can also apply the model jointly to the data from both subjects. The latter option is preferable, because it will allow us to test various aspects of the subjects' performance in the experiment. We can test, for instance, whether one subject paid more attention to the task than the other subject (in other words, whether the two subjects differed in the value of model parameter a). To carry out such a test, I first applied a general model with four parameters. Each subject would have a value of q and a value of a. The best-fitting values of these four parameters were estimated, using the log-likelihood function in Equation 10.5. The results of the parameter estimation procedure were:

q [subject 1] = 2.696

q [subject 2] = 2.935

a [subject 1] = 1.000

a [subject 2] = 0.482.

TABLE 10.3
Fictitious data from cat–dog categorization experiment, for two subjects

	Number correct	
Resolution	*Subject 1*	*Subject 2*
0.5	53	52
0.6	61	58
0.7	67	55
0.8	79	65
0.9	92	67

These parameter values yielded a log-likelihood value of –26.516. From the estimated parameter values, it seems that subject 2 paid less attention to the task than subject 1. However, as in ordinary inferential statistics, a difference in values computed from a sample does not necessarily imply a "true" difference in parameter values. Perhaps both subjects were attending equally to the task, and the difference in the estimated a values is the result of random fluctuations in the data. To test whether the difference in a is reliable, it is necessary to apply a restricted model version to the data, in which the same value of a applies to both subjects. Instead of four parameters (as in the general model), this restricted model version would have only three parameters (two qs and one a). It is a general rule in modelling that restricted versions fit the data worse than the general version from which they are derived. This is true, even if the restricted model is correct. Simply because a more general model has more freedom in fitting, it can pick up some random variability in the data. Therefore, if we set a to the same value for both subjects, we can expect to find a log-likelihood value that is smaller than that from the general model version. The crucial question is whether the difference between the model versions is greater than expected, if the restricted model is correct. If the difference in goodness-of-fit between the restricted and the general version is relatively small, this indicates that the additional degrees of freedom (or parameters) of the general model are not necessary to account for the data, and that the restricted version cannot be rejected. If the general model fits the data considerably better than the restricted version, the conclusion is that the restriction was not justified, and that the restricted model version is therefore not appropriate.

If log-likelihood is used as a measure of goodness-of-fit, a test of the reliability of a difference in goodness-of-fit between a restricted and a general model version is based on the likelihood-ratio statistic (and therefore called a likelihood-ratio test):

$$\chi^2 = -2 \ [\ln L(restricted) - \ln L(general)] \quad \textbf{(10.9)}$$

In this equation, $\ln L$ (restricted) is the log-likelihood value of the restricted version, and $\ln L$ (general) is the log-likelihood of the general version. If the restricted model version is correct, χ^2 has an approximate chi-squared distribution if sample size is sufficiently large. The degrees of freedom of this chi-squared distribution correspond to the number of parameters that were eliminated in the restricted model version, compared to the general version. If χ^2 exceeds the critical value that corresponds to the conventional 95th or 99th percentile under the chi-squared distribution, the null hypothesis that the restricted model is correct is rejected.

A restricted version of the simple categorization model, with two q values (one for each subject) and only one a parameter (which applied to both subjects), was applied to the data in Table 10.3. As expected, this model version fitted the data worse than the 4-parameter version, yielding a log-likelihood value of -28.479. A likelihood-ratio test showed that the difference between the model versions was reliable, $\chi^2 = 3.926$, $P < 0.05$, $df = 1$. The conclusion of the test is therefore that the restricted model is wrong, and that the a values for the two subjects were different. In this example, we tested a hypothesis about the difference between parameters, by setting them equal to each other. Another possibility is to test whether one or more parameters have specific values. We could have tested, for instance, whether a was 0.7 for subject 1 and 0.5 for subject 2, using the same method as before.

If RSS is used as a measure of goodness-of-fit, the likelihood-ratio test has a slightly different form (although the underlying principle is exactly the same). Instead of the previous definition, χ^2 is defined as (Borowiak 1989):

$$\chi^2 = -2 \ln \left[\frac{RSS(general)}{RSS(restricted)} \right]^{n/2} \quad \textbf{(10.10)}$$

in which n is the number of data points. As before, χ^2 has an asymptotic chi-square distribution, with degrees of freedom equal to the number of restricted parameters.

It is important to note that likelihood-ratio tests can only be used to compare model versions that are hierarchically related, in the sense that one version is obtained by restricting the parameter set of the other version, without other modifications. For the comparison of non-hierarchically-related models, other techniques should be used (e.g. Akaike 1974, Read & Cressie 1988).

Tests of overall goodness-of-fit

Once a model has been optimized, one can also ask whether it fits the data well, or whether its predictions differ more from the data than expected on the basis of chance fluctuations. A test of goodness-of-fit is used to answer this question. Although they may seem highly relevant at first, the value of such tests is relative (Wickens 1982). All psychological models are ultimately wrong, in the sense that none of them can capture all possible sources of variation in behaviour. If very reliable and precise measurements of behaviour are made (if sample size is very large, for instance), any model can ultimately be proven false (see Wickens 1982, for an excellent discussion of this point).

Nevertheless, tests of overall goodness-of-fit can be useful. If a model cannot be rejected for a particular data set, there is not much point in trying to refine or change the model further, in order to explain even more of the data. Failure to reject a model does not imply that it is correct, but indicates that the model accounted for most of whatever systematic variation was present in the data. On the other hand, if a model is rejected, this may be an incentive to search for improvements or modifications, because there are obviously systematic aspects of the data that are not explained.

There are many different tests of goodness-of-fit, and which test is appropriate in a given context depends on the characteristics of the data and on the optimization procedure (Read & Cressie 1988, Wickens 1982). If maximum-likelihood is used as the optimization criterion, one possible test of overall goodness-of-fit involves a comparison between the model of interest and a saturated model, which provides the best possible account of the data (and, hence, yields the highest possible likelihood value). Because any substantive model can be considered as a restriction of a saturated model, the same likelihood-ratio tests as those presented in the previous section can be applied. As an illustration, assume that we want to test the goodness-of-fit of the 4-parameter model for the cat–dog categorization experiment. Remember that this model yielded a log-likelihood value of -26.516. A saturated model for the data from the two subjects would have 10 degrees of freedom, because the best possible likelihood value is obtained by simply setting each predicted proportion equal to the corresponding observed proportion. Such a saturated model yields a log-likelihood value of -24.288. A likelihood-ratio test identical to the one used to compare hierarchically related model versions shows that this is not reliably better than the 4-parameter model, $\chi^2 = 4.456$, $df = 6$. Therefore, the 4-parameter model is not rejected.

In the remainder of this chapter I will present an overview of current theorizing about the different stages of perceptual categorization. I will focus mainly on two recent theories. One of these theories primarily addresses the perceptual processing stage, whereas the other one provides a detailed account of the processes in stages 2 and 3. In the final section, I will also present an alternative account of time-related aspects of categorization.

PERCEPTUAL PROCESSING IN CATEGORIZATION

There are no reasons to expect that the perceptual processes in categorization tasks are very different from those in other tasks or processing contexts. Therefore, a complete account of cognitive processing in the first stage of perceptual categorization would amount to a fully-fledged theory of perception. However, it is possible to isolate some aspects of perceptual processing that are particularly relevant for categorization. To understand how people process a stimulus in a categorization task, it is particularly important to know how they establish the stimulus values on the dimensions that are relevant in the task context. A model that I proposed recently, the "extended generalized context model" (EGCM; Lamberts 1995, 1996), provides a detailed description of this process. Before I can introduce the EGCM, however, I will have to present the generalized context model (GCM; Nosofsky 1986, see also Hahn & Chater, this volume), from which it is derived.

The GCM is an exemplar theory of categorization. As I indicated in the introduction, exemplar theories assume that people store individual instances in memory during category learning. Category decisions in the GCM are probabilistic. The model uses the choice rule in Equation 10.2 to compute the probability of the response alternatives. The main difference between the GCM and other exemplar theories is its similarity notion. Similarity in the GCM is an inverse function of the distance between stimuli. The distance concept can be used here, because stimuli can be represented as points in a multidimensional space. Each stimulus dimension defines a dimension of that space, and a stimulus location depends on the values it has on the different dimensions. Figure 10.2 illustrates the case of two stimuli that have two dimensions each.

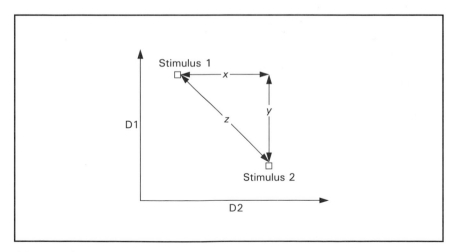

FIG. 10.2.   Spatial representation of two stimuli.

Distance between stimuli is computed as follows:

$$d_{ij} = \left(\sum_{p=1}^{P} w_p \, |x_{ip} - x_{jp}|^r\right)^{1/r} \quad \textbf{(10.11)}$$

In this equation, P is the number of stimulus dimensions, x_{ip} and x_{jp} refer to the values of stimuli i and j on dimension p, w_p is the weight of dimension p, and r is a metric exponent. The weight parameters determine the relative scales of the different dimensions. An increase in the weight of a given dimension, for instance, could be represented by stretching the multidimensional stimulus space in the direction of that dimension. The metric exponent r determines the type of distance measure that is computed. Although r can have any positive value, usually only two special cases are considered. If $r = 1$, distances correspond to a so-called city-block metric. The city-block distance between two stimuli simply equals the sum of the differences between them on all dimensions. In the example in Figure 10.2, the city-block distance between stimuli 1 and 2 is $x + y$. It is easy to see why this is called the city-block metric. If one were to travel from the point corresponding to stimulus 1 to the point of stimulus 2 in a city with a square-grid street layout, the distance travelled would be $x + y$. If $r = 2$ (the other special case), distances are Euclidean. The Euclidean distance between the stimuli in Figure 10.2 is z. According to Pythagoras' theorem, z is equal to the square root of the sum of x and y, and corresponds to the length of a straight line between the two points.

Similarity is negatively related to distance in the stimulus space. In the basic version of the GCM, the relation between distance and similarity is exponential:

$$s_{ij} = \exp(-c \, d_{ij}) \quad \textbf{(10.12)}$$

Nosofsky (1986) has also proposed other relations between distance and similarity, but these are not relevant here. The value of c defines the steepness of the function that relates similarity and distance. In Figure 10.3, I have plotted similarity as a function of distance, for several values of c.

The GCM is defined entirely by the equations that were given in the previous paragraphs. These equations contain several free parameters, such as the dimension weights w_p, the metric exponent r and the generalization value c. Therefore, application of the model to empirical data requires that its parameter values are estimated, using one of the methods outlined in the previous section.

The GCM offers an account of the result of perceptual categorization processes, without saying anything about the time course of these

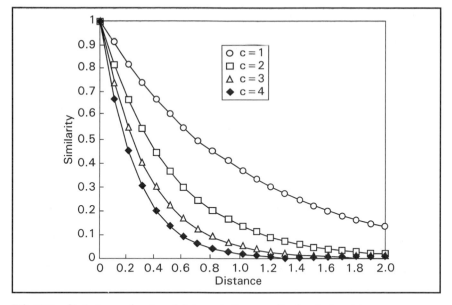

FIG. 10.3.   Similarity as a function of distance in the generalized context model.

processes. The purpose of the EGCM was to enhance the GCM, by providing a more detailed description of the processes in the first stage of categorization (the perceptual processing stage). According to the EGCM, perceptual processing of a stimulus involves the collection of information about the values of the stimulus on its different dimensions. In the model, this sampling process is called the dimensional inclusion process. It is further assumed that the dimensions are processed in parallel, and that it takes a certain, randomly variable amount of time to process each dimension. The probability that a dimension p is processed at or before a given time t after stimulus presentation is called the cumulative inclusion probability for p at t, written as $i_p(t)$, and is given by:

$$i_p(t) = 1 - \exp(-q_p t) \quad \textbf{(10.13)}$$

In this equation, q_p is the inclusion rate of dimension p. The inclusion rate determines how quickly, on average, a dimension is processed. The inclusion rate of a dimension probably depends primarily on the dimension's salience. Salience is a physical characteristic, which determines how easy it is to distinguish the values of a dimension. Dimensions that are highly salient are usually processed faster than dimensions that are less salient (Freeman & Lamberts 1996).

Figure 10.4 shows the cumulative inclusion function over time of two dimensions, one with an inclusion rate of 0.01 and one with a rate of 0.02. After 100 time units, the probability that the first dimension is processed is about 0.63, whereas the probability is higher (about 0.86) for the second dimension.

A consequence of the dimensional inclusion process is that similarity (between the stimulus and stored exemplars) is not static, but changes over time. Specifically, the similarity between a stimulus and an exemplar in memory at time t will depend on the dimensions that have been processed at t. Suppose, for instance, that a stimulus (say, a picture of a car) is identical to an exemplar in memory on the dimensions colour and size, but differs on other dimensions, such as shape of the headlights and number of doors. Colour and overall size are probably very salient dimensions, and they are therefore likely to be processed faster than other, less salient dimensions. Shortly after stimulus presentation, it is possible that only colour and size have been processed. Because the stimulus and the stored exemplar have the same values on these dimensions, their similarity at this point in time will be 1. A little later, when less salient dimensions such as headlight shape and number of doors are processed as well, similarity will decrease, because more differences between the stimulus and the exemplar will become apparent.

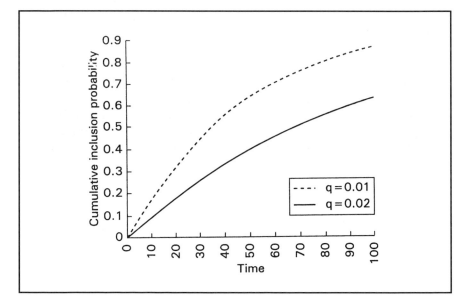

FIG. 10.4.   Cumulative inclusion probability over time as a function of inclusion rate q, according to the EGCM.

Because the dimensional inclusion process alters similarity, the similarity definition in the EGCM is time-dependent:

$$s_{ij}(t) = \exp[-c(\sum_{p=1}^{P} inc_p(t)\, u_p\, |x_{ip} - x_{jp}|^r)^{1/r}] \quad \textbf{(10.14)}$$

This equation is almost identical to the GCM's. The main difference is that the dimension weights w have been replaced by a product of an inclusion indicator $inc_p(t)$ and a utility value u. The inclusion indicator is a binary variable. If its value is 1, the dimension has been processed and will be included in the similarity computation; if $inc_p(t)$ is 0, the dimension is not included. The utility value u_p indicates how important a dimension is in the similarity computation, and can be considered as an attentional weight.

The EGCM is always applied to response proportions that are obtained after aggregation across trials. In applying the model to such data, the probability of occurrence of each possible inclusion pattern is computed, using the cumulative inclusion probabilities of the different dimensions. For each stimulus, the choice probability that corresponds to each inclusion pattern is computed as well, and the mathematical expectation of the choice probabilities for a stimulus is the value predicted by the model for that stimulus.

To test whether the EGCM can effectively account for the earliest stage of perceptual categorization, we have carried out several series of experiments (Freeman & Lamberts 1996, Lamberts 1995, 1996, Lamberts & Brockdorff 1996). The reasoning behind the first series of experiments (Lamberts 1995) was the following. If similarity changes in the perceptual-processing stage of categorization, as postulated in the EGCM, then different categorization behaviour should be observed, dependent on the duration of the perceptual processing stage. If perceptual processing is somehow interrupted, and if people only have the opportunity to sample information about a few stimulus dimensions, their behaviour should differ from a situation in which they can process all relevant dimensions.

The experiments in Lamberts (1995) always consisted of two stages. In the first stage, the subjects learned to classify a number of stimuli (usually about eight) into two categories. The stimuli were simplified, schematic drawings of faces, that varied on four dimensions. Half the stimuli belonged to category A, the other half to category B. On each training trial, a stimulus was selected at random from the set, and presented on a computer screen. The subjects indicated whether they thought the stimulus belonged to category A or to category B by pressing one of two response buttons. After each response, correct–incorrect feedback was given. Training continued until the subjects could classify all training stimuli into the correct category without making any mistakes.

Immediately after the training stage the subjects carried out the transfer task. As in the training stage a stimulus would appear on the screen, and the subjects pressed a button to indicate its category membership (they did not receive feedback in the transfer stage). To manipulate the duration of the perceptual processing stage a response deadline technique was used. Before each block of transfer trials, the subjects were told that they had to respond within a given interval (typically between 600 and 1,500 ms) after every stimulus presentation. There were also blocks of trials without deadline. The subjects were instructed to always respond within the deadline, regardless of whether they thought they had processed the stimulus completely or not. Because the deadlines were short, normal stimulus processing was interrupted, and the subjects were made to respond much faster to the stimuli than they would do in a situation without time pressure. If the EGCM is correct, it should be able to account for the effects of time pressure on people's categorization behaviour.

The dependent variable of interest in these experiments was the proportion of category A responses for each stimulus in the transfer task, under the different response deadlines. The response proportions showed a very regular pattern. Stimuli that belonged to category A during training, yielded a majority of category A responses in the transfer task, as expected. Stimuli from category B yielded relatively few category A responses. However, most important was the finding that the deadline manipulation had a strong effect on these response proportions. When there was no deadline (and the subjects could take all the time they needed), the response proportions tended to be very close to 1 (for the category A stimuli) or very close to 0 (for the category B stimuli), which indicates that the subjects made very consistent choices. When a response deadline applied, the proportions became closer to 0.5, which is the chance level. The shorter the deadline, the less consistent the subjects were. For instance, if they decided on 98 per cent of the trials that stimulus x belonged to category A in the condition without deadline, they would assign the same stimulus to category A on only 70 per cent of the trials if they had to respond within 600 ms. However, this general effect was not always present to the same degree. Whereas the response proportions on some stimuli changed from very consistent (over 0.95 or below 0.05) to near chance level (close to 0.50), performance on other stimuli was hardly affected at all by the deadline. On such stimuli, the subjects would still be very consistent, even if they had very little time. Another remarkable result was that the deadline produced a reversal in category preference for certain stimuli. Some stimuli that were classified mainly in category A without a deadline were categorized mainly in category B when fast responses were required. Overall, the results appeared sufficiently complex to pose a serious challenge to a process model of categorization.

The EGCM was applied to the response proportions. First, a standard version of the model was optimized. Exactly which parameters were estimated is not very important now (see Lamberts 1995, for a detailed discussion), but they included utility values and inclusion rates for all the stimulus dimensions. The duration of the perceptual processing stage (which corresponds to t in the model equations) was assumed to be equal to the average response time in each deadline condition, minus a constant value that represented the combined duration of the memory access and decision stages. The parameter values were estimated using a maximum-likelihood criterion. The log-likelihood function was exactly the same as that for the fictitious cat–dog categorization experiment from the first section of this chapter (see Equation 10.5). In all the experiments, the model fitted the data very well. The EGCM explained all the main trends. Not only did the model predict the general decrease in consistency at shorter deadlines, it also accounted for the differences between the stimuli with remarkable accuracy. The model even accounted for the preference reversal effects for some stimuli. According to the model, these effects occurred because the correct classification of the stimuli that showed a reversal effect required that all their dimensions were processed. If one or two dimensions were left out (as would be the case in the deadline conditions), the stimuli would be confused with stimuli from the opposite category, and thus classified incorrectly. It seemed, therefore, that the EGCM was fully supported by the data.

There is, however, an alternative explanation of the effects of the deadline manipulation that needed to be ruled out. Perhaps subjects simply guessed more when they had little time available. Differential guessing could certainly produce the general tendency of the responses to become less consistent at shorter signal intervals. To test the guessing interpretation, I first applied a version of the EGCM with an additional guessing mechanism. According to this augmented version, the probability of a category A response is:

$$P\ (A)\ _{\text{AUGM}} = (1 - g)\ P\ (A)\ _{\text{EGCM}} + g\ /\ 2\ \textbf{(10.15)}$$

in which g is a guess rate ($0 \le g \le 1$). If g is 1 (in other words, if responses are the result of guessing only), the probability of a category A response is 0.5. If g is 0, the augmented model predicts the same proportion as the basic EGCM. Because it seemed plausible that guess rates differed between deadline conditions, one separate guess-rate parameter was estimated for each deadline condition. In other respects, the augmented model was identical to the standard EGCM. After optimization, the augmented model fitted the data only slightly better than the standard version. A likelihood-ratio test showed that the difference in goodness-of-fit between the model versions was not significant. Therefore, it was not necessary to assume that guessing occurred at all to get a good account of the data. Still, the comparison between the standard version and the augmented version left the possibility that guessing, although not necessary, could be sufficient to explain the deadline effects. Perhaps the dimensional inclusion mechanism of the EGCM was not necessary either, and a model with only differential guessing might account for the data. To test this possibility, I applied yet another model version, from which the dimensional inclusion mechanism was removed, but in which differential guessing could occur (this model was in fact the GCM with an additional guessing mechanism). A likelihood-ratio test showed that this version fitted the data reliably worse than the augmented EGCM, which shows that the dimensional inclusion mechanism cannot be removed without a significant reduction in goodness-of-fit. Therefore, the conclusion was that the dimensional inclusion mechanism postulated in the EGCM was essential in accounting for the data, whereas differential guessing was not relevant. The EGCM's dimensional inclusion mechanism offered a plausible account of the processes in the earliest stage of perceptual categorization.

One potential problem with the response deadline experiments is that the subjects knew in advance how much time was available for each trial. It is quite possible that this knowledge induced changes in processing strategy between deadline conditions. In another series of experiments (Lamberts 1996), I attempted to remedy this shortcoming by using a different technique for imposing time constraints on perceptual processing. Instead of the deadline procedure, these experiments used a variation of Meyer et al.'s (1988) titrated reaction time (TRT) procedure. The TRT procedure allows investigation of the time course of processing, because it randomly combines regular and signal trials in an experimental session. On regular trials, the participants receive a stimulus and try to produce a correct response as quickly as possible. On signal trials, some moment after the stimulus appears, an imperative response signal (a loud auditory tone) is presented. As soon as they detect the response signal, the subjects have to respond immediately, regardless of whether they have completed processing of the stimulus. By varying the time between the onset of the stimulus and the response signal, response patterns can be obtained for various stages of processing. A crucial feature of the TRT procedure is that it induces the subjects to apply the same strategy on all trials, because they cannot predict in advance whether they will hear a response signal or not. In the categorization experiments in which this technique was used, effects were observed that were very similar to those obtained in the deadline experiments (Lamberts 1996). Therefore, it seems unlikely that the deadline effects were entirely due to strategy differences. Again, the EGCM provided a good account of the results of the response signalling experiments, and proved superior to alternative explanations.

In testing formal models with meaningful parameters, it is usually a fruitful strategy to manipulate experimental variables that are supposed to selectively influence one model parameter. The estimated parameter value should change as a result of this manipulation, whereas other aspects of the model should not be affected. This is precisely what we have attempted to do in another series of experiments (Freeman & Lamberts 1996). The purpose of these experiments was to test the hypothesis that dimensional inclusion rates depend on perceptual salience. In the experiments, we used realistic, three-dimensional pictures of objects as stimuli. To manipulate dimensional salience, one feature of the object would be highlighted. The estimated inclusion rates showed that dimensions were included faster if they were highlighted, and likelihood-ratio tests showed that these effects were robust. The conclusion from these experiments was that inclusion rates depended on physical stimulus characteristics, rather than on strategic or attentional factors.

MEMORY ACCESS AND DECISION MAKING

Although the EGCM provides a detailed process account of the first stage of categorization, the model has little to say about the time course of the processes that underlie access to exemplars in memory and the subsequent decision-making process. A detailed process account of these two stages is given by another model that is also derived from the GCM. This model is called the "exemplar-based random walk model" (EBRW;) Nosofsky & Palmeri 1997). Like the GCM and the EGCM, the EBRW assumes that exemplars are stored in memory during category learning, and that subsequent categorization involves comparisons between the stimulus and stored exemplars. The EBRW describes in more detail than the GCM or the EGCM how these comparisons might be carried out, and how they can affect the time course of categorization.

According to the EBRW, the exemplars in memory are activated when a stimulus is presented for categorization. The level of activation of each exemplar corresponds to the product of the strength of the exemplar (which reflects its recency and frequency of presentation) and its similarity to the stimulus:

$$a_{ij} = M_j \cdot s_{ij} \quad \textbf{(10.16)}$$

in which a_{ij} is the activation of exemplar j upon presentation of stimulus i, M_j is the strength of exemplar j, and s_{ij} is the similarity between the stimulus and the exemplar. Similarity is defined in exactly the same way as in the GCM (see Equations 10.11 and 10.12). When a stimulus is presented, the exemplars start to race against each other for retrieval. The time to complete the race for a given exemplar is an exponentially-distributed random variable. The probability density that an exemplar j with activation a_{ij} completes the race at time t is:

$$f(t) = a_{ij} \cdot \exp(-a_{ij} \cdot t) \quad \textbf{(10.17)}$$

The probability that a particular exemplar wins the race and is retrieved thus depends on its activation value (and thereby on its strength and on its similarity to the test stimulus). As soon as an exemplar is retrieved, a new race is initiated and the next exemplar will be retrieved.

The retrieval of exemplars drives a random walk process. If there are two categories to choose between, such a process can be represented by two response boundaries, between which a random walk counter moves (see Figure 10.5).

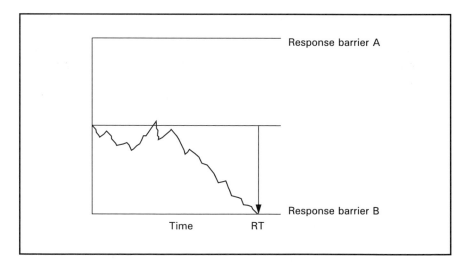

FIG. 10.5.   Illustration of random walk process in EBRW.

The counter starts off in the middle between the barriers. If the retrieved exemplar belongs to category A, the counter moves in the direction of that category barrier. If the exemplar belongs to category B, the counter moves in the opposite direction. The size of each step can depend on the activation of the retrieved exemplar, but in most applications Nosofsky & Palmeri (1997) simplified the model and assumed that the counter moves with constant increments. The random walk process continues until the counter crosses one of the boundaries. When that happens the corresponding response is initiated. As such, the response time on a categorization trial depends on the number of steps that are taken (i.e. the number of exemplars that are retrieved) before a boundary is crossed, and on the duration of each step in the random walk. Each step lasts as long as it takes to retrieve the winning exemplar, plus a constant amount of time.

The EBRW has been used primarily to account for response times in various categorization tasks (Nosofsky & Palmeri 1997, Palmeri 1997). The model makes several testable predictions. First, it predicts that response times will depend on the similarity pattern of a stimulus with respect to the exemplars from both categories. If a stimulus is very typical of one category, it will be highly similar to most exemplars in that category. If that stimulus is also dissimilar to most or all exemplars from the alternative category, the model predicts that the stimulus will be categorized very quickly. The reason for this is that the exemplars from the first category have high activation values, whereas those from the second category have low activation values (see Equation 10.16). As a consequence, almost every race will be won by an exemplar from the first category, and the random walk counter will move consistently towards that category's boundary. This will produce a fast response. However, if a stimulus is about equally similar to exemplars from either category, the random walk will not proceed in such a consistent manner. Instead, the counter will probably move back and forth between the boundaries before it crosses one of them. In such cases, responses will be slow.

A second prediction from the EBRW concerns the effect of exemplar familiarity. Familiar exemplars have been encountered many times, and they will have relatively high strength. Because strength affects activation (Equation 10.16), strong exemplars will tend to have short race times (Equation 10.17). As a result, response times will be shorter when the retrieved exemplars are familiar. This explains why responses will become gradually faster as a result of practice (Nosofsky & Palmeri 1997, Palmeri 1997).

Nosofsky & Palmeri (1997) carried out three experiments, in which they tested various aspects of the EBRW. The model provided good accounts of response times to individual stimuli, and also explained practice effects and the effects of familiarity.

The EGCM and the EBRW complement each other nicely as process models of categorization. The EGCM provides a mechanism for the earliest stage of processing, but does not specify the course of processing in the later stages. The EBRW, on the other hand, has little or nothing to say about the perceptual processing stage, but does provide an account of the time course of memory access and decision making. Probably, the two models could be integrated without too much difficulty. The EGCM's assumptions about the memory access and decision-making stages are compatible with the mechanisms specified in the EBRW. Alternatively, the EBRW assumes that the perceptual processing stage is completed by the time exemplars in memory are activated, and is therefore compatible with the EGCM. A combined model would cover almost the entire range of processes involved in categorization, from the earliest perceptual stages to the final decision making.

ANOTHER MODEL OF RESPONSE TIMES IN CATEGORIZATION

Recently, Ashby et al. (1994, see also Ashby & Maddox 1994) have proposed a theory of response times in categorization that differs fundamentally from the exemplar models I have discussed so far. Although the Ashby et al. (1994) theory is perhaps not a process model in the same sense as the EGCM or the EBRW, it does make predictions about time-related aspects of processing.

Ashby et al.'s (1994) model is based on general recognition theory (GRT; Ashby & Townsend 1986, Ashby & Gott 1988, Ashby & Perrin 1988), and the decision-bound theory of categorization that has been derived from GRT. Like the models based on the GCM, GRT is built on the assumption that stimuli correspond to locations in a multidimensional stimulus space. It is further assumed in the model that the same stimulus does not always produce the same perceptual effect, and therefore the appropriate perceptual description of a stimulus is a multivariate probability distribution rather than a single point in space. Usually, the probability distribution is assumed to be multivariate normal. Figure 10.6 shows a bivariate normal distribution. If the stimulus that produced a perceptual distribution of this form were presented, its perceptual representation could correspond to any point under the distribution. The height of the distribution reflects the probability that the representation falls into a certain area.

To explain categorization, decision-bound theory assumes that the subject divides the perceptual space in as many regions as there are

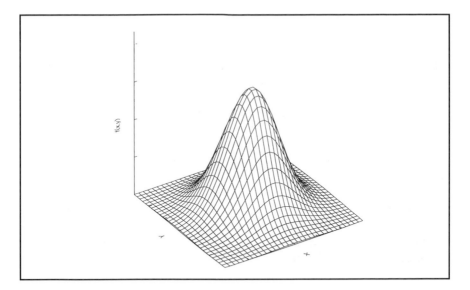

FIG. 10.6.   Bivariate normal distribution.

categories. If the perceptual representation of a stimulus falls into a particular region, the stimulus is assigned to the category that corresponds to that region. Figure 10.7 provides an illustration of a two-dimensional stimulus space, with two regions. The circles in Figure 10.7 are contours of equal likelihood for two stimuli, S1 and S2. These contours connect points in the probability distributions that have the same probability density. They are obtained by drawing the outline of horizontal slices, taken at different heights, from a distribution such as the one in Figure 10.6 (pretty much in the same way as contours are used to construct geographic relief maps).

The diagonal line in Figure 10.7 is a decision bound, which divides the stimulus space into two regions. The upper left hand side of the bound is the region associated with category A, and the lower right hand side is associated with category B. This decision bound is linear, but non-linear decision bounds are also possible. Suppose that stimulus S1 is presented. Most of the time, the perceptual representation of this stimulus will fall into region A, and the stimulus will be classified as a member of category A. Note, however, that a small part of the probability distribution for S1 crosses the decision bound. This implies that there is a small probability that S1 will be classified as a member of the B category.

Ashby and his colleagues have tested GRT and decision-bound theory in numerous experiments. The theory has also been used to explain

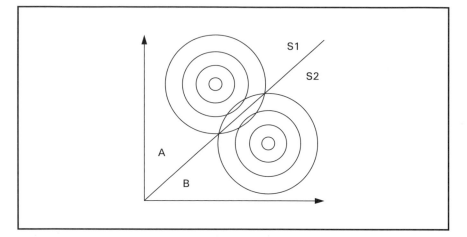

FIG. 10.7.   Contours of equal likelihood for two stimuli (S1 and S2) and linear decision bound.

performance in other tasks, such as identification and preference. In direct experimental comparisons with the GCM, decision-bound theory performed often about equally well, sometimes worse, and sometimes better (e.g. Ashby & Lee 1991, Maddox & Ashby 1993, McKinley & Nosofsky 1995, Nosofsky & Smith 1992). The formal relation between the two models has also been explored in considerable detail (Ashby & Maddox 1993, Ashby & Alfonso-Reese 1995, Myung 1994, Nosofsky 1990).

Based on decision-bound theory, Ashby et al. (1994) proposed a specific model for response times in perceptual classification tasks. Their RT-distance hypothesis states that response time decreases with the distance between the stimulus representation and the decision bound. Stimulus representations that are close to the bound yield slower responses than representations that are far from the bound. This hypothesis also implies that, on average, response times will be shorter for stimuli that are classified correctly than for stimuli that are classified incorrectly. The reason for this difference is shown in Figure 10.8. The two stimuli in the left-hand panel of Figure 10.8 are closer to the decision bound than the stimuli in the right hand panel. Therefore, according to the RT-distance hypothesis, responses will be slower to the stimuli on the left than to the stimuli on the right. However, the probability distributions associated with the stimuli on the left overlap considerably more than those from the stimuli on the right. Therefore, the high-overlap stimuli will produce more errors than the low-overlap stimuli, and hence there will be a correlation between accuracy and response time.

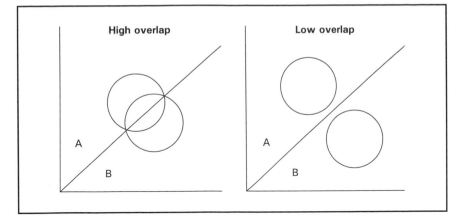

FIG. 10.8.   Contours of equal likelihood for two stimuli close to the decision bound (left panel) and for two stimuli far from the decision bound (right panel).

Ashby et al. (1994) have tested the RT-distance hypothesis in three experiments. They used two-dimensional stimuli that varied continuously along each dimension. In all the experiments, response time was found to increase with distance from the decision bound, confirming the RT-distance hypothesis (see also Ashby & Maddox 1994).

Generally, the EBRW and decision-bound theory make very similar predictions about categorization response times. The EBRW does predict that stimuli that are far from a decision bound will yield the fastest responses, because they are more similar to the exemplars from one category than to those from the other category, leading to a consistent random walk towards a decision boundary (see above). However, the EBRW and the RT-distance hypothesis diverge on one important point. According to the EBRW, the familiarity of a stimulus should affect its categorization time. If an unfamiliar stimulus is encountered, the retrieval times for stored exemplars should be slow. If a stimulus is highly familiar (because it has been encountered many times before), the stored exemplar that corresponds to this stimulus will have high strength, and therefore produce very short retrieval times. The EBRW thus predicts that, all other things being equal, familiar stimuli are classified faster than unfamiliar stimuli (Nosofsky & Palmeri 1997). On the other hand, the RT-distance hypothesis predicts that familiarity should not affect categorization times. Nosofsky & Palmeri (1997) carried out an experiment in which they investigated the effect of stimulus familiarity on categorization response times. They used the category structure shown in Figure 10.9. First, the subjects learned to classify stimuli 1, 2, and 3 in category A, and the other five stimuli in category B. The presentation frequencies of stimuli 7 and 8 during training were manipulated. In condition U7, stimulus 7 was never presented, whereas stimulus 8 was not presented in condition U8. A speeded-classification transfer stage followed training. In the transfer task, the participants carried out speeded classifications of the eight stimuli. Their classification response times were recorded.

The RT-distance hypothesis predicts identical categorization times for stimuli 7 and 8, because they are equally distant from the optimal decision bound (see Figure 10.9). However, contrary to the prediction from the RT-distance hypothesis, there was a significant interaction between presentation condition and response time for stimuli 7 and 8. Responses were faster if the subjects were familiar with the stimulus. In condition U7, where stimulus 7 was not seen during training, responses were faster to stimulus 8 than to stimulus 7. In condition U8, response were faster to stimulus 7 than to stimulus 8. The RT-distance hypothesis cannot readily explain these differences, whereas the EBRW predicts them accurately. Whether and how the RT-distance hypothesis might be extended to account for such results is an issue for future research.

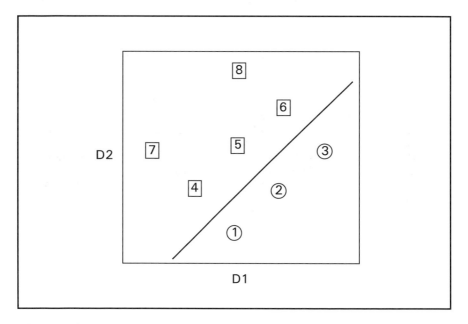

FIG. 10.9.   Stimulus structure in Nosofsky & Palmeri's (1997) Experiment 2. The stimuli represented by circles belong to category A, whereas the square stimuli are members of category B. The oblique line in the graph represents an optimal linear decision bound between the categories.

CONCLUSION

In this chapter, I have tried to give an overview of some recent work on the time course of perceptual categorization. Although interest in this particular issue is fairly recent, several aspects of the processes involved are relatively well understood. In the earliest, perceptual stages of processing, a dimensional sampling process seems to take place, which produces the stimulus representation that drives memory access and decision making. These later stages can be described as a random walk towards barriers that represent the categories, guided by the retrieval of exemplars from memory.

Of course, many questions about the time course of categorization remain unanswered. For instance, does the dimensional inclusion mechanism apply to all kinds of objects? And what precisely is the role of familiarity in the time course of categorization? Another important question has to do with the different processing strategies that people can use in categorization tasks. The exemplar models that I discussed worked fine for certain experiments, but it is clear that people sometimes do use rules (Nosofsky et al. 1994) or prototypes (Hampton 1993) instead of exemplars. Very little is known about the time course of rule-based or prototype-based processing.

REFERENCES

Akaike, H. 1974. A new look at the statistical model identification. *ieee Transactions on Automatic Control* **19**, 716–23.

Ashby, F. G. 1992. Multidimensional models of categorization. In *Multidimensional models of perception and cognition*, F. G. Ashby (ed.), 449–83. Hillsdale, New Jersey: Erlbaum.

Ashby, F. G. & L. A. Alfonso-Reese 1995. Categorization as probability density estimation. *Journal of Mathematical Psychology* **39**, 216–33.

Ashby, F. G., G. Boynton, W. W. Lee 1994. Categorization response time with multidimensional stimuli. *Perception and Psychophysics* **55**, 11–27.

Ashby, F. G. & R. E. Gott 1988. Decision rules in the perception and classification of multidimensional stimuli. *Journal of Experimental Psychology: Learning, Memory, and Cognition* **14**, 33–53.

Ashby, F. G. & W. W. Lee 1991. Predicting similarity and categorization from identification. *Journal of Experimental Psychology: General* **120**, 150–72.

Ashby, F. G. & T. W. Maddox 1993. Relations between prototype, exemplar and decision bound models of categorization. *Journal of Mathematical Psychology* **37**, 372–400.

Ashby, F. G. & T. W. Maddox 1994. A response time theory of separability and integrality in speeded classification. *Journal of Mathematical Psychology* **38**, 423–66.

Ashby, F. G. & N. A. Perrin 1988. Toward a unified theory of similarity and recognition. *Psychological Review* **95**, 124–50.

Ashby, F. G. & J. T. Townsend 1986. Varieties of perceptual independence. *Psychological Review* **93**, 154–79.

Atkinson, R. C., G. H. Bower, E. J. Crothers 1965. *Introduction to mathematical learning theory*. New York: John Wiley.

Atkinson, R. C. & W. K. Estes 1963. Stimulus sampling theory. In *Handbook of mathematical psychology* (vol. 2), R. D. Luce, R. R. Bush, E. Galanter (eds), 326–400. New York: John Wiley.

Borowiak, D. S. 1989. *Model discrimination for nonlinear regression models*. New York: Marcel Dekker.

Estes, W. K. 1986. Array models of category learning. *Cognitive Psychology* **18**, 500–549.

Estes, W. K. 1994. *Classification and cognition*. New York: Oxford University Press.

Freeman, R. P. J. & K. Lamberts 1996. Salience and categorization. Manuscript submitted for publication.

Garner, W. R. 1978. Aspects of a stimulus: features, dimensions, and configurations. In *Cognition and categorization*, E. Rosch & B. B. Lloyd (eds), 99–133. Hillsdale, New Jersey: Erlbaum.

Gluck, M. A. & G. H. Bower 1988. From conditioning to category learning: an adaptive network model. *Journal of Experimental Psychology: General* **117**, 225–44.

Goldstone, R. L. 1994. Influences of categorization on perceptual discrimination. *Journal of Experimental Psychology: General* **123**, 178–200.

Hampton, J. A. 1993. Prototype models of concept representation. In *Categories and concepts: theoretical views and inductive data analysis*, I. Van Mechelen, J. A. Hampton, R. S. Michalski, & P. Theuns (eds), 64–83. London: Academic Press.

Hays, W. L. 1988. *Statistics*. New York: Holt, Rinehart & Winston.

Hintzman, D. L. 1986. Schema abstraction in a multiple-trace memory model. *Psychological Review* **93**, 411–28.

Lamberts, K. 1994. Flexible tuning of similarity in exemplar-based categorization. *Journal of Experimental Psychology: Learning, Memory, and Cognition* **20**, 1003–21.

Lamberts, K. 1995. Categorization under time pressure. *Journal of Experimental Psychology: General* **124**, 161–80.

Lamberts, K. 1996. *The time course of categorization*. Manuscript submitted for publication.

Lamberts, K. & N. Brockdorff 1996. Fast categorization of stimuli with multi-valued dimensions. *Memory, and Cognition*, in press.

Luce, R. D. 1963. Detection and recognition. In *Handbook of mathematical psychology*, R. D. Luce, R. R. Bush, & E. Galanter (eds), 103–189. New York: John Wiley.

Maddox, W. T. & F. G. Ashby 1993. Comparing decision bound and exemplar models of categorization. *Perception and Psychophysics* **53**, 49–70.

McClelland, J. L. 1979. On the time relations of mental processes: an examination of systems of processes in cascade. *Psychological Review* **86**, 287–330.

McKinley, S. C. & R. M. Nosofsky 1995. Investigations of exemplar and decision bound models in large, ill-defined category structures. *Journal of Experimental Psychology: Human Perception and Performance* **21**, 128–48.

Medin, D. L. & M. M. Schaffer 1978. Context theory of classification learning. *Psychological Review* **85**, 207–38.

Medin, D. L., W. D. Wattenmaker, R. S. Michalski 1987. Constraints and preferences in inductive learning: an experimental study of human and machine performance. *Cognitive Science* **11**, 299–339.

Meyer, D. E., D. E. Irwin, A. M. Osman, J. Kounios 1988. The dynamics of cognition and action: mental processes inferred from speed-accuracy decomposition. *Psychological Review* **95**, 183–237.

Murphy, G. L. & D. L. Medin 1985. The role of theories in conceptual coherence. *Psychological Review* **92**, 289–316.

Myung, I. J. 1994. Maximum entropy interpretation of decision bound and context models of categorization. *Journal of Mathematical Psychology* **38**, 335–65.

Nosofsky, R. M. 1986. Attention, similarity, and the identification–categorization relationship. *Journal of Experimental Psychology: General* **115**, 39–57.

Nosofsky, R. M. 1990. Relations between exemplar-similarity and likelihood models of classification. *Journal of Mathematical Psychology* **34**, 393–418.

Nosofsky, R. M. & T. J. Palmeri 1997. An exemplar-based random walk model of speeded classification. *Psychological Review,* **104,** 266–300.

Nosofsky, R. M., T. J. Palmeri, S. C. McKinley 1994. Rule-plus-exception model of classification learning. *Psychological Review* **101**, 53–79.

Nosofsky, R. M. & J. E. K. Smith 1992. Similarity, identification, and categorization: comment on Ashby and Lee (1991). *Journal of Experimental Psychology: General* **121**, 237–45.

Palmeri, T. J. 1997. Exemplar similarity and the development of automaticity. *Journal of Experimental Psychology: Learning, Memory, and Cognition*, **23**, 324–354.

Press, W. H., B. P. Flannery, S. A. Teukolsky, W. T. Vetterling 1989. *Numerical recipes in Pascal*. Cambridge: Cambridge University Press.

Read, T. R. C. & N. A. C. Cressie 1988. *Goodness-of-fit statistics for discrete multivariate data*. New York: Springer.

Riefer, D. M. & W. H. Batchelder 1988. Multinomial modelling and the measurement of cognitive processes. *Psychological Review* **95**, 318–39.

Shepard, R. N. 1958. Stimulus and response generalization: deduction of the generalization gradient from a trace model. *Psychological Review* **65**, 242–256.

Smith, E. E. & D. L. Medin 1981. *Categories and concepts*. Cambridge, Mass.: Harvard University Press.

Wickens, T. D. 1982. *Models for behaviour: stochastic processes in psychology*. San Francisco: Freeman.

NOTE

1.   Preparation of this chapter was supported by a grant from the Economic and Social Research Council. Thanks are due to Noellie Brockdorff, Steve Chong, Richard Freeman, and David Peebles for helpful comments.

CHAPTER ELEVEN

Learning Functional Relations Based on Experience With Input–Output Pairs by Humans and Artificial Neural Networks

Jerome R. Busemeyer, Eunhee Byun,
Edward L. Delosh and Mark A. McDaniel

I. DECISIONS, PREDICTIONS, AND ABSTRACT CONCEPTS

Before making any serious decision, we normally try to anticipate how the effects of our action will vary depending on the action taken. For example, before an anaesthetist can decide the amount of anaesthetic to administer to a patient, she needs to predict how the analgesic effect will vary as a function of the amount injected. Before a father can decide the amount of money to invest in his son's college education, he needs to predict how the return will vary as a function of the size of the investment. The point is that prediction is essential to decision making.

Predictions are thought to be based on knowledge of the *functional relation* between the strength of a cause and the magnitude of an effect. For this reason, there is a large body of empirical research by decision scientists investigating how people learn functional relations (Slovic & Lichtenstein 1971, Klayman 1988). Much of this research, however, has been not been synthesized and integrated into coherent theory, and so this literature remains disconnected from mainstream cognitive psychology.

From a cognitive perspective, functions can be viewed as abstract concepts that summarize cause–effect relationships. Cognitive psychologists have made great progress developing theories of how people learn abstract concepts (see Estes 1994). However, most of this theoretical effort has been restricted to one simple type of concept learning task called *categorization*. It is unclear whether or not theories of category learning can be extended for application to function learning.

The purpose of this chapter is to develop a concept learning model that can account for results from both categorization and function learning tasks. The remainder of the chapter is organized as follows: Section II discusses similarities and differences between category- and function-learning tasks, Section III synthesizes some basic findings on function-learning, Section IV describes an artificial neural network model of category learning and extends this model to function learning, and Section V shows how the extended model reproduces the basic findings from function learning.

II. CATEGORY VERSUS FUNCTION LEARNING PARADIGMS

There is considerable overlap in the basic experimental paradigms used to investigate category and function learning. In both cases, subjects are presented several hundred training trials, each of which consists of (a) the presentation of a stimulus called the *cue* (denoted $x(t)$ on trial t), (b) a response by the subject called the *prediction* (denoted $y(t)$ on trial t) and (c) feedback indicating the correct response called the *criterion* (denoted $z(t)$ on trial t).

For example, Koh & Meyer (1991) trained subjects to learn how to map a tone duration (*cue*) into a movement magnitude (*criterion*). On each trial, a tone duration was presented, the subject made a motor movement, and then the subject was shown the correct motor movement. This example involves mapping one physical continuum (x = tone duration) into a different physical continuum (z = movement magnitude). It is not necessary to employ different physical continua for stimuli and responses. For example, Delosh et al. (1996) trained subjects to map one line length cue into another line length criterion, thus employing a common physical continuum for stimuli and responses. (See Figure 11.1). Other researchers (e.g. Naylor & Clark 1968) used numbers to display the cue and criterion magnitudes.

After subjects learn the cue-criterion mapping for a set of training pairs, they are tested during a transfer phase on new stimuli never seen during training. The transfer test ascertains whether or not subjects can use the newly-learned concepts to interpolate or extrapolate.

For both category and function learning tasks, the mapping from cues to criteria may be probabilistic. In category learning, for example, disease A could occur on 60 per cent of the trials and disease B could occur on 40 per cent of the trials on which the same exact symptom pattern appeared (e.g. Gluck & Bower 1988). In function learning, for

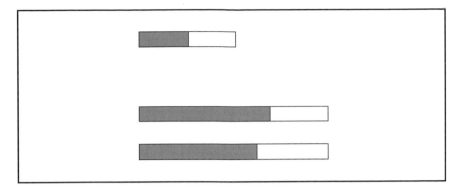

FIG. 11.1.   Illustration of a display of stimulus, response, and criteria feedback for a typical function learning task. First the stimulus bar on the left is displayed, second the response bar in the middle is drawn by the subject, and third the criterion bar on the right is displayed for feedback.

example, infection severity may be proportional to body temperature plus sum random error.

The cue patterns used in category-learning tasks are usually constructed from a small set of binary-valued features (e.g. fever, present or absent; cough, present or absent). The cues used in function learning tasks are constructed from a small set of continuously valued dimensions (e.g. body temperature in centigrade; white blood cell frequency). However, dimensional stimuli have been used in categorization experiments (e.g. Homa 1984, Nosofsky 1986, Ashby & Gott 1988), so this is not the critical property for distinguishing between category- and function-learning tasks.

The responses used in category-learning tasks are usually limited to a small number of nominal categories (e.g. heart disease present or absent). The responses used in function-learning tasks are usually an equally spaced subset of a continuum of criterion magnitudes (e.g. percentage of arterial blockage). However, numbers could be used as category labels (e.g. disease severity levels 1, 2, and 3), and so this is not sufficient for distinguishing between category- and function-learning tasks.

The crucial property for distinguishing category- from function-learning tasks is the nature of the cue–criterion mapping. In category learning, a discontinuous mapping is made from stimuli to categories. In function learning, a continuous function is used to map cues to criteria (i.e. $z(t) = F[x(t)]$ where F is a continuous function). For example, a discontinuous map jumps up or down at some point in an abrupt manner, whereas a continuous map changes gradually at each point in a smooth manner.

Another important difference between category- and function-learning tasks is the way that performance is measured. In category learning, performance is based on the percentage of correct responses. But this would not work in function learning, because responses may be technically incorrect but highly accurate. For example, if the prediction is 78 per cent arterial blockage and the criterion is 79 per cent, then the response is technically incorrect but highly accurate. So in function learning, performance is based on the mean absolute error (MAE) between the subject's prediction and the criterion. (Another measure, called the achievement index, is the correlation between the subject's prediction and the criterion).

III. SUMMARY OF BASIC FINDINGS ON SINGLE-CUE FUNCTION LEARNING

Although function-learning tasks may involve multidimensional stimulus cues (e.g. predict a student's grade point average based on both verbal and math Scholastic Aptitude Test scores), the majority of theoretical work (Carrol 1963, Brehmer 1974, Koh & Meyer 1991) has been limited to single cue tasks (e.g. predict a student's grade point average based on the total SAT score). Accordingly, this chapter is limited to a review of single cue experiments (see Klayman 1988, Slovic & Lichtenstein 1971, for more comprehensive reviews).

The ten basic principles summarized below provide a partial ordering of the difficulty of learning various types of functions from experience. These ten principles are generalizations of well-established experimental results that have been replicated across a variety of conditions.

Principle 1: Continuous functional relations are learned faster than arbitrary categorical relations

See Carrol 1963, Sniezek & Naylor 1978. The mapping from a stimulus set to a criterion set can be formed in two different ways: One is to use a continuous function to form the stimulus–criterion pairs (e.g. using a quadratic function); the second is to use a jagged function (produced by erratic pairings) of the same stimuli and criteria. Thus the stimulus set is identical in both mappings and so is the response set. The only difference is the continuity of the mapping. In this comparison, continuous mappings are learned faster than erratic mappings of the same stimuli and criteria. So far, this result has been obtained with positive linear, negative linear, and quadratic functions, but the results may hold for other continuous functions.

Principle 2: Increasing functions are learned faster than decreasing functions

See Brehmer 1971, 1973, 1974, Brehmer et al. 1974, Naylor & Clark 1968, Naylor & Domine 1981. A function is increasing if its slope (derivative) is always positive, and it is decreasing if its slope is always negative. More specifically, researchers have compared performance for positive and negative linear functions, and they have found that positive linear functions are learned much faster. This finding, however, may not be restricted to linear functions.

Principle 3: Monotonic functions are learned faster than non-monotonic functions

See Carrol 1963, Brehmer 1974, Brehmer et al. 1985, Brehmer et al. 1974, Byun 1995, Deane et al. 1972, Delosh 1995, Sheets & Miller 1974, Sniezek & Naylor 1978. Monotonic functions always increase, or always decrease, but never do both. Non-monotonic functions increase and decrease at different cue values and are generally more difficult to learn. For example, Delosh (1995) has shown that both linearly decreasing functions and exponentially increasing functions are learned more quickly than non-monotonic quadratic functions.

Principle 4: Cyclic functions are more difficult to learn than non-cyclic functions

See Byun 1995. A cyclic function, such as a sine or cosine function, periodically changes directions producing a repeating increasing–decreasing pattern. Non-cyclic functions, such as a quadratic function, do not produce a repeating up–down pattern. To distinguish cyclic from non-cyclic functions within a finite range of cue values, cyclic functions are defined as functions that contain at least two repetitions of an up–down pattern (or two repetitions of a down–up pattern). At this point, only one experiment has been conducted comparing a sine function and a quadratic function, but the results demonstrated such a highly robust difference, that we believe it is safe to conclude that cyclic functions are much more difficult to learn that non-cyclic functions.

Principle 5: Linearly increasing functions are learned faster than nonlinearly increasing functions

See Byun 1995, Delosh et al. 1996. Increasing non-linear functions such as power, exponential, logarithmic, or logistic, always increase, but the rate of increase changes as a function of the cue value. Generally, these non-linear increasing functions are more difficult to learn than linearly-increasing functions. It is important to note that this conclusion depends on the psycho-physical scales used to measure the stimuli and criteria.

For example, Koh & Meyer (1991) found superiority for linear functions only after using a logarithmic scale to measure the continua. Thus the scales used to measure the continua is a key factor for determining the order of difficulty of learning linear versus power functions.

Principle 6: Predictions made at the beginning of training correlate with a linear function

See Sawyer 1991, Summers et al. 1969. When subjects are given a "neutral" cover story, and then they are trained to learn a non-linear function, their responses at the beginning of training correlate most highly with those expected from a linear function. As training progresses, the correlation with the non-linear function steadily grows and exceeds the linear function. This result has been observed with S-shaped logistic functions, but it is likely to hold for a wider class.

Principle 7: Congruent cue labels improve performance

See Byun 1995, Koele 1980, Miller 1971, Muchinsky & Dudycha 1974, 1975, Sniezek 1986, Adelman 1981. The description of the cues elicits prior knowledge about the functional relation that is either congruent, incongruent, or uninformative. For example, suppose subjects are asked to learn a relationship between x = price and y = quality of merchandise (suggesting a positive relation), but then they are trained with a negative linear function. In this case, the cue labels would be incongruent with the training function. Generally, performance is best with congruent labels, and worst with incongruent labels. However, even with incongruent labels, subjects gradually adjust and learn the appropriate cue–criterion relationship.

Principle 8: Systematic training sequences facilitate learning of difficult functions

Byun (1995) and Delosh (1995) trained subjects on a function using either a systematically-increasing sequence of stimulus magnitudes during training, or a randomly-organized sequence of the same magnitudes. Training sequence had no effect on positive linear functions, but it facilitated learning of non-monotonic quadratic functions and cyclic functions, with systematic sequences producing slightly superior performance.

Principle 9: Performance on interpolation test stimuli is almost as accurate as performance on training stimuli

See Carrol 1963, Koh & Meyer 1991, Delosh et al. 1996. During the transfer test phase no feedback is provided, and new cue values are presented that never appeared during training. New transfer cue values that lie inside the range of training values are called *interpolation test stimuli*. On interpolation trials, subjects tend to choose new responses that fall in between the trained criterion values. Previous research with linear, power, exponential, and quadratic functions indicate that predictions on interpolation tests are almost as accurate as the training stimuli.

Principle 10: Subjects can extrapolate, but not as accurately as they interpolate

See Carrol 1963, Surber 1987, Delosh et al. 1996, Wagenaar & Sagaria 1975. An extrapolation test stimulus is a cue value that lies outside the range of the training values. Previous research with linear, exponential, and quadratic functions indicate that subjects generate extrapolation responses, that is responses outside the range of the training criteria values. Their extrapolations are in the appropriate direction with respect to the training function, however, these extrapolations do not come as close to the programmed function as interpolations.

Summary

The first five principles suggest the following tentative order for the difficulty of learning a functional relation from experience: cyclic > non-monotonic > monotonic decreasing > monotonic increasing > linear. Previous researchers have generally explained these findings in terms of prior knowledge or hypotheses about rules used to make predictions (Brehmer 1974, Sniezek 1986, Sawyer 1991). When standard instructions and cue labels are employed, subjects initially expect the cue–criterion relationship to follow a positive linear rule (Principle 6). However, these prior expectations can be modified by changes in prior instructions or by cue labels (Principle 7). The facilitation of learning by systematic as opposed to random stimulus sequences presumably results from the facilitation of hypothesis testing by using systematic sequences (Klayman 1988). Principle 10 has been used to argue that subjects learn abstract rules rather than simple stimulus–response associations (Brehmer 1974, Carrol 1963).

IV. COGNITIVE MODELS OF FUNCTION LEARNING

Theoretical requirements

The ten principles summarized earlier provide guidelines for constructing a model of function learning. However, additional general theoretical constraints must be met as well. First, the model must have the same learning power as humans. For example, a model that approximates all functions by a 3rd degree polynomial is insufficient, because it cannot approximate a cyclic function, which humans can learn (Byun 1995). Secondly, the model must have the same learning speed as humans. For example, a powerful non-linear hidden unit connectionistic network model that requires several thousand feedback trials to learn a simple linear relation is unreasonable because humans can learn this in much less than a hundred trials. Third, we wish to formulate a model of function learning that is consistent with category-learning theory. In other words, we seek a common theoretical explanation for category- and function-learning. Presumably, humans rely on a single common learning process to learn stimulus–response mappings, whether or not the mapping is continuous. There are two quite different approaches to the construction of a model of function learning: one is a *rule-based approach*, and the other is an *associative-learning approach*.

Rule-based Learning Approach

According to this approach (Brehmer 1974, Carrol 1963, Koh & Meyer 1991), the rules that subjects use to make predictions are represented by a linear combination of a basis set of functions:

$$y(t) = b_0 f_0[(t)] + b_1 f_1[x(t)] + b_2 f_2[x(t)] + ... + b_k f_k[x(t)]\ \textbf{(11.1)}$$

The most common choice for the basis set of functions is the polynomial basis, $f_k[x] = x^k$, but other bases are possible such as log polynomial, Fourier, Gaussian, or wavelet. The basis set must be sufficiently powerful to closely approximate all smooth continuous functions.

According to the rule-based approach, learning is represented by a search for the appropriate choice of coefficients $(b_0, b_1, ..., b_k)$ to fit the training function $F[x]$. For example, Brehmer (1974) assumed a cubic polynomial basis, and he assumed that subjects test a linear hypothesis first, followed by a quadratic hypothesis, followed by a cubic hypothesis. Alternatively, Koh and Meyer (1991) assumed a log polynomial basis, and they assumed that subjects gradually adjust all of the coefficients $(b_0, b_1, ..., b_k)$ in a trial by trial manner in the direction of minimizing a loss function.

One problem with these rule-based models is the lack of specification of the trial-by-trial search process. For example, Brehmer (1974) never specified exactly how hypotheses were rejected, nor how the parameters for testing a hypothesis were chosen. A similar shortcoming applies to the Koh & Meyer (1991) model. A second problem is that they do not extrapolate in the same manner as humans.

Delosh et al. (1996) examined the extrapolations produced by polynomial and log polynomial models for linear, quadratic, and exponential training functions, and found that these models failed to reproduce the same pattern of extrapolations as humans. For example, when trained with a negatively-accelerated increasing exponential function, these models generate non-monotonic relations at the upper end of the extrapolation region, contrary to the humans who continued to produce monotonic increasing relations in this region. A third problem is that they are not built from assumptions consistent with current research on category learning. These rule-based models were developed independent of research on category learning, and so they fail to explain category and function learning within a common theoretical framework.

In view of these limitations of rule-based models, the remainder of this chapter will focus on *associative-learning* models (ALMs). This is not to claim that rule-based models can be completely eliminated. We simply leave the question concerning the construction of a successful learning algorithm for them open for future research.

Associative-learning approach

The following associative-learning model is an extension of the artificial neural network model of Knapp & Anderson (1984) and the exemplar-based connectionist model of Kruschke (1992). The latter model is currently a highly successful model of category learning (see Nosofsky & Kruschke 1992, for a rigorous evaluation). The main advantage of this model is that it is built from assumptions that are consistent with the major findings on category learning. Another advantage of this model is that it employs a simple yet powerful learning algorithm. ALM makes the following assumptions (see Figure 11.2).

Assumption 1.   The physical stimulus, $x(t)$, produces a perceptual image represented by a *distribution of activation* across a set of n input nodes:

$$\{x_1, x_2, ..., x_i, ..., x_n\}, \ x_1 < x_2 <... < x_i <... < x_n \ \textbf{(11.2)}$$

Each input node, x_i, corresponds to a real number representing a potential stimulus value, and the index i represents the rank order of the node value. When a cue value, $x(t)$, is presented, it activates input node x_i from the set of n input nodes according to a Gaussian similarity function:

$$a_i[x(t)] = 1 / exp\{ (x_i - \psi_x[x\ (t)]) \ / \ \sigma_x\}_2 \ \textbf{(11.3)}$$

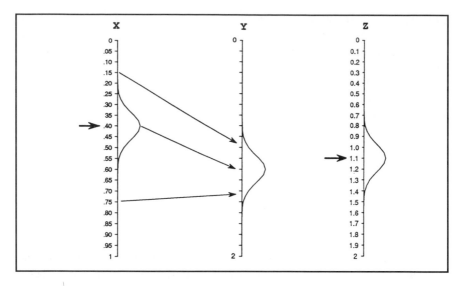

FIG. 11.2. ¹ Illlustration of ALM. The perception of the stimulus is represented by the distribution of activation on the far left. This is mapped onto the output nodes by associations indicated by the arrows (only a few of the many are shown). The subjective response is represented by the distribution of activation shown in the middle. Finally, the perception of the criterion feedback is represented by the distribution of activation on the far right.

The psycho-physical function $\psi_x[x\,(t)]$ represents a subjective scaling of the physical stimulus (e.g. ψ is often approximated by a power function, $\psi(x) = \psi x^\beta$, see Stevens 1961). The parameter σ_x is used to determine the generalization gradient around each input node. For example, in Figure 11.2, the perception of the cue value $x(t) = 40$ is represented by a Gaussian distribution on the left centred at $\psi_x(40) = (0.01) \times 40 = 0.40$, with a standard deviation equal to $\sigma_x = 0.05$.

Assumption 2.   The perceptual image of the criterion value, $z(t)$, is represented by a *distribution of activation* across a set of m criterion nodes,

$$\{z_1,\, z_2,\, ...,\, z_j,\, ...,\, z_m\},\, z_1 < z_2 < ... < z_j < ... < z_m \quad \textbf{(11.4)}$$

Each criterion node, z_j, is a real number, corresponding to a potential response category. When the criterion value, $z(t)$, is presented on trial t, it activates criterion node z_j according to a Gaussian similarity function:

$$c_j[z(t)] = 1/exp\{ (z_j - \psi_z[z(t)])/\sigma_z \}^2 \quad \textbf{(11.5)}$$

In Figure 11.2, the perception of the criterion value $z(t) = 110$ is represented by a Gaussian distribution on the right centred at $\psi_z(110) = (0.01) \times 110 = 1.10$ with a standard deviation equal to $\sigma_z = 0.05$.

Assumption 3. The subjective image of the response, $r(t)$, is represented by a *distribution of activation* across a set of m output nodes:

$$\{r_1, r_2, ..., r_j, ..., r_m\}, \, r_1 < r_2 < ... < r_j < ... < r_m \text{ (11.6)}$$

The activation of output node, r_j, represents the subject's belief that category j is the correct response category. In Figure 11.2, the distribution of output activation in the middle is centred at a response node corresponding to a magnitude of 1.20.

Assumption 4. Each input node x_i is connected to each output node r_j by a weight $w_{ij}(t)$ representing the association between the pair of input and output nodes after t trials of training. The activation pattern distributed across the n input nodes is mapped by the $(m \cdot n)$ connection weights into an activation pattern distributed across the m response nodes. The response node r_j from the set of m response nodes is activated according to the linear associative map:

$$e_j[x(t)] = w_{1j}(t)a_1[x(t)] + w_{2j}(t)a_2[x(t)] + ... + w_{nj}(t)a_n[x(t)] \text{ (11.7)}$$

In Figure 11.2, the arrows indicate a few of the many associations from the inputs to the outputs.

Assumption 5. The distribution of activation across the m criterion nodes provides the feedback for updating the connection weights. The weight, $w_{ij}(t)$, connecting input node x_i to output node r_j is updated on trial t according to the following delta learning rule:

$$w_{ij}(t) = w_{ij}(t-1) + \alpha \cdot a_i[x(t)] \cdot \{c_j[z(t)] - e_j[x(t)]\} \text{ (11.8)}$$

Assumption 6. Prior knowledge is represented by the initial connection weights existing before training and evoked by task instructions, cue labels, and cover stories (cf. Choi et al. 1993). The initial connection weight between input node x_i and output node r_j, is symbolized $w_{ij}(0)$. Two different assumptions concerning the initial weights are examined in the simulations that follow. The first is called the *no-prior-knowledge-assumption*, which is obtained by setting $w_{ij}(0)$ equal to a value randomly sampled from a normal distribution with zero mean. The second is called the *positive-linear-prior-knowledge-*

assumption, which is obtained by teaching the network a positive linear relation prior to experience with the training function. For example, if the initial weights are set to $w_{ij}(0) = 1$ for $i = j$, and zero otherwise, then the network reproduces the identity function, $y = x$.

These six assumptions complete the description of the associative learning process. However, the assumptions concerning response selection have not been made explicit. At this point two different sets of assumptions are introduced: the first set describes a simple ratio rule for selecting responses, and the second set describes a more sophisticated linear interpolation extrapolation response rule.

Ratio response rule

According to previous category learning theories (e.g. Kruschke 1992), the response category is selected probabilistically according to a ratio rule. The probability of choosing output node r_j is assumed to be equal to:

$$Pr[r_j \mid x(t)] = e_j[x(t)] \; / \; \Sigma_{k=1,m} \, e_k[x(t)]. \quad \textbf{(11.9)}$$

The output node r_j is a subjective scale value that needs to be located on the physical criterion scale to produce the observed response, $y(t)$, on trial t. Presumably the subject does this by choosing the physical response value that gives rise to the subjective image, r_j. Mathematically, this is equivalent to taking the inverse of the psycho-physical scaling function to produce the observed response:

$$y(t) = \psi_z^{-1}(r_j). \quad \textbf{(11.10)}$$

This implies that the mean prediction to cue value $x(t) = x_i$ equals:

$$\mu\,(x_i) = \Sigma_{j=1,m} \, Pr[r_j \mid x_i] \cdot \psi_z^{-1}\,(r_j). \quad \textbf{(11.11)}$$

Linear interpolation–extrapolation response rule

Delosh et al. (1996) recently proposed a new model for response selection in function-learning tasks. The essential idea is that predictions are constructed from a linear interpolation–extrapolation rule (see, e.g. Figure 11.3).

First, the transfer test cue, $x(t)$, is matched to one of the previously experienced training values. For example, suppose that the new test cue, $x(t)$, is matched to the previous training value x_i. Consider the case where $x(t) < x_i$, and there is another training value x_{i-1} immediately below x_i. Then these two training values, $x_{i-1} < x_i$, are used to retrieve two outputs, $y(x_{i-1})$ and $y(x_i)$, respectively. Finally,

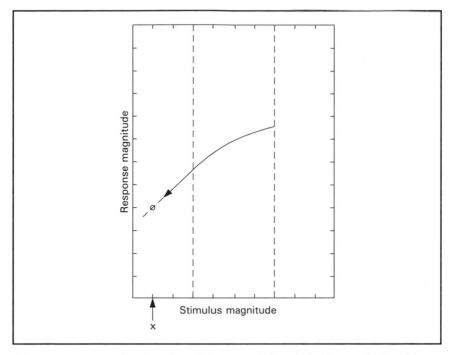

FIG. 11.3.   Illustration of the linear interpolation–extrapolation rule. In this example, the training stimuli on the right are used to form a line that extrapolates down to the left to produce the prediction for the test stimulus indicated by the "x" on the horizontal axis.

the subject's prediction, $y(t)$, for the transfer test cue $x(t)$, is constructed by linear interpolation:

$$y(t) = y(x_{i-1}) + \{[y(x_i) - y(x_{i-1})]/ \; (x_i - x_{i-1})\} \cdot [x_i - x(t)]. \quad \textbf{(11.12a)}$$

If $x(t) < x_i$, and there is no other training stimulus below x_i, then the prediction is linearly extrapolated:

$$y(t) = y(x_i) + \{[y(x_{i+1}) - (x_i)]/ \; (x_{i+1} - x_i)\} \cdot [x(t)\text{-}x_i]. \quad \textbf{(11.12b)}$$

If $x(t) > x_i$, and there is another training stimulus x_{i+1} above x_i, then the prediction is linearly interpolated:

$$y(t) = y(x_i) + \{[y(x_{i+1}) - (x_i)]/ \; (x_{i+1} - x_i)\} \cdot [x(t)\text{-}x_i]. \quad \textbf{(11.12c)}$$

If $x(t) > x_i$, and there is no other training stimulus above x_i, then the prediction is linearly extrapolated:

$y(t) = y(x_i) + \{[y(x_i) - y(x_{i-1})]/ (x_i - x_{i-1})\} \cdot [x(t)-x_i]$ (**11.12d**).

The probability of retrieving the output node $\psi[y(x_i)] = r_j$ using x_i as the retrieval cue is given by Equation 11.9, after substituting x_i for $x(t)$. The mean of $y(t)$ conditioned on matching $x(t)$ to x_i, denoted $\gamma(x_i)$, is obtained from Equation 11.12 by substituting $\mu(x_i)$ for $y(x_i)$ in the equation, where $\mu(x_i)$ is defined in Equation 11.11.

The new cue $x(t)$ is matched to an old training value x_i according to the following process. Training stimuli are identified by the learner as input nodes that produce a strong familiarity response. The familiarity of input node x_i is assumed to be determined by the maximum output activation produced by the input value $x(t)=x$:

$f_i(t) = max[e_1(x), e_2(x), ..., e_m(x)]$ (**11.13**)

(Note: Equation 11.13 is computed with $w_{ij}(0) = 0$ so that prior knowledge is not confused with training experience.) The strength of match of the new cue $x(t)$ to input node x_i, is determined by the product of familiarity and similarity:

$s_i[x(t)] = f_i(t) / exp\{(x_i - \psi_x[x(t)]) / \sigma_s\}^2$ (**11.14**)

where the similarity parameter, σ_s, is an unknown parameter. Finally, the probability of matching input cue $x(t)$ to input node x_i is determined by the ratio rule:

$p_i[x(t)] = s_i[x(t)] / \sum_{k=1,n} s_k[x(t)]$ (**11.15**)

This implies that the mean prediction to cue $x(t)$ is:

$E[y(t)|x(t)] = \sum_{i=1,n} p_i[x(t)] \cdot \gamma(x_i)$ (**11.16**)

In sum, the ratio-response rule uses Equations 11.9 and 11.11 to determine the mean prediction, while the linear interpolation-extrapolation response rule uses Equations 11.12, 11.13, 11.14, 11.15 and 11.16 to determine the mean prediction. The ALM in conjunction with the linear interpolation-extrapolation rule is called by Delosh et al. (1996) the *EXtrapolation Association Model (EXAM)*.

Simulation procedure

ALM involves only three unknown parameters: the generalization gradient for the physical continuum used to display the stimuli (σ_x in Equation 11.6); the generalization gradient for the physical continuum used to display the criteria (σ_z in Equation 11.7); and the learning rate (α in Equation 11.8). The same learning rate ($\alpha = 0.07$) and the same two generalization gradients ($\sigma_x = \sigma_z = 0.05$) were used in all of the simulations reported below. These parameter values were selected to reproduce all of the qualitative aspects of the basic findings, except for the results involving interpolation and extrapolation. The linear interpolation–extrapolation response rule requires an additional generalization gradient parameter (σ_s in Equation 11.14), which was set equal to $\sigma_s = 0.10$.

Several other specifications were necessary for the computer simulations. First, it was necessary to specify the psycho-physical functions, $\psi_x(x)$, $\psi_z(x)$. The simulations reported below were based on experiments that employed line lengths to physically display the stimuli and criteria. Past research has shown that the psycho-physical function for line lengths is approximately a linear function (at least within the limited range of magnitudes used in the experiments that were simulated). The following psycho-physical functions were used for all of the simulations:

$$\psi_x(x) = x/[max(x) - min(x)]$$
$$\psi_z(z) = z/[max(x) - min(x)]$$

where $max(x)$ represents the maximum cue value, and $min(x)$ represents the minumum cue value used in an experiment. This normalizes stimulus magnitudes so that $\psi_x(x)$ ranges from 0.0 to 1.0.

Next the input nodes were chosen to range from 0.0 to 1.0 in 0.01 step units {0.00, 0.01, 0.02, 0.03, . . ., 0.99, 1.0}, providing a dense coverage of the entire range of stimuli. To cover the criteria nodes, a wider range of nodes was employed: {0, 0.01, 0.02, 0.03, . . ., 2.99, 3.0}.

All of the simulations employed the same stimulus magnitudes and number of training trials as were used in the actual experiments. This was essential for reproducing the observed results. Most of the experiments employed randomly ordered stimulus sequences. Unless noted otherwise, the stimulus sequence used in the simulated training was also randomly ordered. The results were robust across different random orders.

V. REPRODUCING THE BASIC FINDINGS OF FUNCTION-LEARNING RESEARCH

The following presentation provides a constructive approach to model building. We begin with the simplest possible version of the ALM, and only introduce complexities as they are demanded by the data. This constructive approach is useful for identifying the importance of each new additional assumption of the model (see also Lamberts, this volume).

Principle 1

Carrol (1963) argued that associative learning models of function learning (such as ALM described earlier) can be ruled out because they fail to explain why continuous functional relations are easier to learn than arbitrary categorical relations. Carrol (1963) did not actually describe any specific associative-learning model, so this claim remains just a conjecture. It is elementary to prove that this conjecture is true for ALM when there is no generalization ($\sigma_x \to 0$). Thus it is interesting to see to what extent this criticism holds when generalization occurs across stimuli (e.g. $\sigma_x = 0.05$).

Carrol (1963) compared two groups of subjects: one trained with a continuous linear function, and another trained with an erratic function of the same stimuli and criteria as the linear function. Carrol (1963) also trained another two groups: one trained with a continuous non-monotonic quadratic function, and another trained with an erratic function of the same stimuli and criteria as the quadratic function.

ALM was trained on the same stimulus–criterion pairs and using the same number of training trials as used by Carrol (1963). The simplest possible version of ALM was employed. In particular, the ratio response rule was used to generate the model predictions and no prior knowledge was assumed. Table 11.1 shows the MAE, averaged across training, obtained from the human learners by Carrol (1963) in comparison with the computer simulation results obtained by ALM. The last two columns present a comparison of the continuous condition with the erratic control for linear and quadratic functions.

TABLE 11.1
Mean absolute error for each condition of Carrol (1963)

Function	Continuous Condition	Erratic Control
Human Data		
Linear	0.03	0.94
Quadratic	0.58	1.29
Simulated Data		
Linear	0.03	0.21
Quadratic	0.13	0.29

The human data was obtained by first computing the absolute error between each subject's prediction and the correction criterion value, and then averaging across subjects. The simulated data was obtained by first computing the average, and then computing the absolute error between the mean prediction and the criterion. The latter procedure produces smaller absolute errors by eliminating individual subject response variability.

As can be seen in Table 11.1, ALM reproduces the correct ordering of MAE across the four conditions. In particular, ALM reproduces the difference between the continuous and erratic functions. This results from the use of an adequate generalization gradient (e.g. $\sigma_x = 0.05$). If the generalization gradient is too narrow (e.g. $\sigma_x = 0.01$), then the ALM no longer produces any difference between the continuous and erratic conditions, just as Carrol (1963) claimed. Thus, the ALM with no prior knowledge, a ratio-response rule, and an adequate generalization gradient is sufficient for explaining Principle 1.

Principle 2

The first simulation did not employ any prior knowledge. However, this assumption fails to account for the fact that decreasing functions are more difficult to learn than increasing functions. If there is no prior knowledge, it is elementary to prove that ALM predicts no difference in rate of learning for decreasing as compared to increasing linear functions (when the same stimulus and criterion sets are used). Thus it is interesting to see to what extent that this problem can be eliminated by incorporating positive linear prior knowledge into the initial connection weights.

Naylor & Clark (1968) compared two groups of subjects: one trained with a positive linear regression equation: $z = 40 + 0.80 \cdot x + error$; and another trained with a negative linear regression equation: $z = 90 - 0.80 \cdot x + error$. The univariate distributions for the stimuli and the criteria were identical across the two conditions. The ALM was trained with the same stimuli and criteria using the ratio-response rule. The initial weights were set to reproduce the identity relation, $y = x$, before experiencing the training function.

Figure 11.4 shows the human results obtained from Naylor & Clark (1968) and Figure 11.5 shows the simulation results from ALM with prior knowledge. Each figure shows the achievement index (the correlation between the prediction and the criterion) plotted as a function of training block. The top curve in each figure represents the positive linear condition, and the bottom curve represents the negative linear condition. Thus, the ALM with adequate generalization, ratio-response rule, and positive linear prior knowledge is sufficient for explaining Principles 1 and 2.

Principles 3 and 4

Recall from the first simulation that even when there is no prior knowledge, the ALM predicts faster learning for linear as compared to quadratic functions (see Table 11.1). It is fairly obvious that the use of positive linear prior knowledge can only facilitate this advantage of

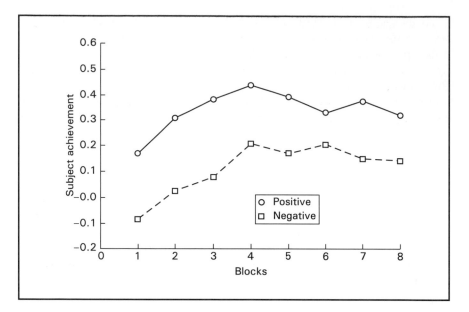

FIG. 11.4.   Achievement index (correlation between prediction and criterion) plotted as a function of training for the positive and negative linear functions. Data from Naylor & Clark (1968).

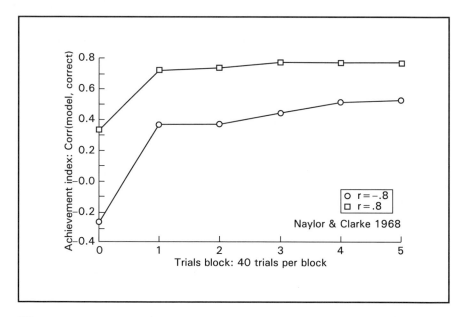

FIG. 11.5.   Achievement index (correlation between prediction and criterion) plotted as a function of training for the positive and negative linear functions. Data from ALM simulation (Naylor & Clark 1968).

positive linear functions over quadratic functions. However, it is not clear that this prior knowledge will produce any advantage for quadratic functions over cyclic functions. Thus it is of interest to see to what extent the ALM can reproduce the differences between quadratic and cyclic functions.

Byun (1995) examined positive linear, non-monotonic quadratic, and cyclic functions as shown in Figure 11.6. The figure shows the criterion plotted as a function of the stimulus magnitude, with a separate curve for each training function. The ALM was trained on the same stimulus –criterion pairs for the same amount of training using the ratio-response rule. The initial weights were set to reproduce the identity relation, $y = x$, as in the previous simulation. The empirical results from Byun (1995) are shown in Figure 11.7, and the simulation results are shown in Figure 11.8. Each figure shows the MAE plotted as a function of training block. As can be seen by comparing Figures 11.7 and 11.8, the ALM reproduces the difficulty ordering: cyclic > non-monotonic > positive linear.

Principle 5

So far, the ALM has succeeded in reproducing the order of learning difficulty for functions that are categorically different in form (e.g. increasing versus decreasing, monotonic versus non-monotonic). A

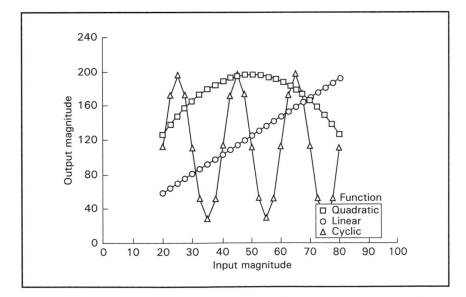

FIG. 11.6.   Criterion plotted as a function of stimulus magnitude for the positive linear, quadratic, and cyclic functions examined by Byun (1995).

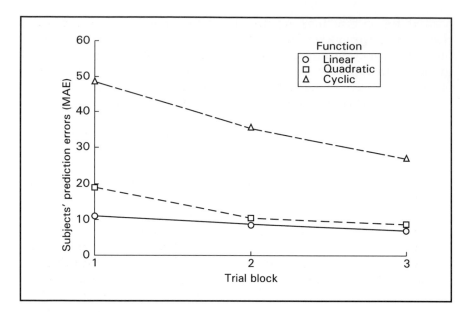

FIG. 11.7.   Mean absolute error plotted as a function of training block separately for the positive linear, quadratic, and cyclic functions. Data from Byun (1995).

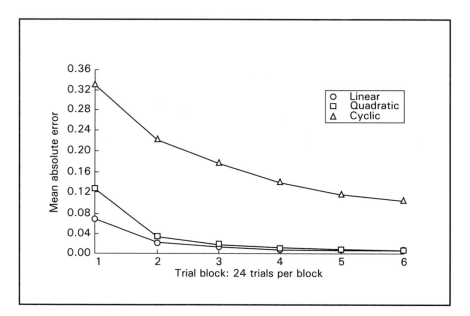

FIG. 11.8.   Mean absolute error plotted as a function of training block separately for the positive linear, quadratic, and cyclic functions. Data from ALM simulation (Byun, Experiment 1).

greater challenge is to see whether or not ALM can reproduce the order of learning difficulty for functions that differ in more subtle quantitative forms. Byun (1995) compared five different monotonically increasing functions as shown in Figure 11.9: positive linear, negatively accelerated power, positively accelerated power, logarithmic, and logistic. The criterion is plotted as a function of the stimulus magnitude, with a separate curve for each of the five functions. The order of learning difficulty obtained from these five functions is shown in Figure 11.10a: logistic > logarithmic > positively accelerated power > negatively accelerated power > positive linear.

When the version of ALM described in the previous two simulations was applied to this data set, the model failed to reproduce the observed order. The main reason was the choice of prior knowledge. In the previous two simulations, the initial weights were set to reproduce the simple positive linear relation, $y = x$. This is a rather crude approximation, but it worked well enough for the categorically different functions that were examined in the previous simulations. However, to capture the subtle differences among the functions shown in Figure 11.9, it is necessary to select the initial weights more carefully. A better selection for the initial weights is to use a *proportional prior-knowledge* assumption, i.e. the minimum cue value is initially mapped onto the

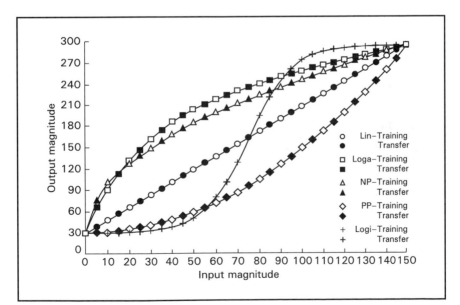

FIG. 11.9.   Criterion plotted as a function of stimulus magnitude for the positive linear (PL), negatively accelerated power (NP), positively accelerated power (PP), logarithmic (LN), and logistic (LG) functions examined by Byun (1995).

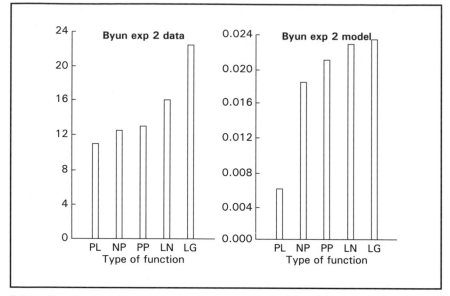

FIG. 11.10.   Mean absolute error produced by each type of function. Panel a on left is data from Byun (1995). Panel b on right is data from ALM simulation. PL = positive linear, NP = negatively accelerated power, PP = positively accelerated power, LN = logarithmic, LG = logistic.

minimum criterion value, the maximum cue value is initially mapped onto the maximum criterion value, and intermediate stimuli are initially mapped proportionally as follows:

$$[y - min\ (z)]/[max\ (z)\ -min\ (z)\ ] = [x\text{-}min(x)]/[max(x) - min(x)] \quad (11.17)$$

The ALM with this proportional prior knowledge assumption reproduces the observed order as shown in Figure 11.10b.

It is informative to examine the reasons why the logarithmic and logistic functions are so difficult to learn compared to the other functions. Figure 11.11 shows the mean predictions (averaged across subjects) as a function of stimulus magnitude produced by the human learners in comparison with the training function, as reported in Byun (1995). As can be seen in the figure, the logarithmic and logistic functions contain more curvature. The human learners underestimate concave (negatively accelerated) sections of these functions, and overestimate convex (positively accelerated) sections of the function. Figures 11.12a and 11.12b shows the predictions produced by ALM in comparison with the training function, for the logarithmic and logistic functions. As can be seen in Figures 11.12a and b, ALM produces the same pattern of errors

– overestimating concave and underestimating convex. This is because of the fact that the generalization gradient of the ALM causes the model to produce an interpolated prediction.

Principles 6 and 7

As illustrated in the three previous simulations, prior knowledge is directly built into the model by the selection of the initial weights. Many so called "neutral" cover stories and cue labels tend to evoke initial weights that conform to the positive linear prior-knowledge assumption. However, cover stories and cue labels can be constructed that evoke quite different initial expectations or initial weights. For example, if subjects are asked to learn a relation between x = sedative amount and z = patient activity, then this would tend to evoke a negative linear set of initial weights, such as for example, $w_{ij}(0) = 1$ if i = -j, and zero otherwise. In

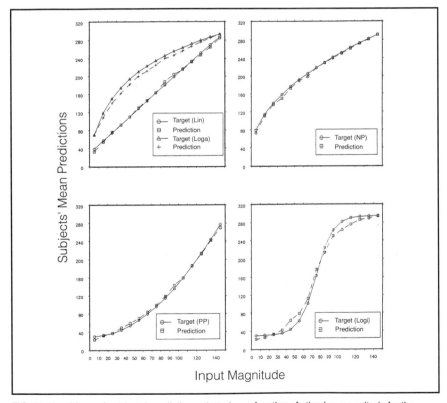

FIG. 11.11.   Mean of subjects' predictions plotted as a function of stimulus magnitude for the logarithmic (top left), negatively accelerated power (top right), positively accelerated power (bottom left), and for the logistic function (bottom right). The training function criterion values are also plotted in each figure.

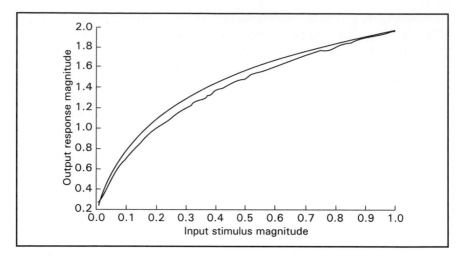

FIG. 11.12a   Predictions of ALM plotted as a function of stimulus magnitude for the logarithmic functions.

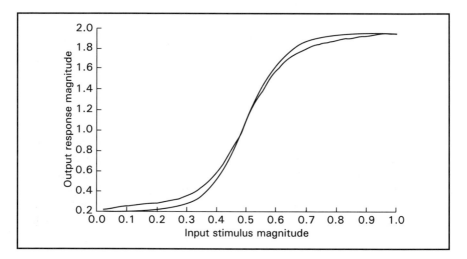

FIG. 11.12b   Predictions of ALM plotted as a function of stimulus magnitude for the logistic function.

this case, the learning curves shown in Figure 11.5 would be produced, except that the top curve would now represent the negative linear training condition (congruent with the prior knowledge).

Principle 8
The effect of systematic as compared to random training sequences provides a very strong challenge to the ALM because there is no specific

mechanism in the model designed to produce such effects. Thus it is quite interesting to see whether or not the ALM can account for the improvement in learning produced by systematic sequences.

Delosh (1995) investigated the order of learning difficulty produced by negative linear as compared to non-monotonic quadratic functions. In addition, he examined the effects of training with systematic versus random stimulus training sequences. The basic results were that negative linear functions were easier to learn than quadratic functions, and furthermore systematic sequences produced better performance than random sequences. The ALM was trained on the same stimulus magnitudes and training sequences as used by Delosh (1995), using the response-ratio rule and the positive linear prior-knowledge assumption. The MAE for each type of function and training sequence produced by the simulation are shown in Table 11.2. As can be seen in the table, the ALM yields better performance with negative linear as compared to quadratic functions, and also there is an advantage produced by training ALM with systematic as compared to random sequences.

The systematic training advantage for ALM is a generally important demonstration. One might not expect that artificial neural networks would be influenced by the organization of the training sequence. Indeed, the advantage of systematic over random training sequences has heretofore been assumed to implicate a hypothesis testing process of function learning. It is now clear that training sequence effects can emerge as well from associative learning processes.

Principles 9 and 10

A number of theorists (Carrol 1963, Brehmer 1974) have argued that the strongest evidence favouring rule-based models over associative-learning models is obtained by examining extrapolation performance. Abstract rules provide systematic guidelines for extrapolating beyond experience, whereas simple associations between stimuli and criteria experienced during training provide no mechanism for extrapolation outside the range of experience (Delosh et al. 1996). This criticism may not apply to ALM because it allows for generalization on both the stimulus and criteria continua, thus it is of interest to see the extent to which ALM can account for interpolation and extrapolation performance.

TABLE 11.2
Mean absolute error produced by ALM for each condition of Delosh (1995)

Function Form	Random Sequence	Systematic Sequence
Negative Linear	0.033	0.028
Quadratic	0.044	0.031

Delosh et al. (1996) trained subjects on the middle range of stimulus magnitudes for linear, exponential, and non-monotonic quadratic functions. Following this training, they later tested subjects on new interpolation test stimuli (new values inside the training range), and new extrapolation test stimuli (new values outside the training range). The ALM was trained on the same stimulus magnitudes and training trials as used by Delosh et al. (1996), using the ratio response rule, and using initial weights that reproduced the simple identity relation ($y = x$). Figure 11.13 shows MAE plotted as a function of training produced by the human subjects, and Figure 11.14 shows the corresponding plot produced by the ALM. Once again, the ALM reproduced the observed order of learning difficulty (quadratic > exponential > positive linear).

Figures 11.15 and 11.16 illustrate the predictions of the ALM for the positive linear training condition. Note that at this point, the predictions are based on the ratio-response rule. Figure 11.15 shows what happens when the generalization gradient is too tight (e.g. $\sigma = 0.01$), and Figure 11.16 illustrates the results for a wider generalization gradient (e.g. $\sigma = 0.05$). The top straight line in both figures represents the linear training function ($z = .3 + 2.2{\cdot}x$, using the normalized stimulus scale). The bottom straight line in both figures represents the prior knowledge identity relation ($y = x$). The jagged line in Figure 11.15 represents the

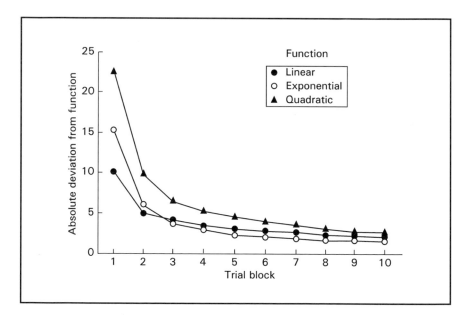

FIG. 11.13.   Mean absolute error plotted as a function of training block separately for the positive linear, exponential, and quadratic functions. Data from Delosh et al. (1996).

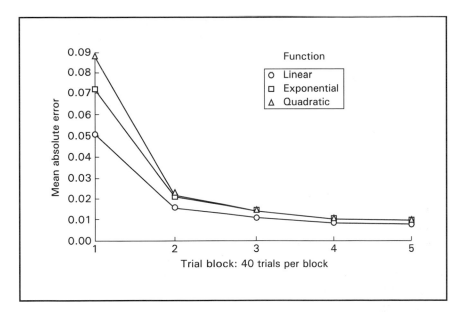

FIG. 11.14.   Mean absolute error plotted as a function of training block separately for the positive linear, exponential, and quadratic functions. Data from ALM simulation (Delosh, Experiment 1).

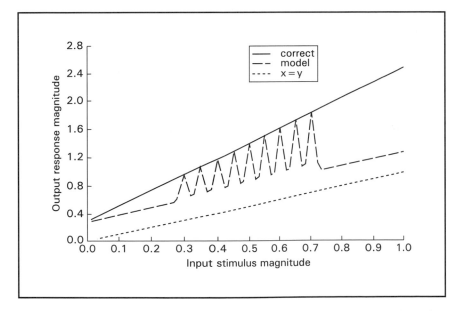

FIG. 11.15.   Predictions produced by ALM plotted as a function of stimulus magnitude for the linear function using a tight generalization gradient.

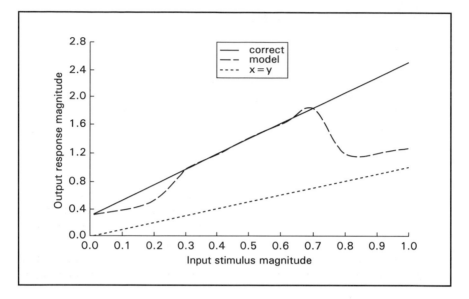

FIG. 11.16.   Predictions produced by ALM plotted as a function of stimulus magnitude for the linear function using a wider generalization gradient.

predictions generated by ALM with no generalization. The training stimulus values produce the predictions by ALM that peak and intersect with the training function criterion values. The sudden drops above and below each peak indicate a failure of the ALM to interpolate when there is no generalization. The smooth curve in Figure 11.16 represents the predictions of ALM with generalization. Now ALM produces appropriate interpolation responses, but it still fails to extrapolate appropriately in the extreme lower and upper transfer test regions – here the predictions of ALM fall back toward the prior knowledge identity function.

In summary, if a ratio-response rule is employed along with a sufficiently wide generalization gradient, then ALM can interpolate but it cannot extrapolate. Thus the criticism of associative learning models by rule-based theorists appears to be partly right. But not entirely, because ALM can be salvaged by adding the linear interpolation–extrapolation response rule. Figure 11.17 illustrates the extrapolation performance by humans in the left panel, and by EXAM in the right panel for the exponential function condition. Figure 11.18 shows the corresponding results produced by a polynomial rule-based model (Equation 11.1). As can be seen in these figures, the extended version of ALM (called EXAM) provides a better account of the pattern of human extrapolation than the rule-based models (see Delosh et al. 1996, for more details).

CONCLUSIONS

The purpose of this chapter was to begin building a bridge between theoretical work on category learning and function learning. Category learning and function learning appear to be closely related, and it seems useful to determine the extent to which it is possible to formulate a common theoretical explanation for both domains of research. Towards this aim, an artificial neural network model originally developed for category learning was extended to make it applicable to function learning. The most important extension was the addition of a linear interpolation–extrapolation response rule. With this extension, the model represents a hybrid or integrated approach to associative and rule-based models. Prior knowledge and learning are represented by simple associations, but rules are evoked during test to construct a sophisticated response from simple associations.

Several important ideas were discovered from this theoretical endeavour. First, artificial neural network models need to carefully

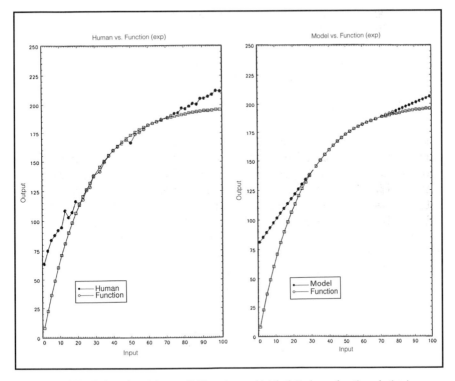

FIG. 11.17.   Predictions from humans (left) and EXAM (right) plotted as a function of stimulus magnitude for the exponential training function.

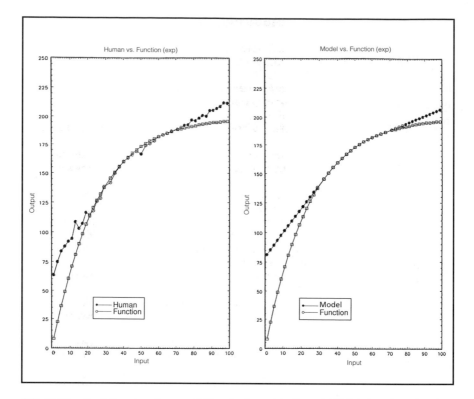

FIG. 11.18.   Predictions from humans (left) and polynomial rule model (right) plotted as a function of stimulus magnitude for the exponential training function.

match the initial associations of the network with the prior knowledge evoked by the task instructions. For example, prior knowledge was necessary to account for the fine grain differences in the difficulty of learning various types of non-linear increasing functions. Secondly, artificial neural network models need to use sophisticated rules to construct responses from the output information retrieved by the network. For example, a linear response rule based on retrieved outputs was necessary to account for extrapolation behaviour in function learning. Thirdly, artificial neural network learning models are sensitive to the organization of the training sequence. For example, a model trained with systematically-increasing stimulus magnitudes produced faster learning than a model trained with randomly-ordered stimulus magnitudes.

Ten basic principles of function learning were synthesized from the empirical literature, and we evaluated the extent to which the model could reproduce these principles. We were successful in finding a common set of model parameters that reproduced all ten principles. (This does not imply that the predictions are insensitive to parameters; on the contrary, the predictions vary dramatically as a function of the generalization gradients.) We conclude that the model provides an excellent starting point for generating simple and parsimonious reproductions of the basic facts from both category and function learning.

REFERENCES

Adelman, L. 1981. The influence of formal, substantive, and contextual task properties on the relative effectiveness of different forms of feedback in multiple-cue probability learning tasks. *Organizational Behavior and Human Performance* **27**, 423–42.

Ashby, F. G. & R. E. Gott 1988. Decision rules in the perception and categorization of multidimensional stimuli. *Journal of Experimental Psychology: Learning, Memory, and Cognition* **14**, 33–53.

Brehmer, B. 1971. Subjects' ability to use functional rules. *Psychonomic Science* **24**, 259–60.

Brehmer, B. 1973. Single-cue probability learning as a function of the sign and magnitude of the correlation between cue and criterion. *Organizational Behavior and Human Performance* **9**, 377–95.

Brehmer, B. 1974. Hypotheses about relations between scaled variables in the learning of probabilistic inference tasks. *Organizational Behavior and Human Performance* **11**, 1–27.

Brehmer, B., H. Alm, L. E. Warg 1985. Learning and hypothesis testing in probabilistic inference tasks. *Scandinavian Journal of Psychology* **26**, 305–13.

Brehmer, B., J. Kuylenstierna, J-E. Liljergren 1974. Effects of function form and cue validity on the subjects' hypothesis in probabilistic inference tasks. *Organizational Behavior and Human Performance* **11**, 338–54.

Byun, E. 1995. *Interaction between prior knowledge and type of nonlinear relationship on function learning.* PhD dissertation, Psychology Dept., Purdue University.

Carrol, J. D. 1963. *Functional learning: the learning of continuous functional mappings relating stimulus and response continua.* Research Bulletin RB–63–26, Educational Testing Service, Princeton, New Jersey.

Choi, S., M. A. McDaniel, J. R. Busemeyer 1993. Evaluation of adaptive network models of conceptual rule learning. *Memory and Cognition* **21**, 413–23.

Deane, D. H., K. R. Hammond, D. A. Summers 1972. Acquisition and application of knowledge in complex inference tasks. *Journal of Experimental Psychology* **92**, 20–26.

Delosh E. L. 1995. *Hypothesis testing in the learning of functional concepts.* Masters thesis, Psychology Dept., Purdue University.

Delosh, E. L., J. R. Busemeyer, M. A. McDaniel 1997. Extrapolation: The *sine qua non* of abstraction. To appear in *Journal of Experimental Psychology: Learning, Memory, Cognition.*

Estes, W. K. 1994. *Classification and cognition.* New York: Oxford University Press.

Gluck, M. A. & G. H. Bower 1988. From conditioning to category learning: an adaptive network model. *Journal of Experimental Psychology: General* **117**, 227–47.

Homa D. 1984. On the nature of categories. In *The psychology of learning and motivation* (vol. 18), G. H. Bower (ed.), 49–94. New York: Academic Press.

Klayman, J. 1988. On the how and why (not) of learning from outcomes. In *Human judgement: the SJT approach*, B. Brehmer & C. R. B. Joyce (eds), 115–62. Amsterdam: North Holland.

Knapp, A. & J. A. Anderson 1984. A signal averaging model for concept formation. *Journal of Experimental Psychology: Learning, Memory, Cognition* **10**, 616–37.

Koele, P. 1980. The influence of labelled stimuli on nonlinear multiple-cue probability learning. *Organizational Behavior and Human Performance* **26**, 22–31.

Koh, K. & D. E. Meyer 1991. Function learning: induction of continuous stimulus–response relations. *Journal of Experimental Psychology: Learning, Memory, Cognition* **17**, 811–36.

Kruschke, J. K. 1992. alcove: an exemplar-based connectionistic model of category learning. *Psychological Review* **99**, 22–44.

Miller, P. M. 1971. Do labels mislead? A multiple cue study, within the framework of Brunswick's probabilistic functionalism. *Organizational Behavior and Human Performance* **6**, 480–500.

Muchinsky, P. M. & A. L. Dudycha 1974. The influence of a suppresser variable and labelled stimuli on MCPL. *Organizational Behavior and Human Performance* **12**, 429–44.

Muchinsky, P. M. & A. L. Dudycha 1975. Human inference behaviour in abstract and meaningful environments. *Organizational Behavior and Human Performance* **13**, 377–91.

Naylor J. C. & R. D. Clark 1968. Intuitive inference strategies in interval learning tasks as a function of magnitude and sign. *Organizational Behavior and Human Performance* **3**, 378–99.

Naylor, J. C. & R. K. Domine 1981. Inferences based on uncertain data: some experiments on the role of slope magnitude, instructions, and stimulus distribution shape on the learning of contingency relations. *Organizational Behavior and Human Performance* **27**, 1–31.

Nosofsky, R. 1986. Attention, similarity, and the identification–categorization relationship. *Journal of Experimental Psychology: General* **115**, 39–57.

Nosofsky, R. & J. K. Kruschke 1992. Investigations of an exemplar-based connectionistic model of category learning. In *The psychology of learning and motivation* (vol. 28), D. L. Medin (ed.), 207–50. New York: Academic Press.

Sawyer, J. E. 1991. Effects of risk and ambiguity on judgments of contingency relations and behavioral resource allocation decisions. *Organizational Behavior and Human Performance* **49**, 124–50.

Sheets, C. A. & M. J. Miller 1974. The effect of cue-criterion function form on multiple cue probability learning. *American Journal of Psychology* **87**, 629–41.

Slovic, P. & S. Lichtenstein 1971. Comparison of Bayesian and regression approaches to the study of information processing in judgment. *Organizational Behavior and Human Performance* **6**, 649–744.

Sniezek, J. A. 1986. The role of variable labels in cue probability learning tasks. *Organizational Behaviour and Human Decision Processes* **38**, 141–61.

Sniezek, J. A. & J. C. Naylor 1978. Cue measurement scale and functional hypothesis testing in cue probability learning. *Organizational Behaviour and Human Decision Processes* **22**, 366–74.

Summers, S. A., R. A. Summers, V. T. Karkau 1969. Judgments based on different functional relations between interacting cues and criterion. *American Journal of Psychology* **82**, 203–11.

Surber, C. F. 1987. Formal representations of qualitative and quantitative reversible operations. In *Formal operations in developmental psychology: progress in cognitive development research*, J. Bisanz, C. J. Brainerd, R. Kail (eds). New York: Springer.

Wagenaar, W. A. & S. D. Sagaria 1975. Misperception of exponential growth. *Perception and Psychophysics* **18**, 416–22.

CHAPTER TWELVE

Formal Models for Intra-categorical Structure that can be Used for Data Analysis

Gert Storms and Paul De Boeck

To most laymen like ourselves, a tomato is just a tomato. We have no knowledge of, nor names for, different sorts of tomatoes. Still, when buying these vegetables, we select our purchases rather carefully, attending to perceptible features such as colour, size and shape, assuming that red tomatoes are usually softer and taste sweeter than green ones. Thus, even although a category such as *tomatoes* is not divided into clear subcategories, we are aware of correlated features, and thus, of structure, within such basic categories. More general categories, such as *vegetables*, are also structured, but at least one important difference is that different sorts of vegetables are lexicalized (as beans, tomatoes, cabbage, etc.).

Within-category structure has been somewhat neglected in the research literature on concepts and categorization. Especially the structure within categories that cannot be divided into common lexicalized subcategories (such as *tomatoes*), has not attracted much attention. Still, detecting within-category structure may be important for the prediction of presence or absence of certain features, such as sweetness, from other features, such as colour. It may explain the ease or difficulty of learning category membership, as some types of within-category structure may be harder to learn than others.

In this chapter, we will first introduce the idea of studying within-category structure starting from an entity by property matrix. The second section reviews the four major views on concepts and categories, with respect to the assumptions made on categorical structure and the implications of these assumptions for the structure of the entity by property matrix. In the third section, empirical studies dealing with the question of whether correlated properties occur in natural categories are reviewed. In the final section, different formal models are presented that assume dependency between properties within categories, and which, in principle, can be used to identify categories through a method for data analysis.

ENTITY BY PROPERTY MATRICES

One way to study within-category structure is to start from an entity by property matrix. In such a matrix, columns represent (possible) examples of the category that is studied and rows represent (possible) features of the category. When analyzing an entity by property matrix, different assumptions can be made regarding the feature relationships within categories of entities. These assumptions are related to the view one has on the nature of concepts and categories. Depending on these assumptions, the basis for recognizing or identifying a category in the matrix will be different.

Two preliminary notes should be made on the nature of the data to be analyzed. The first note concerns the entity by property matrix that is considered when looking for categories. Two questions have to be addressed: which entities and which properties are to be included in the matrix? On the entity side, in principle all entities that belong to the domain to be categorized can be included. On the property side, several kinds of properties for categories exist. (For an elaborate overview, see Smith & Medin 1981.) Garner (1978) distinguished between component and holistic properties. Component properties are parts of entities, without which the entity could still exist (for example, a hat on the head). Holistic properties concern the whole entity and cannot be separated from it (for example, skin colour). Another distinction can be made between dimensional properties (i.e. properties that capture quantitative variations) and featural properties (i.e. properties that either apply to an entity or that do not apply). Since the featural approach has been used most extensively in the psychological study of categorization (Smith & Medin 1981), we will assume here that properties are features of a componential or holistic nature. It should be noted that dimensional information can usually be expressed by a set of nested features (Atkinson & Estes 1963). A continuous variable such as length, for instance, can be expressed as a set of nested features, each of them defined as "is larger than x", with x increasing for consecutive features (see also Hahn & Chater, this volume). Furthermore, Smith & Medin's (1981) triple constraints may be applied when selecting the features: a property is useful if (a) it reveals many relations between concepts, (b) if it applies to many concepts in the domain rather than to a few, and (c) it serves as the input for categorization processes. The features can be either abstract or perceptual.

The second note concerns the level of abstraction at which the categories are defined. Categories are ordered into taxonomies. Higher order categories include lower order categories (see Murphy & Lassaline, this volume). The greater the inclusiveness of a category within the taxonomy, the higher the level of abstraction. For instance, the category of *animals* includes the category of *birds*, and is thus defined at a more abstract level.

The level of abstraction at which a category is defined has important implications for the structure *within* categories. A very concrete category without subcategories (*poodles*, for instance) will obviously have a different within-category structure than a more abstract category that spans two or more subcategories (such as, for instance, *dogs*). More specifically, correlated features are a necessity in categories that span subcategories. Within the category dogs, the features "has curly hair" and "is regularly shaven" will tend to co-occur. These features will thus be correlated. Correlated features are not necessary, but *can* occur, in categories that are not further divided into subcategories. The correlations between features within the larger and abstract category can disappear when studied within the lower level subcategories. For instance, the features "has wings" and "has feathers" are correlated within the category "warm-blooded animals" (although not perfectly), but this correlation may disappear within the category of *birds*, because both features apply to all exemplars of the category. (For an elaboration on this phenomenon, see Rosch et al. 1976.) The reader should keep the relation between abstraction level and intra-category structure in mind in the remainder of this chapter.

INTRA-CATEGORICAL STRUCTURE IN THE MAJOR THEORETICAL VIEWS ON CONCEPTS

A delimitation of the notion of intra-categorical structure strongly depends on how "structure" is defined. In this section, the notion will be considered in its broadest sense of differentiation within the category in the entity by feature matrix. We will concentrate, however, on the kind of differentiation that leads to correlation between features. In what follows, we will largely make abstraction of differentiation between categories. Although isolating intra-categorical structure from inter-categorical structure is rather artificial, we thought that, for the sake of simplicity, it would be better to leave out inter-categorical aspects. We will review the four major theoretical views on semantic concepts: the classical view, the probabilistic view, the exemplar view and finally the theory-based view on categories. We will also derive some implications on how the entity by feature matrix is filled in according to these theories.

The classical view

Smith & Medin (1981) argued that the classical view (e.g. Clark & Clark 1977, Fodor et al. 1974, Miller & Johnson-Laird 1976, Sutcliffe 1993) can be characterized by three assumptions. First, the classical view assumes that the representation of a concept is a summary description of an entire class, rather than a set of descriptions of various subsets or exemplars of that class. Secondly, the features representing a concept are singly necessary and jointly sufficient to define that concept. And finally, if a concept is a subset of another concept, the defining features of the larger of the two categories are nested in the defining features of the smaller category. It has been demonstrated that it is hard to find defining features for most categories used in natural language. The idea, however, can easily be demonstrated with the category of squares, where the necessary and sufficient features are "has four sides", "all sides have equal length", and "has four angles of 90°". The fact that squares are a subset of quadrangles shows that the defining features of the latter category is a subset of the defining features of the category of squares. A large body of empirical evidence against the classical view has been presented in the literature. It is not our aim to evaluate the merits and drawbacks of this theoretical view. For a good overview, see Medin & Smith (1984, Smith & Medin 1981) and Komatsu (1992). Our main concern here is what the implications of the classical view are concerning intra-category structure.

The classical view has no explicit assumptions concerning the pattern of 1s and 0s in the entity by feature matrix for the non-defining features, while the defining features correspond, by definition, to 1-values only. The assumed intra-categorical structure depends on the hierarchical level at which the category is defined. For instance, within a hierarchically higher category, a nested structure of consistent 1-values will be found.

Table 12.1 gives an example of an entity by feature matrix according to the classical view. The rows, labelled with numbers, represent the exemplars; the columns, labelled with letters, represent the features.

TABLE 12.1
Example matrix for the classical view

	A	B	C	D	E	F	G
1	1	1	0	1	1	0	1
2	1	1	0	1	0	1	0
3	1	1	0	1	1	1	0
4	1	1	0	1	1	1	1
5	1	1	0	1	0	0	0
6	1	1	1	0	0	0	1
7	1	1	1	0	1	0	1
8	1	1	1	0	0	0	1
9	1	1	1	0	0	0	0
10	1	1	1	0	0	1	0

Features A and B are defining features and, consequently, all exemplars get 1-values for these features. Features C and D could be defining features for two non-overlapping subcategories (consisting of entities 1 through 5, and entities 6 through 10, respectively), with as a consequence, a negative correlation between C and D. The defining features of the subcategories are nested within the defining features for the overall category. Finally, the non-defining features E, F, and G vary in a non-systematic way over the exemplar set. In Table 12.1, and in all following tables, only one category is presented, as a consequence of the option to concentrate on intra-categorical structure.

The probabilistic view

According to the probabilistic view, semantic categories are abstractions, or summary representations. No necessary and sufficient features are assumed. A feature is included in the representation of the concept if it has a substantial probability of occurring in instances of the concept. It is further assumed that an entity will be categorized as an instance if it possesses some critical number of features, or a sum of weighted features that are included in the representation of the concepts (Medin & Smith 1984). For the category of *games*, for instance, a set of singly necessary and jointly sufficient features does not seem to exist (Wittgenstein 1953), although some features (such as "has rules" or "is played for pleasure") can be considered more critical than others. Activities that are characterized by many of these critical features will more likely be called games than activities that are not.

In its general form, the probabilistic view offers no direct cues concerning the pattern of 1s and 0s in the entity by feature matrix. The absence of necessary and sufficient features implies that not many exemplars exist with all the features associated to the category. The most characteristic features can be expected to result in more dense columns. (Although for a feature to be characteristic, it also needs to be distinctive to some degree, we do not discuss the differentiation between categories here.)

Table 12.2 shows an example of what an entity by feature matrix looks like according to the probabilistic view. None of the features applies to all exemplars of the category, although some features (A, C, D, E, and F) occur frequently and can be considered the characteristic features. None of the exemplars has many 0-values for the characteristic features, since the criterion for inclusion of an exemplar is that it possesses some critical sum of weighted features of the category (Smith & Medin 1981).

In the literature, a number of models have been proposed that have tried to reconcile the classical and the probabilistic view by assuming the existence of defining as well as characteristic features in concept representations. As an example, we will elaborate on the rather influential feature model for semantic decisions, proposed by Smith et al. (1974). The model was designed to account for empirical reaction times in membership verification tasks. Smith et al. assume that the meaning of categories is represented as a set of semantic features, some of which are defining, while others are only characteristic or even accidental. Instances of the category are assumed to have all defining, but not necessarily all characteristic features. Among the facts that an individual may know about *robins*, for instance, are that they are bipeds, have wings, have distinctive colours, are a certain size, and also that they perch in trees and are undomesticated. Smith et al. assume that most people consider the first four of these features as more defining for the concept *robin* than the last two (although the authors admit that people may be uncertain about which of these features are strictly necessary robin features). The assumed distinction between defining and characteristic features imposes some constraints on the

TABLE 12.2
Example matrix for the probabilistic view

	A	B	C	D	E	F	G
1	1	0	1	0	1	1	0
2	1	0	1	1	0	1	0
3	0	1	1	1	1	1	0
4	1	0	1	1	1	0	1
5	1	0	1	1	1	0	1
6	1	1	0	1	1	1	0
7	0	1	1	1	1	1	0
8	1	0	1	1	1	1	1
9	1	0	1	1	1	1	1
10	1	0	1	1	1	1	0

filling of the entity by feature matrix in that they imply that the defining features lead to columns of 1s, characteristic features leads to columns of mainly 1s, and the remaining features result in mainly 0s. A similar argument applies to other theories that combine defining and characteristic features (e.g. Landau 1982, Miller 1978, Miller & Johnson-Laird 1976, Osherson & Smith 1981, Smith 1988).

The exemplar view

This view states that categories are represented by their exemplars rather than by an abstract summary. Membership judgements are assumed to be based on a comparison of the target items with the stored exemplars of the category. For instance, when asked to judge whether a carpet is an example of the category *furniture*, subjects are assumed to compare a carpet with things that are stored as examples of furniture, such as a table, a chair, a sofa, etc. Different conceptions have been proposed concerning the nature of the stored exemplars. At one extreme, an exemplar representation is supposed to be a family resemblance representation that abstracts across different specific instances. This conception of exemplars is called the *multiple prototype approach* by Komatsu (1992). In this conception, the table, chair, sofa, etc., that people are comparing a carpet with, to base their decision on, are not necessarily particular items which they have encountered and stored, but these examples may themselves be abstract notions (that represent categories). Examples of such models can be found, for instance, in Medin & Schaffer (1978), Lakoff (1987a,b) and in Anderson (1990). At the other extreme, exemplar representations are assumed to involve no abstractions, and are a specific memory trace of an instance encountered in the past. The table, chair, and sofa, that come to someone's mind in deciding whether a carpet is an example of furniture are representations of a particular existing table, chair, sofa etc. Such models have been proposed, for instance, by Hintzman (1986), Nosofsky (1984 1986, 1988a,b, 1991), and Rosch (1975).

The two conceptions of the nature of exemplars have different implications for the pattern of 1s and 0s in the entity by feature matrix. For the multiple prototype approach, the implications depend on how the subcategories are regarded: If these subcategories are conceived as in the Smith et al. (1974) model, than an ordering of the entities according to the subcategories will yield sequences of 1s for the defining features; otherwise the pattern in the different regions corresponding to the subcategories will resemble the pattern of categories according to the general probabilistic view, that is, few or no features will occur with only 1s in their column and more 1s will occur the more characteristic a feature is for the subcategory.

The instance approach gives little clues as to how the entity by feature matrix should be filled in. It does, however, imply that features can occur that characterize only one single entity (Komatsu 1992). Table 12.3 shows an example of an entity by feature matrix according to the exemplar view. Features that characterize only one or a few entities such as, for instance, feature B, can occur. The exemplar view also allows entities that are characterized by only a few features (such as entity 3), even if the applying features are not very characteristic for the category as a whole.

More precise constraints can be derived from the best-examples model that is implicitly underlying much of Rosch's work (Rosch 1973, Rosch & Mervis 1975). Although Rosch explicitly disavowed a concern with models (Rosch 1975, 1978) her work can be considered an example of the instance approach (Smith & Medin 1981). Rosch referred explicitly to intra-category structure by arguing that categories are structured internally according to a prototypicality dimension. Prototypical members of a category are described as the "clearest cases, best examples" (Rosch 1973, 1975) and are thus assumed to possess many of the characteristic features of the category. Rosch & Mervis (1975) were able to translate the abstract notion of prototypicality into a concrete operationalization: in a series of experiments, they showed that the members of categories that are considered most prototypical are those with most features in common with other members of the category and with least features in common with members of contrasting categories. When subjects listed features for members of semantic categories which had been previously rated for degree of prototypicality, high positive correlations (around 0.90) showed up between those ratings and the weighted sum of the features of the members, the feature weights being based on the frequency with which these features were generated for the different category members. Similarly, negative correlations

TABLE 12.3
Example matrix for the exemplar view

	A	B	C	D	E	F	G
1	0	0	1	1	0	1	1
2	1	0	1	1	1	0	1
3	1	1	0	0	0	0	0
4	1	0	1	0	0	1	1
5	0	0	1	1	0	1	1
6	0	0	1	0	1	1	0
7	0	0	1	0	1	1	1
8	0	0	0	1	1	0	1
9	0	0	1	1	1	0	1
10	0	0	1	1	1	1	0

(around −0.75) were obtained between prototypicality and the weighted sum of features, the feature weights being based on the extent to which the features characterized members of contrasting categories. This empirically based, derived measure of prototypicality is called *family resemblance* by Rosch & Mervis (1975), after Wittgenstein (1953). The high correlations reported put constraints on the pattern of 1s and 0s in the entity by feature matrix, when external information is available in the form of a vector with prototypicality values for the entities.

Other constraints are imposed by another finding of Rosch & Mervis (1975). They studied, for all the features generated in their study, to how many items these features were considered to apply. For four out of six categories, only one feature was judged to be true for all category members used in the study, but three of these single features were very general and were also true for many non-members. For the remaining two categories, no features characterized all members. The number of features that characterized more than two members decreased as the number of members for which the feature was true increased.

The theory-based view

The three theoretical views described above have been challenged recently by a new view on how concepts are represented. This new theoretical view, generally referred to as the theory-based view (e.g. Carey 1985, Gelman 1988, Keil 1986, Murphy 1993, Murphy & Medin 1985, Rips 1989), is developed to deal with the coherence problem. The three views cannot account for what holds a category together. The classical view relies on the assumption of defining features to solve this problem, but too many empirical studies failed to detect these critical features in a wide variety of categories (Mervis & Rosch 1981, Medin & Smith 1984, Smith & Medin 1981). The remaining two views, the probabilistic view and the exemplar view, explain coherence in a category on the basis of similarity (Komatsu 1992, Medin 1989, Murphy & Medin 1985). However, Murphy & Medin (1985) argued extensively that similarity is too flexible to explain conceptual coherence: any two entities can be arbitrarily similar or dissimilar by changing the criterion of what counts as a relevant feature and thus, similarity does not provide enough constraints on possible concepts (see also Hahn & Chater, this volume). Murphy & Medin further argue that what holds categories together, that is, what makes their members form a comprehensible class, is background knowledge and naïve theories. These theories provide a structural frame of features relevant in the context of the theory. Similarities are argued to be computed given the coherence offered by the theory, rather than being the basis of coherence. In this view, the fact that something comes out of a bird egg, for instance, is more important for the decision that it is a bird than the question whether it has many features in common with an abstract summary representation of a bird or with stored exemplars of the category *bird*. It is thus easy for the theory-based view to explain why a deformed bird without any feathers, wings or legs is still considered a bird, while a toy with a beak, wings, feathers and legs is not considered a real bird.

The theory-based view stresses that features co-occur for reasons that people understand. Having wings correlates with being able to fly because that is what wings usually are used for. The unity of a category is assumed to be based on the meaningfulness of the co-occurence of features. As a consequence, this view relies on the existence of correlated (co-occuring) features within superordinate categories and over more subordinate categories, just like the classical view. What makes the theory-based view different, however, is that it is less stringent with respect to critical features, and that the features that are picked up to be associated with a category are meaningful from the perspective of a theory, as are their correlations. The contribution of the theory-based view lies more in indicating the meaningfulness of feature correlations used to delineate categories than in specifying that there are correlations. As to intra-categorical feature correlations, they may or may not occur, depending on the theory that functions as a basis for the category in question, but also depending on general background knowledge about the world. For example, there should be correlation within the category of *birds*, between flying and building nests in trees. For an extensive overview of the relevant literature, see Murphy & Medin (1985). No separate table representation of the theory-based view is given since not the feature correlations but their meaningfulness is stressed as a basis for the formation of a category.

Conclusions

None of the four views states explicit assumptions on whether the features are stochastically independent or not *within* a category in general, apart from within superordinate categories. In other words, the four views have no explicit stand on whether the occurrence of a particular feature in a certain object can or cannot be predicted from the knowledge that the object is characterized by other particular features. Only in higher level categories that clearly fall apart in a number of lower level categories is this form of predictability explicitly recognized. Perhaps the most important theorizing about this issue stems from Rosch et al. (1976) who defined, in taxonomies of concrete entities, a level of abstraction at which the most basic category cuts are made that capture the correlation between features in a given domain (see also Murphy & Lassaline, this volume). Examples of basic level categories are *piano*, *apple*, *shirt*, *chair*, *car*, *trout*, etc. They showed that these basic level concepts carry the most information. They stated that such categories possess the highest category cue validity (i.e. that membership in such categories can best be predicted given the occurrence of certain features) and that they are therefore the most differentiated from each other. Discerning these basic categories explains the correlational structure of features. Rosch et al. (1976) refer to categories defined at higher taxonomic levels as superordinate categories, and to categories defined at a lower than basic level as subordinates. Within categories, correlated features are, thus, evidently found at the superordinate level categories such as *fish*, that, by definition, fall apart in basic categories at a lower level, such as *salmon*, *trout*, *shark,* and so on. The theory view refines this argument by assuming that the correlated features that are used for categorization are those that fit in people's background knowledge and theories. It is implicitly assumed that these correlations between features disappear within categories at the basic level, although other correlations may remain or even arise within the categories that are defined in this way. Also, these remaining or new correlations can make sense from a theory about the entities involved.

Similarly, a number of models have been proposed in the literature where, implicitly or explicitly, stochastic independence between features within a category is assumed. In the family resemblance model proposed by Rosch & Mervis (1975), for instance, properties are treated as additive and independent (Malt & Smith 1984). The same assumptions of additivity and independence are assumed in Collins & Loftus (1975), in McCloskey & Glucksberg (1979), in the model of Smith et al. (1974), and in Tversky's (1977) contrast model.

EMPIRICAL RESEARCH ON CORRELATED FEATURES WITHIN CATEGORIES

The question whether correlated features occur within categories is, as argued above, intrinsically related to the hierarchical structure of semantic categories. Superordinate categories fall apart into lower level categories due to correlated features (Murphy & Medin 1985, Rosch et al. 1976). It is, therefore, important to keep the scope of the categories under investigation in mind. However, a pattern of feature dependence may also occur in categories at the basic level. Birds that sing, for instance, are usually small, not large.

There is some empirical evidence that correlated features occur *within* categories in general, that is, within categories from basic level as well as from superordinate level. Malt & Smith (1984) explicitly investigated whether salient properties are correlated in natural categories. In a first experiment, subjects generated properties for exemplars of common categories (such as *birds, furniture, fruit,* etc.). The most frequently generated properties were then given to a new group of subjects, who rated how much each property belonged to each category member. For instance, subjects rated, for each of a set of examples of the category bird (*robin, seagull, swallow,* etc.), to what extent features such as "flies", "lays eggs" etc., were present. The results showed that properties of category members occur in systematic relationship to one another rather than independently. In a second experiment, subjects were asked what property pairs (generated in the first experiment) they considered to be related. Overall, one out of three pairs presented were rated as correlated. The number of pairs considered to be correlated ranged widely for the different categories (from 17 per cent for the category *clothing* to 86 per cent for the category *fruit*). Malt & Smith (1984) further investigated whether these property relations influence typicality judgements within the category. Only weak evidence was found for the assumption that particularly salient and functional relationships influence typicality judgements.

Medin et al. (1982) also argued that subjects are sensitive to correlated structure within categories. In a series of experiments, subjects learned about a fictitious disease or about two diseases from hypothetical case studies in which some symptoms (such as swollen eyes, discoloured gums, nose-bleed, etc.) were correlated with each other, while others were independent. After the initial training, subjects were presented either with pairs of new cases and asked to judge which of the two was more likely to have the disease, or with a single case and asked which disease was present. When choosing between pairs of new cases, they tended to choose the case that preserved a correlation over the case that broke the correlation, even when the case with correlated symptoms contained fewer typical symptoms. Similarly, when judging which disease was present in a single case, subjects' diagnoses were determined primarily by the correlated symptoms (i.e. by the co-occurrence of symptoms that tended to co-occur in the cases presented in the learning phase).

INTRA-CATEGORICAL STRUCTURE

As described above, Malt & Smith (1984) found evidence for correlated features in all the categories used in their study. However, the authors did not investigate the specific patterns of co-occurrences that gave rise to the correlations between the properties. They confined themselves to report that properties in their categories occurred mostly in predictable clusters of more than two properties, a finding which suggests that feature clusters exist even within basic categories. However, when features are not completely stochastically independent within categories, the structure of the dependency can be further investigated in a formal way. Different data-analytic models can be used as guidelines for different dependence relations among the features and among the entities. We will first describe latent class analysis as a way to analyze data, and then describe structures based on rectangular blocks, on triangular patterns, and on parallelogram patterns.

Latent class analysis

The latent class model has two basic assumptions. First, it assumes homogeneity at the latent level. All members of the latent class have identical probabilities of having a manifest feature. The probabilities may depend on the feature, but they are identical for all class members. At the manifest level, however, heterogeneity may occur, as the model is probabilistic.

Secondly the latent class model assumes that features are independent within a class. Features depend on class membership of an entity, but given class membership, they are independent among each other, and hence, also uncorrelated within a class. As will be explained later, the latent class model can be enriched so as to allow for structure, but in its classic form, it is restricted to the assumptions given here.

In a way, latent class analysis makes the kind of cuts that Rosch et al. (1976) were thinking of when describing basic categories, since the latent classes are chosen such that they explain all dependency between features, with no dependency left *within* a class. The technique could be used, for instance, to detect different sorts of tomatoes based on the occurrence pattern of features (such as shape, colour, taste, etc.) in tomatoes. In dividing the tomatoes in subcategories, the technique looks for groupings where the different features do not correlate over the exemplars within the subcategories.

Latent class analysis was developed by Lazarsfeld (1950, Lazarsfeld & Henry 1968) and Green (1951). Recent developments of the technique are presented in Langeheime & Rost (1988) and an informal introduction to latent class analysis in the domain of categorization research can be found in De Soete (1993).

The latent class model is a probabilistic model for absence of intra-categorical structure. A non-probabilistic model without intra-categorical structure is the model with categories as rectangles. When, however, a category consists of more than one rectangle, as will be explained, then again structure is obtained.

Rectangular structures

A category can correspond to a rectangle of 1-values, which is a subset of entities having all features from a subset of features. In that case, all features are uncorrelated within the category and there is no structure since the members are not differentiated. Structure within a category may result from the existence of several subcategories that are also basically rectangular in shape. This implies that the subcategories are assumed to be monothetic. The features that are correlated within the broader category are then the features that "define" the rectangular subcategories. Categories at superordinate levels are assumed to fall apart in categories at the basic level in such a way that the correlated structure which characterizes the overall category disappears at the lower level subcategories. A more lenient version of the same kind of structure, which is better in line with what is known about categories, is a rectangular structure with maximal (given the data), but not perfect density. Prototypicality of the different entities may then be related to the number of 1s in the rows corresponding to these entities. Simple rectangular structures, consisting of only one rectangle, cannot account for correlations, not even when they have less than perfect density. In order to obtain correlations, multiple rectangles are needed.

The rectangles that characterize the subcategories may be overlapping or non-overlapping, depending on the nature of the category. Overlapping categories may show overlap in three different ways: on the entity side, on the feature side, or both on the feature and on the entity side. Absence of overlap on the entity side of subcategories is straightforward: a division of mammals into domesticated and wild, for instance, yields no overlap on the entities side. These categories do have an overlap on the feature side. An example of such a structure is given in Table 12.4. Overlap on the entity side is also quite common in natural language: mammals, for instance, can be divided into wild and domesticated, but at the same time into herbivores, carnivores, rodents, etc. These subcategories are certainly overlapping on the entity side. Dividing the category *food* into subcategories such as *vegetables* and *fruits*, for instance, will result in overlap in features. In subcategories with overlapping entities, the entities in the overlap belong to several subtypes.

Radial categories, as described by Lakoff (1987b) can be conceived as a combination of rectangular structures, where each of the subcategories (i.e. each of the "non-central extensions") has a rectangular shape (with or without perfect density) that shares a single feature or a feature set with the central subcategory.

TABLE 12.4
Example matrix with a rectangular structure

	A	B	C	D	E	F	G
1	1	1	1	1	1	0	0
2	1	1	1	1	1	0	0
3	1	1	1	1	1	0	0
4	1	1	1	1	1	0	0
5	1	1	1	1	1	0	0
6	0	0	0	0	0	0	0
7	0	0	0	0	0	0	0

Data-analytic techniques have been proposed in the literature to look for approximate rectangular blocks of 1s in a matrix. Algorithms that allow overlapping rectangles include two-way clustering (Hartigan 1975), block modelling (Arabie et al. 1978), Boolean factor analysis (Mickey et al. 1983), the hierarchical classes model (De Boeck & Rosenberg 1988, De Boeck et al. 1993, Storms et al. 1994) and Gallois lattices (Guénoche & Van Mechelen 1993, Van Mechelen 1993, Wille 1982).

Triangular structures

A different sort of within-category structure that can cause correlation between features is a triangle of 1s. This structure assumes that there are exemplars that only have few features while other exemplars have the same and more features. The features can then be arranged in a linear way according to how many entities within the category are characterized by the features. When starting from an entity by feature matrix where the order of the entities and features is arbitrary, a triangular shape may be obtained after a suitable permutation of the entities and features in the matrix. The resulting triangular shape characterizes a linear implication structure: Table 12.5 shows a matrix that can be rearranged into a perfect triangular structure, as shown in Table 12.6, after suitable permutations of entities and features. To have a less frequent feature implies having all more frequent features. For example, all members of the basic category of *birds* have feathers and wings. Not all of these members can fly. The flying members (that have wings and feathers) are not necessarily small, and among the small birds, only some can sing. Among *birds*, singing implies small, small implies flying, and flying in turn implies wings and feathers.

A triangular structure, even when it consists of only one triangle, can account for correlations between features within a category. Like rectangular structures triangular structures can also be approximate instead of being perfect. Also, different triangles can be combined into

TABLE 12.5
Example matrix with a triangular structure before suitable permutations

	A	B	C	D	E	F	G
7	0	0	1	0	0	0	0
4	1	1	1	1	0	0	0
2	1	1	1	1	1	0	1
3	1	1	1	1	1	0	0
1	1	1	1	1	1	1	1
5	1	1	1	0	0	0	0
6	0	1	1	0	0	0	0

TABLE 12.6
Example matrix with a triangular structure after suitable permutation

	A	B	C	D	E	F	G
1	1	1	1	1	1	1	1
2	1	1	1	1	1	1	0
3	1	1	1	1	1	0	0
4	1	1	1	1	0	0	0
5	1	1	1	0	0	0	0
6	1	1	0	0	0	0	0
7	1	0	0	0	0	0	0

one structure. The different triangles may be defined on different sets of features or on the same set of features, but with a different ordering of the features on the different dimensions underlying the corresponding feature structures. As a hypothesis, the notion of prototypicality can be related to linear implication structures: The more features an entity has in the triangle, the more prototypical it is within the (sub)category.

The data-analytic technique that corresponds to searching for a single linear implication structure in an entities by features matrix is scalogram analysis or Guttman scaling (Guttman 1960). Probabilistic versions of triangular shapes can be obtained by fitting item response models to the entity by features matrix (Hambleton & Swaminathan 1985, Lord 1980). Searching for several, non-overlapping linear implication structures amounts to allocating entities to latent classes that each correspond to a single linear implication structure. A probabilistic version of such a model can be found in Rost (1990).

Parallelogram structures
A third possible sort of within-category structure that results in correlated features is a dimensional zone structure. In such a structure, features can be ordered on a dimension such that, when two of the features apply to an entity, all features from the zone between them will

also apply. This means that, analogous to what was shown for the triangular structure in Tables 12.5 and 12.6, after a suitable permutation of rows and columns of the entity by feature matrix, parallelogram shapes show up. An example of such a parallelogram shape is shown in Table 12.7. Like the other two shapes, the parallelograms can also be imperfect, to account for the rather approximate character of most categories. Dimensional zone structures may be suited for loosely-defined concepts such as sports (Wittgenstein 1953). Table 12.8 gives an example, where, after permutations on the entity and feature side, a parallelogram structure appears. The first entity, billiards, is characterized by the features "is played on a table", "teams consist of only a single person", and "involves balls". The second entity (table tennis) is characterized by the same three features, but also by the feature "is a physical activity". Next, tennis has a 1-value for the last three features, but a zero value for the first feature, etc. Crucial for the dimensional zone structure is that the features can be ordered on an underlying dimension on which the entities can also be situated such that the entities are characterized only by features that form a closed set on the dimensional ordering.

The entity by feature matrix may also be the result of a combination of several dimensional zone structures. These different parallelograms may be defined on different sets of features, or on the same set of

TABLE 12.7
Example matrix with a parallelogram structure

	A	B	C	D	E	F	G
1	1	1	1	0	0	0	0
2	0	1	1	1	0	0	0
3	0	1	1	1	1	0	0
4	0	0	0	1	1	0	0
5	0	0	0	1	1	1	0
6	0	0	0	0	1	1	1
7	0	0	0	0	0	1	1

TABLE 12.8
Example of parallellogram structure

	Played on table	Teams of single persons	Involves balls	Requires physical activity	Played in teams	Played outside
Billiards	1	1	1	0	0	0
Table tennis	1	1	1	1	0	0
Tennis	0	1	1	1	0	0
Volleyball	0	0	1	1	1	0
Football	0	0	1	1	1	1

features, but with a different ordering of the features on the different dimensions underlying the corresponding parallelogram structures.

Unlike a triangle, a parallelogram is not directed. The underlying dimension is called a qualitative dimension, versus a quantitative dimension in the case of an implication structure (Gati & Tversky 1982). Moving along the dimension does not imply more of a quantity, but a different quality instead. Therefore, when the notion of prototype has to be related to the underlying dimension, the relation may be curvilinear, with the highest prototypicality in the middle.

A data-analysis method to look for parallelogram structures has been proposed by Lazarsfeld (1959) and was further developed by Coombs (1964). A probabilistic model and data-analytic method has been developed by Hoijtink (1990). Formal properties of dimensional zone structures have been studied by Gati & Tversky (1982).

CONCLUDING REMARKS

Although intra-categorical structure, in the sense of feature correlations within categories, is a rather neglected topic in theories of concepts and categories, it is clear that such correlations exist and do play a role. Therefore, it is important to reflect on the forms the intra-categorical structure can take. One way to look at the structure is in terms of within-category shapes in an entity by feature matrix. Three types of such shapes were discussed: rectangles, triangles and parallelograms. They each define a kind of structure that corresponds to known models of data analysis that are already used for categorization or that have the potential to be used for that purpose. The three different shapes are also important in two other respects. First, they define a possible coherence principle to delineate a category, not only in data analysis, but possibly also in the mind. Secondly, it might be important for a cognitive psychology of categories and concepts to distinguish between the different forms, for example, because prototypicality might be defined differently, but also because acquisition and identification might depend on the form of a category.

REFERENCES

Anderson, J. R. 1990. *The adaptive character of thought*. Hillsdale, New Jersey: Erlbaum.

Arabie, P., S. A. Boorman, P. R. Levitt 1978. Constructing blockmodels: How and why? *Journal of Mathematical Psychology* **17**, 1–63.

Atkinson, R. C. & W. K. Estes 1963. Stimulus sampling theory. In *Handbook of mathematical psychology* (vol. 2), R. D. Luce, R. R. Bush, E. Galanter (eds), 121–268. New York: John Wiley.

Carey, S. 1985. *Conceptual language in childhood*. Cambridge, Mass.: MIT Press.

Clark, H. H. & E. V. Clark 1977. *Psychology and language*. New York: Harcourt Brace Jovanovich.

Collins, A. M. & E. F. Loftus 1975. A spreading-activation theory of semantic processing. *Psychological Review* 82, 407–28.

Coombs, C. H. 1964. *A theory of data*. New York: John Wiley.

De Boeck, P. & S. Rosenberg 1988. Hierarchical classes: model and data analysis. *Psychometrika* 53, 361–81.

De Boeck, P., S. Rosenberg, & I. Van Mechelen. 1993. The hierarchical classes approach: a review. In *Categories and concepts: theoretical views and inductive data analysis*, I. Van Mechelen, J. Hampton, R. S. Michalski & P. Theuns (eds), 265–286. London: Academic Press.

De Soete, G. 1993. Using latent class analysis in categorization research. In *Categories and concepts: theoretical views and inductive data analysis*, I. Van Mechelen, J. Hampton, R. S. Michalski, & P. Theuns (eds), 309–330. London: Academic Press.

Fodor, J. A., Bever, T. G., & Garrett, M. F. 1974. *The psychology of language: an introduction to psycholinguistics and generative grammar*. New York: McGraw-Hill.

Garner, W. R. 1978. Aspects of a stimulus: features, dimensions, and configurations. In *Cognition and categorization*, E. Rosch & B. B. Lloyd (eds), 99–133. Hillsdale, New Jersey: Erlbaum.

Gati, I. & A. Tversky 1982. Representations of qualitative and quantitative dimensions. *Journal of Experimental Psychology: Human Perception and Emotion* 8, 325–40.

Gelman, S. A. 1988. The development of induction within natural kind and artifact categories. *Cognitive Psychology* 20, 65–95.

Green, B. F. 1951. A general solution for the latent class model of latent structure analysis. *Psychometrika* 16, 151–66.

Guénoche, A. & I. Van Mechelen 1993. Galois approach to the induction of concepts. In *Categories and concepts: theoretical views and inductive data analysis*, I. Van Mechelen, J. Hampton, R. S. Michalski & P. Theuns (eds), 287–308. London: Academic Press.

Guttman, L. A. 1960. The basis of scalogram analysis. In *Measurement and prediction: studies in social psychology in World War ii* (vol. 4), S. A. Stouffer, L. A. Guttman, E. A. Suchman, P. F. Lazarsfeld, S. A. Star & J. A. Clausen (eds), 60–90. Princeton, New Jersey: Princeton University Press.

Hambleton, R. K. & H. Swaminathan 1985. *Item response theory: principles and applications*. Boston, Mass.: Kluwer.

Hartigan, J. A. 1975. *Clustering algorithms*. New York: John Wiley.

Hintzman, D. L. 1986. "Schema abstraction" in a multiple-trace memory model. *Psychological Review* 93, 411–28.

Hoijtink, H. 1990. A latent trait model for dichotomous choice data. *Psychometrika* 55, 641–56.

Keil, F. C. 1986. The acquisition of natural kind and artifact terms. In *Language learning and concept acquisition*, W. Demopoulos & A. Marras (eds), 133–53. Norwood, New Jersey: Ablex.

Komatsu, L. K. 1992. Recent views of conceptual structure. *Psychological Bulletin* **112**, 500–26.

Lakoff, G. 1987a. Cognitive models and prototype theory. In *Concepts and conceptual development*, U. Neisser (ed.), 63–100. New York: Cambridge University Press.

Lakoff, G. 1987b. *Women, fire, and dangerous things: what categories reveal about the mind*. Chicago: University of Chicago Press.

Landau, B. 1982. Will the real grandmother please stand up? The psychological reality of dual meaning representations. *Journal of Psycholinguistic Research* **11**, 47–62.

Langeheine, R. & Rost, J. (eds) 1988. *Latent trait and latent class models*. New York: Plenum.

Lazarsfeld, P. F. 1950b. The interpretation and computation of some latent structures. In *Measurement and prediction*, S. A. Stouffer L. A. Gottman, E. A. Suchman & P. F. Lazarsfeld (eds), 362–412. Princeton, New Jersey: Princeton University Press.

Lazarsfeld, P. F. 1959. Latent structure analysis. In *Psychology: a study of a science* (vol. 3), S. Koch (ed.), 476–543. New York: McGraw-Hill.

Lazarsfeld, P. F. & R. W. Henry 1968. *Latent structure analysis*. Boston, Mass.: Houghton Mifflin.

Lord, F. M. 1980. *Applications of item response theory to practical testing problems*. Hillsdale, New Jersey: Erlbaum.

Malt, B. C. & E. E. Smith 1984. Correlated properties in natural categories. *Journal of Verbal Learning and Verbal Behavior* **23**, 250–69.

McCloskey, M. & S. Glucksberg 1979. Decision processes in verifying category membership statements: implications for models of semantic memory. *Cognitive Psychology* **11**, 1–37.

Medin, D. L. 1989. Concepts and conceptual structure. *Americal Psychologist* **44**, 1469–81.

Medin, D. L., M. W. Altom, S. M. Edelson, D. Freko 1982. Correlated symptoms and simulated medical classification. *Journal of Experimental Psychology: Learning, Memory, and Cognition* **8**, 37–50.

Medin, D. L. & M. M. Schaffer 1978. Context theory of classification learning. *Psychological Review* **85**, 207–38.

Medin, D. L. & E. E. Smith 1984. Concepts and concept formation. *Annual Review of Psychology* **35**, 113–38.

Mervis, C. B. & E. Rosch 1981. Categorization of natural objects. *Annual Review of Psychology* **21**, 129–45.

Mickey, M. R., P. Mundle, L. Engelman 1983. Boolean factor analysis. In BMDP *statistical software*, W. J. Dixon (ed.), 538–45. Berkeley, California: University of California Press.

Miller, G. A. 1978. Practical and lexical knowledge. In *Cognition and categorization*, E. Rosch & B. B. Lloyd (eds), 305–19. Hillsdale, New Jersey: Erlbaum.

Miller, G. A. & P. N. Johnson-Laird 1976. *Language and perception*. Cambridge, Mass.: Harvard University Press.

Murphy, G. L. 1993. Theories and concept formation. In *Categories and concepts: theoretical views and inductive data analysis*, I. Van Mechelen, J. Hampton, R. S. Michalski, P. Theuns (eds), 173–200. London: Academic Press.

Murphy, G. L. & D. L. Medin 1985. The role of theories in conceptual coherence. *Psychological Review* **92**, 289–316.

Nosofsky, R. M. 1984. Choice, similarity, and the context model of classification. *Journal of Experimental Psychology: Learning, Memory, and Cognition* **10**, 104–14.

Nosofsky, R. M. 1986. Attention, similarity, and the identification-categorization relationship. *Journal of Experimental Psychology: General* **115**, 39–57.

Nosofsky, R. M. 1988a. Exemplar based accounts of relations between classification, recognition, and typicality. *Journal of Experimental Psychology: Learning, Memory, and Cognition* **14**, 700–8.

Nosofsky, R. M. 1988b. On exemplar based exemplar representations: reply to Ennis. *Journal of Experimental Psychology: General* **117**, 412–4.

Nosofsky, R. M. 1991. Stimulus bias, asymmetric similarity, and classification. *Cognitive Psychology* **23**, 94–140.

Osherson, D. N. & E. E. Smith 1981. On the adequacy of prototype theory as a theory of concepts. *Cognition* **9**, 35–58.

Rips, L. J. 1989. Similarity, typicality, and categorization. In *Similarity and analogical reasoning*, S. Vosniadou & A. Orthony (eds), 21–59. Cambridge: Cambridge University Press.

Rosch, E. 1973. On the internal structure of perceptual and semantic categories. In *Cognitive development and the acquisition of language*, T. E. Moore (ed.), 111–144. New York: Academic Press.

Rosch, E. 1975. Cognitive representations of semantic categories. *Journal of Experimental Psychology: General* **104**, 192–233.

Rosch, E. 1978. Principles of categorization. In *Cognition and categorization*, E. Rosch & B. B. Lloyd (eds), 27–48. Hillsdale, New Jersey: Erlbaum.

Rosch, E. & C. B. Mervis 1975. Family resemblances: studies in the internal structure of categories. *Cognitive Psychology* **7**, 573–605.

Rosch, E., C. B. Mervis, W. D. Gray, D. M. Johnson, P. Boyes-Braem 1976. Basic objects in natural categories. *Cognitive Psychology* **8**, 382–439.

Rost, J. 1990. Rasch models in latent classes: An integration of two approaches to item analysis. *Applied Psychological Measurement* **3**, 271–82.

Smith, E. E. 1988. Concepts and thought. In *The psychology of human thought*, R. J. Sternberg & E. E. Smith (eds), 19–49. Cambridge: Cambridge University Press.

Smith, E. E. & D. L. Medin 1981. *Categories and concepts*. Cambridge, Mass.: Harvard University Press.

Smith, E. E., E. J. Shoben, L. R. Rips 1974. Structure and process in semantic memory: a featural model for semantic decisions. *Psychological Review* **81**, 214–41.

Storms, G., I. Van Mechelen, P. De Boeck 1994. Structural analysis of the intension and extension of semantic concepts. *European Journal of Cognitive Psychology* **6**, 43–75.

Sutcliffe, J. P. 1993. Concept, class, and category in the tradition of Aristotle. In *Categories and concepts: theoretical views and inductive data analysis*, I. Van Mechelen, J. Hampton, R. S. Michalski, P. Theuns (eds), 35–65. London: Academic Press.

Tversky, A. 1977. Features of similarity. *Psychological Review* **84**, 327–52.

Van Mechelen, I. 1993. Approximate Galois lattices of formal concepts. In *Information and classification*, O. Opitz, B. Lausen, R. Klar (eds), 108–112. Berlin: Springer.

Wille, R. 1982. Restructuring lattice theory: an approach based on hierarchies of concepts. In *Ordered sets*, O. Rival (ed.), 445–70. Boston, Mass.: Reidel.

Wittgenstein, L. 1953. *Philosophical investigations*. Oxford: Blackwell.

Index